A GENIUS FOR PLACE

A GENIUS FOR PLACE

American Landscapes of the Country Place Era

❦

ROBIN KARSON

with photographs by Carol Betsch

For Dick & Marty Jones —

With thanks and all best wishes,

Robin Karson

Feb. 13, 2017

University of Massachusetts Press   Amherst

in association with

Library of American Landscape History   Amherst

LC 2007015083
ISBN 978-1-55849-636-1

Library of Congress Cataloging-in-Publication Data
Karson, Robin S.
    A genius for place : American landscapes of the country place era /
Robin Karson.
        p. cm.
    "In association with Library of American Landscape History, Amherst."
    Includes bibliographical references and index.
    ISBN 978-1-55849-636-1 (cloth : alk. paper)
    1. Landscape architects—United States—Biography. 2.
Horticulturists—United States—Biography. 3. Landscape
architects—United States—History. 4. Horticulturists—United
States—History. 5. Landscape design—History. I. Library of American
Landscape History. II. Title.
SB469.9.K37 2007
712.0973—dc22
                                                            2007015083

British Library Cataloguing in Publication data are available.

Frontispiece: *Bridge in Wild Garden Lagoon*, Stan Hywet Hall, 1997, detail. Photograph by Carol Betsch.

Complete credits for illustration sources abbreviated in the captions are given on page 429.

Publication of this book was generously supported by Mr. and Mrs. Michael Jefcoat and by Nancy R. Turner.
Research and photography were underwritten by Library of American Landscape History, National Endowment for the Arts,
Stanley Smith Horticultural Trust, High Meadow Foundation, and Furthermore, a program of the J. M. Kaplan Fund.

For Carol

CONTENTS

Preface • *ix*
Introduction • *xiii*

Prologue • 3

PART I: AN AMERICAN STYLE, 1900–1919 • 21
1. Warren H. Manning, 1860–1938 • 25
2. Charles A. Platt, 1861–1933 • 47
3. Gwinn, Cleveland, Ohio • 61
4. Stan Hywet Hall, Akron, Ohio • 89
5. Ellen Shipman, 1869–1950 • 117

PART II: INNOVATION AND WILDNESS, 1920–1929 • 129
6. Beatrix Farrand, 1872–1959 • 133
7. Dumbarton Oaks, Washington, D.C. • 149
8. Marian Cruger Coffin, 1876–1957 • 181
9. Winterthur, Winterthur, Delaware • 195
10. Jens Jensen, 1860–1951 • 223
11. Edsel and Eleanor Ford House, Grosse Pointe Shores, Michigan • 239

PART III: DREAMS AND ABSTRACTIONS, 1929–1939 • 265
12. Lockwood de Forest Jr., 1896–1949 • 269
13. Val Verde (Días Felicitas), Santa Barbara, California • 285
14. Fletcher Steele, 1885–1971 • 309
15. Naumkeag, Stockbridge, Massachusetts • 327

Afterword • 355

Notes • *359*
Bibliography • *393*
Acknowledgments • *403*
Index • *407*
Illustration Sources • *429*

PREFACE

The subject of this book is American landscape design from the beginning of the twentieth century through the last years of the Great Depression, a period sometimes referred to as the country place era. I investigate the topic through the examples of seven particularly fine estate designs, all of which retain their fundamental spatial integrity and are now open to visitors. My purpose is to provide an explanation of a complex and interesting phenomenon that has not been well understood—to make vivid this time, these places, and these ideas for both professional and general readers—and in so doing, to provide useful context to the stewards of these landscapes and to others responsible for places that resemble them in spirit and principle. I hope that readers will come away with a sense of the importance of preserving these places, as reflections of history and also as landscapes of transcendent, rejuvenating force.

In choosing among hundreds of potential candidates for the case studies that frame this book, I considered several criteria, primary among which were artistic quality, geographic and chronological distribution, and the talent of the practitioners whose careers these examples represent. Because of the limits of space and the ramifications of working in depth rather than breadth, the works of many fine landscape architects from the period have not been analyzed, a circumstance that might disappoint some readers but that also points the way for future publications. (One could imagine, for example, a survey that covers the work of James L. Greenleaf, Percival Gallagher, Edward Huntsman-Trout, Florence Yoch, Annette Hoyt Flanders, and Marjorie Sewell Cautley.) I believe that nearly all of the period's most imaginative practioners are represented here in some measure, however, and that additional pages would not have furthered my goal, to clarify the central tenets of the larger story.

Potential readers will be helped by knowing something about the book's untraditional organization, and this is best explained by looking at the course of its development. I began writing the manuscript in 1990, the year after the publication of my first book, *Fletcher Steele, Landscape Architect*. It seemed to me that a history that put the work of Steele and his cohorts in context was much needed, as there was little available on the general topic, and as surely as there had been a talent as great as Steele's undiscovered, there must be many others like him. As I began to work out a structure for this book (which initially included one hundred rather than seven projects), I met Carol Betsch, whose black-and-white photographs of American landscapes were deeply stirring and also responsive to the actual spaces depicted. I invited her to join me in the project by photographing the country places with historical and design ideas in mind. One benefit I saw to this approach would be the addition of new, high quality photographs to the archival record of important American places and, I hoped, material for an exhibition that could educate new audiences about the subject.

In the mid-nineties we began traveling to the sites, Carol with her large, wood field camera, and me with my notes and copies of old photographs, drawings, and plans. Soon, the photographs began to accumulate. In 2000, an exhibition, *A Genius for Place: American Landscapes of the Country Place Era*, opened at PaineWebber (now UBS) Art Gallery in New York, sponsored by Library of American Landscape History. The associated book that was to serve as a catalogue to the traveling show was far from complete, though. It had been set aside to work on other books, *The Muses of Gwinn* (1995), *Pioneers of American Landscape Design* (2000), and a new edition of *Fletcher Steele* (2003), the first a monograph about one of the sites in *A Genius for Place*, the second an encyclopedia, and the third a revision of the Steele biography.

As I returned to the country place manuscript, I realized that the discussions of the practitioners' backgrounds were too long to fit comfortably inside the site discussions, and it seemed wise to set up separate chapters for these narratives. I was excited about the potential of gathering detailed biographies of so many important landscape architects into the same volume—a step forward from the encyclopedic intention that had driven earlier compendia such as *Pioneers*. So I wrote the lives of the landscape architects—of whom there were eight, owing to Ellen Shipman's tangential work on two projects—as separate but related stories to alternate with the stories of the landscapes themselves. (This alternating structure had to accommodate Warren H. Manning's involvement in two of the places featured in Part I; readers will quickly understand the logic of the progression.) Each of these

chapters, as well as the introduction and prologue, was conceptualized as an independent essay, but each relates closely to the others, and they are cumulative in impact. The question of how best to integrate Carol's new images with approximately 350 historical plans, photographs, and drawings was solved by Jonathan Lippincott, who came up with a book design that juxtaposes traditionally illustrated text with full-page reproductions of Carol's exhibition photographs.

Many readers will recognize in the title of this book a play on the phrase *genius of the place* or *genius loci*, which was used by the English landscape gardeners of the eighteenth century, in one particularly well-known instance by Alexander Pope, who wrote a poem about the genius of the place—an ancient notion that each setting possesses its own jinn which should be consulted in the matter of design. (The word *genius*, of course, also can mean special talent, and I intend that implication, too.) I use the term *country place era* in the subtitle since it has become familiar as a result of Norman Newton's 1971 text, *Design on the Land*. I prefer it to "Golden Age" or "Gilded Age" because these terms do not address the intensified focus on countryside that sharpened during these years, which I believe lies at the heart of this story. There were other choices about terms that should be addressed here as well.

Throughout the book I have tried to discriminate in my use of the words *garden* and *landscape*, using the former to denote a delineated space given over to ornamental horticulture, and the second to denote a larger area that may or may not have been deliberately designed. These definitions square with those of Warren Manning, who wrote about them in his essay "The Purposes and Practice of Landscape Architecture"—although Manning frequently talked of wild gardens of many hundreds of acres. In his article, he carries the distinction, characteristically, to celestial realms: "The word 'garden' implies reference to a limited defined and exclusive space, and may be used in this way antithetically to the word 'landscape,' the application of which is so comprehensive that it may take in houses, lawns, gardens, orchards, meadows, mountains, and even the sky, with the stars, to the remotest nebulae."

The word *nature* appears on many pages of this book, first in the nineteenth-century incarnation as *Nature*, continuing through the very last essays by Lockwood de Forest and Fletcher Steele. In the writings of Emerson, Pückler, Olmsted, and even Charles Eliot, Nature meant more or less the same thing—a reference to the divine as manifest in the tangible world. But by the end of the century, when some landscape designs were identified as *naturalistic* (largely to distinguish them from *formal* designs), the term had become more variable, depending on context and also the political intention of the writer. I believe that it gained importance among landscape architects largely as a means of contrasting the outdoor world of nature with that of "insistent man-made conditions," as Hubbard and Kimball wrote in *An Introduction to the Study of Landscape Design*. In their 1917 text, these important chroniclers of the profession repeatedly linked *nature* with the word *wild*, and *landscape* with the words *unspoiled*, *untrammeled*, and *untouched*. It was only during the country place era that Americans came to a wide understanding that they could permanently spoil nature, and the implications were profound, given that most believed, as few do today, that only wild, unspoiled nature could "fulfill and complete their being," as Hubbard and Kimball put it.

Among the most eloquent proselytizers of this idea and of the notion that stewardship of nature is humankind's unwavering responsibility was Liberty Hyde Bailey, who wrote about it in his 1915 classic, *The Holy Earth*: "The sacredness to us of the earth is intrinsic and inherent. It lies in our necessary relationship and in the duty imposed upon us to have dominion, and to exercise ourselves even against our own interest. We may not waste that which is not ours. To live in sincere relations with the company of created things and with conscious regard for the support of all men now and yet to come, must be of the essence of righteousness." The landscape architects featured in *A Genius for Place* shared Bailey's belief, and their written and built work express the same Olmstedian regard "for the support of all . . . now and yet to come." My hope is that these practitioners, the landscapes they created, and the ideas motivating them encourage renewed consideration of this perspective.

INTRODUCTION

He was a great lover of God's Out-of-doors & the beauty of Nature, with a technical knowledge & appreciation of native American scenery. Remember that in all these matters that are commonplace to-day, and many others of which I have not spoken, he was practically the first man to think out, and tell the people. From this man's work sprang my profession.

—Fletcher Steele, letter to his father, 1912

When he retired from active practice in 1895, Frederick Law Olmsted (1822–1903) was considered the father of American landscape architecture. In the opinion of the critic and historian Mariana Griswold Van Rensselaer, he could also lay claim to being "the most remarkable artist yet born in America." Olmsted's landscape achievements were well known to Americans. They comprised great urban parks and park systems—including Central Park, in New York City—as well as parkways, suburbs, campuses, institutional grounds, scenic reservations, and private estates throughout the United States and Canada. Olmsted also figured in a diffuse, international Romantic movement that in-

cluded painters, composers, poets, and, in Germany, the landscape gardener Prince Hermann Ludwig Heinrich von Pückler-Muskau (1815–1871). These individuals shared a sense of the divine in nature—or Nature, as even the proto-modernist Fletcher Steele tended to write. Such principles were communicated directly to the practitioners who worked with Olmsted throughout his career and were also expressed in his published reports, correspondence, and in works written about him.

During the four decades that followed Olmsted's death, the art and profession of landscape architecture responded to a host of divergent concerns, primary among which was a sense of America's rising stature as a political and artistic world power. Accompanying this rise was the continuing loss of scenery that had for much of the nineteenth century played a critical role in defining American identity. As increasing numbers of new country estates were commissioned by an expanding upper class, they began to assume importance as artistic vehicles that would aggrandize their owners' cultural status and also, in the tradition of Olmsted, preserve and celebrate passages of distinctive landscape beauty. Throughout this tumultuous period of change and growth, the foundations that had defined the profession in its infancy continued to ground, guide, and inform it.

Residential designs from the American country place era—a period defined by the landscape historian Norman Newton as falling between the late 1890s and the 1930s— have not been studied with much rigor or enthusiasm. American landscape architects, in particular, have been eager to distance themselves from the notion that the profession might be seen, in Newton's words, as "geared solely to magnificence for the opulent few."[1] Other factors have also led to scholarly oversight. Many of era's important practitioners were women, and because women's work in this field was marginalized, their accomplishments have largely been ignored. Newton's own reference to "that great lady Mrs. Farrand" hardly bolstered the stature of Beatrix Jones Farrand, one of the founders of the American Society of Landscape Architects.[2] Then, too, Americans have long struggled with a sense of the inadequacy of their own cultural achievements, particularly in relation to England and Europe. One tendency has been to interpret the landscape designs of the era as pale imitations of European prototypes.

The pendulum of changing taste has also affected our judgment. In the years after World War II, the landscapes of the country place era were rejected by modernist perspectives that favored Bauhaus principles—and thus began an eclipse analogous to the devaluation suffered by the now celebrated paintings of the Hudson River School. Documentation from the period has also served to confuse. Many of the published photographs of its best-known examples emphasized the architectural components that typified geometric passages rather than the natural features, pastoral spatial configurations, and long views that were also vital elements in these designs. Only by studying the full range of photographs, plans, drawings, correspondence, published writings, sequences of development, and the sites themselves has it been possible to assess the scope and integrative complexity of these designs.

The lack of published work on the landscape architecture of the era is striking in comparison with architectural criticism of the period. In addition to several fine monographs on individual architects, three surveys on American country houses have appeared in recent years, two volumes with the title *The American Country House,* one by Clive Aslet and one by Roger W. Moss, and *The Architect and the American Country House* by Mark Alan Hewitt. Hewitt's book is both ambitious and rigorous, and it grapples productively with the complex artistic and intellectual forces that shaped the era. None of these books, however, takes into full account the centrality of landscape to the country place phenomenon.

The first book-length study of an American landscape architect from the country place era was Leonard K. Eaton's 1965 monograph on Jens Jensen, which argued persuasively for Jensen's importance as a great American artist. Eaton's treatment wove together social and political context as a backdrop for understanding artistic principles and, in this regard, set a high standard. (In the years since, Jensen has received more extensive and more measured analysis, notably by Robert E. Grese, whose publications have provided support for the recovery of Jensen's Chicago parks.) Keith N. Morgan's seminal book on Charles A. Platt, published in 1985, illuminated another key figure of the era, and, in its art historical methodology, it, too, set an example. Since then, a small number of monographs of widely varying quality have been published on other practitioners of the time, illuminating aspects of individual careers. *Pioneers of American Landscape Design*, which Charles A. Birnbaum and I coedited, published in 2000, an encyclopedic overview of 160 nineteenth- and early twentieth-century horticulturists, planners, educators, authors, and practitioners, has had a far-ranging impact on the field of American landscape studies by suggesting the scope of the era's achievements.

However, only two surveys have focused specifically on the landscape designs of the period. The first of these is *The Golden Age of American Gardens* (1989) by Mac Griswold and Eleanor Weller, which has provided invaluable support for the preservation of many important gardens and has helped strengthen the landscape preservation movement that began in the National Park Service in the 1970s. The wider time frame of Denise Otis's *Grounds for*

Pleasure (2002) has also yielded information and insight about the history of the era, but this work, too, focuses exclusively on gardens. Neither volume interprets estate landscapes in the context of the broader landscape architectural concerns that shaped the great public parks, institutional grounds, and suburbs during this time. One of my goals in *A Genius for Place* is to illuminate these connections. Another is to propose an understanding of American country place landscape designs as imaginative responses to both the heady artistic atmosphere of the era and the vital, Olmstedian regard for the spirit of the place that endured through it.

By the 1890s American cities were dirty, overcrowded, and rife with disease, circumstances that had developed as factories and sweatshops proliferated and millions of immigrants poured into urban centers that were unprepared to provide decent workplaces or housing for them.[3] Many wealthy citizens sought refuge in new estates constructed in scenic enclaves and on the outskirts of cities made accessible via new rail lines. The estates provided escape from urban squalor, but they also carried ideological weight for their owners—members of a rising and culturally insecure plutocracy which was acquiring property primarily as a manifestation of status, a demonstration of taste and leisure.

The enormous influx of European immigrants that began with waves of Germans and Irish in the mid-nineteenth century not only strained the physical fabric of American cities, it also threatened the cultural hegemony of the descendants of British and Dutch families who had dominated America's social order for decades. As increasing numbers of immigrants, including many European Jews, made their way into positions of economic and political power, country life provided one means of stabilizing exclusionary social networks and reinforcing cultural dominance. Behind the American country life movement was a patrician literary notion that had preoccupied members of the eighteenth-century British and French upper classes, individuals who, as Richard Hofstadter observed, "enjoyed a classical educa-tion, read pastoral poetry, experimented with breeding stock, and owned plantations or country estates."[4] Transplanted to the United States, this ideal had been elaborated by Thomas Jefferson and others who preached the moral benefits of the gentleman-farmer's life and also lived versions of it.[5] Close communion with nature was believed to promote a wholesomeness impossible for the "depraved" population of cities.

By the turn of the twentieth century country life had taken on an aura of romance and nostalgia, a consequence of profound changes in the countryside itself, which was being developed at an increasing pace. Although more Americans still lived on farms than in cities in 1900, twenty years later the opposite would be true. As the nation became increasingly industrialized, the hold of the agrarian myth on its citizens became more tenacious.

The question of where to site the new country estates weighed heavily on the minds of both the prospective owners and the professionals who typically advised them. Landscape architects were drawn to parcels with majestic trees, rich soil, varied natural beauty, and long views to water or mountains.[6] Not surprisingly, practical considerations, such as proximity to urban workplaces and to the estates of family members, friends, and business colleagues, were important to clients. Changing fashions also played a role. The French hauteur of Newport, Rhode Island, which had been favored through the 1890s, lost appeal as other settings acquired specialized chic. Lenox, Massachusetts, attracted literary figures, while Bar Harbor, Maine, drew appreciators of rugged natural beauty. During the 1920s, Gatsbyesque types flocked to Long Island, while bohemian artists mixed with ranch owners in Montecito, California. Some country places were used as weekend retreats, some were occupied seasonally, and others functioned as primary residences—from Long Island, wealthy estate owners could yacht to offices in Manhattan—but all were sited on properties, as the architectural historian Fiske Kimball wrote, "free of the arid blocks and circumscribed 'lots' of the city, where one [could] enjoy the informality of nature out-of-doors."[7]

That great numbers of private estates were built with such rapidity was primarily a consequence of the rise in wealth that accompanied the growth of big business. The large American companies that flourished in the years after the Civil War were generally of three kinds—railroads, manufacturing, and banking—differing markedly from the small, family-run operations that had fueled the antebellum economy. The emerging corporations were funded differently, too, underwritten by huge amounts of capital, particularly after 1890, when it became possible to sell securities, or stock. These new and very successful companies grew in two specific ways, often in combination.

Vertical growth was characterized by the development of related functions—transporting raw material as well as producing it (as did William Gwinn Mather, president of Cleveland-Cliffs Iron Company, who maintained rail lines and a large fleet of steamships as well as mines) or distributing a product as well as manufacturing it (as did Frank A. Seiberling, who opened hundreds of retail outlets to sell his wing-foot brand of tires). In one of the most far-reaching examples of this phenomenon, Henry Ford acquired control of mines, forests, and South American rubber plantations along with shipping lines, railroads, and factories. In one publicity stunt, Ford Motor Company manufactured a car from raw materials in less than five days.

Horizontal growth resulted from mergers among companies that produced the same products or services. These were often accomplished by cutthroat means, as smaller businesses were driven to sell out to large ones. Such deals were carried out under the structure of sprawling trusts, the best known of which was the amalgamation of companies led by John D. Rockefeller, Standard Oil.[8]

The phrase "conspicuous consumption," coined by the economist Thorstein Veblen in his 1899 book *The Theory of the Leisure Class*, characterized the ostentatious display that typically, although not always, accompanied the vast wealth accumulated through these processes. In Veblen's scheme, the descendents of Cornelius Vanderbilt, heirs to a great shipping, railroad, and real estate fortune, qualified as the quintessential consumers, having between 1876 and 1917 constructed seventeen mansions among them—one

of these, Biltmore, near Asheville, North Carolina, the largest American house ever built.[9] Those with more modest fortunes also prospered, and their numbers steadily increased as well. By 1910, Mark Alan Hewitt observes, "there were 15,190 families with incomes of more than $50,000—an amount defining an urban-industrial upper class capable of having country houses."[10]

The first book on the subject of the architectural phenomenon was *American Estates and Gardens*, published in 1904. The author, Barr Ferree, described the new American country house as "sumptuous . . . built at large expense, often palatial in its dimensions, furnished in the richest manner and placed on an estate, perhaps large enough to admit of independent farming operations, and in most cases with a garden which is an integral part of the architectural scheme."[11] By 1915 some authors, like Samuel Howe, who wrote *American Country Houses of To-Day*, were emphasizing landscape. "Probably the one word 'setting,' has done more to revolutionize the architectural outlook than any other," Howe noted. In his view, "An [architect] says to his client, 'We divide your money into two parts. We call one part the pudding, the other the sauce. The pudding is the house, whatever style you desire; the sauce is that which goes to make it palatable, the little piquancy, the perfume, the immeasurable romance and the big sweep of the thing, that is known as the setting.'"[12]

The design of the new American houses was the purview of architects, many of whom had been trained at the École des Beaux-Arts in a method that manipulated line, mass, and ornament independently of style. Richard Morris Hunt, the first American architect to train in Paris, designed Biltmore according to Beaux-Arts principles using a stylistic vocabulary defined as Modern French. But Hunt and his American colleagues were capable of designing in a wide range of historical idioms that presented clients with a bewildering array of choices. Aspects of divergent styles were sometimes commingled into a blend that conveyed a sophisticated awareness, an approach often applied by Charles Platt, whose versatility enabled him to design both residences and grounds.

In most cases, however, the services of landscape architects were sought for the complex tasks associated with the design, building, and planting of the surrounding landscape. These included advising on the purchase of property; siting new residences; creating general plans for the arrangement of the grounds, including roads, bridges, formal and wild gardens, reflecting pools, fountains, terraces, bowling greens, golf courses, tennis courts, swimming pools, greenhouses, garages, barns, stables, and worker cottages; designing landscape features such as meadows, promontories, ponds, and lakes; designing planting compositions; and locating nursery stock and supervising the installation of plants.

The increasingly complicated compositional goals of American landscape architects depended on an ability to predict growth in shrubs and trees and the resultant visual effects through different seasons, so it is not surprising that most practitioners became extremely knowledgeable about plants. Many clients were also horticulturally sophisticated; women in particular were often accomplished gardeners who demanded large gardens in which to showcase their specialties. As hundreds of new species were made available through plant-hunting expeditions in Asia and the western United States, American landscape architects eagerly expanded their horticultural repertories. Most followed the lead of Olmsted's office in using both natives and imports, but even among those practitioners who preferred native plants, compositions typically included a wide range of species. American wild gardens became popular during the era, in part because they could accommodate such large numbers of species.

The work of designing, building, and planting American estates was spelled out in detailed plans, often numbering in the hundreds, undertaken with an eye to overall artistic intention. Often projects stretched over years, or even decades. In the most ambitious commissions, such as George Washington Vanderbilt's Biltmore or Frank A. Seiberling's Stan Hywet Hall in Akron, Ohio, huge contingents of workers needed to be housed, construction crews supervised, temporary railroads built, and nurseries installed. Budgets were often immense, and administrative acumen in managing costs and schedules was critical to success.

The term *landscape architect* was adopted by Olmsted and Vaux in 1865 when they formed Olmsted, Vaux & Co., Landscape Architects, and they continued to use it in their reports until 1872, when they dissolved their partnership. The following year, H. W. S. Cleveland published *Landscape Architecture, as Applied to the Wants of the West*, a small book whose cover was emblazoned with large gold letters that seemed to announce the ascendancy of the profession.[13] The term was still a subject of heated discussion when the first professional organization in the United States convened in 1899. Among the ten charter members of the American Society of Landscape Architects, both Warren H. Manning and Beatrix Jones (later Farrand) referred to themselves as landscape gardeners, and Farrand continued to do so her entire life. That the profession welcomed her—and, soon afterward, one other woman, Elizabeth Bullard—into its ranks was an indicator of the field's unusual openness to women, as well as the prominent professional status that Farrand and many other women were able to achieve at the time.[14]

The era's landscape practitioners, both men and women, considered themselves artists as well as business people, and they regarded the work they produced—estates, parks, playgrounds, campuses, boulevard systems, and even town and city plans—as fine art, of the same stature as painting, sculpture, and architecture. The first university programs for landscape architecture were established in 1900 at Harvard University and Massachusetts Institute of Technology (MIT), and others soon followed, most of them founded in conjunction with agricultural programs at land-grant colleges in the Midwest. While these new programs increased the numbers of trained professionals, they had a formulizing effect on the work of their graduates. Many of the era's most stylistically adventurous practitioners were products of apprenticeships rather than degree-granting institutions.

Competition among landscape architects for wealthy clients was keen, and one of the most effective methods of attracting them was by publishing in specialized magazines lavishly illustrated with photographs (made possible by the new halftone printing technology), often commissioned by the practitioners themselves. Residential work was avidly sought because it paid well, but landscape architects valued it for other reasons too. Estate commissions were typically less constricted than civic or institutional projects, which were invariably overseen by committees representing wide ranging, sometimes conflicting points of view. With their broad scope, large budgets, and sites of transcendent beauty, country places provided laboratories where, in collaboration with willing clients, practitioners could experiment with design ideas. For those eager to explore aesthetic frontiers, this appeal was particularly strong.

Reform motives had a role as well. Throughout the nineteenth century, landscape design was regarded as a mechanism for improving moral character and, thereby, American civilization. This notion, forcefully articulated by A. J. Downing in his 1841 *Treatise on the Theory and Practice of Landscape Gardening*, was also reflected in such initiatives as rural or garden cemeteries, village improvement societies, and new urban parks. The idea lay at the very heart of all of Olmsted's landscape designs, even those undertaken for private clients. At the close of his long career and despite failing health, Olmsted took on the demands of the Biltmore commission because he considered it to be "a private work of very rare public interest in many ways, of much greater public interest—utility, industrial, political, educational and otherwise . . . than we can define to ourselves."[15]

In the years after Olmsted's retirement, progressive landscape architects frequently utilized the social and business networks of the private clients for whom they were creating country estates to achieve civic work that embodied principles associated with the "Great Awakening," a movement that aimed to ameliorate grim conditions in American cities and to create salutary settings for citizens' lives. With both reform and profit motives in mind, practitioners secured commissions for model subdivisions, company towns, parks and park systems, campuses, asylums, and municipal planning projects—initiatives that had the potential to transform American society.

American landscape architects of the Progressive era also attempted to effect positive social change through publications and lectures aimed at broad audiences. Many were involved in civic organizations that advised on landscape improvements. Many became impassioned conservationists and participated in initiatives to set aside land for public use. On the local level, they argued the benefits of street trees, neighborhood parks, horticultural societies, and "tasteful" design of public buildings. In the tradition of Olmsted, many felt a sharp sense of responsibility about the future of American civilization and were committed to guiding it. Most shared Downing's and Olmsted's sense that the future of America depended on its citizens' connection to land.

By the turn of the century, country life was considered not only salutary but also very fashionable. In 1902 *Architectural Record* reported, somewhat wryly, on its growing appeal: "[Americans] have decided that they do not take enough interest in the country, and now with perhaps even greater enthusiasm, they are preparing to make themselves more familiar with nature. Bird books are being published by the score and sell as well as romantic novels. Books about all kinds of gardens are almost equally in demand, and a hot fight is on between the advocates of the formal and the so-called 'natural' garden. Within the last six months two periodicals devoted to different aspects of country life have been started, and will, we hope, have a most prosperous existence."[16] The magazines were *House and Garden* and *Country Life in America*, and both were indicators of the increasing importance of the new country place commissions from ideological as well economic points of view.[17]

Although it was not founded with the goal in mind, *Country Life* soon became the most influential taste-shaping periodical of the day. Its first editor was Liberty Hyde Bailey, horticulturist, author, and professor at Cornell University, who later edited the massive *Standard Cyclopedia of Horticulture* (1914–1917). Bailey was also editor of the Rural Science Series, an outgrowth of Theodore Roosevelt's Commission on Country Life, which included titles that ranged from *Landscape-Gardening* to *The Potato*. As editor, Bailey explained the purposes of the new publication: "*Country Life in America* is a country magazine for the country man, and for the city man who wants to know the country; it is not a city magazine that sees the country afar off and takes it for granted. We hope that the smell of the soil will be on its pages." Despite this earnest beginning, the magazine was soon publishing articles like "Polo, Ancient and Modern" and "Yachting, A Personal Experience." Within two years Bailey resigned, as the historian Christopher Vernon notes, because "the smell of 'old money,' not the 'smell of the soil,' had come to dominate [its] pages."[18] However, Wilhelm Miller, a young horticulturist who had studied under Bailey at Cornell, continued to work for *Country Life* and wrote frequently on topics related to gardening and design.

Many other magazines, including several from England, such as the English edition of *Country Life*, provided conduits for information about new developments in landscape design. Books by the opinionated magazine editor and proselytizer for wild gardening William Robinson and, later, by the doyenne of the Arts and Crafts garden, Gertrude Jekyll, were also avidly read in America, by general enthusiasts and professionals alike, as was Thomas H. Mawson's *The Art and Craft of Garden Making* (1900).[19]

Charles Platt's *Italian Gardens*, published in 1894, helped propel Italianate formality toward general acceptance, particularly in opposition to Victorian layouts associated with the gardenesque methods derived from J. C. Loudon and his disciple in America, A. J. Downing. One of the most influential books of the period was *American Gardens*, published in 1902 by Guy Lowell, head of the new program of landscape architecture at MIT. An accomplished architect who had graduated from MIT's architecture program and then studied at the École des Beaux-Arts, Lowell was also the son-in-law of Charles Sprague Sargent, founder of the Arnold Arboretum.[20]

Lowell's book added fuel to a rising controversy that lay behind the "hot fight" to which *Architectural Record* referred. It was the first published on American gardens, and although his examples ranged from the Colonial to the neoclassical, all were derived from the "ancient" or geometric tradition of cross-axial plans, symmetrically arranged ornament, clipped hedges, and artificial water features.

Most of the contemporary examples Lowell included were the work of architects closely associated with the American Renaissance, a movement whose crowning moment was the World's Columbian Exposition of 1893. Among the architects represented were McKim, Mead & White, Wilson Eyre Jr., Carrère & Hastings, Little & Browne, Cope & Stewardson, and Frank Miles Day, although Charles Platt received more thorough coverage than any other practitioner.[21]

When *American Gardens* appeared, the dominant professional approach to landscape design in the United States was still closely identified with Olmsted and others who are less well known today. These included H. W. S. Cleveland and Robert Morris Copeland, Cleveland's professional partner and author of *Country Life: A Handbook of Agriculture and Landscape Gardening* (1859), as well as Olmsted's later business partner Jacob Weidenmann, author of *Beautifying Country Homes: A Handbook of Landscape Gardening* (1870).

Among the next half-generation of American practitioners who continued to design in the Olmstedian tradition were Olmsted's brilliant associates Henry Sargent Codman and Charles Eliot (both tragically short-lived, Codman dying in 1893 and Eliot in 1897); Samuel B. Parsons Jr. (a partner in Vaux & Company and landscape architect for the New York City Department of Parks); Ossian Cole Simonds, superintendent of Graceland Cemetery in Chicago and later author of *Landscape-Gardening*; Olmsted's stepson and partner, John Charles Olmsted; his son, Frederick Law Olmsted Jr.; and Downing Vaux, son of Olmsted's first partner, Calvert Vaux. Two influential Olmstedian practitioners who established their own firms at the end of the nineteenth century were Warren H. Manning, who had worked as an assistant to Olmsted, and Jens Jensen, an ardent advocate of native plants soon to be associated with the Prairie School of landscape design. Significant differences existed among these practitioners, but all shared a compositional vocabulary based on tenets of the English school of the Picturesque, a belief that the study of nature was fundamental to their art, and a sense of landscape design as an ameliorative force for the individual psyche.

Lowell, by contrast, traced the inspiration for the gardens in his book to early Rome and then to a second flowering in Renaissance Italy, when Lorenzo de' Medici made his garden into "a museum of sculpture and decoration, so that the grounds became a decorative adjunct to the house." Many of the new American princes of commerce were drawn to this analogy, even if their houses were designed to emulate French châteaux or Tudor mansions. Landscape schemes in these projects were created by clearing and then grading expanses of land into flat planes and connecting the resulting terraces through flights of steps. The terraces, which functionally echoed interior rooms, were defined by architecturally determined features, such as balustrades, walls, and sheared hedges. Sculptural decoration was often lavish. In the most fashionable examples, flower beds filled with old varieties softened insistent geometry. The resulting designs were highly photogenic, and to many new homeowners held in the thrall of the charms of Europe, they spelled cultural authority.[22]

In an influential 1896 article for *Garden and Forest*, Charles Eliot parodied the extremists who were emerging on either side of the stylistic divide, chastising both the "pretentious landscape-gardeners, who prescribe curves for paths . . . as being more 'natural' than straight lines" and the architects who browbeat hapless clients with their recommendations for "straight avenues, terraces, and balustrades, a 'rampe douce' at your door." Eliot observed sympathetically, "It is no wonder that the inquiring public is bewildered. How absurd all this quarreling seems." In his sophisticated view, neither approach addressed the guiding principle of fitness, which Eliot considered fundamental to good design. "Success in achieving the beautiful is to be hoped for only when we bow to the law of nature and follow the appointed way. Special purpose is the root, and fitness for purpose the main stem, of the plant of which beauty is the flower," he concluded.[23] Yet amid the rising tide of estate commissions, Eliot's notion of fitness must have seemed a bit abstract. What was the "special purpose" of the new country places other than to reflect the social stature of their owners?

In *The Art of Landscape Architecture* (1915), one the first books to wrestle comprehensively with the goals and methods of the modern profession, Samuel Parsons proposed an answer that responded to both Olmsted's and Eliot's perspectives. He adhered to the Olmstedian notion that an "undying vitality" in landscape design was to be achieved through studying nature. "Above most other arts," Parsons wrote, "landscape architecture is based on nature, and my own particular function in this book I conceive to be to point out how and why the art should be practiced on natural lines, and something of the degree to which this course, in spite of much seeming divergence, is supported by well-recognized authorities."[24] Parsons, however, also proposed that American practitioners include "personal and human" elements in their work, an idea that he traced to Prince Pückler, whose great park at Muskau Parsons had recently visited and whose *Hints on Landscape Gardening* was soon to be published in an English translation, with an introduction by Parsons. "A natural scene may be beautiful in itself, without change," Parsons wrote, "but change, if it be personal and human in its origin, increases the charm of the place for most people, tenfold. What would Wordsworth's descriptions of nature be without the human note?"[25]

Parsons illustrated his book with many photographs of Muskau and also with shots of Central Park, Goethe's cottage at Weimar, the Boboli gardens, the Villa d'Este (an unusual view that made the villa look as though it were nestled in wilderness), Durham Cathedral, a garden in Japan, several American estates including one of his own design, Skylands, in Ringwood, New Jersey, and "A Picturesque Effect of the Native Dogwood" from the Robert Weeks de Forest estate on Long Island. Throughout, Parsons liberally quotes poets, philosophers, and landscape authorities, many of them German, none at greater length than Pückler.[26]

Parsons concludes his chapter "The Laying Out of a Park or Estate" with an example from Bedford, New York, which he believed perfectly exemplified his point. Although the estate's owner had lived in Italy, Parsons wrote,

> her respect . . . for the thoroughly American quality of the place, its simplicity and quaint natural beauty is great. . . . No Italian gardens and pergolas mar the essentially American beauty of the scene.

Just the little grove, the Bosca, with its rude table and benches and quaint oven in the open made of a few stones, and the herb garden, scarcely anything else Italian, and yet you feel that the owner loves Italy, and remembers Italy, but yet loves America still more with its brave simplicity and its absolutely natural charm.

This makes only one more instance of the supreme value of the application of the good landscape-gardening ideas to "the genius of the place" in all countries and times provided the personality of the owner and his other idiosyncrasies receive due consideration. In this way, one may achieve, at lesser or greater expense, a home the result of many aspirations born of diverse experiences. One may have an English or American or French home bearing evidence of the effects of a strong personality, and yet it may have a touch, by no means overpowering, of a more alien, and possibly more desirable style, whether it be Italian, or Japanese, or clearly semi-tropical in effect. The landscape gardening thus becomes basic and universal in its essential quality, and is at the same time full of personality and human feeling.[27]

In essence, Parsons was recommending an approach inspired in some measure by the personality of the owner—and his or her other idiosyncrasies—grounded in an Olmstedian regard for nature.

Two years later, in their *Introduction to the Study of Landscape Design*, Henry Vincent Hubbard, then an assistant professor at Harvard, and Theodora Kimbell, librarian at Harvard's school of landscape architecture, elaborated Parsons's ideas and christened a true modern "American style." They traced its Picturesque tenets to Humphry Repton and other eighteenth-century English landscape gardeners but distinguished the American approach by its emphasis on a "little-humanized Nature in which a man might lose his consciousness of self," finding in it "much more appreciation [of] the preservation and interpretation of natural character" than the English approach evidenced.[28] Like Parsons, the authors advised landscape ar-

chitects to arrange "natural materials" so that they would express both "the natural character of the landscape" and "harmonies of form, of color, of texture, harmonies of repetition and sequence and balance." They advised that these arrangements should be "as far as is humanly possible, both interpretations of natural character and effective pictorial compositions."[29]

At the conclusion of their chapter "Styles of Landscape Design," the authors turned their attention to the question of adapting foreign styles to American settings, and on this point, also like Parsons, they emphasized the enriching potential of human qualities. "An arrangement of an American country place which suggests an English pastoral landscape has to a man familiar with England an added delight, because it calls to his mind additional remembered beauties; and the recent designs of estates inspired by Italian examples hold for lovers of Italy a pleasure and a unity through association which is no small part of their charm."[30] For Hubbard and Kimbell, however, as for most of the era's twentieth-century practitioners, landscape design was above all an art of composition, a question of arranging elements into an ordered whole. The most philosophically detailed chapter of their book is devoted to this topic, and Denman W. Ross, author of *A Theory of Pure Design* (1907) and *On Drawing and Painting* (1912), is cited as the modern authority on it.

Even before the turn of the century, many American landscape practitioners—including Olmsted—had come to recognize the spatial elegance and artistic versatility of Beaux-Arts design and had begun to grapple with the challenge of integrating elements of this system into designs that also expressed the natural character of a place. They saw that by accommodating a rich sampling of architectural and landscape forms, their clients' estates would reflect owners' personalities, histories, and collections, and thereby achieve the human note recommended by authorities from Wordsworth to Pückler, Parsons, and, eventually, Hubbard and Kimbell. Such passages would satisfy the tastes of well-traveled clients, and European borrowings would also express a brash confidence in the right of American designers to appropriate new forms, a claim that had been forcefully announced by the resplendent example of the Chicago World's Columbian Exposition, whose Beaux-Arts plan was the work of Olmsted and his associate Henry Codman. Passages of geometrically ordered space were also more appropriate to the larger size and mass of Beaux-Arts–influenced residences, which benefited from architectural support on the ground. American practitioners were likewise coming to understand the strong aesthetic and emotional appeal of volumetric space in the landscape, regardless of its form— from the outdoor room to the meadow.

Even as they integrated stylistic influences that kept pace with their clients' and their own evolving tastes, American landscape architects continued to respond to nature in their designs. In laying out new estates of great imaginative force, they preserved and in many cases planted noble trees suggestive of the forests that once covered the continent. They dammed streams to create falls, dug lakes where land was marshy, and flooded quarries to make lagoons. They framed striking vistas and panoramas—to mountains, lakes, oceans, and tree-covered countryside—from sites chosen for such potential. Their designs were the products of an inquiring, experimental spirit that continued through the era, and in some measure helped define it for the profession. The trajectory of these stylistic explorations over the first four decades of the twentieth century is the subject of this book.

A Genius for Place begins with a prologue that traces the design principles and professional lives of Downing, Olmsted, and other nineteenth-century figures as a basis for understanding subsequent generations of American landscape practice. The prologue also includes a discussion of the impact of the gardenesque and its rise through a popular interest in horticulture. Part I chronicles two early American country places, Gwinn in Cleveland, Ohio (c. 1907), and Stan Hywet Hall, in Akron (c. 1914), and the professional backgrounds of their designers, Warren H. Manning (1860–1938), Charles A. Platt (1861–1933), and Ellen Shipman (1869–1950), in a chapter that also looks briefly at the topic of women in the profession. In these projects, nature was deliberately brought into the heart of

the design by framing spectacular views and, conversely, through the extension of geometric features into the surrounding "wildness." Two strong-minded clients, William Gwinn Mather and Frank A. Seiberling, both successful industrialists, played important parts in shaping these landscapes. Their wives, Elizabeth Ring Mather and Gertrude Seiberling, also influenced the designs, in more circumscribed roles related to the flower gardens that were a feature of each.

In Part II, readers will find discussions of three estates from the 1920s, a period that continued to bring wealth to many Americans and a sense of increased artistic possibility in landscape design. Over the course of this decade, American estates began to reflect more specifically the tastes, collections, and travels of their owners. At Dumbarton Oaks in Washington, D.C., Italianate and Beaux-Arts principles were expanded with imaginative Arts and Crafts details and plantings by Beatrix Farrand (1872–1959) for her patrons, Robert Woods and Mildred Barnes Bliss. At Winterthur, outside Wilmington, Delaware, Marian Cruger Coffin (1876–1957) worked with Henry Francis du Pont on a design that merged an ingenious Italianate plan with an expansive wild garden. At the Edsel and Eleanor Ford House, in Grosse Pointe Shores, Michigan, Jens Jensen (1860–1951) designed the most extensive residential landscape of his career, adapting his nature-based approach in some measure to the modernist tastes of Edsel Ford. Increasing familiarity with Beaux-Arts principles allowed these practitioners to integrate complex spatial constructions with passages of nature. Long views over countryside enlivened landscape designs that also featured elements from European architectural traditions imaginatively adapted and recombined.

Part III includes discussions of two landscapes that had their origins in the nineteenth century. The first, Val Verde in Santa Barbara, California, was initially laid out as Días Felicitas by Bertram Grosvenor Goodhue and later developed in the 1920s and 1930s by the California-based landscape architect Lockwood de Forest Jr. (1896–1949) for his client Wright S. Ludington, a painter and collector who saw in Val Verde the potential for a Hadrianic villa. The book's culminating discussion focuses on Naumkeag in Stockbridge, Massachusetts, originally designed by Nathan Franklin Barrett for the family of Joseph Hodges Choate, with continuing developments from the 1920s through the 1950s by Fletcher Steele (1885–1971) for Choate's daughter Mabel—a New Woman, gardener, and antique collector who was Steele's artistic partner in the design process. In these projects, both de Forest and Steele began experimenting with deliberately abstract forms in designs that struck a vibrant balance between modernism and a response to the spirit of the place.

A GENIUS FOR PLACE

PROLOGUE

Neither the professional Landscape Gardener, nor the amateur, can hope for much success in realizing the nobler effects of the art, unless he first make himself master of the natural character, or prevailing expression of the place to be improved.

—A. J. Downing, *A Treatise on the Theory and Practice of Landscape Gardening*, 1841

I n the American colonies, wealthy landowners laying out the grounds of stately new homes inevitably turned to England for inspiration. In particular, they looked to the late seventeenth-century gardens of William and Mary, the symmetrical layouts of which were amalgamations of Dutch, French, and Italian traditions. From the Governor's Palace in Williamsburg, Virginia, to the governor's garden in Milton, Massachusetts, to Middleton Place, near Charleston, South Carolina, similar combinations of cross-axial plans, sharply delineated beds, and close-clipped ornamentals structured the layouts of colonial estates. The most authoritative design guide of the period was *The Gardener's Dictionary* written by Phillip Miller in 1731. Alice G. B. Lockwood, author of *Gardens of Colony and State*, pointed to Miller's frontispiece—a symmetrical layout, bisected by a canal, with walled orchards and beds—as "the ideal of many a colonial garden."[1] Such models continued to guide high-style American landscape design well into the nineteenth century, even as gardening fashions in England evolved toward the softer lines of the Picturesque. (Fig. P.1)

There were occasional exceptions to these general stylistic preferences. The garden historian Therese O'Malley, for example, notes that a set of drawings for prospective layouts of the grounds of the Elias Hasket Derby house in Salem, Massachusetts, c. 1799, offered three alternatives, "a range of possibilities . . . from the bilaterally symmetrical garden to the wilderness outside the door."[2] Elements of George Washington's layout for Mount Vernon also departed from the widespread preference for the geometric, as did Thomas Jefferson's Monticello, which, too, emphasized aspects of the Picturesque integrated with a treatment suitable to the American setting and climate.[3] (Fig. P.2) Monticello was sited with a view of many thousands of acres of Virginia forest, "a rich mantle under the eye, mountains, forests, rocks, rivers," as Jefferson wrote. "How sublime to look down upon the

P.1. Frontispiece to *The Gardener's Dictionary* by Phillip Miller. From Alice G. B. Lockwood, *Gardens of Colony and State,* vol. 1, 1931.

P.2. Monticello, aerial view from southwest. Courtesy Monticello/Thomas Jefferson Foundation, Inc.

workhouse of Nature to see her clouds, hail, snow, rain, thunder, all fabricated at our feet."[4]

Over the course of the nineteenth century, the preference for naturalistic design grew in the United States, supported by Transcendentalist notions that regarded Nature as morally edifying—as Emerson wrote, "the organ through which the universal spirit speaks to the individual, and strives to lead back the individual to it."[5] Nature worship was not strictly an American phenomenon, of course. Emerson's concept of God's immanence in the natural world was similar to the Romantic ideas expressed in the work of Wordsworth, Rousseau, Goethe, Friedrich, and many other contemporary poets, painters, and philosophers. In England, France, and Germany realignments in landscape design were also taking place,

also in response to rising industrialization and the concomitant loss of wilderness.

In 1831 the layout of a new cemetery, Mount Auburn, outside Boston, was overseen by General Henry A. S. Dearborn, who devised a Picturesque plan that accentuated the views and varied, hilly terrain of the site. (Fig. P.3) Forest settings with great trees and sylvan ponds made a startling contrast to typical American graveyards, which were filled with rows of slate slabs marked by Death's-head skulls. Soon other American communities followed Boston's lead, creating their own "rural" cemeteries: Laurel Hill in Philadelphia (1836), Green-Wood in Brooklyn (1838), Spring Grove in Cincinnati (1845), and Cave Hill in Louisville (1848)—and the trend continued through the nineteenth century.[6]

In addition to the expected mourners (and the graves' celebrity residents), each of these wooded havens attracted throngs of less melancholic visitors, ordinary citizens seeking relief from crowded and dirty cities. Their picnics and solitary, soul-replenishing walks presaged a role for the large urban parks whose value would soon be argued in the New York press by the poet and journalist William Cullen Bryant and others. Another leading voice in the campaign for a park for America's largest city was A. J. Downing—the nurseryman, landscape gardener, and horticulturist from Newburgh whose 1841 *Treatise on the The-*

ory and Practice of Landscape Gardening had become the most influential book on landscape design in America.

Downing had begun his book as a series of essays on trees, but he came to realize, as he wrote in the preface, the "want of some *leading principles*" for those Americans who wished to "embellish" their country places. These he felt a strong imperative to provide, for, in his opinion, the future of the young country was at stake.[7] Keenly aware of the restlessness of America's population, which was even then beginning to abandon the countryside for more prosperous lives in cities, Downing believed that the "great tendency towards constant change" opposed social and domestic happiness and that a return to country life should be actively fostered. Attractive landscapes would encourage this return. "Whatever, therefore, leads man to assemble the comforts and elegancies of life around his habitation," Downing reasoned, "tends to increase local attachments, and renders domestic life more delightful; thus not only augmenting his own enjoyment, but strengthening his patriotism, and making him a better citizen."[8] In taste, Downing saw a civilizing force and the future of America.

Downing envisioned the ideal domesticated landscape as a villa that inhabited a middle ground between the city, with its frenzied pace and moral dangers, and the still-wild frontier. New railroads and other transportation technologies such as the steam engine had made the separation of workplace and home feasible for the first time, and merchants, doctors, and lawyers began to populate new rural communities outside larger cities. One such community was Newburgh, where Downing and his neighbors lived in villas on the Hudson River and new train and steamboat lines provided access to Manhattan.

The landscape style that Downing's prescribed for America was the "Modern, Natural, or Irregular," an adaptation of the Picturesque that had risen to favor in England in the second half of the eighteenth century, in which an estate landscape is laid out as a series of pastoral and forest scenes—the same approach, in broad strokes, that had inspired Dearborn at Mount Auburn. Downing sought to adapt the principles of this movement to horticultural conditions in the United States, at a scale appro-

P.3. *Cemetery of Mount Auburn*, engraving by W. H. Bartlett, 1839. From *American Scenery; or, Land, Lake, and River Illustrations of Transatlantic Nature* (London: George Virtue, 1840). Courtesy Mount Auburn Cemetery Archives.

priate to an emerging middle class, with an emphasis on practical use or "fitness." Downing identified the English landscape gardener William Kent as the "leader of the class," a spokesman for the complete reform in taste that had been proposed in theory by the essayist Joseph Addison. Downing cites the well-known verse Alexander Pope sent to Richard Boyle, then earl of Burlington, who was laying out his land at Chiswick (with Kent's help). Pope's lines emphasized, in Downing's words, "the study of *nature*, the genius of the place."[9]

> Consult the Genius of the Place in all,
> That tells the Waters or to rise, or fall,
> Or helps th'ambitious Hill the heav'ns to scale,
> Or scoops in circling Theatres the Vale,
> Calls in the Country, catches opening Glades,
> Joins Willing Woods, and varies Shades from Shades,
> Now breaks, or now directs, th'intending Lines,
> Paints as you plant, and as you work, Designs.

Downing did not spell out the precise application of these theories. Like Jefferson, he alluded to a vision of the garden already extant in the landscape—in Downing's case, the lush growth along the Hudson River valley—which he believed could be revealed through removal of excess plants. "Much of the effect of the finest park, carefully laid out and planted in the modern style, is obtained, by judiciously managing the materials, of which nature has here been so extremely prodigal."[10] Downing, however, was also a successful nursery owner, so it is not surprising that he also felt a strong rapport with the ideas of John Claudius Loudon (1783–1843), a Scottish landscape gardener and author who promoted a gardenesque method of planting that prescribed wide spacing which would facilitate the growth of perfect specimens. Engravings in the *Treatise* demonstrate various conjunctions of this method with the Picturesque, all of them emphasizing the importance of setting and view. (Fig. P. 4)

Downing argued his case for the new Modern style by

P.4. Frontispiece to A. J. Downing, *A Treatise on the Theory and Practice of Landscape Gardening,* 1841.

P.5. "The Geometric style, from an old print," from Downing, *Treatise.*

posing its virtues against the staid rigors of the "ancient" approach. "The beauties elicited by the ancient style of gardening were those of regularity, symmetry, and the display of laboured art," he wrote dismissively. "These were attained in a merely mechanical manner, and usually involved little or no theory. The geometrical form and lines of the buildings, were only extended and carried out, in the garden. . . . In short, to lay out a garden in the geometric style, was little more than a formal routine."[11] (Fig. P.5) Like many of his American contemporaries, Downing also saw imperialistic overtones in formal design. "The value of art, of power, and of wealth, were at once easily and strongly shown by an artificial arrangement of all the materials; an arrangement the more striking, as it differed most widely from nature."[12] Later, he elaborated, "It was only after the superior interest of a more natural manner was enforced by men of genius, that beauty of expression was recognized, and Landscape Gardening was raised to the rank of fine art."[13] Downing's emphasis on the patrician origins of the Modern approach undoubtedly appealed to his upper-class readers, in particular. He traced its roots to "the poet, the painter, and the tasteful scholar, rather than . . . the practical man," pointing to the Vaucluse of Petrarch, Tasso's garden of Armida, and the Vale of Tempe as described by Aelian.[14]

Soon many Picturesque landscapes were laid out along the Hudson River. Some were designed by professionals like Downing. Others were the work of staff gardeners, such as Ferdinand Mangold, who was employed at Lyndhurst (then known as The Knoll), near Tarrytown, where he created a Picturesque setting for the Gothic revival mansion designed years earlier, by A. J. Davis. (Fig. P.6) The argument for nature-based design in America was coming from other quarters, too.

One who shared Downing's keen interest in a new landscape style was the poet and essayist Ralph Waldo Emerson, who even more than Downing distrusted the geometric as an expression of power and wealth. Emerson had been instrumental in the development of an "organic" approach at Sleepy Hollow Cemetery in Concord, Massachusetts, where, in 1855, Horace William Shaler Cleveland (1814–1900), in collaboration with his partner

P.7. Minnehaha Falls, c. 1880. Courtesy Minnesota Historical Society.

P.6. Lyndhurst, Tarrytown, N.Y., view of Hudson River from roof. Library of Congress, Prints and Photographs Division, HABS NY, 60-TARY, 1A-32.

Robert Morris Copeland, consciously attempted to conserve the wooded landscape as part of the design. Emerson's consecration address informed the audience that "the 'lay and the look of the land' had suggested the cemetery's design, and that art had been employed only to bring out the site's 'natural advantages.'"[15] Cleveland would go on to apply this aesthetic approach in suburban grounds, parks, park systems, and subdivisions, moving westward over the years, to Chicago and eventually to Minneapolis. There he continued to promote the principle of "natural advantages," such as Minnehaha Falls, which he used as the centerpiece of his design for the city's largest park. (Fig. P.7)

Cleveland's approach, grounded in a respect for natural conditions and a celebration of American scenery,

closely reflected the views of another New England associate, Henry Wadsworth Longfellow, whose book-length poem *The Song of Hiawatha* (written in 1855, the same year Sleepy Hollow was consecrated) spoke to the potency of the native landscape in shaping American spirit and identity.[16] American Romanticism, which saw the physical realities of the landscape—soil, rock, trees, and water—as manifestations of the divine, would continue to influence landscape design.

Nine years after the publication of the *Treatise*, Downing traveled to England to search for an architectural partner for his expanding practice. (He had attempted to persuade A. J. Davis to join him in this role, regularizing their informal association, but Davis had declined.) In London he met Calvert Vaux (1824–1895), a young architect who had cultivated a strong feeling for landscape through hiking and sketching the English countryside. The two felt an immediate rapport, and Vaux agreed to accompany Downing back to Newburgh, where he became his assistant and, a year later, his professional partner. At this junc-

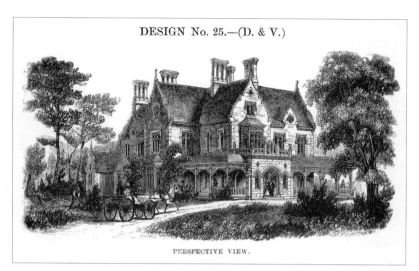

DESIGN No. 25.—(D. & V.)

PERSPECTIVE VIEW.

P.8. Springside, Matthew Vassar estate, Poughkeepsie, N.Y. From Calvert Vaux, *Villas and Cottages,* 1857.

ture, the prolific Downing had published three books in addition to the *Treatise,* one on fruit culture and two on the architecture of country houses.

By 1852 the thriving partnership had secured several important private and public commissions, including improvements to Springside, the estate of Matthew Vassar, in Poughkeepsie, New York, several country houses and grounds in the Hudson River valley, and houses in Newport and Washington, D.C. (Fig. P.8) Downing also continued work on an earlier commission for the public grounds between the Capitol and the White House. His remarkably promising career came to a tragic end that year when, en route to Washington, the steamboat he was aboard caught fire and he drowned in the Hudson attempting to rescue other passengers.

In the years after Downing's widely mourned death, Vaux continued to practice, designing both private and public works, guided, in some measure, by ideas he had developed with his former partner. In 1856 he moved his family and his practice to New York City, and the following year he approached Frederick Law Olmsted, the recently appointed superintendent of the as yet undeveloped Central Park, to invite him to collaborate on an entry.[17] (Although the park would be open to people of all classes, many citizens were dislocated in the process of clearing the landscape to prepare for it.[18]) Olmsted and Vaux had met only once, at Newburgh, but they found their ideas

in sympathy and, over the next several months, they worked together on what they called the "Greensward" plan. (Fig. P.9)

Their layout comprised several remarkable features including emotionally transporting scenery reminiscent of rural landscapes in England and Olmsted's native New England. The partners relied particularly on the effect of pastoral meadows, grassy clearings with undulating boundaries defined by masses of trees. Olmsted also designed passages of irregular, picturesque beauty, rocky hillsides topped with soaring trees and cloaked with vines, the largest of which was the Ramble. (Fig. P.10) "By exploiting such optical characteristics as the play of light and shade in the shadows cast by trees across a sunlit meadow, the atmospheric haze of a distant umbrageous horizon line, and the mystery suggested by an intricate fringe of vines screening a shadowy entrance to a grotto," the landscape historian Elizabeth Barlow Rogers observes, "[Olmsted] created a design idiom that was both naturalistic and Romantic."[19] The partners also worked out an ingenious circulation system that separated horses, carriages, and pedestrians—facilitated by many bridges and underpasses designed by Vaux—providing visitors escape from the commotion and dangers of horse traffic.[20] (Fig. P.11) Central Park soon began attracting throngs of pleasure-seekers, few of whom were knowledgeable about landscape style but who found in the new park welcome relief from the pressures of the crowded city. The first public park in the United States, it was also, remarkably, Olmsted's first professional landscape effort. In the years following the Civil War, many other North American cities would commission Olmsted and Vaux to design similar urban oases. Other types of parks were being created, too.

In 1865 Olmsted was called upon to write a report on the newly acquired Yosemite Valley and Mariposa Big Tree Grove, which Abraham Lincoln had authorized to be transferred to the state of California for "public use, resort and recreation." As chairman of the board of commissioners established to oversee administration of the new parklands, Olmsted presented both a theory of use and a philosophy of leisure, one based on the notion that con-

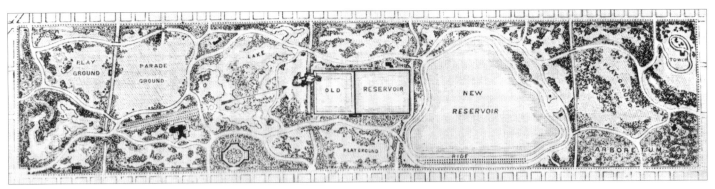

P.9. Olmsted and Vaux Greensward Plan for Central Park, 1857. From Norman T. Newton, *Design on the Land*, 1971.

P.11. Central Park, bridge designed by Calvert Vaux. Harvard GSD.

P.10. Central Park, Ramble. NYPL.

tact with nature was critically important for the character of people in a rapidly urbanizing society. In vivid and moving terms, he describes a valley "with a series of groves of magnificent trees, and meadows of the most varied, luxuriant and exquisite herbage, through which meanders a broad stream of the clearest water, rippling over a pebbly bottom, and eddying among banks of ferns and rushes; sometimes narrowed into sparkling rapids and sometimes expanding into placid pools which reflect the wondrous heights on either side."[21] In this and other reports, Olmsted was not advocating for wilderness for its own sake but rather the principle of making beautiful scenery accessible to the nation's citizens. The complexities in store for America's national parks might have taxed

even Olmsted's imagination. At midcentury, the U.S. population stood at about 31 million; by the time Congress established the National Park Service in 1916, it had tripled. The agrarian nation was well on its way to becoming an urban one.

The young man who would be known as the father of American landscape architecture had had a restless coming of age. After an unhappy period as a clerk in a dry-goods store, he journeyed to China and then apprenticed on a farm in western New York state. In time, his father bought him his own spread at Sachem's Head, near New Haven, Connecticut, but he soon traded it for another on

Staten Island, where the soil was more promising for the practice of scientific agriculture, his vocation at the time. Olmsted was not a particularly happy farmer, and in 1850 he leaped at the chance to travel to England with his brother, John, then a student at Yale, and their mutual friend Charles Brace. That spring the three young men set out on a walking tour of southern England and Wales, an experience that proved life-altering for Frederick.

He chronicled the trip in a series of letters, published in 1852 as a book, *Walks and Talks of an American Farmer in England*. One of the highlights of the text is Olmsted's encounter with the English countryside after a spring rain, a passage that provides a glimpse into a soul transported by Wordsworthian emotion:

> There we were right in the midst of it! The country—and such a country!—green, dripping, glistening, gorgeous! We stood dumbstricken by its loveliness, as, from the bleak April and bare boughs we had left at home, broke on us that English May—sunny, leafy, blooming May—in an English lane; with hedges, English hedges, hawthorn hedges, all in blossom; homely old farmhouses, quaint farm stables and haystacks; the old church spire over the distant trees; the mild sun beaming through the watery atmosphere.[22]

The English countryside had reawakened Olmsted's early memories of the Connecticut River valley, landscapes that he had explored during long walks with his family. (Fig. P.12) The Connecticut Yankee would consciously integrate the memory of such scenes into his landscape commissions. "In effect," wrote the historian Charles C. McLaughlin, "Olmsted remolded portions of the American landscape into idealized versions of the beautiful countryside of Victorian England."[23]

In *Walks and Talks*, Olmsted outlined the important idea that scenes of landscape beauty could salve the troubled human psyche through "*unconscious* or indirect recreation," and this idea would provide the basis of his theory of landscape architecture. As the Olmsted scholar and biographer Charles E. Beveridge writes, "Characteristically,

he did not look to past canons of taste or the rules of particular gardening styles for his basic approach. . . . His emphasis on the psychological effects of scenery gave his design principles a firm base independent of the 'battle of the styles.' Not aesthetic theory but the very health of the human organism became the touchstone of his art."[24] Olmsted felt that such experiences not only provided respite and bolstered physical well-being, they also improved moral character. This idea became a guiding inspiration in his career as a landscape architect and a motivating force in his residential as well as his park and institutional work.

The trip to England seems also to have invigorated the reformer's conscience that would propel Olmsted's considerable journalistic and administrative achievements.[25] In *Walks and Talks* he writes at length about public education, prison reform, poaching, enclosure, and repeal of the Corn Laws, even while discussing scientific farming, his main theme. His impressions of Eaton Hall, a large estate near Chester, were ambivalent, charged with both excitement about the high-style elements in the landscape design and discomfort at the show of wealth behind it. At Birkenhead Park near Liverpool, newly laid out by Joseph Paxton and Edward Kemp, Olmsted discovered an undertaking better suited to his egalitarian principles.

P.12. Farmington River, near Hartford, Conn., Olmsted's childhood home. Photograph by R. S. De Lamater. NYPL.

As he later wrote, "We want a ground to which people may easily go after their day's work is done, and where they may stroll for an hour, seeing, hearing, and feeling nothing of the bustle and jar of the city put far away from them."[26]

Like Horace Cleveland, Olmsted was part of a middle-class reform movement preoccupied by questions of national identity and cultural self-definition. The leaders of this movement, most of them New England Protestants, possessed a strong and abiding faith in the capacity of the built environment to shape human character. They envisioned urban solutions to the problems of the rapidly emerging industrial city—a product of the new railroad—where increasing disparity between wealth and poverty and dire public health issues threatened the well-being of citizens.[27] In pursuit of change, they made sweeping, at times paternalistic, judgments regarding the future of American civilization.

Underlying all of Olmsted's park work was the notion that the natural or "present" character of a landscape should serve as a basis for its improvement. In formulating this principle, Olmsted saw himself following Humphry Repton and other landscape gardeners of the English Picturesque school. Repton's well-known *Sketches and Hints on Landscape Gardening* opened with a statement that Olmsted and Downing, too, both embraced: "All rational improvement of grounds, is, necessarily, founded on a due attention to the character and situation of the place to be improved." Beveridge points out that at the end of his long life, Olmsted was still reflecting on this principle when he confided to Vaux, "The great merit of all the works you and I have done is that in them the larger opportunities of the topography have not been wasted. . . . We have 'let it alone' more than most gardeners can."[28]

Olmsted addressed this belief in many of his reports and published articles as well. "The type of scenery to be preserved or created ought to be that which is developed naturally from the local circumstances in each case. . . . Rocky or steep slopes suggest tangled thickets or forests. Smooth hollows of good soil hint at open or 'park-like' scenery. Swamps and an abundant water supply suggest ponds, pools, or lagoons."[29] In how to manipulate such elements into a cohesive design, Olmsted had been most

influenced by the approach to composition outlined in Uvedale Price's *Essay on the Picturesque* (1794) and William Gilpin's *Practical Hints upon Landscape Gardening* (1832), which he had read as a young man. Downing's *Treatise* had played a part too, with its emphasis on principles of unity, harmony, and variety, a sense of the landscape as a composition.

In 1868–69 Olmsted, collaborating with Vaux, applied these principles in the design of Riverside, a middle-class suburb, north of Chicago. The preservation of scenery along the Des Plaines River was an important consideration in this design, one of the earliest examples of a planned American commuter suburb linked to an urban center by carriage roads and a rail line. The Olmsted–Vaux plan, which was implemented by Willam Le Baron Jenney, featured winding streets rather than the rectilinear grid that typified midwestern towns, resulting in a village like appearance, with triangular greens developed as neighborhood parks. The scheme was never fully implemented, but many of Olmsted & Vaux's guidelines were instituted there; houses were to have a thirty-foot setback from the street and each homeowner was required to plant at least two trees in the front lawn, determinations that contributed to a countrified feel that still exists. (Fig. P.13)

Olmsted's approach to park, institutional, and residen-

P.13. Riverside street scene, early twentieth century. Courtesy Village of Riverside, Riverside Historical Commission.

P.14. Franklin Park, Boston. Harvard GSD.

tial design ran counter to lingering American preferences for decorative display, and his planting *methods* differed markedly from those of Downing, who had, after all, begun his career as a nurseryman. Olmsted had little interest in individual plant species and their characteristics, except insofar as they contributed to broadly composed scenes. The compositions that structured his designs depended on vegetative masses for spatial definition. The meadow, a featured associated with the Beautiful and carrying democratic, egalitarian meaning, became a fundamental compositional element in all his work. (Fig. P.14) Olmsted particularly objected to bright floral displays, believing that jarring visual incidents, however horticulturally interesting, were exciting rather than calming and therefore destructive to the tranquilizing effect of scenes of serene beauty. Not everyone, however, shared Olmsted's tastes.

The aesthetic preferences of some Americans were more closely allied with those of Henry Shaw (1800–1889), who had emigrated from Sheffield, England, while still a young man and made a great fortune importing precision implements to the United States. In 1850 Shaw began laying out his new country estate, Tower Grove, on a site of undulating prairie outside the boomtown of St. Louis on the Missouri and Mississippi rivers. He wanted a design

that would ornament his property and so distinguish it from the surrounding prairie, which he considered raw and uncivilized. Like Downing, Shaw turned to Loudon's writings, and there he found support for an approach that would suit his passion: plants.

Plant-hunting expeditions in the eighteenth and nineteenth centuries had greatly increased the number of known species, and the classification system devised by Linnaeus had made the subject of botany accessible to nonscientists for the first time. As amateurs in England and the United States quickly took it up, botanical study became a vehicle for diverse reform initiatives, used to promote physical fitness, intellectual development, mental discipline, and even to teach human sexuality. The hot colors and exotic forms of new species found their way into literature, too, titillating Victorian readers of erotic poems such as Erasmus Darwin's *Loves of the Plants* (1789), a volume Shaw owned. "The study of botany," writes the art historian Carol Grove, "was seen as a means of improving the young and the poor, of making wiser people and better citizens, of elevating society. It was in this nineteenth-century context . . . that botany, the science that combined 'pleasure with improvement,' had its greatest impact."[30]

In pursuit of bettering the citizenry of St. Louis, Shaw acquired every species he could procure—thousands of herbaceous plants, shrubs, and trees—and installed them in geometric beds that emphasized their scientific as well as their decorative qualities. (Fig. P.15) Within two years of breaking ground, he traveled to England to see the Crystal Palace, Joseph Paxton's glass-and-iron exhibition hall at the first world's fair, the Great Exhibition of the Works of Industry of All Nations, and he visited Chatsworth, the private estate of William Spencer Cavendish, the sixth duke of Devonshire, where the first *Victoria regia* water lily in England had recently bloomed in one of the new glasshouses.[31] Shaw determined that he would bring such marvels to St. Louis and, through them, educate his countrymen. He would turn his estate into a public botanical garden of greater scope than any before attempted in the United States.

To help in the endeavor, Shaw enlisted George Engel-

P.15. Missouri Botanical Garden, main gate with Shaw's cactus collection, 1897. Courtesy Missouri Botanical Garden.

P.16. Botanizing at the Missouri Botanical Garden, 1890. Courtesy Missouri Botanical Garden.

mann, a St. Louis physician, amateur plant hunter, and cactus specialist, whom he sent abroad for study. Shaw also read widely and corresponded with botanical experts such as Asa Gray, author of the *Manual of Botany in the Northern United States* (soon known simply as Gray's *Manual*), and William Jackson Hooker, director of London's Kew Gardens. He expanded the range of his buying, and, to attract the public, he created extravagant ornamental beds—displays based on examples at Kew and elsewhere—and filled them with colorful exotics as well as curious new species.

Tourists came to "Shaw's Garden" by the tens of thousands to see the vividly colored parterres, to "botanize" among the rare exotics, and to pose on the giant pads of the *Victoria regia* lily, overwintered in the conservatories built with new iron-and-glass technology pioneered in England. (Fig. P.16) Horace Greeley visited, and so did P. T. Barnum, Mark Twain, Louis Agassiz, and Asa Gray. Frederick Law Olmsted, then serving as the newly appointed secretary of the U.S. Sanitary Commission (the forerunner of the American Red Cross), also came on one trip through the Middle West. He later confessed that he found the six-hundred-acre garden a "dwarfish and paltry affair"—he was far more enthusiastic about the large park that Shaw was beginning to plan on adjacent land.[32]

By the second half of the nineteenth century other wealthy plant collectors across the country began assem-

bling large holdings of exotics to adorn their grounds. Advancements in greenhouse technology, which were making it possible to raise rare and tender species, also facilitated the production of great quantities of annuals for parterre displays, and the construction of private greenhouses rose sharply among the wealthy. The largest single example in America was built by robber baron Jay Gould, the new owner of Lyndhurst. There (as in Shaw's Garden) ornamental beds were filled with newly discovered cactus species. (Fig. P. 17)

Some of the most extravagant landscapes planted in the gardenesque method were in California, where the gentle climate and new irrigation techniques made it possible to grow a wide range of species, including many recent discoveries from the tropics. Rudolph Ulrich, who had been trained in Germany and Italy, designed extensive and flamboyant gardens for several resort hotels—the Rafel (San Rafael), the Raymond (South Pasadena), and the Hotel del Monte (Monterey)—and several large estates. One of Ulrich's most remarkable works was Linden Towers in Menlo Park (for James Flood), whose grounds

P.17. Lyndhurst greenhouse with cactus planting. Library of Congress, Prints and Photographs Division, HABS NY, 60-TARY, 1B-23.

P.18. Engraving of Linden Towers, Menlo Park, Calif., 1876. From David C. Streatfield, *California Gardens*, 1994.

were captured in an 1876 print that shows a riot of forms not unlike Shaw's Garden. (Fig. P.18) Large tubs of aloe specimens, palms, monkey puzzle trees, Norfolk Island pine, and paths edged with elaborate parterres of succulents created a botanical cacophony that could scarcely have differed more from the quiet reserve of Olmsted and Vaux's Central Park.

Bedding out also offered a means to showcase the bright colors of the expanding palette of tropical species,

and these displays appeared in public parks as well as on private estates, sometimes set into otherwise Picturesque layouts. Elements of formality also survived in the form of topiary, a method of clipping plants into ornamental forms which both Downing and Olmsted scorned. One of the largest collections of topiary was featured at Wellesley, in Waban, Massachusetts, in the c. 1854 estate of Horatio Hollis Hunnewell, who vowed to "plant every conifer, native or foreign, that will be found sufficiently hardy to thrive in our cold New England climate."[33] But the Picturesque thrived at Wellesley, too, where the terraces of clipped conifers were surrounded by rolling, tree-studded lawns. (Fig. P. 19)

Among those highly critical of the widespread use of exotic specimens and gaudy carpet bedding was Mariana Griswold Van Rensselaer, the prolific author and historian whose writings would help make Olmsted's name and principles familiar to the American public. Van Rensselaer had begun her career publishing on topics related to architecture in *Century Magazine*, *American Architect and Building News*, and *Harper's Monthly Magazine* and then turned to landscape and a range of other subjects, from suffrage to the history of New York City. Her first major work (1888) was a biography of Henry Hobson Richardson. In 1893 she published *Art Out-of-Doors*, largely to oppose current gardenesque planting fashions. Subtitled *Hints on Good Taste in Gardening*, her book found wide and appreciative audiences among new homeowners and the burgeoning ranks of professionals.

Van Rensselaer saw an inherent conflict between horticultural variety and good composition. She could well have had the estate of James Flood or Henry Shaw in mind when she wrote: "The more a man loves, in an unreasoning way, the works of Nature, the more likely he is to think that he cannot have too many of them in his grounds, and no error is so fatal as this to a good general result. And the stronger his horticultural passion, the more apt he is to care about novelties and eccentricities—about conspicuous plants as such; and the profuse use of these gives a last fatal touch to the inartistic disorder of the usual overcrowded domain."[34]

Van Rensselaer was also one of the first to promote

landscape architecture as a profession and a fine art.[35] In *Art Out-of-Doors* she emphasized a fundamental tenet of Olmsted's approach, the primary role of composition in landscape design, particularly on smaller sites where forced rusticity had become increasingly mannered through the introduction of artificial curves and home-spun artifacts—cast-iron woodstoves planted with geraniums were a particular favorite. "We should decide upon some scheme of design," she wrote, "whether our acres be many or our square rods be few; make sure that, given our special site and our special tastes, it is a good scheme; and then consider our plants and other materials, not chiefly for their individual charms, but for their value as factors in the general picture we desire. I fear I shall say this very often; but if it could be said a hundred times a year to every owner of American ground, it would be a good thing for all the people who live in America."[36] A revised edition of *Art Out-of-Doors* was issued in 1916 and another in 1925. Students in the graduate program of landscape architecture at Harvard were tested on its contents.

Expanding plant collections were not limited to exotics. Many of plants in Shaw's Garden were of American origin, discovered during expeditions in the West. Other repositories, too, were amassing large numbers of indigenous species, including the Arnold Arboretum, founded in Jamaica Plain, Massachusetts, in 1872 and directed for the next fifty-four years by the botanist Charles Sprague Sargent. An unusual agreement between Harvard University and the City of Boston incorporated the Harvard-owned property into the city's park system. Olmsted was commissioned to design several elements of the new arboretum, including the path and roadway system, and he also selected areas within the arboretum for specific groups of plants. These were organized according to family and genus yet integrated into a Picturesque treatment that would, according to Sargent's wish, "facilitate the comprehensive study of the collections, both in their scientific and picturesque aspects."[37](Fig. P. 20)

In 1881 Olmsted moved to Brookline, Massachusetts, a suburb of Boston that Downing had once praised as "a kind of landscape garden" itself.[38] The business was based at Olmsted's home, Fairsted, a welcoming wood-frame house surrounded by Picturesque grounds that were also the site of horticultural experiments.[39] (Fig. P. 21) By this time, Olmsted's firm had completed hundreds of proj-

P.19. Horatio Hollis Hunnewell estate, Wellesley, Mass., c. 1880. Courtesy Massachusetts Horticultural Society.

P.20. Arnold Arboretum, visitors admiring mountain laurel, c. 1900. Library of Congress.

ects—private estates, cemeteries, parks and park systems, entire planned communities—throughout the United States. The company would soon include as full partners Olmsted's stepson, John Charles Olmsted, and Charles Eliot; somewhat later, a young Warren Manning would work there, too. Olmsted had been drawn to Brookline by Henry Hobson Richardson, who had become a close friend after the Civil War. Richardson figured importantly

P.21. Fairsted, estate of Frederick Law Olmsted, Brookline, Mass., view across lawn to conservatory. NPS/FLO.

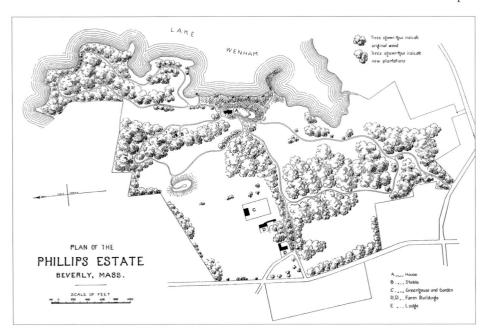

P.22. Moraine Farm, estate of John C. Phillips, Beverly, Mass., plan. From *Garden and Forest,* March 30, 1892.

in Olmsted's artistic development. "He was the greatest comfort and the most potent stimulus that has ever come into my artistic life," Olmsted wrote to Van Rensselaer after Richardson's death in 1886.[40] The two had collaborated on several commissions, including the New York State Capitol in Albany in 1875 and various projects for the Ames family in nearby North Easton, Massachusetts. Richardson's massive neo-Romanesque style likely encouraged Olmsted to begin using large fieldstones in his designs, a striking alternative to the elegant carved forms of Vaux. Olmsted used boulders in the handsome rustic arches in Franklin Park (1875), considered one of the "jewels" of Boston's Emerald Necklace of parks. Bold rockwork was also prominent at Moraine Farm, a 275-acre country place that Olmsted laid out for Mr. and Mrs. John C. Phillips beginning in 1880 in Beverly, Massachusetts (with a house by Peabody & Stearns).[41]

Despite the elegance of the residence, Olmsted wrote to the Phillipses that he wanted their estate to have a "forest character with all its possibilities of forest beauty," and for it to "appear to have been found and not made."[42] The terrace provided bucolic views over Wenham Great Pond, which Olmsted used as the scenic centerpiece of his design. The plan was intended both to satisfy aesthetic goals and to provide the traditional recreational uses of a summer place. Less conventionally, it also offered opportunities for scientific agriculture and experimental forestry, foreshadowing similar programs at Biltmore, which Olmsted began a few years later.

Olmsted's layout included three loop carriage drives, one of which led to an overlook to the lake. (Fig. P.22) Many new trees were added to the existing woods to delineate flowing meadows and to control views along the entry drive. Olmsted told his clients that he wanted the large house terrace "boldly projected, following natural lines, 'country-made' and highly picturesque in its outlines and material." Below the massive terrace walls, he laid out a wild garden planted with ferns, perennials, and small trees, including sumac, dogwood, and Mugho pine, which Olmsted believed "appeared to advantage when looked down upon."[43] Even at this point in his very successful career, however, Olmsted did not find all clients in complete sympathy with his naturalistic approach. Mrs. Phillips, like many other homeowners, wanted an old-fashioned garden filled with colorful flowers, and this he supplied—at a distance from the house, warning Phillips, "If the gardener shows himself outside the walls, off with his head." He once complained, "I design with a view to a passage of quietly composed, soft, subdued pensive character, come back in a year and find—destruction; why? 'My wife is so fond of roses' 'I had a present of some large Norway Spruces' 'I have a weakness for white birch trees—there was one in my father's yard when I was a boy.'"[44]

But strong-minded clients were a persistent reality for American landscape architects, and they would continue to influence projects, for better and for worse. In the 1880s the Olmsted firm was invited to Stockbridge, Massachusetts, to advise on the layout of a new country estate for Mr. and Mrs. Joseph Hodges Choate, who were contemplating building a house on a hillside parcel they owned near the village center. After visiting the site, the firm's representative (it may have been Olmsted himself) suggested that the house be located halfway down the hill, where it would not loom over the new landscape development. Unfortunately, this was precisely the spot where an old oak stood, under which the Choates had been picnicking for years. When they heard that it would have to be sacrificed to see the Olmsted plan through, they began looking for another landscape architect. They found more sympathy for the tree and, perhaps, for more recently evolved fashions in Nathan Franklin Barrett (1845–1919), whom they subsequently hired for the job.[45]

Barrett was a leading figure in the resurgence of formal gardens that began in the 1880s (and some years later a founding member of the American Society of Landscape Architects). At Naumkeag, he terraced the land north of house as a large, shield-shaped garden, bounded on the upper side by a gravel path and on the lower by a curving edge that gave a panoramic view of the Berkshire mountains. (Fig. P. 23) In continuous cultivation af-

ter Barrett laid it out in about 1885, Naumkeag's formal garden successfully absorbed waves of changing fashion. Such a separation of planting design from the architectural framework held obvious advantages for owners who wanted to keep up with evolving horticultural trends, and it also reflected the strong professional distinction that was emerging between landscape architecture and horticulture.

The massive forms of Beaux-Arts residences that became popular during the 1880s and 1890s required more geometrically determined settings than had the Victorian Gothic cottages designed by Downing, Davis, and Vaux. In time, many architects, including Stanford White, the designer of Naumkeag's "cottage," began to lay out formal gardens in conjunction with their houses which would provide these lines. Their goal was cohesiveness and unity of expression, characteristics that were closely associated with neoclassical ideals. These principles would affect the designs of many American landscape architects, even those with long-standing ties to a Picturesque approach, including Olmsted.

The two stylistic treatments were closely juxtaposed at the 1893 World's Columbian Exposition, whose plan was designed by Olmsted and his associate Henry Sargent Codman. The neoclassical grandeur of the Central Basin was amplified by the imposing Beaux-Arts buildings sur-

P.23. Naumkeag, Stockbridge, Mass., formal garden, c. 1885. Naumkeag.

P.24. World's Columbian Exposition, view across lagoon to the Manufactures Building. From J. W. Buel, *The Magic City,* 1894.

Massachusetts, and more importantly described a strategy for holding scenic parcels of land free of taxes, "just as the Public Library holds books and the Art Museum pictures—for the use and enjoyment of the public." As a result of this article and other persuasive writings, Eliot laid groundwork for the Massachusetts Trustees of Public Reservations, the first regional land preservation organization in the world.

Until his own sudden death in 1897, at age thirty-eight, Eliot continued to publish eloquent essays about the American landscape. Many of these appeared in *Garden and Forest,* a magazine noted both for the caliber of its contributors and for its unique role in helping to shape the emerging profession of landscape architecture as a "broad and catholic art," as one editorial described it—"as useful in the preservation of the Yosemite Valley or the scenery of Niagara as it is in planning a pastoral park or

rounding it, while relief from the architectural imperiousness (and raucous crowds) could be found nearby, on the heavily planted shores of the lagoon and the wooded island, where sinuous paths wound through apparently natural growth—all of it newly installed for the occasion. Van Rensselaer told prospective visitors, "Looking over this ground now—here with its straight, stately, wide canals and architectonic terraces, and there with its irregularly-shaped lagoons and islands—you will understand how a great artist like Mr. Olmsted can absolutely create in a way which almost equals Nature's own."[46] (Fig. P. 24)

Harry Codman died from an infected appendix before the exposition opened and thus never saw the completed grounds. His death dealt a blow to the firm, and the very talented young Charles Eliot was soon invited to join as a full partner. Already an independent professional with a keen interest in planning, Eliot was also a passionate advocate for scenic preservation. His now-famous 1890 letter published in *Garden and Forest,* titled "Waverly Oaks: A Plan for Their Preservation for the People," argued for the preservation of a stand of ancient oaks in Belmont,

P.25. Fürst-Pückler-Park, Muskau, photograph by Thomas Sears. From Samuel B. Parsons, *Art of Landscape Architecture,* 1915.

the grounds about a country house."[47] Another of Eliot's well-known articles took as its subject the great park at Muskau, which he praised as "nothing less than the transformation of the almost ugly valley of the Neisse into a vale of beauty and delight." In Eliot's analysis, Pückler had accomplished this "not by extending architectural works throughout the valley . . . but by quietly inducing Nature to transform herself."[48] Eliot's enthusiasm for Pückler's work would motivate several other American practitioners to make their own trips to Muskau, among them Samuel Parsons, Thomas Sears, and Henry Vincent Hubbard. Through their writings, Pückler's notion of landscape design as an expression of personality as well as of Nature would become increasingly familiar to American landscape architects. (Fig. P.25)

P.26. Biltmore, George Washington Vanderbilt estate, house and esplanade. Harvard GSD.

One persistent topic in *Garden and Forest* was the ongoing controversy—the so-called hot fight—between proponents of the formal and informal styles of the landscape design, which the editors found both tiresome and naïve. (They were particularly impatient with the assumption that the rural landscape, the product of many years of cultural habitation, somehow reflected truly "natural" conditions.) Van Rensselaer, Eliot, and others argued strenuously for reasoned principles of landscape architecture that avoided dogma. "True art is not the servant of some temporary fashion," wrote Charles Sargent, the magazine's "conductor," in one editorial, "but something that is to endure, and must, therefore, have a permanent basis in the necessities and aspirations of human life."[49]

Olmsted's last private work was clearly created with such aspirations in mind. Although initially uncomfortable with the pretension and scope of the enterprise, Olmsted was enthusiastic about working with George Washington Vanderbilt, a shy, somewhat retiring collector of books and art who was only twenty-five years old at the time the project began in 1888. "I feel a good deal of ardor about it," Olmsted confided, "and it is increased by the obviously exacting yet frank, trustful, confiding and cordially friendly disposition toward all of us which Mr. Vanderbilt manifests."[50] Even from the outset, Olmsted

made it clear that his purposes at Biltmore were not primarily aesthetic; as he wrote to one associate, "This is to be a private work of very rare public interest in many ways."[51] Olmsted had in mind the potential impact of Biltmore's woods to the emerging study of scientific forestry, and he would also propose an arboretum, which he intended to be "better and *greater*, more comprehensive, than any existing Arboretum in the world."[52]

The commission paired Olmsted with the country's leading proponent of Beaux-Arts design, the architect Richard Morris Hunt, whom Vanderbilt accompanied to Europe in search of architectural inspiration. Over the course of the trip, the size and pretensions of the proposed house grew, to a 250-room mansion that would borrow elements from the early Renaissance châteaux of Chambord, Chenonceaux, and Blois. (Fig. P.26) Soon a three-mile railway spur had been laid down to bring Indiana limestone to the mountain site, and several hundred workmen and a brick factory were fully engaged in construction. Completed in the time for Christmas 1895, Biltmore was the largest American home ever constructed—yet despite its size and opulence, as Mark Alan Hewitt points out, the castle also retained a certain hominess. "The interiors ranged in character from rich, European, and cosmopolitan pastiches to comfortable and slightly passé Victorian confections," Hewitt observes. "Hunt gave his client both a palace and a summer cottage,

P.27. Biltmore, aerial view. Harvard GSD.

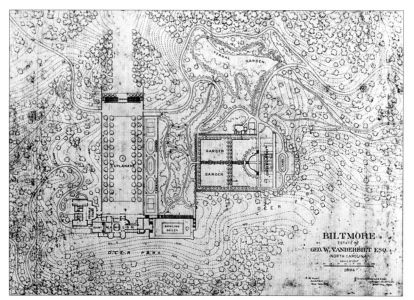

P. 28. Biltmore estate plan, 1894. Harvard GSD.

a synthesis that left anomalies barely under the surface."[53]

The grounds were a hybrid as well. Olmsted's landscape plan responded directly to the lines of Hunt's looming château and, equally, to the mountain setting—a remarkable achievement, given the stark contrast between the colossal edifice and near wilderness surrounding. (In Henry James's description, the American castle seemed a "patch of old brocade" set into "the woof of the native homespun."[54]) (Fig. P.27) The plan set up a choreographed sequence of impressions which begins with a long approach road winding through heavy forest, planted to evoke a sensation of near-tropical wilderness. The road suddenly breaks from the shadowed woodland into sunlight, and a view of the house opens down a long, formal lawn panel and esplanade of yellow poplars. From the forecourt, a flight of steps leads to a series of gardens on descending levels. On the first is an expansive, austere terrace with reflecting pools and parterre gardens. Below is a sloping, shrubby ramble, planted in Loudon's gardenesque approach, a middle ground between formality and woods. From the ramble (later renamed the Shrub Garden), a path leads under a bridge to a glen, a pond, and wilderness. The mountain view is withheld from visitors until they emerge from the house onto a large terrace on the south side of the château, where it is revealed full force, framed by the architecture. Biltmore estate also included extensive cutting and vegetable gardens, a woodland where experiments in scientific forestry were conducted, a dairy, a large farm, lake, and workers' village, all of which were incorporated into Olmsted's plan. (Fig. P. 28)

Biltmore recalled aspects of Olmsted's layout for the World's Columbian Exposition, which was under construction at the same time. Both were apt reflections of a watershed moment in American culture—brilliant and hopeful articulations of a nineteenth-century attitude toward Nature but also expressions of neoclassical elegance, even bravado. Biltmore estate also proved a persuasive model, both as a monument to taste and as a means of achieving a deliberate, sophisticated country life. Many other country places would soon be under way for America's new elite, and these would provide the next generation of landscape architects with fertile ground for experiment.

PART I

AN AMERICAN STYLE

1900–1919

Landscape designs from the first two decades of the twentieth century built on the American style developed by Frederick Law Olmsted and his associates, which reflected the principles of the English Picturesque and a response to nature as a guide to design. Warren H. Manning, among others, remained closely allied with these principles in creating estate landscapes in which large wild gardens and parklike meadows were intended to provide clients with restorative experiences to counteract the stresses of urban life. The geometric approach that became fashionable in the United States during the 1880s was promoted primarily by American architects, including Charles A. Platt, who also laid out landscapes as part of their country house commissions. Underlying these projects was an intention to convey cultural authority through knowing manipulation of Italian Renaissance and Beaux-Arts methods. Unusually vital and highly original designs resulted from practitioners' striving to span both sets of concerns. During the early part of the century, English Arts and Crafts principles, which offered a combination of the two, were also widely in evidence.

ONE

WARREN H. MANNING

1860–1938

It is likely that the next special interest in the development of the
smaller home grounds, estates, parks, club holdings and hunting preserves . . . will be more and more along the wild garden naturalistic
lines and less along the big lawn, expensive formal gardens and the
rockeries that require much upkeep cost and that show lack of attention very conspicuously.

—Warren H. Manning, "History of Walden Estate of
Cyrus H. McCormick," July 1933

Manning was one of the period's most prolific
practitioners and also one of the very few
whose career began in horticulture and expanded to land use planning. (Fig. 1.1) He was born on
the eve of Abraham Lincoln's election to the presidency,
November 7, 1860, in Reading, Massachusetts, a small
manufacturing town twelve miles northwest of Boston,
at the headwaters of the Mystic River. As a child, Manning remembered watching Union soldiers with "glistening guns" depart from the local rail station, but he
was most influenced by his father, a peaceable nurseryman who planted an elm to celebrate his first son's

birth. "I think that there should be a tree planted at the
birth of every child," the older man wrote in his diary,
"so that in the after times, it may be seen which is the
most useful."[1]

Jacob Warren Manning was regarded as the dean of
the nursery trade in New England and was known nationally, too, for his introductions of important fruits and
ornamentals to commercial cultivation, including the
Concord and Dracut Amber grape, Cutter's Seedling
Strawberry, and Woodward arborvitae. Jacob's nursery
also specialized in hardy species marketed for their ornamental qualities, such as white pine and Adam's needle
(*Yucca filamentosa*). Many of these natives were collected
in the wild, according to practices common at the time.[2]
Jacob was a staunch believer, too, in associated effort—as
his son would be—and a member of many horticultural
organizations, among them the Massachusetts Horticultural Society and the American Forestry Association.[3] By
the time he was six, Warren was licking stamps for the
catalogs sent to Reading Nursery customers throughout
the United States and Europe.

Manning's mother, Lydia Chandler Manning, was an
amateur watercolorist whom he tenderly remembered in-

1.1. Warren H. Manning as a young man. WHM, UML.

stilling in him and his four younger brothers a desire to "make America a finer place to live."[4] He wrote of his mother leading him about the home garden showing him birds and flowers, toads, butterflies, and beetles. Manning also remembered playing there alone, modeling "hills, valleys, tunnels, houses, roads, and gardens with pools," using "branchy weed tops" to make trees. As a young boy, he explored miles of open countryside along mill streams with their waterfalls and dams. These interests—the working of nature and the improvement of American civilization—set the stage for Manning's expansive career.[5]

Born and raised a Unitarian, he maintained Transcendentalist perspectives similar to those of his New England neighbors. (These included Ralph Waldo Emerson, who lived nearby in Concord, and Henry Wadsworth Longfellow, with whom Manning once shared a train ride, at age six.) Manning was nonetheless pressured into making a public proclamation of faith at one of the many religious revivals then sweeping the region. He later wrote that he regretted it almost immediately, having come to the conclusion that the "Infinite Power that was responsible for

the creation and direction of the Universe and all life in it" could not, by any stretch of logic, be tied to one church group.[6] He would never waver in this belief.

Manning spent many summers with his maternal grandfather, Abial Chandler, in Concord, New Hampshire, where he worked in the farm fields and greenhouses, and one summer on his uncle Solomon Manning's farm, in Bedford, where his father had been reared. He accompanied his father on plant collecting trips through New England and on walking tours through the South, in New York State, and in Canada, learning firsthand the habits of diverse plant groups. Manning and his father also visited commercial nurseries, including that of Charles Downing, brother of the late A. J. Downing, in Newburgh, New York. Manning had two uncles who were nurserymen and lived on Lake Pepin (bordering Wisconsin and Minnesota), and he spent one summer there, botanizing.[7]

At Reading Nursery, Manning and his four younger brothers learned the practical skills of the trade, and he often spent Saturdays at the Arnold Arboretum, where he could observe every plant hardy to the climate and also talk with Jackson Dawson, the plant propagator. When he was seventeen, his family moved into a fashionable Stick-style home at 142 High Street in Reading. He was educated for one year at General Russell's military school in New Haven and graduated from Reading public high school in 1879. For one semester he attended French's Business School in Boston.

At age twenty-one, Manning helped found the Middlesex Institute, a club that sponsored local botanizing excursions with the foremost authorities in the field, and he became a contributor to *The Flora of Middlesex County*, published in 1888, an exhaustive inventory of the plants growing there. Manning also served on a commission with Charles Sprague Sargent, director of the Arnold Arboretum, and other local preservationists to secure the Middlesex Fells as a public reservation. (Fig. 1.2) It was a time of rapidly rising interest in horticulture, and Manning found himself in demand as a lecturer to groups such as the Massachusetts Horticultural Society and the Rhode Island Society for Domestic Industry. In 1882 he had achieved wide enough renown to be invited to deliver a

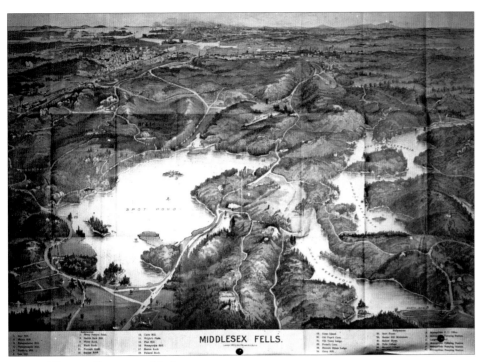

1.2. Middlesex Fells topographical map. WHM, Iowa State.

MIDDLESEX FELLS.

Olmsted's own horticultural skills were limited, and he saw promise in the background the letter described. The following February he hired Manning as superintendent of planting at $50 per month.

Manning's memories of his years with the Olmsted firm are enlivened with details that ranged from the senior partner's love of animals (his cat received attention while important clients waited) to descriptions of his working methods.[10] Manning's primary role was to recommend plants that would provide the visual effects Olmsted and the other partners sought. Manning recorded examples of such exchanges, one of which centered on a choice of ground cover to give "glinting light effects on leaf tops and wide leaf shadows" on the approach road at Biltmore.

"Rhubarb?" [Manning] suggested.
"No Leaf too coarse and wrinkled."
"Hellebore?"
"No. Leaf too deeply cut and dull."
"Large-leaved Saxafrage?"
"Yes. That's the ideal plant for the place."[11]

Manning stayed eight years with the firm, and during that time assisted on a wide a range of projects—he later estimated 125 in 22 states.[12] One of his early assignments was at Pointe d'Acadie, George Washington Vanderbilt's summer home in Bar Harbor, Maine, where Vanderbilt wanted "natural conditions reproduced."[13] In Hopedale, Massachusetts, Manning gained his first experience with company towns, later a specialty in his practice. He also assisted Olmsted Sr. and John Charles Olmsted in developing the planting plan for the Muddy River Improvement, a section of the Boston Metropolitan Park system, in a plan that precipitated a clash between Olmsted Sr. and Charles Sargent, whose acreage abutted the waterway.

speech to the American Academy for the Advancement of Science in Montreal. Manning also judged horticultural exhibits, and he began publishing articles in *Vick's Monthly* and other popular magazines. By 1884 he had begun to design landscapes—a Reading Nursery circular from that year announced Manning's services as a landscape gardener to his father's customers.[8]

In 1885, at age twenty-five, Manning married Henrietta Hamblin Pratt, also of Reading, and decided it was time to leave his father's business. He and Nettie moved to Boston, and he took a job in a music publisher's office (F. H. Gilson, in Fort Hill Square), where he prepared illustrated booklets of popular songs, a task that seems to have included both writing and graphic design. But Manning soon decided to return to the work he loved best, and in November 1887 he wrote to Frederick Law Olmsted to inquire about a job in the famous Brookline firm. His letter touted "knowledge of hardy trees, shrubs, and herbaceous plants & their treatment & the effects produced by them, the common & botanical names & botanical relationships."[9] Manning also pointed to his success in moving large shade trees, a much-valued skill in estate work at a time when immediate effects were in demand.

Sargent was adamant that new plantings should be limited to indigenous species, while Olmsted advocated adding ornamentals for greater color and floral interest, a practice that Manning would soon adopt.[14] (The battle was a draw; each practitioner planted one side of the river in his preferred approach.) (Fig. 1.3) The Boston project also brought Manning into contact with the pioneer mapping techniques of Charles Eliot. Eliot had developed a method

1.3. Muddy River, view upstream from Longwood Avenue Bridge, 1920. NPS/FLO.

1.4. *Woodland Scene in Cherokee Park*, from *Art Work of Louisville*, 1903. Courtesy The Filson Historical Society, Louisville, Ky.

for collecting data—such as soil type, hydrology, vegetation, and scenic views—which were recorded on overlay maps and then analyzed and integrated as a basis for design.

Manning worked on planting plans for several other large park systems, in Buffalo, Chicago, Milwaukee, Trenton (New Jersey), Rochester (New York), and Louisville (Kentucky), some of the most important projects in the firm at the time. (Fig. 1.4) He also designed plantings for the National Zoo in Washington, D.C., and for several residential properties, including the home of Charles W. Eliot, Harvard president and father of Olmsted's young partner. Manning's work on midwestern commissions for the firm was particularly important; through them, he acquired contacts that would provide a cornerstone for his later practice.[15] Over the course of his years with Olmsted, two projects were of outstanding significance, one in Chicago and the second in the Piedmont of North Carolina.

The World's Columbian Exposition of 1893 was the most influential cultural event of the era, and it was also the site of Manning's most prominent work to date. Daniel Hudson Burnham, of Burnham & Root, was the consulting architect for the exposition; Olmsted, assisted by Henry Sargent Codman, was appointed consulting landscape architect. The site selected was Jackson Park, a lakeside parcel for which the Olmsted office had created a c. 1870 design that had never been implemented. The White City was larger than any of the eleven world's fairs that had preceded it, including the 1851 London exposition, which featured Sir Joseph Paxton's Crystal Palace, and the 1889 Exposition Universelle in Paris, for which the Eiffel Tower had been built. (The nickname "White City" derived from the temporary whitewashed pavilions constructed of staff, a mixture of plaster and fiber over wood, but the term might equally have been applied to men involved in the event. As Frederick Douglass noted, not one of the eight million African Americans living in the United States was invited to the opening ceremonies.[16]) The scale, even of the individual buildings, was mind-boggling—the Manufactures and Liberal Arts Building, the largest of several monumental Beaux-Arts edifices there, for example, covered forty-four acres.[17]

The six-hundred-acre plan, devised by Olmsted and Codman, incorporated these structures into a citylike layout, grouped around a large, central basin, with a naturalistic lagoon to the north. (Figs. 1.5, 1.6) The concordance effected by the strength of the plan was perhaps its most striking characteristic, and the impression it left was profound. "For the first time, hundreds of thousands of Americans saw a large group of buildings harmoniously and powerfully arranged in a plan of great variety, perfect balance, and strong climax effect," the historian Talbot Hamlin observed. "This vision of harmonious power was such a contrast to the typical confusion of the average American town that the visitors were almost stunned."[18] Yet, even in this urban project, Olmsted had responded to the genius of the place, using water—a recapitulation of the lake—as a dominant theme.[19] Political wrangling compressed the time allotted for construction to two years, a circumstance that made close cooperation among the various principals involved critical. But cooperate they did, with astonishing results.

The opulence of the display was multiplied by the still novel use of incandescent lights. Visitors could scarcely find the words to praise the "new Venice of the Western world"—one characterized it as "a fairy scene of inexpressible splendor."[20] Even the sophisticated Mariana Van Rensselaer proclaimed that the White City had had no equal "since the Rome of the emperors stood intact."[21] In Liberty Hyde Bailey's view, the display "exceeded in boldness, originality, and artistic merit anything heretofore attempted in the New World."[22] By the time the exposition closed, 27 million visitors had been there to experience its marvels.

The horticultural program was also unprecedented and, like the building program, it was accomplished under great pressure. Olmsted had appointed Rudolph Ulrich as landscape superintendent and was also relying on Henry Codman to coordinate many aspects of the installation. When Codman died from an infected appendix in January of 1893, Olmsted sent Manning to Chicago to help supervise the mammoth planting effort. He later estimated that more than a million specimens were used in the design: "one hundred thousand small willows; seventy-five large railway platform [rail]carloads of collected herbaceous aquatic plants, taken from the wild; one hundred and forty thousand other aquatic plants, . . . two hundred and eighty-five thousand ferns and other perennial herbaceous plants."[23] The most heavily planted section of the layout was the Wooded Island, whose landscape provided a lush alternative to the formality of the core. The "apparently natural scenery," in Olmsted's words, offered a "quieting influence . . . counteractive to the effect of the artificial grandeur, and the crowds, pomp, splendor, and bustle of the rest of the Exposition."[24]

The brilliantly illuminated White City contrasted

1.5. Honor Court of the World's Columbian Exposition. From J. W. Buel, *The Magic City*, 1894.

1.6. Panorama of the Northwest Lagoon, World's Columbian Exposition, Wooded Island in foreground. From Buel, *The Magic City*.

sharply with the slums of the real city a few blocks away, and, for many visitors, the plazas and basins, wide boulevards, fountains, and sculpture represented a model for change, a demonstration of the transformative potential of Beaux-Arts planning—the classical ideal employed as a device for social control. Despite his pivotal role in the Chicago event and his own increasingly fervent progressive values, however, Manning never ascribed to the idea. His own city planning efforts would advocate multiple neighborhood-based urban centers rather than the grand civic concourses that dominated the Chicago fair, or those showcased in similar City Beautiful projects such as the McMillan Plan for Washington, D.C. (1901), or Burnham's plan for Chicago (1909). Manning's opposition to Beaux-Arts planning would also be evident in such initiatives as "Community Days," a method of improvisational, citizen-generated design. Nonetheless, his involvement in the Chicago exposition stimulated his interest in planning, and it could not have failed to shore up his confidence in his own abilities. It also led to important professional contacts with midwestern colleagues, future clients, and venues for publishing.

One other monumental project was under way in the Brookline office at the time. In 1888 Olmsted began laying out Biltmore, George Washington Vanderbilt's country estate in the mountains near Asheville, North Carolina. At the outset, Olmsted urged his client to add to the original 2,000 acres he had already purchased and to devote most of it to scientific forestry. (The soil was poor as a result of over-farming and not suitable to the English landscape park Vanderbilt had initially envisioned.) Manning was among the group that climbed Mount Pisgah to advise on the acquisitions that eventually totaled 125,000 acres, noting wild pigs on his way to summit.

Manning also served as the Olmsted firm's superintendent for planting, directing hundreds of workers who used a small-gauge railroad and horse- and mule-powered vehicles to do the work. Most of the rhododendron and other broad-leaf evergreens dominant in the design were collected from the wild.[25] The years that the Vanderbilt commission was in the Brookline office were the same as those of Manning's tenure with the firm, during which time the project offered a vivid example of private wealth applied to public good.

Manning collaborated closely with Olmsted on planting compositions throughout, including the three-mile approach road, where his intention was to use plantings of almost tropical density in order to amplify the genius loci. Ten thousand *Rhododendron maximum* were installed in the rich, dense woodland to create an impression that was consistent, in Olmsted's words, "with the sensation of passing through the remote depths of a natural forest."[26] (Fig. 1.7) He was calling on his memories of the jungles of Panama, where he had traveled many years before, and also recalling the "green, dripping, glistening, glorious" English countryside he had first encountered at age twenty-eight. Manning would soon be applying these techniques in parks and estate landscapes of his own. He was also involved in planning Biltmore's arboretum, and he assisted Gifford Pinchot in planting the forest. "Mr. O. is taking me into his consultations in a way that makes it of the greatest value to me," Manning wrote to his wife from Biltmore in November 1893. "My position here is a much more satisfactory one than at any other time, for I am recognized as Mr. O's representative and get about what I want."[27]

1.7. Biltmore estate, pool near approach road, with plantings by Olmsted and Manning. Harvard GSD.

Despite the confidence this letter expressed, within two years Manning would tender his resignation from the firm. This decision came close on the heels of Olmsted's formal retirement in 1895 and, not coincidentally, the addition of Frederick Law Olmsted Jr. to the firm. At the time, the younger Olmsted, known as Rick, was twenty-five years old, with no formal training and little practical experience outside Biltmore, where he had served as assistant to his ailing father and Manning. During his months in Asheville, he had weighed with considerable anguish the ponderous professional mantle the increasingly debilitated Olmsted Sr. was urging him to accept.[28] But in the end, the decision to offer Jr. a place in the firm rested, at Sr.'s insistence, with his two partners, John Charles Olmsted and Charles Eliot. They probably did not have to deliberate very long.

These men shared with the younger Olmsted a network of family and social ties, Ivy League educations, and privileged backgrounds that included close working relationships with the era's leading architects and familiarity with important works of architecture and landscape architecture in England and Europe as well as the United States. This mosaic of experiences differed in important respects from those in the background of Manning, a nurseryman's son who had never traveled beyond Canada. The invitation could not have surprised Manning—Olmsted Jr.'s extraordinary talent was evident from the start—but it made the prospect of continuing work in the office difficult. Warren and Nettie had their own son by then, Warren Harold, and, at age thirty-five, Manning was eager to pursue his own ideas.

A congenial parting of ways permitted him to take about fifteen clients with him.[29] Olmsted Sr.'s retirement was likely a factor in some of these transfers, but Manning had clearly won the confidence of many customers. His apprenticeship in Brookline had given him resources that would contribute mightily to his future success. Through his association with Olmsted, Olmsted & Eliot, Manning had strengthened his attachment to the Yankee principle of fitness and his Emersonian regard for the genius loci. He had also gained sophisticated design skills, primary among them an approach to laying out landscapes that in-

tegrated a response to nature with strong spatial planning. He had mastered a technique for pictorial composition in which plants were used as media in creating pictures. He had planted a foot in the future too, having gained an insider's view of the practical operations of America's first national landscape architectural firm. Exposure to Eliot's mapping and planning techniques would provide him with the methodology to guide innovative land use planning initiatives of his own.[30] Under Olmsted, Manning had also observed the deft straddling of private and public benefit in projects such as Biltmore, where individual wealth was directed toward social good, and he, too, would implement sprawling projects that attempted to reconcile complex natural systems with progressive social goals. Throughout his long and prolific career, Manning would practice landscape architecture as a fine art, as his mentors had.[31]

Yet despite the expansive scope of the work that filled his Brookline years, Manning did not lose his fascination with the habits of plants, from trees to near microscopic lichen. Similarly seismic shifts in focus would shape Manning's practice. As he laid out vast park systems and city plans, he was also creating wild gardens for his private clients, refuges that offered life-affirming contact with nature on a personal scale. Manning did not distinguish between the principles that guided these two types of projects. In his published writings and in letters to clients, he frequently invoked Transcendentalist perspectives on the connections between intimate natural phenomena and "the power that creates and controls the Universe." In one Emersonian essay, "The Nature Garden," he juxtaposed the surging power of Niagara Falls with strands of bright green algae swaying gently at the brink, an image that also captured the extremes in Manning's character.[32]

In January 1897 he launched his new business on Tremont Street in Boston. One of his first commissions was for James W. Tufts for the new resort village of Pinehurst, North Carolina, a project that had begun with Olmsted. He would develop several additional projects related to Pinehurst, ranging from parks to subdivisions.[33] Another

1.8. Carriage road, Tranquillity Farm, J. H. Whittemore estate. WMH, UML.

important early project was a series of lakeside estates begun in 1896 for John H. Whittemore, of Middlebury, Connecticut, where miles of carriage roads were lined with great boulders. (Fig. 1.8) (This too came from Olmsted, started under the auspices of Charles Eliot.) The Middlebury job led to subsequent clusters of commissions for the wealthy Whittemore family, there and in nearby Naugatuck. Altogether Manning completed twenty-six projects for the Whittemores, including an amusement park laid out for the benefit of railroad employees, a landscape type that became a specialty for him. From the Olmsted firm, he also transferred important park projects in Milwaukee. Work on these stretched from 1896, when Manning identified himself on one plan as "landscape architect and engineer," until 1904.[34]

In 1896 Manning was commissioned to design Highcroft, a summer home on Lake Minnetonka (Minnesota) for Frank H. Peavy, a Maine native and owner of vast networks of grain elevators and terminals in the region. That high-profile commission led to an eventual forty-five jobs for private clients near the Twin Cities and to improvements to the Minneapolis park system, much of which had been laid out by H. W. S. Cleveland in the 1880s and 1890s. (Fig. 1.9) In the introduction to his 1900 "Report on the Minneapolis Parks," Manning recalled the vision of his predecessor, whose roots also lay in New England: "I would have the city itself as such a work of art as may be a fitting abode of a race of men and women whose lives are devoted to a nobler end than money-getting and whose efforts shall be inspired and sustained by the grandeur and beauty of the scenes in which their lives are passed." Like Cleveland, Manning saw the large river park as an emblem of nature, but, as the historian Lance M. Neckar also notes, Manning was quick to point out to his savvy busi-

1.9. Plan of Minneapolis and St. Paul, n.d., Warren H. Manning. WHM, Iowa State.

ness clients that there was commercial value in beauty, too.[35]

One especially propitious commission that came to Manning during these early years was a c. 1899 landscape design for William Gwinn Mather's summer cottage in Ishpeming, in Michigan's Upper Peninsula—an unassuming start to a subsequent fifty-nine projects for the Cleveland iron magnate in a number of states. These jobs included company towns, mines, schools, hotels, worker subdivisions, and Mather's private estate outside Cleveland, known as Gwinn.[36] (Fig. 1.10)

A "wild gardening estate," Dolobran, for the president of the American Steamship Company, Clement A. Griscom, near Haverford, Pennsylvania, undertaken about the same time, gave Manning's reputation a different sort of boost. Dolobran was the subject of two admiring articles by J. Horace McFarland, a visionary conservationist and civic leader who soon also became an enthusiastic client. In the first article, in the *Outlook* (1899), McFarland praised Manning's design as an example of a "real" American garden, noting that "there are in our broad land not many real American gardens."[37] As McFarland observed, "It was natural that our forefathers, when they began, as Bacon puts it, to 'garden wisely,' should look for models to their old homes across the Atlantic." But the time had arrived, the author argued, for Americans to look to "the glory of our own woods and hills, and discover the gems of our meadows and roadsides," to utilize "the free beauty of native woodland, marsh, and copse . . . the natural beauty of American plants, located cunningly where they love to grow, unrestrained, untrimmed."[38] Of all the estate's features, McFarland was most passionate about the large wild garden Manning had created in an abandoned quarry, a "wonderland," the like of which, he wrote, "does not exist elsewhere in America."[39] The garden sheltered hundreds of species of native wildflowers—McFarland cites an improbable 1,200—nestled into crevices along rock walls and spread through swampy bottomland, planted to provide a continuous sequence of bloom. (Figs. 1.11, 1.12, 1.13)

McFarland was not alone in his enthusiasm for the "natural" beauty of American plants. Illustrated with photographs reproduced with new halftone technology, a

1.10. Town of Gwinn, Mich., showing mine buildings. Postcard.

number of new magazines featured articles on American wild gardens.[40] Some of these supported a view of the wild garden as a place of introspection and divine revelation; others suggested it as a patriotic endeavor. (*Lippincott's Magazine* told its readers that "national pride ought to influence us to choose native plants instead of foreign ones."[41]) Most of these authors emphasized the apparent artlessness of wild gardens and the ease with which they could be created by middle-class homeowners, but McFarland described a professional effort, crediting Dolobran's designer by name. Manning would refer often to this seminal design as he promoted wild gardens to other clients.

In 1896 Manning began working at Walden, the Lake Forest, Illinois, home of Harriet and Cyrus McCormick Jr. The estate was sited on a 103-acre parcel on a high bluff above Lake Michigan, selected for its dramatic outlooks. The design (whose plan was conceived with John Charles Olmsted) was laid out in response to the lake and to the great ravines that gave the land its unique character. The decision to transfer the work to Manning seems to have occurred after a dispute over the house site with Olmsted, who had proposed a location very near the high bluff. Manning persuaded the McCormicks to locate it farther from the edge, where they would see the water over a foreground of "quiet turf."[42] (Fig. 1.14)

1.11. Quarry after planting, Dolobran, Clement A. Griscom estate, Haverford, Pa., 1897. WHM, Iowa State.

1.12. Carriage road, Dolobran, 1897. WHM, Iowa State.

1.13. Moss carpet in old quarry, Dolobran, 1897. WHM, Iowa State.

The design had been influenced, in part, by a nearby development, Highland Park, where the McCormicks had lived previously (and which had been laid out by H. W. S. Cleveland).[43] "From the beginning," wrote Manning, "the exclusion of formality in the naturalistic surroundings of an informal house designed to be an integral part of its landscapes has been rigidly adhered to."[44]

Walden's design would serve as a model for some of his later projects, including both Gwinn and Stan Hywet Hall, and it would also lead to several other commissions for the wealthy family of the inventor of the reaper, Cyrus McCormick Sr.[45]

Securing the eroded clay bluff became an immediate priority. Manning cut the sharp slope back about twenty-five feet and installed diagonal drains throughout, introducing many different kinds of plants to hold the soil in place, including black locusts along the bluff top.[46] Working closely with McCormick Jr. over several years, he laid out an intricate system of roads and trails through the woodland, linked by eleven bridges, all of which McCormick designed himself. The largest of these was constructed of wood salvaged from the 1893 Chicago fair.[47]

McCormick also played a dominant role in the vista-cutting that determined views through the woodland and out to the lake, keeping axes and saws in the front closet so he could open them himself. Each new view was carefully plotted before it was cut, each named according to its character and the plants growing near it. "[These] must accord entirely with the quiet, restful, natural, unobtrusive look of the place," McCormick directed, "with an abundance of green foliage, and the absence of artificial effects."[48] (Fig. 1.15) One suggestion by Manning, for a vista of orange daylilies, was "assassinated" by the midwestern landscape architect Wilhelm Miller, who argued that it would clash with the sunset.[49] The views were considered so successful that in 1915 the Garden Club of America came to Walden to see a vista-opening demonstration.[50]

The Walden plan also emphasized topographical idiosyncrasies and great forest trees. Old photographs show masses of woods and sweeps of meadow, passages combined with rolling lawns and more formal features near the house. Detailed in meticulous lists, plantings included hundreds of native and non-native species. These were secured through several sources, including Thoreau's original Walden, in Concord, Massachusetts. Many were dug from the wild.[51] Manning experimented with several introductions, reassuring his clients that Thoreau at the original Walden had also introduced "non-native" plants.[52] At their request, he shipped a carload of stones from the Concord site for a stepping-stone path on the new estate, as a totemic gesture of connection. The emphatically naturalistic design contrasted sharply with the studied Italian grandiosity of the Villa Turicum next door, which Charles A. Platt had created for Cyrus Jr.'s brother Harold and Edith Rockefeller McCormick in 1908. (Manning was commissioned to advise on siting that house as well.)

Walden also had a formal flower garden. The original plantings were revised by Louise Shelton in 1915, and in

1.14. Ravello and overlook, Walden, Cyrus McCormick Jr. estate, Lake Forest, Ill. From Harriet Hammond McCormick, *Landscape Art, Past and Present*, 1923.

1.15. Carriage road, Walden. From McCormick, *Landscape Art, Past and Present*.

1921 again redone by Helen Bullard (then an employee in Manning's office). In 1931 Ralph Griswold, a well-known landscape architect based in Pittsburgh, was hired to create an entirely new formal garden, a prospect, he confessed he found "terrifying . . . in the midst of this peaceful and harmonious landscape"—though Manning considered the result a masterpiece of its kind, owing largely to the good proportions.[53]

Photographs of Walden were included in Miller's *Prairie Spirit in Landscape Gardening* (1915) in a chapter titled "Restoring the Romantic Types of Illinois Scenery." Before-and-after views demonstrated the effect of Manning's treatment of the wave-ravaged bluff—the caption notes 150 plant species. The estate was also the subject of a richly illustrated book by Harriet McCormick, *Landscape Art, Past and Present*, published posthumously in 1923.[54] Manning wrote at length about the decades-long project in his magazine *Billerica: The North Shore Edition*,[55] and he also described his work there in a private report.[56] He would create wild gardens for other Lake Forest clients, including Stanley Field and Clyde M. Carr, but none at the scale of Walden.

By the turn of the century, Manning had become well known through a national network of prominent clients, including several in the Midwest. These included the beer purveyor Gustav Pabst, whose Milwaukee estate Manning designed in 1898, and the founder of Standard Oil, John D. Rockefeller Sr., who solicited advice from Manning for both his Cleveland and his Tarrytown, New York, country places.[57] Manning was also achieving renown as author, lecturer, and founder of important civic and professional associations. One of these was the American Park and Outdoor Association (soon to become the American Civic Association), established in Louisville, Kentucky, in 1897, by Manning, O. C. Simonds, J. Horace McFarland, and several others. The association served as a precursor to the American Society of Landscape Architects, founded two years later by Manning, Samuel Parsons Jr., and eight other leaders in profession.

During these years, extended absences from Boston became the norm, and letters to far-flung locales record Nettie's frustrations. But Manning thrived on the pace, working throughout long nights on trains, in a pattern that reflected his strong physical constitution and near-manic personality. In these efforts, Manning was propelled by a zeal for reform that resembled his mentor's in his epic career as planner, designer, publisher, author, and administrator. As had Olmsted, Manning held great hope for the young nation, and he, too, felt an unquestioned, sometimes grandiose, authority to guide it.

In 1901, in a short-lived partnership with his brother J. Woodward, Manning began a new park system for Harrisburg, Pennsylvania, where his friend McFarland lived. From the first, Manning worked closely with McFarland and other civic leaders to convince landowners to donate acreage for the new park, much of which was sited along the polluted Susquehanna River. Manning's scheme included dredging the river to restore it to health and instituting flood controls to regulate water levels—an initiative in which he was undoubtedly inspired by the Olmsted firm's pioneering work in Boston's Back Bay and by that of Cleveland in Minneapolis. He was also motivated by his own sense of the river's beauty and variety, which his new plan preserved. "A splendid strip of green more than a mile long," McFarland wrote of Manning's new riverfront park, "giving a superb view over the unsurpassed panorama of river, island and mountains to the west and affording easily reached breathing spaces for a vast multitude of people."[58] (Fig. 1.16) Manning's new parks also included a lake (transformed from a typhoid-infested swamp), described by Manning's employee Egbert Hans as "a unique wild garden," and parkways that bordered small streams winding through wooded valleys.[59] (Fig. 1.17) McFarland took the Harrisburg plan to cities across the United States, delivering slide lectures about Manning's work and the general advantages of park and town planning.[60]

After Jacob Manning's death, Woodward returned to Reading to manage the family nursery, and the brothers dissolved their partnership. One of many large commissions that came to Manning in the years following was the Gwinn estate. In 1906, the year he listed the Gwinn proj-

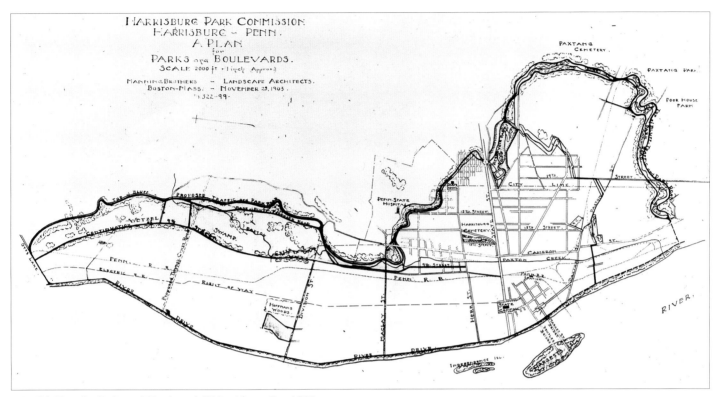

1.16. "A Plan for Parks and Boulevards," Harrisburg, Pa., 1903. WHM, Iowa State.

ect, he also added clients from several other regions, including Illinois, Arizona, Wisconsin, Massachusetts, New York, Rhode Island, Virginia, Pennsylvania, Minnesota, Connecticut, and Alabama—forty-nine commissions altogether.

Despite the demands of these projects, Manning continued to write frequently for popular magazines.[61] In 1903 he published "How to Make a Formal Garden at a Moderate Cost" in *Country Life*. Manning's article contrasted the layout of a formal garden—his ostensible subject—with that of "a distinctly informal garden." He praised the "peculiar beauty" of the latter, describing the appeal of "native shrubbery already established on the thin soil of ridges and ledges," noting that "a person having such a lot, who can appreciate the beauty of natural conditions, . . . may excite the mild derision of his neighbors for buying a 'rubbish hole' and saving 'brush,' but in the end he will turn derision into congratulation and emulation."[62]

In his other published writings, too, Manning advocated wild gardens. Liberty Hyde Bailey invited him to contribute an article on the topic to the 1906 edition of

1.17. Stream in Harrisburg Parks. WHM, Iowa State.

the *Cyclopedia of American Horticulture*. "No form of gardening gives greater and more lasting pleasure, than that which aims to naturalize wild or garden plants," Manning wrote, quoting William A. Stiles. He observed that wild

1.18. Wild garden, G. W. Crile estate, Cleveland, designed 1916. WHM, UML.

1.19. Wild garden, E. S. Burke estate, Chagrin Falls, Ohio, designed 1919–20. WHM, UML.

1.20. Wild garden, Clyde M. Carr estate, Lake Forest, Ill., after 1911. WHM, UML.

gardens were "steadily gaining in America," and that they appealed to "all persons who delight in making nature-like pictures with the help of plants." His article credits the Irish gardener and author William Robinson with originating "both the idea and the name."[63]

Like Robinson, Manning promoted the wild garden as an alternative both to the Victorian displays of showy exotics that had dominated the late nineteenth century and to the geometry of the formal garden that had become increasingly fashionable by the turn of the century. Also like Robinson, he urged planning in a "nature-like manner" to give an "appearance of untamed luxuriance, of careless and unstudied grace which suggests perfect freedom." Manning maintained an ecumenical view of plants, identifying the wild garden spirit as "essentially cosmopolitan," arguing that it could rightfully include imports, particularly leading border favorites such as peonies, phlox, and iris, growing in "lusty colonies."[64]

Even more than Robinson, Manning promoted outcasts from mainstream floriculture for use in such gardens. He admired species that were disdained by gardeners because they were too coarse, insignificant, or, in Manning's words, "ill-smelling, sticky or prickly."[65] His horticultural repertory was vast and continued to expand—his interest in experimenting with new species, from creeping mosses to great trees, did not flag as the years passed. In a 1908 article for *Country Life*, Manning described the swamp and bog gardens he created at his own summer place in Billerica, Massachusetts, where he grew rare mosses, wild orchids, and carnivorous plants. He recommended such endeavors as "easy, simple, natural, tasteful, economical"[66] and continued to link wild gardens to "the highest intelligence and taste," encouraging even his wealthiest clients to pursue them.[67] Transcendently beautiful photographs taken on country places from Chagrin Falls, Ohio, to Chicago's North Shore attest to his success. (Figs. 1.18, 1.19, 1.20)

Manning believed that there were three tasks in developing a wild garden. The first was to evaluate the "the beauty of existing conditions"; the second, to eliminate unwanted plants; the third, to introduce new plants, improve the ground, and add circulation systems.[68] Even on a backyard scale, Manning applied these steps, carefully inventorying existing conditions and then judiciously removing extraneous material and incongruous "incidents." He once compared his approach with that of Thomas Jefferson, whose buildings and landscapes were the subject of a book that Manning coauthored in 1913. In it he quoted Jefferson's observation that the United States is "the country of all others where the noblest gardens may be made without expense. We have only to cut out the superabundant plants."[69] Manning repeatedly emphasized that wild gardens required an intimate knowledge of native species and a sensitive reading of existing conditions, noting particularly the cycles of growth and decay that characterized gardens of this type.[70]

Manning also believed that formal gardens had a legitimate role in American country places—indeed, no landscape practice could have survived without them. In his layouts, they were often planted by specialists, such as Ellen Biddle Shipman, with whom he worked on several commissions.[71] But Manning adamantly discouraged his clients from making formal gardens the centerpieces of their landscapes, arguing that "nature's garden offers another type of beauty that is infinitely more varied in detail and in interest."[72] By 1911, when Miller published his influential book *What England Can Teach Us about Garden-*

1.21. Elon Hooker estate, Greenwich, Conn., designed 1909–14. WHM, UML.

ing, Manning had become well known for his opinions on the subject of strong-hued exotics, which he believed were appropriate only in the formal garden. In Miller's paraphrase of "Manning's law," "horticultural forms originated in the garden; they should be restricted to it, and not allowed to dominate the landscape."[73]

Manning's typical estate layout comprised many of the elements of the Olmstedian formula that had become standard on American country places. These features included winding approach drives, lawns and meadows, massed plantings of trees and shrubs, reflective water features, garden structures, terraces, orchards, vegetable, cutting and ornamental gardens, bridle paths, bridges, and greenhouses, farm buildings, and stables. (Fig. 1.21) In Manning's designs, as in Olmsted's, circulation systems were laid out in response to natural topography and important views, and spatial structure was achieved primarily through richly planted compositions. But wild gardens were Manning's passion, and he continued to encourage his clients to commission them as prominent features.

Manning's business grew rapidly via dense clusters of jobs, as wealthy industrialists commissioned residences and then returned with business-related projects—connections to both Mather and Seiberling would spawn such net-

1.22. Plan for Rock City amusement park, Olean, N.Y., 1907. WHM, Iowa State.

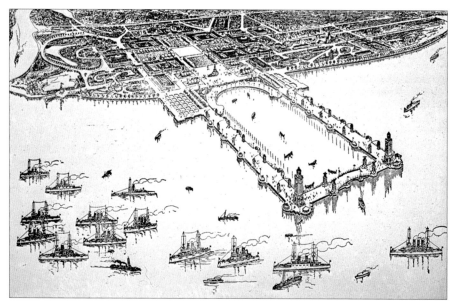

1.23. Aerial drawing of Jamestown Exposition, near Norfolk, Va. WHM, Iowa State.

works. On Manning's side, these designs were motivated by concerns that went beyond the artistic or even the horticultural. He remained a staunch advocate of enlightened city and regional land use planning, public parks, and company towns that provided residents with amenities such as community gardens and large expanses of open space, and he used his increasing network of contacts to secure commissions with these goals in mind. Neckar aptly describes Manning as an agent of "progressive transformation" whose aim was "to democratize wealth without substantially undermining its societal foundations."[74]

As Manning's reach spread, he moved through rapidly expanding webs of commissions, planning his trips to cover as many sites as possible in arcing sweeps through the nation. In 1902 he wrote Nettie that he had made sixteen site visits in two weeks, three in one day in Cincinnati.[75] Unlike many design professionals, Manning preferred to stay in hotels rather than in clients' homes, where he might be expected to socialize. He was typically on the ground at dawn, in hiking boots, with notebook and sketch pad in hand.

Manning's opinionated and garrulous manner served him well with plain-speaking midwestern civic leaders and businessmen, but this trait did not appeal to every client. The architect Theodate Pope (later Riddle), who hired Manning for advice on her new country estate, Hill-Stead, in Farmington, Connecticut, complained in one letter to her father about Manning's tendency to "butt in" where his opinions were not wanted.[76] (Privately, Fletcher Steele once observed that Manning "has no understanding, & consequently no patience with any point of view that does not coincide with his own."[77]) But many clients came to love him. "Warren Manning was like a wonderful farmer-neighbor," recalled Irene Seiberling Harrison, daughter of F. A. and Gertrude. "Mutual, humble in spirit. Charming, filled with wonderful stories about things he had discovered in the nature world."[78]

Manning's growing practice included every conceivable landscape type, including amusement parks, fairs, and expositions. (Fig. 1.22) He was the chief landscape architect of the Jamestown Exposition, planned in 1904 in conjunction with the three hundredth anniversary of the founding of the Virginia settlement. The ambitious event featured an extensive display of navy ships and, like the Chicago World's Fair, used a great lagoon as it its centerpiece. (Fig. 1.23) Unfortunately, the exposition was almost immediately beset by disaster when its president, former Virginia governor Fitzhugh Lee (nephew of Robert E. Lee), died. Additionally, few of the new roads, streetcar lines, piers, and hotels necessary to service the site on its isolated stretch of waterfront, Sewell's Point, were completed on schedule. Opening day in 1907 was an operational nightmare, and the resulting negative publicity discouraged attendance. By the time the exposition was over, only three million people had attended, a dismal contrast to the twenty-seven million who had flocked to Chicago. Although Manning's disappointment was undoubtedly keen, he successfully developed many new commissions in Virginia through contacts made during the project.[79]

He continued to expand his business aggressively into the other areas of the nation.[80] Client records for the period between 1910 and 1913, when he was also working at Gwinn and Stan Hywet, list 202 new projects—estates, hospitals, parks, mines, river improvements, school grounds, campuses, golf courses, cemetery lots, stores, city plans, state fairs, churches, and one island (Mackinac, in upper Michigan). These projects were distributed over a wide geographic range, with dense clusters in Richmond and Norfolk, Virginia, central Connecticut, and central and upper Michigan, where Manning had continuing work for Cleveland-Cliffs Iron Company.[81] In 1912 he began work on Goodyear Heights in Akron, a workers' subdivision that utilized forward-looking planning methods that also depended on a response to setting.

To meet the demands of this work, Manning added several new employees to his firm. In 1908 he took on Fletcher Steele as an unpaid apprentice, and within a year had given him a staggering load of responsibilities for which Steele was scarcely prepared, leaving Manning free to travel and acquire new projects.[82] In the years following, Manning hired several other highly capable men and

women who also became intrinsic to his success. Albert D. Taylor joined his staff in 1909 (Taylor would work at both Gwinn and Stan Hywet); Charles F. Gillette and Herbert Flint came in 1910 (Gillette later established a thriving practice in Richmond); John Noyes (who went on to become the superintendent of the Missouri Botanical Garden) joined in 1911; Stephen Hamblin came in 1912.[83] All these practitioners eventually left Manning's office, and most, including Steele, who departed in 1913, took their own clients with them, as Manning had when he left Olmsted.

In 1914 Manning moved his business office from Boston to the grounds of the Manning Manse in Billerica, a house that had been converted from a tavern by his ancestors which he restored as a summer place.[84] (Figs.

1.24. Manning Manse, North Billerica, Mass., 1921. WHM, UML.

1.25. Warren Manning and Rex, probably at Manning Manse. WHM, UML.

1.26. Plan for Billerica Garden Suburb by Arthur C. Comey and Warren H. Manning, 1914. WHM, UML.

1.24, 1.25) He built a three-story octagonal office for his growing firm, which at its peak included thirty workers. That same year, Manning was elected president of the American Society of Landscape Architects, and he used his client base, as well as his professional contacts, to promote the creation of the National Park Service, established two years later.

Billerica offered a continuing testing ground for some of Manning's most important ideas. There he helped found the Billerica Improvement Association, modeled on the village improvement societies begun throughout New England in the nineteenth century. In 1912 he created a town plan, based on data collected by local citizens he had recruited.[85] Manning also advised on the Billerica Garden Suburb, a low-cost worker housing development that was the first example of co-ownership of homes in the United States. (Fig. 1.26) And it was in Billerica that Manning first experimented with Community Days, during which citizens participated in creating a local park.

As World War I broke out in Europe, many of the era's Progressive ideals were increasingly colored by nationalistic sentiments, and the call for indigenous American plants intensified. Manning's views on plants became more ideologically charged, too. In his entry for the 1916 edition of Bailey's *Cyclopedia*, "The Art of Making Landscape Gardens," he cast exotics in strikingly unwholesome terms, as "garish" and "peculiar" with "variously blotched, dissected and twisted foliage."[86] The fervid language recalled that

of Miller, whose *Prairie Spirit in Landscape Gardening*, published a year earlier, dismissed colorful exotics as "variegated rubbish," quoting the opinionated William Robinson.[87] Too, it evoked the strong views of Jens Jensen, whose recommendations of native over foreign "invaders" had acquired ideological intensity.

Manning's articles during these years increasingly emphasized "distinction" in American landscape design. "The artists of the profession [of landscape architecture]," Manning wrote, "as well as artists among painters of landscape are striving to give a quality of distinction to each of their productions. . . . This distinction comes from a study of the distinctive beauty of the locality in which they work."[88] Like Downing and many American artists and writers of the nineteenth century, Manning was disdainful of European imitation. He dismissed the work of "mere copyists who, in all their problems duplicate or adapt with minor variations, styles, plans and patterns originated by others," and he specifically criticized those who forced the land "to fit the plan." His article took aim at the "big formal gardens of today filled with architectural structures . . . and sculptural bric-a-brac," whose forms he found "rigid."[89] In its fundamental tension, the hot fight had not changed much since 1901.[90]

Through the century's second decade, Manning continued to find new work from wealthy and well-connected

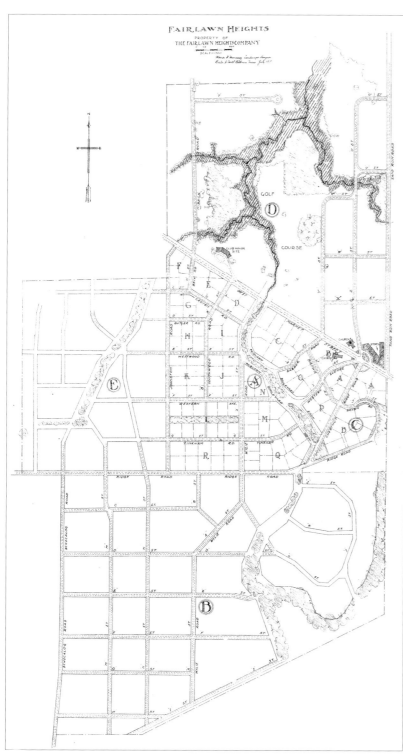

1.27. Plan for Fairlawn Heights, Akron, Ohio, 1917. SHH.

Plan, a mammoth land use study that utilized the same data-gathering techniques and resource-based planning principles that were guiding his park and estate designs. Over the course of several years, he and his staff collected and synthesized more than two thousand sources of governmental data. Never before had so much information about the country been so exhaustively retrieved and coordinated.

Many of Manning's recommendations were visionary, as was the intended result—a long-term plan that would assure the future well-being of the nation. But some of the ideas Manning put forward were extreme even for their day, skewed by nativist ideology, particularly notions of geographical determinism that led to xenophobic recommendations, such as the relocation of ethnic types. There is little question, however, that the initiative was propelled by Progressive-era zeal, as Manning concluded, "There can be no higher patriotism than this planning and working to help the United States of today and of our children's children to lead the world in its progress."[91]

At 927 pages, it is not surprising that the plan's final version never found a publisher, although Manning did manage to get a condensed version into the July 1923 issue of *Landscape Architecture* as a special supplement, and through it reached his professional colleagues. In Neckar's view, the article likely provided an impetus for innovative planning initiatives undertaken by the National Resources Planning Board during the Roosevelt administrations.[92]

Concurrently with his work on the National Plan, Manning designed a city plan for Birmingham, Alabama, published by private subscription in 1919. It was the first comprehensive planning effort undertaken by the rapidly growing city and the most innovative plan of Manning's career.[93] (Fig. 1.28) It was forward-looking in conception, based on the same methods of resource analysis that Manning was using in other ef-

clients. In 1917 he laid out an upscale development and country club, Fairlawn Heights, in Akron, underwritten with capital from F. A. Seiberling. (Fig. 1.27) After the United States entered World War I, business slowed and Manning devoted increasing time to writing a National

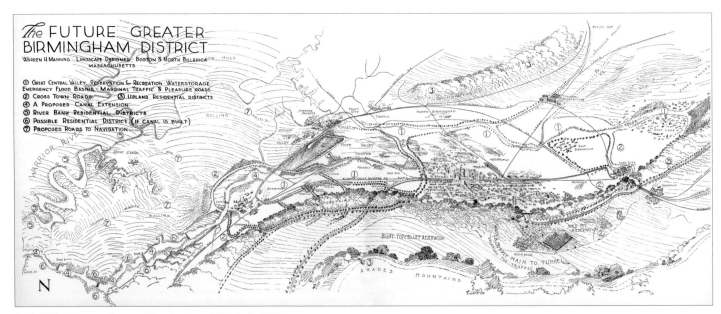

The FUTURE GREATER
BIRMINGHAM DISTRICT
WARREN H MANNING · LANDSCAPE DESIGNER · BOSTON & NORTH BILLERICA
MASSACHUSETTS

① Great Central Valley · Reservation & Recreation · Waterstorage
Emergency Flood Basins · Marginal Traffic & Pleasure roads
② Cross Town Roads   ③ Upland Residential districts
④ A Proposed Canal Extension
⑤ River Bank Residential Districts
⑥ Possible Residential District (if canal is built)
⑦ Proposed Roads to Navigation

1.28. "The Future Greater Birmingham District," 1919. From Philip A. Morris and Marjorie Longenecker White, eds., *Designs on Birmingham*, 1989.

forts. Among the many modern recommendations Manning put forward were reservations for flood detention which could, during periods of low precipitation, function as airplane landing strips, and a water system that provided gray water for industrial cooling.

Manning's plan also urged development of multiple neighborhood-based centers, a striking contrast to the monumental civic centers that had ushered in the City Beautiful movement. Although several factors prevented the Birmingham plan from being fully implemented, it did inspire new studies for zoning and parks, the need for which the report had flagged. The experience in Birmingham reinforced Manning's belief in the importance of community involvement.[94] He would not find planning projects on this scale again, however. Such jobs would go to younger and ultimately more practical men who were better equipped, philosophically and temperamentally, to work for change within existing urban parameters.[95]

During the war, Manning had cut back his office staff as a result of shrinking numbers of commissions and his work on the National Plan, which he had subsidized with his own money. Many of the smaller firm's projects in the years after the war were for Cleveland-Cliffs executives, billed to the company at William Mather's direction. By 1923 business picked up again, and Manning moved his operation to Cambridge.

In the mid-twenties he found new enclaves of private clients in St. Louis, Lookout Mountain, Tennessee, Lake Forest, Illinois, and several in Birmingham, including, in 1926, a large luxury suburb, Mountain Brook Estates, developed by Robert Jemison Jr. Manning's scheme for the development relied on the same responsiveness to topography and scenic principles that were guiding his private work. He was also commissioned to design Jemison's 550-acre estate, Spring Lake Farm, one of the last private country places on this scale in Manning's practice.[96] He continued to find sustaining work through his old clients as well. In 1928 Seiberling commissioned him to undertake a restoration of the Akron estate and provide plans for subdividing a thousand acres into new home sites. Mather commissioned an "Upper Michigan Land Use Study," a report that covered eleven million acres, based on characteristically exhaustive research.[97]

Manning's office was hard hit by the financial decline that began with the collapse of the stock market in 1929. In 1932 he hired his last assistant, Daniel Urban Kiley, although there were few projects in the office at the time.[98] Kiley admired Manning's work and came to incorporate elements of its repertory into his own designs. The ornamental orchard, a standard feature of Manning's estates, became a mainstay in Kiley's gardens and parks.

As the Depression wore on, Manning proposed several

modest jobs to William Mather related to his company, some of which Mather did commission. With time on his hands, Manning wrote an illustrated narrative of the Gwinn estate, for which he asked Mather to underwrite publishing costs (Mather declined, citing dwindling finances). Manning's last letters to his most enduring client, written shortly before his own death from heart failure in 1938, focused on the question of Gwinn's future and his strong wish that the estate should be preserved and made accessible to the public. Manning regarded Gwinn as one of his most important projects and believed that it could serve as a prototype for future designers.

"The ideal estate of the future," he wrote in his unpublished autobiography, "will be large wild land areas with much variation in surface conditions—hills with far-reaching views—valleys—streams—ponds—the great lakes and the sea—and much forest area."[99] Mather's Cleveland estate featured precisely such landscapes. (Fig. 1.29) At Gwinn, as at Stan Hywet Hall and each of the approximately 1,200 residential jobs he undertook over the course of his career, Manning focused on the restorative appeal of well-designed landscapes and the good to American society that might follow.

Fig. 1.29. Ferns and rhododendron, wild garden, Gwinn, c. 1930.
Photograph by Warren H. Manning office. Gwinn.

TWO

CHARLES A. PLATT

1861–1933

By clipped flat planes of turf, terrace walls and balustrades and steps, columns and arbours and colonnades, pools and fountains, cropped shrubs and well-groomed trees, the architecture insinuates itself into the surrounding nature while this in its turn creeps delicately towards the central architecture, where it finally ceases.

—Ralph Adams Cram, "Faulkner Farm," *House and Garden*, 1901

Charles Adams Platt, Manning's design collaborator at Gwinn, was born just one year after his New England colleague, but in many respects their backgrounds could not have differed more.[1] (Fig. 2.1) The place of Platt's birth was New York, America's fastest growing city as well as its most important port and the site of its most influential banks and stock exchanges. Platt's father, John, a corporate lawyer in the pioneering firm of Hutchins & Platt, was also a charter member of the Century Association, New York's most prestigious club for artists and writers, whose ranks also included Frederick Law Olmsted and several landscape painters.[2] The Platts entertained frequently at their home at 90 Lexington Avenue, welcoming prominent guests such as the poet

William Cullen Bryant—who had campaigned doggedly on behalf of Central Park—George Palmer Putnam, publisher of Olmsted's 1852 book about discovering the English countryside, and Horace Greeley, editor of the *Tribune*. According to Platt's biographer Keith N. Morgan, the family, which included three sons and one daughter in addition to Charles, was both prosperous and happy.[3]

Although he suffered from shyness so extreme that public speaking was almost impossible for him, John Platt was nonetheless very successful in his work, noted for his "unfailing fund of humor" and "extremely brilliant and effective" conversation.[4] Charles was also reserved, but he had his father's dry wit, which would serve him well in his profession too. Platt's mother, Mary Elizabeth Cheney, was remembered somewhat less vividly, as "kind and sympathetic."[5] She was the descendant of a clockmaker whose sons established a thriving silk manufacturing business in Manchester, New Hampshire. Two of Mary's uncles, John and Seth Wells Cheney, were artists in addition to mill owners, and Charles knew both well.[6] Even as a boy, Platt wanted to be an artist too. He later remembered the unusual childhood diversion of creating country houses "with the surroundings including inhabitants" all in

2.1. *Portrait of Charles A. Platt,* Thomas Wilmer Dewing, 1893, oil on panel. Courtesy members of the Platt family.

paper, an enterprise that foreshadowed his profession as surely as Manning's constructions with "branchy weed tops" had his.

Platt's role in the landscape design development of the era was unique. He would become the most influential country house architect of his time and the progenitor of a new model for the American house and garden. In certain respects, he was, like Manning, a reformer, stopping well short of the overblown opulence to which many of his contemporaries succumbed. Platt successfully achieved a creative synthesis of historical country house types, bounded by a sense of contained, classical calm. He approached the sites of his commissions pragmatically, from the outside in, deferring to existing scenery and, always, with a view to comprehensive effect.

Platt's pervasive influence on American landscape architecture can be traced both to the landscape model

that he evolved, which featured compartmentalized grounds linked axially to rooms in the house, and to the more abstract principles underlying such designs. Primary among these was sympathy to fitness and to setting—a regard for the genius loci. Second, arguably, was Platt's sense of landscape design as a forum for artistic ideas. The geometry of the outdoor room appealed to many wealthy industrialists as an expression of cultural status; it would appeal to Platt and his colleagues, from Ellen Shipman to Fletcher Steele, as a spatial vehicle that could accommodate a rich store of artistic response. Their designs would be vitalized by the challenge of integrating this geometry into an Olmstedian framework, grounded in nature-based principles.

As Morgan points out, Platt had the opportunity to see enlightened landscape planning at an early age. John and Seth Wells Cheney had attempted to create a model industrial village in conjunction with their silk business, with mills and worker housing that emphasized light and ventilation, set into parklike grounds that appeared as "unchanged natural forest, traversed by picturesque walks."[7] He also had early experience of avant-garde forms in architecture. In Hartford, he saw the Cheney Block (designed by Henry Hobson Richardson in 1875–76), and he may have met Stanford White, who later became a good friend, as he was commissioned to design houses for Platt's uncles in South Manchester. (These were never built, however.)

At age seventeen, Platt enrolled in the National Academy of Design, where he studied drawing with Lemuel Wilmarth, who taught a rapid sketching technique that emphasized light and shadow rather than studied draftsmanship.[8] Platt also joined the Art Students League, and there he received painting instruction from Walter Shirlaw and the American Impressionist William Merritt Chase. During summers, Platt sketched scenery on travels with his family. On vacation in 1879 at Bolton's Landing, New York, he met Stephen Parrish, a printmaker (and the father of Maxfield), who convinced Platt to take up etching, a commercial medium that had only recently been turned to the purpose of fine art. Parrish gave the younger man some informal instruction in the demanding technique, and the lessons picked up again the next summer when Platt joined the Parrishes in the seaside village of Gloucester, Massachusetts. Soon, Platt was turning out spare and strongly composed seascapes reminiscent of the work of James McNeil Whistler, and his father's friends were referring to him as "boy-etcher."[9]

Despite his unusual skill, however, Charles was determined to learn to paint. In 1882, at age twenty-one, Platt set off for Europe, where he remained for the next five years, alternating winter studio study in Paris with summer sketching trips. The first summer, he traveled to England and spent time on the northern coast of France. (Fig. 2.2) The next, he went to Holland, where he studied the work of the Hague School, which combined stylistic influences from the French Barbizon painters and Hals and Van Dyke with the landscape subjects of Hobbema, Cuyp, and Ruysdael. Platt's paintings changed as a result. He began focusing on turbulent sky effects, painted loosely with thick, broad, almost monochromatic strokes.[10]

He spent the following summer in Larmor, a small fishing village in Brittany, and there his painting underwent another change, likely in response to the influence of Dennis Bunker, an American friend and painter who had joined him for the season. The historian Erica E. Hirshler points out that, at this juncture, Platt raised the horizon lines in his paintings, a shift that gave more space to foreground and also led to more tautly structured compositions. She notes a rising tension "between spatial recession and the surface design of abstract shapes."[11] This shift in perspective also forecast the brilliant stroke that would characterize Platt's gardens—a strong balance between foreground composition and view. (Fig. 2.3)

Platt's studies at the Académie Julian in Paris gave his paintings increased compositional strength. There too, he found friendships with several American artists who would figure in his life back in the United States. One of Platt's letters from this period mentions preparation for the entry exam to the architectural division of the École des Beaux-Arts, but apparently he did not follow through with his application, or it was rejected.[12] He continued to paint and to etch, turning frequently to architectural subjects as well as landscapes.

In Paris, Platt met and fell in love with a young

2.2. *Mud Boats on the Thames,* Charles A. Platt, 1883, etching. Private collection.

2.3. *Orchard, East Hampton,* Charles A. Platt, c. 1885, oil on canvas. Photograph courtesy Spanierman Gallery LLC, New York.

woman from the Bronx, Annie Corbin Hoe, and in the months following, he traveled with her and her parents through Italy.[13] The next spring, in April 1886, they were married in Florence—Platt was recovering from typhoid fever at the time—and, within a few months, she became pregnant. Their happiness was short-lived, however, for Annie died in childbirth in the spring of 1887, along with her and Charles's newborn twin daughters. Grief-stricken, Platt returned to the United States. He spent the summer in Gloucester, painting with friends he had made in Paris, and the next summer he returned to Holland to paint, alone.

———

In the summer of 1889, at the encouragement of his friend Henry Walker, Platt went to New Hampshire to see the Cornish artists colony that had been founded by the sculptor Augustus Saint-Gaudens four years before. (Fig. 2.4) He fell in love with the lush landscape of the Connecticut River valley, which many observers have remarked bears a strong resemblance to Tuscany.[14] Maxfield Parrish, who also moved to Cornish about this time, described it as "an ideal country, so paintable and beautiful, . . . a place to dream one's life away."[15] Platt's attachment to the idyllic New England countryside proved lasting.

Continuing to paint and to etch over the course of the summer, Platt also designed a house for Walker—not, in Morgan's view, a particularly remarkable effort.[16] The following year, he returned to Cornish, bought a beautiful piece of property, and designed a handsome clapboard house for himself sited in an old orchard where pastureland and the Connecticut River provided the dominant view. (Figs. 2.5, 2.6) The parlor and the dining room had large triple windows that reached to the floor, and through Greek Doric columns of the large piazza at the west end of the house was the view to Mount Ascutney. Once, when asked by his son Geoffrey how he had learned to be an architect, Platt answered playfully, "by trying it on the dog."[17]

While there were drawbacks to learning architecture

through a trial-and-error method, in Platt's case there were also distinct advantages. "By first dabbling in architecture," Mark Hewitt notes, "[Platt] learned the pragmatic, constructive, and formal aspects of the profession without indoctrination in any theory or philosophy of design."[18] He was peculiarly free to follow his own course. In time, an extensive architectural library, including folios from the Italian and French Renaissance, seventeenth- and eighteenth-century England, and classical ancient sources, would provide Platt with his working vocabulary. In this material he would find a relevant starting point and, after studying it exhaustively, would modify and

2.5. Plan of Charles A. Platt estate, Cornish, N.H. From *Monograph of the Work of Charles A. Platt*, 1913.

2.4. View to mountains from Aspet, Augustus Saint-Gaudens estate, Cornish, N.H. Photograph by Jack E. Boucher. Library of Congress, HABS NH, 10-CORN, 1A-5.

2.6. View of terrace and garden, Charles A. Platt estate. From *Monograph of the Work of Charles A. Platt.*

2.7. High Court, Annie Lazarus estate, Cornish, N.H. From *Monograph of the Work of Charles A. Platt.*

adapt it. Through this method, Platt's houses and gardens would achieve pleasing proportions and a sense of fitness, as well as distinctive character.

In 1890 the philanthropist and art patron Annie Lazarus commissioned Platt to design a villa for her on Plainfield Stage Road, across from Platt's own Cornish home. It was a more ambitious prospect than Platt had previously faced, and he turned to Stanford White for advice. The resulting two-story, U-shaped plan Platt created closely recalled McKim, Mead & White's 1883 plan for the Villard mansion in New York City, a house, as Morgan notes, that was one of the earliest indicators of the return to classical formality that would soon dominate American architecture.[19] (Fig. 2.7) Platt used White's approach innovatively, siting the Cornish house at the very crest of the hill so that the prospect would be revealed at a single sweep. He placed the formal garden on axis with the library at the side of the house, where it would not interfere with the view. (Fig. 2.8) His plan closely related interior and exterior space, through proportion and lines of sight, in a method that was both elegant and practical. Platt later wrote about this design and its sources: "To a house set high upon a hill, the ground falling away from it with some abruptness, the whole site chosen for the view, the landscape gardener will give surroundings of the utmost simplicity that they may not compete with or disturb the larger without. This was recognized in the

2.8. *Larkspur (Garden at High Court, Cornish),* Charles A. Platt, oil on canvas, c. 1895. Courtesy members of the Platt family.

Frascati villas of Italy, which were terraced to give a view of the distant Campagna, and in America there was an example in High Court."[20]

The decade of the 1890s was one of intense cultural

tumult as the nation strained at its agrarian roots and spun with increasing speed toward a system of corporate-capitalist industrialism. For Platt, Cornish and its convivial artist-residents offered a refuge from these dizzying transformations. The bucolic colony had been founded in 1885, when Augustus Saint-Gaudens began renting a house to escape the summer heat of Manhattan. Five years later, the sculptor bought an old farmhouse with a grand view of Mount Ascutney and "classicized" it with a colonnaded front porch—one skeptical neighbor remarked that the building looked as if it were wearing false teeth. Inspired by recent trends in garden design, Saint-Gaudens developed geometric beds in relation to his remodeled house, using rectilinear layouts filled with old-fashioned, hardy flowers, enlivening them with classical ornament and statuary. (Fig. 2.9) The rural setting and Saint-Gaudens's friendly presence drew other, mostly New York–based artists.[21]

In Cornish, serious art-making mixed with serious play, and lively cross-fertilization occurred among the artists and writers who summered there. In addition to Saint-Gaudens, these included the painters Thomas and Maria Oakey Dewing (the Cornish colony's first passionate flower gardeners), Stephen Parrish and his son Maxfield (who came at Platt's urging; both father and son would create strikingly original gardens); the muralist Kenyon Cox; the painter George de Forest Brush; the sculptor Herbert Adams; Rose Standish Nichols, author, landscape architect (and Saint-Gaudens's niece); the novelist Winston Churchill; Ellen Biddle Shipman and her husband Louis (she an ardent gardener and soon-to-be landscape architect, he a playwright), the critic and author Herbert Croly and his wife Louise; Dennis and Edith Hardy Bunker (he a painter, she one of the colony's best gardeners); and, briefly, the sculptor Paul Manship. Virtually all of them lived country lives, bringing verve and imagination to the design of their homes. (Fig. 2.10) Many Cornishites were avid and accomplished gardeners, and they eagerly traded seeds, plants, and advice.[22] So often did dinner party conversation turn to gardening, Ellen Shipman remembered, that one evening before dinner Maxfield Parrish playfully bowed his head and murmured, "Let us spray."[23]

The artistic activities of the group occurred against the backdrop of the American Renaissance, a sprawling movement with roots in the 1880s, a time of great industrial advancement, rising cultural pride, and a sweeping embrace of the classical ideal—a trajectory that led to the Chicago World's Fair in 1893. Among Cornish artists,

2.9. Aspet, Saint-Gaudens estate, Cornish, N.H. Saint-Gaudens NHS.

2.10. Northcote, Stephen Parrish estate, Cornish, N.H. Saint-Gaudens NHS.

many of whom, including Platt, were involved in the Chicago event, allegiance to the classical ideal was tempered by other influences, particularly an appreciation for Arts and Crafts principles. The houses and gardens Platt created for himself and others there were in a sense a laboratory for developing the mixture.[24] In these early experiments, Platt was staunchly supported by his progressive friend and neighbor Herbert Croly, for whom he also designed a house in 1899. (Fig. 2.11)

Croly had also grown up in New York City, reared by distinguished parents—David Goodman Croly, an iconoclastic liberal thinker and editor of the *New York World*, and Jane Cunningham Croly, an ardent feminist and well-known journalist. Herbert, who suffered a nervous breakdown before he could graduate from Harvard, became an architectural critic at a time when most published criticism did not even include designers' names—important houses were identified by their owners.

Croly shared his parents' liberal values, and he wrote several influential articles and books on the topic of the new American country house which reflected them.[25] He believed that Charles Platt's houses and gardens, in particular, offered vital, pragmatic alternatives to the showy eclecticism that characterized the work of many of Platt's colleagues. Further, Croly believed that artists and architects had a responsibility to take the lead in improving American taste, in the service of improving American civilization. Platt, who would change his vocational listing from "artist" to "architect" in the New York Directory of 1899, held views closely aligned with Croly's, likewise equating good taste with good citizenship.

In a 1904 interview Platt commented, "In so far as we get our ideas of country places from our own untrained taste, from slavish imitation of our neighbors, and from our spectacular invention, we are like any other bad citizen, indifferent to the progress of science or political institutions. And in so far as our country places are built with careful use of the best historic models, we are keeping pace with the unmistakably forward march of American rural architecture, and are helping it on its way."[26] Both men saw this process as cumulative and collaborative. Collaboration was to be achieved through friendship

2.11. Herbert Croly estate, Cornish, N.H. From Guy Lowell, *American Gardens*, 1902.

and social intercourse among a diverse group of leaders in various fields, as Hewitt notes, "an enlightened community of educated artists and intellectuals."[27] This was precisely the situation in Cornish.

In 1892 Platt's growing interest in landscape design had been bolstered by a trip to Italy undertaken with his brother William, who was then an assistant in the Olmsted firm.[28] Platt later remarked that he had arranged the tour specifically to "subvert" the teachings of Olmsted, whose emphasis neglected, as he wrote, "the side of landscape architecture which interested me most, . . . that is, the purely architectural side of it."[29] Olmsted had been equally clear about his disapproval of Charles Platt's position: "I am afraid that I do not think much of the fine and costly gardening of Italy," he told William as he prepared for his trip. Olmsted instead encouraged him to pay special attention to roadside scenery, "in which nature contends with and is gaining upon the art of man. I urge you again to hunt for beauty in commonplace and pleasant conditions; . . . and all of such things as are made lovely by growths that seem to be natural and spontaneous to the place."[30]

Over the course of several months, Charles and William visited twenty-four villas in and around Rome, Florence, Siena, and Verona.[31] Most were surrounded by neglected but still beautiful gardens—outdoor rooms with crumbling walls and overgrown hedges, with ceilings of sky vaulted with arching branches of giant ilex and syca-more. Haunting photographs by Charles record poignant moments of discovery, and they also capture exquisitely wrought spaces. (Fig. 2.12) These images were featured in a two-part article for *Harper's* magazine, and, the follow-ing year, published with several sketches in a book, *Italian Gardens*, whose text, Platt admitted, put aside "the matter of research altogether." Nonetheless, Platt's narrative of-fered deft analysis of spatial configuration, lines of sight, perspective, and composition. One passage stands out as his core reading of the Italian idea, soon to become a guiding principle in his work:

> The evident harmony of arrangement between the house and the surrounding landscape is what first strikes one in Italian landscape architecture—the design as a whole, including the gardens, terraces, grove, and their necessary surroundings and em-bellishments, it being clear that no one of these component parts was ever considered independ-ently, the architect of the house being the architect of the garden and the rest of the villa. The problem being to take a piece of land and make it habitable,

the architect proceeded with the idea that not only was the house to be lived in, but that one still wished to be at home while out-of-doors; so the garden was designed as another *apartment*, the ter-races and groves still others, where one might walk about and find a place suitable to the house of the day and feeling of the moment, and still be in that sacred portion of the globe dedicated to one's self.[32]

Platt concludes the book with a statement of his pur-pose in writing it—to provide "a more thorough under-standing and appreciation of the reasons which led to a formal treatment . . . that it might lead to a revival of the same method [in America]."[33] Tragically, William had little opportunity to experiment with any of the influences from the trip; he died in a drowning accident in Maine soon after he returned, a circumstance that added to Charles's already considerable burden of grief.

Reactions to Platt's book were mixed. Charles Eliot, writing for the *Nation*, criticized it for weak scholarship and lack of plans.[34] A reviewer in *Garden and Forest* (likely Charles Eliot again) dismissed the subject as unworthy of serious study, noting that these gardens were examples of "beauty for its own sake," and that such designs do "not address . . . the nobler part of our nature as simple natural scenery does."[35] But, for many readers, *Italian Gardens* res-onated with the romantic appeal of Italy and also with the rising sense of the formal garden as an expression of cul-tural authority.[36] John Elliot, a physician from Needham, Massachusetts, was one of those impressed by Platt's "knowledge and flair for the subject," and on this basis hired him to design a new house, Platt's first job beyond Cornish.[37] Soon there would be others, one of which would catapult Platt into the public eye.

Charles Sprague, a lawyer and U.S. congressman, and his wife, Mary Pratt Sprague, were exasperated with progress at Faulkner Farm, their Brookline country place. Herbert Browne (of Little, Browne & Moore) had de-signed the new house, and the firm of Olmsted, Olmsted & Eliot was overseeing development of the landscape. Almost from the first, Sprague seems perversely to have

2.12. Flower garden at the Villa Pamfili. Photograph by Charles A. Platt. From *Italian Gardens,* 1894.

done his best to create impossible conditions between the two offices until tempers had frayed on every front.[38] When Platt's recent client Elliot (who was also the Spragues' physician) learned of the turmoil, he recommended that they bring in Platt to replace the Olmsted firm. In Platt's hands, the Spragues became surprisingly docile, approving all of the architect's recommendations—even his initial one, to rip up the newly installed curving drive and replace it with a straight approach.

Platt's c. 1897 plan borrowed heavily from the Villa Gamberaia, whose formal garden was also sited to command long views of surrounding countryside. It, too, featured a woodland garden on a nearby hilltop, an allée laid out across the front of the house terminating in a monumental statue, lawn terraces behind the house, and a formal garden adjacent, with geometric beds, semicircular pools, and apselike curving porticos. (Fig. 2.13) The casino at Faulkner Farm recalled an architectural form from another well-known Italian garden, the Villa Lante. (Fig. 2.14) Herms, wellheads, urns, large terra-cotta pots, and bay trees drawn from a standard repertory of Italian ornaments were placed axially throughout the space, and ebullient plantings of flowers filled the beds. By 1898, the design was complete. (Figs. 2.15, 2.16)

At Faulkner Farm, as in his early Cornish gardens, Platt had worked from the outside in, designing a landscape that would take best advantage of setting, even as it responded to the architectural lines and proportions of the house. In this regard, Platt differed from his Beaux-Arts–trained colleagues, including Stanford White, who focused primarily on the design of houses and then developed landscape schemes, with varying degrees of sympathy for the landscape setting. On a much smaller scale, Platt's new garden at Faulkner Farm also evoked the pristine Beaux-Arts classicism of the Columbian Exposition, where plan, structures, planting, and ornament had dazzled visitors with an otherworldly concordance. Like that display, Platt's layout was also remarkably photogenic, which may have been a factor in the garden's almost immediate publication in nu-

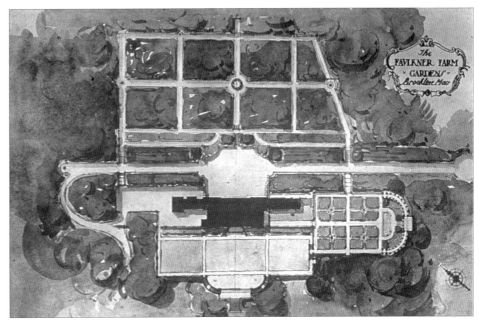

2.13. Plan of Faulkner Farm, Charles F. Sprague estate, Brookline Mass. From *Monograph of the Work of Charles A. Platt.*

2.14. Casino at Faulkner Farm. Harvard GSD.

merous articles. All of them, with one British exception, were filled with exuberant praise.[39]

Among the most enthusiastic was a two-part piece in *House and Garden* published in 1901 by Ralph Adams Cram, an architect whose own idiosyncratic career bore certain resemblances to Platt's. In Cram's view, Platt's new gardens were "thoroughly modern and original."[40] It is

2.15. Flower beds at Faulkner Farm. Harvard GSD.

2.16. Formal garden at Faulkner Farm. From Lowell, *American Gardens.*

ployed, but we must have something, and an architectural style of our own is denied us, so we borrow of course, and in the present instance we have borrowed from Italy."[41] A few years later, Platt explained his reasons for emphasizing the Italian model. "If the American country place . . . be constructed upon the models of the Italian villa of the Renaissance, it will not fall below the best standards. For the basis of taste in these Renaissance villas was that love of formal beauty and propriety in architecture which is architectural classicism. And since formal beauty and propriety are exact things, they may be followed and loved today in America as they were in Italy in the fifteenth century."[42]

In his influential book *American Gardens* (1902), Guy Lowell also praised Faulkner Farm, both featuring it in his introductory essay and concluding the main text with sixteen photographs of it. (Fig. 2.16) Other admiring articles rapidly appeared, in *Country Life in America*, *New England Magazine*, and *Harper's*. In 1904 Herbert Croly included the project along with several other Platt designs in a two-part article for *Architectural Record*. That same year, the garden was featured in Barr Ferree's *American Estates and Gardens*.[43] In 1906 John Cordis Baker ran a large spread on it in *American Country Homes and Their Gardens*.

On the heels of this very successful commission came another opportunity to work in Brookline, at Weld, the country estate of Mrs. Sprague's cousin Isabel Anderson and her husband, Larz. Platt's new garden there would rely on many of the same elements he had used at Faulkner Farm, but the Weld design was arguably more assured than the earlier effort.[44] Its plan was less cluttered, and the various strong elements, which included a large Italianate fountain at the east end, were held together by a central greensward flanked by large flower borders. (Figs. 2.17, 2.18, 2.19) In subsequent designs for formal gardens, including that at Gwinn, Platt would often provide open space in the center of his plan. Within a few years, Weld was extensively published in many of the same magazines and books that had trumpeted the success of Faulkner Farm.[45] One of the most enthusiastic of these accounts was "An 'Italian Garden' That Is Full of Flowers" by the prolific Wilhelm Miller, in which Miller detailed the four

not surprising that Platt's designs appealed to Cram's complex sensibilities, which, too, straddled modern and historical concerns. He contrasted Faulkner Farm both with "sweetly picturesque" designs that had dominated the nineteenth century and with the Victorian predilection for "foolish blots" spattered over a green lawn. He argued that, by focusing on underlying principles, Platt had also escaped "stolid copyism"—that Platt's new gardens were in no sense imitative: "they make no pretense at deceiving one into thinking he has been suddenly transferred to some unfamiliar Italian villa. . . . Whatever flavour of Italy they give is due to the architectural style em-

2.17. Fountain at Weld, Larz Anderson estate, Brookline, Mass., c.1904.
Photograph by Thomas E. Marr. Courtesy Historic New England.

2.18. View of greensward, Weld. Harvard GSD.

2.19. Plan of Weld. From *Monograph of the Work of Charles A. Platt.*

principles he believed led to the garden's "charm": seclusion, changes in level, water, and plenty of flowers. It was not long before the formula found its way into the work of many of the era's practitioners.[46]

With his stature rising, Platt was soon in a position to set his own terms with clients—including the stipulation that the scope of the job include both house and garden. In this way, he could create comprehensive environments that would give his superb compositional talents full expression. Honed during many years' training in the pictorial arts, Platt's abilities were, in Morgan's view, unique among his generation. His distinctive sense of spatial order and visual coherence led to "compositions of carefully integrated forms that functioned effectively in both two and three dimensions."[47]

Platt's spatial approach also proved flexible. It fit a range of scales and budgets, and it yielded a modern residence designed to accommodate the life that was to be lived in it. (Platt once playfully observed that it was "essential that 'the punishment fit the crime.'"[48]) He would borrow from several different architectural repertories besides the Italian—particularly Georgian and Colonial Revival—according to the demands of the client, site, and budget. (Fig. 2.20) In many instances, "he appropriated elements of all of these influences into a blended classicism, a gentle adjustment of familiar prototypes," writes the architect and historian Charles D. Warren, ". . . but even projects that combine styles create a smooth synthesis of disparate antecedents to evoke the long, nearly continuous tradition of classical architecture."[49]

The 1904 publication of Edith Wharton's *Italian Villas and Their Gardens*, jauntily illustrated by Platt's Cornish neighbor Maxfield Parrish, likely benefited Platt's career. Although she reiterated many of the same principles that the architect had set out in his earlier book, Wharton differed from Platt on certain points of interpretation, one of which was the role of bloom in the gardens of the Italian Renaissance. "Though it is an exaggeration to say that there are no flowers in Italian gardens," she wrote authoritatively in her opening sentence, "one must always bear in mind that [Italian garden craft] is independent of floriculture."[50] Platt and his brother had seen very few tended flower beds in the villas they visited, but he nevertheless conjured them up throughout his book, mentioning them on almost every page. Cornish, of course, was filled with gardens, and Platt realized that a landscape approach that married the cachet of classicism with bountiful bloom would dovetail perfectly with America's new passion. It is not surprising that he chose to emphasize this aspect of the formal garden, particularly after his 1893 marriage to Edith Bunker, who was known as the colony's best gardener.

By the turn of the century, interest in flower garden-ing was growing rapidly in response to nostalgia for old-fashioned plants and for the simple "grandmothers' gardens" in which they grew, encouraged by new, richly illustrated magazines and books.[51] Louise Shelton's *Beautiful Gardens in America*, published in 1915, was perhaps most widely read.[52] Interest in bountiful borders, vines, and shrubberies was also sparked by British publications. The earliest and most important of these was William Robinson's classic *The English Flower Garden* (1883); Thomas Mawson's *The Art and Craft of Garden-Making* (1901) and Gertrude Jekyll's somewhat later books on the topic were also widely read in the United States. Wilhelm Miller's various articles in *Country Life* and *Garden Magazine* appeared throughout the early years of the century, and in 1911 they were revised and collected into his book *What England Can Teach Us about Gardening*.

Platt's country place layouts would continue to feature formal gardens with ebullient herbaceous borders, and as his practice developed, he sought out collaborations with landscape practitioners who could bring horticultural expertise and imagination to this feature. About 1910 Platt began working with his Cornish neighbor Ellen Biddle Shipman, whom Judith B. Tankard, Shipman's biographer, estimates designed plantings for forty-nine of Platt's projects.[53] One highly successful and widely published pairing was at The Moorings, a c. 1908 lakeside estate for Russell A. Alger Jr., in Grosse Pointe, outside Detroit. (Fig. 2.21) There Platt's studied classicism provided a foil for Shipman's luxuriant planting combinations, added some years later. He placed the formal garden at the side of the house, as at High Court, and he used a pergola to frame views to Lake St. Clair. Shipman filled the wide beds that ran along the garden's central axis with tea rose standards, lilies, Japanese anemone, columbine, monkshood, delphinium, and evergreen specimens.

Platt also collaborated with less well known planting consultants in his formal garden compositions. One of these was Paul Rubens Frost, who worked at Gwinn in this capacity in 1907. In some projects, Platt was assisted by landscape practitioners in site planning—at the W. Hinckle Smith estate, Timberline, in Bryn Mawr, for example, where Olmsted Brothers were consulted, and at

2.20. Eastover, George T. Palmer estate, New London, Conn. From *Monograph of the Work of Charles A. Platt.*

Villa Turicum, in Lake Forest, where Manning sited the house.[54] (Fig. 2.22)

Platt's early clientele had included many of his mother's relatives and members of the Cornish colony, but he quickly attracted scores of customers beyond this circle.[55] His expanding network included the Maxwells of Rockville, Connecticut (1903), William Mather (Gwinn, 1907), and Harold and Edith Rockefeller McCormick (who rejected a scheme by Frank Lloyd Wright to work with him in Lake Forest, Illinois, in 1908). As he was finishing his plans for Gwinn, Platt was commissioned by Mrs. James S. Roosevelt to design the Manhattan townhouse she would share with Franklin and Eleanor. Charles Lang Freer hired Platt for three projects: a suburban de-

2.21. Gardens at The Moorings, Russell A. Alger Jr. estate, Grosse Pointe, Mich. RMC-Cornell Univ. Library.

velopment he planned Freer's business partner, Col. Frank J. Hecker, in Detroit, with which was never built; a residence in Great Barrington, Massachusetts; and, several years later, the Freer Gallery in Washington, D.C. Between his first professional commission at High Court and his last adjustments to Villa Turicum in Lake Forest, Platt completed more than one hundred landscape projects.[56] International critics sometimes compared him to the British architect Sir Edward Lutyens, although Platt was not a fan of Lutyens's work.[57]

Like many of his American architectural colleagues, Platt routinely designed the interiors of his houses, and here, too, his approach yielded fresh amalgamations. He also frequently selected the wall coverings, draperies, furniture, carpets, and, in some cases, art for these interiors, choosing his own works or sometimes those of his fellow Cornishites. (At Gwinn, he hung several landscapes by Thomas Dewing.) Rather than limit his recommendations to a single period or style, Platt mixed them, relying on his own confident sense of taste. This approach earned the approval of Platt's friend Royal Cortissoz, art critic for the *Tribune*, who contrasted it with the historically driven assemblages that still filled many American country houses—"instances of foolish extravagance and vulgar

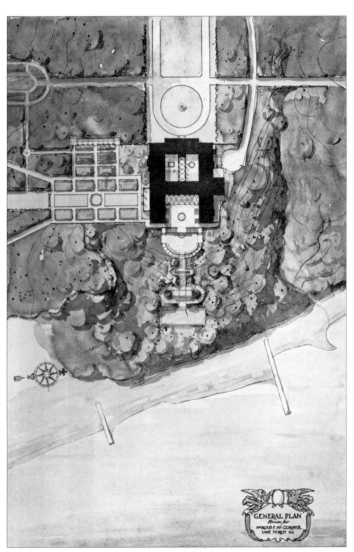

GENERAL PLAN
House for
HAROLD F McCORMICK
LAKE FOREST ILL.

2.22. Plan of Villa Turicum, Harold F. McCormick estate, Lake Forest, Ill., gardens designed 1912–13. From *Monograph of the Work of Charles A. Platt.*

taste. . . . As we turn from them to one of Platt's rooms the contrast is wonderfully illuminating."[58]

Platt's personality was also a boon to his business. He was amusing and articulate, and he shared many of the interests of his rich clients, to whom he related on an equal social footing. He enjoyed travel, appreciated fine food and drink, spoke fluent French, and played golf, bridge, and, during Cornish summers, croquet. He continued to paint for his own enjoyment, maintaining a private studio above his New York office at 101 Park Avenue South, to which he retired from the demands of the day. He was the sole principal in his firm, which meant a limited number of projects and higher than usual fees.

It was a measure of Platt's prominence that in 1912 he was featured in an interview in *Landscape Architecture*. The author, Charles Downing Lay, introduced Platt as a man "who has mastered, as has hardly any other man of modern times, certain parts of the domain of both architecture and landscape architecture.[59] Lay also noted: "one thing in Mr. Platt's point of view which landscape architects would do well to consider is his independence of spirit, his refusal to be bound too closely by the natural conditions of the site, but rather to remold them nearer to the heart's desire."[60]

Herein lay a difference between Platt and Manning, whose approach was decidedly to not "force the land to fit the plan."[61] While Herbert Croly had ebulliently praised Platt's "appreciation of the proper landscape values," Manning and some of his fellow landscape architects saw Platt's work in more partisan terms, as a reflection of a design trend that they believed threatened the robust regard for nature with which they were closely identified.[62] At Gwinn, this debate took to the field, a blue-clay bluff overlooking Lake Erie, and there it shaped a remarkably successful collaboration between two leading figures in the profession.

THREE

GWINN

Cleveland, Ohio

Like many patriotic Americans of the day—including Warren H. Manning—William Gwinn Mather was fascinated by the accomplishments of his colonial forebears. In Mather's case (as in Manning's) they were a distinguished group. Richard Mather had landed in Massachusetts in 1635 and produced the first book in the New World, a translation of Hebrew psalms, and several of his descendants, including Richard's son Increase and Increase's son Cotton, also published important works, most of which William would eventually acquire for his private library. In time, the family's interests turned west, toward more earthly concerns. One of these was the three-million-acre Western Reserve of the Connecticut Land Company, of which William's great-grandfather was a charter member.[1]

In 1843 William's father, Samuel Livingston Mather, traveled to Ohio to sell some of this land, and he decided to settle in Cleveland. The city had gotten a boost fifteen years earlier when the northern section of the Ohio and Erie Canal was completed, making it a prime shipping outlet for mineral and agricultural products. Samuel was ambitious, and when he learned that precious metals had been discovered in Michigan's Upper Peninsula, he and a group of local investors hired a scientist to investigate. Their agent came back with reports of unfriendly Indians and massive deposits of iron ore—not the hoped-for gold or copper—and most of the other speculators lost interest. But Samuel saw promise, and he invested heavily in a new mining operation that would soon require housing for workers in remote locales and, after locks were built at Sault Ste. Marie, a fleet of steamers to ship the ore across the Great Lakes. Despite several financial setbacks, Samuel's Cleveland Iron Mining Company prospered.

William was born in 1857 during a panic that closed down Cleveland's iron works entirely. But this crisis passed, and the company rallied to become one of the city's most successful. When Samuel died in 1890, William took over as president of his father's business, having by then earned a master's degree from Trinity College. He soon presided over a merger with the rival Iron Cliffs Company which gave rise to the largest mining operation in the Upper Peninsula—Cleveland-Cliffs Iron Company. As president, William began to introduce reforms.

He created an open-land policy that permitted people to camp, hunt, fish, and bird-watch on corporation property.[2] Increasing benefits to his workers and introducing

3.1. Gwinn site before construction. Gwinn.

practices to manage relief funds, he also established improved housing in the new company towns, as well as parks, cooperative stores, schools, and recreational facilities. In later years, he added life insurance associations, a welfare department, pension plans, a safety department, and a modern hospital.[3] A violent miners' strike in 1895 was undoubtedly a factor in Mather's growing attention to his workers' well-being; he was also influenced by the progressive ideas of the landscape architect who became involved in company developments in 1896, Warren H. Manning.[4]

Cleveland-Cliffs Iron grew rapidly under William's direction. Business holdings came to include six hundred thousand acres of virgin timber in the Upper Peninsula, 75 percent interest in the Lake Superior and Ishpeming Railroad, several hydroelectric plants, docks in three states, and a fleet of twenty-three iron ore steamers. By the turn of the century, Mather had become a very wealthy man. Though nearing fifty and still a bachelor, he began thinking about building a country estate in the same neighborhood as Shoreby, the country place of his older half-brother Samuel, east of the city. In 1906 he wrote to ask Manning for his opinion about a parcel on Lake Erie that he was considering buying. (Fig. 3.1)

Manning was a busy man when Mather's letter arrived, but he responded to it immediately. He liked the description of the lot, particularly its proximity to the lake and the resulting "outlook," and he offered some advice about the proposed house, recommending that Mather pursue the English cottage style, which was, in his view, "more domestic and homelike than any of the types that have been the fad in times past." Manning also recommended that Mather see some examples of fine American landscape design, mentioning a large wild garden he had designed for Percival Roberts in Narbeth, Pennsylvania. And he proposed that Mather retain him for the job even before hiring an architect so that he could site the house.[5] Mather did not respond directly to Manning's advice or his bid for the job, but asked him to come to Cleveland to see the various properties he was considering, having added two to the list.

Within five days, Manning came west and submitted a six-page report on the three lots, evaluating views, soil, vegetation, shore conditions, location, subdivision potential, garden and lawn potential, and cost, in his typical method. He reasserted his opinion that Mather should buy "Lot C," citing the water view and the unusual curve of the amphitheater-like bluff. Manning also submitted sketchy plans for potential estate layouts for all three properties, and he closed his letter with another request for the job and an offer to secure competitive proposals from architects that he and Mather could review together.[6]

Mather wrote again, this time to inquire about recent examples of American country houses. Manning sent photos of several examples, among which was the Cornish house Charles Platt had designed for Herbert and Louis Croly, which he described as "rather original and rather distinctively American." (The phrase "distinctively American" appears seven times in Manning's four-page letter.[7]) Mather then wrote again to ask Manning for his opinion of Platt, perhaps also remembering a letter from his friend Charles Lang Freer, who was a client of Platt's.[8] The easy exchange took on a more guarded tone as Manning explained that while he found Platt's gardens "more consistent and satisfactory than any others," he also considered them "rather overloaded with architectural objects." In his view, in Platt's gardens "flowers are an incident or rather a decorative feature that is made subordinate to the architectural features."[9]

Despite the lukewarm endorsement, Mather's interest in Platt grew, buoyed by glowing articles in leading magazines and books and favorable reports from previous clients, and by May of 1907 he had decided to hire Platt to design his new house.[10] He wrote to Manning to tell him of his decision, noting that it was Platt's "custom" (it was actually Platt's requirement) "to plan the arrangement of grounds as well as the house." But Mather did not throw Manning over entirely. "Mr. Platt and I will both be pleased," he wrote, "if you will collaborate with him."[11]

Manning was no doubt disappointed at this turn of events, but his response showed less of this than his characteristic doggedness. He requested a conference with Platt before his sketches were too far advanced because he felt certain (on no particular evidence) that Platt would agree "that neither one of us can consider any of the details of the proposed plan unless each one is in close touch with the other from the beginning."[12] And so the project began, guided by a shrewd businessman who had engineered an arrangement that promised to take best advantage of each man's talent.

Though Mather was vacationing at the time of Platt's first visit to Cleveland in March 1907—a circumstance the architect preferred[13]—he had left Platt a note about the house, indicating that he wanted "an effect of more color and lightness than is possible with natural brick and stone,—something of the Italian or Riviera effect." He also listed his practical requirements: "a stable and garage accommodations for two horses; three or four carriages, three automobiles. A tennis court, vegetable and kitchen garden and of course principally the pleasure garden."[14] Platt, too, had reviewed the three properties under consideration, and he agreed with Manning's opinion that Lot C was superior to the others, primarily because the roughly rectangular parcel could support a cohesive plan, his specialty.

On the basis of both designers' approval, Mather bought the 505-foot shorefront parcel on Lake Shore Boulevard. He planned to retain only the middle section, about five and a half acres, and he asked Platt to proceed with a design, instructing him that he wanted to limit the rest of his spending, including interior decoration but not furniture, to $55,000. Platt was pessimistic about keeping to that figure and warned Mather that it would likely need to be revised substantially.

The design proceeded quickly. As was his method, Platt had conceived the landscape plan as a whole, determining the location and proportions of each component in relation to the others. (Fig. 3.2) The most unusual feature of the proposed scheme was a 200-foot curving seawall that would

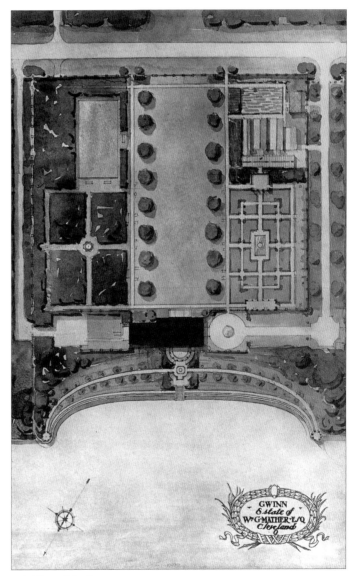

3.2. Plan of Gwinn. From *Monograph of the Work of Charles A. Platt*, 1913.

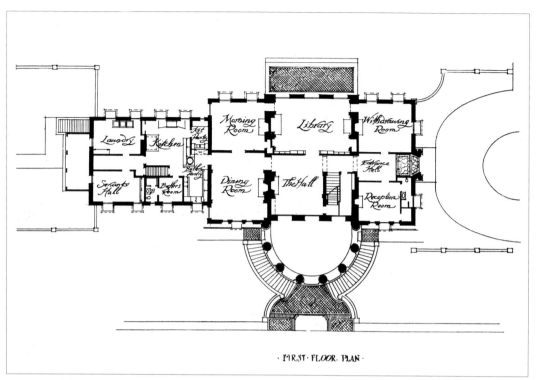

3.3. Plan of first floor. From *Monograph of the Work of Charles A. Platt.*

3.4. Construction of fountain terrace, 1907. Gwinn.

Platt seems never to have considered any other location for the house but the edge of the bluff, where the impact of the lake was sharp and spare. In his design, the lake would first be revealed from inside the house, through French doors in a large central hall, and then from a large portico on the north facade, in the Italian tradition. The curving form, which replaced a square version he had proposed initially, resembles the portico on the south façade of the White House, which in turn recalls the Temple of Vesta at Tivoli—classical examples all. Herbert Croly later wrote that Platt's design "comes, as it were, to a head in this portico, which is both the one ornamental member of the house itself, and the member which will be of most use and pleasure to the inhabitants thereof."[17] (Fig. 3.3) Curving stairways from the portico lead to a terrace below, and there, a broad view of the lake. Another set of curving stairs leads to a lower terrace, and from there a flight of steps descends to the narrow beach and the water itself. Two curving walks take visitors to the end of the seawall. Each of these elements takes its proportions from the house. (Fig. 3.4)

From this vantage point, lake views are austere, in the manner of Whistler. Water and sky appear almost as changing planes of color and light, abstract compositions in keeping with Platt's preference for clarity and balance. At the same time, a vivid sense of the lake's expanse and force is heightened by this enframement, which delivers the water view into the heart of the design. Platt's scheme provided both an architecturally elegant space and transcendent views, the hallmark of his best work. (Fig. 3.5)

trace the natural contour of the cove and thereby frame the lake panorama. Within this embrace, Lake Erie would seem almost to belong to the garden. Samuel Howe, one of many critics to write about Gwinn, later described the force of the appropriation: "Think of having a lake of your own a hundred miles long, the boundaries of which no eye can determine, and to know that it is yours for ever, and that it cannot be taken from you."[15] Few of Platt's houses would have the advantage of such dramatic, scenic splendor.[16]

3.5. *Boy with Dolphin from East Staircase,* 1995. Photograph by Carol Betsch.

In contrast to the drama of the lake terraces Platt designed a parklike expanse for the south side of the property, where a flat, tree-shadowed lawn is flanked by a grove on the east and a formal garden on the west. (Fig. 3.6) The formal garden is bounded by a loggia to the north, a teahouse to the south, and a long wall along its western edge that separates it from the approach drive. At the center is a reflecting pool, surrounded by herbaceous borders edged by wide gravel paths. The garden's geometric layout and axial placement of ornaments, including tubs of bay trees, recalled other formal gardens by Platt, such as Weld, which also featured an open expanse in its center. Practical concerns were addressed, too. Platt included a gardener's cottage and greenhouses extending from the teahouse at the south of the formal garden. (Figs. 3.7, 3.8) The grove on the east side of the lawn offers nearly the opposite experience of shade and seclusion. In the Italian tradition, Platt had provided a range of garden settings—theatrical, calming, intimate, and grand—suitable to any mood. Chauffeur's quarters, garage, stable, and farm buildings were located on a parcel across Lake Shore Boulevard.

An arrival sequence from the street brought guests along a straight approach drive at the west side of the property and a right-hand turn to an intimately scaled forecourt. (Fig. 3.9) The sequence is mirrored at the east end of the property by a service drive and court. The front door is located on the west end of the house, where it opens into a modest entrance hall. The south side of the property, freed of the necessity of a drive, provides an uninterrupted expanse for the large lawn and gardens. The plan is balanced, cohesive, and concise.[18]

Platt's Georgian-influenced concrete and stucco house was stately but not extravagant by the standards of the day—the design would be praised for its "sincerity, direct-

3.7. Construction of teahouse, greenhouse foundations, and gardener's house, view across formal garden, 1908. Gwinn.

3.8. Formal garden after planting, with George Jacques, c. 1909. Gwinn.

ness of purpose, wholesome construction, and restraint."[19] The house included sixteen rooms, six of which were bedrooms, including one for Katharine, William's older half-sister, who lived at Gwinn and, in the tradition of the time, served as his hostess.[20] A two-story wing at the east end of the house provided servants' rooms upstairs, kitchen and service areas downstairs. A parapet concealed windows on the third floor, which was used as an attic.[21]

As the design process went forward, prices for the project climbed. By June 1907, Platt's estimate for the house and

garden structures, not including the cost of the seawall or property itself, had reached $146,500, about three times the initial budget.[22] Mather was a moderate man—almost to an extreme—and he was uneasy about the growing grandeur of Platt's ideas, perhaps more than the cost itself. "I would be careful not to have it in the slightest degree extravagant," he wrote Platt about the garden, adding anxiously, however, that "it should be commensurate with the dignity and style of the house."[23] After suggesting a flurry of cost-cutting measures—all of which Platt dismissed—Mather resigned himself to the much larger sum required and launched into the enterprise with new enthusiasm, reviewing each plan in detail and contributing suggestions of his own, many of which Platt did adopt. By mid-July the site plan and the house designs had been approved, and construction began almost immediately.[24]

Manning's planting schemes were recorded on large plans that corresponded to detailed lists of species and quantities, in methods learned from Olmsted. Manning also had to locate sources for the plants needed and to acquire them. As was customary, many were dug from other properties and from the wild. It was Manning's responsibility to secure the health of the existing large elms, beeches, and maples that were critical to the character of the front lawn, and to improve and lighten the heavy, clay soil throughout the landscape, to prepare it for new plantings.[25] Platt suggested specific plantings for two areas—American elms to line the entry drive, an idea that Manning heartily approved, and an elaborate mix, primarily of annuals, for the formal garden, a responsibility overseen by Platt's assistant Paul Rubens Frost.[26]

From the beginning, Manning emphasized that originality would be critical to design success at Gwinn. "If your place is to have the personality that you wish it to have, it must grow out of your own taste and the taste of your advisors," he wrote to Mather in 1908. In the same

3.10. North facade with mature plantings. Gwinn.

letter, Manning expressed his view that Gwinn's gardens "will be distinguished from other of Mr. Platt's gardens . . . by less of the piling of architectural detail which architects so like to include." In this, too, he proved correct. Both men agreed that the feature that would give the place the its "greatest distinction" was the curving shoreline.[27]

Determining plantings for the amphitheater-shaped cove presented a challenge, owing to the large area to be covered and the proximity of the water and strong winds. For the slope, Manning decided on a carpet of Japanese barberry, anticipating that its thick matted roots would stand up to the wind and waves. The textured foliage offered a rich upholstery of green until autumn, when it turned scarlet-orange. (Fig. 3.10) On either side of the central stairs down to the lake, he planted white fringe tree (*Chionanthus virginicus*), which would grow to form an enclosure. To reiterate the vertical elements in the portico, he added Lombardy poplars (which were used to similar effect near the pergola in the formal garden). At the ends of the two curving walks, Manning planted an apple tree and a golden bark willow. Both had strong horizontal lines, and in time became weathered, softening the impact of the small pavilions that were later added.

3.9. *Forecourt,* 1995. Photograph by Carol Betsch.

Mather and his sister wintered in Pasadena, so the lack of winter foliage was a not a concern at Gwinn.[28]

For the understory of the elm-lined approach to the estate, Manning recommended a "nearly continuous mass

3.11. Entry drive with mature elms. Gwinn.

3.12. Forecourt from house. Gwinn.

of the native Viburnum dentatum" which, he explained to Mather, "has good foliage, grows well in shade, will face down to the turf in an attractive manner, is attractive in flowers and fruits, is free from disease and can be secured in good sized plants."[29] (Fig. 3.11) For variety, he mixed in a few *Viburnum opulus*. At the end of the drive, he planted a grove of white birch and Scotch pine. (The white birch died in the heavy clay and were replaced by gray birch; the Scotch pine also faltered on the exposed site and were replaced by white pine. In 1909 yellowwood were added to the tree planting.) An understory mix of raspberry, maple-leaved viburnum, hydrangea (*arborescens* and *nivea*), teabush, and sweet briar rose formed a delicate, idealized woodland composition.

Where the approach drive made a right-hand turn, Manning discontinued the elms and began large groups of lilacs and mock orange to screen the garden wall to the south and the lake to the north. These were faced down with smaller plants, jetbead (*Rhodotypos scandens*) and fragrant honeysuckle. Manning's planting instructions also included fifty snowberry, which were "to be used sparingly on the main drive, to be increased in the road to the forecourt." A few "were to be planted irregularly along the wall on the north side of the court."[30] (Fig. 3.12)

At Gwinn, as elsewhere, Manning was often influenced in his planting compositions by the coincident availability of fine plants. As he explained to Mather, he was always actively searching for those "with character."[31] He had been watching a big lot of "rather unusually good" lilacs on an old Brookline estate for a long time and bought one hundred of them for a hedge between Gwinn's lawn and the formal garden. Views through the hedge were framed by the arching forms of wrought iron trellises. (Fig. 3.13)

The bosco, on the other side of the lawn from the formal garden, presented Manning with the type of setting most inspiring to his artist's imagination. In 1908 he wrote to Mather at length about the varieties of wildflowers he wanted to try under the trees

3.13. View from formal garden through lilac hedge, 1995. Photograph by Carol Betsch.

3.14. Rhododendron in small wild garden (bosco), view toward house. Gwinn.

there—waterleaf, wood violet, Indian and California strawberry, lily-of-the-valley, trillium, creeping Jenny, lungwort, mistflower, hepatica, and many different ferns—a mix of wild, cultivated, and weedy. This scheme would be changed several times over the years to accommodate different uses of the area, Manning's interest in experiment, and Mather's request for bolder effects.

In 1909 Manning added more natives to the little woods, including *Clematis verticillata, Cornus canadensis, Pyrola,* mayflower, *Clintonia borealis, Polygala pauciflora, Prenanthes, Epilobium angustifolium, Petasites, Aralia nudicaulis,* and several varieties of ferns. The long lists sent to Mather were typical for Manning. The 1909 nursery orders were supplemented by twelve crates of wildflowers dug in the Up-

per Peninsula and shipped in the hold of one of Mather's Cleveland-Cliffs steamers. Thick stands of rhododendron under the mature tree canopy gave the area seclusion, though the shrubs tended to sulk on the cold clay bluff and had to be replaced frequently. They were generally dug from the wild, many in North Carolina, near Asheville, and shipped via train in boxcars. (Fig. 3.14)

During the planting phase of Gwinn, Manning was in close contact with Mather's gardener, George Jacques. Even during construction, each American country place supported its own landscape crew, directed by the head gardener or superintendent. For big jobs, Manning often supplied a representative from his own firm, and his man in Ohio was Albert Davis Taylor.[32] But Jacques would be key to the success of the operation, from its implementation through long-term care.

By May 1909 construction of the house was complete and many of the plantings listed on Manning's plan were in. Manning was confident that he had achieved his aim—to clothe Platt's "rigid design" with a "graceful and attractive drapery of foliage and flowers."[33] But Mather was dissatisfied. He told Manning he wanted his new

3.15. Gwinn library, looking toward vista. Gwinn.

3.16. Fountain in small wild garden, 1957. Photograph by Walter P. Bruning. Gwinn.

gardens to possess the age-old feel of those he had visited in England, such as Hampton Court. He was also disgruntled with Platt about the house interior, which seemed to him "cold and bare."[34] It would, in fact, take Platt several years and several trips to Europe to assemble the rich, eclectic ensemble for which he was known.[35] (Fig. 3.15) Manning reiterated his confidence in the eventual success of his planting design, and he counseled Mather to be patient.

In September Mather wrote to both men to complain about the wild garden on the east side of Gwinn's front lawn. "One walks into it with the feeling that he is going to see something particularly attractive," he wrote Manning, "but there is a measure, to me at least, of disappointment. It is indefinite."[36] In response, Manning recommended greater numbers of bulbs and wildflowers, and he offered to design a small drip fountain that would encourage interesting mosses. He also suggested adding stepping stones imprinted with the forms of plant species growing there. Convinced that the problem stemmed from Mather's lack of appreciation for the understated beauties of nature, Manning explained that such designs were for "the comparatively few people who can fully appreciate the . . . quiet tone of green and inconspicuous flowers." He contrasted these effects with the "brilliant masses of color that you can get in the flower garden."

Manning blamed some share of the problem on Jacques, too, who "does not know well and probably does not care much for the wild garden." He concluded, "I believe that you will find this garden will grow upon you in interest even more than the flower garden as you watch it through the year."[37]

Platt's bolder remedy—a monumental fountain—was more what Mather had in mind, and Mather quickly told him to go ahead and make the drawings for it. The fountain was an amalgamation of elements from several different Italian models, including a finial from the Fountain of the Moors at the Villa Lante and dolphins from a villa at Giusti, near Verona. (Fig. 3.16) Platt's drawings were approved and sent to Blum & Delbridge, stonecutters in Amherst, Ohio, for fabrication. When the various pieces of the big fountain arrived (one weighed five tons), Mather was at a loss where to site them. Platt's travel and work schedule prevented his being in Cleveland at the time.

Once installed—per Mather's engineer's calculations—the new fountain completely dominated the setting. (Fig. 3.17) The addition of sandstone seats and a marble-columned pergola a few years later completed

3.17. *Fountain in Small Wild Garden, View toward Lawn,* 1995. Photograph by Carol Betsch.

the furnishings for what had become an out-door room.[38] (Fig. 3.18) Manning's wild plantings were simplified and paths added, further contributing to the architectural effect. The revised design echoed the layout of the formal garden across the lawn. It, too, included a central water feature, pergola, and paths. Mather commissioned Manning to develop his drip fountain for his summer home in Ishpeming.

Mather also expressed dissatisfaction with the lawn plantings (most of them elms, oaks, and maples), complaining to Manning about the lack of evergreens. In one letter he announced his plan to bring in a "couple of splendid, fully-developed spruce at each corner." Manning objected strenuously, writing that he found the blue form of spruce so pronounced that it would be obtrusive. "It seems to me that you have rather more variety in the foliage . . . than one would expect on a small place."[39] Lingering gardenesque tastes would continue to dog Manning as they had Olmsted.

Despite the paradigmatic conflict in the woodland garden and somewhat unilateral resolution, Mather had not lost interest in Manning's idea that nature-based design could play an important role at his estate. In 1910 he purchased twenty-one additional acres across the boulevard from Gwinn and turned most of it over to Manning for a wild garden. Manning had created such gardens for other clients, but few would achieve the complexity or refinement of the one he began that year.[40]

Manning hired a local man to map the area, paying particular attention to the course of Nine-Mile Creek, a small watercourse that he later credited with "carving out a picturesque and varied lay of the land . . . and for laying down rich soils."[41] His decision to use the creek as the organizing element in the new design recalled his park work in Harrisburg and elsewhere. Per Manning's directions,

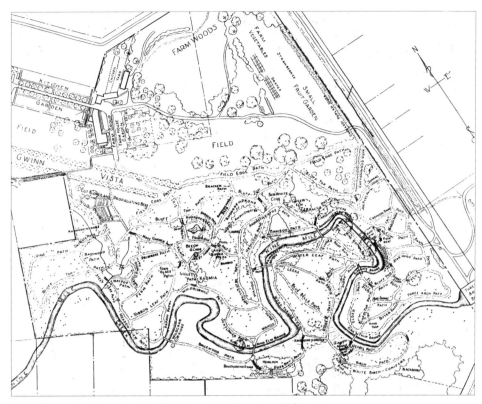

3.19. Plan of wild garden (detail), Warren H. Manning, 1931. Gwinn.

the existing-conditions map was also to include "steep slopes, gradual slopes, small gullies, . . . glades, locations of important trees, and masses of shrubbery."[42]

In response to this detailed information, Manning devised miles of foot and bridle trail systems that offered optimum scenic variety and plant habitat—the settings ranged from bogs to open fields. (Fig. 3.19) Jacques was directed to spade out uninteresting herbaceous material but leave "all tree seedlings as well as Sumachs and other shrubs."[43] A workforce of forty men, overseen by Jacques and E. J. Cotter, Manning's supervisor brought down from Ishpeming, cleared and planted the new garden in about three months. Manning told Mather that he thought they had performed a miracle.[44]

The quantities and varieties of new plants for the project were extraordinary. In the first year, sixteen railway boxcar loads of five hundred large rhododendron each were dug in Damascus, Virginia, and planted along with mountain laurel and thousands of square feet of wild ginger and maidenhair fern. Japanese honeysuckle, Grecian silk vine, and cutleaf blackberry were set out

3.18. *Pergola in Small Wild Garden*, 1995. Photograph by Carol Betsch.

3.20. Bog in wild garden, c. 1930. Photograph by Warren H. Manning office. Gwinn.

3.21. *Rhododendron maximum* and *carolinianum* in wild garden, c. 1930. Photograph by Warren H. Manning office. Gwinn.

3.22. Field edged with *Hemerocallis fulva,* wild garden, c. 1930. Photograph by Warren H. Manning office. Gwinn.

common grape hyacinth, white grape hyacinth, and tiger lily.) Five hundred plants each of crested iris and Crimean iris were planted. One thousand shooting-star came from Wisconsin. Tawny daylily and iris, in variety, were planted along the easterly side of one field. Manning also had Jacques propagate five thousand plants of Oswego bee-balm, sunflower, and red sneezewort. (Figs. 3.20, 3.21, 3.22)

In the spring of 1914 five hundred butterfly weed dug in New Jersey were introduced. Climbing hempweed was put in along the stream edge where silk vine and blackberry had failed. Great, small, and false Solomon's-seal and *Mertensia* were added. Double tansy was brought from North Carolina, walking fern from Virginia. The following spring, American spikenard and American gin-seng came from Illinois. Orange groundsel was planted from seed provided by Cyrus H. McCormick, and Man-

along the stream banks. Three thousand blue marsh vio-lets from Ishpeming were planted in the woods, as were spring flowering bulbs from Holland. (These were or-dered in lots from one to five thousand; they included lily leek, Siberian squill, Spanish squill, common Star-of-Bethlehem, common snowdrop, Poet's Narcissus, crocus,

ning brought spike speedwell from his summer place in Billerica.

Three species of leeks were planted, along with native *allium*, and mock cucumber installed along the steam. Groundsel bush, aster, marshmallows, and one dozen varieties of goldenrod were put in, along with Joe-pye weed and other thoroughworts. On the western bank, Carolina poplar, graceful sunflower, giant sunflower, prairie and showy coneflower, and musk mallow were planted, and cutleaf grape fern and adder's-tongue fern were added, too. Manning's final list contains more than two hundred fifty different species of plants.[45] In time, each bridge, glade, set of steps, and path was named—Pawpaw, Hemlock, Rosebay, Water Leaf, Stag Horn, Bluff Top, Bittersweet, Primrose, Spicewood, Field Edge, Wood Thrush, Blue Bell, Ginger Root, and Bamboo. Eventually, the web of trails crisscrossed the stream with six bridges, one of which, along with a summerhouse, was designed by Charles Platt.

Period photographs record the garden's intricate, layered beauty, which Cornelia Ireland, Mather's stepdaughter-in-law, recalled many decades later. "Each rill needle-pointed in fern or bulb was of the greatest delicacy—like the effect of meticulously plumaged wild birds," she remembered. "What you would gasp at today, I think—is how breathlessly refined all the species were, compared to today's hybrids and developments—and how perilously sheer the little banks were. The meticulous early laying out eventuated in pure Quails' Breast fern, multiplying by—it had to be!—heaven's grace. It was very, truly awe inspiring to walk through in May and June . . . then high weeds cloaked everything over."[46] Manning's horticultural prowess had provided the means to create pictorial compositions of transporting impact; his years with Olmsted had provided the method. The wild garden also recalled the ideal set forth by J. Horace McFarland in his 1899 *Outlook* article: "free beauty of native woodland, marsh, and copse . . . the natural beauty of American plants, located cunningly where they love to grow, unrestrained, untrimmed."[47] (Figs. 3.23, 3.24)

Through the years, Manning continued to refine the wild garden plantings and added small trees for overhead

3.23. Clearing edged with rhododendron, wild garden, c. 1930. Photograph by Warren H. Manning office. Gwinn.

3.24. Rhododendron glade, wild garden, c. 1930. Photograph by Warren H. Manning office. Gwinn.

floral display, including dogwood, redbud, apple, crabapple, peach, and apricots, golden rain tree, and hawthorn. He also planted Chinese wisteria at the base of old trees, to shower the woodland edge with panicles of lavender. Beginning in 1910 Mather added several structures to the farm group, along with vegetable gardens, an orchard and a meadow. One of these buildings functioned as an orangerie, providing winter protection for the bay trees from the formal garden.[48] (Fig. 3.25) These improvements and the area's resulting leap in charm recalled similar developments on other American *fermes ornées* at the time. After Mather returned from a trip to Europe in 1912, he suggested adding an allée of Lombardy poplar to the field adjacent to the new wild garden. The nine-hundred-foot vista, on axis with the center of the house, conveyed the impression of a great contiguous expanse. (Fig. 3.26)

3.26. Poplar vista across Lake Shore Boulevard. Gwinn.

As the wild garden developed, Platt was concurrently suggesting improvements for the home grounds.[49] In 1910, the same year that the large fountain went in, he designed a new fountain for the formal garden pool which featured a large stone basin (subsequently removed because it blocked views through the garden) and a near life-size bronze of Fortuna, copied from an original in Fano, Italy, fabricated by Tiffany & Company. A third fountain, a basin and pool with cherub, after Verrocchio's *Boy with Dolphin*, was added to the lakeside terrace. Platt also oversaw a Pompeiian scheme for the interior of the teahouse, a garden room attached to the large greenhouses, including amorous wall paintings by J. Alden Twachtman that Mather found rather alarming.[50]

For a "weak" spot along the drive, Mather commissioned a large marble vase from Platt's fellow Cornishite Paul Manship, who decorated the classical form with bas-reliefs of Plains Indians hunting pronghorn antelope.

(Mather was disgruntled when he discovered that the rear of the expensive vase was out of view, so Platt designed a turntable to rotate it periodically.) Gwinn's sculptural program had come to figure among the finest of any garden in the United States. (Fig. 3.27)

A pair of life-size sandstone lions based on originals at the stairs of the Campidoglio in Rome were carved to flank the staircase to Lake Erie, and a wall fountain of Bacchus was set into the base of the portico. (Fig. 3.28) The forecourt island was fitted with a low basin with central jet and small lion's-head fountains around the perimeter.

In 1912 Platt designed twin gazebos for the ends of the seawall. The open-sided shelters projected over the water, offering a wilder experience of the wave-tossed lake than even the portico gave. (Fig. 3.29) The new features prompted another stylistic tug-of-war between the two designers. Manning suggested lining the curving walks leading to the gazebos with small spruce trees that would, in time, be weathered into irregular shapes; Platt argued for conifers trimmed into pyramids, in the French classical style. Mather rejected both ideas, opting instead for a pleached allée based on a linden walk he had re-

3.25. *Farm Buildings,* 1995. Photograph by Carol Betsch.

3.27. Vase by Paul Manship. Gwinn.

3.30. Norway maple allée. Gwinn.

cently seen in Europe. Manning guided the choice of tree, the tough (and now ubiquitous) *Acer platinoides*, Norway maple, which he knew could stand up to the weather coming off the lake. (Figs. 3.30, 3.31)

Although it did not excite the same publishing frenzy as Faulkner Farm or Weld, Gwinn achieved modest and lasting national renown.[51] In 1909, just months after the house was completed, a long account was included in an issue of *Architectural Record* devoted to new phases of American domestic architecture. There Gwinn was praised by the anonymous writer (almost surely Herbert Croly) as "an admirable example of the successful and spirited carrying out of one dominant idea"—a celebration of the lake. In 1912 *National Architect*, *Architecture*, and *Country Life in America* all published articles, the last by Phil M. Riley, who included Gwinn with two other lakeside examples by Platt. Three years later, Samuel Howe included the estate in his book *American Country Houses of To-day*. Gwinn was also prominently featured in a 1913 monograph, in which Royal Cortissoz wrote, "The old Italian ideal is so tactfully and with such sincerity adjusted to local conditions that the completed work becomes part and parcel of a veritable characteristic American house."[52]

The most effusive article on the design, written by Samuel Howe, appeared in the British edition of *Country Life*. There Howe praised Platt's restraint, which he found "refreshing to the average citizen who has become wearied of . . . fantastic methods of representing old traditions," and he also praised the choice of the setting: "Glorious in summer, willful in winter, useful at all times, the lake is a wonderful luminant which must impress every eye." Howe's appreciation for the landscape design was keener than other writers'. "Gwinn is a many-sided, many-coloured place, varying in its texture, full of an aesthetic magnetism," he wrote, appearing to struggle to define the source of this quality. He continued, "We should also remember with thankfulness the fine grove of elm trees whose reflections have coloured the shore line for several generations. Some of these elms are a century old. It is by this grove and still more to the maple, Lombardy poplars, birch and sycamore, and to the underbrush and shrubbery that the glare so disastrous to a water front is

3.28. *Lions on Seawall*, 1995. Photograph by Carol Betsch.

avoided." Without acknowledging Manning by name—indeed, he attributed the success of these plantings to Platt—Howe concluded, "Ordinarily trees of this size do not grow at the very edge of lakes. Here they flourish. The architect in conceiving his picture knew that it would prosper and grow more beautiful day by day. It is that which delights the visitors. It is that which places Gwinn in a distinctive class."[53]

During the 1920s, Manning made regular visits to monitor developments throughout the grounds. When George Jacques died in 1923, Manning suggested that Mather hire Jacques's daughter, Lillie, to replace him. Her tenure was a success and also, by one reckoning, unique: the local newspaper claimed that she was the only woman estate superintendent in the world. Articles featured Lillie's prize chrysanthemums and the dwarf peaches she trained on trellises as table centerpieces. ("Mr. Mather likes to pick his dinner fruits from the tree," she explained to one reporter.[54]) She remained in the job even after her marriage in the early 1930s, continuing to work closely with Manning managing all the landscapes of Gwinn.

Platt returned to Gwinn on occasion, too, and in 1927 Mather asked him to design a gate in the garden wall between his estate and that of his widowed neighbor, Elizabeth Ring Ireland (who by strange coincidence had spent part of her childhood in one of Platt's first houses, designed for her parents in Saginaw, Michigan). (Fig. 3.32) The gate reflected more than neighborliness. Within two years, William and Elizabeth were married at a small ceremony at Cleveland's Trinity Episcopal Church. The match caused a stir—there was a thirty-three-year difference in their ages—and some confusion. One elderly uncle thought that the service was a memorial for Elizabeth's first husband and sent a wreath.[55] After the ceremony the newlyweds left for their honeymoon aboard the *William G. Mather*, the flagship of the Cleveland-Cliffs fleet. At 618 feet, with a carrying capacity of fifteen thousand tons, the steamer was one of the two largest freighters on the lake,

3.31. Lakeside terraces, 1957. Photograph by Walter P. Bruning. Gwinn.

3.32. Elizabeth Ring Mather on lakeside terrace. Gwinn.

recognizable by its size and its distinctive color scheme—olive green on the pilot house and a red *C* on the rear smokestack—designed by Charles Platt.

Within one month of the wedding, the stock market

3.29. *West Gazebo before Storm,* 1995. Photograph by Carol Betsch.

collapsed, and, as the nation's economic picture wors-
ened, maintenance at Gwinn was substantially reduced.
Manning returned to offer advice on where expenses
might be pared. "Encourage the creepers," he wrote
Mather in May 1933, "especially the nearly evergreens,
such as the Speedwells or Veronicas, Bugle, Creeping
Dandelion, English Daisy, . . . all of which can be walked
on comfortably. . . . Then keep a limited area near the terrace in perfect grass."[56] Even in reduced circumstances,
Mather found the idea of a lawn full of dandelions appalling. Instead, he took the dramatic step of selling most
of his beloved Mather library. The year brought other
changes, too. In September 1933 Charles Platt, who had
just announced a new partnership with his sons, Geoffrey
and William (despite the fact that there was no work in
the New York office), died at age seventy-one. His reputation had already entered the slow eclipse that would not
be reversed for the next half century.[57]

By 1935 the Mathers' finances had stabilized, and they
decided to commission a revision of the formal garden
with more up-to-date plantings than the stiff design
Frost had created thirty years earlier. They contacted Ellen
Shipman, whose career Platt had helped launch and whom
Manning had once described as one of the "best Flower
Garden makers in America." (Shipman had actually been
hired in 1914 to design plantings for Gwinn's formal
garden, but tension between her and Jacques over his
penchant for red geraniums had prevented their being
implemented.[58])

Shipman's 1935 plans called for a complete redesign of
the big herbaceous beds, an installation of Japanese cherry
trees and tree lilacs around the pool, and vines on the loggia and teahouse. (Figs. 3.33, 3.34) The garden became
more interesting with these additions, particularly the
trees, whose long shadows made the space seem larger and
more complex. Shipman also reconfigured the beds, filling them with thousands of perennials and annuals to create a robust display, adding pale pink and apricot tones to
the original color palette of blue, yellow, and white. In
time, the character of the garden gradually shifted from

3.34. View to loggia, formal garden. Photograph by Walter P. Bruning. Gwinn.

the sunny expanse of Platt's tenure to a shade-dappled
grove, an effect that was, ironically, more in keeping with
the Italian examples Platt and his brother had visited
many years before. (Fig. 3.35) The garden came to serve as
a living connector between Elizabeth and an extensive
network of women gardeners in Cleveland and beyond,
through the Garden Club of America.[59]

Shipman returned to Gwinn twice more with additional designs for the formal garden. In 1940 she created
a parterre of ageratum in the form of an interlocking *W*
and *E*, William's and Elizabeth's initials. (Fig. 3.36) The
parterre still, dependably, excited a sense of privilege in
America's elite. In 1946 Shipman designed new plantings
in the beds in front of the loggia based on a three-season
plan for spring bulbs, summer annuals, and fall chrysanthemums, reflecting a post–World War II intensification of
color that differed from the softer Jekyllian approach that
had guided her earlier work.

The talent and divergent aesthetic perspectives of

3.33. *Teahouse in Formal Garden,* 1995. Photograph by Carol Betsch.

Gwinn's designers had resulted in a landscape of original-ity and expressive force. Platt's seawall had deftly appropri-ated the lake, and the three fountains he had added in 1910 (in the wild garden, formal garden, and lake terrace) brought water to play throughout the designed landscape. The fountains trace an isosceles triangle, a spatial echo of—and classically themed response to—the panoramic views north from the lakeside portico. The poplar allée, on axis with the pivotal portico, added another spatial vector that led directly into the heart of Manning's wild garden. (Figs. 3.37, 3.38)

There the water theme was revived playfully. The creek rushed through the hilly terrain, doubling back on itself, and paths laid out by Manning and Jacques answered its winding course. Throughout the wild garden, compo-sitions overlapped, both temporally and spatially. Light warmed and shadows lengthened as the day progressed; high summer ferns gradually overtook spring bloom. From one walking perspective to the next, views shifted and picturelike compositions emerged and dissolved. Cor-nelia Ireland remembered her father-in-law's attachment to this landscape: "You may well believe each bank was Mr. Mather's joy—I think, almost more than the formal garden beds, much as he loved fountains and the architec-tural detail . . . —with its beeches, birches, and clouds of fern and (cursed) aegepodium, it was extraordinary, just as one might expect in painting, rather than nature alone."[60]

Art, of course, had figured in Manning's inspiration for the wild garden, as he and Jacques laid out these painterly compositions. And nature, epitomized by the windswept lake, had inspired Charles Platt. Sharp awareness of the two poles of influence had guided both men throughout the collaboration. (Fig. 3.39)

3.35. *Formal Garden,* 1995. Photograph by Carol Betsch.

3.36. Formal garden, 1957. Photograph by Walter P. Bruning. Gwinn.

3.37. Aerial view of Gwinn estate, looking southeast. Gwinn.

Mather took a keen interest in all the gardens of Gwinn, but Manning agreed with Ireland that he grew to love the wild garden best. Toward the end of his life Manning wrote, "How well I remember our walks through the woods and wild gardens of his home. There would be the rippling of the stream, the whispering of the winds through the tree tops, the chirping of the crickets, the whirring wings of a startled bird, . . . the constantly changing colors, shadows, the far-reaching lake and sky colors and cloud patterns, the ripple and varying wave action on the sandy beach and rock-rimmed shore of Lake Erie."[61] Manning may have concluded that Mather's enlightened company policies and philanthropic endeav-ors were, in some measure, a result of the well-being he

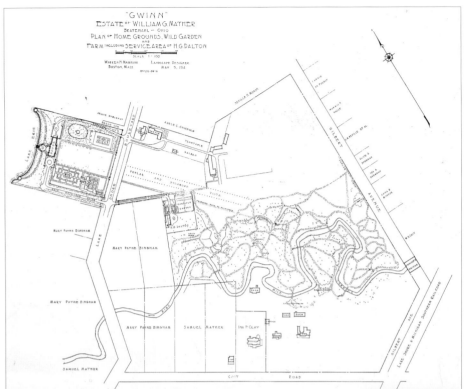

3.38. "Plan of Home Grounds, Wild Garden," by Warren H. Manning, 1931. Gwinn.

3.39. Warren Manning (center) with Lillie Jacques on viewing platform in wild garden. Gwinn.

found at Gwinn.[62] He came to envision Gwinn as a prototype for other developments of its kind.

In Manning's resilient, progressive worldview, the boundary between private resources and public good remained blurred. He continued to believe that private estates could function as preserves, safeguarding land as a scenic resource for future generations. And although he was unable to convince Mather to transform Gwinn into a public or "semi-public" reservation, despite arguing for it in his last letters to his patron, his ideas proved persuasive to the next generation.[63] William Mather died at Gwinn in 1951, at the remarkable age of ninety-seven, and Elizabeth, despite her relative youth, followed six years later. Elizabeth's son, James D. Ireland, and his wife, Cornelia, took the steps necessary to transform Gwinn into a nonprofit conference center, and a new role for the estate began.

FOUR

STAN HYWET HALL

Akron, Ohio

It was Gertrude Seiberling's idea to commission a country estate from Warren Manning—probably she knew of him through his many articles in *Country Life*. However, Manning's first letters about the project and most of the hundreds that followed were addressed to Frank A. Seiberling, founder of Goodyear Tire and Rubber Company, a brand familiar to many Americans.

Seiberling's meteoric business career began in 1898, when he was thirty-nine and looking for opportunities to regain financial footing lost in the depression of 1893. According to company lore, he saw an old factory for sale in downtown Akron, quickly bought it with borrowed funds, and within days decided that his new business would be rubber. Akron was already home to the B. F. Goodrich Company, which had incorporated there in 1870, and to Diamond Rubber, founded by the owner of the Diamond Match Company. Seiberling's own father had founded the India Rubber Company, where F. A. had worked for a few years. Despite the inland location, which made importing raw materials expensive, Akron would continue to attract rubber entrepreneurs, including Harvey Firestone, who launched the Firestone Tire and Rubber Company there in 1900.[1]

Perhaps hoping to profit from confusion with Goodrich's successful company, Seiberling named his business "Goodyear" after Charles Goodyear (1800–1860), the scientist who had discovered vulcanization, a process that transformed raw, sticky rubber into a pliable, hard-wearing material that was suitable for rubber bands, horseshoe pads, or, more lucratively, tires for horse-drawn carriages. Seiberling soon settled on the wing-footed Mercury as his trademark, and he began to sell stock in the new company, held in partnership with his brother Charles. He recovered two boilers from the scrap heap of his family's defunct street car business, retrofitted the factory, and started taking orders. The bicycle boom of the 1890s gave the business a sure start.[2]

With growing numbers of automobiles on the road, Seiberling's new company prospered. He ran it imaginatively, hiring innovative engineers, and he also personally filed hundreds of patents, including the first tire manufacturing machine and the detachable rim. As Goodyear sales outlets multiplied, profits soared. They continued to climb as the company began manufacturing tires for trucks and then for airplanes. F. A. was said to have "great talents of persuasion, courage that flamed high when things were at

their worst, and above all, was quick to recognize an opportunity and act on it."[3] Without hesitation, he also hired
the most talented men available. This last principle served
him well, both in business and in the enterprise of building a new country estate.[4]

By the century's early years, increasing wealth and a growing family were prompting F. A. to think about moving
from a house on East Market Street, next door to his elderly mother, to the countryside.[5] The Seiberlings were
no strangers to country life. Since 1900 the family had
spent long periods each summer at Cedar Lodge, Michigan, a rustic camp on an island in Lake Huron, where they
swam, hiked, and fished, and their children played with
Chippewa natives whose parents served as camp caretak-
ers and private boatsmen. Gertrude, an enthusiastic proponent of the Arts and Crafts, furnished the lodge interior
with her own birch-bark furniture.[6]

Outdoor life was to play an important role on their
new Akron estate too. The Seiberlings wanted plenty of
land for sports. They also required a large house that
would provide indoor facilities for their six children to
bowl, play basketball and tennis, and swim year round.
Gertrude, who was a fine amateur singer, wanted a music
room large enough to accommodate performances, bedrooms for anticipated guests, and a large dining room
where everyone could sit down at the same table.

In 1910 F. A. wrote to Manning for his opinion about
some land he had recently purchased with a new estate
in mind. (Figs. 4.1, 4.2) He was not concerned about an
architectural style for the mansion—he and Gertrude
already knew what they wanted. Not the "low rambling
house with broad piazzas for shade" Manning was about
to recommend to them, or a restrained Georgian residence, like the one Platt had just designed for Mather, but
a sprawling castle of the sort that Manning disdained. Despite these differences in taste, the two men soon discovered a deep rapport based on their enthusiasm for country
life. Both envisioned a landscape development that would
emphasize the rural, American beauty of the land.

After visiting the property, Manning wrote to Seiber-

4.1. Old quarry on undeveloped Seiberling property, c. 1911. SHH.

4.2. Farm buildings on developed Seiberling property, c. 1911. SHH.

ling approvingly, "I will at the outset say that very few of
the thousand or more properties that I have examined and
made plans for, offer within a hundred acres so many and
such varied incidents."[7] The land comprised several old
farms with apple, peach, and plum orchards that would, in
Manning's words, "give profitable crops"; old woods with
"favorable conditions for the addition of the woodland
plants"; open forest with "very fine individual specimens"; and springs and wetlands at the base of an escarpment.[8] The feature that would give the estate its "greatest
distinction," in Manning's assessment, was the sandstone
quarry, "a great, irregular pan, with one side a perpendi-
cular rough wall face, capped by an old peach orchard."
This feature would also give the estate its name, Stan
Hywet, Old English for "stone quarry."

On Manning's first visit to the site he envisioned

flooding the depression to create lagoons and clothing the rock walls with honeysuckle and the slopes with wildflowers. The sandstone pan had springs cold enough for trout, and lagoons would also provide opportunities for boating, swimming, and F. A.'s particular boyhood talent, ice skating.[9] Bridges would link small islands with miles of hiking and bridle trails. Manning knew just the man to oversee the job, he wrote Seiberling—a Mr. Barclay, who had "worked out" the Griscom quarry garden in the 1890s. Ten years after its publication in *Country Life,* Manning was still encouraging clients to visit the pivotal Haverford commission that had been identified as a real "American garden."[10]

Immediately after his visit, Manning sent a plan of existing conditions overlaid with a proposed landscape development that included roads and a site for the house, and he urged Seiberling to add to his initial holdings—they would eventually comprise about three thousand non-contiguous acres.[11] (Fig. 4.3) Manning's rough layout divided the property into three general areas, a large lawn east of the house; the wild garden to the west; and, northeast of the house site, a section marked "Farm." He encouraged Seiberling to retain some of the existing farm buildings here, arguing that they "will be decided additions from a picturesque point of view."[12] They would, however, be removed to make space for vegetable and cutting gardens, a conservatory, and the carriage house.[13]

Manning's plan put the house at the edge of the escarpment, where it would have the most commanding view. (This arrangement recalled that at Gwinn, where the house also perched at the edge of a bluff.) His scheme reflected two broad stylistic ideas. The large wild garden, vistas, and many acres of improved woodland emphasized American plants and scenery. The rolling lawns and winding drives derived from the English Picturesque tradition.

Gertrude and F. A. interviewed several architects and

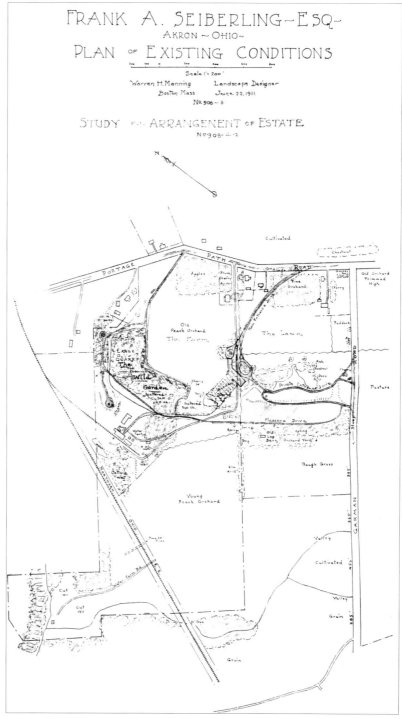

4.3. "Plan of Existing Conditions," by Warren H. Manning, 1911. SHH.

reviewed their proposals for the house before selecting George B. Post & Sons of New York for the job. Charles S. Schneider, the firm's Ohio representative and a Cleveland native, was assigned the project. In preparation for this very moment, Gertrude had studied architectural history, interior design, and landscape gardening at Buchtel

College in Akron, and she was eager to apply her education. In the spring of 1912 she, F. A., their daughter Irene, and Schneider embarked on a tour of England and France to look for models. Their return voyage, which had been booked on the *Titanic*, was postponed for a few weeks after the ship sank.

The Seiberlings developed friendly bonds with Schneider, which was fortunate, for soon after their return he had a falling out with George Post and by the end of 1912 had resigned from the prestigious firm to open his own Cleveland practice. The Seiberlings decided to retain him, although they were also required by contract to continue with Post.[14] Despite the two-pronged arrangement, plans for the new house progressed rapidly, and by December 1912 the design of the sixty-five-room mansion was substantially complete. Ground had actually been broken earlier that year.

Schneider's design borrowed liberally from Compton Wynates, a widely imitated sixteenth-century Tudor house in Warwickshire he and the Seiberlings had visited; its jutting chimneys and unexpected projections suggested cumulative growth, an impression that appealed to new Americans homeowners eager to convey long-standing ties to the land. The design was influenced by other British examples, too, including Ockwells Manor in Berkshire and Haddon Hall in Derbyshire. However, the new house avoided strict replication of any of them—as Schneider explained to Seiberling, "I prefer not to take things too straight."[15] Unlike its fortified predecessors, Schneider's structure would stretch into the landscape with a kind of relaxed midwestern self-assurance, the same expansive quality, as one historian has noted, seen in Frank Lloyd Wright's contemporaneous architecture.[16]

The Tudor Revival style was particularly well suited to the palatial scale at which the Seiberlings and many of their wealthy compatriots chose to build. The alternative frequently used for such grandiose undertakings at the time was the chillier "Modern French" exemplified by Hunt at Biltmore and in several houses in Newport, such as The Elms, by Horace Trumbauer.[17] But the Seiberlings would have found French formality unfamiliar and pretentious. Undoubtedly they identified with the Anglo-Saxon ethos of Tudor Revival, a vague signifier of land, history, and learning. And they were enthusiastic about the romantic appeal of the English manor home and its potential as a setting for rambling domesticity. Of this Warren Manning approved, even if his own taste conflicted with the imperial scale of the Seiberlings' architectural program.

One senses, from Seiberling's exasperated letters to Schneider, that the enterprise soon took on a life of its own.[18] Harvey S. Firestone, Seiberling's friendly competitor in the tire business, reflected on the mysterious forces behind his own enormous Akron home, where a large addition was under construction at the same time as Stan Hywet Hall—Firestone was adding an indoor swimming pool in an attempt to keep pace with his colleague. His home, too, was Tudor Revival. "I built a house in Akron many times larger than I have the least use for," Firestone wrote in one letter. "I have another house at Miami Beach, which is also much larger than I need. I suppose that before I die I shall buy or build other houses which also will be larger than I need. I do not know why I do it—the houses are only a burden. But I have done it, and all my friends who have acquired wealth have big houses. . . . I wonder why it is."[19]

Herbert Croly notwithstanding, most of America's captains of industry believed that bigger *was* better, and the competition among them was keen. Many regarded their manorial homes as a sort of national product, a reflection of national achievement. As *Architectural Record* put it, "These buildings are the registers and, let us hope, enduring chronicles of our very latest days, of our rapidly accumulating wealth, of the prodigious rewards of high finance, and the extraordinary degree of luxury that has become compatible with American life."[20] In Seiberling's view, a large country house was patriotic—as he explained to his daughter Irene, it would keep "the family strong . . . for the country."[21]

Gertrude would see to it that Stan Hywet Hall also provided every modern convenience. These included central heat and vacuum, three elevators, a thirty-seven-station telephone system, twenty-five bathrooms, and an indoor heated swimming pool and sauna. Despite these amenities, the interior decoration was to be insistently, paradoxically, historical. Interior design was overseen by H. F. Huber of New York, who traveled to England with the Seiberlings to select furnishings. Schneider was anxious about this arrangement and sent a long letter to his clients, already aboard the *Lusitania*, urging them to exercise the most refined taste in their purchases.[22] The interior of the new home occupied hundreds of workers over several years, at extraordinary, eventually unmanageable expense.

Each room was conceived and executed as a set piece, a backdrop for anticipated patterns of living and entertainment that matched Frank and Gertrude's cultural aspirations—the leap from the old wooden frame house on East Market Street was to be a grand one. Woodwork, carved stone, ironwork, leaded glass, carpets, and molded plaster ceilings throughout would be crafted by fine artisans and leading firms—Hayden Company, Thorton Smith, Samuel Yellin, Heinigke & Bowen, Donnelly & Ricci, and the Beloochistan Rug Weaving Company of India. The Music Room was the largest and most opulent of the rooms at Stan Hywet Hall, outfitted with seventeenth- and eighteenth-century English furniture, French tapestries, a nine-foot concert Steinway, an Aeolian organ, and a harpsichord, bought from Ockwells Manor as war was breaking out and prices were dropping precipitously. Gertrude was a talented contralto and she would perform here, as would others

4.4. Music Room, Stan Hywet Hall. SHH.

with wider reputations, including Helen Jepson, Ignace Paderewski, and Leopold Stokowski.[23] (Fig. 4.4)

The year ground was broken, 1912, Goodyear acquired the Diamond Rubber Company and achieved fourth place nationally in the highly competitive rubber business. Company earnings were approaching $33 million, and, thanks to aggressive new advertising in the *Saturday Evening Post* and other magazines, the "wing-foot" brand had become as well known as Ivory Soap, Heinz 57 Varieties, and Eastman Kodak.[24] In 1913 Goodyear began manufacturing the fabric that was a key ingredient in corded tires. In 1915 it added sales branches in Australia and Argentina. In 1916 it became the world's largest tire company and acquired a 20,000-acre rubber plantation in Sumatra.

Seiberling's original Akron plant grew, too, eventually employing 6,800 laborers, most of whom lived in a grimy area of the city known locally as Cinder World, where revolving shifts of men lived in boarding houses, sleeping in the same unchanged beds. As F. A. watched his own Tudor castle taking form, he grew increasingly uneasy about the lack of decent housing for his workers. Like his colleague Mather, he knew that inadequate living conditions would eventually undermine job stability, and, also like Mather, he approached Manning for a solution. The result was a new suburban development, Goodyear Heights, commissioned at his own expense, where attractive, low-cost homes would be available to all company employees.

The neighborhood was located within one-quarter mile of the factories and two and one-half miles from the business center of Akron. (Within a few years, Seiberling would put the nation's second bus line in operation to connect them.) The land was "composed of hills and valleys," according to the sales prospectus, "which make attractive home sites with pleasant views."[25] Manning's scheme borrowed other ideas from previous company towns he had planned.[26] Like those in Upper Michigan, Goodyear Heights also included small parks and lots planted with fruit trees and space for flower and vegetable gardens. Seiberling hired the architectural firm of Mann & McNeille of New York to design several different house

4.5. Construction showing small-gauge rail, house in background, c. 1912. SHH.

4.6. Laborers working on house terrace, c. 1912. SHH.

models, all of them stucco or dark red brick, each with its own fireplace, sold to workers at cost, with no down payment.[27] (Harvey Firestone soon created a similar development for his workers, Firestone Park.[28])

Construction of Stan Hywet Hall recalled a similar process at Biltmore, where a narrow-gauge railroad had also brought building materials from the local rail line. (Fig. 4.5) In Akron, too, city roads were paved for the convoys of trucks that transported materials to the site. Municipal water lines were extended. The ambitious construction operation required extensive coordination—

both Manning and Seiberling were intent on efficiency, and the latter kept a close eye on expenses. Sandstone excavated from the quarry was to be mixed in the concrete foundation, for example, and stone from the basement excavation was used in new retaining walls. Despite such measures, costs were ultimately estimated to be about $3 million, beyond what Seiberling could actually afford.

Manning's representative on the job was A. D. Taylor, who had supervised work at Gwinn. Taylor, in turn, directed Seiberling's superintendent, G. B. Edwards, who oversaw large crews of workers. Many of them were transients, housed in a camp built near the orchard. (In one 1912 letter Taylor suggested paying the "hobo labor" only every two weeks, so they might stay on the job longer and drink less.[29]) Highly skilled laborers were also employed. (Fig. 4.6) Some aspects of the landscape scheme had been settled early, but Manning anticipated that installation of several individual garden areas could not proceed until house construction was substantially complete, and correspondence shows that this turned out to be the case. Despite the demands of this project and several others of similar scope in the office at the time, Manning wrote to Seiberling in October to ask for a letter of introduction to Henry Ford, who was thinking about a country place outside Detroit.[30]

The estate outbuildings (which included the carriage house, stables, gate lodge, poultryman's house, and gardener's cottage) were designed by Schneider, primarily in the same Tudor style as the house. Schneider would also design the house terraces and overlooks, in collaboration with Manning.[31] The location of each of these features on approximately seventy acres of home grounds was determined by Manning, in close consultation with the Seiberlings, who were involved with landscape decisions throughout.

Manning located the approach road to Stan Hywet Hall at the southeast corner of the property, at the intersection of Garman Road and North Portage Path. (Fig. 4.7) The curving drive passed first through large wrought-iron gates and by a half-timbered gate lodge, planted in the English cottage style, then wound through an old apple orchard that Manning retained, as he wrote Seiberling, to "give the property a rural beauty and long-established character."[32] (Fig. 4.8) The orchard also provided a shady prelude to the sudden Reptonian view of rolling lawn with its carefully sited chestnut trees. Arriving guests got a glimpse of the mansion, which then disappeared as the road entered another grove of trees. (Fig. 4.9) When the house appeared again, it loomed large and imposingly close at hand. Manning's restrained

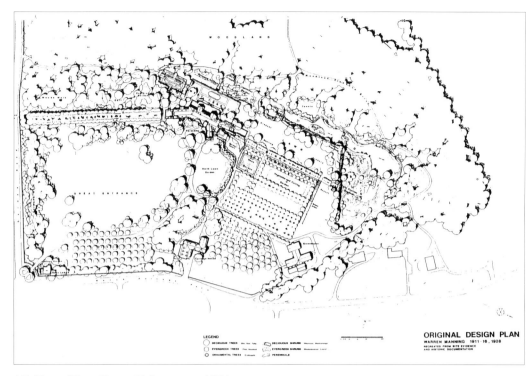

4.7. Plan of Stan Hywet Hall property, 1984. Child, Hornbeck Associates.

planting scheme for the front facade featured several towering American elms.[33]

Manning had argued against a large formal garden sited in the middle of the front lawn, which had been one of Schneider's early suggestions. "A garden to interrupt the turf passage . . . would seem to me as much out of place as an imitation garden would be in a picture gallery on the floor between you and a fine landscape canvas of some great artist," he wrote to Seiberling. He wanted to preserve the turf as "a foreground of your distant views, a quiet, naturalesque place which you can enjoy without the blaze of color and the hard formal lines that make up a summer garden."[34]

A proposed garden near the front of the house in an area known as the Ellipse was one early compromise. A 1914 plan shows this layout and long, narrow, geometric flower beds projecting from the north wing of the house, bordered by an allée. (Fig. 4.10) Manning seems to have persuaded the Seiberlings to eliminate the gardens but retain the allée. Two allées were eventually planted: one from the north wing of the house, a long tunnel of white birch, *Betula papyfera,* and one from the south wing, of London plane. (In Manning's records these are listed as sycamore,

4.8. Gatehouse at Stan Hywet Hall. SHH.

but they have since been identified as *Platanus* x *acerifolia*.) The two double rows of trees extend almost like great arms, grounding the sprawling mansion in the landscape. Frank A. Seiberling Jr., the Seiberlings' youngest son, who later developed a keen interest in landscape design, observed that the lines of trees defined a division—the wild garden on the quarry side and high-style lawns on the other.[35]

The 650-foot plane tree allée, laid out on axis with the Music Room and visible from it, brings a sense of land and vitality into the domestic sphere. Conversely, the giant trees frame a view back toward the house, appearing to shelter and protect it. (Figs. 4.11, 4.12) The trees also create a defining wall of foliage edging the English lawn, and on their western side, they demarcate a natural amphitheater. They are under-planted with pale pink rhododendron and azaleas that have grown to great size in the high shade.

At the opposite, north, end of the house, the 550-foot long pleached birch allée leads to a high lookout and long views over the wild garden to the Cuyahoga Valley. (Fig. 4.13) Loosely paved with granite stepping stones and underplanted with lily-of-the-valley, the feature offers a backdrop to the rose garden and orchards to the east. Rhythmically alternating pools of light and shadow fill the long tunnel. The birch allée evokes Arts and Crafts principles as it deftly straddles the poles of formal and naturalistic design—the era's sticky wicket.

Among all the new gardens under way, the wild garden engaged Manning's imagination most vividly. From the start, he envisioned it as the centerpiece of the landscape scheme. After his 1911 site visit, he wrote to Seiberling, "Imagine the rock walls clothed with the Honeysuckle for the spring flowers, Rambler and Prairie Roses for the summer, Japanese Clematis for the fall flowers and the Japanese Bittersweet for the winter fruits; the steep earth slopes clothed with the Yellow, and the Tawny Day Lilies, the Blue Speedwells, the Pink and White Hibiscus, the Scarlet Lychnis, and the Bee Balm; and the bottom of the

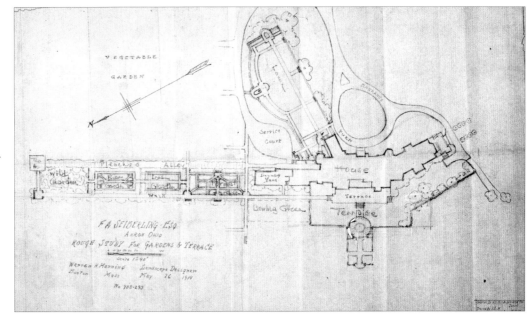

4.10. Plan of proposed development, by Warren H. Manning, 1914. SHH.

4.12. View down plane tree allée from Music Room. SHH.

pan carpeted with the yellow flowered Sedums . . . great carpets of color instead of little garden bunches."[36]

Years before, Manning had compared his approach with the work of a painter who "uses his pigments, to secure certain landscape effects." In Manning's method, as in Olmsted's, the landscape architect "does not select a plant

4.9. *Front Lawn, View toward House*, 1997. Photograph by Carol Betsch.

FOLLOWING PAGES:
4.11. *London Plane Allée, View toward House*, 1997. Photograph by Carol Betsch.

4.13. *Birch Allée*, 1997. Photograph by Carol Betsch.

4.15. Wild garden. SHH.

4.14. Quarry wall (escarpment) in wild garden, shortly after planting, c. 1920. SHH.

4.16. Wild garden, 1940. SHH.

for a position because it is rare, but because it gives just the shade of color, texture, or outline to complete the ideal picture he has formed in his mind."[37] The Seiberlings' estate provided opportunities to create many such "ideal pictures."

For a silver edge along the lagoon shore, Manning used native *Elaeagnus augustifolia* (Russian olive), and to provide a sharp accent, he used the swordlike form of iris. Plants with vertical form, such as arborvitae, were used to anchor and to frame. Others with fountainlike arches, such as prairie rose and *Forsythia suspensa,* softened the lagoon's rocky edge. In this design, as in the wild garden at Gwinn, the incidental and the intimate were celebrated over the classical ideal. (Figs. 4.14, 4.15, 4.17)

At the same time that he was developing the Seiberlings' wild garden, Manning published an entry in Bailey's *Cyclopedia of Horticulture* that drew a further comparison with landscape painting. In it, he likened his and his colleagues' efforts to define a distinctive approach to American landscape design to those of nineteenth-century landscape painters who had also persevered in striving to define a distinctive American style. At Stan Hywet Hall, the parallels became tangible, as scenes recalling Hudson River School canvases unfolded along miles of trails.[38] (Fig. 4.16)

Realizing these scenes required significant skill—to eradicate unwanted plants, prepare soil, locate and propa-

4.17. *Escarpment in Wild Garden,* 1997. Photograph by Carol Betsch.

gate new plants, coax them to grow in the varied terrain, and, in some cases, to keep them in scale. Manning wrote to Seiberling that he was purposely using shallow soil in some areas to stunt growth so trees would not block views. As at Gwinn, some existing plants were retained, and new ones were raised from seed or cuttings, purchased from nurseries, and dug from the wild. Native and imported species were mixed throughout. As work progressed and the lagoons were filled, bridges were constructed to join small islands with the irregular banks. (Figs. 4.18, 4.19) The resulting compositions recalled Olmsted's approach road at

4.18. Bridge in wild garden lagoon, c. 1920. SHH.

4.20. Outlook. SHH.

Biltmore, where he had achieved "a natural and comparatively wild and secluded character . . . with incidents growing out of the vicinity of springs and streams and pools, steep banks and rocks."[39]

As Seiberling's support for Manning's "pond plan" grew, confrontations between architect and landscape architect recalled similar disputes at Gwinn. On Stan Hywet's home grounds, however, the authority was reversed: Seiberling's growing appreciation for an American style supported Manning's perspectives. In 1916 the outlook, a circular extension at the center of the house terrace, became the subject of an argument between Schneider and Seiberling. "I don't want a sub-plaza of stone put out in front of the terrace," Seiberling wrote Schneider. "So don't send down any sketches that mean a large structure in front, as I will have none of it."[40] But Schneider persisted. "I am positive I am right about it. [The outlook] should not be made very small and out of keeping and harmony with the general magnitude of the house and the upper terrace. It is on the main axis line carrying through the Great Hall and should be a final focal point. I had hoped that in the center of it you would someday put a beautiful piece of marble or bronze sculpture."[41]

Yet, precisely because the outlook was to be aligned with the Great Hall and also, by virtue of Manning's siting of the house, exactly on axis with the summer sunset, neither Manning nor Seiberling wanted a large piece of sculpture to block the view—one of the most important in the estate's landscape design.[42] Manning clearly envisioned that his clients would walk out and sit in this space. As he wrote to one workman, "Both Mr. and Mrs. Seiberling feel that it ought to be out as far as possible, so one would have the feeling of the great height possible under them, . . . and also feel they were out in the middle of the landscape rather [than] detached from the top of the bluff."[43] Manning prevailed in the argument and developed the outlook as an elegantly bounded viewing platform. From this vantage point, tall stands of trees frame a long vista that brings an experience of reach, quiet expanse, and sky into the designed landscape. (Fig. 4.20)

4.19. *Bridge in Wild Garden Lagoon,* 1997. Photograph by Carol Betsch.

4.21. Fountain at end of birch allée, 1990. Photograph by Robin Karson.

4.22. Twin pavilions at end of birch allée, 1997. Photograph by Carol Betsch.

4.23. Formal terrace, 1997. Photograph by Carol Betsch.

Like the plane tree allée, the birch allée was visible from inside the house, and it, too, linked the domestic space to the countryside. Schneider also proposed a structure at the end of it, but it soon became apparent that a building of any size would block the prospect. Seiberling suggested instead "a little Japanese roof effect, without much of the appearance of a building."[44] Eventually twin pavilions were designed which framed an open vista across a low stone basin and fountain spray.[45] From this precipice, views stretch many miles to the north, and the wild garden spreads below. (Figs. 4.21, 4.22) A flight of steps against the stone retaining wall brings visitors down into it.

Despite his dominant role in the design process, Manning did not prevail on every debate at Stan Hywet Hall. He had argued for a small house terrace and pool, but the Seiberlings wanted an expanse that would accommodate many guests.[46] But Seiberling did agree with Manning's opinion that the terrace, whatever its dimensions, should remain flowerless. (Fig. 4.23) "The more I think of the situation viewed from the terrace side," F. A. wrote to him, "the more I grow in sympathy with your idea that there should be no view of color to any appreciable extent, certainly

4.24. *Formal Terrace Wall and Herbaceous Border*, 1997. Photograph by Carol Betsch.

4.25. Gertrude Seiberling in Japanese garden. SHH.

nothing that would catch the eye first; that the grandeur [sic] view, after all, is the over-mastering result to attain, and the flowers near at hand do not help it."[47] Instead, long English-inspired herbaceous borders were located at the bottom of the terrace retaining wall. (Fig. 4.24)

At the Seiberlings' request, several specialized gardens were designed for the grounds. In one 1914 letter F. A. noted, not too enthusiastically, that Gertrude was "strong" for a Japanese feature.[48] Manning offered to design the garden himself and sent a series of proposals for it. The Seiberlings decided, however, to commission a specialist for the work, T. R. Otsuka, who had designed the Japanese garden on the Wooded Island at the 1893 World's Columbian Exposition.[49] Otsuka may have been Manning's own suggestion—the two likely met in Chicago. According to his business circular, his approach emphasized the use of local "naturally fitted rocks and trees," and clients were to furnish their own laborers, whom Otsuka supervised on site. He selected his own ornaments and furniture.[50]

Period photographs of the Seiberlings' Japanese garden show a waterfall, meandering stream, stepping-stone paths, and small trees and shrubs. The miniaturized design owed more to Victorian England than Japan, but it seemed to suit Gertrude's Japanese idea. (Fig. 4.25) Manning sited the garden over a large underground cistern, west of the

house terrace and out of view from it. Over the years, as trees and shrubs grew and shade deepened, the character of the garden softened and in time it became indistinguishable from the wild garden surrounding. (Fig. 4.26)

The English Garden, begun in 1915, was also Gertrude's request. Typically, wives oversaw the development of such features, which were often delineated—somewhat metaphorically—by an enclosure such as a wall. The idea appealed to Gertrude, who had confided to Manning that she was looking for a refuge from the demands of six children and would be happy for a secluded one like that in Frances Hodgson Burnett's *The Secret Garden,* published in 1911. After several discussions about where to site it, Manning located the feature below and south of the house terrace, where it would not interfere with the view.

The elements in the 60-by-120-foot walled garden, designed by Schneider in collaboration with Manning, were structurally almost identical to those Platt had used in the formal garden at Gwinn, in the Italianate formula of the day: walls, central reflecting pool, geometric flower beds, intersecting paths, and figurative sculpture. At Stan Hywet the sculpture was *The Garden of the Water Goddess,* a delicately scaled nude by Willard D. Paddock. The purposes of the two gardens were also identical—to provide intimate, sunny, flower-filled retreats that would serve as counterpoints to wilder landscape passages. But Manning's use of local stone, dark purplish brick, and a strong color palette resulted in an Arts and Crafts design rather than the classically themed layout at Gwinn. (Fig. 4.27)

Manning's 1915 plant list included familiar, old-fashioned garden varieties and a wide range of annuals, bulbs, lilies, and vines, grouped by color. He specified maroon, pink, rose, white, scarlet, gray, violet, blue, yellow, and orange—an unusual combination by any standard—listing

4.26. *Formal Terrace from Japanese garden,* 1997. Photograph by Carol Betsch.

FOLLOWING PAGES:
4.27. *English Garden,* 1997. Photograph by Carol Betsch.

4.29. *View to Rose Garden,* 1996. Photograph by Carol Betsch.

4.28. Gertrude Seiberling in English Garden. SHH.

hollyhock, peony, Sweet William, *Fritillaria persica*, marta-gon lily, petunia, verbena, snapdragon, phlox, yarrow, di-anthus, tulip, hosta, poppy, salvia, *Lobelia cardinalis*, aster, campanula, rose, and many others. The title of this docu-ment, "List of Plants for Panels in English Garden," and the definitive color groupings suggest that individual pan-els were devoted to specific hues.[51] (The plan for their arrangement, no. 908-307, has been lost, as have most of the landscape plans for Stan Hywet Hall.) Period photo-graphs show that Manning's design also featured Dutch-man's pipe, whose broad leaves were in scale with the strong architectural proportions of the walls and lych-gate entryway.[52] (Fig. 4.28)

Among the other specialized gardens on the estate was a small terrace adjacent to the Breakfast Room, where the family typically ate their meals. Manning had suggested a moss garden for this spot, but this rather subtle idea was overruled in favor of a more conventional brick terrace and small fountain.[53] Surrounding beds were planted to correspond to the interior color scheme, canary yellow and Delft china blue. (Gertrude kept real canaries in the Breakfast Room, too.)

In the area east of the birch allée, a large rose garden was laid out, its square form and intersecting paths based on traditional English prototypes. This area (the site of the original farm buildings) supported large vegetable and

cutting gardens as well, and a long grape-covered pergola along the northern edge. (Fig. 4.29) A greenhouse com-plex and carriage house were also built here, the latter at the edge of North Portage Path. Elsewhere on the prop-erty, new farm buildings were located and meadows fenced for Seiberling's large herd of dairy cows and horses. Crops were raised elsewhere on the large parcel, at Portage Path Farm and White Sands Farm, to keep the household provided with fresh vegetables and fruit.

Formal entertainment on the Akron estate was lavish and, like the house, it was also Tudor-toned. On June 16, 1916, an elaborate Shakespearean housewarming took place to celebrate the barely finished home. The festivi-ties required period dress, overseen by a theatrical com-pany based in New York, which made all the costumes. Gertrude came as Queen Elizabeth, and F. A. was Mark Antony. Mrs. H. F. Huber, the decorator's wife, appeared as Cleopatra. Professionals also guided the evening's en-tertainment, providing scripts that were based on ex-cerpts from Shakespeare's plays. Photographs attest to the elaborate resolve with which the Seiberlings were cata-pulting themselves into Akron society. (Figs. 4.30, 4.31)

By the following year, Stan Hywet Hall was substan-tially complete, and Schneider was eager to publish his work in *Architectural Record,* still the leading periodical on country house design. Seiberling refused, claiming that the plantings needed more time to mature. Before this could happen, World War I intervened and building stopped altogether. When general construction resumed after the war, tastes had changed. Fewer clients sought houses of the audacious size and style of Stan Hywet Hall, and Schnei-der's imaginative design never got the publicity it de-served. The architect did go on to create several school and civic buildings, as well as homes in Shaker Heights and other posh Cleveland neighborhoods, but none were as ambitious or artistically distinctive as the Seiberlings'.

Manning's landscape design was never published ei-ther. In the years after his work in Akron, he was engulfed by a host of divergent professional concerns: a term as president of the ASLA, his new office in Billerica, research

4.30. Guards at front door in Shakespearean dress, 1918. SHH.

4.31. The Seiberlings and guests at Shakespearean housewarming (Gertrude center left, F. A. center right), 1918. SHH.

for his National Plan, dozens of articles, and his book on the landscape architecture of Thomas Jefferson. During this period, he listed 328 new projects in twenty states and Canada. Among these was another housing development for Seiberling, Fairlawn Heights. This elite suburb with country club, constructed in 1917, was aimed at company executives and other successful Akron businessmen—a wealthy man's Goodyear Heights. The enclave was built on 1,000 undeveloped acres south of West Market Street, with $1.5 million in improvements.[54] There Manning applied planning methods similar to those he had used in other suburbs, including Goodyear Heights. His design responded closely to existing topographic features, retain-

ing important trees and providing large lots that offered maximum scenic variety. His representative on the job was Harold S. Wagner, who was also advising on developments at Stan Hywet Hall at the time. Wagner grew to like Akron and, within a few years, he had left Manning's office and accepted a job as director of Akron's city parks.

Goodyear company profits declined sharply during the war, but Seiberling anticipated a surge in business after it was over, and he began amassing a large inventory of raw materials, all of it acquired on credit. When the boom failed to materialize and a depression descended instead, Goodyear's finances collapsed. In 1921 F. A. and Charles were forced to resign from the company they had founded twenty-three years before. But the brothers proved as resilient as the product they had pioneered, and they soon began another business, the Seiberling Rubber Company. It too would prosper, but it would never provide Seiberling with the kind of private income he had enjoyed before the war. He and Gertrude were able to hold onto Stan Hywet Hall only by drastically reducing the size of the staff and relaxing maintenance on many parts of the landscape.

Still, recreation remained central to life on the estate in the 1920s. Guests had access to horses and more than ten miles of bridle paths. (Fig. 4.32) Two tennis courts were maintained, one near the lagoon for the family and one near the carriage house for staff. In the North Meadow there were courts for lawn bowling, croquet courts, and an archery range, and in the Great Meadow there were two golf courses, one a four-hole links and the other a clock course. Visitors could still ice skate, fish, canoe, and swim in the lagoon. Children were married in the English garden and grandchildren splashed in the formal pool. Musical performances, family dinners, and wedding celebrations filled the years. (Figs. 4.33, 4.34)

In 1923 F. A. Seiberling and two other area businessmen had taken the lead in founding the Akron Metropolitan District Commission, a regional park system modeled after the very successful example created in Cleveland by Olmsted Brothers a few years before. In 1925 F. A. donated almost one thousand acres of Stan Hywet Hall property to form the Sand Hill Reservation, the first sec-

4.32. Bridle trail, c. 1920. SHH.

4.33. Seiberling children swimming in lagoon, 1920s. SHH.

4.34. Wedding of Virginia Seiberling, 1919. SHH.

tion of the new system. He and Harold Wagner (by then director of the park commission) convinced the city to bring in the Olmsted firm to plan the new parks.[55] Olmsted Brothers' 1925 report in support of the initiative eloquently describes the beauty of the region, the same that had inspired Manning's estate design fourteen years before: "There is a wealth of beautiful scenery in your county—the wonderful and impressive landscape of the Cuyahoga Valley north of Akron, the many and varied wooded ravines running up from this main valley to the plateau land on either side, and large stretches of gently rolling pastoral landscape, streams and lakes, occasional gorges and picturesque ravines where the streams have worn through the sandstone strata, and some hills of a more or less rugged character commanding broad outlooks over the countryside."[56]

At Manning's encouragement, Seiberling had acquired thousands of acres for his estate, and it was likely at Manning's encouragement that much of this land, held in a private trust, as it were, was later transferred to public use. As the end of the decade approached, Manning could see that few American country places would survive intact, even during the lifetimes of their original owners, and he was encouraging his private clients to bequeath private acres for the public good. By the end of the 1920s, a significant portion of Stan Hywet Hall was providing Akron

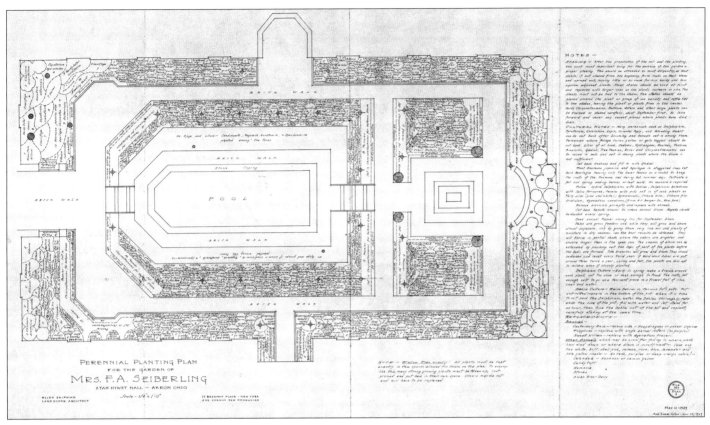

4.35. Plan for plantings in English Garden, by Ellen Shipman, 1929. SHH.

park visitors with opportunities to hike, swim, drive, and bicycle—much as it had for the Seiberlings when the land was all their own.[57]

The reduction in size—and ideological purposes—of American country places was not limited to Akron. Although wealthy Americans would continue to build country estates, even through the depths of the Depression, they would never again achieve the scope of those created during the boom years of the country place era.

In 1928 Gertrude and F. A. commissioned Manning to return to the estate to advise on a restoration of the home grounds. His sixteen-page report recommended substantial tree-cutting of volunteers, pruning, and replacement of plants that had died.[58] The following year Manning returned again, this time to advise on subdividing an additional thousand acres into parcels to be sold to individual homeowners. Perhaps in compensation for the anticipated loss, Gertrude had already begun planning a revision to the plantings in the English Garden.

For the artistic goals Gertrude had in mind, Manning

recommended Ellen Shipman, who was at that time at the height of her fame. Manning knew her work well because they had collaborated on several projects in which Shipman's role was identical to the one she would undertake at Stan Hywet Hall, designing new plantings for an existing garden framework.[59] Irene Seiberling remembered Shipman's lofty bearing and celebrity as the country's foremost flower garden designer, a reputation secured by years of published work and lectures for various civic and garden organizations, especially the powerful Garden Club of America.[60] Gertrude was an integral part of this network, too; in 1924 she had founded and become first president of the Akron Garden Club, later a GCA affiliate.[61]

Shipman's 1929 plan retained the existing architecture and Paddock's sculpture but replaced most of the plants. (Fig. 4.35) She mixed herbaceous and woody species in wide borders and added several flowering shrubs and trees, climbing rose, and buddleia standards. She introduced a yew hedge around the lower pool, interplanted with tall stands of lilies. The margins of Shipman's plans carried

4.36. Restored Shipman plantings in English Garden, 1997. Photograph by Carol Betsch.

meticulously penned notes on cultivation and maintenance, a trademark feature that was a critical component of her flower garden designs. These notes outline strategies for keeping flowers in good health, staked, and for filling gaps with potted annuals where plants died back or bloom was insufficient for the abundant effects Shipman sought. In this design, as in others, Shipman permitted substitutions of specific varieties as long as color harmonies were observed. "Use only the white, buff, shell-pink, salmon, rose, blue, lavender and pale yellow shades," she wrote, "no reds, purples or deep orange colors."[62]

The addition of pear trees, laburnum, dogwood, hawthorn, flowering crab, cherry, and cedars gave the garden new three-dimensional heft and interest, the same transformation Shipman would effect at Gwinn. The new beds offered a "glittering mosaic" of color, a departure from the Impressionistic washes that Shipman typically wrought, a choice that may have been influenced by the bold architectural framework.[63] The plantings gave the English Garden vitality and a feeling of seclusion that typified Shipman's best work.[64] Gertrude tended this garden until her death in 1946. (Fig. 4.36)

F. A. lived at Stan Hywet Hall another nine years, enjoying robust health into his eighties. After his death in

1955, his six children established the seventy-acre core of the property as a house museum and historic landscape, and, with the help of other Akron residents, raised an endowment to maintain the estate as a nonprofit cultural institution. According to Frank Seiberling Jr., all were adamant that the "artistic character of the land and the buildings remain unaltered."[65]

In the decades that followed, public taste for bright floral display led to the planting of brilliantly colored gardens on the wide English lawns. During these years, Seiberling Jr., who had by then become chair of the art history department at University of Iowa, began a study of Manning's design principles and became convinced of the nearly forgotten landscape architect's pivotal significance in the history of American landscape architecture. His persuasive lectures on Manning's importance, in conjunction with new research within the field of landscape studies, laid important groundwork for the reclamation of the original landscape design which began in the 1980s. Obtrusive flower beds were removed from the lawns, views were opened, elms replanted, and drives that had been widened to accommodate visitor traffic narrowed to original proportions—all with the intention of recapturing the spirit of the land that had guided Manning in his design of the estate.[66]

Like his mentors, Manning understood design and planning as contiguous endeavors, and this Olmstedian perspective, which links present-day decisions with future good, laid firm groundwork for Stan Hywet Hall's second life as a public garden and parklike refuge. It is difficult today to imagine the sense of possibility Manning felt as he explored the rough, rural parcel for the first time—in retrospect, it seems an age of almost impossible innocence. The landscape architect's response to the spirit of this place remains vivid, however, preserved in the eloquence of his design and the long views that still cradle it in the rolling landscape. (Figs. 4.37, 4.38)

4.37. *View over Lagoon*, 1996. Photograph by Carol Betsch.

FOLLOWING PAGE:
4.38. *Formal Terrace from the East*, 1996. Photograph by Carol Betsch.

FIVE

ELLEN SHIPMAN

1869–1950

Some gardens, like some homes, afford little more privacy than a shop window. Better one room that is your own than a whole house exposed to the world, better a tiny plot where you can be alone than a great expanse without this essential attribute of the real garden.

—ELLEN SHIPMAN, "A Landscape Architect Discusses Gardens," *Better Homes and Gardens,* November 1930

American women's close association with gardens began in the Colonial era when settlers brought seeds and cuttings from England and carefully tended plants for cooking and healing, and as remembrances of places left behind.[1] During the nineteenth century, women were still considered temperamentally suited to horticulture as part of their work in the domestic sphere, even believed to be endowed with natural talents for it.[2] The idea had been eloquently expressed in Jane Loudon's *Gardening for Ladies* (1840) and continued as a theme through Ella Rodman Church's *The Home Gardener* (1881). It was still apparent when *What Girls Can Do* was published in 1926.[3] As Guy Lowell once observed, in a rather backhanded compliment, "A woman will *fuss*

with a garden in a way that no man will ever have the patience to do."[4]

During the 1890s, American women discovered that landscape gardening also offered them the potential of paid work, largely through the example of Beatrix Jones (later Farrand). In 1896 Jones's professional progress was reported in the *Bar Harbor Record* as "a decidedly new and quite ambitious departure." The author was enthusiastic about the "young, attractive society girl . . . taking upon herself such a mammoth task," noting that "she is certainly carrying it through most commendably, shirking none of the hard and disagreeable details, and handling big crews of men with great tact and dignity."[5]

A 1908 article in the *Outlook*, published just as Ellen Shipman was creating her first commissioned designs, was less ebullient about the prospects for fair aspirants arming themselves for careers in the garden, sketching a rather bleak picture of the demands of the work.[6] The author interviewed Beatrix Jones, Marian Coffin, and Martha Brookes Brown, the three best-known women practitioners at the time. All of them advised caution before embarking on the arduous vocational journey, citing constant travel, extreme weather conditions, surly crews, and low pay. Still, there was rising interest in the field and in women pursuing professional lives generally.

During the second half of the nineteenth century women made enormous gains in expanding their rights, particularly through the efforts of the early suffragists, many of whom took on prominent public roles that transgressed accepted gender stereotypes. From Susan B. Anthony to Jane Addams, women found more or less confrontational methods to widen their influence.[7] As the turn of the century approached, however, and gender roles continued to loosen, new prohibitions developed to keep women out of the workforce and tethered to traditional identities as wives and mothers, safe in the "haven" of the home.

Women who insisted on doing "brain work" were believed to be prone to nervousness, itself a subject of growing interest. Females so afflicted were treated as infants, sent to bed in darkened rooms and spoon-fed milk.[8] In striking contrast, male neurasthenics—of whom there were also considerable numbers—were advised to go west and pursue rugged, outdoor lives. Among the men who recovered their health through these means were Owen Wister, who went on to write *The Virginian,* and Theodore Roosevelt, who became a hero in the Spanish-American War. Patriotism also was enlisted in the effort to curtail women's entry into the professional workforce. In his presidential address of 1903, Roosevelt—cured of his neurasthenia—denounced any woman who chose not to have children as "a criminal against the race."[9] Nevertheless, he graciously welcomed a childless Beatrix Jones to the White House on several occasions, where she met important clients.

New Women who did manage to establish landscape architectural practices—often with the help of sympathetic men such as Charles Platt, Warren Manning, and even Theodore Roosevelt—soon discovered other obstacles. Shipman and her female colleagues were repeatedly passed over for estate and institutional work because it was assumed that they did not possess the authority to supervise male construction crews. On occasion, male friends and colleagues intervened on their behalf, and this support, coupled with women practitioners' own increasing

cultural authority, provided them with a small number of institutional projects where they did, indeed, successfully supervise construction, with "tact and dignity."[10] Still, among all the types of projects available to the burgeoning ranks of landscape architects throughout the United States—from parks and parkways, to campuses and institutional grounds, to company towns and new suburbs—flower gardens continued to provide American women practitioners their greatest source of commissions.[11] Ellen Shipman was the most celebrated practitioner in this specialized and demanding genre.

That she and her compatriots are not better known today, as the historian Rebecca Warren Davidson points out, is largely owing to the scarcity of public commissions that were given to women. Another reason why women's role in the history of American landscape architecture has only recently begun to be examined, in Davidson's words, "has to do with the way we have written our history." She argues that the design history of the domestic garden in the United States has been marginalized in the general literature of the profession, both because of its perceived lack of social relevance and its continued association with "women's work."[12]

American men, by contrast, are rarely identified with flower gardens. (This is not the case in England, where several prominent men created important gardens—Lawrence Johnston at Hidcote Manor, for example, and Harold Nicolson at Sissinghurst.) Even H. F. du Pont, who loved flowers passionately, soon took his plant trials into the surrounding woods. The other well-known du Pont who gardened at this scale, Pierre, specialized in fountains. In this sense they were typical of American men who focused on the broad effects that could be achieved through grading, water works, road building, bridge building, and tree and massed planting. Male landscape architects who did design flower borders rarely evidenced much enthusiasm for them—Warren Manning's odd plantings for Stan Hywet's English Garden offer a case in point.[13]

Shipman's designs deserve more serious recognition than history has awarded them—no American practitioner explored the aesthetic potential of the flower garden more extensively than she. In their imaginativeness and sheer beauty, Shipman's gardens rivaled those of her British contemporary Gertrude Jekyll, whose planting methods and attention to color and texture had strongly influenced her. Shipman's style also reflected the influence of the Arts and Crafts gardens of Cornish, where inventive use of old-fashioned perennials was paired with traditional Colonial plans and classically inspired architectural features. Shipman was further influenced by American landscape architects whose emphasis on composition reflected Olmstedian purposes. In words that recall Olmsted, she once explained that she used plants "as a painter uses the colors from his palette."[14] Most of Shipman's gardens disappeared during the 1940s, when maintenance of large formal gardens was generally abandoned. Even so, in her 1950 obituary, the *New York Times* identified Shipman as "one of the leading landscape architects of the United States." (Fig. 5.1)

Ellen McGowan Biddle was born in 1869 in Philadelphia, on the military rather than the banking side of the Biddle family. Described by her mother as a "tall, fearless girl," she loved the great wild spaces of the Arizona territory where she spent her early childhood and was distraught when her family moved east, to New Jersey. Once settled, however, she grew to love dooryard gardens and the traditional flowers that flourished in them—which she apparently found irresistible. "A rose to hold all the way to school," she later remembered, "seemed well worth the punishment."[15] Dispatched to boarding school in Baltimore as an adolescent, she was encouraged in her interest in design by a teacher's gift of an architectural dictionary.

After graduating, Biddle briefly attended Radcliffe College (then an annex of Harvard) and in 1893 married Louis Shipman, an aspiring young playwright whose career seemed to hold great promise. A year later, the Shipmans moved to Plainfield, New Hampshire, near Cornish, considered by many the "most beautifully gardened village in all America."[16] They rented a house with Herbert and Louise Croly (Ellen's roommate at Radcliffe), and became friendly with Eleanor and Charles Platt, both prominent gardeners in the colony. Shipman vividly re-

membered her first night in Cornish, at a dinner party at High Court, Annie Lazarus's country house designed by Platt a few years before. "Below, where we stood upon a terrace, was a Sunken Garden with rows bathed in moonlight of white lilies standing as an altar for Ascutney," she wrote. "As I look back I realize it was at that moment that a garden became for me the most essential part of a home."[17]

She planted her first garden a few years later, at Poins House, a simple backyard layout that was noticed and admired by many of her neighbors, including Platt. (Fig. 5.2) One day he came across some sketches Shipman had done

5.1. Ellen Shipman in her Beekman Place office, New York, N.Y., 1920s. Photograph by Bradley Studio. Courtesy Nancy Angell Streeter Collection.

5.2. Ellen Shipman in her Poins House garden, Plainfield, N.H. Courtesy Nancy Angell Streeter Collection.

and made her a gift of some drafting tools, with a vastly encouraging note, "you better keep on."[18] By 1910 Louis Shipman's career was floundering and so was the marriage. (He would soon depart, leaving Ellen with three children to rear on her own; the couple would eventually divorce.) About this same time, Platt suggested that Shipman assist him on some of his garden projects. The prospect of working with the architect was probably thrilling, but she was unsure of her abilities and requested drafting instruction from one of Platt's assistants. Their early unrecorded collaborations seemed to have been a success because Platt continued to recommend her work to his clients. Shipman also launched a solo career, largely as a means to achieve financial security.

Her preparation for the demands of the new profession had been rather sketchy, but women had limited training options at the time. Female applicants were not admitted to Harvard's professional program, the first in the United States, or to any other such university program except those at Cornell and MIT, where they could enroll only as special students. There were a few special schools for women—Lowthorpe School of Landscape Architecture for Women, founded in Groton, Massachusetts, in 1901, the Pennsylvania School of Horticulture for Women in Ambler, founded in 1910, and the Cambridge School of Architecture and Landscape Architecture, founded in 1916; however, Shipman was not in a financial position to attend any of them.[19] Ironically, this circumstance may have served her well, as had Platt's unusual preparation for his career. The combination of Shipman's architectural tutoring, her horticultural expertise (gained from hands-on experience), her exposure to the Arts and Crafts sensibilities of her artistic neighbors, and her independent intellect, which sought out authoritative books on the topic, gave rise to her distinctive approach.[20] Indeed, no formal program produced so original a talent among the female practitioners of the day except MIT, where Marian Coffin received a Beaux-Arts education that was robustly supplemented by her horticultural association with H. F. du Pont.[21]

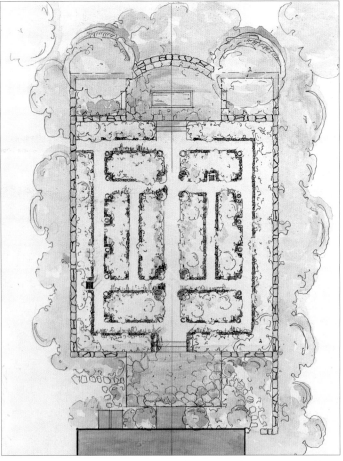

5.3. Sketch plan for walled garden, Old Farms, Alanson L. Daniels estate, Wenham, Mass., ink and wash on paper, March 1913. RMC-Cornell Univ. Library.

One of Shipman's earliest recorded projects, a 1913 garden for Alanson L. Daniels, at Old Farms in Wenham, Massachusetts, announced a repertory of features that came to structure much of her later work, nearly six hundred projects in all. The design was based on a geometric plan and included a reflecting pool, stone terrace, and abundant plantings arranged in a strong, simple composition. The design's most remarkable element was the imaginative planting scheme, a combination of groundcovers, perennials, annuals, bulbs, shrubs, and trees in a composition that evoked Colonial gardens in New England, as well as new developments in old England. The Daniels garden struck the note of quiet, self-contained charm that typified Shipman's best work, a sense of the garden as a private world, a haven. (Figs. 5.3, 5.4)

In 1913 Platt recommended Shipman to James Fenimore Cooper II for work at Fynmere in Cooperstown,

5.4. Daniels garden, 1913. Photograph by Edith Hastings Tracy. RMC-Cornell Univ. Library.

5.5. View from the terrace, Fynmere, James Fenimore Cooper estate, Cooperstown, N.Y., 1912. RMC-Cornell Univ. Library.

of these projects featured complex plantings set in counterpoint to substantial architectural features—pergolas, arbors, and pavilions designed by Platt in relation to the proportions and styles of the houses associated with them. (Figs. 5.6, 5.7, 5.8) Shipman also collaborated with Warren Manning on several projects, usually in similarly gender-divided arrangements that focused her work within the formal garden wall.[22] One of the most distinctive of these projects was a walled garden for Halfred Farms in Chagrin Falls, Ohio, where Charles A. Lindbergh landed his plane and offered a her lift back to New York. (Fig. 5.9)

5.6. Walled garden, The Causeway, James Parmelee estate, Washington, D.C., c. 1917. Photograph by Frances Benjamin Johnston. RMC-Cornell Univ. Library.

5.7. Pool and pavilion, Girdle Ridge, William F. Fahnestock estate, Katonah, N.Y., c. 1912. Photograph by Jessie Tarbox Beals. RMC-Cornell Univ. Library.

New York, where she had considerable responsibility for architectural features. (At this point, Platt was accepting garden commissions only in conjunction with houses, and he seems to have been diverting garden jobs to Shipman.) Her secure handling of the plan and the new garden buildings testifies to the success of her training under Platt. (Fig. 5.5)

She soon began working with Platt on other jobs including the James Parmelee estate in Washington, D.C., which featured extensive brickwork, and a collaboration at Girdle Ridge, the Katonah, New York, estate of William F. Fahnestock. In 1919 Shipman became involved at The Moorings, the estate Platt had designed for Russell A. Alger Jr., in Grosse Pointe, Michigan, a decade before. Each

5.8. Pool garden, The Moorings, Russell A. Alger estate, Grosse Pointe, Mich., 1930s. Photograph by Thomas Ellison. RMC-Cornell Univ. Library.

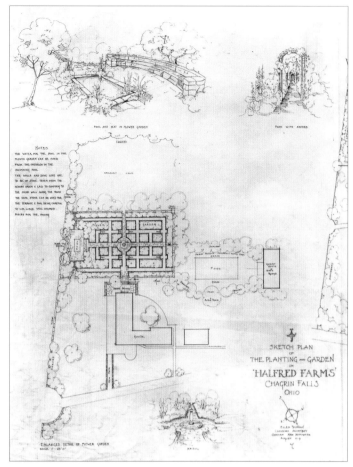

5.9. Sketch plan of Halfred Farms, Windsor T. White estate, Chagrin Falls, Ohio, ink on linen, August 1919. RMC-Cornell Univ. Library.

In an independent design for a Greenport, New York, garden for Julia Fish (1916), Shipman used the herbaceous border as a primary focus, a compositional technique that recalled the approach of other Cornish gardeners, including Platt, although here, as in most of her gardens, Shipman utilized far fewer architectural elements than Platt typically employed. On the featureless Long Island site, she laid out a pair of 300-foot borders set against a backing of cedars, dogwood, beach plum, flowering crabs, and cherries, planting the beds in an Impressionistic wash of color that ranged from lavender to pink to white. The modest central ornament in the design, where the long and short garden axes crossed, was a small reflecting pool. Shipman's detailed plan included views within the garden but none from the garden to the surrounding countryside. (Fig. 5.10)

In a Colonial Revival design a few years later (c. 1919) for the sisters Mary and Neltje Pruyn, in East Hampton, New York, Shipman again used big herbaceous beds as the centerpiece of the layout. Photographs by Mattie Edwards Hewitt capture imaginative juxtapositions that relied on strong foliage as well as bloom— swords of German iris, shiny-leaved peony, square-cut box, clouds of baby's breath, and bursts of white phlox.

A photograph of the Pruyn place was among the illustrations in "Design of the Small Place," Fletcher Steele's chapter in the *House Beautiful Gardening Manual*; his caption praised "the unusually successful Colonial feeling" Shipman had achieved, "due to the fact that stiff accuracy has been avoided."[23] (Fig. 5.11) As nativist sentiments surged and American architecture and design rose in the estimation of the cultural elite, Shipman's close association with the Colonial Revival movement served her career well.

By 1920, when she moved her office to New York City, Shipman had begun to secure larger commissions. As a result of the increased publicity about her work, her well-attended lectures, and her continued association with prominent landscape architects, Shipman's client base had spread throughout the eastern half of United States and beyond, to the Midwest and the South.[24] At the

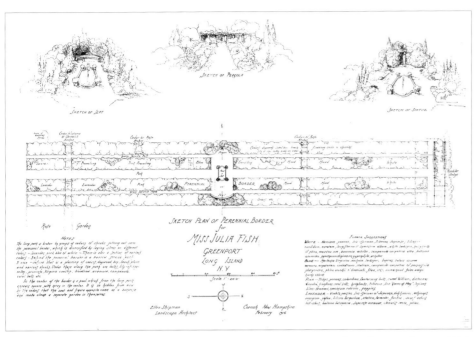

5.10. Sketch of perennial border, Julia Fish garden, Greenport, N.Y., ink on linen, February 1916. RMC-Cornell Univ. Library.

height of her career, she employed several full-time workers, all of them women, most of them educated at the Lowthorpe School. Among the best known were Elizabeth Lord and Edith Schryver, who later established a joint practice in Salem, Oregon.[25] Unlike her wealthier colleagues, Shipman did not travel to Europe to gather design ideas, though she did eventually see England, France, and Spain in 1929. Her gardens were frequently published in prominent design periodicals, where they were illustrated with photographs by Mattie Edwards Hewitt, Samuel Gottscho, Harry G. Healy, Jessie Tarbox Beals, and others of equal stature. She was not a particularly fluid writer and rarely published herself.

In the 1920s Shipman's projects grew in size and architectural complexity. Typical was Penwood, the estate of Carll Tucker, in Mount Kisco, New York, begun in

5.11. Mary and Neltje Pruyn garden, 1920, East Hampton, N.Y., c. 1923. Photograph by Mattie Edwards Hewitt. RMC-Cornell Univ. Library.

5.12. Pool, Penwood, Carll Tucker estate, Mount Kisco, N.Y., late 1930s. Photograph by Harry G. Healy. RMC-Cornell Univ. Library.

1926. Shipman's design featured Italianate forms, including a massive pergola, realized in an Arts and Crafts style.[26] (Fig. 5.12) There were also charming details. An error in measurement for the plumbing of a small pool resulted in a stepped, flagstone coping that provided opportunities for bits of varied plantings. Shipman repeated the distinctive pool treatment in several other projects, including her own garden, Brook Place, in Plainfield. That same year, 1926, she began work on her most extensive project, Rynwood, the estate of Samuel A. Salvage in Glen Head, New York, where she combined a Cotswold-inspired teahouse, a slate-roofed dovecote, and an apple orchard in a layout that featured masses of perennials. Roger H. Bullard was the architect of the Tudor house, which was awarded the Gold Medal of Better Homes in America in 1933.[27] (Figs. 5.13, 5.14) Both of these country estates, though large in acreage, were nevertheless structured by domestically scaled gardens linked in a classical grid. Only a few of Shipman's works made the leap to broader spatial treatment.[28]

Among her more ambitious projects were a limited number of institutional commissions that brought her talents before a wider public. In 1928 Shipman was invited to design the Women's Advisory Council Border for the New York Botanical Garden, a 254-foot-long bed that included a mix of shrubs, perennials, and standards.[29] (Fig. 5.15) A 1930 job of unusual scope for Aetna Life and Casualty Insurance Company in Hartford, Connecticut, included planning the twenty-two-acre site and designing lawns, formal courtyards, and a roof garden for the company president, who was also a private client. James Gamble Rogers was the architect for what was billed as "America's largest Colonial-style office building." (Fig. 5.16) In 1936 Shipman was given a prominent commission for the Sarah P. Duke Gardens at

5.13. Dovecote, Rynwood, Samuel A. Salvage estate, Glen Head, N.Y., 1935. Photograph by Harry G. Healy. RMC-Cornell Univ. Library.

5.14. Plan for Rynwood, Salvage estate, ink on linen, February 1926. RMC-Cornell Univ. Library.

5.15. Women's Advisory Council Border, New York Botanical Garden, Bronx, N.Y., 1928. RMC-Cornell Univ. Library.

5.16. Roof garden, Aetna Life, Hartford, Conn, 1931. Photograph by Fred Jones. Courtesy Aetna Life and Casualty.

5.17. Sarah P. Duke Gardens, Durham, N.C., 1940. Duke University Archives.

beds down to a pond at the bottom.[30] (Fig. 5.17) Even on a public scale, Shipman's work was distinguished by an unusual intimacy and a sense of privacy.

Along with these big jobs were commissions for new plantings in formal gardens whose architectural frameworks had been previously designed by other practitioners. In 1927 Clara Ford hired Shipman to create a new planting for the rose garden at Fair Lane originally designed by Jens Jensen for the c. 1914 estate. As did other women clients of the day, Clara wanted swaths of spring bloom and ample color through summer and fall—which Shipman provided.[31] Two years later, Gertrude Seiberling commissioned her to redesign the plantings in the English Garden at Stan Hywet Hall, a project that brought Shipman's Arts and Crafts methods alongside Manning's. (Fig. 5.18) In 1935 she worked in a similar capacity for Elizabeth

Duke University, in Durham, North Carolina, secured through her friendship with Dr. Frederick M. Hanes, whose large family provided the landscape architect with many private jobs. At Duke, she designed seven curving stone terraces that were planted with a mix of Japanese cherries, crabs, shrubs, and perennials. The uppermost terrace was crowned with a garden structure not unlike the one Platt designed for the seawalls at Gwinn. Wide steps of rose-tinged flagstone brought visitors past brimming

5.18. English Garden, Stan Hywet Hall, Akron, Ohio, with restored Shipman plantings, 1997. Photograph by Carol Betsch.

Mather at Gwinn, where she designed new plantings for Platt's formal layout. These circumscribed commissions would continue throughout her long working life.

Shipman would also find opportunities to continue to explore design at the scale of Penwood and Rynwood, even during the depth of the Great Depression. In 1934 she began what became one of her best-known projects,

Longue Vue, in New Orleans, for Edith and Edgar B. Stern. Initially, the scope of Shipman's work was to include the design of the Sterns' house, but she soon discovered that she did not have the requisite skills, and William and Geoffrey Platt, the sons of Charles Platt, who had recently died, stepped in to help. They designed a handsome three-story Classical Revival house that was based in part on Shadows-on-the-Teche in New Iberia. Shipman worked closely with the Platts on the house and also designed the interiors, which were closely related to the gardens.[32]

Her concise and intricate landscape plan featured a formal approach drive, parterre gardens off the south portico planted for spring and fall display, a magnolia-bordered vista terminating in a garden pavilion and long pool, a big, octagonal kitchen garden, and a wild garden, planted in consultation with noted naturalist and native plant expert Caroline Dorman. In its balance of expansive and intimate spaces, views and detail, Longue Vue was one of Shipman's most artistically successful landscapes and, after Edith Stern's death, one of her few private works open to visitors.[33] (Figs. 5.19, 5.20)

Shipman's most compelling gardens, like Longue Vue, were layered and complex, charged with a sense of mystery as well as charm.[34] Few, however, were guided by the breadth and spirit of nature that would inspire Shipman's colleagues Beatrix Farrand and Marian Coffin. These slightly younger women had come to the field through less domestic routes than the one available to Ellen Shipman. Each would, rather brilliantly, explore new means of responding to the genius loci.

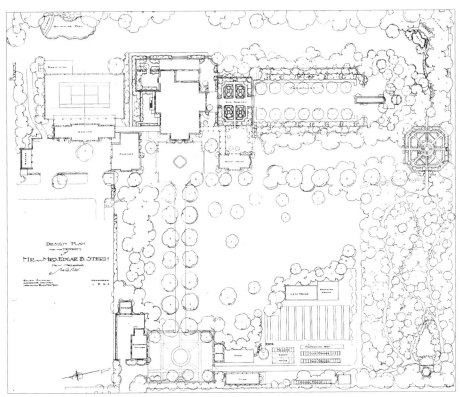

5.19. "Design Plan," Longue Vue, Edgar B. Stern estate, New Orleans, La., December 1942. RMC-Cornell Univ. Library.

5.20. Reflecting pool to house, Longue Vue. Photograph by Shipman office. RMC-Cornell Univ. Library.

PART II

INNOVATION AND WILDNESS

1920–1929

American landscape design in the 1920s was characterized by increasingly far-ranging experimentation. Landscape practitioners became adept at integrating clearly defined outdoor spaces with the fundamental precepts of the Olmstedian Picturesque, finding ingenious means to combine outdoor rooms with borrowed views and other strongly articulated responses to the genius loci—a principle expressed by one of the era's great landscape architects, Beatrix Farrand, as "keeping step with the great stride of Nature." Other themes emerged during this innovative decade. As practitioners gained sophistication, so, too, did clients, many of whom were active partners in the design process. Extended and frequent travel to Europe provided a stream of ideas to both practitioners and their clients, and the ability to confidently mix historical influences, even within a single landscape passage, grew. As designs became more varied and more secure, they also became more idiosyncratic. In particular, the notion that landscapes could achieve distinction by reflecting individual client personalities gained footing.

SIX

BEATRIX FARRAND

1872–1959

Every lover of nature must have noticed how beautiful the edge of a woods is in early summer, when the dark branch of an evergreen throws out the paler green of some deciduous neighbor. In the clearing and planting which are necessary on some places every year, should we not try to get like effects?

—Beatrix Jones, "Nature's Landscape-gardening in Maine," *Garden and Forest*, September 1893

Beatrix Cadwalader Jones was born in New York City—the product, as she later wrote, of several generations of gardeners. Her parents were Mary Cadwalader Rawle, from Philadelphia, and the very wealthy Frederic Rhinelander Jones, of New York. Mary and Frederic married in 1870 but separated when Beatrix was still very young and divorced before she was twelve. Despite this circumstance, Mary continued her close friendship with Frederic's sister, the novelist Edith Wharton, who would figure importantly in Beatrix's life, too. As Farrand's biographers have noted, while her childhood may have been challenging in certain respects, it did offer a liberating alternative to the strictures of the typical Vic-

torian family. In combination with her unusually strong character, privileged background, and artistic gifts, her outsider's perspective may have opened fresh perspectives on her art. She would make several innovative contributions to it.[1] (Fig. 6.1)

As a young girl, Beatrix spent summers with her family in the resort village of Bar Harbor, Maine, where the Joneses had built a large cottage on a few acres near the shore.[2] Mary preferred native to imported species, and her daughter also came to love the trillium, lilies, and shadblow that grew in the island wilds near Reef Point. (Fig. 6.2) There Beatrix gardened by her mother's side, coming to love the feel of the soil and know the ways of plants. In this regard, she resembled Ellen Shipman and other young women who would turn an early pastime into a professional career. But unlike Shipman, Beatrix Jones witnessed several women's professional lives at close range. Mary Jones was a social reformer who worked to improve conditions for nurses in New York City, and, as financial necessity grew, a literary agent for her sister-in-law and Henry James's representative in the United States. Edith Wharton was the author of several highly esteemed novels, including *The Age of Innocence*, for which she received

6.1. Beatrix Farrand. Dumbarton Oaks.

6.2. Shore front of Reef Point gardens. Photograph by Sewall Brown. From *Reef Point Gardens Bulletin,* November 1947. Courtesy Patrick Chassé.

a Pulitzer Prize in 1921—the same year that Farrand began her largest and most compelling work, Dumbarton Oaks.

In winters, the Joneses lived in Washington Square, where they enjoyed sure knowledge of their privileged place in the stratified, stultifying world that formed the backdrop of Wharton's incisive novels. Beatrix frequently traveled abroad with her mother, often in the company of her aunt, who was just ten years her senior. In addition to her reform work, Mary Jones presided over a salon that brought together many of the leading literary and artistic figures of the American Renaissance—Brooks and Henry Adams, Francis Marion Crawford, John La Farge, Maud Howe Elliot, Augustus Saint-Gaudens, John Singer Sargent, and Henry James among them. James became an older, somewhat avuncular friend of Beatrix's, too.

A more fatherly presence in Beatrix's life, and the person to whom she seems to have been closest emotionally,

was her mother's cousin John Lambert Cadwalader, a distinguished lawyer, trustee of the Metropolitan Museum of Art, and founder of the New York Public Library.[3] Cadwalader regularly took Beatrix to Scotland, where she learned to shoot on the moors and also to "keep time with nature." He manifested unusually staunch support for his young cousin's vocational aspirations, later remarking, "Let her be a gardener or, for that matter, anything she wants to be. What she wishes to do will be well done."[4]

It may have been Mariana Van Rensselaer, a family friend as well as a strong advocate for women entering the profession, who suggested that young Beatrix consider becoming a landscape architect. By the time she was twenty-one Jones had set her sights on this goal, abandoning an earlier idea of pursuing a career in vocal music. She advanced rapidly, sped by propitious circumstances and her own indomitable will. By 1908, when an article about women and landscape architecture appeared in the *Out-*

look, Beatrix Jones was considered the doyenne of the profession.[5]

Her horticultural training began in 1893, when she was twenty-one and moved to Brookline, Massachusetts, to study with Charles Sprague Sargent, founder and director of the Arnold Arboretum. The invitation had come through Sargent's wife, Mary Robeson, a talented amateur painter, who met young Beatrix through Mary Jones. Over many years, Charles Sargent had developed his 150-acre country estate, Holm Lea, into a landscape garden in the tradition of the American Picturesque. It was a beautiful place, graced with open pastoral views framed by groves of native trees and a pond on whose shores cattle grazed. (Fig. 6.3) Each spring great banks of rhododendron bloomed amid magnolias, ornamental cherries, and mountain laurel, and crowds from the city flocked to see the display. At the nearby Arnold Arboretum, Beatrix had the opportunity to become acquainted with an even greater range of plants, every species known to be hardy to the climate.

In her last piece of autobiographical writing—her obituary—Farrand recalled Sargent's influence, noting especially his advice to "make the plan fit the ground and not to twist the ground to fit a plan."[6] She would heed her mentor's counsel, but she would also make important modifications to it by aligning herself almost equally with Charles Platt's "refusal to be bound too closely by the natural conditions of the site, . . . to remold them nearer to the heart's desire."[7] Farrand was one of the first American landscape architects to successfully fuse a deep response to nature with highly expressive designs, to commingle with confidence passages evoking a sense of wildness with passages of artistic invention.

In 1893, when Jones's first article, "Nature's Landscape-gardening in Maine," was published, she had already developed a fairly specific perspective on landscape design. She wrote in praise of the principle of nature inspiration, and she also emphasized the importance of study and knowledge of the pictorial principles Olmsted had adapted to an American style:

6.3. Holm Lea, Charles Sprague Sargent estate, Jamaica Plain, Mass. From Samuel Parsons, *Art of Landscape Architecture,* 1915.

In driving along the wooded roads in the district where the grounds lie which are to be developed, one who notes which are the handsomest of the native trees can get an idea as to which ones to plant and how these should be grouped; but the appropriate massing of foliage, so as to secure the best effect from soft harmonies or bold contrasts of color, requires much study and critical knowledge. After the varieties have been decided upon comes the serious question of grouping for contrasting color, and the arrangement of those colors for different seasons of the years and varying lights demands close observation and study.[8]

In October 1893 Jones, her mentor Sargent, and his wife spent a week at the Chicago World's Columbian Exposition—the subject of several articles Sargent was writing for *Garden and Forest*. There Jones took extensive notes on the plan and plantings of the exposition and also recorded her responses to the design of the buildings. She was drawn to Peabody & Stearns's Massachusetts State Building, for example, where Jacob Manning's planting design had been awarded a prize. Other pivotal experiences followed rapidly.

The next spring Beatrix, her mother, and the Sargents traveled to Biltmore in George Washington Vanderbilt's private rail car, the "Swannanoa." Sargent's purpose was to discuss plans for Vanderbilt's arboretum with Olmsted.

Jones likely knew both Vanderbilt and Gifford Pinchot, who was charged with planting the Biltmore forest, as both were summer residents of Bar Harbor, but she had evidently never met Olmsted. In Asheville she saw his last great private work firsthand—the densely planted approach road, sunlit formal terraces, shrubby ramble, cutting and vegetable gardens, and momentous views to mountains and lake—and she saw the beginnings of what was to have been the most ambitious tree collection in the world. Olmsted was not much impressed by Jones, whom he dismissed as someone "inclined to dabble in landscape architecture"; however, he extended an invitation to her to visit Fairsted. She went in June.[9] (Fig. 6.4)

Jones toured the rambling Brookline house whose accretions chronicled the growth of the firm, and she took extensive notes on the workings of the business. She also recorded her opinions of the plantings on the grounds: that the azaleas on the front lawn clashed, and "two brilliantly white and evidently cultivated spireas in a quasi-natural shrubbery seemed rather out of place."[10] But Jones's mind was open to Olmsted's working methods, such as the use of tracing paper overlaid on site surveys and a system of delineating plants on plans keyed to detailed lists. The delegation of professional responsibilities, the basis of the complex, modern landscape architectural practice that Olmsted had pioneered, would provide her with a model that she would soon adopt in her own practice.

As a next step in her education, Jones planned an extended European tour to see influential examples of landscape architecture and also to seek out important landscape paintings, so that she might, as Sargent advised, "learn from all the great arts, as all art is akin."[11] Accompanied by her mother and armed with letters of introduction from Charles Eliot and others, she left the following spring.[12] The Joneses' itinerary began in Gibraltar and included Rome and several of the most important villas of Italy, the great gardens and parks of Germany (among these Nymphenburg and Dr. Carl Bolle's island plantation, Schwarfenberg), and the parks and botanical gardens of London. London also provided a base for excursions to the Surrey Hills, Sussex, Cumbria, and Scotland. The three-month tour concluded with the parks and gardens of Paris.

The lessons Jones absorbed pacing out Italian villas left particularly strong impressions (there were about twenty on their tour), and her notes on them presaged artistic

6.5. Villa Lante, 1895. Photograph by Beatrix Jones. EDA, Berkeley.

6.4 Fairsted, Frederick Law Olmsted estate, Brookline, Mass., 1894, as Jones would have seen it on her June visit. NPS/FLO.

6.6. William Robinson's Gravetye Manor, from Wilhelm Miller, *What England Can Teach Us*, 1911.

6.7 Bridge over the River Kent, Levens Hall, Cumbria, 1895. Photograph by Beatrix Jones. EDA, Berkeley.

concerns that would soon inform her work. Of Io Viterbo she wrote, for example, "the grounds seemed the best combination I had seen of the landscape and the architectural styles. The transition was almost imperceptible, and from a formal fountain one walked into a deep wood and then out on a grassy lawn with a tennis court on it."[13] She thought the Villa Lante the "most charming" of those visited—an assessment that Fletcher Steele would echo after his 1913 visit, two decades later. (Fig. 6.5)

The English sites on the tour also made a strong impact. Jones and her mother visited Munstead Wood, the Sussex country home of Gertrude Jekyll, where she met the gardener. They also visited William Robinson's one-thousand-acre estate, Gravetye Manor, and there Jones met the Irish gardener and author. (Fig. 6.6) She remained in contact with Robinson for many years and

made several return visits to Gravetye. The Joneses also visited Penshurst, a Tudor garden that had recently been redesigned in the Italianate style then being promoted in opposition to Robinson's wild gardening approach. Jones was particularly inspired by the park at Levens Hall and wrote an article about the stone bridge there which was published in *Garden and Forest* the following year.[14] (Fig. 6.7)

By the autumn of 1895 her informal course of education was almost complete. She set up a professional office on the third floor of her mother's house on East Eleventh Street (in her own nursery, converted for the purpose) and enrolled in a drafting course taught by William Ware at the School of Mines.[15] Jones soon had several jobs in hand from family friends in Bar Harbor, most of them small and tightly circumscribed. One of these was advising on draining a swamp for Anna Dorinda Blaksley Barnes Bliss, mother of her future client Mildred Bliss. Mount Desert Island would provide her with a greater number of commissions than any other locale—of the approximately two hundred projects eventually recorded in her archives, about one-quarter were for summer residents of the island.[16]

6.8. "Sketch for Grounds," William R. Garrison estate, Tuxedo, N.Y., 1896. EDA, Berkeley.

Her most substantial early project came in 1896 from William R. Garrison for his new house at Tuxedo Park, a resort community north of Manhattan that had been planned by Ernest W. Bowditch. In her design Jones retained existing trees—hickory, oak, maple, and birch—and added others to frame a view out to Tuxedo Lake, the centerpiece of the development. A large terrace at the rear of the house, designed by the architect William A. Bates, offered an architectural framework to the broad view. (Fig. 6.8) The sources of Jones's design ideas for this early project are not difficult to trace: Olmsted and Sargent's American approach is apparent in the structure of the grounds; Jekyll's influence was evident in the planting around the house, a mix of lilac, honeysuckle, and other fragrant shrubs and languid roses.

The following year, Jones published a second article in *Garden and Forest*, "The Garden in Relation to the House," a review of a paper presented by landscape gardener H. E. Milner to the Royal Institute of British Architects. Jones's piece offered an earnest assessment of Milner's ideas on landscape design and sympathy toward his approval of the "happy mean," whereby the "art of

both schools [architecture and landscape architecture] . . . go hand in hand." It also opens a window into her sensitivity to "the spirit of the beauty of nature . . . her majesty, simplicity, peacefulness, sweetness, repose, refinement, strength, and variety in form, color, abundance," and Jones's desire that these be "brought into juxtaposition." She closed her article with a quote from Milner which emphasizes the value of topographic drama: "When the ground is broken or undulating (either natural or created), advantage should be seized by marking the eminences." Jones would follow this advice in her own work, too.[17]

In 1897 she was the subject of an interview in the *New York Sun* that focused on the young society woman's unusual choice of profession. The article also reported on her love of sport, her "majestic" beauty, and her choice of clothes—a bicycling suit. Clearly a patrician woman landscape gardener who wore pantaloons on the job was a sensation.[18] According to the article, Jones had already amassed a professional library of three hundred volumes, and she was confidently at work on several commissions.[19]

The *Sun*'s admiring feature may have brought her more private clients—Jones soon listed new jobs in several locations, all of which were residential—but her interest in public projects is chronicled, too. In 1898 she wrote an article for the *Journal of the Committee on Municipal Administration*, in which she promoted small neighborhood parks—in Jones's words, "open air gymnasiums"—for New York City children. She may have imagined that park work would come to her as a result of this publication, but no such commissions followed. American women's roles in the new profession were still securely tied to flower gardens, and even though parks often included such gardens, parks also required engineering, road building, and city politics, none of which were considered remotely suitable for women at the time. Nevertheless, the article did provide an important vocational boost.

Prior to its publication, Jones's piece was reviewed by

Samuel Parsons, who maintained strong control of New York's parks in his position as superintendent. Parsons was impressed by what he read, and he recommended Jones as a charter member in the professional organization then being developed by himself, Warren Manning, and a somewhat reluctant John Charles Olmsted, who was not convinced that the field was ready for this step—the American Society of Landscape Architects.[20] Jones was the only woman invited to join the group, and the least experienced among its members. Yet, by virtue of her determined course of study, her earnest and clear-headed publications, and her success with her early jobs, she had rapidly achieved prominence. She did not take the profession's name, however; Jones continued to use the term *landscape gardener*, with its horticultural emphasis, for her entire career.

A c. 1901 job for her first cousin Clement B. Newbold in Jenkintown, Pennsylvania, marked an important professional step.[21] Jones had begun analyzing the 190-acre site of Crosswicks in 1891, even before she had decided to become a landscape architect. The designer of the Georgian-influenced house was the prominent author and architect Guy Lowell, the son-in-law of Jones's mentor, Sargent. The work is significant as Jones's first recorded use of classical lines, and at Crosswicks she created what seems to have been her first wild garden.

The house was sited at the brink of an abandoned quarry, and the richly planted garden Jones created there provided the dominant foreground view. Her analysis of the quarry area recorded "fibrous loam, limestone, peat bog, and sand, as well as areas in intense shade."[22] Drifts of plants were nestled into rocky crevices and a winding stone path that led to a rustic summer house. (In these passages, Jones may have been influenced by the quarry garden Manning had created for Clement Griscom in nearby Haverford, which had been published in the *Outlook* and *Country Life*.) Beyond the garden stretched the farm fields and forest of the Delaware Valley. Jones retained an existing mass of trees as a screen between the wild garden and the large formal garden, laid out to the east along

the central axis of the house. Here, densely planted beds recalled the drift arrangements of Jekyll. In the center, Jones created a sunken rose garden. Her interest in local material was evident in the native stone, combined with brick in the garden walls, which focused views back toward the wild garden and out to the surrounding landscape. (Figs. 6.9, 6.10) Jones's beautifully rendered ink and

6.9. Crosswicks, Clement B. Newbold estate, Jenkintown, Pa., rose garden, c. 1903. EDA, Berkeley.

6.10. Crosswicks, wall of formal garden. EDA, Berkeley.

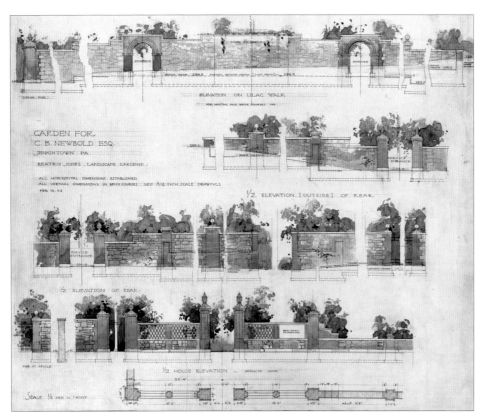

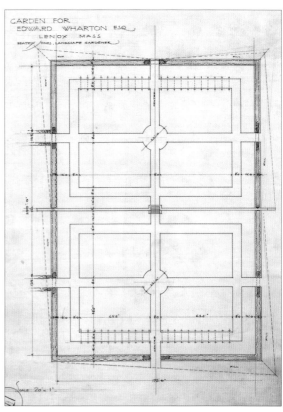

6.11. "Garden for C. B. Newbold, Esq.," 1903, presentation drawing (detail). EDA, Berkeley.

6.12. "Garden for Edward Wharton, Esq." (plan for kitchen garden), Lenox, Mass., 1901. EDA, Berkeley.

watercolor presentation drawing emphasizes the play of lines against the country setting. (Fig. 6.11)

Concurrently, Jones was designing a plan for a kitchen garden and the layout of the approach drive for The Mount, Edith and Edward Wharton's new home in Lenox, Massachusetts, and there, too, formal and wild gardens were juxtaposed. (Fig. 6.12) Wharton herself was designing the layout of the 128-acre estate, a task that occupied her intensely and gave her great satisfaction over many years.[23] (Fig. 6.13) "I am amazed at the success of my efforts," Wharton wrote immodestly to her lover, Morton Fullerton, in 1911. "Decidedly, I'm a better landscape gardener than novelist, and this place, every line of which is my own work, far surpasses *The House of Mirth*."[24] She also designed the outbuildings in a c. 1901 collaboration with Francis L.V. Hoppin, of Hoppin & Koen. For the interior, Wharton collaborated with Ogden Codman Jr., her coauthor on *The Decoration of Houses* (1897).

Despite the scope of the enterprise and Wharton's enthusiasm for it, her country idyll would be relatively brief—ten years, after which time, she, like her sister-in-law Mary, divorced.[25] Nevertheless, the place loomed large in Wharton's imagination. "The Mount," she later wrote, "was to give me country cares and joys, long happy rides and drives through the wooded lanes of that loveliest region, the companionship of a few dear friends, and the freedom from trivial obligations which was necessary if I was to go on with my writing."[26]

The incisive classical taste expressed at The Mount had coalesced in Edith years earlier. Her and Edward's first home, Land's End, in Newport (begun in 1892), also had an Italianate garden, developed by Edith, apparently with advice from Ogden Codman Jr.[27] Wharton's enthusiasm for Italy had also been made apparent throughout *The Decoration of Houses*, which praised the "moderation, fitness, relevance" of the Italian Renaissance model.[28] Her devotion to these principles was even more explicit in her *Italian Villas and Their Gardens*, published in 1904. During these years, Jones would also have seen photographs of Charles Platt's highly publicized gardens in Brookline (and those featured in his 1894 book), and she would have known similar designs in Lowell's 1902 book, *American Gardens*, as well as dozens of Italianate examples published in *Architectural Record*, *Country Life*, and other periodicals. It is not surprising that she began to turn to the "ancient" model with increasing frequency, integrating it, cautiously at first, with the Olmstedian methods that she had absorbed from Sargent.

Jones's practice grew slowly in comparison with those of colleagues such as Warren Manning or Ellen Shipman, who sought publicity in popular magazines and through exhibitions and lectures.[29] Of the three jobs that came to her in 1906, two held particular promise. John D. Rockefeller commissioned her for work at Kykuit, his Pocantico Hills estate, near Tarrytown, New York. (Her work there, however, appears to have been limited to plantings for an existing border.) A more extensive job for Edward F. Whitney, in Oyster Bay, Long Island, involved several new gardens. A schematic plan for the project shows a layout similar to the one Jones created at Crosswicks, which also paired a large formal garden with a wild garden. In the Whitneys' wild garden, she planted shrubs and iris amid existing forest trees and groups of cedar. (Fig. 6. 14)

In 1907 Jones published "The Garden as a Picture," in which she set forth one of the central tenets of a design philosophy that was coming to guide her work: "The artist must try to keep step with the great stride of Nature and copy as far as possible her breadth and simplicity." A few lines further on, she amended this principle: "We must keep time with Nature, and follow her forms of expression in different places *while we carry out our own ideas or adaptations*."[30] Jones's sense of the importance of her own artistic ideas would continue to grow.

Her article sheds light on many of the quandaries that were occupying her at the time, particularly the drawbacks inherent in a pictorial method, and this uneasiness presaged changes that were about to occur in her own work. Jones expresses envy of the painter who can control the perspective from which his work is seen and

6.13. The Mount, Edith and Edward Wharton estate, 2004. Photograph by Kevin Sprague.

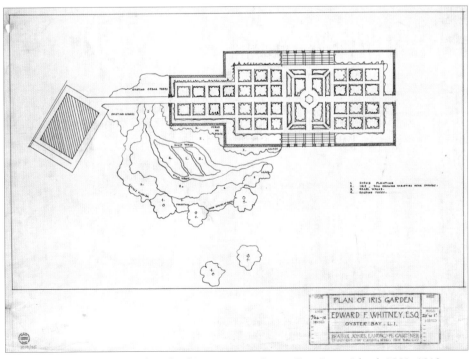

6.14. Schematic plan for Edward Whitney estate, Oyster Bay, Long Island, N.Y., 1912. EDA, Berkeley.

6.15. Quandrangle, Graduate College, Princeton University, 1984. Photograph by Alan Ward.

"follow his own bent." And she voices her frustration with the compositional challenge of the "so-called natural garden," which was, in her view, the most difficult of all. "There is no set line to act as a backbone to the composition, and the whole effect must be obtained from masses of color, contrasting heights, and varieties of texture without any straight line as an axis, without any architectural accessory for emphasis, without anything but an inchoate mass of trees or shrubs of a nondescript shape in which to put something that will look like a thought-out composition."

Jones draws a parallel between landscape design and musical composition, and this metaphor would come to inform her designs, in which attention to color values was particularly important. "There is the same difference in quality of color between a landscape and a garden that there is between an old orchestra and a modern one of nearly double its size, where the parts are much more sub-divided and the sound consequently more complicated. In the same way the vibrations of color from a garden, being more closely brought together, are much more exciting than in an ordinary landscape."[31] Jones extended the anal-

ogy to include the principle of rhythm, and this notion would shape her methods as well. She would continue to adhere to the goal of "keeping time with Nature."

In 1912 Jones listed eight new commissions, more than any previous year. Some of these were large jobs, requiring hundreds of plans, drawings, and plant lists. She moved her office to 124 East 40th Street, where she employed several assistants, all of them women, each with a specialized role in the practice. To accommodate Jones's schedule, her assistants often met her on the train, boarding in New York and getting off when business was done, and then taking the next train back. Arrangements for travel and meetings with clients were meticulous, scheduled by secretaries weeks in advance. Correspondence was precise, even with clients who were intimate friends. Like Manning, Jones preferred to stay in hotels rather than the homes of her clients, fearing that she was an "agitated" guest with her long hours and late nights.[32] On occasion, her tendency to overwork led to physical exhaustion and periods of convalescence.[33]

Among the commissions that came to her in 1912 was a landscape design for the new Graduate College at Princeton. It was her most important work to date and, arguably, the most significant job yet offered a woman landscape practitioner. Jones may have been recommended for the work by Sargent, who was a friend of Andrew Fleming West, dean of the new college, but she remembered it coming from Mr. and Mrs. Moses Taylor Pyne, whom she had met at the White House while visiting Theodore Roosevelt. The Pynes were the owners of Drumthwacket, a Princeton estate that Jones was brought in to "reorganize"—reportedly because the Pynes' superintendent was so often intoxicated.[34]

In her restrained and monumental design for the new campus, Jones would consciously restrict the landscape elements to trees and shrubs rather than feature colorful garden bloom. (Fig. 6.15) She would respond directly to the distinguished architectural elements in the scheme and to the spaces these elements defined. The commission would also prod her to stake out and defend her professional ground, leaving her permanently emboldened in her dealings with other design professionals. Each of these developments would figure importantly in her later work at Dumbarton Oaks.

Almost immediately, conflict sprang up between Jones and the formidable Ralph Adams Cram, consulting architect for Princeton and the designer of the new buildings in the graduate college. "I am very strongly of the opinion," Cram wrote to the Building and Grounds Committee, "that the landscape treatment around a given building should be determined by the architect thereof; . . . no landscape gardener, however competent, can be expected to see the thing as he sees it." He went on condescendingly, "When it comes to the preparation of the soil, the selection of trees and shrubs, etc. the landscape gardener is invaluable."[35]

Cram did not hold back on his criticism of Jones's proposed design either. "The new roads on the plan are to a great extent curvilinear and are too frequently double curves. . . . for my part I prefer straight runs and unmechanical curves." Nor did he approve of the heavy planting along roads and paths, which provided shady glimpses but "no vistas through." Cram was also agitated—and this, no doubt, was the crux of his disgruntlement—about her proposed plant groups because they would obscure his buildings. "My first impression is that the thicket of pines and hemlocks as shown would be most objectionable as it would, in time, practically cut off the entire view of the east side of the Graduate College from the main line of approach. This is the most important 'prospect' of the buildings, and I should consider it unfortunate if they were masked so completely at this point."[36]

Jones stood her ground, however, and, with the trustees' support, she carried through on a scheme that introduced massed plantings and extended walks and lines of sight from the new college to link it to the main campus. Her distinctive treatment limited lawn plantings to large native trees, including red oak, sweet gum, and tulip poplars, and screens of selected evergreens. By avoiding detailed planting incidents, she created spaces of majestic calm and, by virtue of the great trees, canopies that evoked an idealized sense of forest. (Fig. 6.16)

Despite the conflict, Jones had clearly been inspired by Cram's handsome buildings and the knowing spatial rela-

6.16. Courtyard, Graduate College, Princeton University, 1984. Photograph by Alan Ward.

tionships among them. In the courtyards, she adapted European techniques for training trees and shrubs as wall plantings, attaching them to the stone surfaces and clipping them to forms that harmonized with and enhanced the complex Gothic forms. In the view of the landscape architect Diana Balmori, these plantings seem almost like "the sculpted, crafted pieces in the Gothic edifice; each was a specific contribution to the design."[37] Pointing to the Arts and Crafts aspect of Cram's architecture, Balmori also suggests that the buildings were a factor in Jones's establishing a large nursery of hardy shrubs and trees at Princeton—an enterprise in which she sees an Arts and Crafts emphasis on high-quality local material.

As a result of this success, Jones (by then, Farrand) was offered the post of Consulting Landscape Architect to Princeton in 1915, a position she successfully retained for twenty-six years. But further challenges to her authority would arise.[38] In 1925 Cyrus McCormick Jr., a university trustee, offered to engage Warrren Manning, at his own expense, to review her work. McCormick felt, in the words of the trustee chairman, Henry Thompson, that Farrand "depends for her efforts too much on shrubbery and does not plant a sufficient number of trees." Thompson, who seems to have been caught in the middle, wrote congenially, "Personally I think that the Campus under her control has improved as vistas have been opened up and a good deal of 'unplanting' done by the removal of meaningless groups of shrubbery, etc."[39]

6.17. "Garden at the White House," presentation drawing. EDA, Berkeley.

6.18. "Sketch of Middle Arbours," Willard Straight estate, Old Westbury, N.Y., 1914. EDA, Berkeley.

Within a few days of his visit to the site, Manning had issued a report. In it he suggested various ways to improve the health of the "old patriarchs" already in place and also advised removing some aging shrubs. But Manning pointedly absolved Farrand of any inadequacy, noting that the offending shrub plantings (most of which were barberry, ironically a species that Manning had planted in abundance at Gwinn) predated Farrand's involvement at Princeton by several years. He praised her use of flowering shrubs on building walls and more unusual choices, such as inkberry. After reviewing Manning's sympathetic report, the board decided to continue the existing arrangement with Farrand. If Manning had harbored hopes of acquiring the Princeton consulting job, his integrity carried the day.[40]

In 1912, the same year that she began her Princeton work, Jones met Max Farrand (1869–1945), an eminent historian and the chair of the history department at Yale. At the time, Farrand was completing his magnum opus, *The Framing of the Constitution of the United States*, a work that would be considered one of the great scholarly achievements of the period. At ages forty and forty-three, Beatrix and Max discovered that they shared similar inter-

6.19. Perspective view, Straight estate, 1914. EDA, Berkeley.

ests, in particular, an appreciation of outdoor life. The following December, they were married in a small, private ceremony.

It was, for its day, an unconventional arrangement. Beatrix continued to practice, working out of her office in New York, where she kept an apartment, and they also had a place in New Haven, where Max continued to teach. Beatrix also set up an office at Reef Point, where she and Max spent time each summer, fishing, golfing, and, increasingly, gardening. (In 1917 Mary Jones transferred ownership of Reef Point to her daughter.) Beatrix also continued to travel widely during this time, and she came to rely increasingly on her staff to keep the New York office functioning smoothly. Among her prominent mid-decade clients were J. Pierpont Morgan, for his New York townhouse (later the Pierpont Morgan Library) and Ellen Axson Wilson, wife of President Woodrow Wilson, for a new rose garden at the White House. (Fig. 6.17) It was a period of growing assurance and expanding artistic horizons.

In 1914 Farrand began one of her most experimental projects, a garden for Dorothy and Willard Straight in Old Westbury, Long Island. She quickly developed an affectionate relationship with both Straights, who stood out among the conservative financiers who made up much of her clientele. An international banker with many connections to China, Willard had been deeply influenced by Herbert Croly's *The Promise of American Life*, and together he and Dorothy had founded the liberal political journal the *New Republic*, with Croly as its first editor. The Straights also founded *Asia* magazine. In close consultation with her clients (recently returned from a diplomatic posting in Beijing), Farrand created a walled Chinese garden, one of the first examples of its kind in the United States.[41] Her design also evoked the geometry of Italy and the coloristic effects of Gertrude Jekyll, but it was distinctive for its exotic architectural treatment, which included a moon gate. In this respect, the plan diverged from Farrand's previous work and likely opened her imagination to new possibilities.[42] (Figs. 6.18, 6.19)

A walled garden with many Asian elements, The Eyrie, for Abby Aldrich and John D. Rockefeller Jr., be-

gun in 1926 in Seal Harbor, Maine, would carry this line of exploration still further. Few of Farrand's landscape designs would offer such a bold reconceptualization of the herbaceous border as this one in the Maine woods, where it expanded to the scale of a meadow, defined by a wall and entered through a moon gate. In a passage adjacent to the walled garden, Farrand created a setting for the Rockefellers' collection of Korean sculpture, the Guardian Walk (later, the Spirit Path), where large figures are set into native sod against a backdrop of forest wall. The sense of the Maine forest is vivid here, intensified (as in a Japanese garden) by the spareness of the elements and the solemn restraint of the arrangement. (Figs. 6.20, 6.21, 6.22)

As the United States entered World War I, work became scarce for Farrand and other landscape architects who were not engaged in government planning projects, but after the war her practice resumed with vigor. Commissions came from Mrs. Samuel G. Colt (Pittsfield, Mass.) and Mrs. Zenas Crane (Dalton, Mass.). Farrand also produced designs at Eolia, for Edward S. and Mary Harkness

6.20. The sunken garden, The Eyrie, Abby Aldrich Rockefeller estate, Seal Harbor, Maine, c. 1930. Photograph courtesy Patrick Chassé.

in New London, Connecticut, where James Gamble Rogers had designed large Beaux-Arts gardens for an earlier house. She remained involved at Eolia until 1932, and her work there eventually expanded to include many new and rather playful garden areas and structures.[43] (Fig. 6.23)

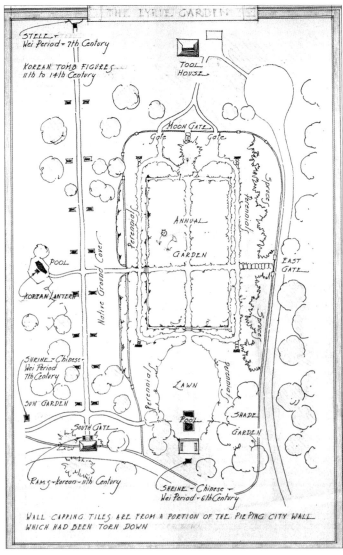

6.21. The Spirit Path (formerly Guardian Walk), The Eyrie, c. 1930.
Photograph courtesy Patrick Chassé.

6.22. General plan (redesign of 1926 plan), The Eyrie. EDA, Berkeley.

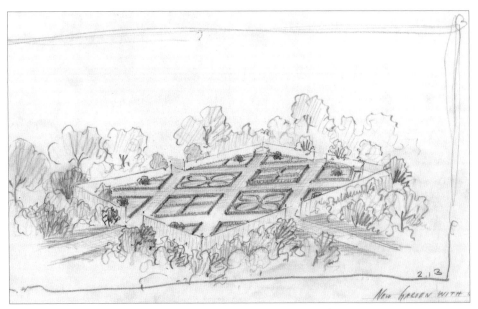

6.23. "New Garden with Box Design," Eolia, Edward S. Harkness estate, New London, Conn.
EDA, Berkeley.

In 1920 a commission came from Otto H. Kahn, for Oheka (by Delano & Aldrich), whose overall landscape plan was by Olmsted Brothers. Farrand would continue to work there until 1928, adding to the existing gardens with a series of outdoor rooms. Oheka was one of several commissions she found on Long Island, where she had earlier worked for the architect Thomas Hastings (of Carrère & Hastings) in Roslyn (1915). She also worked for S. Vernon Mann at Great Neck (1918–30) and for the architect William Adams Delano in Syosett (1921).

The most commanding prospect during these years was a new estate for Mildred

Barnes and Robert Woods Bliss in Washington, D.C., a project Farrand would later describe as the "best and most deeply felt" of her career.[44] She began the design shortly after the Blisses bought the Georgetown property in 1920 and remained involved there until 1947, seven years after Dumbarton Oaks had been donated to Harvard University. No other commission would approach this one in scope, expressiveness, or emotional depth.

DUMBARTON OAKS

Washington, D.C.

Mildred Barnes was born in 1879, the only child of Anna Dorinda Blaksley and Demas Barnes, U.S. congressman from New York. Anna was heir to her father's fortune, one of the largest in St. Louis, and her husband's stake in a new product, Fletcher's Castoria (cod liver oil), along with other prudent investments, had also produced great wealth. When Demas died in 1888, his widow and nine-year-old Mildred were among New York's wealthiest residents, members of the celebrated "Four Hundred."[1]

Nine years later Anna remarried. Her new husband was William Henry Bliss, a successful attorney, formerly of her hometown of St. Louis, and vice president of the St. Paul and Duluth Railroad Company. Bliss was also widowed, with two children. His son, Robert, had graduated from Harvard and then entered the diplomatic corps, serving in San Juan, Venice, St. Petersburg, and Brussels. In the decade following his father's remarriage, Robert's interest in art and travel grew, and so did his interest in his stepsister Mildred, who had been "finished" in Paris. Although she was initially unmoved by Robert's persistent wooing, Mildred rather abruptly gave in, and in 1908, while he was home on leave from his assignment in Bel-

gium, she married him, throwing over a plan to elope with a rival suitor. The unusual match was met with some disdain in the national press—"Weds His Father's Wife's Daughter" read one Baltimore headline—however, the alliance kept the fortune in the family.

The newlyweds lived first in Belgium and then, after Robert was reassigned, in Buenos Aires. Mildred was delighted when her husband was transferred to Paris in 1912, where he served as secretary of the American embassy. There the Blisses' lives were filled with nights of dancing and frequent visits from artists and writers. Among them was Edith Wharton, who moved to Paris in 1913, in the process of divorcing her husband and having just completed *The Custom of the Country*. It was one of Wharton's most savage and gripping novels, the story of Undine Spragg, an ambitious young midwestern woman, who forces her way into the top echelon of society through a series of calculated marriages and culturally advantageous pursuits, primary among them art collecting.

In Paris the Blisses would begin their own art collections at a scale and with a focus only a few of their peers matched. There Robert made his first acquisition, a pre-

Columbian Olmec jade figure, a purchase that marked the beginning of an enterprise that would come to engage his deepest passions. Mildred specialized in Byzantine antiquities, acquired with advice from several authorities, including Bernard Berenson and Royall Tyler (her former suitor). Through these collections, the Blisses would secure their place in society, and in history, too. Their combined holdings, of great importance in their respective fields, would form the future museum at Dumbarton Oaks (of which Tyler's son William would become director).

When World War I brutally interrupted the swirl of life in Paris, Mildred turned her energies to fund-raising among her wealthy American friends. She and Robert also contributed several ambulances and cars to the French relief effort. "I suppose this nightmare will cease some day," she wrote to friends in America, "but our snap is gone and our hearts broken and the wounded young men and the wreckage of the horses are an open sore."[2] Edith Wharton also worked prodigiously on behalf of the French, taking supplies to the front and founding several hospitals and the Children of Flanders Rescue Committee. For their efforts, both she and the Blisses were decorated with the French Legion of Honor. During the war, Mildred and Edith served on many of the same committees and their paths crossed often, but their meetings were not always pleasant. Edith did not elicit the best from

7.1. Front facade of house, c. 1920. Dumbarton Oaks.

Mildred, who chafed at Wharton's imperiousness and, undoubtedly, her perspective on members of the recently arrived American elite.[3]

After the war ended, Robert accepted a post as chief of the Division of Western European Affairs in the U.S. Department of State and steered his reluctant wife back to the United States. Mildred was distraught over leaving Paris and particularly unhappy about the idea of living in Washington, D.C., which offered few of the cultural advantages of the City of Light, but Robert was adamant about satisfying his dream, as he put it, of finding a "country house in the city." He located a somewhat shabby Georgetown estate with a c. 1801 Federal-style residence known as The Oaks which he thought would suit their needs, and in 1920 the Blisses bought it for $150,000. (Fig. 7.1)

The first owner of the property had been Colonel Ninian Beall, a Scotsman who named it "Rock of Dumbarton" after a castle near his home in the Highlands. The estate had changed hands several times before Lucretia and Colonel Henry Fitch Blount acquired it in 1891. During their tenure, the Blounts hosted several important events there, including the founding of the Federation of Women's Clubs and the National Society of the Daughters of the American Revolution. Many prominent political and cultural figures had been their guests, as well, including Hawaii's Queen Liliuokalani, President William Howard Taft, Susan B. Anthony, and Alexander Graham Bell, Henry Blount's closest friend.[4] Over the years, the Blounts made few exterior changes to the house, but they had terraced some of the sixty-five acres of land in the back and planted several large boxwood purchased from neighboring estates.

When Mildred Bliss asked Beatrix Farrand to make a professional visit to the estate in 1921, Farrand was one of the most highly regarded landscape architects in the nation. This stature, along with her ties to Mount Desert and Mildred's family, would certainly have appealed to Mildred, who took up the garden project with great verve. Undoubtedly Bliss was inspired by similarly grand ventures under way elsewhere at the time and, perhaps, by some of the people associated with them. Edith Wharton, of course, was well known for her ardent interest in gardens, evidenced by her 1904 book and the extensive landscape she had laid out at The Mount. (And Wharton had continued her gardenmaking after she left Lenox, at the Pavillon Colombe, an eighteenth-century villa near the Forêt de Montmorency outside Paris she had purchased immediately after the war, and at an old monastery she acquired, outside Hyères in the south of France.)

Another catalyst for the ambitious landscape project may have been Mildred's own mother, who had just commissioned Montecito's most opulent estate, Casa Dorinda, which Robert and Mildred visited just before settling in Washington.[5] Forty-eight acres of gardens surrounded an eighty-room house, designed by Carleton M. Winslow—the largest estate in an area renowned for grand places and famous personalities. In October 1919 even the king and queen of Belgium came to stay at Casa Dorinda (and were welcomed by a crowd of 5,000 well-wishers at the tiny Santa Barbara rail station).[6] Mildred and Robert had also visited country houses in Europe, England, and the United States, and these, along with hundreds of examples publicized in the pages of *Country Life* and other taste-making magazines, were likewise stimulating Mildred's imagination.

Arguably the single most important force behind the development of Dumbarton Oaks, however, was Mildred's own sense of aesthetic possibility. This had been made explicit years earlier, in an essay from 1908 in which she had rhetorically posed the question, "What is man's duty?" and answered, "To inculcate a love of Beauty so true and so deep that passion, caprice and public opinion can never pervert it."[7] Supported by this philosophy, her sharp administrative tactics, her drive, and the Bliss fortune, Mildred's garden project rapidly assumed substance.

On her first visit to the site, Farrand noted that the house, a "solid, ugly brick construction," was nevertheless far enough back from the adjoining streets to still keep a semi-rural air, and this circumstance would prove key to her plan.[8] The land also retained a few farm buildings, a cow pond and paths, a scattering of the old boxwood, and several impressive trees, including many great oaks. A large

7.2 Barn and house from west, c. 1920. Dumbarton Oaks.

7.3 House and orangery, from southeast, c. 1920. Dumbarton Oaks.

orangery east of the house supported an enormous fig vine, *Ficus pumila*, which had been growing there since 1860. (Figs. 7.2, 7.3) The beginnings of a landscape plan had resulted in a terrace in the area north of house, designed by George Burnap just months before. (Fig. 7.4) (He apparently had been removed from the job in favor of Farrand.)[9] The land sloped sharply, dropping fifty feet toward the east and about one hundred feet to the north,

7.4. Cypress planting in North Vista, according to Burnap design, c. 1921. Dumbarton Oaks.

toward woods, meadows, and a tributary of Rock Creek that once powered a small mill.

When Farrand returned for a second visit in August, she met the local architect who was renovating the house, Frederick H. Brooke, and she also met Samuel Yellin, the renowned metalworker who was creating fanciful ironwork for the interior staircases. She envisioned much of the garden's new layout on these first visits, walking the steeply sloping land with Mildred and listening to her ideas. In June of the following year, 1922, Farrand conveyed her proposed scheme in a seven-page letter. The specificity of her recommendations even at this preliminary stage was remarkable.

She turned her attention first to the south side of the property. "No planting should be countenanced which in any way would distract one's attention from the simple and beautiful lines of the grades and the magnificent oak trees which surround the house."[10] Her letter went on to sketch out many ideas for the development to the north, including a "green garden" off the library and the addition of heavy-textured planting on the looming house, "such

as the large-leaved ivy or the evergreen magnolia pinned to the wall as it is often grown in England." Farrand recommended that the ground cover be "very fine in leaf, as every effort should be made to exaggerate the already large scale of the oak." She listed specific plant palettes for both the north and the south sides of the orangery and new plants (wisteria, climbing roses, and early daphne and cherry) to grow inside it.

Farrand's letter also described a rose garden terrace that "must be practically flat in appearance," with a large stone retaining wall on its west side that was to be a vital part of the plan. (A rose garden already existed in this location, but the grade tilted sharply.) A herbaceous garden just below the rose garden was to have a "very much less prim design . . . with considerable masses of perennials, none of them large in size, but giving a sort of general friendly mixture of color and form and entirely different in type from the upper level." Farrand enclosed a detailed list of suggested plants and groupings.

She went on to propose a pool below the herbaceous garden with grassy seats and slopes, so "entirely romantic in type that all sorts of plants of the weeping-willowish variety will be appropriate." And she outlined a scheme for a kitchen garden and its attendant cutting garden, with "small fruit and large, planted on either side of the walks and also on the hillsides sloping down from the terraces to the garden." Farrand added, "This would seem to tie the whole scheme of house, terrace and green garden, swimming pool and kitchen garden, into a unit."

Her letter also suggested a "large mass of forsythia planted on one of the hillsides." "In the writer's mind," Farrand continued, "the development of the north part of the place should be on the lines of a series of interesting plantations, each thought out for a certain season, and easily reached by a good walk and yet not conspicuously in view when it was not at its best." She described a plan for the wooded acres and stream at the north of the property. "The brook certainly could be widened and dammed up at various points and used as a mirror in which to reflect large plantations of azaleas and iris, or overhanging dark masses of hemlock, with water-loving plants growing on the still surface, and walks arranged on the different levels so that the plantations could be seen from above as well as from their own level."

In sum, Farrand's letter evoked a vision of terraces amid tall trees, connected by paths and flights of stairs, cascades of yellow forsythia, curtains of weeping willow, cushions of boxwood, hillsides of flowering crabs and cherries, and an idealized woodland that provided a view-shed for the upper gardens—all part of a cohesive plan that would eventually be realized. (Fig. 7.5) Her suggestions were greeted with approval by her new client. "Your letter and its enclosures have made us purr with content-ment," Mildred Bliss wrote a few weeks later. "You have got it exactly: in every respect, and I can't be patient un-til you get back here and start to realize your and our mu-tual dream."[11]

The notion of Dumbarton Oaks as a "mutual dream" was repeated many times in the correspondence between Bliss and Farrand, as were expressions of shared affection and excitement about the venture. Letters between them were typically addressed "Dearest dear," "Dear Dumbar-ton Twin," or "Dearest-est."[12] Farrand sounded rather swept off her feet in one note from 1923. "It is not only that I've grown very fond of you," she wrote Bliss, "and admire you immensely, your courage, self-control, clear-headedness and character, with their accompanying ele-gance and looks, but I feel personally bereft that you are going away and will try to prove it to you in making a good out-door understudy for the really controlling per-son." (Farrand's meaning here was more diplomatic than a first reading suggests: a sense of the design as Mildred's own.) She went on, "Somehow there will be a rather drab feeling in the Oaks without you, and it is going to be very hard to find it empty of you on my next visit, and not to be able to look forward to your little crow and laugh as you appear around a corner."[13] Mildred eventually re-sponded to Beatrix's "beguiling letter" to say that "we are both happy to know that you still love 'The Oaks' and your devoted Blisses."[14]

The 1920s were a heady period for American women, who felt growing authority to exercise artistic as well as political opinion. However, the sense of mutuality and in-timacy that characterized Farrand and Bliss's exchanges

7.5. Box Walk, c. 1930, with Farrand's plantings at maturity. Dumbarton Oaks.

was evident in other patron-artist friendships that took root during the decade, regardless of sex. Wealthy Ameri-cans of Mildred and Robert Bliss's generation were gen-erally more sophisticated than their parents had been, and the relationships that evolved between them and the de-signers who were laying out their new country places were often more intimate and also more collaborative than the tutorial ones that had characterized the genera-tion before. Mildred Bliss, who was born into great wealth and lived abroad for many years, differed strikingly from Gertrude Seiberling, whose first exposure to art came during her Buchtel courses in Akron. Each was, in her way, typical of her generation.

In planning a treatment for the sharply sloping George-town site, Farrand and Bliss were cognizant of the two ob-vious spatial alternatives available to them. A passage from Wharton's *Italian Villas and Their Gardens* illuminates the choice they faced:

[While] the modern gardener's one idea of pro-ducing an effect of space is to annihilate his boundaries, and not only to merge into one an-

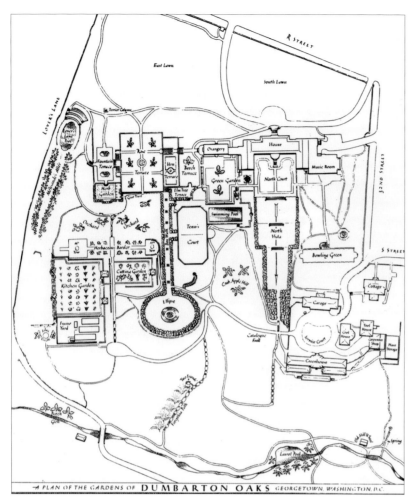

7.6. "Plan of the Gardens of Dumbarton Oaks," detail, Rudolph Ruzicka, 1935. Dumbarton Oaks.

other the necessary divisions of the garden, but also to blend this vague whole with the landscape, the old garden-architect proceeded on the opposite principle, arguing that, as the garden is but the prolongation of the house, and as a house containing a single huge room would be less interesting and less serviceable than one divided according to the varied requirements of its inmates, so a garden which is merely one huge outdoor room is also less interesting and less serviceable than one which has its logical divisions.[15]

Bliss had already settled on an approach that would yield many "logical divisions," and Farrand would embrace this principle, integrating it within her own response to the setting. (Fig 7.6) Her design would marry

the underlying structure of an Italian plan with an American regard for a feeling of expanse and country. She would provide unity among disparate outdoor rooms by enlivening them with "the great stride of Nature," acknowledging throughout the genius loci.

Although it has often been remarked that the gardens at Dumbarton Oaks become less formal as the distance from the house increases, in the tradition of the eighteenth-century English landscape garden, this is not quite the case. Farrand's plan accommodated many great trees already growing on the site, some of them very near the residence. She also set broad hillsides of informally massed plantings within the formal scheme and designed one area close to the house, the Copse, as "a distinct piece of forest." Throughout the landscape plan, curving paths wind across and down sharply sloping hillsides in lines that are neither Italian nor Beaux-Arts inspired, nor derived from the Arts and Crafts tradition. They are American, inspired by the rural tracings on the land, by Farrand's lyrical imagination, and by her response to the topography of the site. These dynamic curves and commanding views over billowing canopies are convincingly woven into the Italian grid: a synthetic masterstroke. (Figs. 7.7, 7.8)

By screening views from one area to the next and using changes in level to create moments of surprise, Farrand disguised the geometry of her plan. As the historian Michel Conan observes, she "plays with the crossing of the axes so you fail to see where they intersect."[16] "Rarely is the entire composition understood at once," writes the historian Eleanor M. McPeck. "Often, when resolution is expected, a sudden turn in the walk leads to some unseen arbor, some unanticipated part."[17] Such moments make good garden theater, too—very much in the Italian tradition. Henry Wotton's 1624 playful account of the gardens he had seen while serving as ambassador to Venice captures the spirit of Farrand and Bliss's idea precisely.

I have seene a *Garden* . . . into which the first Accesse was a high walke like a *Tarrace*, from whence might bee taken a general view of the whole *Plott*

7.7. *Goat Trail,* 1999. Photograph by Carol Betsch.

below but rather in a delightfull confusion, then with any plaine distinction of the pieces. From this the *Beholder* descending many steps, was afterwards conveyed againe, by several *mountings* and *valings*, to various entertainements of his *sent*, and *sight:* which I shall not neede to describe (for that were poeticall) let me only note this, that every one of these diversities, was as if hee had beene *Magically* transported into a new Garden.[18]

Even before Farrand was engaged for the landscape, Frederick H. Brooke had been commissioned to remodel the house. He focused first on removing Victorian accretions to the Federal structure and stripping off layers of paint to reveal the original warm tones of the brick. Soon, the role of consulting architect was turned over to Lawrence White, son of the late Stanford White, who maintained an office in New York not far from Farrand's. It was the Blisses' decision to bring White into the landscape design process too, a move that circumvented a role for Farrand's own consulting architect and that also kept the clients at the center of the design process and firmly in control of it.[19] While still working on the revision to the house, he set to work almost immediately designing a tennis court and swimming pool. Still, it was clear that in matters relating to landscape White was to answer to Farrand. Her authority had grown since her clash with Ralph Cram at Princeton, and it is evident in the many letters chronicling White's proposals at Dumbarton Oaks.

One of the first areas to occupy Farrand was the Rose Garden, a large (123' x 88') terrace reached by a long flight of steps descending from the orangery. By virtue of its position and scale, it was the most important of the new outdoor rooms. Nowhere else is space so forcibly wrought or its impact so sublime as here. The exquisitely proportioned room seems to hover—suspended, almost—over the landscape below. It is defined on the west by a looming stone wall planted with climbing roses, jasmine, and "a wispy veil of *Forsythia suspensa*."[20] (Fig. 7.9) The

7.8. *Path to Grape Arbor,* 1999. Photograph by Carol Betsch.

7.9. West wall of Rose Garden, view toward orangery and Beech Terrace, 1999. Photograph by Carol Betsch.

7.10. Rose Garden, c. 1930. Dumbarton Oaks.

north and east sides open to views across the orchards, the trim fields of the kitchen garden, and below, the treetops of Dumbarton Oaks Park. (Fig. 7.10) The geometric layout of the beds is enlivened by large boxwood specimens that provide an evergreen foil for the roses. The architec-

tural components were completed by 1922, and planting was under way within a year.

Farrand specified that the northern third of the beds was to be filled with yellow shades; the center third, with salmon and yellow-pink; and the southern third, pink and salmon with a few red varieties. She identified this Jekyllian treatment as "a wash of color . . . deepening in hue from north to south." As the landscape architect Diane Kostial McGuire has observed, in June the garden becomes a "grand ballroom," the roses appearing as "figures in bright costume gracefully moving in the late afternoon breeze."[21] McGuire also notes that the blossoms were secondary to the general design of the garden and its form and mass. Because the garden was always thought likely to be often seen in winter, it was designed, in Farrand's words, with regard to "enduring outlines and form."[22] (Fig. 7. 11)

The layout of the Rose Garden had been determined, as so many others at Dumbarton Oaks would be, through a process of detailed exchanges between the landscape architect and her client. One began with a letter dated September 11, 1922, in which Farrand carefully explained a problem to Mildred Bliss: if the steps leading down to the Rose Garden from the terrace above (the Box Terrace[23]) were built to the width Farrand considered necessary, about fifteen inches, they would reach beyond the Rose Garden's west retaining wall. Farrand enclosed blueprints and described various solutions to resolve this awkwardness. Bliss wrote back to approve the solution that Farrand also preferred—changing the dimensions of the terrace above. But it is clear from the correspondence that the choice was Mildred's to make.

In the same package, Farrand sent three different patterns for the brick walks in the Rose Garden and four alternative sets of plans for the beds. She supplied a descriptive paragraph on each of the four layouts, citing a range of design sources from Italy, eighteenth-century England, and, playfully, Babylon. Any of these would work, she explained to Bliss, and any could be adapted to any other. "The whole thing is fluid," she wrote. "And I

want your help arranging it." She closed with still more direct encouragement: "Do tear up the designs as much as you will—mark them up and return them to me with your comments. I eagerly await your sharp criticism."[24]

That the design process at Dumbarton Oaks involved Mildred Bliss in such a central role did not hinder Farrand. On the contrary, this dynamic seems to have inspired her. Neither does it, from a current vantage point, call into question Farrand's authorship of the design. Simply put, the two women sparked each other, and the design of Dumbarton Oaks benefited as a result. The collaborative process evident in the Rose Garden would be applied throughout, and when the general spatial framework of the layout had been settled, it would be applied again, as plantings were refined, and again, as the decorative arts program was addressed. Attention to these various layers of design would overlap and intermingle over many years.

By the mid-1920s, the terraces nearest the house were substantially completed, and most of their plantings had been determined. Many of these were evergreen, such as great *Magnolia grandiflora* trained against the house and the *Hedera helix* (Baltic ivy) that covered the ground and also clothed architectural forms. The Green Garden, overlooking the swimming pool, was most simply planted, dominated by two large oaks. (Fig. 7.12) The Star Terrace, the smallest area near the house, is tucked near it, surrounded by a hedge of white azaleas.[25] The Beech Terrace, named for the enormous *Fagus sylvatica* that once shaded it (later replaced by a *Fagus grandifolia*), is enlivened by the views it provides over the gardens and park beyond. (Fig. 7.13)

A long, forced-perspective lawn known as the North Vista was laid out in relation to the architectural lines of the house. The largest and most commanding of the spaces near the residence, it terminated in a soft boxwood apse backed by lofty canopies of tulip trees and other towering species that brought a sense of expanse to the landscape.[26] (Fig. 7. 14) One of the earliest plant purchases Farrand made was the pair of towering Cedar-of-Lebanon that framed the view out, acquired from Charles Sargent at the Arnold Arboretum for $300 each. The char-

7.11. *Rose Garden, 1999.* Photograph by Carol Betsch.

7.12. Green Garden, looking northeast, c. 1935. Dumbarton Oaks.

7.14. North Vista, planted with boxwood, c. 1930. Dumbarton Oaks.

7.13. *Fagus grandifolia,* Beech Terrace, 1979. Photograph by Ursula Pariser. Dumbarton Oaks.

acter of this space and of the other terraces near the house is more restrained than that in the outlying gardens. From the start, these areas were intended to provide settings for the "semi-public" gatherings that were an anticipated part of the Blisses' lives as members of the diplomatic corps. Farrand's treatment of them recalls aspects of her work at Princeton and on other campuses, particularly her use of strongly defined space, large trees, massive wall plantings, and avoidance of strong color effects.[27] (Fig. 7.15)

In Farrand's original layout, the North Vista was bordered to the west by a densely planted woodland known

as the Copse, whose "poetic and delicate" appearance made it "the sort of place," she wrote, "in which thrushes sing and in which dreams are dreamt." She regarded this intimate area as "a distinct piece of forest" and specified that visitors seated in the music room at the west end of the house should "feel themselves in an open woodland."[28] (Fig. 7.16) Farrand's several allusions to forest and woodland in describing this area indicate her purpose—to bring an experience of wildness into the scheme. The woodland had the more pragmatic function, as well, to serve as a dense visual screen between the garden and 32nd Street, where several houses stood. The woods also provided opportunities for layered plantings unlike any others in the gardens near the house.

Here Farrand mixed an overstory of oaks (white and black), red maple, hackberry, beech, and American elm with a mid-height planting of white dogwood, in great quantity, "as this seems to float in the air under the shadow of the big trees," she noted. Among other mid-height trees and shrubs, she recommended spicebush, *Magnolia stellata, Magnolia kobus* (to be "cherished and replaced," she directed, since it is rather tender), and Japanese maple in abundance, for "the delicacy of its foliage in spring and summer adds distinct lightness and grace." Farrand also

7.15. *North Vista, View toward House,* 1999. Photograph by Carol Betsch.

7.16. The Copse, detail of topographical watercolor by Ernest Clegg, 1935. Dumbarton Oaks.

included less refined species, such as common black cherry (*Prunus seritona*), arguing that "as it is much liked by the birds, its disadvantage as a collector of caterpillars must be accepted." The woodland floor was to be green year round, carpeted with Japanese honeysuckle, myrtle, lily-of-the-valley, and white violets, except in spring, when it was washed with the hues of spring bulbs, including old-fashioned *Leedsii* daffodils (Farrand's plant book specifies 'Mrs. Langtry' and 'White Lady'), whose woodland character she considered fitting for the design.[29]

The stylistic and metaphorical opposite of the woodland copse was the sunny, open Fountain Terrace, located east of the Rose Garden and reached down a double flight

of stairs. The diminutive setting comprises a lawn, a pair of pools with antique fountains, colorful herbaceous borders, and a framework of tall trees, including a magnificent English beech. (Fig. 7.17) Farrand recommended that the borders here be filled with a "revolving series of flowers" in a scheme guided by color rather than exact species. After the brilliant show of tulips she directed that summer annuals be planted in shades of "yellows, bronzes, blues, and primrose . . . rather than shades of pink, lavender, or crimson." For autumn she recommended chrysanthemums of yellow, bronze, deep brown, and maroon . . . but no pinks or whites."[30]

She also specified plantings to address a problem of scale, suggesting *Parthenocissus heterophylla* "to cover the heavy wall enclosing the steps, as this wall, if unclothed, is overmassive," or alternatively, two espaliered *Magnolia grandiflora* and two large yews (*Taxus cuspidata*), "both to clothe and hide the heavy wall and to reduce the size of the border."[31] Discovered from above, the glittering flower beds heighten the impact of the jewellike island of green, which had an importance Farrand also anticipated: "The transition from the brick walks of the Beech Terrace to the flagged walks of the Rose Garden and again to the grass walks of the Fountain Terrace has all been carefully thought out."[32]

Below and to the east of the Fountain Garden is Lovers' Lane pool, one of the most transporting of the landscape passages at Dumbarton Oaks. Farrand cited the open-air theater at the Accademia degli Arcadi Bosco Parrasio in Rome as her inspiration for the seats and the shape of the small theater. The secluded, shady retreat was surrounded by cast-stone columns of Italian baroque design connected with wood lattice, laced with honeysuckle, ivy, and jasmine. A large silver maple and large walnut arched over the quiet surface of the shallow pool, edged with curving walks of brick. A weeping willow was planted at the north. A thick stand of bamboo and privet screened the area from the east. (Fig. 7.18)

Lover's Lane provides a passage to Mélisande's Allée, a wide lane bordered by silver maples underplanted with

7.17. *Fountain Terrace,* 1999. Photograph by Carol Betsch.

7.18. Lover's Lane pool and amphitheater. Dumbarton Oaks.

7.19. Mélisande's Allée. Dumbarton Oaks.

7.20. Lilac Circle, 1999. Photograph by Carol Betsch.

swaths of naturalized daffodils, squill, grape hyacinth, and other spring bulbs, in the manner recommended by Jekyll and Robinson. (Fig. 7.19) The lane traces the route of an old cow path and eventually leads to a grape arbor at the eastern edge of the kitchen garden. Below the arbor is the Lilac Circle, whose original shrubs were later replaced with mock orange. Intimate and unexpected, the circle

extends the geometry of the plan into the outmost corner of the gardens. (Fig. 7.20) Throughout the design process, Farrand's creative impulses operated on several planes— horticultural, spatial, and, not least, imaginative.

Her design for the cutting and kitchen gardens and the long herbaceous borders that define the southern boundaries of these two large areas recall English Arts and Crafts models. Noting that the borders in the Fountain Terrace were planted with orange, yellow, bronze, and ma- roon, Farrand felt it prudent to turn to shades of pink, red, lavender, and pale blue for the larger ones below. Her plant list includes a wide range of perennials and annuals, with phlox and pincushion flower predominating. The traditional mix of flowers, in borders separated by a wide grass path, was set off by hedges of dark yew. Arts and Crafts–inspired wooden gates divide the long borders into more intimate sections. (Fig. 7.21) The western edge of the cutting garden was defined by a long and very tall

7.21. Herbaceous borders, view north, with toolhouses at right, 1938. Dumbarton Oaks.

7.22. The Forsythia Dell, 1959. Dumbarton Oaks.

stone retaining wall into which were built two "amusements," garden pavilions, whose models, as the historian Jane Brown points out, can be found in the ogee-roofed garden houses in the seventeenth-century gardens at Traquair House, near Peebles, Scotland.[33]

Unlike the layers of historical reference embedded in these garden rooms, Farrand's planting of informal areas was characterized by "simplicity of intention and directness of purpose."[34] The most remarkable of these is the Forsythia Dell, where one acre of *F. intermedia* 'Spectabilis' bursts into color each spring, a golden tangle that covers the hillside and reaches to the creek in the park below. Farrand instructed that the planting be kept to one variety and the shrubs be pruned to reveal the modeling of the hill. (Fig. 7.22) She created two other such massed plantings. Crabapple Hill is located above (south of) the Forsythia Dell, between the North Vista and the tennis court. Farrand suggested that it be planted with a limited number of varieties (*Malus spectabilis, floribunda, Malus ioen-*

sis 'Plena,' and *Malus hupehensis* and *toringoides*). "The attractiveness of this part of the design," she wrote, "should consist of the mass of flowering trees in the early season—each one having at least room enough to develop adequately, if not completely—and the hanging fruit in the autumn."[35] The third informal planting is Cherry Hill, located north of the kitchen garden. "It is purposely isolated from the rest of the plantations," Farrand wrote, "so that the area may be devoted to a display beautiful at one specific time of year and not a conspicuous part of the design in constant view." Even when the trees are not in bloom, their curving trunks trace compelling patterns against the strong slope. (Fig. 7.23)

Between the Forsythia Dell and Cherry Hill is the Ellipse, a secluded oval "constructed out of series of curves" that was originally bordered by an encircling, rumpled wall of box twenty feet tall. Farrand considered it "one of the quietest and most peaceful parts of the garden." Old photographs capture the repose of this area, enlivened by a single jet in an ivy-bordered pool that brought, in Farrand's words, "a spot of light" to the end of the walk.[36] (Fig. 7.25) In 1958 the Ellipse was

FOLLOWING PAGES:
7.23. *Cherry Hill*, 1999. Photograph by Carol Betsch.

7.24. *Swimming Pool*, 1999. Photograph by Carol Betsch.

7.25. The Ellipse, planted with boxwood according to Farrand design, view south, c. 1930. Dumbarton Oaks.

7.26. The Ellipse, planted with hornbeam according to Hopkins design, view north, 1999. Photograph by Carol Betsch.

redesigned by the architect Alden Hopkins, who replaced the box with a clipped hornbeam hedge, altering the oval from a softly enclosing bower to a crisp, architecturally defined space, a change that Farrand had foreseen years earlier, anticipating that the boxwood might some day die out.[37] (Fig. 7.26)

Each of these garden areas possesses its own character, and the experience of each is affected by what precedes and follows it. The garden unfolds sequentially, in time as well as space. "It is the chambered nautilus of gardens," McPeck observes, "suggesting at every turn deeper levels of meaning and experience."[38] In laying out these garden spaces, Farrand was guided both by architectural principles and by the more abstract musical principle of theme and variation. "A garden should be a series of variations on an air," she wrote in one undated essay, "through which one feels the lilt of the original melody and throbs of the original rhythm."[39] At Dumbarton Oaks, as elsewhere in Farrand's work, the rhythm would be provided by the genius loci.

A number of diverse planting influences are apparent throughout the gardens. Gertrude Jekyll's ideas are evident in compositions for the beds at the west edge of the Rose Garden, where Farrand combined forsythia with climbing roses and *Clematis paniculata*, and in the frequent use of vines and trees trained against stone and brick walls. Jekyll's influence is also reflected in the plantings in the herbaceous borders, the kitchen garden, and the ornamental orchards that cover the hillsides above it. (Fig. 7.28) Jekyll and William Robinson were undoubtedly the inspiration for Mélisande's Allée and other compositions that combine layers of foliage and bloom, such as those in the Copse. Farrand also made use of classic French and Italian planting techniques in certain passages, such as the north edge of the Herb Garden Terrace, where the Tuscan-inspired Keiffer pears are planted as a raised double hedge.[40] Here she included a handsome wisteria-covered arbor, based on a design by the French architect Androuet du Cerceau. (Fig. 7.29) Farrand's notes reflect pragmatic motives for plant choices too, as in those for the west retaining wall by the swimming pool, where she "lifted" problematic grades with willows, weeping cherries, and silver maples. (Fig. 7.24)

Farrand's plantings also manifest strong American in-

7.27 *Box Walk to Ellipse*, 1999. Photograph by Carol Betsch.

7.28. Orchards and view to cutting and kitchen gardens, 1999. Photograph by Carol Betsch.

7.29. Arbor on Herb Garden Terrace, c. 1935. Dumbarton Oaks.

7.30. Box (later, Urn) Terrace, looking south, 1931. Photograph by Stewart Brothers. Dumbarton Oaks.

fluences. She retained large specimen trees—oaks, maples, and tulip poplars—already growing on the site, a decision that emphasized the robust character of the land. The location and character of these trees, in turn, influenced the rhythms of her plan by determining divisions of various garden areas. The towering forms became anchors for terrace rooms, providing canopies to planting compositions that were created to complement them. A grove of giant silver maples (*Acer saccharinum*) was underplanted with a mass of forsythia, as McGuire notes, because "the graceful swaying movement of the silver maple harmonizes with the billowing of forsythia."[41]

Farrand used many broad-leaved evergreens in the design of Dumbarton Oaks, including magnolia, holly, and boxwood, which is the landscape's dominant shrub. Its cushioned forms establish spatial definition and character throughout. Large conical specimens of box are featured

in the Rose Garden, and a small-leaved variety (*Buxus sempervirens* 'Suffruticosa') once hedged the beds there. Box was the featured plant on the Box Terrace. (Fig. 7.30) It was used to define the Ellipse, and box once edged the North Vista. Box is featured to particularly memorable effect along the long brick path known as the Box Walk, which despite its simplicity, Farrand considered the "loveliest feature of the garden."[42] (Fig. 7.27)

Buxus has many historical associations. It was used extensively in Italian Renaissance villa gardens, and it was a mainstay of Edwardian gardens in England. Box was an important ingredient in Colonial Revival gardens in the United States, used extensively in the American South, and also in the Arts and Crafts gardens of Cornish, including Ellen Shipman's own Brook Place. Shipman installed box in large estates from Grosse Pointe to Long Island. Marian Coffin also used it in her estate work, at Winterthur, where its cloudlike forms bordered an imposing staircase, and on Long Island, where it was sheared into fanciful forms. At Dumbarton Oaks, Farrand relied on box to provide a quiet and strong framework against which showier plants could burst forth in seasonal displays.[43]

At the northern edge of the parcel, Farrand developed an extensive section into a naturalistic parkland that stretches along either side of the small creek. She created the woodland and its accompanying meadows as a wild counterpart to the formal gardens, specifying that it was to be

7.31. Stream and dams in the wild garden. Dumbarton Oaks.

7.32. Meadow near rustic arbor in the wild garden, 1938. Dumbarton Oaks.

7.33. Path in the wild garden, 1938. Dumbarton Oaks.

carefully managed, despite its wild appearance. A path system ran through the park and connected it with the home grounds, so that a tour of the property would include both. The woodland is integral to the gardens above in one other important regard: it provides views of billowing treetops from almost every vantage point within the garden rooms. More than any other element at Dumbarton

Oaks, the park gives the gardens a feeling of breadth, expanse, and vitality. In later years, this heavily planted area also came to provide a critical buffer against encroaching development.

Farrand's methods in designing this feature recall those of Warren Manning in laying out his wild gardens. "The whole scheme," she wrote Mildred Bliss in her early letter, "should properly be studied from the ground itself rather than from any plan, as the contours and expressions of the ground will control the plantations more strongly than any other feature."[44] As Manning often did, Farrand relied on a water feature as the organizing spatial element in her layout. (In Bliss's view, the little brook, along with the tennis court and swimming pool, also completed the "illusion of country life" at Dumbarton Oaks.[45]) To increase its drama, Farrand added eighteen dams that created a series of waterfalls and pools. (Fig. 7.31)

Parallel to the stream, she laid out five meadows, each with its own planting theme and character. A wooded slope north of these served as a boundary and a backdrop for the park as a whole. (Fig. 7.32) Farrand's design also incorporated existing features—an old farm building, bridge, spring house, and pet cemetery. For character and interest, however, the landscape relied primarily on its plantings—a hillside of mountain laurel, another of gray birch, great stands of hollyhocks, a copse of white dogwood. Overlooking a small pond was a rustic arbor, whose proportions, as McGuire has aptly noted, were as elegant as the most exquisitely detailed structures in the formal areas above. Bridle trails in the woodland connected to adjacent trails in Rock Creek Park. Throughout the wild garden, Farrand mixed exotics with native species in gentle, pictorial scenes in an American style, evoking idealized passages of countryside. (Fig. 7.33)

By 1923, when Robert Bliss was appointed minister to Sweden, work on many sections of the landscape of Dumbarton Oaks was well under way. Lawrence White had begun plans for a quadrangle of new buildings northwest of the house that comprised a garage, stable, machine shop, heating plant, greenhouse, and orangery. When a

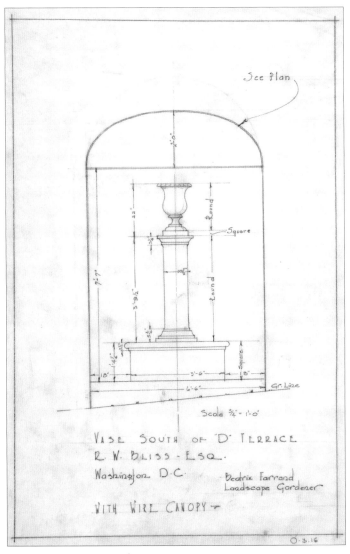

7.34. Measured drawing for Terrior Column. Dumbarton Oaks.

rather cursory note from Robert threatened to eliminate the stable, Farrand stepped in to mediate and prevented the collapse of the entire scheme. That same year, White began plans for the new music room addition to the main house, suitable for large crowds. Several locations were considered, including the site of the new swimming pool, before, at Farrand's urging, a less obtrusive one was selected at the west end of the house.

After a three-year absence, Mildred Bliss returned to review progress at Dumbarton Oaks in May 1926, and she was pleased with what she found. Despite her long stay

7.35. *Terrior Column,* 1999. Photograph by Carol Betsch.

7.36. Bench in Rose Garden. 1999. Photograph by Carol Betsch.

7.37. Pineapple finial and gate post for Rose Garden, drawing by Armand-Albert Rateau. Dumbarton Oaks.

abroad, Bliss had remained involved with all aspects of the garden's development by regularly reviewing plans, draw-ings, and photographs of full-scale mock-ups in wood and plaster, on which she communicated comments and crit-

7.38. Dummy of Rateau's pineapple finial in Rose Garden. Dumbarton Oaks.

icisms. These extensive visual records document a design process characterized by precise, almost obsessive atten-tion to detail, applied to proposals for each wall, balus-trade, urn, seat, post, pilaster, gate, and finial. (Figs. 7.34, 7.35, 7.37, 7.38, 7.39) In addition to many drawings and photographs, at least one model survives. Doll-house size, it depicts the walled Rose Garden, with interchangeable, stylistically alternative pilasters.[46]

Many of the architectural details at Dumbarton Oaks were inspired by elements in European gardens, adapted by Farrand and her assistants, Anne Baker, Margaret H. Baile, and (somewhat later) Ruth Havey. The gardens also featured several antique pieces, purchased directly from dealers, or replicas of antiques, such as the finials on the Rose Garden bench based on models at Gayhurst and Montacute. (Fig. 7.36) Some of the most striking orna-ments were adapted from designs by Armand-Albert Rateau (1882–1938), a French "ensemblier," who worked in an eclectic range of styles, including Art Deco.[47] In 1924 White asked Rateau, who was based in Paris, to

7.39. *North Gate to Rose Garden*, 1999. Photograph by Carol Betsch.

scout for interesting ornaments and furniture for the garden, and four years later, Rateau came to Dumbarton Oaks to oversee the installation of the ceiling he had designed for the Music Room. Mildred Bliss was so pleased with it that she asked Rateau to submit designs for new ornaments for the garden rooms. He sent several the following year, many of which were adapted by Farrand and her staff. The pineapple finial in the Rose Garden gate, for example, was based on a Rateau drawing, as were the "Pepper Pot" vase near the swimming pool and the horseshoe stairway and fountain leading from the orangery.[48]

Refinements to the gardens at Dumbarton Oaks were carried out through the twenties, during which time the Blisses continued to live in Sweden. In 1927 Robert was appointed ambassador to Argentina by President Coolidge, a reward for paying his dues at relatively minor posts over so many years, and he and Mildred moved to Buenos Aires. Max and Beatrix Farrand moved in 1927, too, relocating from New Haven to San Marino, California, where Max had accepted a prestigious post as the first director of the Huntington Art Gallery and Library.

In Pasadena, the Farrands lived in a modest house on the lavish estate of Henry Huntington whose grounds were in the "obsessive grip" of Huntington's territorial gardener, William Hertrich. Consequently, Farrand had no influence on them.[49] From her new winter base in California, she continued work on several projects, including Dumbarton Oaks and the large garden she had begun in 1926 for Abby and John D. Rockefeller Jr. in Seal Harbor, Maine.[50]

Only two residential jobs from Southern California are listed in her archives. One of these was for consulting work at Casa Dorinda, which the Blisses had inherited from Mildred's mother. An unfortunate clash with the California landscape architect Lockwood de Forest Jr. erupted over a design Farrand proposed for the Blaksley (later Santa Barbara) Botanic Garden, which had also been underwritten by Anna Bliss. The contretemps probably strained collegial relations and may have added to

Farrand's trouble in finding work. At age fifty-six, with her patrician background and bearing, adjustment to life in Southern California must have been difficult. She did eventually attract some institutional projects there, however, and she also was commissioned for a later project at the Santa Barbara Botanic Garden while de Forest was serving in World War II.[51]

Soon after the Farrands' move, Beatrix's assistant Ruth Havey assumed control of several aspects of design development at Dumbarton Oaks. Havey's taste, particularly her preoccupation with decorative detail, diverged from Farrand's in important regards. In truth, it more resembled that of Mildred Bliss, whose growing admiration for "the great sweeps and smaller excitements of baroque art," as McGuire tactfully observed, was not entirely sympathetic to the bolder Arts and Crafts aesthetic Farrand brought to Dumbarton Oaks.[52] Although Farrand approved many of Havey's proposals, some provoked sharply negative responses. "You can imagine how my eyes popped out of my head when this typical merry-go-round seat appeared," Farrand wrote to Mildred Bliss about one of them.[53] The blush that had suffused the letters exchanged during the first years of their friendship faded as differences of aesthetic judgment arose with increasing frequency.

Throughout the gardens of Dumbarton Oaks, ornament proliferated, and in some passages architectural elements and materials were substituted for plantings. Mildred Bliss began to add increasing numbers of plaques throughout the garden, too, inscribed with quotations culled from historical texts, and translated by scholars into ancient languages. Although these changes did not compromise the general spatial integrity of Farrand's design, they modified the character of the landscape, diminishing the sense of country ease that had once suffused it.

After Franklin Roosevelt assumed the presidency, Robert retired from the diplomatic service, and in 1933 the Blisses, both of whom were Republicans, moved back to Washington to live at Dumbarton Oaks for the first time. (Fig. 7.40) Still, Robert continued his travels to the wilds of Mexico and Central America in search of pre-Columbian artifacts for his ever-expanding collection.

During the Depression, the size of the gardening staff was reduced, but minor embellishments continued. In 1934 a new plaque was installed in the Green Garden, dedicated to "the friendship of Beatrix Farrand." Translated from the Latin, the inscription reads, in part, *May kindly stars guard the dreams born beneath the spreading branches of Dumbarton Oaks.*

In the summer of 1937 Edith Wharton suffered a stroke, and Beatrix, her closest living relative, traveled to Paris to be with her. The meeting was strained, and Farrand was on the steamer returning to the United States when her aunt died. Having lost her mother only a few years before, she felt Edith's death sharply. "We shall find it an empty, queer world without her," she wrote to Wharton's literary executor, "and already one feels the void where one could ever before rely on her wisdom, keenness, appreciation and justice." Farrand's note conveyed more complicated feelings, too: "What an example she is of a beautiful construction built around a great gift."[54]

In 1938 the Blisses celebrated their thirtieth wedding anniversary at the Oaks with a performance of a concerto by Igor Stravinsky they had commissioned for the event. That same year they opened the gardens to the public for the first time. Within months, rumors began to circulate that the estate was to be given to Harvard University, and it soon became apparent that this was the case. Opening the gardens and collections to the public for cultural and educational purposes had been the Blisses' plan for years, but the date of the transfer was quickly moved up as war in Europe became a certainty.[55]

Two years later Harvard accepted the sixteen-and-one-quarter-acre core of the property for use as a library, museum, and research center. John S. Thacher was appointed the first director, charged with overseeing the grounds as well as administering the new institution's scholarly affairs.[56] The remaining twenty-seven acres of the estate, the large wild garden, were turned over to the National Park Service for use as a public park. Having lived at Dumbarton Oaks for only seven of the twenty years they had owned their country place, the Blisses

7.40. Robert and Mildred Bliss near herbaceous borders, c. 1936. Harvard University Archives, HUGFP 76.74p, Box 10.

moved into a smaller house in the neighborhood nearby.[57]

The decision to sever the estate and home grounds from the park made administrative sense, but it did violence to the whole, permanently altering both the circulation patterns of Farrand's layout and her broader design intentions. She had conceived of the upper gardens and the park in relation to each other—visually and experientially. In effect, the division had the effect of orphaning the park, whose design was not well understood by the Park Service and subsequently not well maintained, so that many sections of it became derelict. Fortunately, even in its most degraded state, Dumbarton Oaks Park continued to provide a heavily treed canopy, a viewshed for the gardens above. (Fig. 7.41)

Max Farrand retired from his post at the Huntington in 1940, and the Farrands moved back to Reef Point, where they became year-round residents for the first time. Beatrix's practice was sharply reduced as a consequence of the war and her health had declined; however, at Thacher's request, she took on the task of writing a plant book for Dumbarton Oaks to guide future upkeep of the garden. She addressed the complexities of planting design throughout, offering advice about long-term care and horticultural alternatives. The book also contains forty-

7.41. View from Rose Garden toward Dumbarton Oaks Park, 2000. Photograph by Carol Betsch.

two plant lists of the species represented in the gardens the year it was published, 1941. It has provided critical advice to successive garden superintendents.

Max Farrand's death from cancer in 1945 was a severe blow to Beatrix. Her files list no further professional jobs except one a few years later for a guest house for David Rockefeller in Seal Harbor. In 1947 she came to the conclusion that she had exhausted her commitment to Dumbarton Oaks, and in February of that year she tendered her resignation as landscape adviser to the garden. "Making this decision is a good deal like tearing off an arm or a leg or cutting out one's heart," she wrote Mildred Bliss, "but the change has got to come some day and Dumbarton develop on lines that I might not be able to approve or follow."[58] Bliss tried to dissuade her, but Farrand was adamant. Her last letter in her official role recalled years of collaboration and intimate memories: "Thank you for so many hours of common work, and common delight, the spring days and summer evenings, full of thrush song and moonlight, and the autumn days of color and blue skies."[59]

Farrand did not cut ties with Dumbarton Oaks en-

tirely, however. The same year she resigned, she suggested that Mildred Bliss begin developing a garden studies library to include "prints, monographs, and plans of well-designed gardens."[60] Bliss responded enthusiastically to this idea and proceeded with her typical administrative acumen, relying heavily on Farrand's recommendations. The project seemed to mark a resurgence in the collaborative ardor that had guided the early development of the gardens. Bliss also continued to make changes to the landscape design, several of which were seen through under Havey's professional direction.[61]

Back at Reef Point, Farrand was turning her energies to the project that she had begun several years earlier, transforming the large house and surrounding six acres into a horticultural study center. As part of this effort, she began publishing the *Reef Point Gardens Bulletin*, a periodical that addressed horticultural topics related to the display gardens there. The first issue was printed in August 1946, the year after Max's death. Farrand's introduction to the new bulletin echoed the Progressive-era principles that had once spurred her to urge new "open-air gymnasiums" in New York City. "The object at Reef Point," she wrote, "is primarily to show what outdoor beauty can contribute to those who have the interest and perception. . . . Wise use of leisure is a problem for each individual to solve, but Reef Point Gardens hopes to be of use as a living example of at least one of the many solutions."[62]

Farrand continued to publish the journal, and she continued to add to her extensive private library and to the plantings at Reef Point.[63] "Rhododendrons and azaleas from many parts of the world have found a home," she noted in the first issue, "and surprising success has been achieved with Chinese and Asian shrubs and creepers."[64] Indigenous plants were encouraged too. Farrand also gathered a large collection of single hybrid tea roses, displaying the blossoms indoors in clusters of bud vases, each of which held one stem.

Reef Point escaped the raging fires that destroyed

much of Bar Harbor in 1948, but economic uncertainty followed, and Farrand ultimately abandoned the ambitious study center project. In 1955 she made the grueling, and to many baffling, decision to dismantle her extensive gardens, donate her private library to the University of California at Berkeley, and sell her beloved home. These were severe actions, and Farrand's resolve in seeing them through reflected the most unbending aspects of her nature.

She moved into a small cottage adjacent to the farmhouse at nearby Garland Farm, commissioning the struc-

ture from Robert Whiteley Patterson, a professional associate who had also maintained an office at Reef Point. She brought many of her favorite plants with her and began a new series of gardens, laid out close to the house. Farrand also brought with her the motto that had been inscribed in the hallway at Reef Point and had it inscribed in her new home: *Intellectum da mihi et vivam*, "Give me understanding and I shall live." In 1959, after a brief illness, Beatrix Farrand died in Bar Harbor at the age of eighty-seven. Her life had come to a close much as it had begun—gardening, and surrounded by the plants she loved.[65]

MARIAN CRUGER COFFIN

1876–1957

Nature is endlessly and untiringly presenting wonderful landscape and gardening compositions to our unseeing eyes. She is always trying to teach us the value of bigness, unity and simplicity of effect in her own large scale, which lessons, if we have but wit to see, we can follow in principle and reduce in scale for our own home grounds.

—Marian Coffin, in *Garden Club of America Bulletin*, May 1920

Marian Coffin was born in 1876 in Scarborough, New York, the only child of Alice Church and Julian Ravenel Coffin.[1] Her maternal family lines went back through the Churches and the Schuylers of New York State, and the Trumbulls and Sillimans of Connecticut. Among her distinguished forebears were the owners of a large estate, Belvedere, in Hudson, New York—a fact deemed so significant that it was included in Coffin's obituary in *Landscape Architecture*, where her contributions to the field were also commemorated. (Fig. 8.1) Marian's father's people had descended from the Nantucket branch of the Coffins, plantation owners in North Carolina who lost everything during the Civil War. Alice and Julian were married in the decade

after the South surrendered, but they were not married long. Coffin abandoned his wife and daughter when Marian was two years old and died five years later.

Not financially able to keep their own home, Marian and her mother moved among various relatives, eventually settling with Alice's wealthy brother, John Barker Church IV, in Geneva, on Seneca Lake, the largest of the Finger Lakes, midway between Syracuse and Rochester. The town was surrounded by rich farmland, vineyards, orchards, meadow, and woods—"a paradise," as one resident described it, "a proud street along the lake, with its sloping gardens and distant views."[2] Marian was more interested in the views. "Even as a small girl," she wrote, "I loved the country, not so much gardens and growing things, for I had no experience with these . . . but simply the great outdoor world."[3]

Despite the family's strained finances, Coffin was tutored at home and enjoyed other benefits of an upper-class life, including exposure to fine music and art. Like Shipman, she became an accomplished horsewoman, learning to ride with ease and grace. As a young girl, Coffin loved stories of the explorers of the Middle East, and under other circumstances, in one close friend's opinion,

8.1. Portrait of Marian Cruger Coffin, c. 1904. Winterthur Archives.

might have become a Gertrude Bell or a Freya Stark. Coffin did become an inveterate traveler, later penetrating to remote parts of Mexico and Guatemala.[4] Her boldest explorations, however, would be in the realm of landscape design.

Coffin quickly developed a sense of her family's cultural heft, a perspective that helped her in her later dealings with privileged and powerful clients, primary among whom was Henry Francis du Pont, the scion of a large and wealthy family who emigrated from France in the eighteenth century to settle in the Brandywine Valley, near Wilmington. The du Ponts had been friends with Marion's Church relatives for generations, and there were contemporary ties as well.[5] Two years before Marian was born, Alice had been a bridesmaid at the wedding of du Pont's parents, Mary Pauline Foster (whose family had also owned a house on Seneca Lake) and Colonel Henry Algernon du Pont. Alice and Mary Pauline had remained

close friends through the years, and Alice had been a visitor at the du Pont estate, Winterthur. Scrapbook photographs capture images of a young Marian Coffin there, too.

Bright, strong-willed, and striking, Marian dreamed as a young girl of becoming a great artist and was disappointed that she did not possess significant talent in any of the traditional arts. When she learned of Beatrix Jones's "novel" profession and the success she was making of it, she decided to become a landscape architect. Marian's uncle Benjamin Church, an engineer who had worked for Olmsted in laying out Central Park, may also have offered vocational inspiration. There is little question that the decision was propelled by economic as well as artistic concerns, and that it was also made with an understanding of its probable implications regarding marriage and family. As Coffin's colleague Martha Brookes (Brown) Hutcheson noted, for a woman to pursue a career at the time meant "almost social suicide and distinctly matrimonial suicide."[6]

In 1900 Coffin applied to the new program of landscape architecture at Massachusetts Institute of Technology in Cambridge, one of the two university programs that would accept women. Coffin's genteel education had left her ill-prepared for anything so rigorous. "When it was reluctantly dragged from me that I had had only a smattering [of] algebra and hardly knew the meaning of the word 'geometry,'" she later wrote, "the authorities turned from me in calm contempt." She would have abandoned her plan without the encouragement of the head of the architecture school, Professor Joseph Chandler, and that of Guy Lowell, founder and director of the new program. Coffin also found strong support in Farrand's mentor, Charles Sprague Sargent.

After a year of tutoring in mathematics, she was admitted to MIT in 1901 as a special student, permitted to attend regular courses but not eligible for a degree—a somewhat dubious arrangement, but the only one available at the time. Coffin was one of four women among five hundred men, a situation that would have intimated a less tenacious personality. Martha Brookes Brown had enrolled in the new program the year before, also as a special student—inspired to improve hospital grounds through planting—but she withdrew after two years because she was disappointed in the lack of horticultural emphasis in the new program. "I saw at once that the curriculum did not give nearly enough time to what must be known of the plant world," she later explained.[7]

The program Lowell had set up at MIT taught landscape design in the Beaux-Arts method, an approach that emphasized composition in three dimensions, primarily in relation to architectural line and mass. Coffin's coursework included drawing and drafting, surveying, geology, biology, architectural design, and mathematics. She also independently obtained supplemental drafting instruction, and, after her second year, traveled to Europe with her mother to visit important gardens.[8] During this time, she also studied watercolor painting. (Despite her early misgivings about a career in art, Coffin developed a substantial talent for it.)

As part of her studies, Coffin also attended horticultural classes at the Arnold Arboretum twice weekly with John G. Jack, and she toured area nurseries and gardens, among them Faulkner Farm, Holm Lea, Green Hill (the Brookline estate of Isabella Stewart Gardner), and the Arnold Arboretum.[9] It is unclear how much of this touring was done under the auspices of the MIT program and how much she undertook on her own and with friends, one of whom was Harry du Pont, then a student at Harvard.

After Coffin arrived in Cambridge, du Pont's interest in horticulture and design grew rapidly. They met often, to dine and to visit gardens, and they exchanged ideas and books. For Christmas in 1901, du Pont presented Coffin with a handsome volume on French gardens, and the following year Harry and his sister, Louise, together surprised her with three volumes of L. H. Bailey's *Cyclopedia of Horticulture*. Coffin continued to correspond about gardens with du Pont even after he graduated in 1902 and moved back to Winterthur. She also remained friends with Louise, who moved to Marblehead, Massachusetts, after marrying the wealthy yachtsman Francis Crowninshield.[10]

In May 1903 Coffin wrote to du Pont about a recent visit to Green Hill, and the architectural background she was gaining at MIT was evident, even in her first sentence: "I didn't think the place itself nearly as fine as the Sargents—no such sense of space, but some bits are charming." Among those she noted were a "large grass oval" and "a most fascinating brick wall covered with stucco which is peeled off in places & every now & then fragments of sculpture set in." She also admired "a little forged out seat with a superb view and along each side pots of glorious flame colored azaleas—really a splendid color effect." Coffin concluded, "I was enchanted with the garden though it wasn't especially well designed it had a great charm of its own which I dare say one finds in some of the small private gardens in Italy."[11]

By doubling up on coursework, Coffin was able to squeeze the four-year program into three. Her last year of study at MIT (1903–4) was given over to pure landscape problems, where she excelled. She considered her training "splendid," she wrote many years later, "three years of such hard work as I fancy few of the schools now insist upon."[12] After her graduation, she and her mother set out again for Europe, where they would return on several subsequent trips. These travels included visits to well-known gardens and stays with family and friends. Walter Berry, Edith Wharton's close friend, was a cousin and introduced the Coffins to Wharton, who, in turn, introduced them to Henry James. "A more exciting visit (to her)," remembered Coffin's friend Warren Hunting Smith, "was a call upon Miss Gertrude Jekyll."[13]

Marian Coffin's education, which began a few years after Beatrix Jones's, offers almost a mirror image of it. While Jones had made her base Holm Lea and supplemented Charles Sargent's strong horticultural orientation with private drafting instruction and rigorous, self-directed study of European gardens, Coffin's starting point was the architecturally oriented education at MIT, which she supplemented with self-directed horticultural study, much of it undertaken with Harry du Pont. Despite these different paths, the artistic methods the two women developed were similar in several respects.

Both would utilize an approach to spatial composition based on principles of Beaux-Arts design but that also integrated a strong response to setting. Both would experiment with imaginative planting design, utilizing many English principles (learned primarily from Jekyll and Robinson) and also incorporating a wide range of native American plants. Farrand's approach was somewhat more conservative, grounded in the American tradition of Olmsted but frequently integrating other historical idioms, particularly the Arts and Crafts. Coffin's training at MIT had given her a thorough grounding in architectural concepts, and she had quickly become an assured designer of space and forms in space. As her career progressed, her planting designs became increasingly abstract and her experiments with spatial layout more adventurous.

After returning from Europe in 1904, Marian and her mother moved to New York City, where Alice's brother Benjamin and his wife lived, and took rooms at the National Arts Club at 15 Gramercy Park. Poised to embark on her professional life, Coffin encountered a set of obstacles that she may not have anticipated, one of which was the lack of an apprenticeship. "The idea of taking a woman into an office was unheard of [at the time]," Coffin later wrote. "'My dear young lady, what will you do about supervising the work on the ground?' became such a constant and discouraging query that the only thing seemed to be for me to hang out my shingle and see what I *would* do about it."[14] She set up her own office in two rooms in the apartment and began to attract small jobs, most of them for flower gardens. To boost her practice, Coffin joined the ASLA, which had two other women members at the time, Beatrix Jones and Elizabeth Bullard.

Her earliest recorded project was a 1906 suburban garden for the Edward Spragues, and despite its modest scale, the job marked an auspicious start. Coffin wrote about the design a few years later in *Country Life in America*, and it was also featured in Elsa Rehmann's 1918 book, *The Small Place: Its Landscape Architecture*.[15] The Spragues' house was situated on a modest (150' x 300') lot in a new neighborhood in the village of Flushing, a commuter suburb on Long Island. The property was typical of many under development at the time, clustered outside large urban centers and linked to them with new roads and rail lines. Coffin directed her article toward the "moderately well-to-do" homeowner, arguing that a large and handsome garden could be created and maintained at a lower cost than the initial expenditure and annual upkeep for a moderately priced car. The comparison was undoubtedly inspired by Henry Ford's Model T, introduced two years earlier.

Coffin's notion that interest, beauty, and variety could be achieved through imaginative plantings held particular value for suburban layouts like the Spragues', because most were sited on practically featureless lots. "We certainly cannot create a magnificent view," Coffin wrote of the project, "but we can plan and plant beautiful screens and backgrounds that will be interesting at all seasons of the year. We may not easily be able to construct a picturesque diversity of ground level, but we can plant so as to have much height and variety in our flower and shrub groups." The principle would also serve her on a much larger scale, especially on Long Island, where varied natural features were not abundant. Generally, it would provide the basis for her distinctive approach, one that emphasized planting design.

Her plan for the Spragues' garden was structured around two long gravel paths that formed a T, centered on the midpoint of the house. The design became informal on the far side of the cross path, where a roughly circular expanse of lawn opened up, backed by trees and shrubs and rimmed with large drifts of tulips and perennials grouped by color. The unusual layout set it apart from hundreds of more formulaic examples then being published in the new design magazines. Even at this early stage in her career, Coffin defined space with conviction and verve. (Figs. 8.2, 8.3)

The geometry of the long paths also provided ample planting opportunities, and it was this aspect of the design that caught Elsa Rehmann's attention. Rehmann was particularly impressed with Coffin's use of sequence, in which borders given over to specific color schemes were separated "but not into hard and distinct sections."[16] Rehmann also noted Coffin's color pairings between trees and spring bulbs (*Pyrus floribunda* and the brilliant rose tulip 'Clara

8.2. Intersection of paths in garden, Edward E. Sprague estate, Flushing, N.Y., c. 1906. Winterthur Archives.

8.3. Flower-rimmed lawn, Sprague estate, c. 1906. Winterthur Archives.

Butt,' for example), remarking, "This is a field of artistic opportunity which we are just beginning to grasp."[17] Coffin's attentiveness to the visual interplay between plants at all scales (herbs, shrubs, and trees) is evident in many of the photographs of the design, which emphasize the unusual space as well as horticultural diversity.

When the Coffins returned to Europe with Henry du Pont in 1907, their travels included a visit to the "wild, lonely, and impressive" coast of Dalmatia. Coffin wrote evocatively about the beauty of the mountains for *National Geographic*, illustrating her article with thirty of her own black-and-white photographs. She was back in Europe in 1909, again with du Pont, and together they toured English gardens, including Munstead Wood, where they visited Jekyll.[18] Coffin had become an ardent student of plants and their visual effects; however, her work would rarely reflect the Arts and Crafts principles that characterized Jekyll's gardens.

In 1909 a commission from William Marshall Bullitt in Glenview, Kentucky, came to Coffin, almost certainly on du Pont's recommendation. (He would continue to offer stalwart support for Coffin's career and to recommend her services to many of his wealthy friends.) Her design utilized a variation of the T-shaped plan she had created for the Spragues. In a meadow setting, long (100-foot) borders edged a path leading to an imposing elm, beyond which lay a grass tennis court. A small formal garden that included several circular beds was tucked close against the house. (Figs. 8.4, 8.5)

The Bullitt job led to two others nearby, one of which, for Charles T. Ballard (1911), shows an imaginative spatial leap. In this design Coffin made use of an Italianate approach that had, by then, become standard in the repertory of many landscape architects, but she broke it up with circular forms. (Fig. 8.6) These included the forecourt, curving paths, and a curving terminus to the for-

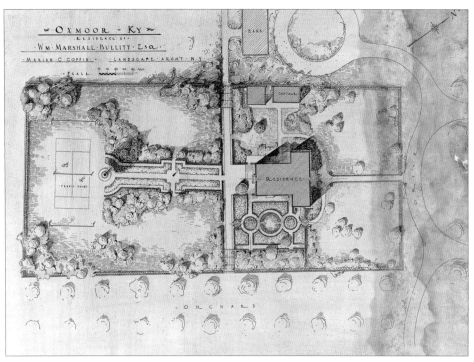

8.4. Plan for Oxmoor, William Marshall Bullitt estate, 1910, Oxmoor, Ky. Winterthur Archives.

8.5. View to elm, Oxmoor. Winterthur Archives.

mal garden. Another commission from this time, a large garden for Albert Boardman in Southampton, Long Island, was also emphatically geometric—and like most of Coffin's designs of this period, filled with floriferous beds.[19] In a c. 1910 garden for Coffin's friend Elizabeth E. Farnum, in Norfolk, Connecticut, circular forms also figured prominently. The feeling of intimacy and charm

captured in old photographs of this design recalls contemporaneous gardens by Ellen Shipman.[20] (Fig. 8.7)

By 1911 Coffin's practice was large enough to support an assistant, and that year she dispatched Elizabeth F. Colwell to Winterthur to record trial plantings in du Pont's formal garden.[21] A more substantial job in the region came in 1916 from H. Rodney Sharp, who with his wife, Isabella (Harry du Pont's cousin), had enlarged their 1844 stone house, Gibraltar, taking care to preserve its original core. Coffin added plantings to a terrace with a swimming pool and a large, curving staircase to link the feature to upper terraces that overlooked it. She also developed a series of architecturally determined spaces leading away from the house and a large wild garden to enfold and screen them from the lawn and street beyond. (Figs. 8.8, 8.9)

Two years later, Coffin invited the architect James Scheiner, formerly an assistant to John Russell Pope, to join her office as an associate, and he soon became key to Coffin's operation, playing an important role in jobs that involved large-scale grading and construction. Scheiner was also available to supervise work on the ground, a circumstance that seems to have opened the way to a host of new, larger commissions in the 1920s. (Fig. 8.10) That none of Coffin's colleagues had such an arrangement is hardly surprising; it would have been impossible without the architectural authority she had accrued during her studies at MIT. In September 1919 she wrote du Pont that she was going to open a "real little office, now that my Scheiner is back from the War."[22]

In the same letter Coffin asked du Pont to recommend her to Harry Milliken, a Chicago architect he knew well. She was eager to expand her practice, and the Midwest seemed to hold potential. However, the wide reputations of several very successful landscape architects based in Chicago (particularly Jens Jensen) stood in the way, and Coffin does not appear to have found work west of Mansfield, Ohio. Still, she had enough business in the firm to support an office at 830 Lexington Avenue, and she added another employee, Ethel D. Nevius, to her staff. In 1919 she began the most extensive job of her career to date, a landscape design for the new conjoined campuses of the Delaware State College. She had been recommended for the job by Sharp, who was chairman of the Buildings and Grounds Committee.

A master plan for the college had been completed in 1918 by Frank Miles Day and Charles Z. Klauder of Philadelphia. (Earlier campus plantings had been overseen by Coffin's colleague Elsa Rehmann, perhaps through connections with Rehmann's father, who was an architect.) Coffin's general plan was accompanied by a five-page report that included detailed planting schemes for existing and proposed buildings. (Fig. 8.11) It also described several new features that would provide circulation between the two campuses. The central element of Coffin's plan was a large oval that ingeniously disguised a bend in the long axis that ran through the two campuses. She bracketed this space with gardens and a large grove of trees.[23] Coffin detailed two planting schemes of generally differing character for the two campuses. The palette for the men's dormitories was confined largely to evergreens, some of which were trained on walls, in the same manner Farrand had used at Princeton. The plantings for the women's college were lyrical, colorful, and floriferous. In later years, she added allées of paulownia to border walks leading to the central oval.

Adamant about protecting her design and maintaining oversight of its implementation, Coffin asked Sharp for a contract which specified that ongoing work was to be carried out solely under her direction and through her office.[24] The agreement was soon in place, as was considerable financial support from Sharp as well as from du Pont, who had become a college trustee in 1919. Yet Coffin's recommendations encountered resistance from the college architects. A series of letters record criticism of her design for new library terraces and presented an alternative that the architects argued would supply a "much

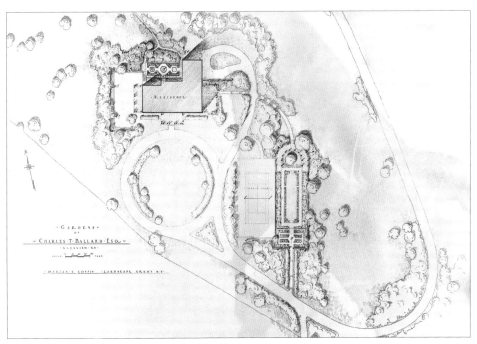

8.6. Plan for Charles T. Ballard estate, Glenview, Ky. Winterthur Archives.

8.7. Elizabeth E. Farnum estate, Norfolk, Conn. Photograph by Harry G. Healy. Winterthur Archives.

8.8. Gibraltar, H. Rodney Sharp estate, Wilmington, Del. Winterthur Archives.

more dignified and formal setting."[25] Coffin prevailed in her recommendations, however, as Farrand had at Princeton.

A letter from Coffin to Sharp the following year makes clear that tensions over the dispute lingered. "If you were surprised at the 'tone' of my letter," she wrote Sharp, "I was surprised you found any tone in it, as I had meant none. I am always glad to get suggestions from you, the architects, and other friends of the college. I am not, however, willing to let contractors or other workmen make suggestions or go on with work without consulting first with me."[26] Coffin's strong resolve served her well in these conflicts. Her professional relationship with the college lasted until 1953, her entire working life.

Starting in 1920, Coffin undertook a number of strategies aimed at expanding her client base. That year she joined the Garden Club of America as a member-at-large and began to publish articles in the club's *Bulletin*, aimed at the powerful and wealthy women who filled the GCA's rosters. There she also advertised the titles of five slide lectures. She began to publish her designs more frequently in other venues, too, including *House and Garden*, *Country Life in America*, *Garden Magazine*, *House Beautiful*, and *Garden and Home Builder*, illustrating these articles with evocative photographs commissioned from the country's most talented landscape photographers, includ-

8.9. Stone path and spring beds, Gibraltar. Winterthur Archives.

8.10. James M. Scheiner at Winterthur, 1929. Winterthur Archives.

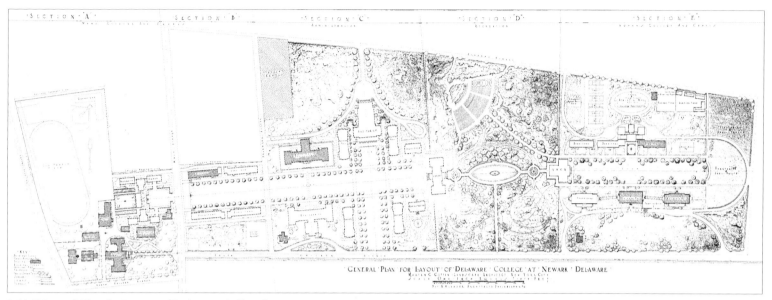

8.11. "General Plan for Layout of Delaware College," 1919. Courtesy University of Delaware Archives.

ing Mattie Edwards Hewitt, Jessie Tarbox Beals, and Harry G. Healy. These efforts led to a surge in both the number and the scope of her projects. Coffin, however, like all her female colleagues, continued to accept circumscribed assignments, one of which, in 1919, was a planting design for Mrs. Joseph Choate's garden at Naumkeag in Stockbridge, Massachusetts.[27]

In 1920 Coffin published an article in the GCA *Bulletin* that captured several of her professional concerns of the moment. First among them was raising the embargo on imported plants which was preventing American landscape architects from ordering from nurseries abroad. Coffin addressed more philosophical matters too, urging her female audience toward a more expansive involvement in landscape-related concerns. "Beyond the high wall of your gardens proper, lies a wide field that is in need of just such interest and good work as you have been doing within," she wrote. "Many Garden Club members are so keen about flowers and have so concentrated upon them that they do not realize they are but a part of all the fine plant material we have to draw from."[28]

Coffin had been named a Fellow of the American Society of Landscape Architects in 1918 (the same year that Fletcher Steele was so honored), and she was keen to promote the profession to her readers. Her article continued, "We want you to work with us in the making of more

lovely gardens, the laying out of Country Places, big or little, and of suburban plots or even tiny backyards, to the planning of City Parks, Play Grounds, and of Cemeteries." Her scope of vision, like her colleagues', extended further still, to conservation of public lands: "We want your interest and cooperation for the preservation of fine woods, groups of trees and other natural scenery."[29]

Coffin's broadening reputation reflected more than marketing savvy. Her bold and spare designs were a good match for the more adventurous tastes of many younger clients who had tired of distinctly European models. She was also increasingly responsive to the idiosyncrasies of her customers as sources of artistic inspiration, a quality that further appealed to the new generation. In her 1918 book, Elsa Rehmann had articulated the idea that a garden should be a "manifestation of distinctive individuality, an expression of personality," a principle that many of Coffin's designs of the 1920s emphasized. The sense of the garden as a vehicle for expressing the private self was taking sure hold in many of the designs of the period.

But Rehmann's notion of "distinction" differed strongly from that of Manning and Coffin's older colleagues, who, during these years, continued to promote the beauty of "locality" as a guiding principle in landscape design. It also differed subtly from the perspective of Farrand, who would continue to explore a balance between the "stride of

Nature" and authoritative principles gleaned from Italy and England. As distinctive settings for new country places became increasingly rare, emphasis on natural scenery lessened, in part because expansive pleasure grounds were out of the economic reach of all but the very rich.

One of Coffin's most original commissions during the productive period after the war was Bayberryland, in Shinnecock Hills. The project bought her out to the Gold

8.12. Lower flower garden, Bayberryland, Charles H. Sabin estate, Shinnecock Hills, N.Y. Winterthur Archives.

8.13. Path to house with torch lilies (*Kniphofia*), Bayberryland. Photograph by John Wallace Gillies. Winterthur Archives.

Coast of Long Island, which had attracted the country's largest concentration of wealthy clients, drawn to the region by the water views, country clubs, polo fields, yacht-filled harbors, and the one-hour commute to New York City. Mac Griswold and Eleanor Weller estimate that nine hundred estates were built on Long Island between 1865 and 1940, many of them almost "principalities."[30] Amid the building frenzy, Coffin found wealthy patrons and new inspiration too.

Her clients at Bayberryland were Charles H. Sabin, chairman of the board of Morgan Guarantee Trust, and Pauline Sabin, heir to the Morton Salt fortune. The house, by Cross & Cross, was a low, sprawling English cottage type. Coffin's design, however, was not traditional. She laid out a richly planted series of walled gardens that set up a strong ocean view over broad planes of grass and reflecting pools. (Fig. 8.12) Below these, a curving stone walk, bordered by a wild garden of *Kniphofia uvaria* (Red-hot poker) and other shore-loving plants, wound in a dynamic arc to the water's edge.[31] (Fig. 8.13) The juxtaposition of the two bold landscape gestures—the descending rectangular planes and the strong curve—diverged noticeably from the historicizing treatments that were still dominant in other new estates in the region. Smart, athletic, and chic, as Griswold and Weller point out, Bayberryland was the first real beach garden on Long Island.

In 1920 E. F. Hutton and Marjorie Merriweather Post, heir to the Postum Cereal Company fortune, commissioned a landscape design for Hillwood, their new, several-hundred-acre estate in nearby Wheaton Hills. The scale and style of the almost childlike "Tuderbethan" house, designed by Charles M. Hart, inspired Coffin to lay out a series of playful gardens that differed markedly from one another, each with its own narrative tone.[32] The flat Long Island site offered little dramatic potential, so she generated interest internally, through geometric, almost fantastical plantings. The landscape unfolded scene by scene. (Fig. 8.14) A large topiary garden was set into a clearing surrounded by dense woodland, almost like an oversize version of a child's board game. A nearby lawn was edged with a long, scalloped privet hedge. A garden walk was bordered with an allée of Chinese magnolias. Each of these

8.14. Hillwood, E. F. Hutton estate, Wheatley Hills, N.Y. Photograph by
Mattie Edwards Hewitt. Winterthur Archives.

8.15. Clayton, Childs Frick estate, Roslyn Harbor, N.Y. Photograph by Samuel H. Gottscho.
Winterthur Archives.

whimsical features utilized plants almost as pure form, a reflection of the increasingly abstract direction Coffin's designs were taking. These spatial units were nestled into a
sprawling landscape of open meadows and woods. The
Huttons' garden was publicized in *House and Garden*
(1924), *Garden and Home Builder* (1926), and, later, Coffin's
1940 book, *Trees and Shrubs for Landscape Effects*.

It was a measure of Coffin's stature that in 1920 she
was invited to participate in one of the largest estate projects on Long Island. The client was Marshall Field III,
who worked closely with his architect, John Russell Pope
(James Scheiner's former employer) on the layout of his
2,300-acre Caumsett. Only one other Long Island estate
approached this scale—Oheka, in Woodbury, commissioned by Otto Kahn (where Farrand had worked extensively). At Caumsett, large portions of the woods were
left intact, and preservation principles were apparent as
well in the restoration of a Revolutionary War–vintage
house, which was adapted as a gate lodge.[33] Most of the
gardens on the estate had been designed by the talented
superintendent, George H. Gillies, and laid out under the
keen eye of the owner. Coffin was hired to create a wild
garden for the Winter Cottage, where she made a forest
glade and a pool of ivy, one of the most understated
works in the region.

At the other extreme of the stylistic continuum was

8.16. Borders to pool, Clayton. Photograph by Samuel H. Gottscho. Winterthur
Archives.

Coffin's design for Clayton, in Roslyn Harbor, for the
Childs Fricks, where she was commissioned to redo the
formal garden in 1925. (The house, originally built for
Lloyd Stephen Bryce c. 1893, was designed by Ogden
Codman Jr.) Coffin's design introduced a large, round
pool located at the crossing of major axes, where the water redoubled the effect of a looming Roman arch of
clipped privet. Surrounding the pool were large beds that
mixed herbaceous material with shrubs and small flowering trees. (Figs. 8.15, 8.16) Flower borders lining a long
path to the pool were arranged by color, from "lightest of

pinks to the hottest of scarlets and oranges, with blues and yellows" providing a transition.[34] Areas of lawn and dense woodland offered more informal planting opportunities. (Fig. 8.17) Although the job ended in conflict with Mrs. Frick, Coffin considered Clayton to be one of her finest works. Photographs by Samuel H. Gottscho attest to its exuberant, almost muscular design, as well as its passages of transcendent landscape beauty.[35]

A year earlier, Coffin had been commissioned to lay out the grounds for Ruth and Harry du Pont's new summer place, Chestertown House, in Southampton. That design featured a spare, geometric lawn terrace

8.18. Chestertown House, Henry Francis du Pont estate, Southampton, N.Y. Photograph by Amemya. Winterthur Archives.

8.17. Woods, Clayton. Photograph by Mattie Edwards Hewitt. Winterthur Archives.

that overlooked wild grasses and man-made dunes. (Fig. 8.18) Du Pont's summer estate reflected a notion of the country place as haven and preserve, an understated manifestation of culture and taste. These fundamental principles were guiding development at Winterthur, too, where Coffin was already advising informally.

Commissions continued to come to Coffin through the end of the decade, among them large projects in New Jersey, Connecticut, upstate New York, and Long Island. One of the most successful of these was begun c. 1927 for the Edgar W. Bassicks, in Bridgeport, Connecticut. There, Coffin exposed rock ledge as a major motive in the naturalistic design and piped water to trickle into a small pool and rill, then into a larger pool below. A spare woodland underplanted with great masses of narcissus recalled work that du Pont was undertaking at Winterthur. (Fig. 8.19) Her handling of space in the layout also brings to mind that of a slightly earlier design, for Joseph Morgan Wing, in Millbrook, New York, where she used a lake as the centerpiece of the plan. (Fig. 8.20) Both projects would be cited by the Architectural League of New York, which awarded Coffin the Gold Medal of Honor in 1930.

8.19. The Oaks, Edgar W. Bassick estate, Bridgeport, Conn. Photograph by Harry G. Healy. Winterthur Archives.

In 1926 Coffin was stricken with a serious hip infection that limited her physical activity and eventually forced her into the hospital for a long convalescence. The

8.20. Joseph Morgan Wing estate, Millbrook, N.Y. Photograph by Amemya. Winterthur Archives.

following year she came into a substantial inheritance from a cousin and was able to buy a handsome house in New Haven, which she furnished in Edwardian style. She laid out a beautiful, suburban-scale garden in the back, rimmed with an overstory of large shade trees and mid-story layer of magnolia and dogwood, fenced to keep out children and dogs (to her neighbors' consternation). By interesting coincidence, this was the same year Beatrix Farrand moved from New Haven to Pasadena, a circumstance that gave Coffin an opportunity to add several Connecticut clients to her practice.[36]

According to Warren Hunting Smith, who boarded in Coffin's house for many years, she entertained often and in great style. "Innumerable teas, cocktail parties, musicales, and buffet suppers" took place in the big living room, and, in the summer, the garden became a setting for her parties. He remembers Coffin befriending architects, artists, musicians, and writers, reportedly preferring young men and women to "stodgy" middle-aged people. Smith also recalled Coffin's bold interpersonal style, evident during one lunch with the imperious author Hilaire Belloc, whom she unhesitantly snubbed when he grilled her about which of his books she had read.[37] During these years Coffin also kept an office in New York, commuting each day and spending weekends in Connecticut and summers at Wendover, in Watch Hill, Rhode Island, a small country place that she and Scheiner renovated during the 1920s.[38] (Fig. 8.21)

8.21. Marian Coffin at her county estate, Wendover, Watch Hill, R.I. Winterthur Archives.

The job for Harry and Ruth du Pont at Winterthur began two years after Coffin's move to New Haven, and it became the most extensive of her career. Fortuitously timed, the commission occupied her through the Depression, when estate work became increasingly scarce and private practices shrank in numbers of clients as well as sizes of projects. The job provided handsome fees that, together with Coffin's adventurous and—to some friends—alarming stock investments made it possible for her to keep two homes, a maid, and a chauffeur even through the economic decline. The scale of the du Pont project had been determined before the stock market crashed, and the family's enormous gunpowder fortune would see it through to completion.

NINE

WINTERTHUR

Winterthur, Delaware

Henry F. du Pont's great-great-grandfather, Pierre Samuel du Pont de Nemours (1739–1817), was an outspoken critic of the corrupt government that had risen to power in France after the Revolution, and in a violent uprising in 1797, his print shop was ransacked and he and his son Eleuthère Irénée were briefly imprisoned.[1] After his release, Pierre retreated to Bois-des-Fossés, his family's country estate south of Paris, and there began to lay plans to settle in the United States, where free speech was protected by a new constitution. Inspired by *Observations sur la Virginie*, written by his friend Thomas Jefferson, he set his sights on Virginia. Pierre saw great advantages in the state's warm climate, rich soil, abundant acres, and proximity to Washington, D.C., where the national government was soon to relocate.[2]

On October 2, 1799, du Pont and his two sons, their wives, and their children sailed for the United States on the *American Eagle*. On landing in Newport, Rhode Island, they were welcomed by an affectionate note from Jefferson, who also warned them of predators waiting to pounce on land speculators. In fact, tales of cheap land in the young nation had been grossly exaggerated, and after three years at Good Stay, New Jersey, du Pont returned to France without realizing his dream. Both sons remained, however, and set up businesses.

Victor established a commission house in New York City, and Eleuthère Irénée bought land four miles north of Wilmington, Delaware, on the Brandywine Creek. In rolling woods and fertile meadows, he established Eleutherian Mills, part gunpowder factory, part farm, financed by private investors in Paris. The area was primitive, Eleuthère wrote to a friend in 1802, with "no road, no decent house, no garden."[3] He considered the last his greatest deprivation, and it was one of the first projects to occupy his time. In 1804 he received a large shipment of seeds and plants from Paris—three large cases contained "grapevines, nut trees, linden and mulberry trees; four varieties of roses; seeds of melons and artichokes; bundles of lavender and tarragon with roots; clumps of violets; raspberries . . . and almost two hundred fruit trees."[4] With them, he planted a *potager*, a reminiscence of his family's farm in France. (Fig. 9.1)

Du Pont soon became an active participant in the circle of prominent Philadelphians who shared his interests in agriculture, animal husbandry, and horticulture. He proved both a good farmer and a good businessman, and

9.1. Eleutherian Mills garden, by Theophilus P. Chandler, 1873, ink wash on paper. Courtesy Hagley Museum and Library.

9.2. Old carriage drive. Winterthur Archives.

his fortune grew, aided by speculative trading in merino sheep. Before long the gunpowder business began to crowd out his prize herd, and du Pont started acquiring contiguous farms along Kennett Turnpike where he could relocate his animals. In the rich soil of these fields he also planted clover, rye, and other American grains, and he experimented with millet imported from Europe. In time, cattle replaced sheep. The family's horticultural interests continued to deepen and their wealth continued to grow. Scientists from Philadelphia, including many Frenchmen, came to Eleutherian Mills to botanize in the Brandywine woods and to socialize in the sophisticated du Pont household, where fine wine was served and literature and politics, as well as plants, were frequent topics of conversation.[5]

Irénée's daughter Evelina and her husband, Jacques Bidermann, built a twelve-room house on 450 acres of this property and named the estate Winterthur after Jacques's

ancestral home in Switzerland. In 1867 this land was purchased by Irénée's son (Evelina's brother) General Henry du Pont. Under the general's stewardship, the property continued to expand, encompassing more than one thousand acres of pasture, farm, and garden. In 1889 the estate came to his son—yet another Henry, Colonel Henry Algernon du Pont, a graduate of West Point who had performed heroically in the Civil War and, after his 1874 marriage to Mary Pauline Foster, assumed the presidency of the Wilmington and Northern Railroad. The Colonel also, each morning, went to work at the family gunpowder business at Eleutherian Mills.

The Colonel was as passionate about the landscape of Winterthur as his forebears had been. He added hundreds of acres to the estate and laid out many miles of carriage drives through the woods. He planted groves of trees, flowers, and vegetables and built new greenhouses. The evolution of this landscape had been overseen by four generations of du Ponts, but it was the looming example of Frederick Law Olmsted's American Picturesque which gave it more definitive shape during these years. (Fig. 9.2)

Winterthur provided the du Ponts with solace as well as joy. Of the seven children born to them there, only two survived infancy, Louise Evelina, born in 1877, and her brother Henry Francis, known as Harry, born three years later. (Fig. 9.3) Pauline and the Colonel were avid, somewhat stereotypical, gardeners—he more involved with trees, she more devoted to flowers. Ac-

9.3. Henry Francis du Pont. Winterthur Archives.   9.4. Meadow at dawn, 1990. Photograph by Carol Betsch.

cording to Louise, she and Harry were required to memorize botanical names and sent to bed without supper if they failed.[6] There is other evidence of stern, although perhaps not unusual, Victorian fathering on the part of the Colonel and a strong attachment, on Harry's part, to his mother.

Shy and severely homesick at boarding school in Groton, Massachusetts, where his academic performance was poor—hampered, some have suggested, by his being forced to write with his right hand—young du Pont sent his parents heart-wrenching letters. "If someone doesn't come to see me soon I will die of grief. I cry sometimes so that I cannot write."[7] In time, he adjusted to the separation. When Harry was sixteen, he wrote excitedly to tell his mother about having recognized one of his favorite wildflowers, "Brandywine bulbs," in Gray's *Botany.* "Their Latin name is 'Mertensia virginica,'" he informed her.[8] He was cheered, too, by sprays of lily-of-the-valley that she sent from Winterthur (these came by rail, carefully wrapped in sphagnum moss), and he also began tending his own small garden at school. He found a job working part-time for Herman Huebner, a local Connecticut florist whose specialty was violets.

Long summers spent at Winterthur were a relief and a joy. Harry roamed through acres of meadowland, botanizing, and also visiting the estates of other du Ponts, many of whom were gifted gardeners. (Fig. 9.4) The country places of his great aunt Victorine du Pont Foster and Sophie Madeline du Pont were especially fine. The family had retained its enthusiasm for horticulture, and the flowering of any particularly interesting specimen on any of the du Pont estates would be called to the attention of the entire clan.[9] Harry also hung about watching farmworkers at their jobs and sometimes helped out, learning practical skills unusual for someone of his social class.[10]

Du Pont graduated from Groton in 1899 and was privately tutored, then admitted to Harvard with his freshman requirements already fulfilled. In Cambridge, he found himself at the center of a horticultural world of almost unimaginable richness, amplified by connections to Boston's elite through his sister's marriage to Francis Crowninshield. Du Pont's horizons were further broadened in 1901 by a trip to Europe with his parents—his first—which also included visits to many gardens. Soon Harry began spending time with Marian

Coffin, who had started her own coursework at MIT in 1901.

In October du Pont wrote home to say that he had decided to enroll in the Bussey Institution, Harvard's college of agriculture and horticulture for gardeners, florists, farmers, and estate managers. "College life is nice enough," he told his mother, "but I want something more than it can give me. In fact flowers etc. are the only real interests I have." He credited Coffin's influence (she, too, was taking courses at the Bussey, although not the same ones as he), but du Pont embraced the new vocational direction as his own. "I do not think I am too impulsive," he explained, "[I] merely think it is the mouldering of latent thought which has burst into flame."[11]

Courses at the Bussey emphasized theory, obtained through reading and lectures, and practical expertise, acquired in the greenhouse and the field. One of du Pont's instructors was Benjamin M. Watson, a widely respected horticulturalist and author of many important articles.[12] Du Pont was also introduced to the color theories of Gertrude Jekyll and, in a course taught under the auspices of Harvard, to the "Theory and Principles of Landscape Design," through the work of William Kent, William Shenstone, Capability Brown, Humphry Repton, J. C. Loudon, and Reginald Blomfield, among others.[13]

Du Pont's horticultural biographer, Valencia Libby, who has written eloquently on these early years, sees evidence of his future approach to landscape design in an essay, "The Development of a Country Place, 1878–1902," whose subject was his great-aunt Victorine Foster's estate, Virieux. In it, du Pont praised the Olmstedian principles his aunt had employed, which depended on preserving, in his words, "the original characteristics and natural beauty of the place." He noted the picturesque effect of dogwood and redbud branches reaching down into a clearing in the woods. And he praised the decision to avoid the ubiquitous Victorian convention of boulders made into "raised round flower beds planted with the ever prominent red geranium." These he found "in shockingly bad taste."[14]

The Bussey Institution was adjacent to the Arnold Arboretum, which essentially provided a four-hundred-acre classroom for its students. Du Pont visited often, some-

times with Coffin, and he also began visiting other well-known area gardens, including Charles Sargent's Holm Lea, which he saw for the first time in 1902.[15] During these years, too, he started collecting volumes by Gertrude Jekyll and William Robinson.[16] He graduated in the spring of 1902 and applied to the School of Practical Agriculture and Horticulture in Briarcliff Manor, New York, where he was admitted for the fall semester.

At Winterthur that summer, he threw himself into an experimental planting of forty-two cultivars of dahlias, observing their bloom and meticulously recording information such as color, date, and size. It was, in Libby's opinion, du Pont's first horticultural initiative at Winterthur and the harbinger of several other trials that would, within a few years, include daffodils, gladiolus, iris, and tulips. In these trials, du Pont immersed himself in one flower at a time, exhaustively investigating it before moving on to another. His methods were painstakingly exact, obsessively precise.[17]

In September 1902 du Pont's mother died while she was visiting Louise and Frank in Marblehead, and Harry, grief stricken, abruptly changed his plans. Instead of going to Briarcliff Manor, he stayed at Winterthur to help his father oversee the estate. The former director of Winterthur Gardens, C. Gordon Tyrrell, dates du Pont's first bulb plantings to that fall, when du Pont installed a trial plot of 54 species of *Narcissus*, listing their names alphabetically under their floral type ("trumpet-flowered," "double-flowered"), just as he had done with the dahlias. He was already contemplating wide-scale naturalizing of the bulbs, and these early trials were clearly undertaken to determine which would perennialize most successfully.[18]

At this juncture, du Pont also began to supervise many of the domestic responsibilities that his mother once had, such as changing the curtains with the seasons and cutting and arranging flowers. These tasks were unusual for a man, then as now, but du Pont maintained them and, in fact, continued to expand them even after his 1916 marriage to Ruth Wales, applying the same attention to detail that he was bringing to his gardening. In time, these domestic rituals would be integrated into the larger project of designing the house interior as a series of museum installa-

tions. Many of du Pont's interests, including those associated with gardening, underwent similar transformations
from domestic, feminine roots to more male-identified,
quasi-professional endeavors.

In 1902 du Pont also began to design plantings for a
new formal garden that had been created at Winterthur
the year before.[19] The garden comprised four terraces surrounded by low walls of local stone set at a distance southeast of the residence, reached by a flight of stairs. The
upper terrace supported a pool, twin pavilions, and a wall
fountain; the second, a lawn and wide herbaceous borders
edged with stone paths; the third, flower beds and wisteria-covered arbors; and the lowest, a rose garden and a
small pool for water lilies. (Figs., 9.5, 9.6, 9.7)

The geometric layout was a variation of the Italianate
prototype Charles Platt and others were popularizing at
the time, the progeny of which were appearing in country places throughout the United States.[20] Statuary, urns,
cisterns, and sundials ornamented the architecturally determined outdoor rooms, and stone walls, terraces, walks,
pool, and pergola provided foils for lush plantings. None
of this was unusual, as Libby points out: "the formal garden was a symbol of wealth, taste, and culture for American estate owners, and in this aspect, Winterthur was
typical."[21]

More unusual was the intensity of the horticultural
experiments du Pont conducted in these gardens, as he attempted to secure effects similar to those he was discovering through his reading and travels. England provided
particular inspiration. There is no doubt of Jekyll's influence on du Pont's horticultural experiments—he referred
to her by name in his notebooks as he recorded attempts
at exact replications of her designs, with limited success
owing to differences between the cool, moist climate of
England and the hot, dry summers of Delaware. He
adopted certain of her trademark practices, such as using
clematis to cover spent delphinium foliage, and he emulated many of her color combinations, such as "white and
pale yellow fls with . . . pale blue Delphiniums." He also
emulated Jekyll's precise methods of recording successes
and failures, which were temperamentally suited to his
own obsessive nature.[22]

9.5 Formal garden. Photograph by Strohmeyer. Winterthur Archives.

9.6. Wisteria arbor in formal garden. Photograph by Strohmeyer. Winterthur
Archives.

9.7. Rose garden and reflecting pool in formal garden. Winterthur Archives.

To track his plantings in the twenty beds of the formal garden, du Pont commissioned Marian Coffin's office to record and annually revise plans of the area.[23] Coffin's assistant generated plans that du Pont cross-referenced with lists of hundreds of species of perennials, annuals, and bulbs, annotated with observations concerning color, time of bloom, and habit. Du Pont found inspiration in *The Garden Month by Month* by Mabel Cabot Sedgwick. Three of his notebooks from these years are labeled Color Schemes, Combinations, Month Gardens.[24] In these, he listed plants suitable for single-color borders or combinations—"blue-white-yellow" or "brown-yellow" borders, for example.

Du Pont was intent on exact hues and forms and he exhaustively queried plant growers throughout the United States and Europe to find the precise cultivars he needed.[25] Often his aims were thwarted; letters record his frustrations at having color schemes "deranged" by nurserymen who carelessly mislabeled seedlings.[26] Yet du Pont's scientific approach did not undermine the artistry of his achievement—even by the exacting standards of the day, these gardens were beautiful. Old autochromes record luxuriant vines and languid roses reflected in quiet pools. The compositions in the formal garden would occupy du Pont for decades, holding his attention as fully as the wild garden experiments he was conducting at the same time.[27]

Du Pont's first naturalistic plantings date to 1903, when he began introducing drifts of daffodils into the woods, guided by the results obtained in the trial beds. Inspired chiefly by William Robinson's 1870 book, *The Wild Garden*, du Pont took Robinson's horticultural principles into a new realm, conceptualizing the plantings as broad, sequential sheets of color—a "superbly calculated choreography," in the words of the landscape architect William H. Frederick, who has studied du Pont's work carefully.[28] By the time he was given official charge of the grounds of Winterthur, du Pont had begun to naturalize several species of bulbs, among them snowdrops, crocus, *colchicum* (autumn crocus), grape hyacinths, wood hyacinths, and winter aconite, in addition to narcissus. In 1909 he ordered 25,000 bulbs, most of them for a slope north of the house, known later (and still today) as the March Bank. (Fig. 9.8) By 1913 the annual order had grown to 39,000 bulbs. This included flowers for house arrangements and for the formal garden.

Du Pont obtained bulbs from leading growers in England and Holland, many for only a few cents apiece, arranging them in irregular drifts so that they would emerge in naturalistic masses.[29] He used tree branches to guide these layouts, marking the placement of each bulb with a wooden label. In the filtered light of the woods, he preferred to use smaller, delicate species; in the strong light of open meadows, he turned to the bolder shapes of large-cupped narcissus. The massed plantings continued unabated for many years, and du Pont also continued testing individual varieties in experimental beds, closely observing color and form, imagining these characteristics multiplied into great swaths throughout the woods, where they would amplify the grandeur of the setting.

Beginning in late February, winding down in September, broad sheets of bloom cloak the swells of the March Bank, each in its season. In February white snowdrops appear with winter aconite, and then both yield to *Adonis amurensis*. Spring snowflakes are succeeded by yellow and gold crocus, glory-of-the snow, and blue scilla. In late spring, Brandywine bluebells and roving bellflower emerge, and in summer white snakeroot and meadow-rue. Finally, plantainlily—today's hosta. Remarkable in the intensity of its color and scope, the display also emphasizes the lay of the land. The woodland's connection to the surrounding farmland was established by vistas cut throughout the woods. (Figs. 9.9, 9.11)

Each of du Pont's two ambitious horticultural initiatives at Winterthur represented one side of the stylistic dichotomy that was informing landscape design throughout the United States at the time. Spatially, the endeavors were disjunctive—like the formal and wild gardens at Gwinn—but at Winterthur the artistic goals were intertwined, inspired by the same fervid investigation of color.

———

Du Pont began to naturalize azaleas in 1906, at a time when the floriferous shrubs were grown chiefly as forced specimens for conservatory displays.[30] A turning point came in 1917, when du Pont visited Robert T. Brown of Cottage Gardens Companies in Queens Village, Long Island, and bought seventeen small Japanese hybrids, known as Kurume azaleas, from a collection that Brown had purchased at the Panama Pacific International Exposition two years before. He brought them back to Winterthur and planted them in the woods, choosing clearings that had resulted from a chestnut blight.[31]

The Kurumes thrived in the dappled sunlight and eventually produced many new hybrids whose blooming times differed slightly from their parents'. Intrigued by the idea of extending the fleeting display, du Pont selected several that blossomed one week apart and tested various arrangements of them, using branches held in milk bottles borrowed from Winterthur's dairy, or, less efficiently, directing his gardeners to move entire plants from hole to hole. In time, the Azalea Woods grew to cover eight acres. Du Pont added many new species, including the Asian types hybridized by Charles O. Dexter and "torch" species that had been collected in Japan by Sargent. "I wish you could have been here to have seen the hardy Azaleas," Sargent wrote to him in 1919 about a recent rush of bloom at the Arnold Arboretum. "The red-flowered A. Kaempferi have never been so fine before and just now A. Japonicum is splendid. All these hardy Azaleas will do well, I am sure, at Winterthur and I should like to think of them growing there in the thousands."[32] In time, du Pont augmented the display with great masses of other species of shrubs, flowering trees, and wildflowers.[33] (Fig. 9.10)

The vivid sheets of color he orchestrated under the forest canopy were pure artifice, but the plants adapted to their surroundings and came to look at home there, claiming the woods as garden. Many of du Pont's color harmonies were sonorous, but he also experimented with precipitous clashes. After one visit, Coffin wrote to him, "I can shut my eyes and see it all and am still undecided which Azalea effect was the loveliest. You certainly handled the discords or near discords . . . with consummate skill,

9.8. March Bank and view to house, c. 1908. Winterthur Archives.

9.9. March Bank and view to meadow, 1932. Photograph by Gottscho-Schleisner, Inc. Winterthur Archives.

9.11 Azaleas and view to meadow, 1938. Winterthur Archives.

9.12. Latimeria gates at entrance to the young pinetum. Photograph by Samuel Gottscho. Winterthur Archives.

and with those vibrant pinks and magentas that is no mean feat. Still I think I loved best the ledifoliums (or were they Kurumes?) with the foreground of the bluer white of the Trillium and the creamy yellow of the Primroses. Each glimpse was better than the last, so after all I am not sure!"[34] Du Pont went on to create naturalized plantings in other areas of Winterthur, using the same principles he employed on the March Bank and in the Azalea Woods, achieving broad color effects with plants as disparate as winterhazel and quince, and later, lilacs and primrose.

Other horticultural initiatives were under way at Winterthur as well. In 1914 du Pont and his father visited England together, and among the estates they saw was Dropmore, in Buckinghamshire, which had a fine ornamental pine forest. Before returning, they had decided to create a similar feature at Winterthur, a large pinetum that would include species hardy to the climate.[35] They decided on a site northeast of the house, beyond the March Bank, where the new plantings would extend the general sense of woodland.

Development of the collection was overseen by the Colonel, who had lost his U.S. Senate seat in 1917 and found himself with time to devote to the project. Harry's marriage to Ruth Wales in 1916, coupled with his deepening involvement in the large farm operation at Winterthur, may also have contributed to the Colonel's dedication to the new project. Charles Sargent took a lively interest in the pinetum, too—seeing it as a patriotic endeavor—and supplied many of the rarest trees from the Arnold Arboretum. Eventually, more than fifty species were planted.[36] (Figs. 9.12, 9.13. 9.14, 9.15)

In the decade after World War I, Harry and Ruth visited Europe annually and also traveled widely throughout the United States, where du Pont sought out nurseries, botanical gardens, and private gardens in his relentless search for new plants and landscape effects. In 1919 he visited Stan Hywet Hall, where he discussed dairying with F. A. Seiberling, who also had a fine herd, writing afterward in praise of Seiberling's "beautiful place."[37] Streams of guests

9.10 *Trillium in Azalea Woods,* 1990. Photograph by Carol Betsch.

FOLLOWING PAGES:

9.13. *Latimeria Gates (Entrance to Pinetum),* 1999. Photograph by Carol Betsch.

9.14. *Steps to Blue Atlas Cedar Circle,* 1999. Photograph by Carol Betsch.

9.15. Winterthur from the air, c. 1920, with newly planted pinetum upper right. Photograph by Victor Dallin. Winterthur Archives.

at Winterthur are also recorded, their presence providing welcome distraction from family tensions, particularly between Ruth and her imperious father-in-law.

The concern with bloom and color that dominated du Pont's work in the gardens of Winterthur came to play a role indoors as well. A 1924 inventory lists eight greenhouses that supplied flowers for the house, including roses, lilies, callas, hibiscus, orchids, begonias, gesnera, poinsettias, chrysanthemums, lantanas, sweet peas, snapdragons, buddleia, freesia, and primula. The scope of these plantings was not unusual—virtually every country estate maintained extensive greenhouses for this same purpose—but the scale was extreme. At Winterthur one entire greenhouse was devoted to hibiscus, which were brought into the conservatory when their bright, dinnerplate-size blooms appeared.

The glasshouses and cutting gardens also provided the flowers for table arrangements, which du Pont determined each day, along with choosing place settings from among fifty-eight sets of linens and china. In a recent book about her childhood on the estate, Ruth Lord describes the exhaustive, sixty-year record her father kept of the combinations of flowers and tableware: ageratum in "white wicker" china, Gloire de Lorraine begonias in Norwegian silver, paperwhites with Copenhagen china, Iceland poppies with Green Leaf Wedgwood, yellow roses with silver luster. "A flower to be used on the table was not to be seen anywhere else in the house that day," Lord recalled, "for its drama would have been undermined."[38]

Du Pont's fascination with American decorative arts can be traced to these years. By his own reckoning, it began with an aesthetic epiphany he had during a 1923 visit to the Shelburne, Vermont, estate of Electra Havemayer Webb.[39] Touring the imaginative interiors Webb had created there, du Pont came under the spell of a row of Staffordshire plates on a pine dresser, and he became transported by the combination of the pink-toned porcelain and the warm hues of the wood. The excitement of this vision was reignited a few days later when he visited Beauport, a restored home in Gloucester, Massachusetts, whose American interiors were the work of the owner, the Boston architect Henry Davis Sleeper. Sleeper's rooms, even more than Webb's, were arranged with an eye to color and dramatic effect, and their harmonies made a strong and lasting impression. Du Pont's own eye had been finely tuned through years of observing bloom.

Almost immediately, he began acquiring furniture for his new summer home, Chestertown House, in Southampton, Long Island, planning its interiors along the same quasi-historical lines as Beauport. (Marian Coffin's design for the Chestertown House landscape was, by contrast, assertively abstract.) Among his first purchases were a walnut high case and a mantel embellished with a scene of the Battle of Lake Erie—according to the art historian Jay Cantor, both forecast du Pont's lifelong preference for pieces that were both beautiful and well documented. By the end of 1923, he had purchased an additional one hundred pieces of furniture. The following year, he acquired seven hundred, and the next, twelve hundred. According to du Pont's own calculation, Chestertown House came to include three times as many pieces as the American collection at the Metropolitan Museum of Art.[40]

Du Pont was not alone in his enthusiasm. The fervor for American antiques—a relatively new subject for serious art collectors—swept the country in the years immediately following World War I. As had been the case in the years immediately following the nation's centennial, the simplicity of Colonial forms was praised over the "decadence" of Victoriana, and the earlier period came to symbolize ethnic purity and moral superiority.[41] The phenomenon gained momentum as multitudes of European immigrants flooded the United States in the 1920s, and, in the minds of many Americans, threatened the cultural status quo. Widespread collecting among the wealthy was furthered by several institutional initiatives. The *Magazine Antiques*, founded in 1922, brought the craze to national attention and vastly expanded the customer base for new dealers. The new American Wing of the Metropolitan Museum, which opened in 1924, further sanctioned the endeavor for well-to-do connoisseurs.[42]

The appeal of Americana also reached the middle classes. In 1926 the Reverend W. A. R. Goodwin convinced John D. Rockefeller Jr. to underwrite the rescue of Colonial Williamsburg, and eventually large numbers of visitors were touring the creatively restored buildings and grounds of that Colonial-era village. During these same years, Henry Ford began amassing the collection of American objects and buildings that he would later display under the auspices of the Henry Ford Museum and Greenfield Village.

A concern with enshrining American values and traditions underlay all of this activity, and du Pont was no doubt inspired by this sentiment as well as by his own aesthetic preoccupations. By 1927 he had begun to explore the idea of turning Chestertown House into a museum that would be open to the public, and he went so far as to draft a prospectus for the operation. He changed his mind, though, and soon refocused his collecting passion on new rooms he began to imagine at Winterthur. When du Pont's father died on the last day of 1926, Harry had already collected a great many of these, taken from their original locations, and he was ready to install them.[43]

Du Pont wrote to Coffin in May to tell her about the large wing he was about to build to accommodate his purchases—it would more than double the size of the mansion—and to enlist her services for changes to the landscape associated with it. He told her that he wanted to "rearrange the grounds at the back . . . entirely."[44] Du Pont's oversight of the ambitious house and landscape revision would be characteristically thorough, chronicled in densely detailed letters that ran to several pages each, writ-

9.16. House, from northwest, c. 1880. Winterthur Archives.

9.17. House reconstruction, from northwest, 1930. Winterthur Archives.

9.18. House after reconstruction, from northwest. Photograph by Samuel Gottscho. Winterthur Archives.

9.19. Aerial view of house and formal garden from southeast, after reconstruction. Winterthur Archives.

ten on an almost daily basis over the course of the three-year building campaign.

The house renovation was massive. Du Pont decided to rotate the existing structure's orientation ninety degrees (from north to west), relocating the front entry and transforming the old porte cochere into a conservatory. (Figs. 9.16, 9.17) Each room in the new nine-story wing was to have windows on the outside wall to provide views to the surrounding lawns and gardens. (Ruth's and Harry's bed-

room suites were located on the seventh floor, Ruth's on the west, Harry's on the east; their daughters, Pauline Louise, born in 1918, and Ruth Ellen, in 1922, also had bedrooms on this floor.) Existing trees were to be saved, whenever possible. These stipulations resulted in an oddly narrow and very tall structure, designed by the Wilmington-based architect Albert Ely Ives. Coffin, with assistance from her associate James Scheiner, was in charge of the landscape. One of her first recommendations was to lay out a new approach drive to give visitors a view of the tall wing as they neared the house. She would soon plan a forecourt large enough to accommodate the Garden Club of America buses du Pont was already anticipating.

The style of the house was also redefined. Victorian ornamentation was stripped (as at Dumbarton Oaks) and, at the front, roof lines simplified; new dormers were added, their design based on an eighteenth-century house outside Philadelphia, Port Royal, from which interiors were also taken.[45] The design borrowed elements as well from Woodlands, a country place built in 1788 for William Hamilton outside Philadelphia. Pilasters from the north front of Hamilton's house were adapted for use on Winterthur's new conservatory; great Tuscan columns, entablature, and pilasters based on models from the south facade at Woodlands appeared as part of the new three-story porch off Winterthur's dining room. The almost featureless public (west) facade was less interesting than the garden side of the house, where a conjunction of loggia, pavilions, and porches was crowned by a variety of roof lines, accentuated by tall chimneys. (Figs. 9.18, 9.19)

Coffin's charge would be to integrate several aspects of the landscape—the 1902 formal garden, important views to the southeast, and du Pont's woodland plantings—with several new elements, including the redesigned house. Not since her work at Delaware College had she faced a design proposition with so many contingencies. The Long Island commissions that filled her practice during the 1920s had taken place on largely undeveloped sites, a circumstance that gave her imagination comparatively free rein. At Winterthur, her design would require deft and complex responses in order to relate it to the new architectural forms, already magnificent plantings, and surrounding views. After studying Coffin's plan, du Pont approved it in December 1928.[46] Construction began the following year and, by 1930, plants were going in.

The primary architectural elements of Coffin's scheme were a large house terrace, a grand staircase, and a swimming pool at the base, flanked by twin pavilions. (Fig. 9.20) Coffin sited these new elements in relation to the lines of the house architecture, according to Italianate principles (the axis of the staircase, for example, aligned with that of du Pont's bedroom), and through the addition of terraces, paths, gardens, and water features defined several garden rooms, in the Italian tradition. The new features took their architectural cues from both the house and the old garden, and they served to connect the two. (Figs. 9.21, 9.22)

As an ingenious cross axis to the major line of development, Coffin designed an American-inspired passage— a waterfall, stream, and two pools planted with more than forty species of herbaceous plants and shrubs. The waterfall was constructed of one hundred

tons of imported limestone, made to look like a natural spring emerging from the steep escarpment. (Fig. 9.23) Water, used naturalistically in these features, and formally in the fountain on the stair descent and new swimming pool, provided the landscape with an enlivening theme. The cross axis where the two stylistic treatments met

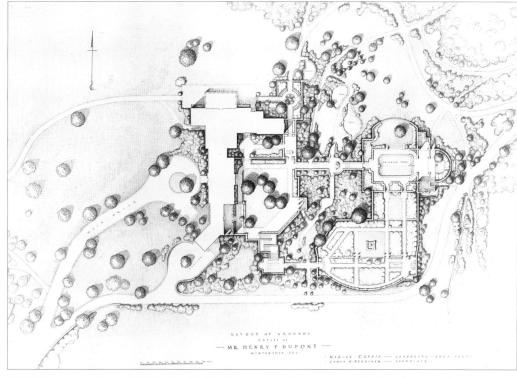

9.20. "Layout of Grounds," Marian Coffin, landscape architect, James. M. Scheiner, architect. Winterthur Archives.

9.21. Construction of swimming pool, view west to house, 1930. Winterthur Archives.

9.22. View to swimming pool, 1932. Photograph by Gottscho-Schleisner, Inc. Winterthur Archives.

9.24. View from steps to fountain and house under construction. Winterthur Archives.

9.26. Garden house on east terrace, view toward Oak Hill. Photograph by Samuel Gottscho. Winterthur Archives.

effectively integrated them, bringing the wildness of the woods into the heart of the formal plan.

Coffin incorporated large, existing trees into the design of the terrace and staircase, and she planted boxwood (*Buxus sempervirens* 'Suffruticosa') in abundance to structure subsidiary garden spaces and to border the steps. The boxwood eventually grew to great cushions of green that merged into cloudlike forms.[47] In the area between the staircase and the formal garden, to the southeast, she mixed small trees, conifers, shrubs, and herbaceous plants to give the impression of an idealized meadow. Along the staircase she added vines of akebia, pink *Clematis montana*, and English ivy, which came to soften the bold architectural elements. The view down the steps emphasizes the geometry of the staircase and its satisfying conclusion in the rectangular plane of the pool, backed by a semicircular retaining wall. The view from below, up through tall trees, strikes a deeper imaginative chord. From here, the lush cloak of foliage reaches from the ground up through the tops of the leafy canopies. The house is barely visible through branches of the trees that grow in close proximity to it. (Figs. 9.24, 9.25)

The most dynamic of the outdoor spaces is the house terrace itself, where giant tulip poplars, remnants of the old forest, rise from the lawn in defiance of conventional

9.27. View north to house and terrace. Photograph by Samuel Gottscho. Winterthur Archives.

practices that placed domestic, garden-scale plantings near the house and relegated large trees to more distant locations. The wildness of the trees is exaggerated against the trim forms of lawn, garden house, and balustrade. The powerful trunks support a canopy of staggering height, a space of soaring impact. The terrace provided the loom-

FOLLOWING PAGES:
9.25. *Staircase to East Terrace,* 1999. Photograph by Carol Betsch.

9.28. *East Terrace,* 1999. Photograph by Carol Betsch.

9.23. *Overlook above Glade Garden,* 1999. Photograph by Carol Betsch.

9.30 Boxwood Scroll Garden, under construction, view north, c. 1930. Winterthur Archives.

9.31. Boxwood Scroll Garden, view south, 1932. Photograph by Gottscho-Schleisner, Inc. Winterthur Archives.

ing house with an architectural setting to match its scale and presence. (Figs. 9.26, 9.27, 9.28)

Coffin's classical forms reach into the surrounding woodland, too. On the banks of the long valley to the north, she created formal overlooks in the woods, platforms defined by balustrades similar to the one on the southern edge of the house terrace. (Fig. 9.29) These architecturally determined spaces contrast with the rolling landforms of the wooded valley and set up views through them. Curving paths and drives cut across the upper banks of these woods (one road, laid out generations before, makes a full circuit), moving in counterpoint to the linearity of the two powerful landscape vectors of staircase and stream.

Coffin designed several other features at Winterthur as part of the c. 1930 renovation. The Boxwood Scroll Garden, a small circular terrace at the northeast corner of the house, was developed to mark an intersection of major paths, one from the conservatory terrace and the other from the March Bank, the most prominent of the wild areas visible from the house. The beds were edged with low-growing box and filled with early tulips, begonias in summer, and species lilies in autumn. The trim precision of the circular space holds its own against the big trees and spread of lawn to the north. (As at Dumbarton Oaks, dummy forms had been employed to deter-

9.32. Iris garden, 1932. Photograph by Gottscho-Schleisner, Inc. Winterthur Archives.

mine the scale of the new garden's components.) (Figs. 9.30, 9.31)

West of the house, in view of Ruth's bedroom window, Coffin created a large garden of German iris planted in curving drifts unlike any borders of the time, their contours laid out in response to the undulating land as abstract streams of shimmering color.[48] (Fig. 9.32) Architectural elements in the new garden included paths and a summerhouse that du Pont purchased from Latimeria, a Colonial-era estate in Wilmington. Coffin's plant list also indicates

9.29. *Icewell Terrace,* 1999. Photograph by Carol Betsch.

9.33. Winterthur Farms, with Holsteins. Photograph by Strohmeyer. Winterthur Archives.

9.34. H. F. du Pont with Bess Burke Best, a prize bull from his Holstein herd. Winterthur Archives.

mixed shrub borders in the area. These were diverse and, according to a memo from September 1929, decided on the ground. Plants include mock orange and lilac, blue clematis, Scotch rose, *Perovskia*, and one climber, 'Dr. Van Fleet,' for the area near the summerhouse, *Kolkwitzia*, honeysuckle, and *Weigela*. During this same period, Coffin laid out the plan and plantings for a new croquet court, in the vicinity of the pinetum. Here, too, boxwood was used to determine spatial divisions and, as in the Boxwood Scroll Garden, Coffin's strong lines successfully held against the great trees and surrounding space.

In 1931 du Pont wrote to tell Coffin that the house was nearly finished, "every curtain material and chair material is settled upon and ordered . . . every color of paint has been selected, and every piece of furniture put in place." The grounds had also been completed with great speed. "Everyone thinks the grounds, walls, garden houses, planting, etc. a great success," he added. "I think you will get a lot of free advertising."[49] One of the first to receive an invitation to the newly finished house and grounds was Mabel Choate, whose interest in American antiques and gardens was well known to du Pont. She approved, and so did the hundreds of other visitors who came to see the redesigned house and garden. Later that year du Pont wrote

to Coffin, "Everyone who comes to the place is very keen about the terrace, etc. etc., and we have used it constantly ourselves. No one can believe that the house is just finished and the planting just put in."[50]

Over the 1930s, Winterthur grew to cover more than 2,200 acres of rolling farmland. The estate also included a ten-hole golf course, post office, railroad station, employee housing, clubhouse with theater, blacksmith, carpenter and butcher shops, and laundry, supporting two hundred and fifty workers, most of them at Winterthur Farms, which du Pont managed in the paternalistic tradition of Biltmore. Du Pont's farming and animal husbandry skills were prodigious, and he was relentlessly seeking to improve his techniques. The Winterthur Holsteins set new records for milk production, reaching over one thousand pounds apiece per month.[51] Cows grazing in wide meadows, fertile fields, and handsome farm buildings were vital components of the scenery, and views throughout the garden took in this rural grandeur. (Figs. 9.33, 9.34, 9.35) Beyond his singular achievements as horticulturist, connoisseur, collector, and farmer, du Pont also possessed the administrative acumen to run four separate households simultaneously.

The family moved with the seasons—spring in the Brandywine River valley, summer in Southampton, fall weekends in New York, and winter in Florida. The du

9.35. *Fireflies in Old Meadow, Midnight,* 1990. Photograph by Carol Betsch.

Ponts were also often in Washington, D.C., socializing in a circle that also included Robert and Mildred Bliss. In New York, Harry and Ruth sometimes saw Mabel Choate, who maintained a house there, and they also met up with Marian Coffin, who had an apartment and office on Lexington Avenue. Both Coffin and Ruth du Pont were members of the Colony Club, one of the city's most prestigious private establishments for women.[52] Despite these connections, Ruth and Marian did not enjoy a particularly warm friendship. Ruth was a deeply traditional wife and mother, and the freedom with which Coffin conducted her life seemed both to alarm and to intrigue her. On one occasion she wrote in mixed admiration, "she may not be everything *morally* but she sure has the eye and the ability."[53]

Coffin was a frequent visitor to Winterthur through the 1930s, and affectionate letters between her and du Pont chronicle shared interests, travel, and a persistent preoccupation with plants. "I was so sorry you could not arrange to stop here on your way North as it was a perfect weekend," he wrote one February, continuing in typical horticultural detail, "the terrace was abloom with Jasminum Nudiflorum, two large Hamamelis Mollis, numerous Snowdrops, big patches of Adonis Amurensis,

9.36. North edge of pinetum, 1932. Photograph by Gottscho-Schleisner, Inc. Winterthur Archives.

some yellow Crocus, and the sweet scented Lonicera Fragrantissima."[54] The two gardening friends appreciated middlebrow culture too. Du Pont wrote in April 1932 about a new play by Janet Beecher and lunch at Winterthur with a young actress friend of hers, an "awfully attractive little girl" named Jane Wyatt, whom he enjoyed showing around. Then he added, "Did you see the hemlocks and the elm tree in the meadow near the service entrance and did you like them?"[55]

There is no doubt that Coffin continued to exert a strong impact on the evolving landscape of Winterthur, as both a friend and a paid professional. She visited frequently and, according to du Pont's letters, was expected to give advice. For example, "In a moment of folly the other day," he wrote to her on February 16, 1931, "I invested in three enormous magnolias. . . . I should like to have you tell me where I am to put them. They are beautiful trees and I could not resist them." Five days later, he returned to the subject. "I wish . . . that when you are here you would spend a great deal of time with Humphries and stamp about and see just where those three magnolias must go. . . . Also do you think it would be a good idea to have a thick planting of Abelias on each side of the stone walk going from the driveway to the garden gate? . . . Also cast your eye on the layout I have made for the Azaleas on the edge of the lawn where we moved out the big hemlock, and if you do not like the contour, change it."[56] (Fig. 9.36)

Du Pont was also interested in furthering Coffin's reputation. He publicly credited her contributions to Winterthur's design on several occasions, and he also supported her in the competitive jostling for wealthy clients throughout her career. Once he wrote to her gleefully about a new garden room in Mrs. (Frances) Randal Morgan's Chestnut Hill, Pennsylvania, home, where Coffin had earlier done work. "Someone said she had a little pool in the middle of it and that almost everybody fell into it. I trust the latter was not designed by Miss M. C. C."[57] (In fact, Fletcher

Steele had designed the fantastical pool and room, whose corners were filled with glass cases of white orchids, illuminated by Lucite rods.)

During the Depression, even du Pont felt the impact of the economic decline. After one visit, Coffin declined payment for her professional time, telling du Pont to consider her advice "love taps to Winterthur." (He had written to Coffin three months before to ask her if any of her other clients were buying plants, offering spider lily bulbs for $12 per 100 and amaryllis at $8 per dozen.[58]) She was enthusiastic about some primroses she had just seen in the garden of another client, "the Munsteads, Blue . . . and Gold laced as well as Cashmerianium, all Sutton seeds," and encouraged du Pont to try some at Winterthur, as a low-cost alternative to shrubs and trees. She also, in this same letter, expressed her thanks for this work. "You have been such an extraordinarily understanding client and have given me such a marvelous opportunity to help in creating the new development of the grounds that I can never be grateful enough."[59]

As World War II broke out in Europe, further developments in the gardens of Winterthur were curtailed, and Coffin's liberal sympathies with Roosevelt's New Deal took precedence over garden news in the letters that passed between them. In 1940 du Pont, a staunch Republican, wrote to her in frustration, "I cannot but feel that if the President is reelected for a third term, this country will have gone under forever," but he signed the letter "your old friend." As the impact of the world war intensified, Coffin looked to Winterthur as a source of reassurance and a refuge. "These days I know that I for one absolutely require beauty to keep going at all and Winterthur both inside and out is so entirely soul satisfying that I feel that seeing it has given me an uplift for days to come."[60] The exchange of gifts, news, and affection continued.

In the years after the war, the du Ponts moved from the main house to a smaller residence they had built on the grounds, and there, too, they turned to Coffin for a design.[61] The estate's transition from private home to public museum had been anticipated for many years, and it occurred much as it had been planned. In 1955 du Pont contacted Coffin, then seventy-nine years old, about creating still one more garden for Winterthur, a transformation of the old tennis court into a shrub garden that would offer growing crowds of visitors extended spring display. "This is a permanent planting," he instructed, "not for immediate effect."[62]

She responded with a bold design, a marriage of a concise, geometric plan with painterly blooms of kerria, quince, spiraea, viburnum, lilac, and pearlbush in great cushions and sprays.[63] (Fig. 9.37) Coffin's classical format brought order to the intricate, rapidly changing display. Her ability to compose at a large scale and to articulate architectural line and form through plantings had guided the design. In her 1940 book, *Trees and Shrubs for Landscape Effects*, she described the complexity of the undertaking and her sense of the importance of relating the design to the landscape setting.

In architecture the plan and the elevation are so interrelated, that in a well-thought-out scheme it is

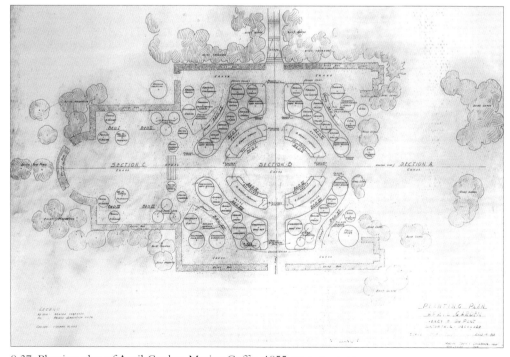

9.37. Planting plan of April Garden, Marian Coffin, 1955. Winterthur Archives.

impossible to imagine any separation of the parts. A good landscape plan, like a good architectural plan, should also be expressed in its elevation, but besides this, many intangible elements go into making or marring the success of its application. It must be, or seem to be, primarily a part of its surroundings, and the beauty which lies beyond must be brought into the picture. The landscape designer should not only have the architect's sense of form and line but also the artist's perception of color and texture. He should be sensitive to the play of light and shadow on his composition, in order that the woody plants that he uses to express his elevation may appear to the best advantage. This elevation, after it is achieved, unlike the architect's is not static but is composed of living material, always growing and changing.[64]

By October, the plantings in the April Garden were complete. Du Pont had taken the lead in selecting species,

relying on Coffin's lines to guide the arrangement. "Never have I had a more satisfactory time at Winterthur than this last week," Coffin wrote to him, "getting all your attention about the planting, and seeing the garden so well laid out. . . . You are a wonder! The more I see of Winterthur the more I think so."[65]

The beauty of the April Garden is most vivid viewed from the meadow, looking west toward the Colonel's pinetum, where gothic spires of spruce, pine, and blue Atlas cedar have grown to commanding height. (Fig. 9.38) From this vantage point, the trees form an immense curtain of glaucous green and silvery blue, a backdrop to the embroidery of bloom that emerges each spring. Here, the genius of Marian Coffin is fully revealed—her capacity to plan in time and in three dimensions while responding to the "bigness, unity and simplicity" of nature. Many threads of experience, including two young friends' early wanderings through the Arnold Arboretum, are woven together in this garden, Coffin's last for Winterthur.

9.38. *April Garden and Pinetum,* 1999. Photograph by Carol Betsch.

TEN

JENS JENSEN

1860–1951

The landscaper belongs to the future. It is he who will weave the works of man and of the primitive into one harmonious whole, counteracting the scars made on mother earth through ignorance. He will oppose the enslaved thoughts of our machine age by singing with the freedom of . . . our poets of hills and valleys, of far-reaching plains, of intimate brooks, and of sea-going streams.

—Jens Jensen, *Siftings,* 1939

Jens Jensen was born near Dybbøl, in Slesvig, Denmark, on a prosperous farm near the North Sea. As a child, Jensen developed a keen awareness of the pleasures of nature—in this regard he resembled Warren Manning, born the same year in rural Massachusetts. Like Manning, Jensen often hiked with his father, taking in broad views over the countryside as he learned the names of the flowers that grew in the meadows. (Fig. 10.1) On his own, he spent long afternoons exploring the thick hedgerows that traced patterns on the land near his family's farm and later wrote of his sense of the sure balance between nature and culture dating to "the dawn of history."[1] Enlivened with ancient folk stories of the myster-

ies of the sea and lands across the fjord, Jensen experienced the awakening of a poetic imagination and a certain belief that Nature was the mother of all things, even Art.[2] (Fig. 10.2)

When Jensen was four, the German army invaded and annexed Slesvig, initiating a battle that resulted in the burning of his family's farm. The war soon ended with an accord known as the Peace of Vienna, but the attacking forces continued to occupy Holstein, Slesvig, and Lauenburg provinces, and Danish nationalism intensified in the face of the German presence. Folk schools, like the one Jensen attended at Vindig, assumed new importance as conduits of Danish culture. Curricula included Nordic folklore as well as the liberal arts, conveyed through stories, songs, and dramatic presentations that celebrated the seasons. Classes were often held outdoors, sometimes around a blazing fire. In these teachings, writes Jensen's biographer Robert E. Grese, "soil was viewed as the source of all life."[3]

After Jensen completed his folk school studies, he enrolled in Tune Agricultural School outside Copenhagen, where he received training in botany, chemistry, and soil analysis, all of which continued to emphasize the funda-

10.1. Jens Jensen standing beside the Dunes Memorial Fountain (his own design), Indiana Dunes State Park. Courtesy Prairie Club Archives, Westchester Township History Museum, Chesterton, Ind.

mental importance of land. After graduating, he was required to join the German army and, because of his height—over six feet—was made a member of the Imperial Guard. In Berlin, Jensen saw expansive urban parks by Baron Georges-Eugène Haussmann under construction, and he came to associate their vast plazas and arrow-straight avenues with imperialism and autocracy. He also saw new English-style parks, which he deemed more in keeping with the needs of the lower classes. His most vivid memory of Germany was of a meadow, "full of sweet grasses and multitudes of flowers," where he picnicked with friends and discovered a sense of freedom through the camaraderie. He traced the beginnings of his professional life to this experience.[4]

After completing his military service, Jensen became engaged to Anne Marie Hansen, a young woman of the cottager class. His parents, who were landed gentry, disapproved of the match, and in 1884 the couple eloped to the United States, living first in Florida and then in Iowa, where Jensen found agricultural work.[5] They eventually settled in Chicago, a center of economic activity where many other Nordic immigrants were also establishing new homes. The Jensens lived near Humboldt Park, where Swedes, Norwegians, and Danes often met, to picnic and to listen to band music. "From the very beginning of his life in Chicago," the historian and landscape architect Leonard K. Eaton notes, "Jensen was identified with the parks."[6] Jens and Anne Marie became intimately acquainted with the surrounding countryside, too.

From Chicago the Jensens sometimes boarded the train and rode it to its last stops, where they could take long walks through undeveloped land. They explored the bluffs along Lake Michigan and the bogs of northern Illinois, and discovered the giant oaks and wild roses of the prairie.[7] (Fig. 10.3) Jensen was both inspired and comforted by the broad and mysterious prairie landscape, whose expanse recalled the sea of his childhood.[8] Through these trips, he forged a deep attachment to the

10.2. View from the backyard of the Jensen family farm, with the Dybbøl mill in the background. Bentley.

American countryside and a commitment to preserving it that would inform his entire professional life.

In 1886 Jensen got a job as a street sweeper for the West Parks District, and during winters in these lean years he also worked part-time for Swain Nelson, a Swedish landscape gardener who did occasional jobs for the Chicago parks. At some point during the 1880s Jensen acquired responsibility for tending gardens in the parks and was, in time, permitted to "tinker" (in Grese's word) with a corner of Union Park, whose popularity had ebbed after a zoo was moved from it.[9] There Jensen created the American Garden, using collected wildflowers set against native trees and shrubs. The new feature drew approving crowds.

In an interview published years later in the *Saturday Evening Post*, Jensen claimed that the American Garden was "the first natural garden in Chicago," but this was not quite accurate. Although nurseries did not yet stock them, native plants were held in high regard by many Chicagoans, and educating the public about them had become something of a municipal goal. In 1888 city commissioners ordered Garfield (formerly Central) Park planted with every kind of tree that grew in the region—oak, elm, maple, basswood, wild cherry, and several nut-bearing species—labeled with their scientific names, "to familiarize the public with the names of trees, shrubs, and vines growing wild in this climate."[10] There were other examples of native and naturalistic plantings in Chicago as well.

The most heavily visited of these was Graceland Cemetery, laid out by William Saunders in the early 1870s, with additional work by H. W. S. Cleveland and William Le Baron Jenney, and extensive plantings by Ossian Cole Simonds, who became superintendent there in 1881.[11] (Fig. 10.4) Simonds had been encouraged in his initial efforts by the Chicago philanthropist Bryan Lathrop to create passages that emulated naturally occurring plant groupings evoking the Illinois countryside. The cemetery's native plants, pastoral meadows, and tree-bordered lake drew praise from visitors still more accustomed to American burying grounds dominated by large monuments. (Graceland drew international praise too. The

10.3. Limestone bluffs of the Rock River, Illinois. Photograph by Jens Jensen. Courtesy Jensen Collection, The Sterling Morton Library, The Morton Arboretum, Lisle, Ill.

10.4 Lake Hazelmere, Graceland Cemetery, designed by O. C. Simonds. Courtesy Landscape Architecture Program, School of Natural Resources, University of Michigan, Ann Arbor.

cemetery was awarded a Silver Medal at the Paris Exposition of 1900, the same year Jensen established his private practice in Chicago.[12]) Simonds also created dozens of residential designs in the region—twenty-seven in Winnetka, Illinois, alone—relying on a nature-based method of design.[13]

After his work at Graceland, H. W. S. Cleveland, who was also based in Chicago, continued to promote other applications of what has been identified as an "organic"

10.5. Henry Babson house, Riverside, Ill. Harvard GSD.

approach to design. Cleveland had moved to the city in 1869 and over the next five years laid out the Lake Forest suburb of Highland Park, utilizing the principle of relying on existing plants and scenery to guide design. (His partner in the venture was William M. R. French, brother of the famous sculptor and later the first director of the Art Institute of Chicago.) The 1,200-acre development was sited in the wooded ravines above Lake Michigan, where it responded to the rugged topography and views out to the lake below. Cleveland had also been commissioned for design work in Washington Park, where he introduced many hardy, common plants.

Jensen undoubtedly knew these projects, and he may have known Cleveland's 1869 pamphlet, *The Public Grounds of Chicago: How to Give Them Character and Expression*, which promoted conservation as well as a nature-based treatment of landscape, and an 1870 article for *Atlantic Monthly*, in which Cleveland addressed the problems, and great potential, presented by the influx of people and capital to the Middle West. His *Landscape Architecture, as Applied to the Wants of the West*, published four years later, offered a more comprehensive description of his approach, which could be applied at every scale, from the backyard garden to parks and park systems. This book, too, would have been available to Jensen.[14]

Jensen was also likely familiar with the region's landscapes designed by Olmsted & Vaux. Riverside, the northern commuter suburb linked to the city by rail, was designed by the partners in 1868. The contiguous landscape featured pastoral scenery and provided large lawns, parks, and open space along the Des Plaines River. (Jensen would create two important residential designs at Riverside in 1909, for Henry Babson, whose house was designed by Louis Sullivan, and for Avery Coonley, where Frank Lloyd Wright was the architect. [Fig. 10.5])

The Olmsted firm had also created a plan for Jackson Park with a 165-acre lagoon, years before the design was realized as part of the World's Columbian Exposition of 1893. "The thing is to make it appear that we *found* this body of water and its shores," Olmsted had explained during his work on the exposition, "and have done nothing to them except at the landings and bridges. They were rich, rank, luxurious, crowded with vegetation, like the banks of some tropical rivers that I have seen on Louisiana bayous."[15] Tropical richness—a quality that Olmsted once described as the "profuse careless utterance of Nature"—informed his approach to planting design generally. It is clear that Olmsted saw no disjunction between his desire to heighten the impact of existing scenery and his attachment to the genius loci. As his plantings for the exposition showed, he believed that lushness could amplify even the restrained scenery of the American prairie. The Olmsted scholar Charles E. Beveridge goes so far as to identify Olmsted's plantings for the Chicago fair as "the first fully realized demonstrations of the prairie-river landscape that became such an icon for the prairie landscape school of the Midwest in the following years."[16] The teeming plantings on the Wooded Island, in particular, may have left an impression on Jensen; the park and private landscapes he designed after this time closely resembled them.

Jensen's developing views about nature-based landscape design and its potential for improving the lives of American citizens also closely accorded with the goals underlying Olmsted's park work: pure air, "pleasant openings and outlooks," and "distance from the jar, noise, confusion, and bustle of commercial thoroughfares," as Olmsted had described it.[17] Like Olmsted, Jensen considered "play . . . at all times subservient" to the more passive pleasures of enjoying scenery. In his view, park users, most of them physical laborers, were very active during the course of their workday, but they lacked mental stimulation. "They need the out of doors," Jensen wrote, "as expressed in beauty and art and a broader interest in life. They need the quietude of the pastoral meadow and the soothing green of grove and woodland in contrast with the noise and the glare of the great city."[18] Again, like Olmsted, Jensen would make little distinction between his goals for his parks and residential projects. Beyond their function as refuges from urban life, his gardens also served as preserves for native plants and vehicles for teaching owners to appreciate local landscapes so that they might conserve them.

Jensen may have been familiar with the work Warren Manning was doing for Cyrus and Harriet McCormick in the 1890s. Manning's design for Walden, one of his most extensive wild gardens, was the topic of lectures by Harriet McCormick as early as 1903. There is no question that the McCormicks knew Jensen, as they later supported his efforts to preserve the area's high lake bluffs. Jensen also knew Manning, although the date of their first meeting is not recorded. In 1929 Manning spoke publicly in admiration of Jensen's conservation initiatives, which corresponded closely to his own.[19]

Like his Boston-based colleague, Jensen was strongly critical of the Beaux-Arts approach to city planning that had gained traction in Chicago in the wake of the 1893 exposition. He wrote disdainfully of Burnham & Bennett's 1909 plan for Chicago, which he found "distinctly imperialistic" and "destructive to the morals of its people."[20] Jensen believed that planners should look to the home as the vital basic unit of organization rather than focus on the formal public spaces that were a hallmark of the Beaux-Arts method. His 1911 article "Regulating City Building" offers a forceful critique: "On the face of it, this idea of city planning is a fine thing—broad boulevards, ornate arches, formal promenades, all give one a feeling of excitement, as of being dressed in one's best clothes for

some festive occasion. But right here is one of the most salient evils of such a city. It is too often a show city; it is at once the city of palaces and of box-like houses where humanity is packed together like cattle in railroad cars. To build civic centers and magnificent boulevards, leaving the greatest part of the city in filth and squalor, is to tell an untruth, to put on a false front."[21]

Despite his strong antipathy toward this aspect of the City Beautiful movement, Jensen (again, like Manning) was clearly invigorated by the spirit of progress that had taken hold in Chicago at the turn of the century as a result of several factors, including the success of the 1893 Columbian Exposition. Jensen's progressive social ideas had been influenced by many reform-minded Chicagoans, several of whom taught at the University of Chicago. One of the most outspoken of these was the economist Thorstein Veblen, who came to teach at the university in 1892 and seven years later wrote *The Theory of the Leisure Class*, a provocative and widely discussed social commentary. In precise, sardonic prose, Veblen inveighed against the greed and pretentiousness of America's new ruling class, piercing the veil of custom with an incisiveness made possible by his outsider's perspective. (Although he was born in Iowa, Veblen's parents were Norwegian immigrants who maintained strong cultural traditions, and his family associated almost exclusively with other immigrants. Like Jensen, he too was reared with stories from Nordic myths.) Jensen would issue similarly passionate diatribes against pretension and wealth and the elaborate show gardens that were often the consequence.

The social activist Jane Addams—who maintained close ties to Manning's clients the McCormicks—had a forceful impact on Jensen's developing ideas as well. Addams's Hull House, founded in 1889, provided housing for immigrants and was also a center for arts and crafts classes and dramatic presentations by residents who performed in native languages, presentations that would have reminded Jensen of those in his youth. He soon began to include facilities for similar pageantry in his parks, and some of the features associated with storytelling, notably council rings (stone circles bordering fire pits) and players' greens, would also find their way into his private gardens. The settlement house program also spurred Jensen's ideas about the importance of providing facilities for urban recreation.[22]

Jensen's interest in studying plant associations was strongly influenced by Henry C. Cowles, also of the University of Chicago, a botanist and author of "The Ecological Relations of the Vegetation on the Sand Dunes of Lake Michigan."[23] Together Jensen and Cowles hiked across dunes, prairie, woods, and wetlands in Illinois and Indiana to observe plant communities firsthand. Cowles's notions about "plant sociology" helped shape Jensen's views on the functional and aesthetic advantages of keeping "friends" together. Jensen also used these hikes to observe plants in transitional zones, particularly those between the prairie and forest edge, where one species gives way to another. His ability to create compelling compositions for such passages in his landscape designs grew out of these observational forays.

Jensen's ideas regarding plant ecology had also been influenced by German colleagues, many of whom were developing notions about a scientific basis for garden design. One of the most influential of these was Willy Lange, who developed the concept of "biological aesthetics." In Lange's view, the nature garden was to be designed solely according to the laws of nature—as the historians Gert Groening and Joachim Wolschke-Bulmahn noted ironically, "a place for a nearly religious presentation of nature, a place where nature was not only protected, but also might be worshipped."[24] Lange's ideas had a particularly strong impact on the Massachusetts Agricultural College professor Frank A. Waugh, who studied with him in Germany and wrote in admiration of his work. Waugh was also a staunch admirer of Jensen, whose garden designs he actively promoted.

Despite both men's attachment to the principle of plant sociology as a force in design, neither Waugh nor Jensen saw it as a basis for a political role for gardens—as would Heinrich Friedrich Wiepking-Jürgensmann, chairman for landscape design under Himmler and author of "The Greening of the New Town of Auschwitz," or Reinhold Tüxen, who supported "a war of extermination" against *Impatiens parviflora*, a small forest plant that he believed was endangering the purity of the German forest.[25] That said, Jensen later developed appalling ideas about the racial superiority of "northern" peoples. In one letter, he argued that the introduction of southern Europeans into the American workforce would reduce "vitality and intellect," an example of the same rabid nativism that had tainted Warren Manning's national planning efforts.[26]

10.6. Plan for Union Park, between 1888 and 1894. Courtesy Special Collections, Chicago Park District.

In 1895 Jensen was promoted to the position of superintendent of Union Park, and the following year he was named to the same post at Humboldt Park. (Fig. 10.6) But his rise through the park administration was abruptly halted five years later when he refused to accept a short order of coal and was fired for exposing the corruption. (Chicago was run by ward bosses whose power depended on the votes of immigrants, to whom they supplied jobs in exchange. The system depended on graft to function, and disrupting it took courage, as it almost certainly meant dismissal.) To support his family, which had come to include three daughters and a son, Jensen launched a private practice out of his home, drafting on his kitchen table. He was forty years old at the time.

Although he would turn increasingly to residential projects during the next few years, Jensen did not lose interest in the Chicago parks. The proceedings of the Sixth Annual Meeting of the American Park and Outdoor Art Association in 1902 record his tirade against "statuary of questionable art," "buildings of ugly and ill-fitting architecture," an elephant "whose sudden appearance to the timid and unwary park visitor may cause hysterical convulsions," and "floral designs of the most ridiculous and fantastic kinds." In Jensen's view, these conditions were "misleading the uneducated as to what a park should be—a place of natural scenery and sylvan beauty brought to his very doorstep in which his weary body and overworked nerves can find needed rest and comfort."[27] These goals were soon guiding design in his gardens too.

One of Jensen's earliest projects in private practice was a design for the grounds of St. Ann's Hospital in Chicago, which specialized in the care of tubercular patients. He wrote about the design in *Park and Cemetery* in 1901, emphasizing the area of the garden that was a "miniature park, with plenty of walks, pretty scenery, abundance of sunlight . . . which will have a healthy influence upon the sick."[28] The plan more resembled a gardenesque scheme than one of the understated naturalistic designs that would soon become typical of Jensen's work; it featured insistent loops along the path system, a spiral maze, lozenge-shaped flower bed, and exotic tree specimens. (Fig. 10.7) But the lagoon and its plantings hint at Jensen's future approach: he lists alder, arrowhead, cattails, dogwood, grasses, hawthorn, iris, cinquefoil, blackberry, rushes, tamarack, and viburnum.[29]

In 1903 Jensen began a small place for Harry Rubens, in Glencoe, Illinois, using stratified rock at the edge of a pool filled with native water lilies and edged with ferns and indigenous grasses.[30] (Fig. 10.8) At this juncture, he had several aspects of his signature "prairie" approach in

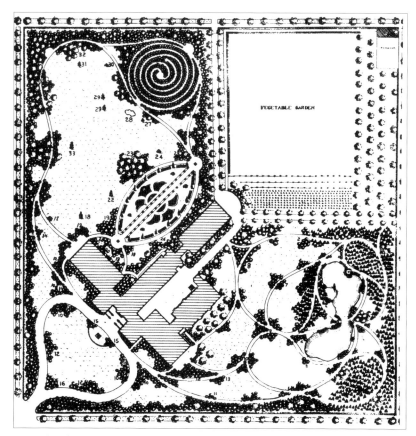

10.7. Plan for St. Ann's Hospital, Chicago. From *Park and Cemetery*, December 1901.

10.8. Harry Rubens estate, Glencoe, Ill. Photograph by Frank A. Waugh. Courtesy Special Collections, W. E. B. Du Bois Library, University of Massachusetts Amherst.

place.[31] The design reflects the pictorial as well as the horticultural underpinnings of his developing style, in which carefully composed landscape scenes played a pivotal role. (Jensen later remarked that many influences had shaped

10.9. Humboldt Park meadow, 1918. Courtesy Special Collections, Chicago Park District.

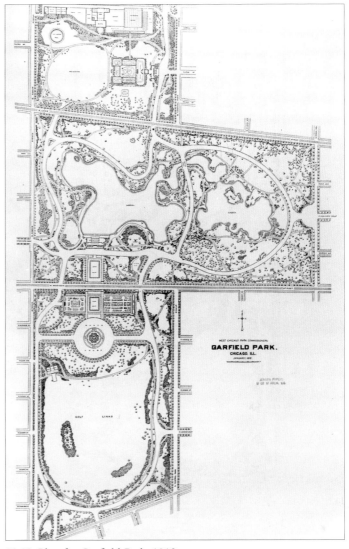

10.10. Plan for Garfield Park, 1912. Bentley.

the Rubens landscape composition, and alluded, rather mysteriously, to Franz Schubert's *Unfinished Symphony*.[32]) The lushly planted garden was published by Waugh in his 1910 book, *The Landscape Beautiful*, and five years later Wilhelm Miller featured it prominently in *The Prairie Spirit in Landscape Gardening*.[33]

In 1905 Jensen was re-hired as superintendent and landscape architect of the West Parks, and he turned his attention to reshaping areas of Humboldt, Garfield, and Douglas parks, which had been laid out by William Le Baron Jenney several years before.[34] (Figs. 10.9, 10.10) His work during the period was facilitated by the enlightened Parks Commission chairman, Bernard A. Eckhart (the very successful owner of B. A. Eckhart Milling Company and the director of several banks), who had hired him for the position. Over the next several years Jensen made improvements to these and to a number of small neighborhood parks which had a profound, transformative impact on the city.

During this period, Jensen also began his personal campaign to survey the land around Chicago for what would become the Cook Country Forest Preserve, one of his many significant conservation accomplishments. (Fig. 10.11) In 1909 he was forced, once again, to resign from his official position in the Chicago Parks—the result of

continuing conflict with corrupt political bosses—but this time he was retained as Consulting Landscape Architect, a job that also left him free to pursue private commissions. From this point on, Jensen worked in both the public and private sectors simultaneously.

Although he often expressed disdain for wealth and privilege, residential jobs for prominent citizens were adding social cachet to Jensen's reputation and his gardens were increasingly sought after by Chicago's fashion-minded elite. Like Manning, Jensen used these commissions to gain access to an expanding network of powerful businessmen and civic leaders who were not only building estates but developing and improving parks and preserving public lands as well.[35]

Among Jensen's most conservation-minded clients were Julius Rosenwald, chairman of the board of Sears, Roebuck and Company, and his wife, Augusta. The Rosenwalds generously supported Jensen's preservation initiatives and were charter members of the Friends of Our Native Landscape, of which Augusta also served as first vice president.[36] Jensen designed two residential landscapes for the couple, the first of which was in Chicago's Hyde Park. The project was chronicled by Miller in *Country Life in America*, illustrated by photographs of characteristically luxuriant plantings and a very tall Arts and Crafts–style birdhouse.[37] In 1911 Jensen began a design for the Rosenwalds' new home in Highland Park. Jensen's layout there was so spare that Julius reportedly did not see any design at all and playfully challenged him about the high fees he charged for the work.[38]

As Jensen's reputation grew, his client base expanded geographically. In 1911 he was working in Spring Station, Kentucky, on three large jobs, for W. E. Simms, E. F. Simms, and Kenneth D. Alexander. These projects involved extensive stonework meant to evoke the high bluffs bordering the Illinois, Rock, and Mississippi rivers and also featured artificial pools, falls, and, characteristically, rich plantings. (Fig. 10.12) Pictorial arrangements of these elements reflected the nineteenth-century sensibilities that would continue to guide Jensen's work.[39] His commissions at the time also included projects in Benton Harbor, Michigan; Indianapolis; Lake Geneva, Wisconsin; Decatur, Illinois; Kansas; Iowa; and even in few in California. Chicago and its environs, however, would provide the greatest concentration of clients over the course of his career.

As he came to rely more exclusively on native plants, Jensen began to refer to his approach as the "Prairie Style," linking it specifically to a midwestern plant palette—particularly hawthorns, crabs, and other horizon-

10.11. "Proposed System of Forest Parks and Country Pleasure Road[s]," Cook County, Ill., hand-drawn map, 1903. Bentley.

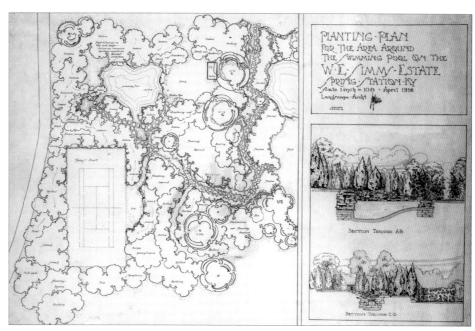

10.12. "Planting Plan for the Area Around the Swimming Pool," W. E. Simms estate, Spring Station, Ky., April 1916. Bentley.

tally branched trees—and to specific landscape forms, such as prairie rivers and stratified rock formations typical of the Midwest. (Fig. 10.13) His emerging prairie vocabulary and the stylistic approach that it represented were shaped in some measure by the harsh midwestern climate, but they also reflected the desire for a distinctive style that would set midwestern clients apart from Eurocentric Northeasterners.

10.13. Humboldt Park, prairie river. From Wilhelm Miller, *The Prairie Spirit in Landscape Gardening*, 1915.

The first reference in Jensen's writings to the native landscape as a source of design inspiration occurred in his 1906 essay "Landscape Art—An Inspiration from the Western Plains," his first published writing, which was illustrated with photographs of his seminal 1902–3 design for Harry Rubens, in Glencoe.[40] But Jensen does not appear to have used the specific word *prairie* in conjunction with his work before 1910, when he was quoted in Waugh's book *The Landscape Beautiful* as tracing his design inspiration to "the flat, level prairies." (According to Waugh, Jensen also cited the Zuni Indians as providing inspiration.[41]) The book featured several other projects by Jensen in addition to the Rubens garden, which Waugh praised as "original" and "novel," and "clear away from the formulas now familiar in America."[42] *The Landscape Beautiful* boosted Jensen's national reputation and likely brought him to the attention of Wilhelm Miller, who two years later began to promote Jensen's career with relentless enthusiasm.

Jensen's evocation of the prairie as a source for land-

scape design was actually predated by almost a full decade by Frank Lloyd Wright's "prairie house," which was featured in a 1901 *Ladies' Home Journal* article. Wright claimed a direct relationship between the prairie landscape and the architectural elements he used in this house: "gently sloping roofs, low proportions, quiet sky lines, suppressed heavy-set chimneys and sheltering overhangs, low terraces and out-reaching walls sequestering private gardens," elements that stressed horizontality, as Jensen's designs soon would.[43]

Robert Spencer, another Chicago architect with whom Jensen worked (and who, along with Jensen, Dwight Perkins, Myron Hunt, Wright, and others, maintained offices in Steinway Hall), had also drawn attention to the prairie connection in Wright's work, well before Jensen began referring to it.[44] In a 1900 article for *Architectural Review* Spencer wrote that Wright swung "easily along amid the beauties of the forests and flower-sown prairies of his own country." Continuing his vegetative metaphor, he emphasized the potential of regional, land-based expression to an emerging national style of architecture: "If we are to have a real basis for a great national architecture, our beautiful buildings must not be the forced fruits of an artificial civilization, but must be the natural bloom of a hardy native growth with its roots deep in the soil."[45]

George W. Maher, architect of the Rubens house, also saw the regional landscape as inspiration for a new American architecture. In his 1906 essay "The Western Spirit," Maher wrote, "Must it be said that the nature which surrounds us is unworthy of art expression? That the men and women we meet must admire the Greek leafage and flora and not the flower of our fields? Does nature around us ape that of the Greek or Goth? Is not our landscape beautiful, grand beyond expression?"[46] The historian Christopher Vernon points out that Jensen may have heard Maher deliver his essay as a lecture to the Chicago Architectural Club in March that year and taken away specific inspiration from it.[47]

The celebration of the term *prairie spirit* was most emphatically expressed in Miller's 1915 publication *The Prairie Spirit in Landscape Gardening*, which linked Jensen's work with that of O. C. Simonds, Warren H. Manning, and Walter Burley Griffin (although none of these other practitioners were as eager as Jensen to be associated with a regional style—Simonds believed that many of the features Miller was proclaiming as distinctively midwestern were equally appropriate for other regions of the country[48]). In the end, it is not surprising that midwestern clients found the prairie appealing, both visually and ideologically, and that an approach which emphasized a connection to it, however metaphorical, would emerge in both architecture and, somewhat later, landscape architecture. That Jensen followed the lead of his architectural colleagues made good sense—artistically, philosophically, and financially.[49]

Jensen's distinctive style was based on a combination of several signature elements sited with acute sensitivity to the lay of the land—the genius loci. These included prairie lagoons and rivers; striated rockwork; fire or council rings; flower lanes; small cascades and waterfalls that brought the sound of trickling water into the designed landscape, and meadows bordered by horizontally branched midsize trees, such as hawthorn and crab.[50] Most significant in Jensen's designs were the flowing meadows that structured their spatial organization; adapting this feature to a residential, even a backyard, scale became a cornerstone of his approach.

Jensen's childhood experience of walking through meadows near the sea, and later along the edge of the prairie, formed the basis of the prodigious spatial skill that enabled him to lay out meadows of great size and varying configurations with poetic conviction and to link them in such a way as to create series of dissolving pictures. In this remarkable ability, Jensen had no equal—arguably, not even Olmsted. Although Jensen's meadows did not literally resemble prairies—they more closely resembled the meadows in Olmsted & Vaux's urban parks—these features brought to his landscapes a calm reminiscent of the prairie, and, like the prairie, they opened expanses of the sky. The interaction between landscape and sky held philosophical as well as visual importance to Jensen, who encouraged his clients to observe the heavens as a reminder of nature's cycles. In Jensen's progressive worldview, as in Manning's, such experiences improved character.

Jensen's meadows fell into two categories, "broad" and "long" views.[51] Broad views borrowed techniques not only from Olmsted and Olmsted's English forebears, particularly Humphry Repton, but also from the German landscape gardener and author Prince Hermann Ludwig Heinrich von Pückler-Muskau, who had also relied on irregular masses to define open spaces at his great park, begun in 1816. Pückler created such spaces throughout the park's 1,350 acres, aiming for the "character of untrammeled Nature," a concept that reappears throughout his 1834 book, *Hints on Landscape Gardening.*

To establish viewing points that yielded a series of changing perspectives into his meadows, Jensen typically laid out approach roads and walkways around their perimeters. Smaller subsidiary spaces, which O. C. Simonds identified as "sylvan living rooms," offered a sense of enclosure and discovery. These areas were sited adjacent to the main meadow or linked to one another in such a way as to encourage movement. Long views were narrow, sinuous openings that terminated in "a hazy ridge or misty piece of the woods" (according to a description by Miller), vistas that evoked a feeling of limitlessness.[52] As focal points in the long views Jensen selected plants that would catch the low-angled rays of the setting or rising sun to dramatic effect—goldenrod, for example, or sugar maple.

Jensen rarely indicated the exact location of individual plants on his plans but, rather, demarcated intricately shaped masses of single types. He preferred to supervise the placement of plants on the ground or leave it to trusted foremen, such as Alfred Caldwell, who worked for him between 1917 and 1932. Toward the end of his life, Jensen forewent plans and simply indicated where plants should be located as he walked through the landscape. After analyzing individual sites carefully, he planted accord-

10.14. House and power house, Fair Lane, estate of Henry Ford, Dearborn, Mich. The Henry Ford.

10.15. Dam and rockwork along Rouge River, Fair Lane. Photograph by Robert E. Grese.

ing to existing conditions, often adding large native trees to bolster the dominant framework.

Although Jensen utilized a wide range of plants, he turned to hawthorn more often than any other small tree, using it to establish a midstory layer, typically in combination with alternate-leaf dogwood, prairie crabapple, sumac, and American plum, all of which provide glowing

fall color. In the South, he also included redbud and flowering dogwood. To Jensen, these trees symbolized the prairie—their branching structure recalling the open horizon, and their rounded tops, the rolling land. Stratified-branching trees also provided a visual transition to larger trees in woodland borders, such as oaks and maples, and helped to guide rather than interrupt views down the open turf of meadow. Jensen scattered small trees inside the meadow space as they might have sown themselves, reiterating patterns he had observed in the wild.

Jensen was more emphatic in his preference for native plants than any of his contemporaries, and this tendency grew over the course of his long career. However, it was not absolute.[53] Admiring lilac, hollyhock, rose, daylily, and other species that had acquired strong cultural associations through long use, he continued to include them in his designs, often near the house. Alfred Caldwell noted that nurserymen were eager to work with Jensen because he planted in such great variety and quantity.[54]

In 1914 Jensen was contacted by the automotive entrepreneur Henry Ford to consult on the siting of Ford's new mansion, Fair Lane, then under construction outside Dearborn, Michigan, because the structure appeared to be sliding downhill.[55] Ford was impressed by Jensen's deft solution to the problem, which involved regrading the site, and he soon offered him the job of creating a new landscape layout for the 3,000-acre estate. Jensen at first refused, anticipating conflict—presciently, as it turned out—but he could not resist the challenge the big job presented. It would be one of his most extensive private commissions and, at the height of development, the largest private landscape project then under way in the United States.[56]

Jensen's design included extensive striated rockwork along the Rouge River, which heightened the impact of the river, and a dam that powered a hydroelectric plant, which Ford designed himself. (Figs. 10.14, 10.15) Along either side of the river, Jensen laid out large meadows and planted them in compositions evoking aspects of the native landscape. He made extensive use of outdoor living

10.16. Fair Lane, peony garden. The Henry Ford.

10.18. Fair Lane meadow with rose garden by Kellaway and Foote, aerial view. The Henry Ford.

10.17. Fair Lane, view toward river from gardens. The Henry Ford.

rooms, set adjacent to the meadows, planting them with the same shrubs and wildflowers that grow at the woodland edge. (Figs. 10.16, 10.17)

Jensen later claimed that his goal in the project had been to put "the land back to what it was when the American Indians skied down the banks of the River Rouge."[57] The statement was completely disingenuous—

all of Jensen's landscapes were highly idealized compositions—but it did accurately represent his intention to preserve a feeling of the history of the site and Ford's own country roots, which had become increasingly important to the wealthy industrialist. Native shrubs and trees and bird-houses throughout provided habitat for the species Henry and Clara loved.[58]

The course of the project was stormy, and Jensen reportedly resigned from it three times. His work on the commission ended after an intense disagreement with Clara Ford, who had never been happy with the small rose garden Jensen had provided and in 1925 brought in Herbert J. Kellaway and Harriet R. Foote to lay out an alternative, hiring Ellen Biddle Shipman to replant the first one with a mix of perennials and annuals.[59] If the size of the new feature accurately reflected Clara's pent-up frustrations with Jensen, they must have been extreme—it was 1,200 feet long, sited directly in the center of one of Jensen's primary meadows, where it completely dominated the design and essentially ruined a significant part of it.[60] (Fig. 10.18) Jensen's temper erupted in a long letter to Clara Ford, and he also wrote to the American Society of Landscape Architects, demanding that Kellaway be censured for interfering. When the ASLA refused, Jensen resigned in protest.

10.19. Jefferson Avenue garden of Edsel and Eleanor Ford, stepping stones and naturalistic garden, pool at right. The Henry Ford.

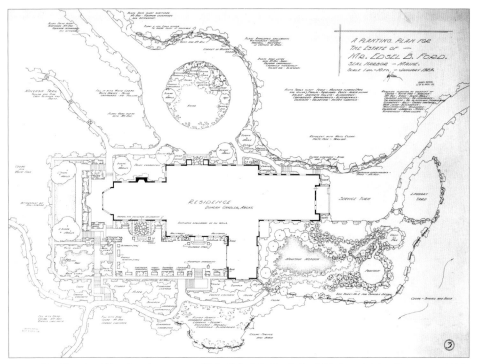

10.20. "A Planting Plan for the Estate of Mr. Edsel B. Ford, Seal Harbor–Maine," January 1925. Bentley.

Despite the intensity of the conflict, Jensen continued to work on several projects relating to the Ford Motor Company, including Henry Ford Hospital in Detroit, Greenfield Village, the Dearborn Inn, and the Rotunda. (The latter, designed by Walter Dorwin Teague, had been originally built for the 1933 Chicago Century of Progress Exposition; it was later relocated to Dearborn.) Jensen also worked on residential designs for several Ford executives.[61] Neither does the dispute seem to have had much effect on Jensen's relationship with Edsel Bryant Ford, Henry and Clara's son, who, by the time of the break, had become one of Jensen's most devoted clients. With his wife, Eleanor, Edsel hired the landscape architect for four separate residential commissions.

The long professional association began in 1920, the year after Edsel became president of Ford Motor Company, when Edsel and Eleanor (with their sons Benson and Henry II) moved from a house in the Detroit neighborhood of Indian Village to a new one on East Jefferson Avenue, where Jensen designed a new layout for it.[62] (Fig. 10.19) Jensen's plans record a narrow site reaching down to the Detroit River and a design incorporating many of his trademark features. The spatial core of his plan was a long meadow bounded on one side by a flower lane and on the other by a naturalistic swimming pool, playhouse, tennis courts, vegetable garden, and a council ring. Jensen's design also included intricate rockwork, spring-blooming trees, and an idealized cedar grove, planted to look as though the old meadow were returning to forest. Edsel's favorite feature was the swimming pool crafted of striated rock.

Two years later, the Fords commissioned Jensen to design a landscape for Skylands, as it was later known, their new summer home in Seal Harbor, Maine, where extensive rockwork and plantings blended with the shorefront location to fit into "the ruggedness and mystery" of the ancient cliffs.[63] Jensen successfully redesigned key elements in architect Duncan Candler's extensive terraces to allow more space for landscape features. The most important of these was a small "mountain meadow" laid out in view of the dining room windows, with a carpet of heather and a backing of largely native trees and shrubs, more than fifty species in all. Jensen designed a trickling waterfall and small rock-edged pool that added to the sense of calm, telling the Fords that it was the only really "restful place you will have, . . . in sharp contrast with the great out-of-doors all around you."[64] (Fig. 10.20)

The same year, 1922, Eleanor and Edsel bought 2,400 acres of land in Oakland County, Michigan, and Jensen worked there, too. Although Haven Hill, as the country estate was known, never had the high-style design that the Fords' other properties did, it became Edsel's preferred getaway—he called it his "nerve retreat," an indication of the stress that cast a pall over much of Edsel's adult life.[65]

The paths of Jensen and Edsel Ford crossed several times, too, during work on the Lincoln Highway, brainchild of the Indianapolis businessman Carl Fisher, who also sponsored the Indianapolis Speedway. Fisher began promoting the idea of a cross-country highway in 1912 because he believed that the future success of the automobile depended on good roads. Although Henry Ford declined to help with the venture (Ford wanted nothing to do with a scheme for a privately funded highway—he was adamant that the federal government should take the lead), Fisher was able to enlist the support of Henry B. Joy, president of the Packard Motor Company, and F. A. Seiberling, founder of Goodyear Rubber and Tire Company, whose stakes in good roads for America were obvious. Edsel was also an enthusiastic backer of the project and took great interest in the physical design of the road, arguing for grass shoulders and no curbs, to give the general appearance of a country road. Progress was slow, however, owing largely to conflicts about the proposed route.

By 1920, when O. C. Simonds published his major work, *Book of Landscape-Gardening*, roadside development and increasing numbers of

billboards had become a source of growing concern to him and many American landscape architects.[66] Because of his interest in the topic, Simonds was appointed as an adviser to the Lincoln Highway Association. In 1921 the

10.21 Pathway along "ideal section" of Lincoln Highway. Courtesy Transportation History Collection, Special Collections Library, University of Michigan, Ann Arbor.

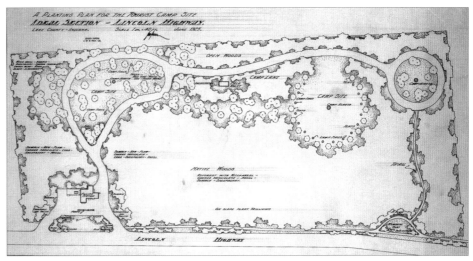

10.22. "A Planting Plan for the Tourist Camp Site, Ideal Section–Lincoln Highway," 1925. Bentley.

group selected a one-and-one-third-mile stretch between Schererville and Dyer, Indiana, which they designated an "ideal section," where they would demonstrate the latest innovations in lighting, paving, and planting design.[67] On Simonds's recommendation, Jensen was commissioned to plan the landscape for it. (Fig. 10.21)

Jensen followed the committee's advice to avoid "formal or regular planting" and instead to use "natural grouping[s] of native trees and shrubs to frame roadside views."[68] His plan added native grasses, wildflowers, and clusters of hawthorns to the existing plantings, and he laid out a hiking trail, sited to provide views into the woods. In 1925 he also designed a prototype rest area, comprising campsites, council ring, filling station, store, and restrooms. (Fig. 10.22) Edsel Ford offered $25,000 to fund construction of Jensen's model rest area, but when cost estimates for the feature almost tripled, Ford decided against pursuing it and it was never realized.

In 1926 Edsel and Eleanor turned to Jensen for one last residential project, a new estate in Grosse Pointe Shores, Michigan. The story of this landscape—Jensen's largest and, arguably, his finest work—is closely intertwined with Edsel's own strong aesthetic and, to some degree, the modern changes in American culture that were occurring in the wake of Henry's automobiles.

EDSEL AND ELEANOR FORD HOUSE

Grosse Pointe Shores, Michigan

In October 1908 the first advertisements for the Model T appeared in newspapers throughout the United States. The price was $850, roughly the equivalent of a school teacher's annual salary. Despite the high cost, almost a thousand inquiries arrived at Henry Ford's office the following day, and within a year, ten thousand of the cars had been sold. Owing to improvements in manufacturing efficiency, the price fell steadily, and soon the simple, dependable vehicle was within economic reach of the American middle class. By the time the Ford Motor Company stopped producing the model in 1927, 15 million Tin Lizzies had come off the assembly line, and Henry Ford was one of the richest men in the world.[1]

Money, however, had not been Ford's motivation for developing the Model T. A few years before unveiling it, he explained his goals: using honest materials, "the best workmen that money can hire," and "the simplest designs that modern engineering can devise." Ford's mission was to make a car so low in price that "the man of moderate means may own one and enjoy with his family the blessings of happy hours spent in God's great open spaces."[2] Most of these egalitarian aims were realized, with one ironic twist.

The automobile did make it easier to get to "God's great open spaces," but in the end it imperiled them, irrevocably altering the American landscape, transforming acres of green into acres of pavement, and changing how and where Americans lived, worked, and played. Ford's car and the rise in industrialization associated with it undermined the very agrarian values he so cherished. Ford was not blind to the change. In 1924 he told the journalist Drew Pearson, "The city has taught us much, but the overhead expense of living in such places is becoming unbearable."[3] Even as he continued the expansion of his automotive empire, Ford began to seek ways to counterbalance it. Certainly his work with Jensen at Fair Lane was born from this desire.

Four years later, and within one year of breaking ground for the River Rouge plant, the largest factory in the world, Ford had initiated another ambitious rural enterprise, the Ford Company village industries.[4] Between 1918 and 1944, Ford constructed nineteen small-scale decentralized factory enclaves within sixty miles of Dearborn headquarters. Nestled into pastoral river settings, the little plants were sited "in leafy bowers and surrounded with flowering shrubs, green bushes and trees, . . . spots,"

11.1. Ypsilanti, Michigan, Ford Motor Company Plant, Albert Kahn, 1936, the largest of Ford's Village Industries. The Henry Ford.

according to one Ford publicist, "you would select for a picnic."[5] (Fig. 11.1) Many of the village factories were integrated into actual historic structures that had been retrofitted to accommodate and disguise their industrial purposes. Nankin Mills, which opened on the Rouge River in 1922, for example, occupied an old gristmill.[6]

Life magazine described Ford's venture and the contradictions of the personality behind it: "Henry Ford would be less than the man he is if, walking by the River Rouge, he did not thrill at the sight of his huge plant growing huger and huger by the day. But the old man's dearest dream is no longer of piling building on building in metropolitan congestion. A farm boy who has kept his love of the land, Ford now visions the 'little factory in a meadow' as the future shape of American industry."[7] In fact, the village industries would embody precisely the opposite principle of the mammoth Rouge plant—the Jeffersonian ideal of decentralized production.

The fervid embrace of rural values that fueled Ford's village industries was also a force behind the collection of Americana which he began to amass during these same years.[8] In 1919 Ford had rescued his family's old farmhouse (ironically, from an impending road development) and had it moved. He restored every detail, down to his

mother's china, and was so satisfied with the result that he soon turned to saving other buildings. He also began collecting decorative, household, and industrial artifacts of every description—ploughs, cars, butter churns, cigar store Indians, scrubbing boards, furniture, milk bottles, spinning wheels (he had five hundred of these), and clocks, as well as machines and vehicles. Not one shred of aesthetic concern shaped this collection, which, in this regard, was almost the antithesis of H. F. du Pont's, although the two were similar in scale.

Ford's acquisitions soon filled several warehouses, and by the mid-1920s he had begun to plan a venue to exhibit them, in this regard also resembling du Pont. Ford's Edison Institute would not only showcase the objects but transmit the patriotic values inherent in the material accumulation. The venture was to have two components. Greenfield Village would feature the actual buildings associated with the men Ford most admired—Stephen Foster, Abraham Lincoln, Thomas Edison, Luther Burbank, and others less renowned (among them Ford's dentist)—transplanted and arranged around a New England–style green.[9] The Henry Ford Museum, located adjacent, would present objects in more traditional gallery settings, 350,000 square feet of exhibition space. The museum's facade was an architectural amalgamation of Philadelphia's Independence Hall, Congress Hall, and Old City Hall, designed by a Detroit architect, Robert O. Derrick. The two initiatives grew to dominate Ford's imagination and eventually consumed a substantial portion of his fortune.

The opening of Greenfield Village took place on October 21, 1929, a date chosen to commemorate the fiftieth anniversary of the invention of the incandescent light bulb. (Less propitiously, it fell exactly one week before the crash of the New York Stock Exchange.) Thomas Edison, age eighty-two, came to Dearborn to throw the switch that would illuminate the laboratory where he had created the bulb—which Ford had moved from Menlo Park, New Jersey. The guest list reflected Ford's stature as the most famous man in the world and the seriousness with which his venture was greeted. Among those present were President and Mrs. Herbert Hoover, John D. Rockefeller Jr., Orville Wright, J. P. Morgan, Will Rogers, George

Eastman, Marie Curie, Charles Schwab, Adolph Ochs, and Albert Einstein. Henry's son, Edsel, and Edsel's wife, Eleanor, however, did not attend. They were home in bed that night with the flu, quarantined from the historical pageant.[10]

Edsel Ford (1893–1943) was cut from very different cloth than his father.[11] (Fig. 11.2) Edsel loved the countryside, but he was not concerned about waning rural values in America or burgeoning factories. In fact, he regarded the modern factory as a beautiful object, a source of aesthetic stimulation. It was his idea, in 1927, to invite the artist Charles Sheeler to come to Detroit to photograph the River Rouge plant. (Fig. 11.3) And although he, too, sought time in nature, perhaps even more avidly than Henry, to Edsel rural America was less the urgent transmitter of Jeffersonian values than a source of respite and relaxation. In this regard, he was typical of his generation.

A talented automotive designer, Edsel was also an art patron and collector, aviator, philanthropist, photographer, and yachtsman.[12] With his wife Eleanor and their urbane, Gatsbyesque contemporaries, Edsel appreciated tennis, speed boats, jazz, and a highball at the end of the day. A passionate advocate of modern art and one of the first trustees of the Museum of Modern Art in New York, he participated in an *Art in Our Time* radio broadcast with MOMA chairman Nelson Rockefeller, during which he told the audience, "The time is come when we are ashamed to copy styles inherited from the past and imported from abroad."[13] In 1932 Ford brought the Marxist artist Diego Rivera from Mexico to the Detroit Institute of Arts to paint *Detroit Industry*, a fresco cycle that depicted the city's auto workers on the factory assembly line.[14] When the murals were unveiled and the public balked at both the style and the political content of the paintings, Ford staunchly defended them. By contrast, and despite almost unimaginable wealth, Edsel's parents were teetotaling homebodies. Henry's tastes in food, entertainment, and decor were so conservative they were almost rustic. He once announced, "I wouldn't give five cents for all the finest art in the world."[15]

11.2. Henry and Edsel Ford with Model A, 1927. The Henry Ford.

11.3. *Criss-Crossed Conveyors, River Rouge Plant, Ford Motor Company,* Charles Sheeler, 1927, photograph. The Henry Ford.

As a child, Edsel spent many hours at his father's side, watching him develop the car that would make the family's fortune, and, in time, he was permitted to stamp envelopes and deliver memos to Henry's business associates. After graduating from high school, he was given an office next to Henry's at the Highland Park plant. In 1919 Henry made him president of the company. While Henry's primary focus was on mechanical innovation, Edsel's interest was design. His first efforts were directed toward a new model of the Lincoln, an ailing company that Henry bought in 1922. Edsel's successful redesign established the luxury car as one of the most fashionable in the world. He was also one of the primary designers of the Model A, the 1927 replacement for the utilitarian Model T. Sleek, curved fenders and a graceful radiator shell set the new model apart from its clunky predecessor, as did the range of exotic colors that replaced the cheap and fast-drying black that Henry had used for the Flivver—"Niagara Blue," "Arabian Sand," and "Dawn Gray" among them. (The Cartier brothers once joked that they would like to mount up a few as miniatures on brooches and bracelets.[16])

There is little question that Henry loved his son, but as Edsel began to develop his own ideas, Henry could not let go. Nor could he relinquish control of the company he had founded, and at times he brutally undermined Edsel's administration of it. The economic cataclysm of the Depression was a nightmare for the younger Ford, whose management was continually second-guessed and sometimes overridden by his father, to the detriment of the company's earnings and, eventually, the welfare of Ford workers. In the end, Henry's actions eroded Edsel's well-being and compromised his health.

Yet Edsel admired many aspects of this towering and problematic figure, whose life was so closely intertwined with his own. In particular, he had inherited from Henry a love of the American countryside and the wildlife inhabiting it. (It was largely owing to Henry Ford's support for the Weeks-McLean Migratory Bird Act that the legislation was passed by Congress in 1913; Henry also supported the Migratory Bird Treaty with Canada of 1918.) Father and son also shared an admiration for Jens Jensen, who by 1914 was known nationally for his nature-based approach to landscape design. Both would work closely with Jensen on the designs of their family

estates, among the most quiescently beautiful of the era. These designs would, nonetheless, be stamped with important differences

Letters between Jensen and the younger Ford over the course of four residential projects track Edsel's rising interest in design and his growing authority in matters relating to it. In 1922, for example, during construction of the Jefferson Avenue landscape, Jensen became outraged about a disagreement that had erupted with the Fords' architect over some alteration of his plan (not an unusual event owing to Jensen's fiery temper). He wrote to Ford at length about the controversy, thundering about Edsel's role in it, scolding him, and finally questioning his honor: "If any changes of my plans were desired, a gentleman would notify me thereof."[17] The tension was resolved somehow, and Jensen's letters never again assumed such an imperious tone toward Ford.

Correspondence about the design of Skylands chronicles aesthetic disagreements, too, which were handled with increasing authority on Ford's part. In 1924 he wrote to ask Jensen to revise several aspects of the plan, including his rockwork frame for it: "We feel that inasmuch as the whole country-side is rock around Seal Harbor and the house and its surroundings are made of stone, that the garden should carry as much green as possible."[18] A subsequent letter from Ford questioned Jensen's planting plan for the front court, which he and Eleanor found "too hot." "Rather than Asters, Golden Rod, etc.," Edsel wrote, "we would prefer a blue cast suggesting Lupine, Delphinium, etc."[19] (In fact, the asters Jensen was recommending were blue.) But the following week Ford wrote to Jensen about other "detailed alterations which we took occasion to make," including the elimination of the proposed council ring.[20] None of these requests were unusual—some of the best clients of the era were argumentative—and Jensen's accommodation of them was also within expected bounds, but Ford's deepening involvement reveals an increasingly collaborative stance.

At Grosse Pointe Shores, where Jensen designed his fourth and final landscape for the Fords, Edsel would have an even more forceful role, and, as a consequence, the landscape would differ in important respects from Jensen's characteristic work. Jensen's assured spatial abilities and deep response to land would shape this landscape, but his typically lush plantings and naturalistic handling of grades would be tempered by Ford's leaner, more abstract aesthetic. Letters from the project illuminate the extent of Ford's role in developing the design and his specific requests for it. Primary among these were expanses of smooth lawn, irregularly and widely spaced trees, and uninterrupted views of the lake.

By 1926, when Edsel and Eleanor decided to build a large estate on the outskirts of Detroit, they had four children and were looking for a spot where they could enjoy a sense of country and find ample privacy.[21] At the time, Henry owned a parcel in Grosse Pointe Shores on Gaukler Point, about eight miles northeast of the city, where he had intended to build. He had instead bought land west of the city, in Dearborn, and developed it with Jensen's help as Fair Lane, hoping that Edsel would build there too. When it became clear that this was never going to happen, Henry agreed to sell his son the lakefront parcel. It covered about sixty acres, most of which were heavily treed

According to Samuel Howe's account in *American Country Houses of To-Day*, Grosse Pointe was famous for its woods. Several prominent citizens whose businesses were based in Detroit were drawn to the area, in part, because of the trees.[22] In 1908 Russell A. Alger commissioned The Moorings from Charles Platt, and in 1926 Standish Backus, president of National Cash Register Company, and his wife, Dorothy, were beginning to develop an estate designed by Ralph Adams Cram with a new landscape by Fletcher Steele.[23] During the 1920s and 1930s, Ellen Shipman would list forty-four commissions in Grosse Pointe alone.

The Fords' new property occupied a small point of land that protruded from the western shore of Lake St. Clair, perhaps once a lookout for the tribes who inhabited the area. (Fig. 11.4) French farmers divided this land into narrow strips that led down to the lake and planted them with pear, apple, peach, and cherry orchards; English settlers built roads through the property and lined them with

silver maple and Norway spruce. Several of these trees and many willows and self-sown poplars were growing on the land when Jensen first visited it in 1926.

Edsel was distressed at having to leave the rockwork pool behind on Jefferson Avenue and asked Jensen if it could be moved to the lakefront property. But Jensen wanted a fresh start; having visited several quarries, he assured Ford that he "could beat the old pool in beauty and practicality."[24] Other ideas from previous designs for the Fords would be carried over to the Lake St. Clair estate, too, including habitat to attract birds. A deep regard for the subtle beauties of nature, shared by Jensen and the Fords, would provide the theme.

The house, by contrast, struck a historical note. Edsel undoubtedly knew the architect Albert Kahn through his father, who had first hired him in 1917 to design the Rouge plant. Since then, Kahn had become the main architect of Ford's automotive empire, designing hundreds of company projects.[25] Kahn was versatile, moving gracefully from the Bauhaus efficiency of the modern factory to the Art Deco eloquence of the skyscraper to the Arts and Crafts charm of the Cotswold manor, the style that Edsel and Eleanor settled on for their Grosse Pointe home after several trips abroad to review alternatives.

Faced with Briarhill sandstone and roofed with limestone tiles, the sixty-room residence combined elements of several different English houses clustered in a way that helped disguise the size of the structure. (Fig. 11.5) Here the Fords differed from their Akron counterparts, as they preferred to downplay the scope of their wealth. But like the Seiberlings' architect—and H. F. du Pont—Kahn integrated several actual pieces of English country houses into his American one: a Caen stone chimneypiece from Deene Park, eighteenth-century pine paneling from Spitalfields, and a c. 1600 staircase from Lyveden Old Bield Manor in Northamptonshire among them. The rooms were furnished with a mix of French and English furniture, ancient Persian and Chinese ceramics, medieval ivories, and African art. In addition to portraits by Reynolds and Raeburn, selected with help from the well-known art dealer Joseph Duveen, there were more daring choices by van Gogh, Cézanne, Matisse, Renoir, and Chagall, guided by Eleanor's

cousin Robert Hudson Tannahill, later a major benefactor of the Detroit Institute of Arts.

There were modernist notes, too, in Ford's bedroom and, somewhat later, in the boys' bedrooms, sitting room, and game room, which were designed by the industrial designer Walter Dorwin Teague. (Teague also designed the interior of Kahn's streamlined Rotunda for the Chicago Century of Progress Exposition in 1933 and the Ford Motor Company pavilion for the 1939 New York World's Fair.) No expense was spared in the custom-made moderne furnishings—a Steinway piano of bubinga wood, recessed lighting, and leather-paneled walls hung with paintings by Lionel Feininger and Juan Gris. Radios were built into Formica-topped tables and seating integrated into the walls. (Fig. 11.6)

By 1928 plans for the estate grounds were nearing completion. Several changes had occurred since Jensen's first proposals were recorded. An early design for a naturalistic swimming pool had been replaced by a sinuous poured-concrete form, and a site plan that included a water channel which left the big house on a small island had been revised to eliminate the channel. (Fig. 11.7) The Fords had rejected Jensen's design for the rose garden. A letter from Edsel that year instructed, "In your new layout . . . do not make the rose garden very large, but Mrs. Ford wants it quite formal." Ford also included a long list of shrubs, many of them exotics, which he instructed Jensen to work into the design of the flower lanes. (These included smokebush, *Viburnum carlesi*, lilacs, pink hawthorn, *Deutzia*, devil's walking stick, forsythia, and cherry, plum, and pear trees.[26]) Jensen wrote back immediately that he intended to "comply with Mrs. F.'s wishes and also add the plants she desires in the planting scheme."[27] Ford had also informed Jensen that he was "sorry to say that we have abandoned the terrace that connected the two buildings in the garden," which had been replaced by a single, larger building of Kahn's design, with changing rooms for swimmers and a squash court.

11.5 *Courtyard*, 1998. Photograph by Carol Betsch.

11.4. Gaukler Point, aerial view, 1929, before sandbars were removed from the lake. The Henry Ford.

11.6. Ford boys' game room, Ford House. Designed by Walter Dorwin Teague. Ford House.

A subsequent series of letters from 1927–29 addresses more subtle aspects of the new layout—particularly grade, a subject that clearly interested Ford, who was just completing work on the Model A. In December he wrote Jensen that he and Eleanor found a proposed ravine between the house and the free-form pool unacceptable. "We have always wanted to have the effect of a lawn running away from the house towards the pool and playhouse, with the large trees placed at random," Ford explained, "and I feel that the ravine which is being dug will take away this effect which we desire so much." He continued, "We are also much against the high grade down on the point where so much ground has been filled in. We want that point to be somewhat lower in grade than the lawn around the house, and as you have it

planned there is an abrupt rise when you get out near the lake shore."[28] Ford was also concerned with views through and across the landscape. "We did not want to look over this hill out to the lake. The natural grade on that point before any work was done was the nearest to our idea as to what it should be, and every foot of fill on top of that original grade makes it worse, to our minds."[29]

The grading of Bird Island, an important determinant in the plan, involved an extended discussion. In March 1928 Ford asked his personal secretary, A. J. Lepine, to write on his behalf. "Mr. Ford became greatly concerned today on learning . . . that the island built up off Gaukler Point is about nine feet above water level, whereas the roadway paralleling the island is four feet, and the average of the mainland near the residence is eight feet. He wants to be able to see the lake over the island." Lepine continued, "[Mr. Ford] was also surprised to hear that a thick planting of grove and shrubbery was contemplated. He wanted a sufficiently thin planting of trees so that a view could be had between the trunks."[30] (Fig. 11.8)

Over 80,000 cubic yards of lake bottom had been dug and transported to create the island from an existing sandbar, making this the most expensive design Jensen had ever created. As a consequence of this engineering operation, the property's shoreline had grown to more than 3,000 feet. Jensen's motives in rearranging the shoreline were the same as Platt's at Gwinn: to create a sense of the landscape as a world unto itself. (Fig. 11.9) The harbor between the new island and the shoreline was practical, too. It sheltered Ford's speed- and sailboats and the yacht he used to commute to his office on the Rouge River.

Jensen's ability to envision sequential landscape experiences is particularly evi-

11.7. "A Planting Plan for the South Portion of the Estate," March 1928. Ford House.

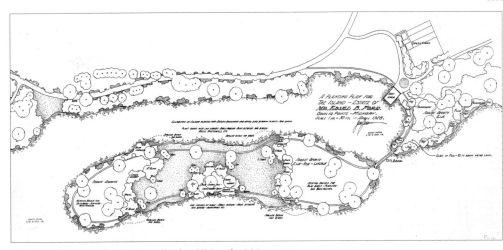

11.8. "A Planting Plan for [Bird] Island," April 1928. Ford House.

dent in the design for the approach drive. Visitors turning off Lake Shore Drive enter the landscape through the massive stone arch of the gatehouse and then proceed past a small grove of sugar maples. (Fig. 11.10) A glimpse of the house is revealed to the east, across the length of the Great Meadow. The road then enters a grove of American elms and begins to curve toward the house. Bird Island is visible offshore, to the north (left). (Fig. 11.11) The house disappears until the road curves again, and then it is close at hand, and a long view of the meadow opens back to the west. The approach road is sunk slightly, so that it is invisible from the house. "The sequence provides a sense of anticipation and ceremony," Robert E. Grese observes, "as one proceeds past the end of the meadow, through the woods at the edge of the meadow, and finally to the house. Yet the house does not assume extreme prominence as it

11.9. View to Lake St. Clair through harbor, Bird Island at left, 1998. Photograph by Carol Betsch.

might have, had it been situated on an axis with the long drive leading through the center of the meadow. Instead [it] is situated to take advantage of the view without ever dominating the landscape."[31] (Figs. 11.12, 11.13)

A central feature of Jensen's plan, the Great Meadow, stretches from east to west, defined along its southern edge by a planting of old silver maples faced down by hawthorns and crabs, and along the north by American elm, maple, ash, linden, oak, and a few Norway spruce that were retained at Ford's insistence from existing plantings. These, too, are fronted by smaller trees, primarily crabs. (Fig. 11.14) Jensen's plan indicated a dense layer of herbaceous and shrub plantings (*ilex*, *Cornus paniculata*, *Rosa carolina*, ninebark, sheepberry, native plum, sumac, and shad), but these were apparently never installed. (Figs. 11.15, 11.16) The resulting planting is more open than Jensen's typical composition, a contrast in lawn and staggering height of magnificent trees. Views across this immense, sunlit space are layered and changing, owing to the transparency of the plantings that define it and the mist that often rolls in from the lake. The meadow is visible from almost any point in the land-

11.10. Gatehouse, 1998. Photograph by Carol Betsch.

scape, each view different from the next. None is as transfixing as the slow series of pictures obtained from the approach road, where shifting alignments of trees and shadow-crossed lawn slowly unfold outside the window of a car.

The flowing spaces that Jensen used throughout this design closely resemble those in his park work, a spatial

approach that differed considerably from the Beaux-Arts principles Fletcher Steele was employing nearby at the much smaller Backus estate.[32] Jensen's meadows were organized in relation to the overall plan yet closely attuned to the exigencies of the site. His response to place is evident in the rhythm and flow of these spaces, the groupings of trees that define them, and the patterns of light and shadow that cycle through them.

Jensen typically laid out his meadows from east to west so that the summer sun rose and set along them. He curved the axes of these spaces slightly so that one end was not visible from the other, making them seem mysterious, and he made the edges irregular, marked by "coves and promontories," which also contributed to a sense of the infinite.[33] The qualities inherent in Jensen's meadows—mystery, complexity, and movement—were the virtual opposites of the clarity, order, and stasis that characterized the classical ideal, and Jensen saw the opportunity to realize all of them at the meadow edge. "The bold leap that nature often makes from haws and crabs down to the prairie flowers," he once remarked, "reminds me of some powerful and beautiful animal, slipping silently from forest shade into a sea of grasses.[34]

While irregular curves provided opportunities for massed plantings—another hallmark of Jensen's work—they also resonated with ideological associations that Jensen emphasized in his writings. "Straight lines spell autocracy," he wrote in *Siftings*, "of which most European gardens are an expression, and their course points to intellectual decay, which soon develops a prison from which the mind can never escape."[35] Curves "full of mystery and beauty" thus seemed most appropriate to democratic ideals. (Jensen did, however, use straight lines in his rose, kitchen, and

11.12. View from house to Great Meadow, 1998. Photograph by Carol Betsch.

11.13. View up Great Meadow to house. Ford House.

cutting gardens, forms that had long-standing associations with cultural traditions.)

In the Fords' landscape, as in others he designed, Jensen emphasized the experience of viewing sunlight

11.11. *View to Bird Island,* 1996. Photograph by Carol Betsch.

from shadow. (Figs. 11.17, 11.18, 11.19) In his 1906 article "Landscape Art," he described this event in almost religious terms: "Nothing is so fascinating as the light behind the immediate shade; the lining to the cloud; to some, the hope beyond, which may be the greatest part of life itself; with its allurement of mystery, its enticement for reaching the goal beyond, yet withal, the futility of the effort, the inborn, onward striving of the soul toward the unattainable."[36] To achieve this end, most of Jensen's landscapes included small "sun openings," clearings that were visible from the shadows.

Grese, in fact, suggests that "the spatial framework for many of Jensen's designs had as much to do with sunlight and shadow as with the physical expression of space."[37] (Figs. 11.20, 11.21, 11.22) Others have argued that Jensen's preoccupation with patterns of light and shadow and with the brilliant colors of the midwestern landscape stemmed from the deprivation of his childhood in Denmark, where skies were often overcast and winters long.[38] Jensen's favorite painter was George Inness, who included "a ray of light in every picture he painted"—he once remarked that he felt "refreshed" after visiting the Inness paintings at the Chicago Art Institute.[39]

Traditional flowers were also given a place in the Fords' landscape, primarily in the wide, grass path that adjoins the meadow. At Eleanor's request, the inner edges of the passage were designed to provide planting pockets for spring, early summer, and late fall color. (The Fords spent July and August at Skylands.) *Anchusa*, delphinium, veronica, daylilies, peonies, hollyhocks, lupines, shasta daisies, and others are listed on Jensen's plan. The Flower Lane also incorporated old fruit trees from the

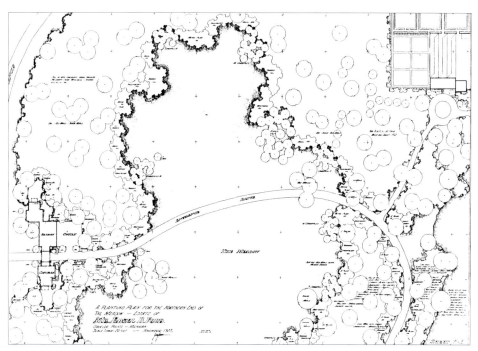

11.15. "A Planting Plan for the Northern End of the Meadow," November 1927. Ford House.

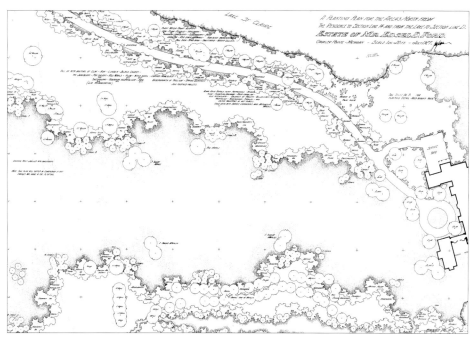

11.16. "A Planting Plan for the Areas North from the Residence," July 1927. Ford House.

French strip farms, to which Jensen added dogwood, haws, and other small trees. Several ornamental shrubs Eleanor Ford requested were integrated into this area as well. (Fig. 11.23)

The creamy white, yellow, and blue color scheme of the Flower Lane is reiterated in the Rose Garden, located

11.14. *Crabapple at Edge of Great Meadow*, 1996. Photograph by Carol Betsch.

11.17. Silver maples at meadow edge, 1996. Photograph by Carol Betsch.

11.18. Shadows on lawn near lagoon, 1998. Photograph by Carol Betsch.

11.19. View across west end of meadow from entry drive, 1998. Photograph by Carol Betsch.

to the south. An early plan by Jensen for this area took the form of a large, intricately detailed form that resembled a fish skeleton. At Eleanor's request, he simplified this into an English wagon-wheel layout with eight spokes, walled with limestone. The main entrance is located at the north, opposite an eighteenth-century English lead cistern and wall fountain. The planting plan for this area was also Eleanor's choice. She specified white and yellow tea roses, with blue forget-me-nots and periwinkle around the rose beds. (The garden's central ornament, a water lily mounted on a low fountain and pool, was reworked by one of Jensen's assistants when Eleanor objected to the snake that he had first proposed.[40]) Jensen's spatial mastery is evident in the location as well as the proportions of this outdoor room. In its conception and functional role, the garden resembles the formal garden at Gwinn and the

11.20. *View to Great Meadow,* 1998. Photograph by Carol Betsch.

11.22. Shadows under old Austrian pine, 1998. Photograph by Carol Betsch.

11.23. Flower Lane, next to Great Meadow, 1998. Photograph by Carol Betsch.

English Garden at Stan Hywet. Jensen's placement of it within the larger plantings and contours of the site responds to subtle spatial underpinnings of the overall scheme. (Fig. 11.24, 11.25)

Closest in style to Jensen's traditional planting approach is the area surrounding the naturalistic lagoon, which is cloaked with native spruce, hemlock, birch, ferns, and several species of wildflowers in an evocation of the Michigan woods.[41] (Figs. 11.26, 11.27) The lagoon edge was constructed of stone like the exposed ledge of northern Michigan, an irregular contrast to the flowing concrete edge of the swimming pool, which lies adjacent. The vista over the pool and lagoon out to Lake St. Clair is one of most dramatic in the landscape. Framed by stands of trees on either side, it brings the spirit of the lake into the design. (Fig. 11.28)

On the lawn bordering the lagoon, trees are scattered across a subtle, rolling grade, a spare abstraction of a birch grove. On the east side of the house, near the lake, a grassy expanse retains trees from the old plantings. Here,

Austrian pine, willows, and pear frame views to the water, and several elms added by Jensen still stand too. (Fig. 11.29) More traditional shrubs were planted by the Fords to enclose the house terrace, which also held great tubs of oleander, Eleanor's favorite flower. (Fig. 11.30) Other trees from previous plantings continue along the point at the northern edge of the property, framing views to Bird Island.

In Jensen's 1928 plan the island was to be connected to the mainland by a seventy-five-foot bridge, but a narrow isthmus linked it to the shore instead, making it a peninsula. At either end of the landform, Jensen specified forest growth of American elm, ash, and linden, and a shrub understory of fruit-bearing plants, including American plum, gray dogwood, chokeberry, native roses, and crabs. Clearings were planted with asters, goldenrod, and other seed-bearing plants, and shallow beaches created to attract migrating birds.[42]

Jensen's earlier design for Henry and Clara Ford at Fair Lane had produced a landscape that provided the experi-

11.21. *Path to Swimming Pool*, 1998. Photograph by Carol Betsch.

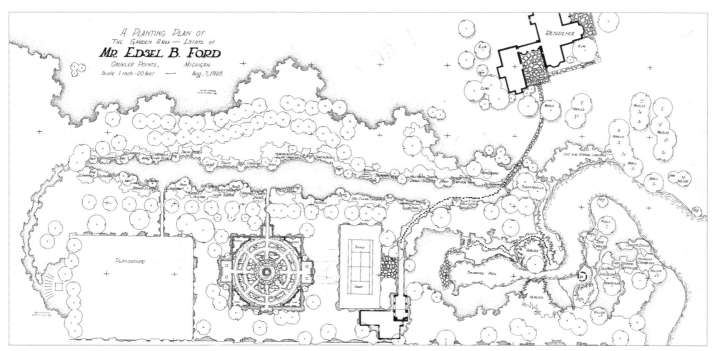

11.25. "A Planting Plan of the Garden Area," August 1928. Ford House.

11.26. Stepping stones across water near lagoon with Jensen plantings. Ford House.

11.27. View from lagoon to swimming pool. Ford House.

ence of an idealized walk in the country—photographs show abundant textured plantings, disappearing vistas, winding country roads, and dappled shade, compositions

---

11.24. *Rose Garden,* 1998. Photograph by Carol Betsch.

FOLLOWING PAGES:

11.28 *Lagoon and Lake St. Clair,* 1998. Photograph by Carol Betsch.

11.29. *Old Pines on Point,* 1998. Photograph by Carol Betsch.

that evoked the rapidly vanishing rural feel of southeastern Michigan. (Fig. 11.31) By contrast, the plantings at Gaukler Point are transparent and, in some respects, rather stark.[43] Spare and abstract, their forms change continuously with movement—of the sun and shifting shadows and of the viewer, whose perception is altered with every step. (Fig. 11.32)

By the late 1920s, when Edsel and Eleanor Ford's new landscape was under construction, modern painters from

11.30. Lake terrace, 1998. Photograph by Carol Betsch.

11.31. Road at Fair Lane. The Henry Ford.

Juan Gris to Diego Rivera—the same artists whom the Fords were collecting—had firmly challenged the classical notion that perspective could exist independently of the viewer. That American landscape design was shifting from an evocation of idealized nature—or, alternatively, a celebration of classical formality—to a frank acknowledgment of the interdependence of the seer and the seen is not surprising. The estate at Gaukler Point, arguably one of the first abstract landscapes created in the United States, was the product of two imaginations, one firmly rooted in the workings of nature and the other fixed on the beauty of pure line and form—freed, as Edsel Ford observed in the MOMA broadcast, of "styles inherited from the past and imported from abroad."

On a practical level, the Fords' estate functioned as a domestic enterprise that required a large staff and several service buildings to maintain it.

11.32. Great Meadow from entry drive, view southeast. Photograph by Carol Betsch.

11.33. *Playhouse,* 1998. Photograph by Carol Betsch.

11.34. View east to swimming pool and Lake St. Clair. Ford House.

advise, this was not the Fords' approach.) Jensen sent a bill for $55,000, identified as the balance of his design fee. Despite Jensen's substantial charges and the cost of building and plantings, estimated to be more than $2 million, Edsel and Eleanor were well satisfied with their estate. In December of that year they sent Jensen an album of professional photographs they had commissioned, with an enclosure from Edsel: "I am sure these pictures will recall to you the splendid layout and attractiveness of our grounds, for which we are most appreciative of your good work."[44] Jensen responded philosophically. "It will be interesting for you to note the changes that will take place as things now in youth grow into maturity. It is really in maturity that life is most beautiful—when it has run its journey and speaks its story complete."[45]

Jensen remained in contact with the Fords

Among these were a Cotswold-style power house, extensive greenhouses, garages, and servants' cottages. The garage and chauffeur's cottage were combined in a massive gatehouse whose proportions reflected the security concerns of the day, when kidnappings were often in the headlines. A playhouse built for their daughter Josephine's seventh birthday (a gift from the children's grandmother, designed by Robert O. Derrick in 1934) took the form of a diminutive cottage at three-quarter scale. (Fig. 11.33)

From an outsider's perspective, the Ford children led storybook lives on the estate, swimming in the kidney-shaped pool, boating in the lagoons, and driving miniature motorized cars built for them by their doting grandfather. (Figs. 11.34, 11.35, 11.36) Edsel was a sports fan, part of the syndicate that brought the Red Wings franchise to Detroit, and he often organized impromptu baseball games on the lawn with his kids. More stylish entertainment also took place there. When William Clay Ford turned twenty-one, his parents threw him a party that featured young Frank Sinatra and Tommy Dorsey.

By 1930 the landscape design was substantially complete, and Ford's secretary wrote to Jensen to suggest that the business arrangement be terminated. (Although some clients retained their landscape architects indefinitely to

11.35. View west to swimming pool and pool house (chimneys visible in trees at left). Ford House.

during the 1930s, informing them about the development of an untraditional landscape design school, The Clearing, he was creating in Ellison Bay, in Door County, Wisconsin, where he had moved after his wife's death in 1934. He had hoped to enlist the Fords' support in the venture, but they were feeling heavy obligations to local charitable and cultural institutions and did not send the cash Jensen requested, though Edsel did contribute a Ford truck and tractor. When the Fords wanted a design for a small area west of the Rose Garden, the "New Garden," about 1935, Jensen referred them to his son-in-law, Marshall Johnson, who had taken over his practice.

11.36. Edsel and Eleanor Ford (left), with children. The Henry Ford.

Despite Jensen's hope that his clients would someday see the maturing landscape at its most beautiful, when it "spoke its story complete," for Edsel this was not to be. He died in 1943, at age forty-nine, from complications arising from the ulcers he had developed during his most stressful years at Ford. Three years later Edsel's "nerve retreat," Haven Hill, was sold to the Michigan Department of Conservation and became a designated Natural Landmark.[46] Eleanor lived at Ford House until 1976, when she died at the age of eighty.

Eleanor had arranged that after her death the estate would be open to the public as a historic house museum and landscape, its maintenance and preservation supported by a large endowment left for that purpose, and this transition took place much as she imagined it would. Research by Robert E. Grese and others continues to guide preservation policy there.[47] (Fig. 11.37)

Jensen's long and richly productive life continued until 1951, when he died at age ninety-one. (At that time, his secretary, Mertha Fulkerson, assumed responsibility for The Clearing. The school still exists today.) Unlike many of his American colleagues, Jensen did not imagine that his landscape designs would, or should, endure. "It matters little if the garden disappears with its maker," Jensen wrote in *Siftings*. "Its record is not essential to those who follow because it is for them to solve their own problem, or art will soon decay. . . . Let the garden disappear in the bosom of nature of which it is a part, and although the hand of

man is not visible, his spirit remains as long as the plants he planted grow and scatter their seed."[48]

In this respect, Jensen's philosophies stood a distance apart from those of his American colleagues, none of whom viewed the relationship between their gardens and "the bosom of nature" as an ebb and flow. Most American landscape architects of the period, including Manning, were acutely aware of the designed space of the garden as distinct from the setting surrounding it, even as they experimented with methods to connect the two, philosophically and visually. Jensen's perspective was the product of a different culture, born of a different sense of humankind's place in the cosmic order.[49]

That Jensen's work for Edsel and Eleanor Ford achieved the harmonious balance it did—between a focused response to nature and the taste of one very modern man—speaks to the strength of Jensen's talent and his sensitivity to the genius loci. In their increasingly secular attitudes toward nature and ardent appreciation of abstract form and line, the next generation of American landscape architects would have more in common with the younger Ford.

FOLLOWING PAGE:
11.37. *View East to Lake St. Clair,* 1998. Photograph by Carol Betsch.

PART III

DREAMS AND ABSTRACTIONS

1929–1939

In the late 1920s and early 1930s new conceptual frameworks coalesced which emphasized three-dimensional space over pictorial composition. Largely as a result of articles by Fletcher Steele, American landscape practitioners began to find sources of design inspiration in modern painting and sculpture, and in modernist gardens in France and Germany. Attributes of these gardens—new uses of abstract form, bent or shattered axes, and untraditional materials—appeared in Steele's work and, somewhat later on, that of his colleagues. The most artistically vital landscape designs of the period merged these modernist experiments with a persistent American response to the spirit of place.

LOCKWOOD DE FOREST JR.

1896–1949

Nothing ever aggravates us quite so much as after showing a stranger over one of the very beautiful but very formal Montecito estates to have him say, "This is all very well, but I like a naturalistic garden myself." Our savage thought is, "Why does he waste our time, then? Why doesn't he just wander up Sycamore Cañon?"

—Lockwood de Forest Jr., "Comportment," *Santa Barbara Gardener*, August 1936

In 1887 the Southern Pacific Railroad laid tracks from Los Angeles to Santa Barbara, and soon waves of wealthy easterners began to arrive, seeking warmth, beauty, pleasure, and a sense of possibility.[1] They stayed in luxury hotels, such as the Arlington (1887), the Miramar (1889), and the Potter (1903), amusing themselves on new polo fields and at the Montecito Golf and Country Club. Some bought ranch spreads in the Santa Ynez Valley or in nearby Goleta and Carpinteria. Some built large estates in the countryside, with views of the Pacific and the orchard-covered slopes of the Santa Ynez Mountains. (Fig. 12.1)

Santa Barbara County is host to the southern oak woodland plant community, dominated by *Quercus agrifolia*, live oak. Inland, these great trees give way to grassland and, in the mountains, to chaparral and a dusty palette of silver-toned plants that are transformed by winter rains into carpets of brilliant wildflowers. The region's temperate, dry climate closely resembles that of the Mediterranean basin, a consequence of the unusual south-facing orientation and the 4,000-foot mountains that provide protection from the north. Despite this climatic reality, some early developers promoted the region as a subtropical paradise, and many came to the area expecting to see palms, gem-toned orchids, and even exotic animals.[2] The jungle metaphor took on particular significance at Días Felicitas, a well-irrigated Montecito estate later known as Val Verde.

Among the easterners putting down roots in what had been Chumash Indian land (and after the Indians were forced out, Spanish missions and presidios) were Meta and Lockwood de Forest II, who began wintering in Santa Barbara in 1902, when their son the future landscape architect was seven years old. The New York de Forests were

12.1. Hotel Potter, Santa Barbara, c. 1909. Haines Photo Company. Library of Congress.

descended from Jesse De Forest, a French Protestant to whom the Dutch West Indies Company granted the original charter to settle in New Amsterdam. The Walloons, as they were known, landed in 1624 and established Manhattan Island's first colony. Lockwood de Forest II—painter, interior designer, and amateur architect—was born there in 1850.

De Forest II had been encouraged in his painting career by Frederic Edwin Church, his maternal great-uncle, with whom he traveled in Europe and at whose Persian-influenced country house, Olana, in Hudson, New York, he sometimes stayed, enjoying long views to the Hudson River and access to Church's enormous art library.[3] (De Forest's formal training had taken place in Rome with Hermann Corrodi and James Hart; it lasted only about six months.[4]) Like Church, de Forest became an inexhaustible traveler, journeying to Egypt, Syria, Greece, India, and beyond. In 1881—the year after he married Meta Kemble (H. F. du Pont's cousin)—de Forest returned to India to set up a woodcarving workshop in Ahmedabad to preserve local craft traditions. Workshop panels made there were imported to the United States and sold through Associated Artists, an interior design firm that de Forest established with his childhood friend Louis Comfort Tiffany.[5]

Meta shared her husband's appetite for travel. They honeymooned in Bombay, trekked through Nepal, and sought out other far-flung locales, even after the births of their three children.[6] In 1885 de Forest published a book, *Indian Domestic Architecture*, and two years later he collaborated on the design of a house for himself and Meta in Greenwich Village, which used carved Indian panels on the exterior (featured in 1900 in *House Beautiful* as "The Most Indian House in America"[7]). Like Charles Platt, born one decade later, de Forest painted landscapes that depicted stirring effects of weather and sky, and, also like Platt, he was sharply attuned to the power of abstraction in his compositions. A love of fine objects, appreciation of line and form, and an imaginative exoticism permeated the household where the de Forests' son Lockwood III (later known as Jr.), was born in 1896. Two godfathers were present at his christening, Rudyard Kipling, his father's friend from India, and Robert Weeks de Forest, the painter's older brother.

Robert has been described as the personification of the "gentleman-activist" of the Progressive era, a leader in every major philanthropic, charitable, and cultural organization in New York.[8] He served as president of the Metropolitan Museum of Art from 1913 to 1931 and was one of its major benefactors. Robert and his wife, Emily, were also passionate collectors of American antiques and the prime forces behind the building of the museum's American Wing in 1924. A younger brother, Henry Wheeler de Forest, president of the Southern Pacific Railroad Company and an avid gardener, also served as president of the board of trustees of the New York Botanic Garden. (He, too, wintered in Santa Barbara, migrating seasonally in his private rail car.) Their sister, Julia Brasher, collected photographs of European works of art and wrote a history of art in 1881. For a boy inclined toward both nature and art, it was a stimulating group of relatives.

After an unpromising start at Pomfret, an exclusive prep school in Connecticut, "Lock" began attending

Thacher, a boarding school set in a remote area of the Ojai Valley, outside Santa Barbara. (Fig. 12.2) The program drew students who had failed to thrive in traditional schools and those whose parents, like de Forest's, were looking for a robust outdoor experience for their sons. Thacher required each pupil to keep his own horse and featured excursions into the mountains with overnight stays in shacks the boys built themselves. De Forest loved the place. He spent long stretches of time in the silver-toned landscape and painted it, too, having learned the requisite skills from his father, who was an avid proponent of plein-air oil sketching.[9] At Thacher, Lock also got to know his melancholy younger cousin Wright Ludington, who was homesick for his family in Connecticut. He took Wright under his wing, introducing him to the beauties of the California desert and the pleasures of making art.[10]

De Forest graduated from Thacher in 1916 and, not possessing the academic grades to be admitted to Yale (the de Forest school of choice), enrolled in Williams College in Williamstown, Massachusetts. He withdrew after just one year, finding the program too regimented after his years in the desert. The following year, he enrolled in a summer program in landscape architecture at Harvard but also found that unsatisfying and withdrew. During World War I, de Forest served as a volunteer in the 144th Field Artillery, and afterward got a job with a construction firm at Roland Park, in Baltimore. For a brief time, he worked for the landscape architect Thomas W. Sears in Philadelphia.[11]

In 1919 de Forest returned to California and began studying in the landscape architecture program at University of California, Berkeley, enrolling in "Theory and Aesthetics of Landscape Gardening" and "Advanced Landscape Gardening." He stayed at Berkeley just one year, however, later recalling that only "Plant Materials" taught by Miss Katherine Jones had "something of value to offer."[12] The historian David C. Streatfield points out that de Forest's abiding professional interest in horticulture might be traced to Jones; he remained in contact with her for many years and sought her advice on plants for his designs.[13]

The restless de Forest returned again to Santa Barbara

12.2. Lockwood de Forest Jr. at Thacher School. Photograph courtesy Kellam de Forest.

in 1920, where his parents had built an Indian-themed house five years before, and secured a job in the landscape design office of Ralph Stevens, one of the region's preeminent designers.[14] But de Forest found Stevens difficult and his work conventional, and he left the firm after six months, though he continued to draw for Stevens on a freelance basis. Within a year, he opened his own fledgling practice, listing his parents' Santa Barbara address at 1815 Laguna Street as his place of business. By then, de Forest senior had become an avid gardener, too. "My house and garden [provide] the greatest pleasure," he wrote, "as I am entirely shut out from every thing that is ugly and I get the long distance view."[15]

An opportunity to further expand design horizons came to Lock in the spring of 1921, when he and Wright Ludington decided to embark on a grand tour of Europe. The journey was sponsored by Ludington's father primarily as a means of recovery for his son, who was deeply affected by his mother's recent death from tuberculosis. The two young men also saw it as an opportunity to immerse themselves in classical art and architecture, in the artistic tradition of the day. De Forest was clearly the guide, as Ludington later wrote of the adventure, "we had a marvelous trip. . . . What tremendous taste and imagination [Lock] had."[16]

They landed at Palermo and sailed to Naples and then toured the ruins of Pompeii. De Forest's scrapbook records visits to several other well-known sites—churches,

12.3. Title page from "Italy: Summer of 1921" scrapbook.   12.4. Amalfi, at twilight. Photograph by Lockwood de Forest Jr., courtesy Kellam de Forest.
Courtesy Kellam de Forest.

12.5. Temple of Neptune, Paestum. Photograph by Lockwood de Forest Jr., courtesy Kellam de Forest.

12.6. Wright Ludington at the Villa d'Este, "depressed by coming storm," according to de Forest's caption. Photograph by Lockwood de Forest Jr., courtesy Kellam de Forest.

museums, and villas, including the Villa Rufolo in Ra-vello, Villa d'Este, Villa Lante, and Villa Gamberaia, which de Forest considered the most beautiful of all and where they had tea with the Berensons.[17] His snapshots capture looming columns and framed views that foreshadowed features in his own later design work. De Forest's painter's eye was informing his perceptions of the countryside. He later put these lyrical photographs into a scrapbook titled "Italy." (Figs. 12.3, 12.4, 12.5, 12.6)

The travelers journeyed on to Venice and then to Lake Como, where they visited Villa Balbaniello, whose design, Streatfield suggests, had a particularly strong influence on de Forest's later work.[18] They continued to Lake Maggiore and Isola Bella, then to Genoa and Marseilles, where their routes diverged. (Figs. 12.7, 12.8) Lock went to Barcelona, Madrid, and Granada, where he became entranced by Moorish tiles, pools, and fountains, and then to Malaga, Cordoba, and Seville, where he saw Maria Luisa Park, by

the modernist designer J. C. N. Forestier, back to Madrid, and then to Paris and London, and visited Kew Gardens, noting especially the display of California plants. Ludington headed to Paris, and there discovered a silver lining to the cloud of his grief as he began to buy art with the fortune left to him by his mother. Even from the start, his acquisitions were remarkably choice, guided by a connoisseur's sense of line, form, and color. Collecting came to dominate Ludington's imaginative life, and it would soon influence his art-making and eventually the design of the houses and gardens that he would commission during his lifetime.

After the trip, de Forest returned to Santa Barbara and his nascent practice, changing his business address to Soule, Murphy & Hastings, an architectural firm in which his future brother-in-law, Windsor Soule, was a partner. He advanced his drafting skills by assisting with the firm's projects during these early years, but he was also beginning to attract his own clients. Among the most important of these were George and Carrie Steedman, young retirees who had recently moved to the Southland from St. Louis.

The Steedmans' Montecito estate, Casa del Herrero ("home of the blacksmith," an allusion to George Steedman's prodigious talents as an amateur metalworker), included a 1925 Spanish Colonial house by George Washington Smith and a Beaux-Arts layout by Ralph Stevens,

12.7. View from Villa Balbaniello to Lake Como. Photograph by Lockwood de Forest Jr., courtesy Kellam de Forest.

12.8. Ludington and friends, Montefiascone. Photograph by Lockwood de Forest Jr., courtesy Kellam de Forest.

de Forest's former employer. By this time, Smith had become California's leading proponent of Spanish Colonial Revival architecture, and his influence was pervasive, particularly in Santa Barbara, where many clients shared his preference for "intimacy and mystery" over "formality and grandeur," as he once put it. Smith especially valued the qualities of romance and surprise in a Spanish garden, noting that "one is never overcome by seeing it all at once."[19]

De Forest's improvements for the Steedmans' property included new plantings for the south lawn and a redesign of the motor court that featured a black-and-white pebble paving modeled after the Patio de la Reja at the Alhambra. He may also have overseen the addition of subtropical plantings to the main vista, a plunging view from a small, exquisitely detailed terrace. According to notes on his drawings, these changes were approved by Francis T. Underhill, a distinguished Santa Barbara architect who was also advising the Steedmans.[20]

Casa del Herrero was one of the region's finest landscape designs, owing not only to the talents of the professional designers but to the clients' own abilities and taste. They were involved in every aspect of the estate's development, including the metalwork, which Steedman executed himself.[21] Over the course of the project, the Steedmans traveled to Spain with fellow Santa Barbarans Arthur and Mildred Stapley Byne, great authorities on Spanish houses and gardens, who guided their acquisitions of decorative objects, including the Spanish and Algerian tiles they incorporated into the house interior and into the several outdoor rooms of the gardens.[22] The job offered de Forest a compelling example of clients in the role of enlightened collaborators, and it also demonstrated the adaptability of a Beaux-Arts spatial layout to subtropical plantings and exotic materials.

De Forest's familiarity with other designed landscapes in the region added to the rich store of design ideas he was rapidly assimilating. Most influential, in Streatfield's view, was Underhill's Montecito garden for Willis Ward, a bold forty-acre scheme of "astonishing" simplicity laid out about 1916. It comprised a water garden of three oval pools above a large meadow, extensive beds of ivy, a forest of redwoods, giant arborvitae, and several old oaks. The quiescent landscape also made superb use of views north to San Ysidro Canyon. De Forest's future landscape compositions would also tend toward the spare and monumental, and they, too, would take dramatic advantage of view.[23]

More typical of the region's landscape designs was Las Tejas (The Tiles), whose c. 1918 layout was largely the creation of its owner, Mrs. Oakleigh (Helen) Thorne. Her eclectic scheme included, as Streatfield describes it, "a wildflower field, a small masonry gazebo with brick arches and fifteenth-century Romanesque-style columns from southern France, a knot garden, a heliotrope garden, a Spanish garden, a Japanese garden, a rock garden, orange and apricot orchards, and a small cactus garden."[24] The main vista recalled the Casino at Caprarola. De Forest would reject the insistent stylistic mix that characterized Las Tejas, but, like Helen Thorne, he would turn to drought-resistant plants and often forgo the convention of the well-irrigated lawn.[25] De Forest would also have been aware of Montecito's largest estate, Casa Dorinda, the home of Anna Blaksley and William Bliss, constructed the same year as Las Tejas (1918).

One estate that would have loomed particularly large in de Forest's imagination was El Fureidis, whose Persian-influenced grounds had been laid out by the architect Bertram Goodhue for his client J. Waldron Gillespie just after the turn of the century. (Fig. 12.9) The palm-filled estate had been published repeatedly in the national design press (in 1915 *Country Life* featured it as one of the "Best Twelve Country Houses in America"), and it was open to visitors on a regular basis. The grounds had also been featured in a film, *The Adventures of Jacques*, released by the Flying A Studio in 1913. The adjoining estate, Días Felicitas, also designed by Goodhue c. 1915, was less ostentatiously exotic in its landscape (and less well publicized), but it, too, was architecturally fine. It was to become the site of the most extensive landscape project of de Forest's career, beginning in 1926.

Hundreds of other country places were being developed in Southern California during the period. Most comprised grounds with designs derived from the combination of the American Picturesque and Beaux-Arts principles

12.9. El Fureidis, view from the house. Photograph by Lockwood de Forest Jr., courtesy Kellam de Forest.

12.10. Frederick S. Gould estate, Santa Barbara. From P. H. Elwood Jr., *American Landscape Architecture*, 1924.

that was structuring estates in the eastern United States, given a regional cast with local plants. In San Diego a focus on indigenous species was actively promoted by the horticulturist Kate Sessions; Theodore Payne, who had emigrated to Los Angeles from England in 1898, maintained a nursery that featured native plants. Arts and Crafts principles were strong in the designs of the Pasadena-based architects Myron Hunt and Charles and Henry Greene, who laid out residential grounds with a new emphasis on local materials and craftsmanship. Lloyd Wright (son of Frank Lloyd Wright), who was both an architect and a landscape architect, created designs that reflected modernist trends emphasizing an architectonic treatment of space. Other important California landscape architects active during this period were Paul Thiene (Lloyd Wright's partner from

1914 to 1916), Stephen Child, A. E. Hanson, Edward Huntsman-Trout, and Florence Yoch and her partner Lucille Council.[26] By the 1920s a recurring approach featured a standard Italianate repertory—formal water treatment, axial layout, crisp architectural detailing—arranged with an eye to the view. Stephen Child's design for Frederick S. Gould was, in this respect, typical. (Fig. 12.10) A few easterners ventured out (notably Warren Manning in 1897 and Beatrix Farrand in 1927), but few were successful in finding significant commissions, in large part because knowledge of local plants was critically important.[27]

The region's fascination with horticulture had begun decades earlier. One of the first nurserymen in Santa Barbara was Dana B. Clark, whose display of yearling plants, according to an 1872 report, included "several hundred Assyrian date palms in a healthy condition, a large lot of white maple, osage orange, white ash, black walnut, persimmon, pineapple, tea plants and choice orange trees."[28] Other early Santa Barbara nurseries were developed by Joseph Sexton, Ellwood Cooper, and Kinton Stevens (father of the landscape architect Ralph Stevens), who was the first to sell tropical and subtropical plants.[29] The area's most influential horticulturist, however, was Dr. Francisco Franceschi. Born Emanuele Orazio Fenzi in Florence, Italy, he had trained as a lawyer and then emigrated in 1893 to Santa Barbara, where he co-founded the Southern California Acclimatizing Association, a group that systematically recorded every plant that could be grown in the region. Franceschi reportedly raised 150 different species of palms, as many conifers, 50 species of bamboo, 300 vines, and 2,000 species of other trees, shrubs, and perennials.[30] By the mid-1920s, there were scores of growers in Santa Barbara, and the number of imports available continued to increase, shaping the designs of rising numbers of landscape architects, including those of Lockwood de Forest Jr.

Witty, urbane, personable, and feisty, de Forest was fascinated by new developments in architecture and horticul-

12.11. De Forest in the "Buffalo," 1935. Photograph courtesy Kellam de Forest.

12.12. County Court House, Santa Barbara. Postcard.

ture as well as landscape architecture. With his unusual looks and dapper, casual dress (which featured Bermuda shorts), he cut a memorable figure. Like his contemporary Edsel Ford, Lock was intrigued by speed and by cars.[31] One he owned was the "Buffalo" (named for its buffalo-hide seats), a yellow convertible adapted from a Model A, with an open platform in the back for transporting plants.[32] (Fig. 12.11)

In 1925 de Forest married Elizabeth Kellam, whose San Franciscan parents, like de Forest's, also appreciated art and horticulture. Elizabeth was a graduate of Vassar College and had gone on to earn a master's degree in child psychology from Stanford University, where she also took a single course in botany, a modest precursor to a career that would be almost as accomplished as her husband's.[33] She had striking blue eyes, which she reportedly emphasized with jean jackets, worn casually over tailored dresses and strands of pearls. Like Lock, she was a maverick, not afraid to speak her mind.[34] "They read Willa Cather and Aldous Huxley and Evelyn Waugh," the journalist Trish Reynales writes. "They wallpapered their hallway with massive maps of London. They made their own light fixtures out of old car parts and lampshades out of old maps or parchment."[35] The vibrant pair was also intimately connected to the community in which they lived, and they contributed significantly to the sophisticated design culture that came to distinguish it.

The year the de Forests married, 1925, much of downtown Santa Barbara was leveled by an earthquake, a disaster that provided an ironic opportunity. The Community Arts Association, through its Plans and Planting Committee, already had in place a scheme to establish Spanish Colonial Revival as the town's dominant architectural style—a response to the romantic, albeit mythical, idea of a Spanish past, spun by such novels as Helen Hunt Jackson's popular *Ramona* (1884)—and the damage from the earthquake set the transformation in motion.[36] The Architectural Board of Review began vetting plans for intimately scaled, tile-roofed civic buildings, and charming examples soon came to line shady courtyards and pedestrian-friendly streets. (Fig. 12.12) De Forest designed one of the new buildings, a studio for the Community Arts Association, and he also designed a garden for the director of the association, Bernhard Hoffman.

That same year, Elizabeth's parents purchased property in Mission Canyon, north of Santa Barbara, and they hired the Los Angeles architect William Wurster to design a new house and their son-in-law to design a landscape for it. They gave a portion of the parcel to Elizabeth and Lock for their own home, the cost of which they also under-wrote. Two years later Lock began working on a design for it and the surrounding landscape. The project pro-vided a testing ground for emerging ideas that foreshad-owed aspects of several subsequent designs.

De Forest's one-story, ocher-washed, stucco house was devoid of historical reference. Its rooms were ar-ranged around a brick-paved courtyard that sheltered a basin of ancient tiles used for flower-arranging, shaded by a single olive tree. Each corridor had access to the court-yard and was cooled through large glazed doors that opened onto it. The kitchen featured an enormous fire-place and a work island with overhead rails for utensils. (The avant-garde arrangement was the subject of a 1935 article in *American Home*.[37]) Guests were served exotic curries in a silver dining room with walls coated with ra-diator paint and windows draped with silk.[38] When the weather was warm, the de Forests entertained under the spreading branches of live oaks in the "Horse Corral," one of several garden areas that provided outdoor living space.

The landscape design, like the house, was guided by concerns for efficiency as well as Arts and Crafts charm, and featured many drought-resistant plants including a lawn of kikuyu grass (*Pennisetum clandestinum*). Local stone was used throughout, and the wide-ranging and sophisticated plant palette evoked the subdued hues of the native landscape. The garden rooms were intimate, arranged along paths and joined one to the other, much as the interior rooms were linked. (Fig. 12.13) Each cor-responded to a room in the house, in both location and purpose. A kitchen garden with a small flagstone terrace and pool provided space for herbs and vegetables. The dining room garden was filled with herbaceous beds and

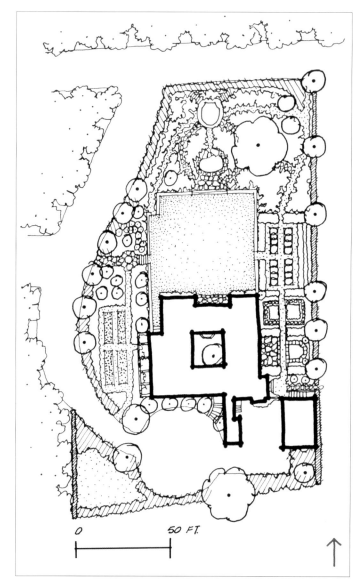

12.13. Plan of de Forest garden, Santa Barbara. Courtesy William Frederick Peters.

featured a small reflecting pool backed by dark-toned yews. The geometric beds of the rose garden (later planted with lavender) stretched beyond the east side of the library–living room.[39] Each of these small gardens was visible from indoors.

On the west side of the house were a geometric cut-ting garden and a garden designed to attract birds. The north side of the house opens to a large square lawn edged on three sides by an eighteen-inch stone wall that sets it off sharply from the surrounding tangle of vege-tation. De Forest created a berm to screen Todos Santos Lane, and laid out a naturalistic scene comprising two

12.14. De Forest garden, view toward house. Photograph by Lockwood de Forest Jr., courtesy Kellam de Forest.

12.15. Pool and berm, de Forest garden, 1978. Photograph by William Frederick Peters.

12.16. View to Mission Ridge Peak through lavender beds, de Forest garden, 1978. Photograph by William Frederick Peters.

the land and plants he knew and the colors he loved. These sources of regional inspiration, coupled with his interest in abstract form and his taste for drama, soon opened new horizons.

small pools and large boulders, planted with South African bulbs and native grasses and shrubs. At one time trees on neighboring properties framed a stark, almost flat view of Mission Ridge Peak, the borrowed scenic centerpiece of the design. (Figs. 12.14, 12.15, 12.16)

De Forest would continue to derive design ideas from

Over the course of his brief career, de Forest would list approximately 270 projects, most of them gardens for private clients.[40] The landscape architect maintained a small office, typically employing no more than eight assistants at a time, most of whom worked in the field. He was actively involved in all of the office's jobs. De Forest's approach to work was, nonetheless, spirited and casual. "It was not unusual on a particularly beautiful day," writes the landscape architect William Peters, "for de Forest to close the office and take his entire staff to the beach for a long, leisurely lunch."[41]

De Forest shunned the elaborately detailed presentation drawings that were still key to many practices, frequently constructing models to work out spatial problems. Unconventionally, he also made many design decisions on-site.[42] He spent long hours browsing in nurseries, searching for the right varieties or specimens, generally preferring permanent trees and shrubs to colorful herbaceous plants and exotics. (A fine prostrate rosemary, *Rosmarinus officinalis* 'Lockwood de Forest,' the result of a propitious cross, came from his own Santa Barbara garden.) During the 1930s, when landscape commissions were scarce, de Forest took on small-scale architectural projects, including several ranch and beach houses in Sandyland Cove, Carpinteria.[43] The sophisticated network of clients who commissioned work from him included artists and middle-class homeowners, as well as the elite.

In 1929 de Forest began work for an estate known as Constantia, aspects of which would exemplify his emerging design philosophies. The grounds were laid out on a relatively small (3.2 acre) parcel for the Arthur Meekers, whose wealth derived from Chicago's great meatpacking business, Armour & Company. The new house was designed by the Meekers' son-in-law Ambrose C. Cramer, in a South African Dutch Colonial style.[44] De Forest sited the residence at the highest point of the landscape and laid out an abstract, roomlike development that extended to the north, consisting of a limited number of strongly articulated elements: a capacious volume of space, a sculpted hedge of Australian brush cherry, a square reflecting pool, a lawn, and a blackwood acacia hedge (*Acacia melanoxylon*).[45] (Fig. 12.17) Like the composition he had devised in back of his own house, these elements set up a framed view to a mountain peak.

Throughout his work, de Forest relied on the framed view as an organizing force, an approach grounded in the long-standing tradition adapted to America by Olmsted. But de Forest's framed views, like the one Platt devised at Gwinn, came to emphasize the abstract as well as pictorial qualities of a scene, and were often bold in impact. In this respect, de Forest's technique of appropriating views may have owed something to Japanese prints, with their compositions that typically feature flat, planar constructions.[46]

12.17. Constantia, Arthur Meeker estate, Montecito, 1939. Photograph by Shreve Ballard, courtesy Kellam de Forest.

The striking mountain views that de Forest set up were sharply illuminated by the setting sun in an effect that also recalls the backdrops of movie sets.[47]

In their simplicity and bold axial emphasis, their abstract use of form and color, de Forest's estate designs stood apart from those of his California colleagues. These characteristics were forcefully demonstrated in one of his most distinctive works, a c. 1928 estate for William Dickinson at Hope Ranch in Santa Barbara. In this project, de Forest sited the new house in such a way as to preserve the great live oaks in an old grove, treating the main lawn as a visual field against which he accentuated their sculptural forms. In the evening, Streatfield notes, "the low sun threw long shadows on the ground, and silver light haloed the trunks and branches of the trees."[48] (Figs. 12.18, 12.19) Throughout the design, de Forest used color as a unifying force. One memorable passage consisted of an allée of silver trees (*Leucadendron argenteum*) underplanted with the glaucous-toned foliage of Bird-of-Paradise. The path led to a rose garden and a view of the Pacific Ocean, which turned silver as the sun set.

The dramatic framing of distant imagery, spare and powerful arrangement of forms in space, and spectacular lighting effects that distinguished the Dickinson garden became characteristic elements in de Forest's designs, in-

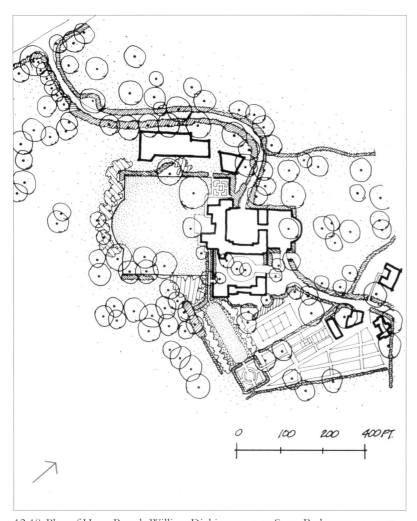

12.18. Plan of Hope Ranch, William Dickinson estate, Santa Barbara. Courtesy William Frederick Peters.

12.19. Hope Ranch, 1938. Photograph by Shreve Ballard, courtesy Kellam de Forest.

12.20. Il Brolino, Mary Stewart estate, Montecito, designed by Florence Yoch, 1926. Photograph by Lockwood de Forest Jr., courtesy Kellam de Forest.

cluding his work for Wright Ludington at Val Verde. Each of these elements also reflected a growing general trend toward theatrical landscape design which was particularly pronounced in Southern California.[49] At its most literal, this trend was exemplified in historically themed, typically Roman, gardens, many belonging to movie moguls and serving as stage sets for lavish parties. These designs tended to rely heavily on props such as marble columns and statuary rather than on distinctive spatial layouts or innovative use of plants. Even the refined work of Florence Yoch became "obviously theatrical, spacious, and expensive," notes the historian James J. Yoch. "Grand perspectives replaced subtle pictorial effects, and unlike the rustic ornaments that decorated [Yoch's] Pasadena gardens, . . . statues, baroque columns, and figured urns were prominently displayed."[50] (Fig. 12.20) By 1926, the year de Forest began working on Val Verde, the film industry had become the state's highest grossing business and the fourth most profitable enterprise in the world. As the business of creating fantastical places came to influence imaginations throughout the Southland, it is not surprising that de Forest and his client Ludington would be caught up in the excitement.

The progression of de Forest's most important design ideas can be traced through the articles he wrote for the *Santa Barbara Gardener.*[51] Lock and Elizabeth founded the unassuming monthly in 1925, with initial funding—

twenty-five dollars—from the town's Community Arts Association. Topics ranged from design to gardening techniques to imported plants suitable for the region, particularly species from South Africa and Australia.[52] The de Forests wrote most of the articles themselves, but there were also contributions from regional plantsmen, including the horticulturist Lester Rowntree and the nurseryman Peter Reidel, who had succeeded Franceschi as director of the Acclimatizing Association.

The first design-oriented article for the publication, "The Fear of the Formal," ran in the March 1927 issue. There de Forest grappled with the still-preoccupying debate between formality and naturalism, and he set out a fundamental principle of his emerging design approach: "We have no desire to start an argument on the relative merits of the formal versus the informal garden," he explained, "but here is a point to bear in mind; it is easier to arrive at a notable effect in a formal garden and easier to maintain such an effect."[53] He returned to the issue in January 1930, in an article titled "Order—Not Stiffness":

There is an elemental garden fact that we are going to preach to our readers during 1930, and preach it early and often because it seems to be so sorely needed, wherever gardens are being made. It is simply this, that the word formal when applied to gardens does not mean stiffness and severity, but rather a sense of order and balance and rhythm. If all of us would only think of a formal garden as an ordered garden in contrast to a naturalistic or wild garden! There is plan and design behind it; one is not attempting, praise Heaven! to imitate nature but to solve a problem in providing a fitting setting for a house which must of necessity always take some sort of form.[54]

De Forest quotes William Morris in support of his argument: "A garden should by no means imitate either the willfulness or the wildness of nature, but should look like a thing never to be seen except near a house." In Morris's view (as de Forest paraphrased it), "no work of art should put on the airs of nature; . . . as houses ought not to be

built to look like caves, so gardens ought not to be designed to look like flowery meadows or stretches of woodland. The beauty of nature is one thing; the beauty of art another."[55] On this point, de Forest was breaking with both his Olmstedian predecessors and many of his contemporaries, who continued to create scenes of Picturesque beauty in their work. But he did create at least one very beautiful meadow, for the Santa Barbara Botanic Garden, co-designed with Beatrix Farrand in 1927.[56]

In a subsequent issue, de Forest took up another topic of current interest: the "disastrous results" that follow from "copying gardens that someone has told us are beautiful," arguing in the same terms used by an older generation, including Warren Manning, who also warned clients against "copyists." Like Manning, and Olmsted too, de Forest instead emphasized locality as the "one great truth." "Every slope of ground, every change of exposure, every varying use suggests a different development, and it is as we are alive to the differences and work them into one well-considered whole then we will grow in garden intellect."[57]

Throughout his articles de Forest continued to recommend an architectural approach to ordering garden space. "Start with space and envisage walls around that space much as an architect should do with his rooms," he wrote in 1932. "After organizing the space, consider the emotional possibilities. If red enchants you plant a garden where red flowering plants will thrive. . . . Create; let your imagination go; anything is possible in your garden space from a completely enclosed, low-ceilinged room to one bordered by the horizon, with the sky as ceiling supported by pillars of palms and pines."[58] (Fig. 12.21) Later pieces suggest similarly vibrant color schemes for garden rooms, including one based on a Chinese robe "embroidered in orange and blue with a cerise lining."[59]

In 1933 de Forest wrote the single example of a garden "review" in the eighteen-year run of the *Santa Barbara Gardener*. The topic was Fletcher Steele's c. 1926 design for the Temple (later, Afternoon) Garden at Naumkeag, and it began, "Have you seen the photographs of The Temple Garden in 'House Beautiful'? Did you get a thrill from them?" The article conveyed de Forest's excitement about the modern approach to spatial composition

12.21. Lotusland, Ganna Walska estate, Montecito, c. 1942. Photograph by Shreve Ballard, courtesy Kellam de Forest.

Steele had employed in the design and about his method for linking garden space to setting, the notion of the "transparent wall." De Forest believed that the example held great potential for Southern California:

> Looking over these pictures detail by detail and reading Fletcher Steele's description of how he worked out this problem, gave us more suggestions of what we could do here in California than any similar number of words or photographs we have read and seen in a long time.
>
> Perhaps the greatest interest in these pictures is the way Mr. Steele has handled the enclosure of his garden to the south and west. It is genius. There is scarcely a garden in California that has not a distant view of hills, mountains or ocean and rarely does the view control the garden design, but here is a fine example of how this may be done.[60]

It would not be long before de Forest was emulating aspects of this design in his own work, at Val Verde and elsewhere.

De Forest's articles continued to address the bold redefinition of garden space that was occurring in his own landscape designs.[61] In 1940 he recommended following the lead of modern painting, which, he believed, had dis-

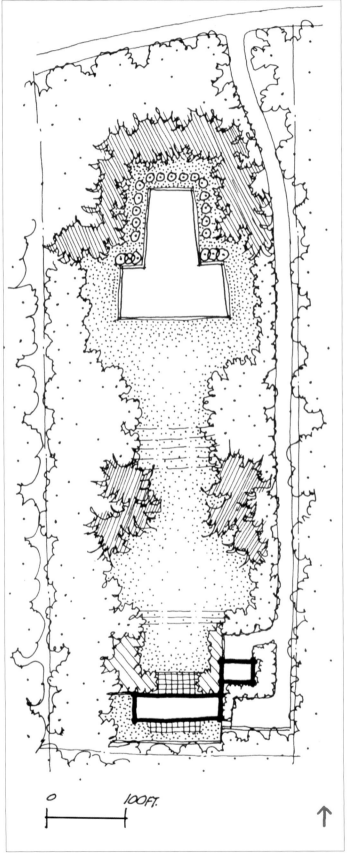

0   100 FT.

12.22. Plan of Sterling Morton estate, Montecito. Courtesy William Frederick Peters.

pensed with a rule from the "old days" that required land-scape paintings to include a foreground, middle distance, and background. De Forest proposed eliminating the middle ground altogether and organizing garden space into an architecturally determined foreground and a long-distance prospect of "mountains or ocean or other peo-ple's trees."[62] In a brief piece for *Landscape Architecture* written after the war, he returned to this idea, observing, "Even the small city garden usually has a glimpse of a dis-tant mountain that can be used as a focal point to give the garden meaning and a feeling of size."[63]

De Forest's final projects continued to balance abstract spatial composition with a framed, or borrowed, view. His c. 1946 landscape for the Sterling Mortons, an enormous outdoor room sited with a view to the Santa Ynez Moun-tains, was one of the most elemental and stripped down of the period.[64] (Figs. 12.22, 12.23) De Forest laid out the garden on an estate that had originally been designed by Charles A. Platt, in 1916–18, for new patrons who were unusually obliging.[65] According to one employee, de For-est worked on-site, entirely without plans, determining the shape and size of the large, spare reflecting pool on the ground. Bordering trees and shrubs define a great plung-ing space on three terraces, the last of which tilts almost imperceptibly upward. The geometric pool narrows at its farthest end to enhance the illusion of distance.[66] De For-est's design was a powerful culmination to a career cut short by his sudden death in 1949.[67]

———

12.23. View to Santa Ynez Mountains, Morton estate, 1978. Photograph by William Frederick Peters.

In their spare, architectonic treatment, emphasis on out-door living, strong functional and visual relationship of exterior and interior, and ease of maintenance, de Forest's gardens would influence a younger group of West Coast designers, among them Thomas Church (1902–1978) and Garrett Eckbo (1910–2000), whose California practices included many suburban gardens.[68] The architectonic ap-proach that de Forest so vigorously promoted was well suited to the compact spaces and the inward focus that resulted as suburban developments gradually obliterated views of mountains and sea. At Val Verde, however, where de Forest worked intermittently from 1926 through the late 1930s, attention to long view would guide design, even as modernist ideas erupted with force.

THIRTEEN

VAL VERDE (DÍAS FELICITAS)

Santa Barbara, California

Wright Ludington returned from his and Lockwood de Forest's 1921 grand tour with a new passion for art and life al fresco. Within two years, his father, Charles H. Ludington Jr. (corporate lawyer, investment banker, and vice president and treasurer of the Curtis Publishing Company), had purchased Días Felicitas, a ten-acre estate in Montecito, as a winter home for himself and his three sons. (Fig. 13.1) Wright could scarcely contain his excitement as he began to imagine improvements to it—Elizabeth and Lock found him sitting on their front porch when they returned from their honeymoon.[1] Both men were undoubtedly aware of the artistic significance of this estate and the one that adjoined it, each the work of architect Bertram Grosvenor Goodhue.

Goodhue had been introduced to Southern California by J. Waldron Gillespie, a well-to-do bachelor who also owned homes in Manhattan, upstate New York, and Cuba. Tempted by the beauty of the landscape and its seemingly unlimited horticultural possibilities, Gillespie had bought sixteen acres near the Montecito coast in the 1890s.[2] (Locally, claims of prodigious horticultural feats were epitomized by an immense grapevine flourishing on Para Grande Lane, where Gillespie's new property was located.[3]) Gillespie laid out his estate to accommodate a large collection of exotic plants, particularly palms and acacias; in 1897 he turned to Warren Manning for advice.[4] (Manning was in Montecito to advise Mrs. Cyrus McCormick Sr. on her nearby estate, Riven Rock.[5]) No record of his suggestions to Gillespie has been found.

According to an article in *Garden Magazine*, "Why Palms Belong in Southern California," Gillespie had seen his first palm at the Centennial Exposition in Philadelphia, and the tree had forcefully brought to his mind the biblical scene of the Garden of Eden. After his move to Southern California, he began avidly promoting it for urban as well as residential settings.[6] Others were promoting the tree as well. The nurseryman R. Kinton Stevens listed 10,000 palms in an 1887 inventory.[7] Gillespie added many to his collection and also began to sell them, as well as their seeds and oils, to world markets.[8]

As the turn of the century approached, Gillespie decided to replace the old wood-frame house on the estate, and he asked Goodhue, who was based in Boston, to design a new house. The young architect was an inspired but curious choice, as he had designed only a few

13.1. Días Felicitas, view northeast, terraces by Bertram Goodhue. Photograph courtesy Kellam de Forest.

13.2. El Fureidis. Postcard. Courtesy William Frederick Peters.

private homes at the time. He was best known for his churches and for his unusual public libraries, built in a range of historically influenced styles.[9] It is possible that Gillespie had learned of him through these projects and was drawn to the fertile imagination they evidenced, or he may have met the charismatic architect through a bohemian network in Boston, in which Goodhue was a lively figure.[10]

At age fifteen, Goodhue had become an apprentice to the Gothic Revival architect James Renwick Jr., designer of St. Patrick's Cathedral in New York City. He remained in Renwick's office (Renwick, Aspinwall & Russell) for almost a decade, during which time he came under the sway of the Arts and Crafts movement, which reinforced many of his nascent interests.[11] In 1891 Goodhue left Renwick and moved to Boston to join forces with Ralph Adams Cram and Charles Francis Wentworth, who were then professional partners. Over the course of the ensuing decade—a period described by Goodhue's biographer, Richard Oliver, as one of "impetuous revelry"—Goodhue gained considerable architectural skill and also continued to develop his prodigious talents as a draftsman and illustrator.[12] As the century drew to a close, he was eager to strike out on his own.

To research ideas for the Montecito house, Goodhue and Gillespie departed on a yearlong journey that began with Spain and Italy and continued through Persia. They traveled on horseback from the Caspian Sea to the Persian Gulf, through Isfahan, Shiraz, and Persepolis, visiting gardens by day and returning to see them in the moonlight. Goodhue's evocative sketches of the trip chronicle many of the gardens they visited and also convey a sense of mystery and, presumably, romance.[13]

Immediately after their return in 1900, Goodhue began plans for Gillespie's new house and the gardens that were to surround it. (Fig. 13.2) The estate would be named El Fureidis, after an Arabic word meaning "pleasant place" or "place of delights." Although essentially geometric, Goodhue's design did not reflect the Italian Renaissance villa tradition that was being promoted so enthusiastically in the East by Platt, Cram, and others, but rather conjured up visions of Persian pleasure gardens, such as those he and Gillespie had just visited.[14] A narrow reflecting pool dominated the brick-paved upper terrace, below which was a parterre of geometric pools surrounding a central fountain, laid out as a "Paradise Garden," a square divided by water representing the four Rivers of Life. A long staircase led down a hill to a series of three shallow pools, bordered by columnar cypress. The walk terminated in a casino overlooking Montecito Creek. Groves of tropical plantings, a naturalistic water garden, a Javanese temple, and meadowlike spaces were laid out at the bottom of the hill. (Francis T. Underhill was engaged to advise on the plantings.[15])

The house peristyle was Greek, enlivened by a bas-relief frieze featuring the Arthurian legends by the sculptor Lee Lawrie, who had collaborated with Goodhue on several previous projects. (Fig. 13.3) Stark white stucco walls on the other three facades, punctuated only by unadorned openings of windows and doors, evoked Mexican Colonial traditions and offered a foil for the lush plantings. The Persian-influenced rooms looked onto a tiled courtyard. The sumptuous, domed bathing room featured a sunken tub.

El Fureidis marked something of a turning point in Goodhue's career, foreshadowing the synthesis of the classical, romantic, and vernacular that would characterize much of his subsequent work, including the neighboring Días Felicitas.[16] A 1903 article in *House and Garden* praised Goodhue's design, especially its avoidance of "the mass of accessory details so frequent in similar work." *Architectural Review* also approved, finding the house "in every way charming, simple."[17] Almost immediately the estate began to influence other residential landscapes in the Santa Barbara area, instilling in particular new interest in Persian-style water gardens.[18]

Other articles, however, were not so positive about the exotic overtones of El Fureidis, especially the junglelike plantings and diverse architectural references. Among the California writers urging less effusive use of tropicals was Charles Keeler, a Berkeley poet, who believed that California gardens should emphasize plantings and designs that harmonized with the local environment.[19] Herbert Croly also expressed concern, arguing in a 1906 article that the region's Mediterranean climate setting called for a "graceful and unaffected architecture and landscape architecture."[20]

In 1911 Goodhue returned to California for work on a master plan for the San Diego Panama-California Exposition.[21] Having come to the conclusion that "the artistic individual mind works to best advantage when alone," he severed his architectural partnership with Cram and Ferguson.[22] The exposition opened in 1915 to rave reviews, many of them praising the romantic, meandering quality

13.3. El Fureidis. Photograph by Ben Foster, courtesy Kellam de Forest.

of Goodhue's unusual arrangement, a striking alternative to the superimposed unity of a City Beautiful approach. The more variegated layout appeared to have grown up over time, the same quality that was soon to inform the architect's residential work.[23]

Gillespie's cousin Henry Dater Jr., a coffee trader and his business partner in the plant and seed export business, had meanwhile decided to build his own house in Montecito, and he and his wife commissioned Goodhue to lay out an estate on a ten-acre parcel that had formerly been part of El Fureidis. Goodhue's c. 1915 design for the new house and grounds, Días Felicitas (Happy Days), avoided the flamboyance that had been criticized by Croly and others, though it continued to reflect the wide mix of influences epitomizing Goodhue's approach in his other architectural works. Here he combined southwestern adobe, North African, Mexican Colonial, Italian, and Persian elements, all realized through stark, modern forms emphatically lacking ornamentation and surface embellishment.[24] Rarely had the American country house been articulated with such subtlety.

The front entry of the stucco residence was com-

13.5. Living room, Val Verde. Photograph courtesy Townsend Ludington.

pletely unpretentious. (Fig. 13.4) A wooden door with wrought-iron fittings opened to a modest, single-story hallway. Beyond was a large courtyard paved with Mexican tiles which sheltered a small pool and fountain, planted with four palms. Interior rooms were arranged around the patio. (Fig. 13.5) The rear facade, two stories rather than the single of the front part of the house, owed more to Italy. Tall windows in the living room and bedrooms and a long house terrace overlooked a large reflecting pool and Montecito Creek. Views from the interior were carefully aligned with natural features, including the creek to the east, Montecito Peak to the north, and the Pacific Ocean to the south. Islamic-inspired roof walkways and a loggia attached to the library on the south end of the house provided intimate contact with the outdoors.

As at El Fureidis, the core of the spatial layout of the landscape plan of Días Felicitas was shaped by Beaux-Arts principles, but there were also oblique, seemingly incidental lines of circulation introduced. (Fig. 13.6) The heavy tangle of palms, bananas, acacias, and other subtropical species also lent an irregularity and exoticism to the grounds. (Fig. 13.7) (Charles Gibbs Adams, who had apprenticed with Goodhue, advised on these.) Goodhue carried the plan through the dense plantings with brick paths.[25] His layout also included flower gardens at the south

13.4. *Forecourt and Front Door*, 1998. Photograph by Carol Betsch.

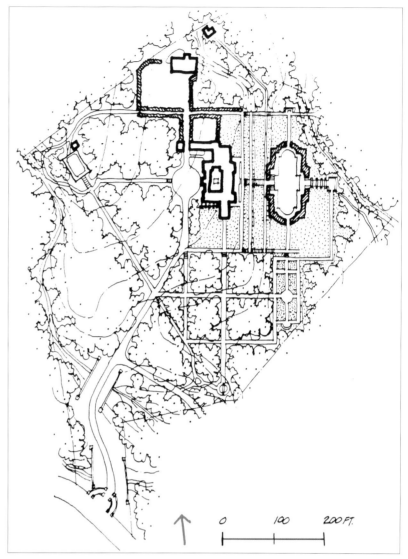

13.6. Plan of Días Felicitas. Courtesy William Frederick Peters.

end of the large central reflecting pool. At the north end of the house, he created a servants' wing and a paddock. Terraces on the east facade were planted with turf, palms, and roses. From them, striking views to the ocean and to the Santa Ynez Mountains brought a feeling of grandeur into the garden. Even in the forecourt, where de Forest would integrate native plants into the tangle of old vegetation, the mountain view was primary. (Fig. 13.8)

The Daters never took much interest in their new estate—some have suggested that Dater was nonplussed by his cousin's fervid love life—and they began renting it almost immediately. Over the years, the house was often used by Goodhue, with whom Gillespie remained good friends.[26] About to embark on construction of his

13.7. Brick steps to keyhole room, 1937. Photograph by Shreve Ballard, courtesy Kellam de Forest.

own new home in Santa Barbara, the architect died from a heart attack in 1924, at age fifty-three. It may have been his sudden demise that prompted the sale of Días Felicitas to Charles Ludington in May the following year.[27]

Lockwood de Forest's initial work on the estate began under Charles Ludington, whose first focus was on modernizing it. He asked de Forest to replace the old paddock with a large service court and add a new garage. De Forest transformed the old service court into cutting and kitchen gardens, enlarged the servants' wing, and created a new brick-paved terrace and Italianate fountain, inspired by the fountain facing the entrance of the Villa Medici in Rome. Arriving guests saw the silhouetted fountain as

13.8. Plantings in forecourt. Photograph by Lockwood de Forest Jr., courtesy Kellam de Forest.

they drove in, absorbing an impression of charming, villagelike development beyond. (Fig. 13.9)

More fantastical features were designed as well. From the fountain terrace, de Forest built a flight of stairs down to a curving brick walk edged by a high stucco wall that was embedded with early Christian bas-reliefs collected by young Ludington. The Gaudi-like flowing form of the wall expressed a modernist sculptural sensibility that was unprecedented in American gardens. With its literal references to the past, the wall also seemed to propose a fluid, almost surreal sense of time. (Fig. 13.10) There were other theatrical passages too. At the edge of the new terrace, de Forest created a stucco wall with a faux-weathered cut-out that accommodated a large branch of a nearby live oak.

De Forest used regional plant species extensively in his work, and he introduced a number of them at the Ludington estate, including live oaks. The wide-branching trees added both a note of wildness to the landscape and new spatial definition, particularly along the entry drive, where they formed a high tunnel. (Fig. 13.11) (Unlike

13.9. *Service Court Fountain*, 1998. Photograph by Carol Betsch.

FOLLOWING PAGES:
13.10 *Stucco Wall with Bas-Reliefs*, 1998. Photograph by Carol Betsch.

13.11. *Entry Drive*, 1998. Photograph by Carol Betsch.

many of his contemporaries, de Forest tended to plant small specimens, arguing that everything grew so fast in Southern California that the risky and expensive procedure of moving large trees was scarcely warranted.[28]) De Forest also added agaves and olives, whose foliage brought the silver and grays of the Mediterranean into the dark, shiny tropical palette.

After Charles H. Ludington died in 1927 and Wright inherited the estate, he almost immediately renamed it Val Verde and embarked on a new series of commissions that would further transform aspects of it. None of these, however, would substantially alter the footprint of Goodhue's original design; inspired by the layout, de Forest would develop the changes in relation to it. The revisions and additions came in waves, as money from Ludington's various trust funds became available. The felicitous, ongoing partnership benefited both men: the scope and importance of the job offered a professional boost to the landscape architect, while the estate provided the young easterner a haven that came to offer far more than the typical summer home.[29] Val Verde was to be an intensely personal and artistic endeavor, inspired by ruins in the Roman campagna and, in some measure, by Hollywood.

For many wealthy owners, villas such as Val Verde provided a means of sustaining East Coast culture in the Southland, particularly during the years when a rapidly expanding population of midwesterners—many associated with Chicago's meatpacking industry—threatened to infiltrate the cultural oligarchy. Ludington's villa un-

13.12. Guest in Roman bath. Courtesy Townsend Ludington.

doubtedly drew vitality from this tradition, and like others of its type shored up the social hegemony of old families whose roots were in New York and New England. At Val Verde, more idiosyncratic purposes were also at work.

The name Ludington chose—Spanish for "green valley"—undoubtedly expressed his sense of his new home as a sylvan retreat, shielded from the encroachments of an increasingly suburban world beyond. The word "green" may also have conveyed particular meaning in the context of the bohemian (homosexual) network that had nurtured Cram and Goodhue in their younger years.[30] The erotic escapades of the painters, set designers, stage and movie directors, composers, actors, and musicians who congregated at Val Verde would have made Ludington's Connecticut forebears blanch. Guests' visits were often followed by gifts of works of art, offerings that reflected gratitude as well a response to the beauty of the place. The most flamboyant of these was a Roman-inspired makeover of Ludington's private bath by the English set designer Oliver Messel, c. 1939.[31] (Fig. 13.12)

In the late 1920s de Forest began working on a design to transform a deep concrete reservoir west of the house into a swimming pool, and to remake the old water tower into a gallery to display a collection of Chinese paintings that had belonged to Ludington's father.[32] Patrons throughout the United States were commissioning swimming pools during these years, and often these features were designed as part of fantastical settings, stage sets for parties as well as more impromptu gatherings. (Fig. 13.13)

Ludington's new pool and exotic gallery were part of a general metamorphosis that was transforming Val Verde into a version of Hadrian's Villa, peopled with a dazzling assortment of nude figures, only some of whom were Greek and Roman statues.[33] De Forest and Ludington had visited the ruins together on their 1921 tour and seem to have absorbed inspiration from them. In particular, new spatial developments at Val Verde resembled aspects of the sprawling estate in the countryside outside Rome. The gridlike structure of Goodhue's c. 1915 plan would soon be overlaid with increasing numbers of diagonal trajectories suggested by the meaning, and use, of particular places. (Fig. 13.14) In de Forest's scheme, architectural features would contrast sharply with a sense of wildness, of luxuriant bounty. At Val Verde, this impression was enhanced by the subtropical species from Gillespie's day and the tangle of native live oaks added by de Forest.

In the 1930s de Forest added two changing rooms to the art gallery tower and created a courtyard that would accommodate a flower garden and several pieces from Ludington's growing collection of Greek and Roman figurative sculpture. The new design drew on vernacular tra-

ditions, but de Forest also used classical elements, executed in sumptuous materials. Pink marble columns in the courtyard were copied from Venetian originals, and sage green marble tiles surrounded a small pool shaded by four olive trees. (Figs. 13.15, 13.16) The new gardens possessed a dreamlike quality that was heightened at night by dramatic lighting. (Fig. 13.17) Although only about two hundred feet from the forecourt of the main house, the complex was screened from the residence and took on the character of a hideaway. Ludington's handwritten notes on de Forest's drawings reveal his deep involvement in the design as well as the playful intimacy that provided a context for the project.[34]

De Forest also used the opportunity of the new pool

13.13. Guest house and old water tower. Photograph by Lockwood de Forest Jr., courtesy Kellam de Forest.

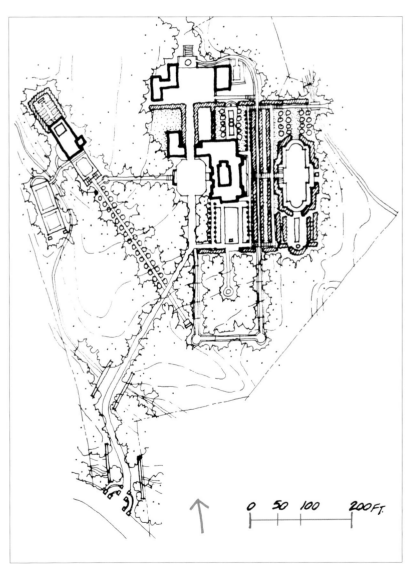

13.14. Plan of Val Verde. Courtesy William Frederick Peters.

13.15. Courtyard with classical sculpture, guesthouse. Courtesy Kellam de Forest.

13.16. Courtyard with classical sculpture, guesthouse. Courtesy Kellam de Forest.

13.17. Guesthouse at night. Courtesy Kellam de Forest.

to introduce some of the Persian spirit that characterized Goodhue's gardens next door. West of the swimming pool and down a small ravine, he laid a bridge over the creek and transformed a pair of shallow pools into a reflective water feature, applying terra-cotta sculptural motifs. (Fig. 13.18) He created a brick terrace adjacent to the upper

pool and thinned the overgrown vegetation, adding native live oaks whose tall canopies offered a leafy roof to the broad sheets of mirror-water. A feeling of pleasure, calm, and unreality suffuses the moment of discovering this hidden grove, when the water's surface brings the sky to the floor of the woods. The setting seems to have been carved out of the wilderness. (Fig. 13.19). It might have been the landscape about which Charles Eliot wrote:

[The] scenery is artificial in the sense that Nature, working alone, would never have produced it; but the art which has here "mended nature," to

13.18. *Reflecting Pools*, 1998. Photograph by Carol Betsch.

13.19. Sculpture by reflecting pools near guesthouse, 1998. Photograph by Carol Betsch.

13.21. View across forecourt toward entry drive, 1998. Photograph by Carol Betsch.

use Shakespeare's phrase, has worked with Nature and not against her. It has, by judicious thinning, helped Nature to grow great trees; it has spread wide carpets of green where Nature hinted she was willing grass should grow; it has in one place induced a screen of foliage to grow thickly, and in another place it has disclosed a hidden vision of blue distance; and so, while it has adapted Nature's landscape to human use, it has also, as it were, concentrated and intensified the expression of each scene.[35]

De Forest marked the connection between the new water gardens and the house with a small six-sided building based on the form of a Spanish baptistery, a reminis-

cence from one of Ludington's European trips. (Fig. 13.20) The "What-Not," as it was known, was sited at the southeast corner of the swimming pool, on axis with the front door of the house. The entry to the path leading to it from the forecourt was marked with a large Italianate archway. The court was also reshaped from an oval into an octagon and repaved with slate. (Fig. 13.21)

New developments by de Forest also enhanced features retained from Goodhue's plan. To a path that connected the swimming pool with a small fountain, he added a Persian water runnel, similar to the feature at El Fureidis, and an allée of cypress. In a square garden, defined by four intersecting paths, de Forest replaced low box hedges with stepped concrete and stucco walls that became a foil for the tropical leaves of bunya-bunya, bird-of-paradise, Moreton bay fig, blue potato bush, western

13.20. *Reservoir and What-Not*, 1998. Photograph by Carol Betsch.

sycamore, golden mimosa, Monterey cypress, and black-wood acacia.[36] The paths intersected in "keyhole rooms" of tall, curving concrete walls, enclosures that served as niches for sculpture as well as for shady seats. The sense of meandering growth which Goodhue had exploited at the San Diego exposition was heightened by the changes de Forest was making. (Fig. 13.22)

The junglelike plantings, tended by a crew of fourteen gardeners, flourished on the sheltered site. From giant agaves to thick carpets of *Vinca minor*, the plants at Val Verde seem to possess an almost surreal vitality. Their health and size owe much to the remarkable climate and, according to some local residents, perhaps to natural chemicals in Montecito Creek, which also supports steelhead trout. The water that rushes through the property constitutes an important counterpart to the geometry of Goodhue's old gardens, too. Massed plantings of clivia and other exotics have naturalized along its banks. (Fig. 13.23) The sound of the torrent, which rages after winter rains, is never far away.

The sheen and abundance of the tropical plantings and thick forms of old oaks and olives also manifest the skill of the Mexican gardeners who cared for this land in Wright Ludington's day and whose descendants care for it still. In one lecture, Elizabeth de Forest credited these workers and their fellow Santa Barbara gardeners—from Scotland, England, Sweden, and Italy as well as Mexico—with a large share of the beauty of gardens in the region.[37] (Fig. 13.24)

During the mid-1930s, new designs by de Forest transformed the core of Val Verde's landscape. At the south end of the house, Goodhue's loggia was replaced by three rectangular reflecting pools, aligned with the edges of the house. Beds along the pools were planted with box, camellias, and orange trees underplanted with yellow lilies. Yellow roses climbed against the house, recalling the fragrant blossoms of Islamic gardens. Set into the largest, central, pool and reflected in it was a Roman marble copy of a fifth-century-B.C. statue of Aphrodite. (Fig. 13.25) A small torso of a Roman youth sat to the side of the large pool.

At the north end of the house, de Forest designed a more intimate water garden that focused on another remarkable sculpture, the Lansdowne Hermes, a Roman work from the second century B.C., backed by an exedra similar to a feature at El Fureidis.[38] (Fig. 13.26) The muscular nude, reflected in the pool and illuminated by spotlight at night, was a focal point for those seated at the dining room table. Two rows of olives were planted on either side of the pool, recalling the olive grove on a nearby hillside and lightening the landscape values with their silver-green leaves. The olives alternate with Corinthian capitals, and a pair of Ionic capitals frames the large window of the dining room.[39] The erotic overtones of the two new gardens were unmistakable. De Forest's powerful and dramatic settings for these works of art heightened their commanding physical presence.

Magnificent sculpture was sited elsewhere in the landscape, too. Among the most splendid was a torso of Herakles (a Roman copy of Lysippos), positioned at the center point of Goodhue's central terrace, where light from the setting sun played over the sensual form. De Forest's restrained backdrop for the sculpture was in keeping with his general predilection for the abstract. A white marble Dioscurus provided a terminus for a smaller reflecting pool and an acacia-hedge maze, built on the site of a former tennis court south of the large pool. (Figs. 13.27, 13.28) De Forest's stylized and highly abstract treatment of the acacia recalled his hedges at the Meeker estate.

When asked about his preference for classical art, Ludington reflected on the landscape that had drawn him to the region initially. "It is well to keep in mind the unusual parallel between California and the Mediterranean and the interest in classical art that adapts so well to this area. The Latin background of both, as well as the climate and the vegetation, all add to the similarities."[40] On the subject of collecting generally, Ludington once explained, "Having always been fond of less theoretical and more instinctive artists, I have retained a preference for the human aspects of the art of our time—for the pictorial and the

13.22. *Path with Banana Plant*, 1998. Photograph by Carol Betsch.

13.24. Gardener and century plant. Photograph by Lockwood de Forest Jr., courtesy Kellam de Forest.

13.25. South pool, with Aphrodite. Photograph by Roy Flamm, courtesy Kellam de Forest.

13.26. North pool, with Lansdowne Hermes. Photograph courtesy Kellam de Forest.

colorful." He added, "I have never bought anything I did not like well enough to own, no matter how important the artist or the work or how opportune the deal."[41] These tenets served him well as he accumulated a collection that included pieces of world-class significance.

Other changes were made to the landscape in the mid-1930s. The long, narrow garden beds and lawns that occupied the steep terraces to the central pool were replaced by clipped box hedges that accentuated their architectural lines. Rather more dramatic was the addition of a gigantic colonnade along the house terrace. The feature consists of pairs of twelve-foot stucco piers, joined by a traditional balustrade below and open at the top. (Fig. 13.29) The columns run the length of the three-hundred-foot terrace expanse. Visible from many vantage points, they charge

the landscape with a sense of drama throughout. The feature is abstract and, at the same time, suggests great age, as if the timbered crossbeams of some enormous pergola had rotted—hinting, in David C. Streatfield's view, at a "mood

13.23. *Montecito Creek*, 1998. Photograph by Carol Betsch.

13.27. Maze with Dioscurus. Photograph courtesy Kellam de Forest.

3.28. View to large reflecting pool. Photograph courtesy Kellam de Forest.

of decay." Mac Griswold and Eleanor Weller see more am-
biguous meaning, "the sense of roofless temples, an inti-
mation of decay, but also of happiness . . . the supreme
paradox of a paradise both lost and regained."[42]

The columns provided a new, vertical dimension to
the core of the landscape, defining it as space separate
from the middle landscape and structuring views out to
it and beyond. They recall the genius stroke of Charles
Platt at Gwinn, using a columned portico to frame views
to Lake Erie, and they also bring to mind de Forest's article about Naumkeag's Afternoon Garden, which he
published in the *Santa Barbara Gardener* the year before he
created his feature at Val Verde. "Of course not many of us
are going to find oak pilings which we can build into
Venetian gondola 'hitching' poles," de Forest had observed, "but pipe is cheap or we could use second hand
telephone poles or even re-enforced [*sic*] concrete to get
the same effect." (The columns at Val Verde are of con-

crete blocks, covered with stucco.) In the end, though, it
was the spatial impact that captured de Forest's attention
more than the material: "the way Mr. Steele has handled
the enclosure of his garden to the south and west. It is
genius."[43]

More than any other feature of the place, the loggia
transformed the landscape of Val Verde into a melancholic Arcadian ruin, like the one Marguerite Yourcenar
so vividly described in *Memoirs of Hadrian*, where its pro-
prietor could retire to "garden pavilions built for privacy
and for repose, to the vestiges of a luxury free of pomp,
and as little imperial as possible, conceived of rather for
the wealthy connoisseur who tries to combine the pleasures of art with the charms of rural life."[44] (Fig. 13.30)

———

13.29. *Formal Reflecting Pool,* 1998. Photograph by Carol Betsch.

De Forest continued to advise at Val Verde during the 1940s, but there were no developments on the scale of the previous decade's. A break between Ludington and his lover, who was inhabiting the art gallery apartment, precipitated his selling off this portion of the property in 1946 in a fit of pique. On the heels of this transition came de Forest's unexpected death in 1949, after a lingering severe cold.

In 1955 Ludington sold Val Verde to Marjorie Buell, a Denver woman who was disappointed to discover that she could not ride her horse into the foyer, and immediately put it back on the market. Ludington moved to Hesperides, an austere and dramatic house in the mountains above Santa Barbara designed for him by Lutah Maria Riggs, and he donated several pieces of sculpture from the grounds of Val Verde to the Santa Barbara Museum of Art. Others he sited on his new estate. Ludington's private physician, Warren R. Austin, continued to rent a cottage on the grounds of Val Verde, and after Buell moved out, Austin and his new wife, Heath "Bunny" Horton, heiress to the Chicago Bridge and Iron Company fortune, became the owners.

Austin proved a colorful successor to Ludington. He was for many years the private physician to the duke and duchess of Windsor, who gave him a rare kind of watercress that still grows on the estate, and he cared for local celebrities too, including Ganna Walska, the imperious opera star and owner of nearby Lotusland, where Lockwood de Forest had briefly worked.[45] Among Austin's close friends were the aviator and author Beryl Markham, who remembered him vividly in her memoirs, and Dame Judith Anderson, who was a frequent houseguest at Val Verde.[46] The Austins were also patrons of local theater and opera, and they generously supported these and other cultural initiatives in Santa Barbara for decades. Bunny died in 1991 after a long illness, and her husband followed in 1999. Austin's will bequeathed the estate and a substantial endowment to the Austin Val Verde Foundation, an organization established to ensure Val Verde's survival as a cultural and educational site. This entity has struggled to gain the approval of neighbors to admit public visitors.

When Wright Ludington died in 1992, at the age of ninety-one, he was remembered by his fellow Santa Barbarans for his exquisite taste and his charitable bequests to the Museum of Art.[47] Primary among them were his collection of Greek and Roman sculpture and the C. H. Ludington Court, an addition to the museum named in memory of his father. Ludington's more unusual and perhaps even more remarkable cultural legacy was Val Verde, a complex and multilayered design that spanned the California years of one of America's most adventurous architects and the entire career of one of the twentieth century's most original landscape architects, early modernists both.

13.30. *Box-bordered Terrace*, 1998. Photograph by Carol Betsch.

FOURTEEN

FLETCHER STEELE

1885–1971

The work of the landscape architect is to balance three tensions. The pull of the land. The pull of the client and the pull of the professional designer himself. His job is to make a pattern of the three. If the balance never wavers and the tensions never turn into a tug of war, then the outcome is apt to be a pretty spider web.

—Fletcher Steele, "Naumkeag Gardens Develop,"
manuscript, May 1947

Many cultural currents of the early twentieth century came together in the far-ranging design experiments of Fletcher Steele. He was born in the prosperous, midsize city of Rochester, New York, near Lake Ontario, in the wide and fertile Genesee Valley, home to George Ellwanger and Patrick Barry, two of America's pioneering nurserymen. The region had been settled years before by holders in the Connecticut Land Company and southerners—a mix, Steele thought, that "burst from time to time like a social geyser." From New England, Steele sensed an "indelible ethical and moral seal," while "the South brought in a generous, easy life, hospitality, and enthusiasm."[1]

These traits were strong in Steele's own personality, too. (Fig. 14.1)

Steele's father, John, was a lawyer descended from New England farmers, lawyers, and Colonial administrators. His mother, Mary, whose forebears were Germans and Yankees, was a talented amateur pianist who tutored Fletcher at home, instilling a lasting love of music in her son, who both sang and played the violin.[2] Although they were traditional in many respects, Mary and John Steele also steadfastly encouraged their son's independent and somewhat contrary nature. "From earliest time," he remembered, "[I] was never satisfied with the place people or nature put things or with their shapes and sizes."[3] Mary's sister, a world traveler who collected Barbizon landscapes, provided a cosmopolitan example to her nephew and a counterpoint to local conservative tastes. "Rochester liked cheerful scenes in pictures reminiscent of that 'trip to Europe' by which all life before and after was measured," Steele remembered disdainfully. "It liked careful, obvious craftsmanship with no uncertainty about what a painting was supposed to 'mean.'"[4]

When Fletcher was ten, his family moved to the nearby village of Pittsford, on the Erie Canal, and into the

14.1. Fletcher Steele, c. 1925. Courtesy American Horticultural Society.

Harvard's master's degree program, founded just one year before, lent academic cachet to the new profession, and this may have mitigated some of the concerns of Steele's parents, who had hoped that he would follow his father into law. Landscape architecture would offer him an opportunity to combine his discerning eye with a deep feeling for land, although Steele once wrote, "I would have gone wholeheartedly into any of the arts."[8] From the first, he regarded the profession as a fine art, "more exacting than painting or sculpture," nearer in human values, Steele often commented, to music.[9]

Steele's first courses at Harvard emphasized drafting, art, and botany, and he was initially inspired by them, but his letters home soon turned to his part-time job singing in a Reform synagogue in Boston. For a time, he contem-

farmhouse that John Steele's parents had built almost fifty years before. He bicycled the eight miles to private school and then home again, to his country life. The Pittsford farm had a garden with big rectangular beds and a grape-laden arbor, where flowers and vegetables intermingled and a stream meandered through. (Fig. 14.2) "There was nothing grand about it—certainly no conceivable axis," Steele remembered. "I doubt if my grandparents had ever heard of such a thing."[5] The earnest values this garden epitomized—charm, fitness, and a sense of nature welcomed—would inform Steele's designs.

After graduating from high school, he attended Williams College, where he sang in the glee club, joined a fraternity, and generally had a good time, much of it, apparently, inebriated. Despite the revelry, Steele earned enough credits in his first three years to take the fourth away with a letter from the dean that prophesied "excellent success in whatever further study he may undertake."[6] He graduated with his class in 1907 and immediately decided to pursue a career in landscape architecture, later explaining dryly, "I was not rich and had to do something."[7]

14.2. Steele family garden, Pittsford, N.Y. SUNY ESF College Archives.

plated converting. His professional aspirations were revitalized by a trip to Warren Manning's office, where he was offered an unpaid apprenticeship on the spot. Steele sent home an exuberant account of the meeting. "Today was the first day and I learned more about landscape proper than I did all last winter. . . . Occasionally I was wrong of course, & [Manning] was constantly there to set me right. It was inspiring."[10]

One of Steele's tests from classes that October posed questions on the theories of Charles Eliot, Mariana Van Rensselaer, and Philip Hamerton, whose 1885 book, *Landscape*, explored the impact of landscape on emotions.[11] As the gulf widened between his Harvard studies and the hands-on experience he was gaining in Manning's office, Steele's impatience with Harvard grew. He complained to his parents about the "old maids" in the program: "I think they spend so much time over details that it becomes puttering instead of working half the time."[12] By the following spring, he had decided to drop out and accept a full-time position with Manning.

Although he left without a degree, Steele's studies at Harvard would serve him well. In particular, they had introduced him to the ideas of Denman W. Ross, who taught aesthetics in the fine arts program. At the time of Steele's enrollment, Ross was advancing a nine-step chart of color values and a theory of pure design, and both would affect Steele's own art-making. It is not surprising that Ross's "scientific" theories on modern painting and sculpture appealed to Steele—the legitimacy of abstract art was a hot topic in the century's early years. Social ties were forged too. Ross hired Steele to dig his vegetable garden, and in the 1920s they traveled to Europe together.

In July 1909 Steele received an offer from Manning to become his private traveling secretary. The post, as Steele described it, would demand working knowledge of every job in the office, extensive travel, client contact, studies on the ground, and writing reports. "This is very much the same experience that Charles Eliot had with the elder Olmsted," he boasted to his parents, "I don't suppose any one else has ever had a like opportunity."[14] Manning also encouraged him to visit the Manse, Manning's country house in Billerica, where he kept his large library. By

August, Steele had assumed major responsibilities for an estate on Buzzards Bay, whose scope anticipated projects in his own future practice; he mentioned "over two miles of beautiful shore & a hundred acres of fine wood and meadow."[14] He soon began to accumulate responsibilities on other jobs, including planting plans for the high school in Hopedale, Massachusetts, and oversight of new development on a large estate for the lumber magnate H. W. Sage in Albany.

Manning's work on the Sage place included an Italianate garden, in the tradition of Charles Platt, with whom Manning was concurrently working at Gwinn. Steele's analysis of the design recalls Platt's description of High Court, from almost twenty years before: "The pattern and color will make a very interesting side outlook from the terrace and not interfere with the view in any way, which is on the other side of the terrace."[15] Steele's charge was to lay out the beds in the new garden (not the overall architectural framework), and he sent rough sketches in his letters home that chronicled his progress. But once the garden was complete, he found the results disappointing, because they lacked "the charm of coziness and delicacy that belong to a private garden." He faulted Manning's lack of enframing design.[16] He was already beginning to sense a difference between himself and his mentor. It was the same divide, in broad strokes, that separated Manning from Platt.

Steele's work in Manning's office continued in a wide range of localities and typologies. It included an Arapaho Indian mission in Laramie, Wyoming, an Arts and Crafts village for North Carolina State Normal School (later the University of North Carolina, Greensboro), a city plan for Bangor, Maine, and several large estates. These commissions honed Steele's emerging technical abilities in several dimensions. In May 1910 he was involved in preparing a map indicating the disposition of all public land, "semi-public" holdings (cemeteries and institutions), estates, and rail lines and roads in Massachusetts.

By October of 1910 Steele had become the link between the "sanctum sanctorum" of Manning's inner office and the drafting department. The new position, Steele wrote, was designed to improve communications between the two aspects of the practice. He was responsible for taking Manning's sketches, making notes, and giving them to the head draftsman. Steele wrote home, "I have complete control of all the plant orders under Mr. Mgs guidance, I do a large part of the estimating for all the work and I check all that I cannot do but turn over to others, I see all the correspondence that is of the slightest importance, and every bit of information that comes from Mr. Mg about any work whatsoever I either overhear, or is given directly to me. It is a big proposition." He added, "Don't you agree that I am fortunate?"[17] The shift in Steele's role was precipitated by the arrival of several new assistants in the office, prominent among them Albert Davis Taylor, who came in 1909 and was also a strong designer. (Taylor was soon assigned oversight of several jobs in the Midwest, including Gwinn and Stan Hywet Hall.) Manning continued to add assistants, and they, too, were given broad responsibilities.[18]

As Steele entered his fifth year in the office, he discovered that Manning was grooming Harold, his sixteen-year-old son, to become his successor. The situation was not unlike the one Manning had faced as a hopeful assistant in Olmsted's office two decades before, and it had a similar effect. Steele began frankly to reassess his position there, weighing his regard for his mentor against his growing ambivalence about future work for him.[19] "While I am warmly in accord with his finest broad minded theories," he wrote his father, "few of them interest me enuf to support with enthusiasm these, and no others, for life." His candid analysis went on:

Designing, with [Manning], is best to fulfill convenience & economy & natural conditions, whence he believes beauty will follow. Well, it usually will, but to my mind [is] all the better for being always consciously considered. . . . So whereas he is regarded as one of the very strong members of the profession, he is also regarded as very one sided. That side in which he excels is the one which would appeal to . . . a horticulturist, and . . . a park superintendent and engineer. But it is not a side which appeals to an architect or an artist.

While it is an invaluable side, it is by no means the expression of the whole profession. And my nature, by training & choice, inclines, if anything, rather to the side which he has not. On this very account, I feel all the stronger that my training with him has been invaluable, but none the less that its value for me is limited.[20]

Steele remained in Manning's office, but he began making plans for a grand tour that would give him exposure to examples of painting, architecture, and landscape architecture on which he could base his own art. The trip took place the following spring, encouraged and to a modest degree underwritten by Manning, who gave him $100 toward it. Manning also paid him to write up his extensive notes into a narrative when it was over and provided a stenographer to type up the account.[21]

Steele's travels took him through Portugal, Spain, North Africa, Italy, France, Germany, and England, to botanical gardens, parks, city squares, museums, and cemeteries, as well as private estates. His narrative chronicles the tour in rich detail, often through impressions of color, a concern that would dominate his future art-making. Remembering his April 1913 departure, Boston Harbor, Steele wrote, "Red ferry boats, bright green or light blue harbor craft scuttled about in the foreground of a splendid landscape, with a red purple city beyond crossed with bands of deep blue, tipped with the gold dome of the State House."[22]

The trip included virtually the entire canon of major Italian villas, and Steele dutifully recorded opinions of many of them. He liked least the Villa Aldobrandini at Frascati, which he thought "very ugly and stupidly designed," and admired most the Villa Lante, which he found "charming." (Fig. 14.3) His wide-ranging attentions focused on art and architecture as frequently as landscape. Steele also closely observed his own emotions, in the tradition of Horace Walpole (and Philip Hamerton, whose work he had just studied at Harvard). "Great masses of mountains have more dignity and grandeur," Steele noted, "but irregular jagged peaks are more inspiring to the imagination."[23] His susceptibility to aesthetic response was

Detail ⅛ octagonal Fountain
Villa Lante – Bagnaia

14.3. Sketch of the Villa Lante from "Europe, 1913."
SUNY ESF College Archives.

wish our work to be."[25] Over the course of the trip, he absorbed many new design ideas, but he also retained a high regard for American tradition, noting, "Too much is frequently said of what is fine and too little about what is bad in Europe."[26]

Years later, Steele recalled that the tour had instilled in him an enduring sense of the garden as an expression of human values, a topic on which would eventually write a book, titled *Gardens and People*.[27] In a letter to his assistant Peter H. Hornbeck, he observed, "It was there I first learned to hunt for the causes underlying human endeavor, whether in landscape architecture or other matters. Far more important than merely what was done. Study gardens all day at Frascati if you will, but always get back to the Piazza Venezia in time for an aperitif and a cake with a passing friend. It is then you will learn."[28]

In the spring of 1914 Steele resigned from his job with Manning to set up his own Boston practice. He took with him a few projects that had been begun under Manning's auspices—as Manning had from Olmsted a generation before—and he quickly secured commissions from friends. One of these was Grahame Wood, a fraternity brother from Williams College, who was creating a new estate, Blossom Hill, in the countryside near Wawa, Pennsylvania.

Steele's plan for Wood's new country place strongly resembled aspects of Manning's layout for Stan Hywet Hall, a commission that had come into the office toward the end of Steele's tenure there, in 1911. (Fig. 14.4) (There is no indication he worked on the project, but he likely knew it.) In both designs, views were determined largely by the lay of the land, gently rolling countryside. In Steele's 1915 plan these views are clearly marked, as are golf links, a feature at Stan Hywet, too, as well as a deer park, meadows, and a wooded ravine. Despite its scope and the wealth behind the job, the estate was characterized by a sense of pastoral country expanse. (Fig.14.5)

The same year, Steele received a commission for a small in-town residence on Oliver Street in Rochester. His clients were Atkinson Allen, whom he knew from

apparent on almost every page: "The Bay of Naples is all in beauty that is said of it. . . . Take the most imaginative castle-covered island rock that Maxfield Parrish ever put in a fairy tale, with a romantic coloring and mystery that he can but faintly approximate, see it from the blue Mediterranean on a summer misty morning, and no more wholly satisfying introduction to the adventure of Europe could be devised."[24]

Steele's report also analyzed the appeal of form and line distinct from emotion. "The Place Vendôme in Paris is perfect," he wrote. "It is the simplest of all in design and execution; its proportions are most majestic; its decoration superb. If it possesses some of the superhuman coldness of perfection which threatens Raphael and chills the Venus de Medici, it is in the company where each of us would

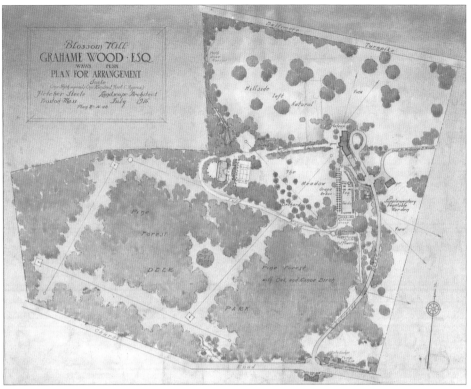

14.4. "Plan for Arrangement," Blossom Hill, Graham Wood estate, Wawa, Pa., 1916. SUNY ESF College Archives.

14.5. Meadow view, Blossom Hill. Photograph by Paul Weber. SUNY ESF College Archives.

high school, and Allen's new wife, Charlotte. Though limited in size, the job would offer a laboratory for design experiments over many years and foreshadow aspects of later work at Naumkeag. Behind the house (the only available space for a garden), Steele used high walls and hedges to define a taut, geometric space. (Fig.14.6) His approach appears to have been inspired by examples of modern "architectural gardens" in Germany that deemphasized plants in favor of masonry construction, treillage, and sculpture.[29] The central feature of Steele's design was a *tapis vert*, laid out on axis with the living room. Beyond the lawn was a small pool and a terrace planted with a beech allée. (Fig. 14.7)

Several years later, Allen commissioned the sculptor Gaston Lachaise to create a standing nude for the garden, modeled (according to local gossip) on Charlotte Allen herself. An enframing arch for the Lachaise sculpture based on a Sussex cemetery gateway and a mobile by Alexander Calder, with whom Steele had recently become friends, were added in the mid-1930s. In 1938 a pool shelter inspired by the form of a medieval campaign tent was installed. (Figs. 14.8, 14.9) These additions increased the garden's complexity and exoticism, but they did not undermine the spatial composition that gave the design its strength and cohesiveness from the first. Assured volumetric handling of space would soon become a central force in Steele's work.[30]

Steele's friendship with Charlotte Allen continued over the years—she eventually divorced Atkinson—weathering distance and, on her side, stiff bills, one of which read "$50 . . . Contemplation on Tree."[31] The letters record shared tastes in travel, food and drink, books, and a circle of friends that included the sculptor Calder (who created a pair of wire earrings for Allen that spelled out "happy" and "birthday") and Joseph Taylor, president of Bausch & Lomb, who also became a client.[32] Steele returned to Oliver Street frequently to attend the "chilled glass hour" and gossip. Work on the garden continued intermittently through the 1960s. He once wrote that he regarded the Allen garden as "in many ways . . . the best place I have ever done, as well as about the smallest."[33]

More explicitly than his colleagues, Fletcher Steele considered the emotional complexities of his clients a primary determinant in design, and it was, in part, this source of inspiration (which included his clients' art collections, horticultural passions, and travel memories) that led to unusually imaginative work. In 1912 he wrote of his desire to achieve "consideration for the more intimate if

generally unexpressed needs of people," tracing the concept to Olmsted.[34] In one (undated) lecture transcript, he described his intention "to bring to other people's lives a suitable inspiration for their contentment, even . . . their happiness," and how this figured in his method.

> To reach this sensitive achievement, he must first study the personality of the people for whom the place is to be created. . . . [He] wanders into the house to see what kind of books she reads, what kind of furniture and bric-a-brac she gathers about her. He gets her talking about her travels and the places she likes the best and ones she does not like. He probes to discover, not what she has, but what she dreams of having: not what she does but what she would like to do.
>
> . . . [W]hat he aims at as a sure prop for contentment is to furnish the best available background for the clients' daydreams. . . . Dreaming enables us to withdraw into ourselves for brief moments and rests us. It is good and if the garden makes it easier and pleasant to dream, then it is a good garden.[35]

Other themes soon emerged in Steele's work. In a 1915 design for Ethan Allen's estate, Rolling Ridge, in North Andover, Massachusetts, diagonal trajectories

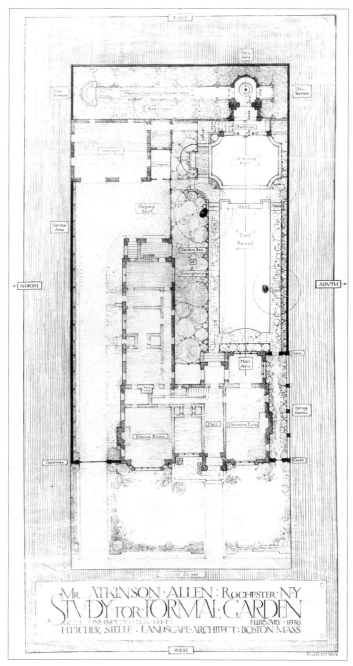

14.6. "Study for Formal Garden," Atkinson Allen garden, Rochester, N.Y., 1916. SUNY ESF College Archives.

14.7. View east, with sculpture by Gaston Lachaise, Allen garden, 1938. Photograph by Fletcher Steele. SUNY ESF College Archives.

14.8. Shelter at swimming pool with furniture by Steele, Allen garden. Photograph by Fletcher Steele. SUNY ESF College Archives.

14.9. Drawing for shelter at swimming pool, Allen garden, 1937, rejected design. SUNY ESF College Archives.

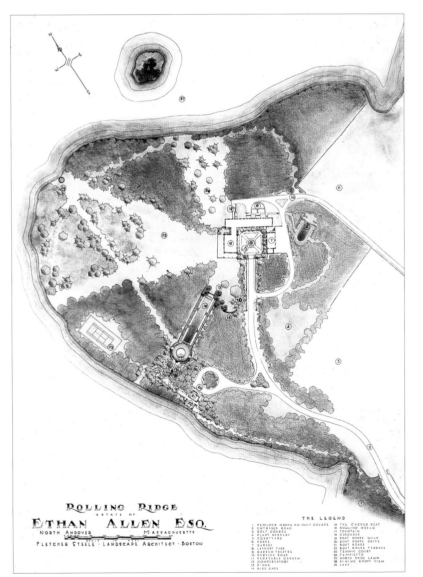

ROLLING RIDGE
ESTATE OF
ETHAN ALLEN ESQ.
NORTH ANDOVER   MASSACHUSETTS
FLETCHER STEELE · LANDSCAPE ARCHITECT · BOSTON

14.10. Plan for Rolling Ridge, Ethan Allen estate, North Andover, Mass. SUNY ESF College Archives.

played a prominent role, an indication of Steele's early interest in exploring spatial layout outside the Beaux-Arts tradition. His plan shows views to Lake Cochichewick through the woods, and he also introduced a sequence of water-themed vignettes. (Fig. 14.10) An Italian pool with a large waterspout was sited at the end of a rhododendron-bordered bowling green; a double staircase along rushing cascades, based on a similar feature at the Villa Torlonia; small shell-shaped fountains modeled after features at the Generalife of the Alhambra, in Granada, Spain, coaxed visitors through the woods to a boathouse terrace, where a stupendous view of the lake was revealed. (Figs.14.11, 14.12) In this progression, artifice led to nature with powerful impact. The sequence would soon be reiterated in other designs.

Despite the wide-ranging influences that were shaping Steele's gardens, he understood this work to be grounded in an American school of ideas. He later wrote of Rolling Ridge, "[It] amuses me . . . to have people say 'It is a perfect Italian garden' and the next 'It is purely Spanish' and another 'It is genuinely English,' according to the European things that they have seen and liked the best. Of

14.11. Bowling green and fountain jet, Rolling Ridge. Photograph by Paul Weber. SUNY ESF College Archives.

14.12. Staircase behind fountain, Rolling Ridge. Photograph by Paul Weber. SUNY ESF College Archives.

course it is nothing but American, although quite unlike any other American place."[36] Steele would continue to respond to the genius loci as a guiding force independent of style. "It does not take the traveler long to find out that hills are hills and valleys [are] valleys all over the world," he wrote toward the end of his life. "In every country man has built on them both well and ill; fitted, and failed to fit, his structures onto the land. When he has had respect for the qualities of the site, then nothing in style or decoration has gone far wrong."[37]

In the years following World War I, Steele's client base expanded northward into New Hampshire and west through New York State to Michigan and Chicago's North Shore. With few exceptions, these jobs were pri-

vate.[38] Many of them were extensive, involving hundreds of plans and drawings. Steele published frequently, in *Landscape Architecture, Garden Magazine, Garden Club of America Bulletin, Country Life, House Beautiful, House and Garden, Horticulture, Ladies' Home Journal, Parks & Recreation*, and many other professional and popular periodicals. His topics ranged from horticulture to war memorials, billboard legislation to garden maintenance, space composition and modernism to suburban design. This writing was done with business goals in mind but from a progressive point of view, with the improvement of American taste as a goal. Color was a subject of persistent interest.

Steele was keenly aware of the structural role color played in his own landscape designs, and he closely observed it in the work of others. In a 1921 article for the

Garden Club of America Bulletin, he wrote appreciatively of Beatrix Farrand's planting composition in a Bar Harbor garden, noting the heightening in color values of the bloom that had been accomplished by hiding "so far as possible the green foliage of the perennials behind the whitish grey leaves of common and uncommon grey-foliage plants."[39] Over time, Steele became interested in bolder use of color. He wrote of attempting strong, "actually ugly" combinations that "would be instantly ripped out when they appeared in any other garden," and noted that he was "pleased when scolded for making dreadful sights which attract the eye with violence," adding provocatively, "There is nothing like a bit of downright ugliness to attract attention away from what one does not want observed."[40] Steele regarded bloom as pure pigment, a means of achieving "sheets of flat, daring color that leave the frantic cubist painter speechless."[41] In pursuit of these goals, he used a wide range of plant species, including the

gaudy exotics that Olmsted had so forcefully dismissed. In 1926 Steele told an interviewer in *Town and Country* magazine, "The chief vice in gardens, as in women, is to be merely pretty."[42]

In 1924 Steele published *Design in the Little Garden*, as part of Louisa Yeoman King's Little Garden series. The genial, conversational volume was a design primer aimed at general readers, and it also found admirers among members of the profession for its pragmatic approach to the small suburban place. George Tobey credits Steele's book with prophesying "the age of functionalism" four years before Clarence Stein and Henry Wright created their influential scheme for Radburn, New Jersey.[43] Many of the ideas outlined in *Design in the Little Garden* were also reflected in Steele's built work, where practicality continued as a defining virtue.

Steele addressed the same principles in his introduction to *The House Beautiful Gardening Manual*, where he observed pragmatically, "Fitness will be the keynote of everything," echoing the fundamental advice of Charles Eliot.[44] Steele, however, added a qualifier that addressed another aspect of his art-making: that an "ability to assimilate all previous knowledge in the creation of a new garden, adjusted to your needs, will prove once more the knack that is yours by right of being an American."[45]

———

14.13. Stairway to circular lawn, Wingfield, John and Nora Towne estate, Mount Kisco, N.Y. Photograph by Mattie Edwards Hewitt. SUNY ESF College Archives.

14.14. View across circular lawn to grotto, Wingfield. Photograph by Mattie Edwards Hewitt. SUNY ESF College Archives.

14.15. View out of circular lawn to meadow, Wingfield. Photograph by Mattie Edwards Hewitt. SUNY ESF College Archives.

14.16. View east across terrace pool to mountains, Lisburne Grange, Samuel and Katherine Sloan estate, Garrison, N.Y. Photograph by Fletcher Steele. SUNY ESF College Archives.

Several of Steele's designs from the early 1920s foreshadow aspects of work at Naumkeag, his most experimental, arguably his most important landscape design. In 1921 Steele began an estate job for John and Nora Towne in Mount Kisco, New York, where there was already an Italianate garden, designed c. 1910 by Arthur Shurcliff, who also ran a Boston-based practice.[46] Steele's additions included a staircase from the house terrace that led down to a circular lawn defined by a stucco exedra. (Figs. 14.13, 14.14) The view continued up into the woods and a hill-

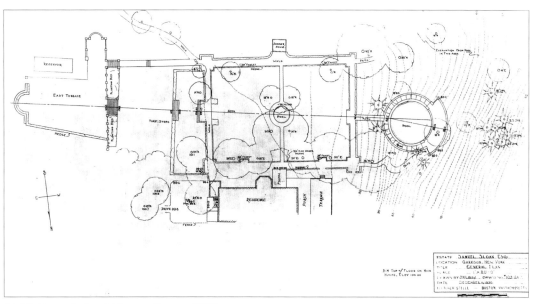

14.17. General plan, Lisburne Grange, 1930. SUNY ESF College Archives.

side grotto. Steele's scheme borrowed distinctive lines from the Villa Falconieri and also quoted elements of the grotto there. He situated these features on axis with Shurcliff's earlier garden, using its lines and proportions to guide them. At the bottom of the hill, Steele created paths from the circular lawn to flower-lined paths and, beyond, to wooded hillsides. (Fig. 14.15) The sequence from house to garden to woods repeated that at Rolling Ridge—artifice led to nature, a progression that would figure in his designs for Mabel Choate, too.

A 1921 commission from Samuel and Katherine Sloan, in Garrison, New York, also incorporated elements of an existing design. Steele wrote admiringly of the mid-nineteenth-century landscape of Lisburne Grange, the "grandeur of the now full-grown trees" and "breadth of . . . naturalistic park scenery."[47] Among the features he added to enhance these elements were a pair of large arborvitae that framed a mountain view and a new terrace that disguised an old water reservoir. (Figs. 14.16, 14.17) Steele was vigilant about protecting the spirit of the old design.

14.18. Swimming pool, Lisburne Grange. Photograph by Paul Weber. SUNY ESF College Archives.

14.19. View south to summer house, Lisburne Grange. Photograph by Fletcher Steele. SUNY ESF College Archives.

14.20. General plan, Ancrum House, Angelica Gerry estate, Delhi, N.Y. SUNY ESF College Archives.

When the Sloans asked him to create a new swimming pool for the estate in 1929, he located it in the side of the hill below the terrace, out of sight of the house and the main terrace. (Fig. 14.18) In the pool design, Steele borrowed forms from the Dragon Fountain at the Villa d'Este and added scrolls of close-clipped privet, in the French style, to frame the new feature. He bent the axis of the orientation, so that the pool faced a broad meadow—in Steele's opinion, the "finest feature of the place." His gardens would continue to include wide-ranging historical references, and view would also play a pivotal role.[48] (Fig. 14.19)

One of Steele's most ambitious projects from the 1920s was a landscape design for Ancrum House (c. 1925), in Delhi, New York, whose intricate plan included landscape passages that alternately concealed and revealed views of the Catskills. (Figs. 14.20, 14.21) Steele also accommodated his client's intense interest in bloom. Among several flower-oriented features were a forced perspective garden, with little drinking pools for Miss Angelica Gerry's dogs, and a mazelike series of beds for her delphinium. Steele devised still bolder uses for flowers in a grand sweep below a large semicircular terrace, where great swaths of iris and peonies appeared in succession. The most innovative aspect of the design was the plan, which accommodated many discrete areas while it set up framed vistas in almost every direction. Steele's colleague and close friend Ralph Adams Cram was the architect of the house (and the nearby church that Gerry

14.21. View east to Catskill Mountains, Ancrum House. Photograph by Fletcher Steele. SUNY ESF College Archives.

14.22. View to Lake St. Clair, Standish and Dorothy Backus estate, Grosse Pointe Shores, Mich. Photograph by Fletcher Steele. SUNY ESF College Archives.

14.23. Long Shot, Backus estate. Photograph by Fletcher Steele. SUNY ESF College Archives.

also commissioned). The job had likely come on his recommendation.

Cram may also have been the source of a concurrent job in Grosse Pointe Shores, Michigan, where Steele worked on a much smaller scale, although not a smaller budget. The clients there were Standish and Dorothy Backus, who also hired Steele to design a modest summer house estate, High Cliffe, in Manchester-by-the-Sea, Massachusetts. In the Michigan project, Steele was held closely to the Elizabethan period of English architecture, working closely with Cram and the client. Like the design for Ancrum House, the Backus place relied on a plan that defined precise garden areas. View was critical here, too, but limited to a single vista of Lake St. Clair, framed by a grading scheme that hid a busy boulevard with a rise in the lawn.[49] (Fig. 14.22) (While the Backuses had chosen to build on a relatively small lot near the village center, Edsel and Eleanor Ford, who were working on their estate project during these same years, were building directly on the lake, about eight miles to the north.) The most innovative feature on the Backus estate was the Long Shot, a forced-perspective modernist feature that comprised twelve bays, each of which displayed its own distinct garden border in a strong palette that kept it from being "merely pretty." (Fig. 14.23) Cram was the architect of the forty-room limestone house, and Robert O. Derrick (who was work-ing on the patriotic architectural amalgamation for Henry Ford's new museum in Dearborn at the time) was the lo-cal architect. Relief portraits of all three men were not too modestly incorporated into one of the piers in the estate's wild garden. (Fig. 14.24)

Ralph Cram was one of Steele's closest Boston friends.[50] The older architect offered him both intellectual

14.24. Post with relief portraits of Steele (left) and Ralph Adams Cram (right), Backus estate. Photograph by Fletcher Steele. SUNY ESF College Archives.

14.25. Ralph Adams Cram estate, Sudbury Center, Mass. Photograph by Fletcher Steele. SUNY ESF College Archives.

and social stimulation, and he shared Steele's respect for tradition as well as modern developments in art, enough to hire Steele to design his own country place landscape in 1926, in a design that mixed New England stone walls and classical columns.[51] (Fig. 14.25) Cram was bet-ter known than the landscape architect—in 1926, he was featured on the cover of *Time*—but Steele's renown was growing. *Town and Country* ran a society profile of him that same year.

At first encouraged by his teachers at Harvard and di-rected by his own philosophical inclinations, Steele con-tinued to embrace the past as a source of design ideas, even as he integrated modernist influences. "Dr. Ross taught me one thing at least," Steele had written to his mother in 1917, "that there is no intrinsic value in what is new or what is old . . . but that all things are valuable for what quality is in them. In that way one escapes try-ing to do a thing because it is new, and tries only for what has promise of beauty."[52] Years later he observed, "All that is permanent of what is being built today grows out of previous thought and deed, even though it is fed con-trivances not hitherto known, like steel and concrete construction."[53]

The freedom to borrow and recombine historical traditions guided Steele's work through the 1920s. The same principle was also evident in the designs of Farrand and Coffin, who, like Steele, also remained keenly alert to the spirit of the land. More explicitly than these colleagues, however, Steele was coming to con-ceptualize the garden as a three-dimensional space occupied by abstract forms. His interest in modernist treatment of garden space in-creased dramatically after he visited the 1925 Exposition des Arts Décoratifs et Industriels Modernes in Paris, where the garden installa-tions had been overseen by J. C. N. Forestier.[54] Among them were several Art Deco–inspired examples, including the "Garden of Water and Light" by Gabriel Guevrekian, which featured a revolving mirror globe, colored gravel, and angled flower beds filled with brightly colored bedding plants. (Fig. 14.26) Steele soon added hand-colored glass slides of this and other modernist designs (by Pierre-Émile Legrain, Albert Laprade, Tony Garnier, André Lurçat, Ernst May, and others) to his repertory of lectures for garden and civic clubs. He was most intrigued by the use of vertical space in these gardens. "The beds are not flat, but pyramidal or tilted at various angles," he wrote of Guevrekian's design, "so that the usual loss of interest in a flat pattern in perspective is minimized and a way indicated by which vertical dimensions may play a major part in future garden design."[55]

Steele's growing interest in modern art also reflected the influence of Alfred H. Barr Jr., who, like Denman Ross, championed abstract principles. "The grandeur of a Poussin is perceived, is read, remains as it were at arm's length," Steele wrote (quoting Barr's introduction to the first catalog of the Museum of Modern Art). "But a great Cézanne is immanent; it grows around one and includes one. What interests me most is the expanded sense,—not a new sense but the expansion of our old sense of dimensions, space, relativity, call it what you will."[56] Two years later, he explained the concept in more detail in an article in *Landscape Architecture*:

Successful space composition has an entity of its own quite independent of the things around and in it. It is felt rather than seen. It houses the spirit and charm of a place. It is intangible yet continually felt. Size—mere smallness or largeness—has nothing to do with it. Whatever the size, the human being *feels* a relation to the space in which he is,—an almost mystical sense of being part of it himself.

Then he drew out the implications for the design process:

A good result depends on designing in three dimensions from the first. Plans and elevations, worked out in two dimensions, no matter how

14.26. "Garden of Water and Light," Gabriel Guevrekian, Exposition Internationale des Arts Décoratifs et Industriels Modernes, Paris, glass slide in Steele's collection. SUNY ESF College Archives.

carefully fitted together, are never sufficient. The spaces must be conceived in volumes and the enclosures made to fit accordingly. . . . Nothing exists for itself nor for its relation to other features alone, but also because it serves to build up this other thing.[57]

By the early 1930s emphasis on three-dimensional treatment of garden space was guiding other American practitioners too, among them Lockwood de Forest.[58] Steele predicted, with accuracy, "that successful space composition will be the next serious preoccupation of landscape architects."[59] At the Paris exposition Steele also saw examples of the "bent" or "broken" axis, and this, too, would affect his methods. He wrote admiringly of Legrain's design for Villa Tachard, where "the dead axis of the past has come to elusive vibrant life."[60]

Steele was soon experimenting with the principle of the bent axis in a 1928 design for the Camden (Maine) Public Library Amphitheater, one of the few public commissions that he took on over his long career. The project was commissioned by Mary Bok, a wealthy summer resident who had simultaneously hired Olmsted Brothers to design a park across the avenue, directly on the harbor.[61] Steele's methods were thus juxtaposed with those of Fred-

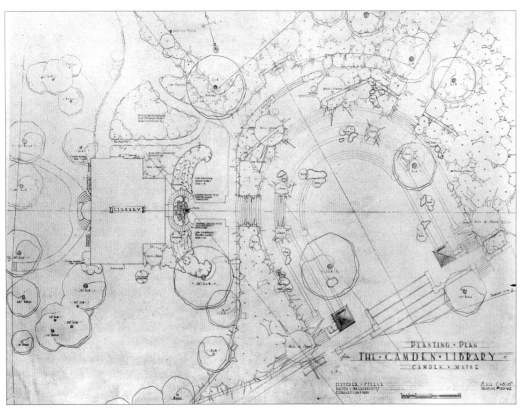

14.27. Plan for Camden (Me.) Public Library Amphitheater, 1930. SUNY ESF College Archives.

14.28. View to harbor, Camden Amphitheater. Photograph by Paul Weber. SUNY ESF College Archives.

erick Law Olmsted Jr.—one of the "old maids" at Harvard he had complained to his parents about. Almost immediately, conflict sprang up over Steele's decision to align the axis of the amphitheater (behind the library) so that it would provide a direct view of the harbor and Olmsted

Jr.'s sense that the arrangement was not, in his word, "normal," that is, the garden did not align, in the Beaux-Arts tradition, with the central axis of the architecture. But Steele persuaded Bok of the advantages of his plan and the building committee approved it.[62] (Fig. 14.27)

Steele's design for Camden was characterized by other quietly revolutionary aspects. Although he relied primarily on native plants for the scheme—American elm, maple, spruce, and birch—they were utilized for strong abstract effect. White birch, in particular, provided a forceful visual counterpoint to the horizontal rock terraces. (At Naumkeag, Steele would again turn to birch for their pungent mix of lithe vertical form and wildness.) Yet Steele's integration of these abstract effects did little to disturb a poetic sense of the amphitheater as an ancient site, a ruin, as it were, going back to nature. (Fig. 14.28)

In Paris, Steele had also become intrigued by the French modernists' new use of materials in gardens—notoriously demonstrated at the exposition by Robert Mallet-Stevens's garden of concrete trees. He would soon begin to experiment in his own projects with colored gravel and other nontraditional materials, Lucite, brass, factory tiles, car headlights, and, most famously at Naumkeag, concrete steps that he painted blue.[63] A few years before creating the Blue Steps, he designed a pink concrete rose garden for Helen Ellwanger, granddaughter of the famous Rochester nurseryman. (Fig. 14.29) The versatile material allowed for the flowing curves that structured many of Steele's works during the decade. In 1929 Steele observed that it was not surprising to see the French take the lead in such experiments, for they had always had "but little real affection for horticulture. . . . A tree to them is not good in itself, but for what can be done with it, as with brick or a thousand gallons of water."[64]

Many of the most important tenets in Steele's garden-making derived from French traditions, including the concept of the "Three Unities of Garden Design," as he identified them: "Floor of earth or water. Walls of marble or of Verdure. Roof of Sky." Steele believed that this principle implied three-dimensional composition, which had become one cornerstone of his theoretical approach. In an essay for the San Francisco Museum of Art exhibition *Contemporary Landscape Architecture and Its Sources* (1936), he explained his sense that awareness of spatial composition trumped the categories of formal and informal design that were still informing the thinking of many of his colleagues: "These two styles are mere surface decoration, each in accord with profound instincts in human character. Composition in landscape design may be achieved by either method or by combination of both. At bottom, the true aim of landscape architecture is one: by use of style, color and form, to create beauty in space composition."[65]

During the 1920s and 1930s, Steele returned to Europe almost every year, and there he found inspiration for new projects. He also continued to add to his extensive library, which came to include many rare folios on which he relied for ideas.[66] Henry Hoover, Steele's assistant from 1926 until 1940, recalled that Steele studied these volumes and then presented him with sketched designs that often combined multiple influences. Hoover used the sketches to produce drawings for client presentations. Another key employee in Steele's practice during these years, Virginia Cavendish, generated planting plans and located sources for plants. Many other assistants, draftsmen, and secretaries worked for Steele, but he was the sole principal, and client contact was almost always directly with him.[67] He eventually listed about seven hundred commissions.

14.29. Staircase in rose garden, Helen Ellwanger estate, Rochester, N.Y. Photograph by Fletcher Steele. SUNY ESF College Archives.

Over the course of his career, Steele built up a reputation as a lively and amusing lecturer. He was inspired by the progressive spirit of the day, but his lectures also became a highly effective means of finding new commissions. Audiences enjoyed hearing advice about street trees and maintenance techniques mixed with humorous jabs at current gardening fashions. It was at one such lecture, for the Lenox, Massachusetts, Garden Club in July 1926, that Steele met Mabel Choate. Her family's summer place, Naumkeag, occupied a hillside in nearby Stockbridge, and over lunch she explained to him that she had recently been to Santa Barbara and was eager to add a California-style outdoor room to her garden. Steele agreed to come for a visit the following day.

FIFTEEN

NAUMKEAG

Stockbridge, Massachusetts

Naumkeag was considerably less grand than the Berkshires' most opulent estates—Shadow Brook, for example, the largest house in America until Biltmore superseded it one year later, or Bellefontaine, whose extensive Beaux-Arts landscape development was overseen by Carrère & Hastings.[1] Both of these estates, and many more like them, were located in Lenox, which was also pretentious in comparison to nearby Stockbridge, a frontier mission village. But Naumkeag possessed a quality these more ostentatious layouts lacked—charm. As Wilhelm Miller advised *Country Life* readers in 1910, "If you like atmosphere, harmony, proportion, balance, permanence, self-mastery, sit here and drink your fill."[2] (Fig. 15.1)

Miller particularly approved of the way that Nathan Barrett had nestled Naumkeag's formal gardens into the steep hillside, where they commanded a broad view of Monument Mountain—ironically, just where Olmsted had pronounced a garden impossible. (The firm had been dismissed after suggesting a location for the house on the site of the Choates' favorite oak.[3]) Miller also admired the design's restraint: "Trees all around the garden—high enough to give seclusion and comfort, but not high enough to spoil the view. Steps descending to the four successive levels, where one may walk without apparent effort. A fountain shimmering in the sunshine. Borders of perennial flowers glowing against the evergreen hedges. A few simple flower beds in stately order. An atmosphere of sunny calm. A benign old garden, modest, self-restrained, wearing its honors with an easy grace. . . . Famous men rarely have good gardens, but Mr. Joseph H. Choate has one that is almost as brilliant, mellow, and simple-hearted as himself."[4]

Miller's description of Joseph Choate scarcely suggests one of the sharpest legal minds of the era, but few would dispute that claim. As partner in the firm of Evarts, Southmayd & Choate, Joseph successfully argued some of the period's most important court cases, including the unconstitutionality of the proposed income tax, which he managed to stave off until 1913. He also prosecuted early Tammany Hall scandals and, from 1899 to 1905, served as ambassador to Great Britain, renting Naumkeag to the Marshall Fields while he and his family lived in London. His wit was widely admired, as was the speed with which he employed it in the courtroom. Still, Joseph's great pleasure seems to have been nature. "What a luxury it will

15.1. Formal garden, design by Nathan Barrett. Naumkeag.

later) Edith Wharton. It drew artists, too, the most prominent being Daniel Chester French, who became so intrigued by the process of designing the property of his studio, Chesterwood, that he began taking on landscape jobs for his neighbors.[7]

Despite these cultural overtones, summers in Berkshire were a recreational frenzy. "Merry-go-rounds . . . at a tally-ho pace" was how one writer described the scene.

> There were lawn parties and picnics in the hills, boating on the Housatonic and veranda tete-a-tetes, horseback riding and bicycling about town, or long expeditions by buggy, coach or Stephen Field's new trolley to such attractions as Bash Bish [Falls]. . . . There were croquet, cricket and tennis tourneys. . . . There were soirees and theatricals, and dances at the Casino. The Lenox Season closed with the gala Tub Parade and that of Stockbridge with the costumed street festivities and bonfire following the mad, torchlight scramble through Ice Glen.[8]

The Choates were typically there through late fall, when they moved back to Manhattan.

In 1884 Joseph and Caroline purchased about fifty acres of steeply sloping hillside pasture where they had been picnicking for a decade, and threw themselves into the project of building a new country estate, approaching Charles McKim, of McKim, Mead & White, to do the work. McKim was getting married, however, so he turned the job over to his young partner Stanford White, who soon became a friend of the family. "Every moment of the building of the house and the laying out of the grounds was watched with excitement by the family and with curiosity by everyone in town," Mabel Choate wrote. "I suspect that my father's old partner, Mr. Southmayd, was voicing public opinion when he asked, 'What all the gimcracks were for.'"[9] (Joseph, who was frugal in his tastes, may have wondered, too. Once, when asked for a donation to build a fence for the village cemetery, he declined, pointing out that "nobody inside can get out, and no one on the outside wants to get in."[10])

be to me to escape from the city," he wrote to his daughter in 1883, "and to roll on the grass, ride over the hills, and float in Stockbridge Bowl."[5]

Caroline Sterling Choate, Joseph's wife, was an amateur artist and ardent promoter of women's higher education. In the 1880s she persuaded a young friend of her son's to found a preparatory school for girls in New York City, Brearley, and enrolled her two daughters in the inaugural class. The curriculum included Greek, Latin, and mathematics, subjects that were required for admittance to most universities. Still not satisfied, Caroline convinced the trustees of Columbia to create Barnard, the first women's college in Manhattan, and was named vice-chairman of the board. Mabel, her elder daughter, enrolled as a student in political science there and later became a trustee.

In 1874 the Choates began summering in western Massachusetts, a four-hour train ride to the north.[6] Berkshire, as the region was then known, combined beautiful mountain scenery with pastoral New England charm, and it drew increasing numbers of tourists eager for such pleasures. Over the course of the nineteenth century the area had also attracted several literary figures, among them Catharine M. Sedgwick, Oliver Wendell Holmes Sr., Nathaniel Hawthorne, Herman Melville, and (somewhat

White designed a large cottage that featured an arrangement of bays, towers, and gables that together conveyed the stalwart impression of a Norman fortress. (Fig. 15.2) The front and north facades are exposed brick and fieldstone, enlivened with shimmering bits of broken glass mixed into the mortar. The simpler south and west facades, which are open to the landscape, feature brick and unpainted shingles. Guests entered from a porte cochere and a thick paneled front door through a looming brick arch into the living hall, a relatively new innovation that had won the approval of Mariana Van Rensselaer, who described the hybrid space as "a spacious yet cozy and informal lounging-place for times when we cannot lounge on our beloved piazzas."[11] (Charles Platt would design a similar room off the portico at Gwinn.) Easy exchange between indoors and out was facilitated by double doors that led to a covered porch and terrace at the rear. (Fig. 15.3)

Naumkeag's forty-four rooms were designed in styles that ranged from Jacobean to Neoclassical to Colonial Revival, furnished in the eclectic mix recommended by the day's leading arbiters of taste. Mabel Choate's later notable additions included a large collection of Chinese export porcelain, oriental rugs, and a pioneering assemblage of early American furniture, deemed "mouthwatering" by Geoffrey Platt, Charles Platt's son, a frequent guest at Naumkeag after his marriage to Mabel's niece Helen.[12] Fletcher Steele also heartily approved of the mix: "Experience had taught that Jacobean settles, modern pianos, Flemish tapestries, oriental rugs and up-to-date French paintings could all be harmonious if well arranged."[13]

Nathan Barrett's design for the grounds, realized at approximately the same time the house was built, was also the subject of great excitement. Mabel remembers that she and her brothers and sister were mystified by Barrett's talk of "features." "We always thought the word meant noses, chins, etc., and were astonished, but we soon learned and 'features' became one of our best family words."[14] Steele thought the design particularly fine, noting that "Barrett had vision at a time when most landscape designers merely fumbled."[15] The strong geometry of the upper and lower gardens, laid out on either side of

15.2. House from southeast, design by Stanford White, 1885. Library of Congress.

15.3. Mabel (left) and Josephine Choate (next), sitting in Naumkeag's covered piazza, view north. Naumkeag.

the entry drive, responded to the lines and the massing of the house. (Fig. 15.4) Both provided views west, to the mountains.

In the four decades between construction of the estate and Steele's first visit to it, the Choate family had been transformed by time and loss. Mabel's brother Ruluff died of a brain aneurysm while home on vacation from Harvard in 1884, just before the house was completed. Effie (Josephine) died in 1896, of then untreatable colitis. A second brother, George, suffered a nervous breakdown shortly after enrolling in Williams College and remained

15.4. Mabel Choate in arborvitae allée, formal garden, view southeast.
Library of Congress.

institutionalized for his entire life. Naumkeag offered respite and renewal in the wake of the family's tragedies.[16]

The country estate, whose name came from the Algonquian word for Joseph's birthplace, Salem, Massachusetts—haven of peace—also provided a retreat from the demands of his urban life. "I do miss Stockbridge and every dear thing in it," he wrote Caroline from Albany in 1894, "wife, children, friends, house, garden, lands, horses, cows, pigs, not to speak of the donkey."[17] Joseph died peacefully in 1917, after a dinner spent discussing the immortality of the soul with his guests, among whom was the philosopher Henri Bergson. Caroline Choate would live to ninety-two. As she aged, her unmarried daughter, Mabel, began to assume increasing responsibility for running the estate.

Although she did not enjoy particularly good health, Mabel Choate possessed a robust spirit that Steele found inspiring. She also had "two remarkably strong instincts pertinent to landscape architecture," he wrote after many years of working with her. "She wants to make and try

things. And she deeply enjoys, analyses and understands beauty in landscape, in detail as in larger aspects."[18] Steele came to enjoy her company immensely, and the feeling was mutual. Geoffrey Platt remembered the two having "a marvelous time together, with much laughter and private conferences."[19] Their collaboration would stretch over three decades, supported by deepening friendship and excitement about Naumkeag's potential as a work of art. Steele's artistic imaginings were never more heartily encouraged.

As Mabel Choate and Fletcher Steele walked around the estate on the July afternoon of his first visit in 1926, she explained her desire for a new outdoor room, as well as her intention to preserve the Victorian feeling of the existing design. Steele agreed "that the bones of what had been first done were good and should not only be preserved where possible but that the old spirit should be followed in all that was to come."[20] This decision laid a firm footing for Steele's future work. Choate also told him that she wanted to reduce the demands of the old flower beds as their upkeep had begun to overwhelm the estate superintendent, Robert Crighton, whose crew had shrunk from the sixteen men who had been in charge of raking the gravel paths, feeding and staking the six-foot delphinium, and trimming up the topiary.[21]

She had sought landscape advice from other well-known landscape practitioners before she turned to Steele. In 1918 Choate had commissioned Marian Coffin to consult on new plantings for the formal garden, and Coffin's recommendations from that visit and over the next two years reflect an intention to bring a more up-to-date mix to the old-fashioned beds.[22] She had also consulted Olmsted Brothers. A 1919 memo from their representative Percival Gallagher recommended new plantings for the steep slope below the house.[23] The division of labor—Coffin advising on the flower gardens, Gallagher on the hillside plantings—neatly captured the profession's enduring gender divide.

Neither of these consultations, however, led to the sort collaborative excitement that would arise with

Steele, whose frank manner and wry sense of humor must have struck the right chord with Choate from the first. He began the tour by pointing out that before anything else happened at Naumkeag, the estate's service entry was going to be redesigned—because, in Steele's words, he "couldn't possibly work for anyone whose back door looked like that."[24] Recently returned from the 1925 Paris exposition, he was probably also impatient to integrate some of the principles he had absorbed there into work for her.

He decided that the new outdoor room should be located on the south side of the house, off the library, where it would get good sun and also provide mountain views. (Fig. 15.5) As at Dumbarton Oaks and in many Italian villa gardens, these views would be facilitated by a sharp drop in grade—at Naumkeag, about one hundred feet. But the first call was for privacy. "The owner felt exposed," Steele explained in a long piece he wrote about the design, "there was no place near the house to find ease on a steamer chair out of view of the constant visitors on her own drive."[25] He decided that a tall wall should separate the drive, and thus, two walls of the room were fixed.

As a focal point in the garden, Steele hit upon the idea of relocating a bronze sculpture that was ensconced in a vine-covered niche at the front of the house, Frederick W. MacMonnies's *Boy with Heron*, whose "handsome, agitated silhouette" he thought wasted in the dark enclosure.[26] A young farm boy (without heron) was asked to stand in for the statue and moved about on a stepladder until he looked right from all angles, and there the sculpture was placed, marking the corner of the new room. (Figs. 15.6, 15.7) The aesthetic experiment was comparable to H. F. du Pont's color trials at Winterthur, as he tested azalea branches held in milk bottles, or Beatrix Farrand's full-size mock-ups at Dumbarton Oaks. But this bit of theater at Naumkeag, undoubtedly invigorated by Margaret's celebrated martinis (which the kitchen maid kept premixed, in the freezer), was as much a goal as a means to an end.

15.5. Plan for Afternoon Garden, 1929. SUNY ESF College Archives.

Developments throughout the estate would be determined by similar experiments, typically conducted as part of the cocktail hour, which in Steele's case began at one in the afternoon.[27]

"To plan an inner wall between a garden and the drive required no thought," he wrote. "But just how to build an enclosed outdoor room with no obstruction of the view on two sides was another matter."[28] Steele arrived at the solution of using columns to define transparent walls for the room—conceived from the start as a well-composed volume of air—by remembering the experience of walking through a colonnade, where he "felt well enclosed, yet could see between the columns all that could be seen." (It was this aspect of the feature that would so excite Lockwood de Forest.) Steele purchased a group of columns that had been dredged out of Boston Harbor and had them carved by Archangelo Cascieri, his office sculptor, in what he described as a "Norwegian" style. Bold capitals were added, painted, Steele said, the colors of medieval manuscript illuminations—gold, dark blue, green, garnet red—and heavy ropes strung between them to add a

15.6. Afternoon Garden from library, view south. Photograph by Paul Weber. SUNY ESF College Archives.

15.7. Afternoon Garden from garden gate, view west. Photograph by Paul Weber. SUNY ESF College Archives.

horizontal dimension. (Fig. 15.8) Woodbine and clematis soon clambered over all.

In furnishing the new room, Steele drew on landscape traditions from Italy, France, Spain, England, and rural New England, responding to Choate's wide-ranging tastes in art, horticulture, and travel locales, as was his method. He introduced four little marble fountains based on shell-shaped prototypes from the Generalife, the same design as those in the woodland walk at Rolling Ridge. Between them he laid an oval of shining black glass, covered by half an inch of water, he said, to bring a reflection of sky into the garden. (Fig. 15.9) "Around the fountains is an old French knot design," Steele explained. "Once the beds were filled with tiny blue and yellow flowers. They were a bother to keep in good condition. So now their places

15.8. Construction, Afternoon Garden, view northwest. SUNY ESF College Archives.

15.9. *Afternoon Garden,* 1998. Photograph by Carol Betsch.

are filled with chips of pink and green marble and blue-black coal. The eye is sufficiently satisfied and the contemptuous horticulturist can look away to dozens of pots of fuchsias, yellow callas, agapanthus and bamboo."[29] Wrought-iron holders, modeled on Spanish prototypes, held Choate's collection of pots. A grapevine-covered lattice roof shaded a portion of the room, in the Italian tradition. The "walls" were scenic views of the Berkshire mountains.

Steele included a model of the garden in an exhibition at the Louvre in 1930. Shaped like a box with viewing holes in the side, it had a sheet of ground glass across the top, with the interior sides painted to resemble a mountain panorama.[30] The Afternoon Garden was also pub-

15.10. South lawn, with fill. Photograph by Fletcher Steele. SUNY ESF College Archives.

15.11. South lawn, after grading. Photograph by Fletcher Steele. SUNY ESF College Archives.

lished in several articles, the first of which appeared in *House Beautiful* in 1933. Among Steele's admirers was John D. Rockefeller Jr., who liked the feature so much, *House Beautiful* reported, "that he referred to it as the kind of garden he would like to see built on one of the elevated terraces of Radio City."[31] Choate felt immediately at home in her new garden room. "One can sit there with a friend, and talk; or alone, and dream; and never have a sensation of loneliness, or feel that it is necessary to find something to do."[32]

By 1930 the vista from the Afternoon Garden to Bear Mountain had been obscured by a stand of trees. Steele decided to top the encroaching grove, shaping the tree line in perfect imitation of the curve of the mountain's silhouette beyond it. The task required a large crew, armed with saws and directed by Steele from the Afternoon Garden, walkie-talkie and field glasses in hand. "Thus," Steele wrote, "the strongest design line furnished by Nature was brought back and made the major motive."[33]

The new contour was an improvement, but the bumpy, uneven lawn that stretched between the Afternoon Garden and the grove was an eyesore, and Steele decided that a new design for it was needed to complete the picture. He weighed two alternatives and dismissed both "a so-called naturalistic affair with a path meandering down hill" and the solution that Edith Wharton would have recommended, "a range of terraces in the Italian Garden manner." The first did not appeal to Steele's designer's instinct, and he rejected the second, he wrote, because "Italian Gardens do not fit Victorian wood houses." His solution would transcend both and offer a revolutionary reframing of the space.

Steele decided to carve the big lawn into a form that recalled contemporary work by Constantin Brancusi and Jean Arp, as he described it, "an abstract form in the manner of modern sculpture, with swinging curves and slopes which would aim to make their impression directly, without calling on the help of associated ideas, whether in nature or art."[34] (Figs. 15.10, 15.11) The curving, sculpted lawn was unprecedented at the time, the first example of a modern earthwork.

Creating the new lawn required a large amount of fill, which Mabel Choate helpfully secured from a convoy of dump trucks she noticed passing the house one day. The grading procedure was painstaking, Steele remembered, "cutting and hauling and scraping, then doing it all over again, because it was necessary to learn what to do while doing it." He added appreciatively, "Most of all it took unbelievable patience on the part of the client, who had to watch men interminably raking a few inches off a ridge for a week or more after the work appeared finished."[35] He directed the work on-site, taking stock of the emerging shape from every angle.

First seen after entering the garden gate, the great swooping curve is sudden and insistent, its impact almost visceral, a consequence of its scale and plastic strength. Once-distant mountains, appropriated by the new contours, are forcefully brought into the garden picture. Foreground and background coalesce into a composition in which Nature's "major motive" is answered with imaginative, abstract force. Designed in the pictorial tradition of Olmsted, the South Lawn is also both meadow and three-dimensional object, a positive and primary spatial entity, shaped with precise, sculptural intention. (Fig. 15.12)

Steele would continue the play of curves by reshaping the contour of the lower edge of the South Lawn to repeat the line of the mountains and distant grove. He laid out a brick path (which also served as a service road) that echoed this trajectory in reverse, and had the office's rockwork expert, Henry Rice, construct a promontory that pulled the eye out toward the mountains to the west. (Fig. 15.13) At the lower edge of the new lawn, he planted a curving row of globe locust trees (*Gleditsia robinia*) to throw "swooping shadows across the modeled earth, marking the minor changes which would otherwise flatten in the harsh light."[36] At the end of the lawn, where it arced out of sight, Steele planted a curl of red Japanese maples, trimmed to form a hedge. The double hemlock

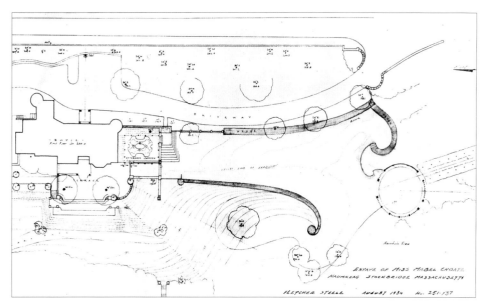

15.12. General plan, Naumkeag, 1934. SUNY ESF College Archives.

hedge at the top of the lawn was Choate's own idea, based on an example she had admired at Courances, outside Paris, which she had visited with the Garden Club of America in 1936.

Still not satisfied, Steele decided that the garden picture needed a focal point. "What finally developed," he wrote, "was dipped out of the American melting pot, like so many other things on the place." He bought a cast-iron verandah that had been salvaged from an old house in Washington, D.C., and made a pavilion from it, which Choate then painted. Inside, they placed a large sacred stone on a carved Ming base, both bought in China. (Fig. 15.14) "Like all good Chinese garden decoration, it appeals strongly to the imagination without any good reason," Steele noted. "It is just a rock, but makes one think of all sorts of romantic things."[37] The resulting composition—mountain vista, curving tree line, sculptural lawn, and pavilion—holds its own against the panoramic view to the west. Steele's curves are compelling, and, in the end, they satisfied the modernist as well as the genius loci, "the pull of the land itself."[38]

The new gardens at Naumkeag were Steele's inventions, but they also owed a great deal to Mabel Choate's taste and imagination. Over decades of travel with the GCA,

she recorded her impressions in club bulletins that out-lined garden tours in Hawaii, France, Japan, China, Chicago, Philadelphia, the Hudson River valley, Rochester, California, and several other locations.[39] She was interested in many aspects of garden design, from architectural detail to less tangible entities, such as charm. Among her notes from a July 1934 trip to Camden, Maine, is a sketch of Steele's bent-axis plan for the library amphitheater, and during a 1933 trip to Lake Forest, Illinois, she made a drawing of Manning's layout for Harriet and Cyrus Mc-Cormick's Walden, marking the important view to Lake Michigan.[40]

Choate was sophisticated about plants too. At Naumkeag, she experimented determinedly with new species to find out which would survive the severe extremes of the climate. Steele noted that she tested eight species of rhododendron, eight heaths and heathers, six box, twenty *Hedera helix*, twenty-nine tree peonies, and fifty-five clematis. Choate also experimented with tender annuals for pot culture, a subject of great interest to Steele, who recorded fifty-one varieties of fuchsia, nineteen "local" pelargonium, and twenty from England.[41] Despite the meticulous record-keeping, gardenmaking at Naumkeag was more often propelled by a sense of fun and shared endeavor. Steele sometimes put Choate's other houseguests to work weeding, watering, and dead-heading. The playfulness Mabel sought in the gardenmaking process was also expressed in games with her grandnieces and -nephews, whom she taught how to belch (a sign of gratitude after a meal in China, she explained) and tucked in at night by tracing planetary addresses on the backs of their pajamas.

Music played an important role at Naumkeag, too. Choate often held small, private performances during her house parties, using musicians from the Boston Symphony Orchestra who were in town to perform at the Tanglewood Music Festival. For these, Steele created the Ronde

15.14. Pavilion and view into Ronde Point. Photograph by Fletcher Steele. Naumkeag.

Point, a little theater adjacent to the newly graded South Lawn, a clearing defined by a curving hedge of arborvitae and, at the east side, a long bench for the audience.[42] The feature had been inspired by the Place de l'Étoile, a convergence of streets in Paris, where Steele and Choate had traveled together in 1932. The Ronde Point also served as a transition to the Linden Allée, which had been planted decades earlier by Caroline Choate. (Fig. 15.15)

Steele's revision of Barrett's landscape layout eventually focused on the geometric flower beds that survived from the c. 1885 design. The upper garden became a site for Choate's plant trials, and the lower one, on the west side of the long arborvitae allée (also retained from Barrett's design), became an evergreen garden, edged with a curving hedge of low box and specimen spruce and faced down with massed plantings of yucca and snakeroot (*Cimicifuga*).[43] (Figs. 15.16, 15.17) The great flower border that once filled the swath of the hillside below the South Lawn was given over to Japanese knotweed.

In 1937 Steele began work on Naumkeag's most exotic feature, the Chinese Temple Garden. Choate had traveled to China and Japan in 1935 (the year after a similar trip by Steele) and then rented a house in Peking for a month, acquiring figures, pots, sacred rocks, and carvings—"without guessing," Steele later noted, "the shudders of her professional landscape advisor whose duty it

15.13. *Oak in South Lawn,* 1998. Photograph by Carol Betsch.

FOLLOWING PAGES:
15.15. *View from Linden Allée,* 1998. Photograph by Carol Betsch.

15.16. *Arborvitae Allée,* 1998. Photograph by Carol Betsch.

15.17. Plantings in evergreen garden. Photograph by Fletcher Steele. SUNY ESF College Archives.

15.18. Construction of Chinese Temple, 1937. Photograph by Fletcher Steele. SUNY ESF College Archives.

was to make them feel at home on a New England hillside."[44] Cram, who visited Naumkeag shortly after Choate's return, suggested creating a garden for them.

Steele said that he worked out the construction details for the new garden on-site, including the temple walls, steps, and marble Spirit Walk. (Fig. 15.18) A wall was built to separate the garden from the drive, the interior of it painted six different shades of red. (Fig. 15.19) A coat of whitewash was applied while the paint was still wet, giving the impression, Henry Hoover remembered, that "it had been raining since Confucius."[45] A Devil's Gate with a blue-tiled roof was installed to provide access through first a right-hand and then a left-hand turn (keeping the Devil out, since he can only travel in a straight line). (Fig. 15.20)

The garden's planting scheme was Chinese-inspired as well. "The marble boxes beside the walk, each guarding a Dianthus plant, are a reminder of the same plant used the same way, in far off Tai Yuan Fu," wrote Steele. "The Peonies in the long narrow shelf at the foot of the Temple wall remind one of Tan Ch'ih Ssu and many another place."[46] The floor of the new garden was covered with moss and a clump of Japanese butterbur (*Petasites japonicus*) planted to evoke lotus. A grove of seven gingko trees was planted, along with large specimen white pine. Ornamental plum and peach grew in oversize porcelain tubs. (Figs. 15.21, 15.22) Steele remembered Mabel Choate's impatience with long-winded discussions about what to plant in the sixteen metal pots in the garden and that she finally set out into the countryside by herself and dug several "stalwart weeds" to fill them.[47] The fantastical setting inspired at least one bit of impromptu theater, too. Frank Crowninshield, Choate's Berkshire neighbor and a frequent guest, sneaked into Naumkeag unseen one evening and later emerged from the Chinese Temple in monk's garb, scaring Steele out of his wits.

The details were fascinating, but the garden's most memorable attribute was its space. Geoffrey Platt considered it the finest garden at Naumkeag, "a masterpiece."[48] Like the Afternoon Garden, the Chinese Garden provides

15.19. *Chinese Garden Wall*, 1998. Photograph by Carol Betsch.

both a feeling of enclosure and a connection to the landscape beyond, set up by the location of the temple at the top of the hillside, where it frames a long view directly west. (Fig. 15.23) That Charles Platt's son—an architect like his father—admired it was no surprise.

Many of Steele's gardens reflected his clients' travel reminiscences, and, conversely, his gardens provided many of the same satisfactions as travel. One of his happiest customers in this regard was Charlotte Whitney Allen, who told Steele that she had stopped going to Europe because her own backyard was so much more satisfactory than anything she ever saw abroad.[49] Naumkeag's Chinese Garden was similarly intended to recollect the exotic atmosphere of places admired and, as Steele

15.21. Chinese Temple. Photograph by Fletcher Steele. SUNY ESF College Archives.

wrote in a nod to progressive tradition, to improve American life: "This is a Traveler's garden," Steele explained, "bringing home to America the best of foreign life and habits to enrich our ways here."[50] To his sister, he privately acknowledged the latitude with which he had interpreted the traditional Chinese form: "Of course it is no more Chinese than an old parlor in Salem filled with Chinese objects."[51]

In 1938 Steele began the best-known of his gardens at Naumkeag, the Blue Steps, built in response to Choate's request for proper stairs to her cutting gardens at the bottom of the steep hill. She told Steele that she didn't care how they looked, but they must be easy to use. He worked out the design, he claimed, from kinesthetic principles. "I figure that comfort in going up a steep hill depends on variety of leg action the lack of which makes a long flight of steps intolerable," he noted. "So I put up four 'divisions,' each one having a couple of steps and turns, two ramps of different steepness and a graduated flight of half a dozen steps to a platform." Steele's description scarcely does justice to the grace of the design, whose curves and rhythms

15.22. Furniture and plantings in Chinese Garden. Photograph by Fletcher Steele. SUNY ESF College Archives.

must have been evident even as the plans for the water staircase took shape on the drafting table. (Fig. 15.24) In fact, the feature's basic form was inspired by an Italian prototype, and the shallow brick runnel that leads to it was derived from Moorish gardens in Spain. Steele's version stripped these forms of their historical associations and realized them in brick and concrete.[52] (Fig. 15.25)

It was only after the staircase was complete that Steele suggested painting it. He, Choate, and her other house-

15.20. *Devil's Gate*, 1998. Photograph by Carol Betsch.

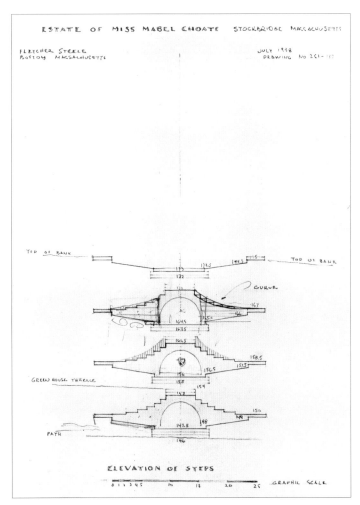

15.24. Construction drawing for steps, 1938. SUNY ESF College Archives.

15.25. Construction of steps, toward cutting garden. Photograph by Fletcher Steele. SUNY ESF College Archives.

15.26. Mabel Choate and Fletcher Steele painting steps, 1938. SUNY ESF College Archives.

guests did the work one weekend, applying a scheme of bright blue, yellow, and barn red that Steele thought was spectacular. (Fig. 15.26) Apparently not everyone agreed because the combination was quickly replaced by a strong, rich blue applied to the inside of the arches. The concrete surrounding eventually weathered to organic shades of gray and brown, warmed by the light that filters through the grove of birch planted to surround the feature.

The trees seem to have been an afterthought as well—Hoover's 1938 presentation drawings show low shrubs instead. (Fig. 15.27) Construction photographs of the site reveal that native birch were growing nearby, and these evidently offered inspiration. Steele would have known

15.23. *View from Chinese Garden,* 1998. Photograph by Carol Betsch.

Manning's use of the tree in the allée at Stan Hywet Hall, and Steele himself had used birch for abstract purposes in his 1929 design for the Camden Library Amphitheater. At Naumkeag, Steele's intention was evidently to suggest natural patterns of growth, for the birch clumps were purchased in several sizes. (Fig. 15.28) Low *Taxus* hedges heighten the decorative impact of both the white trees and the railings.

A walk down the steps requires cutting back and forth at a 180-degree angle, a kinesthetic manifestation of the

Stairs down the Bank
Estate of Miss Mabel Choate
          Stockbridge Massachusetts

Fletcher Steele   June 1938
Boston Massachusetts   No 251–186

15.27. Presentation drawing of steps, 1938. SUNY ESF College Archives.

15.28. Planting birches around steps, 1938. Photograph by Fletcher Steele. SUNY ESF College Archives.

zigzagging axis that Steele had admired in France. The larger landscape, as glimpsed through the birch trunks, becomes a series of changing, faceted views. (Fig. 15.29) But the full beauty of the design is revealed only at the bottom of the steps. From this vantage point, the arched openings appear to widen sequentially, and the space defined by the birches and the transparent planes of railings seems almost to flow down the hill. Most arresting is the visual play between the Art Deco curves of pipe and the arching forms of the birch. Reversing one of the central premises of a field in which art typically seeks to imitate nature, here Steele coaxes nature into imitating art, both blurring the distinction between the two and proposing an inventive reconciliation of them. (Fig. 15.30)

His 1936 essay "Modern Landscape Architecture" anticipated the "progressive" integration:

Now the effort is being made to harmonize the two by mixing the "formal" and "informal" where common sense and true aesthetic satisfaction warrant. . . . The combination is deliberate; a method of relieving the often monotonous stiffness of formal work and of bringing manifest order into nature which in more cases than not, seems to express chaos rather than design.

Further, the progressive designer is trying to blend in each some of the qualities of the other. The old axis is retained in spirit, but changed almost beyond recognition. It is shattered and its fragments moved, duplicated and bent, as is the theoretical axis of any bit of good natural scenery. Formal objects are put thus in occult rather than symmetrical balance. And in informal work, there is no hesitation in assembling divers unique natural forms such as trees, rocks and streams, according to recognized architectural principles of axis, transverse axis, symmetrical balance, etc., though in a good result these methods may well be altogether hidden (but not necessarily so).[53]

Naumkeag was providing Steele with a design laboratory, but, as Choate's visitor book testifies, it was also a setting for an evolving life. From her parents' era, signatures of political luminaries such as Elihu Root and William Lloyd Garrison Jr. survive. By the time she assumed charge of the household in the mid-1920s, there were fewer social callers and greater numbers of family. Over the course of her long friendship with Steele, the "quiet time" Choate preferred was gradually supplanted by more of the "social time" he thrived on. The names of their mutual friends, interspersed with frequent visits from Mabel's nephews and nieces and their children, chronicle many new connections.

Steele's first visit was recorded in 1926 and he returned, with one apparent exception (1927), every subsequent year until Choate's death, several times a season. By 1931 colleagues, friends, and clients of Steele's are re-

corded, and, by 1932, groups of Rochesterians were also coming to stay, some of these (including Steele's sister Esther and her close friend Helen Ellwanger) returning several times even when Steele was not there. One of the most intriguing convergences took place on a weekend in October 1934, when Naumkeag had only two house-guests, Fletcher Steele and Marian Coffin—the sole record of a social meeting between them.[54]

Louisa Yeomans King visited Naumkeag in 1933, and other garden and literary celebrities came as well, including Agnes Selkirk Clark in 1936 (Clark's work was prominently featured in *The House Beautiful Gardening Manual*, written by Steele) and Alice G. B. Lockwood, author of the highly esteemed *Gardens of Colony and State*. The former editor of the *Atlantic Monthly*, Ellery Sedgwick, and his wife, Marjorie, were there in 1948.[55] Marian Coffin returned in 1949 accompanied by a client whom she and Steele shared (for different projects), Frances Biddle Morgan of Chestnut Hill, Pennsylvania.[56] Morgan's visits to Naumkeag were recorded every year for twenty years. She was part of a tight-knit group that convened there every

15.29. View down steps. Photograph by Fletcher Steele. SUNY ESF College Archives.

15.30. Blue Steps, 2003. Photograph by Carol Betsch.

summer to celebrate Steele's birthday, which also included Fairman Furness, the owner of Upper Banks Nursery in Media, Pennsylvania, and Grahame Wood, Steele's old client from Blossom Hill.

One of the most frequently recorded names in the guest book is that of Frank Crowninshield, the urbane editor of *Vanity Fair*, who had a summer place in Lenox. Crowninshield was also a member of the famed Algonquin Round Table, an avid collector of African art, early supporter of the Museum of Modern Art, and friend to Gertrude Whitney, George Gershwin, and many other Jazz Age figures of note, including Gertrude Stein, whose work he published, along with that of Edna St. Vincent Millay. Crowninshield was a figure in the Three Arts Society, an ad hoc committee that purchased the Stockbridge Casino (designed by Stanford White in 1888) from Mabel Choate and had it moved to Yale Hill Road, where it became the Berkshire Playhouse.[57]

One visit of particular landscape architectural significance occurred in 1932, when Dan Kiley came to Naumkeag on Warren Manning's recommendation. Kiley was a new employee of Manning's, and Manning had told him of the imaginative work that Steele, a former employee, was doing there. Kiley remembered that he was

chatting (rather timidly, he said) with Mabel Choate when Steele arrived in his chauffeur-driven Rolls Royce. Just as it was opened for him, the car door fell off. Steele rescued the moment by pretending that nothing had happened, and simply walked over it, a show of sangfroid that impressed the young man. Kiley was even more impressed by the fact that at one point Steele got on Choate's phone, apparently to talk to someone in Paris.[58] Later in his life, Kiley expressed a strong artistic debt to Steele, whom he considered the "only good designer" of the era.[59]

If the weather was fine, Choate's houseguests gathered on the Great Seat to watch the sun set behind Monument Mountain. (Fig. 15.31) Steele had redesigned the terrace in 1931 to create a long seat at the edge of it, incorporating materials from the house into a rich architectural amalgamation. Framing the vista to the southwest (pretentiously called the Perugino View, after the fifteenth-century Italian painter) were tall arborvitae and plantings of *Magnolia tripetala*, buckthorn, and silvery Russian olive. (Fig. 15.32) On the northwest corner of the terrace, Steele planted a large stand of devil's walking stick (*Aralia spinosa*), an unusual spiny native that sends up plumes of ivory flowers in late summer. An espaliered apple hedge provided a railing along the western edge.

Since the 1880s the estate's farm and greenhouses had been supplying the Choates' New York townhouse with fruit, vegetables, and flowers through long winters, and dinners at Naumkeag typically featured produce from the farm—raw peas in season were served as a first course, eaten with spoons. A more important role for the farm may have been as a visual component in the foreground view. (Fig. 15.33) As the sun sank, Mabel Choate sometimes cued the estate farmer to prod the cows to saunter across the fields, Constable-like. For the American country elite, the farm still served as a source of patrician pleasure. (Once when he was asked about what he raised on *his* New England farm, Stormfield, Mark Twain answered, "Really nothing but sunsets and scenery."[60]) With its

15.32. Perugino View, 1931, drawing. SUNY ESF College Archives.

15.31. *View from Terrace*, 1998. Photograph by Carol Betsch.

spruce-lined approach, sloping orchards, and wide meadows, Naumkeag's farm also contributed a patina of time, providing the martini-drinking cosmopolites with a staunch connection to the past and its stabilizing force. No one among them more vociferously disapproved of modern life than Steele. As he told one editor in 1947, "I don't read newspapers nor go to the movies. I see no reason to answer the telephone just because it rings. I like good general conversation and detest being in a room where lots of people are jabbering."[61] Naumkeag would continue to provide the imperious landscape architect with a social and intellectual retreat, and his time there increased over the years.

Steele's association with Mabel Choate also spawned projects that transcended the boundaries of the estate. One of these was the Mission House museum, and it, too, was inspired by a desire to connect to the past. The project got under way soon after Steele met Choate, when she impulsively purchased the oldest house in Stockbridge and arranged to have it moved to the hill below Naumkeag.[62] The eighteenth-century structure was falling apart, but, with Steele advising, she restored it and filled it with a large collection of period furniture. Steele designed beguiling, Colonial-inspired though not historically accurate grounds to surround it. These included a drying yard, grape arbors, and vegetable and flower gardens, arranged with an eye to strong spatial composition.[63] (Fig. 15.34)

John D. Rockefeller Jr. came to visit the house museum in 1943, just missing Choate, who was traveling at the time. He sent a note afterward to express his admiration and to congratulate her on her achievement. "It seemed to me that the result was as nearly perfect as it could possibly be," Rockefeller wrote, continuing in the robust preservation spirit of the day, "You have done a truly beautiful thing, the value of which is infinitely great because beauty has not been sacrificed for authenticity

15.34. Mission House and outbuildings, Stockbridge, Mass. Photograph by Paul Weber. SUNY ESF College Archives.

and historical accuracy."[64] Choate responded by graciously acknowledging Steele's creative role: "I feel that I cannot really take the credit for it myself, as it was Fletcher Steele, a landscape architect, who did the whole thing except the furnishing of the interior. I am afraid if it had not been for him I should have painted it white with apple-green shutters and put umbrellas on the lawn and made it altogether horrible; but through his knowledge and inspiration I learned what really should be done there."[65]

During World War II, landscape commissions became scarce, and Steele devoted much of his time to advising clients about how to maintain large gardens with dwindling funds and manpower.[66] On his recommendation, Choate hired a "farmerette" to oversee the grounds of Naumkeag. After the war Steele's practice gradually resumed, but it only occasionally presented the type of commission that had, even during the Depression, occupied him.

"So [in] my mind," Mabel Choate wrote Steele in 1950, "Naumkeag is now a work of art. Thanks to you. I am more interested in it and excited about it all the time . . .

15.33. *Naumkeag Farm*, 1998. Photograph by Carol Betsch.

15.35. Rose Garden. Photograph by Fletcher Steele. SUNY ESF College Archives.

15.36. Moon gate, China, 1934. Photograph by Fletcher Steele. SUNY ESF College Archives.

15.37. Mabel Choate and visitor (Steele?) in Chinese Garden. Naumkeag.

for you know, I have always wanted to make it a complete whole, like a picture in its frame."[67] But Steele had still more ideas in store. In 1952 he proposed a rose parterre to replace a lawn north of the house terrace, west of the old arborvitae allée. His design featured enormous floribundas that look like big dollops of paint—yellow, white, pink, and red—tucked into scalloped beds at the ends of curving ribbons of pink gravel. (Fig. 15.35) According to Peter H. Hornbeck, Steele's assistant at the time, he based the forms of the ribbons on a stylized motif of the Chinese mushroom in an effort to connect it visually with the Chinese Garden above, but many see in the sleek curves the remembered rhythms of Art Deco. The imaginative garden offers an unexpected picture from the terrace and an exuberant liberation from the stiff geometry of the typical rose garden layout.

Steele's final project at Naumkeag took place in 1955, a recollection of his 1934 trip to China, and to him, it seemed like the last piece of the garden puzzle. (Fig. 15.36) "When the south side of [the Chinese Garden] wall is completed," Steele wrote to his sister in anticipation, "the secret of the whole valley and surrounding hills as seen from this place will be clarified and reduced to one continuous curve. All of Naumkeag and the landscape beyond will be like the unfolding of a seashell whose nucleus is the Chinese Garden itself."[68] For three decades, Steele had focused on the challenge of integrating curves into the setting and finding means to "call in the Country," in Pope's phrase. The new wall and the Chinese moon gate that pierced it would finish the task. Practically, the opening provided a passageway for visitors. Symbolically, the circle represented a close to Steele's design work at Naumkeag and the final episode of a remarkable collaboration. (Fig. 15.37)

Mabel Choate continued to spend summer and fall at Naumkeag, and her visitor book continued to record the names of many old friends, Fletcher Steele often among them. In 1958, the final year that the book was kept, Steele came in September and again in October. Choate's death two months later, at age eighty-eight, brought to an end their artistic partnership and a sustaining friendship. But it did not bring an end to Naumkeag.

Steele had persuaded Choate to bequeath the estate and the Mission House to The Trustees of Reservations, a Massachusetts organization founded in 1891. The gift marked the completion of another kind of circle, one that linked Steele's design with the origins of the profession and the principles that had guided its founders. These included his mentor Warren Manning and Manning's mentor Charles Eliot, whose efforts had led to the founding of the Trustees, the first regional preservation initiative in the world and the model for Britain's National Trust. Steele admired the work of the Trustees and served as a consultant on several properties, including Naumkeag. (Fig. 15.38)

15.38. Naumkeag, west facade, 1959. Photograph by Clemens Kalischer.

"This society has been active for more than half a century in acquiring and preserving places of natural beauty and historic interest," Steele wrote approvingly, in words that echoed those of his teachers. "It has been influential in the establishment of state and city parks, forests and reservations. It has materially assisted many public and private agencies in acquiring their own lands for conservation. It undertakes the education of our people in the use and importance of the conservation of land, flora, and wild life."[69] Steele continued to visit Naumkeag as a professional adviser for the Trustees into the 1960s, bringing his near-impossible standards for maintenance to bear on complicated preservation quandaries, raising the hackles of superintendents who struggled with an aging landscape, limited budgets, and decreasing understanding of the complex design principles of the period.

In 1962 Steele closed his Boston office and moved back to his parents' home in Pittsford and into "semi-retirement." Shortly afterward, he began one of the finest gardens of his career, a late-style work distinguished by a sense of ease and grandeur. The garden's primary feature is a great outdoor room composed of trees and shrubs that stretches behind a handsome Greek Revival house. In-

wardly focused, the design harks back to the simplicity, refinement, and symmetry of a classical French layout, to haunting effect owing to Steele's strong handling of this very large volume of space. He was still working on it when he died in 1971.[70]

Late in life, Steele reflected on the transitory nature of his art in an essay begins, "The last deep pleasure of the spirit to be learned from a garden will lie in its permanence. . . . A good garden abounds in suggestions of the past." He continues:

As we relish the past, so should we prepare for the future and other coming lovers of gardens yet unborn. The true gardener has abiding faith and must express it, if only by planting an acorn where the "Genius loci" calls for an oak. Better still is some imprint of ourselves in imperishable wall, in steps of stone, in a terrace that will be but more beautiful if the neglect of centuries overtakes it perchance. Then will our sound satisfaction lie not in showy flowers, not in exquisite details of the moment, but in knowledge that the charm which has been discovered, the genius of the place which has been revealed and adorned, is safe for all time, a gift to the future more lovely then than even we can now dream.[71]

Since 1959, when Naumkeag was first opened to the public, thousands of visitors have wandered through Stanford White's summer cottage, marveling at the details captured within its walls—the old-fashioned telephone system that links guest rooms with the kitchen, the Turkish hookah on Steele's bedside table, and shelves filled with Mabel Choate's old Garden Club of America *Bulletins*. The table is set with her Chinese porcelain ware, as though friends were just about to arrive.

Outdoors, visitors may perceive deeper stirrings—intimations of laughter, keen intelligence, and a love of the land "so deep," as Steele once put it, "that it hurts to leave home for a day."[72] Here, layers of time and imagination are caught in the roll of big lawns, the shadows of old trees, and fountains that still play against the spread of the Berkshires. Seeds descended from plants sown long ago still sprout from crevices. Japanese butterbur, delirious at having leapt the Chinese Garden wall, erupts from the stream bed each spring. Lichen covers old rocks and moss cushions ground under copper beeches where grass once grew.

"Landscape architecture is part of nature itself," Steele once wrote. "The story does not end. On it goes, getting more and more interesting as we get old and have time to understand."[73] In the landscape of Naumkeag, the story continues, shaped by time and imagination, protected by understanding. There, the people who "worked up" this land are still communicating, with one another and with the genius of the place.

Oak tree, south lawn, 1997. Photograph by Carol Betsch.

AFTERWORD

The dire economic conditions of the 1930s put an end to large-scale estate building, and after the United States became involved in World War II, maintenance on most American country places was curtailed out of a sense of patriotic duty, a circumstance that soon led to the demise of many. When the economy rebounded in the years following the war, home construction soared, but few Americans—even wealthy ones—were inclined to build on a scale or with the elaborateness of earlier times. There were changes in the profession as well.

A new generation of landscape practitioners had emerged, led by a lively triumvirate of intellectual mavericks who regarded the work of their forebears with a mixture of approval and scorn. James Rose, the most radical of this group, considered all American design from the first half of the century derivative and did not hesitate to express this opinion. Both Garrett Eckbo and Dan Kiley, however, admired some of the country place–era practitioners, particularly Fletcher Steele. Eckbo considered Steele a transitional figure "between the old guard and the moderns" and admired his exploratory spirit. "He interested me because he was an experimenter, he wasn't con-

tent to keep repeating the formula—which we were still being taught was the only way to do things. . . . I was also very impressed with him as a human being. He seemed to possess great humanity, to be a leader."[1]

Kiley visited Steele's office often and considered him "without question the best landscape architect during the twenties, thirties, and into the early forties, . . . a brilliant designer who could express himself eloquently, which he did through his articles in *Landscape Quarterly* and other writings." In a 1995 memo, Kiley continued his reminiscences:

In his travels abroad, he became interested in the ideas of the early modern French designers. He wrote lucid essays on their work, and was perhaps the only landscape architect of his time to consider extrapolating these ideas into a practice of "modern landscape design." Although this influence could be seen in his later work, it is unfortunate that he did not completely break with tradition—(in retrospect, maybe not). . . .

I was very taken by the beautiful drawings being produced there. These elegant drawings impressed on me the value of doing clear and sensitive graphic work, and my drafting took on new luster. I believe that I was so inspired by Fletcher Steele's work, especially, that much of my early schemes and plantings were along his lines. In particular, I emulated the classical plantings of trees and simple, unified plant beds.

Steele had many important clients besides Mabel Choate. In particular I remember his work for the Fords in Grosse Pointe, Michigan, where amongst other sculptures, his head appears in granite, with a crew haircut. [Kiley was actually remembering the Backus place, where a bas-relief portrait of Steele appears on a post, along with the faces of Ralph Adams Cram and Robert O. Derrick.] . . . Undoubtedly of great character, and very delightful to me, he was just what the profession needed at the time, *and still needs*. I learned a great deal from Fletcher Steele, and can say that he has been a tremendous inspiration to me throughout my career.[2]

Neither Kiley's nor Eckbo's opinions of the other landscape architects featured in *A Genius for Place* survive—with the exception of Warren Manning, whom Kiley worked for and admired—but it is unlikely either man knew much about the work of any them. By the late 1930s, Platt had died, Farrand's career had ebbed, de Forest had turned to designing small beach houses, and Coffin was semi-retired in New Haven. Jensen's continued insistence on his Prairie moniker, coupled with his fiery dismissal of eastern "pomp," had isolated him from the profession. The popular magazines that once published the work of these designers in the 1920s were no longer promoting estate-scale work. As a result, many of the finest designs of the country place era quickly became invisible to the field. The reputation of Fletcher Steele, who lived until 1971, was eclipsed, too, owing in part to Norman Newton's dismissal of him, expressed to students at Harvard and also manifested by the exclusion of him from Newton's *Design on the Land*, published the year Steele died.

In his landmark book, Newton does cover Platt's work in considerable depth, and he also presents cogent analyses of private work by Jensen as well as other important designers not covered in *A Genius for Place*—James L. Greenleaf, Percival Gallagher, Ferruccio Vitale, Alfred Geiffert Jr., Bryant Fleming, and Annette Hoyt Flanders. But Newton's apologetic references to the size of their estate projects emphasized the work's elitist origins, and the students of the 1970s likely passed over these pages quickly.

Nonetheless, Newton's summary of the design achievements of the era was insightful. He considered it "a period of remarkable progress in quality in landscape architecture," owing largely to the field's intensive preoccupation with problems that "sharply emphasized the necessity of strong design." He also regarded several achievements of the period "fully applicable to . . . current problems in landscape design." Newton cites meticulous care for detail, proportion, and scale; clarity of spatial structure; equal clarity of correspondence between horizontal and vertical; rightness of relation between form and material; restrained plant lists, with materials tending toward firmness; understatement and reserve rather than exaggeration—arguably, characteristics of interest today.[3]

Newton made errors, too, and one of these served to obfuscate the connection between this group of practitioners and their spiritual and professional forebears. In Newton's misunderstanding, Olmsted and his partners worked "almost exclusively" on public projects, a reflection of the "profession's basic value to the whole of society." In fact, the Olmsted firm took on many private commissions, and in these designs applied the same principles that were shaping the great park systems, campuses, and subdivisions concurrently in the office. Chief among these principles was to provide the soothing and salutary effect of nature by designing in relation to prevailing conditions.

Even as they explored the use of space as a "positive and primary" material, the next generation of practitioners carried forward this even more essential Olmstedian principle, too, which they understood as a regard for the genius loci. They also carried forward a desire to improve society through design in both the public and the private spheres, through publications, lectures, professional associations, and preservation advocacy. Newton's book did not describe these efforts, and they, too, became invisible to the new generation.

Nor does his text address the public work of those better known for their private commissions: Farrand's and Coffin's campuses, Manning's far-flung planned communities, Shipman's Duke University Gardens and Aetna Insurance grounds, Jensen's extensive developments in the Chicago parks, or Steele's modernist park in Camden, Maine.

There is little question today that the work of these practitioners, both public and private, deserves study, and that such study will provide rewards for current practitioners, many of whom have little sense of the history of their own profession. I believe that the field of landscape studies is poised to enter a new phase, one that involves less trawling for tangential figures and more application of engaged analysis to the work of practitioners whose significant accomplishments are now apparent.

There is another compelling reason for more intensive study of landscape history. If we are to preserve, conserve, restore, and rehabilitate important historical places, we must first understand them—not just as circulation systems and lines of sight and tree species, but as living, evolving entities expressive of specific principles. To maintain these places is a task of almost unbelievable complexity, owing largely to cycles of growth and decay. In the case of public landscapes, including those explored in this book, this challenge is multiplied by the necessity of accommodating visitors who expect parking, lunch, restrooms, visitor centers, gift shops, plant sales, interpretive signage, and, at the furthest extreme, trams, children's gardens, and lavish settings for once-in-a-lifetime weddings. The need to generate income continues to drive administrative decision-making at many of our finest historic landscapes, with often unfortunate results.

The most successful preservation initiatives are those undertaken by professional staff whose knowledge of the designed landscape encompasses the past as well as the present and whose efforts are guided by long-range plans created by preservation specialists, based on meticulous research and supported by sophisticated parent organizations and educated constituencies. The work of the landscape historian is a critical element in this formula. As greater numbers of significant historical landscapes are recognized, questions about which to preserve and how to preserve them loom large. Sustained investigations that result in thoughtful, clear histories can offer both direction and inspiration.

NOTES

INTRODUCTION

1. Norman T. Newton, *Design on the Land: The Development of Landscape Architecture* (Cambridge, Mass.: Belknap Press of Harvard University Press, 1971), 427.

2. Ibid., 392.

3. Richard Hofstadter, *The Age of Reform* (New York: Random House, 1955). The first waves of immigrants, German, Scandinavian, Irish, and English, began arriving in the United States in the 1840s. After 1900, peasants from southern and eastern Europe came in great numbers. According to Hofstadter, the influx peaked in 1907, when 1,285,000 were recorded, and by 1910, 13,345,000 foreign-born persons were living in the United States.

4. Ibid., 25.

5. See Tamara Plakins Thornton, *Cultivating Gentlemen: The Meaning of Country Life among the Boston Elite, 1785–1860* (New Haven: Yale University Press, 1989).

6. See Melanie Simo, *Garden and Forest: Traces of Wilderness in a Modernizing Land, 1897–1949* (Charlottesville: University of Virginia Press, 2003). Simo's discussion casts interesting light on the notion of wildness in America.

7. Fiske Kimball, "The American Country House," *Architectural Record* 46 (October 1919): 293.

8. By 1910 a long and familiar roster of industrial giants had been formed through both vertical and horizontal corporate integration—Texaco, U.S. Rubber, Goodyear, U.S. Steel, Ford Motor Company, Phelps-Dodge, General Electric, Westinghouse, American Sugar, United Fruit, American Tobacco, DuPont, American Harvester, and Eastman Kodak, for example. The names of the era's business titans are also familiar: these included Andrew Carnegie, Philip Armour, James Duke, Henry Ford, Henry Havemeyer, and John Pierpont Morgan, the richest of them all.

9. Richard Guy Wilson and Dianne H. Pilgrim, eds., *The American Renaissance, 1876–1917* (New York: Pantheon in association with the Brooklyn Museum, 1979), 19.

10. Mark Alan Hewitt, *The Architect and the American Country House* (New Haven: Yale University Press, 1990), 12. Hewitt observes, "In 1892 the *New York Times* listed 4,027 men as millionaires, whereas *Forum* magazine estimated that there were 120 men in the country with fortunes in excess of $10 million" (10). He calculates that an income of $50,000 would have allowed $100,000 worth of house and land and an operating budget of $7,500.

11. Barr Ferree, *American Estates and Gardens* (New York: Munn, 1904), 1.

12. Samuel Howe, *American Country Houses of To-Day*, cited from Hewitt, *The Architect and the American Country House*, 190.

13. Olmsted discussed his use of the term many years later: "We must bear in mind that the word architecture is not limited in application to works of building. The Almighty is referred to as the 'Architect of the Universe.' Plutarch writes of the architecture of a poem, meaning the plotting of it. 'The architect of his own fortune' is an old proverbial term yet commonly used in our newspapers, and is applicable as well to a banker or a miner as to one whose fortune has been made by directing works of building." "The Landscape Architecture of the World's Columbian Exposition," *Inland Architect* 22, no. 2 (September 1893): 18.

14. The phenomenon of the New Woman was an important cultural current in the country place era. Freedom from traditional roles permitted (and, to some degree, encouraged) Beatrix Farrand, Marian Coffin, and Ellen Shipman to pursue full-time careers.

Mabel Choate, an important patron, also enjoyed freedom that would not have been available to her in a traditional marriage. Mariana Griswold Van Rensselaer (1851–1934) wrote her most important work, *Art Out-of-Doors*, after she became a widow. There are many examples of New Women throughout *A Genius for Place*.

15. Frederick Law Olmsted to William A. Thompson, November 6, 1889, quoted from Charles E. Beveridge, "The First Great *Private Work of Our Profession in the Country*: Frederick Law Olmsted, Senior, at Biltmore," in Charles E. Beveridge and Susan L. Klaus, *The Olmsteds at Biltmore* (Bethesda, Md.: National Association for Olmsted Parks, 1995), 1.

16. "American Country Life and Art," *Architectural Record* 11 (January 1902): 112.

17. Magazines were critical to the American country life movement. See Virginia Tuttle Clayton, ed., *The Once and Future Gardener: Garden Writing from the Golden Age of Magazines, 1900–1940* (Boston: David R. Godine, 2000).

18. Christopher Vernon, "Wilhelm Miller: Prairie Spirit in Landscape Gardening," in *Midwestern Landscape Architecture*, ed. William H. Tishler (Urbana: University of Illinois Press in collaboration with Library of American Landscape History, 2000), 177.

19. See Judith B. Tankard, "The Influence of British Garden Literature on American Garden Design during the Country Place Era," in *Masters of American Garden Design IV: Influences on American Garden Design, 1895–1940*, ed. Robin Karson (New York: Garden Conservancy, 1995), 17–29.

20. Sargent was a central figure of the era and had ties to several of the professional and amateur practitioners featured in *A Genius for Place*, particularly Coffin, du Pont, and Farrand.

21. Two gardens by the Olmsted firm were included in Lowell's book, as were two by Nathan Barrett, the original landscape architect of Naumkeag, and one by Daniel W. Langton. Two landscapes were designed by sculptors, an indication of the rising number of amateurs undertaking landscape design—Chesterwood, the garden of Daniel Chester French (1850–1931) in Stockbridge, Mass., and Aspet, Augustus Saint-Gaudens's garden in Cornish, N.H.

22. Olmsted and his followers used formal layouts, too, as Downing had, but these were invariably circumscribed and served traditional purposes—cutting, herb, and vegetable gardens or borders—rather than being the dominant motive in an overall design.

23. Charles Eliot, "What Would Be Fair Must First Be Fit," *Garden and Forest*, April 1, 1896.

24. Samuel Parsons, *The Art of Landscape Architecture* (New York: G. P. Putnam's Sons, 1915), ix.

25. Ibid., 74.

26. Informally, Elizabeth Barlow Rogers has expressed the intriguing idea that Parsons, who was a student of Vaux's, was eager to promote Pückler as a rival to Olmsted because Olmsted's reputation eclipsed that of his mentor.

27. Parsons, *Art of Landscape Architecture*, 76.

28. Henry Vincent Hubbard and Theodora Kimball, *Introduction to the Study of Landscape Design* (New York: Macmillan, 1917), 58.

29. Ibid., 71.

30. Ibid., 61.

PROLOGUE

1. Alice G. B. Lockwood, *Gardens of Colony and State*, 2 vols. (New York: Charles Scribner's Sons, for the Garden Club of America, 1931), 2:6–7.

2. Therese O'Malley, "The Evidence of American Garden History: Interpreting American Gardens through Words and Images," in *Keywords in American Landscape Design*, ed. Therese O'Malley, Elizabeth Kryder-Reid, and Anne Helmreich (New Haven: Yale University Press, forthcoming). Another notable exception to geometric formality was Thomas Lyman's estate in Waltham, Mass. As Charles Eliot observed, "Plainly, English books on landscape gardening, like Repton's or Whately's, had made part of this American gentleman's reading—the low setting of the house and the serpentine curves given to the grass-edged shore of the stream furnish proof of this." See Charles W. Eliot, *Charles Eliot, Landscape Architect*, reprint of 1903 edition (Amherst: University of Massachusetts Press in association with Library of American Landscape History, 1999), 244–45.

3. Jefferson traveled to England in the years after the Revolution and visited many gardens described in Whately's *Observations on Modern Gardening*, a copy of which he owned.

4. William Alexander Lambeth and Warren H. Manning, *Thomas Jefferson as an Architect and a Designer of Landscapes* (Boston: Houghton Mifflin, 1913), 99.

5. Ralph Waldo Emerson, "Nature," in *Essays and Lectures*, ed. Joel Porte (New York: Library of America, 1983), 40.

6. For more on Mount Auburn Cemetery, see Blanche M. G. Linden, *Silent City on a Hill: Picturesque Landscapes of Memory and Boston's Mount Auburn Cemetery*, rev. ed. (Amherst: University of Massachusetts Press in association with Library of American Landscape History, 2007); for a list of rural cemeteries, see appendix 2.

7. Andrew Jackson Downing, *A Treatise on the Theory and Practice of Landscape Gardening, Adapted to North America; with a View to the Improvement of Country Residences*, 2nd ed. (New York: Wiley and Putnam, 1844).

8. Ibid., ix.

9. Ibid., 22.

10. Ibid., 37.

11. Ibid., 48.

12. Ibid., 13.

13. Ibid., 48–49.

14. Ibid., 21.

15. See Daniel J. Nadenicek and Lance M. Neckar, introduction to H. W. S. Cleveland, *Landscape Architecture, as Applied to the Wants of the West*, reprint of 1873 edition (Amherst: University of Massachusetts Press in association with Library of American Landscape History, 2002), xviii–xxi. Cleveland and Copeland's c. 1855 plan was also innovative in pioneering the concept of linked green spaces, an idea that was an important precursor to the Boston Metropolitan Park System. Cleveland's later work in Chicago and Minneapolis and his 1873 book also disseminated these ideas.

16. Ibid., xliii.

17. Vaux had reviewed plans for the new park that had been prepared by Egbert Viele, the engineer who had been hired to survey the land, and he was dismayed by their lack of imaginativeness. He lobbied to organize a design competition, which he then entered with Olmsted.

18. For more on the social context of the creation of Central Park, see Roy Rosenzweig and Elizabeth Blackmar, *The Park and the People: A History of Central Park*. (Ithaca, N.Y.: Cornell University Press, 1992).

19. Elizabeth Barlow Rogers, *Landscape Design: A Cultural and Architectural History* (New York: Harry N. Abrams, 2001), 341.

20. Vaux also designed numerous shelters and several buildings in the park, including the Casino (1862–63), the Mineral Springs (1869), the Dairy (1869–70), and the Belvedere (1867–71). An excellent study of Vaux's career is Francis Kowsky, *Country, Park & City: The Architecture and Life of Calvert Vaux* (New York: Oxford University Press, 1998).

21. Frederick Law Olmsted, "Yosemite and the Mariposa Grove: A Preliminary Report, 1865." http://www.yosemite.ca.us/library/olmsted/report.html.

22. Frederick Law Olmsted, *Walks and Talks of an American Farmer in England*, reprint of 1852 edition (Amherst, Mass.: Library of American Landscape History, 2002), 98.

23. Charles C. McLaughlin, introduction to ibid., ix.

24. Charles E. Beveridge and Paul Rocheleau, *Frederick Law Olmsted: Designing the American Landscape* (New York: Rizzoli, 1995), 34. Beveridge points to three aspects of nature that Olmsted believed led to such experiences: "One was mystery, caused by deep shadows and the play of light and shadow; a second was bounteousness, displayed in richness of foliage and lushness of growth; and a third was peacefulness, as evoked by gentle rolling meadows with scattered shade trees or small bodies of water that reflected trees and sky. In time these scenic features would become the most important elements in the landscapes he created and the emotional responses he sought to produce through them" (33).

25. Olmsted was among the founders of the liberal magazine the *Nation*. His journalistic career had led him to tour the South in the years before the Civil War and to argue fervidly for abolition. This trip is chronicled in *The Cotton Kingdom: A Traveller's Observations on Cotton and Slavery in the American Slave States* (New York: Mason Brothers, 1861).

26. Frederick Law Olmsted, *Public Parks and the Enlargement of Towns*, reprint of 1870 edition (New York: Arno Press and New York Times, 1970).

27. Reuben M. Rainey, "William Le Baron Jenney and Chicago's West Parks: From Prairies to Pleasure Grounds," in *Midwestern Landscape Architecture*, ed. William H. Tishler (Urbana: University of Illinois Press in collaboration with Library of American Landscape History, 2000), 59–60.

28. Frederick Law Olmsted to Calvert Vaux, September 3, 1887, quoted in Beveridge and Rocheleau, *Frederick Law Olmsted*, 36.

29. Frederick Law Olmsted, "Parks, Parkways, and Pleasure Grounds," *Garden and Forest*, May 22, 1895, 202; also in *Engineering Magazine* 9, no. 2 (1895): 253–60. This article was most likely written by Charles Eliot; see *Charles Eliot, Landscape Architect*, 441.

30. Carol Grove, *Henry Shaw's Victorian Landscapes: The Missouri Botanical Garden and Tower Grove Park* (Amherst: University of Massachusetts Press in association with Library of American Landscape History, 2005), 11.

31. Chatsworth featured a fine, Picturesque landscape from earlier generations, and under the supervision of Sir Joseph Paxton (1803–1865), who became head gardener there in 1826, it had acquired spectacular waterworks and an enormous greenhouse known as the Great Stove.

32. Grove, *Henry Shaw's Victorian Landscapes*, 102. Tower Grove Park opened to the public on September 28, 1872. It is one of the best preserved parks of the era, still open to the public, hosting over one million visitors each year.

33. Mac Griswold and Eleanor Weller, *The Golden Age of American Gardens* (New York: Harry N. Abrams, 1991), 25.

34. Mrs. Schuyler [Mariana Griswold] Van Rensselaer, *Art Out-of-Doors* (New York: Charles Scribner's Sons, 1893), 49.

35. Some sections of Van Rensselaer's book were previously published in the *American Architect and Building News*, such as the 1888 series that praised the collaborative example of Henry Hobson Richardson and Olmsted, who strongly influenced Richardson's designs. Many sections had also been published in *Garden and Forest*.

36. Van Rensselaer, *Art Out-of-Doors*, 49–50.

37. See http://www.arboretum.harvard.edu/aboutus/history.html.

38. Downing, *Treatise*, 42.

39. See Mac Griswold, afterword to Cynthia Zaitzevsky, *Fairsted: A Cultural Landscape History* (Boston: National Park Service and Arnold Arboretum, 1997), 123–50.

40. Mariana Griswold Van Rensselaer, *Henry Hobson Richardson and His Works* (1888), quoted in Beveridge and Rocheleau, *Frederick Law Olmsted*, 175.

41. This estate is privately owned and much of the original landscape design is intact.

42. Frederick Law Olmsted to John C. Phillips, September 27, 1881, quoted in Beveridge and Rocheleau, *Frederick Law Olmsted*, 157.

43. Frederick Law Olmsted to John C. Phillips, May 11, 1880, quoted in ibid., 158, 170.

44. Olmsted to Phillips, March 6, 1882; Olmsted to Mariana Griswold Van Rensselaer, May 17, 1887; quoted in ibid., 164, 138.

45. Though well known in his day, Barrett has not received much scholarly attention. In addition to the town of Pullman, Barrett worked on several suburban developments, in Chevy Chase, Md., Fort Worth, Tex., and Birmingham, Ala., and he designed several large country estates, including H. O. Havemeyer's, in Islip, Long Island, and Pullman's own in Elberon, N.J. The latter was part of a large real estate development that included forty miles of ocean frontage. See "Slice of New Jersey Coast Acquired by Syndicate for $3,000,000," *New York Times*, August 25, 1897, 8. Barrett was among the founders of the American Society of Landscape Architects (ASLA) and served as its president in 1903. See Judith Helm Robinson and Stephanie S. Foell, "Nathan Franklin Barrett," in *Pioneers of American Landscape Design*, ed. Charles A. Birnbaum and Robin Karson (New York: McGraw-Hill, 2000), 10–14.

46. Mariana Griswold Van Rensselaer, "The Artistic Triumph of the Fair-Builders," in *Accents as Well as Broad Effects: Writings on Architecture, Landscape, and the Environment, 1876–1925*, ed. David Gebhard (Berkeley: University of California Press, 1996), 71.

47. Editorial, *Garden and Forest*, May 19, 1897, 192. Among the several authorities whose ideas were disseminated through its pages were its editor, William A. Stiles (1837–1897), who was also an editorial writer for the *New York Tribune*, and Charles Sprague Sargent (1841–1927), director of the Arnold Arboretum, who served as "conductor." The large number of correspondents included Olmsted Sr., Codman, and Eliot, as well as Beatrix Jones (later Farrand), Parsons, Frank A. Waugh (1869–1943), O. C. Simonds (1855–1931), Warren Manning, Harold A. Caparn (1864–1945), Wilhelm Miller (1869–1938), and John Charles Olmsted (1852–1920). The magazine was essentially a surrogate journal for the emerging profession of landscape architecture, featuring articles on horticulture, forestry, conservation, and design, its authors crossing gracefully from one field of inquiry to another. When Stiles died in 1897, it was dissolved. No single journal emerged to replace it, although several new taste-shaping magazines, including *Country Life in America*, were begun in its aftermath. For more on *Garden and Forest*, see Ethan Carr, "*Garden and Forest* and 'Landscape Art,'" http://www.loc.gov/preserv/prd/gardfor/essays/carr.html.

48. Charles Eliot, "Muskau: A German Country Park," *Garden and Forest*, January 28, 1891, 38.

49. "Park Work near Boston," *Garden and Forest*, April 29, 1896, 171.

50. Olmsted to William A. Thompson, November 6, 1889, quoted in Beveridge and Rocheleau, *Frederick Law Olmsted*, 225.

51. Ibid.

52. Frederick Law Olmsted Jr. to John C. Olmsted, August 19, 1895, quoted in ibid.

53. Mark Alan Hewitt, *The Architect and the American Country House* (New Haven: Yale University Press, 1990), 3.

54. Henry James, *Collected Travel Writings: Great Britain and America* (New York: Library of America, 1993), 680.

1. WARREN H. MANNING

1. Information for this chapter is drawn from several sources, primary among which is Manning's unpublished autobiography, held in the Warren H. Manning Collection, University of Massachusetts Lowell (hereafter cited as Manning Collection, Lowell). Manning wrote the manuscript (hereafter cited as WHMA) in the last years of his life and planned to submit it to Houghton Mifflin for publication, but this was never done. A second version, prepared by Manning's employee Egbert Hans, is here abbreviated WHMA/Hans. I have also relied on information from several brief biographical articles, including obituaries, from Manning's surviving correspondence, and from documents relating to his practice. These are held in individual repositories (William G. Mather Papers, Gwinn Archives, Gwinn Estate, Cleveland, Ohio, hereafter cited as Gwinn Archives; and Stan Hywet Hall and Gardens, Akron, Ohio, hereafter cited as SHH Archives); the Manning collection at Iowa State University, Ames; and Lowell. At the end of his active career, Manning attempted to return plans and drawings to individual clients; however, most such material, including correspondence and business records, was not returned and was subsequently destroyed. Another rich source of information on Manning is the excellent article by Lance M. Neckar, "Developing Landscape Architecture for the Twentieth Century: The Career of Warren H. Manning," *Landscape Journal* 8 (Fall 1989): 78–91. See also Robin Karson, *The Muses of Gwinn: Art and Nature in a Garden Designed by Warren H. Manning, Charles A. Platt, and Ellen Biddle Shipman* (Sagaponack, N.Y.: Sagapress/Abrams in association with Library of American Landscape History, 1995); Karson, "Warren H. Manning: Pragmatist in the Wild Garden," in *Nature and Ideology: Natural Garden Design in the Twentieth Century*, Dumbarton Oaks Colloquium on the History of Landscape Architecture, ed. Joachim Wolschke-Bulmahn (Washington, D.C.: Dumbarton Oaks Research Library and Collection, 1997), 113–30; and Karson, "Warren H. Manning," in *Pioneers of American Landscape Design*, ed. Charles A. Birnbaum and Robin Karson (New York: McGraw-Hill, 2000), 236–42.

2. These also included Colorado spruce, cutleaf staghorn sumac, and summersweet (*Clethtra*).

3. See "Jacob W. Manning," *American Gardening*, September 24, 1904, 627, and "Jacob Warren Manning," *American Gardening*, October 1, 1904, 636.

4. WHMA, 4.

5. Manning's project list contains approximately seventeen hundred commissions; not all of these were realized. A national survey, conducted by Library of American Landscape History, in Amherst, Mass., is currently under way to assess the scope of his built work.

6. WHMA, 15.

7. See Lance M. Neckar, "Warren H. Manning and His Minnesota Clients: Developing a National Practice in a Landscape of Resources, 1898–1919," in *Midwestern Landscape Architecture*, ed. William H. Tishler (Urbana: University of Illinois Press in collaboration with Library of American Landscape History, 2000), 145.

8. At various times in his career Manning employed the terms *landscape gardener*, *landscape designer*, *landscape architect*, and *landscape planner*.

9. Warren H. Manning to Frederick Law Olmsted, November 7, 1887, Manning Collection, Lowell.

10. Olmsted's business changed its name twice during Manning's tenure, to F. L. Olmsted & Company in 1889, after Henry Sargent Codman became a partner, and to Olmsted, Olmsted & Eliot in 1893, after Codman's death and Charles Eliot's promotion. In his autobiography Manning related an anecdote about Senator Leland Stanford's waiting for Olmsted to finish petting his beloved cat before making himself available to discuss plans for the new university in Palo Alto.

11. WHMA, 30.

12. William Grundmann, "Warren H. Manning," in *American Landscape Architecture*, ed. William Tishler (Washington, D.C.: The Preservation Press, 1989), 56.

13. WHMA, 33.

14. For more on the dispute, see Cynthia Zaitzevsky, *Frederick Law Olmsted and the Boston Park System* (Cambridge, Mass.: Belknap Press of Harvard University Press, 1982), 195–96.

15. For more on the midwestern reach of Manning's practice, see Neckar, "Minnesota Clients," 142–58.

16. David F. Burg, *Chicago's White City of 1893* (Lexington: University of Kentucky Press, 1976), 109.

17. As architect-in-chief, Burnham invited George B. Post (designer of the Manufactures and Liberal Arts Building), McKim, Mead & White, Richard M. Hunt, Peabody & Stearns, and Van Brunt & Howe to design the five major buildings. Five Chicago firms were invited to design less monumental structures.

18. Talbot Hamlin, *Forms and Functions of Twentieth-Century Architecture*, 4 vols. (New York: Columbia University Press, 1952), 1:578–79.

19. The fair was to be "directly associated with the existing grandeur, beauty, and interest of the one distinguishing natural, historic, and poetic feature of this part of the American Continent—its great inland seas." *Report of Joint Committee on Site* (Chicago, 1890), quoted from Norman T. Newton, *Design on the Land: The Development of Landscape Architecture* (Cambridge, Mass.: Belknap Press of Harvard University Press, 1971), 359.

20. James W. Shepp and Daniel B. Shepp, *Shepp's World's Fair Photographed* (Chicago: Globe Bible Publishing, 1893), 8.

21. Mariana Griswold Van Rensselaer, "The Artistic Triumph of the Fair-Builders," in *Accents as Well as Broad Effects: Writings on Architecture, Landscape, and the Environment, 1876–1925*, ed. David Gebhard (Berkeley: University of California Press, 1996), 69.

22. WHMA/Hans, 22.

23. Frederick Law Olmsted, "The Landscape Architecture of the World's Columbian Exposition," *Inland Architect* 22, no. 2 (September 1893): 21. In Chicago, Manning met O. C. Simonds, then superintendent of Graceland Cemetery. They discussed setting up a Chicago practice together, but the scheme never worked out. Jacob Manning was also at the exposition; his landscape design for the Massachusetts State Building won a medal.

24. Daniel H. Burnham and Francis D. Millet, *World's Columbian Exposition: The Book of the Builders* (Chicago: Columbian Memorial Publication Society, 1894).

25. Manning credits his brother William S. Manning with being the first to undertake collecting on a large scale during his tenure in the Olmsted firm. WHMA/Hans, 27.

26. Charles E. Beveridge and Paul Rocheleau, *Frederick Law Olmsted: Designing the American Landscape* (New York: Rizzoli, 1995), 226–28. It was widely believed that tropical environments had a salubrious effect, which also may have been a factor in their appeal to Olmsted. See Daniel J. Nadenicek and Lance M. Neckar, introduction to H. W. S. Cleveland, *Landscape Architecture, as Applied to the Wants of the West*, reprint of 1873 edition (Amherst: University of Massachusetts Press in association with Library of American Landscape History, 2002), lxii n. 11.

27. Manning to Henrietta Manning, November 1893, Manning Collection, Lowell. In 1898 Pinchot left his post at Biltmore to became the first chief of the Division of Forestry of the U.S. Department of Agriculture.

28. Olmsted Jr.'s professional coming of age is described in Susan L. Klaus, *A Modern Arcadia: Frederick Law Olmsted Jr. and the Plan for Forest Hills Gardens* (Amherst: University of Massachusetts Press in association with Library of American Landscape History, 2002), 17–29. A brief, comprehensive account of Olmsted Jr.'s career is Klaus, "Frederick Law Olmsted Jr.," in Birnbaum and Karson, *Pioneers of American Landscape Design*, 273–76.

29. See WHMA, 45.

30. For more on Manning's debt to Eliot, see Neckar, "Developing Landscape Architecture," 80.

31. Warren H. Manning, "The Field of Landscape Design," *Landscape Architecture* 2, no. 3 (April 1912): 108–10.

32. Warren H. Manning, "Gwinn," undated manuscript, 5, Gwinn Archives. Warren Manning, "The Nature Garden," undated manuscript, Manning Collection, Lowell.

33. In the 1890s, Tufts purchased almost six thousand acres of sandy pine barrens, which he transformed into a resort town, Pinehurst. About thirty commissions related to the Tufts family and Pinehurst are listed in Manning's archive.

34. See William Grundmann, "The Early Parks of Milwaukee: Lake, Washington, Mitchell, and Kosciuszko, Warren H. Manning's Legacy," unpublished paper, 1992.

35. Warren H. Manning, "Report on the Minneapolis Parks," January 13, 1900, 1, quoted in Neckar, "Minnesota Clients," 148–49.

36. For more on Manning's projects for Mather, see Karson, *Muses of Gwinn*. Ishpeming, one of several company towns associated with Mather's iron ore business, Cleveland-Cliffs Iron Company, is the location for the film *Anatomy of a Murder* (1958). Director Otto Preminger used the lakeside setting, dominated by the obelisk-like mine buildings in Manning's plan, as a moody backdrop to the murder and trial.

37. J. Horace McFarland, "An American Garden: Dolobran near Philadelphia," *Outlook*, October 7, 1899, 328–29.

38. Ibid., 328. Like most of his contemporaries and many native plant enthusiasts today, McFarland's notion of "American" or native plants was naïve, a combination of "sound biology, invalid ideas, false extensions, ethical implications, and political usage both intended and unanticipated," as Stephen Jay Gould observes. Plant communities are in a continual state of flux owing to many forces, such as changes in climate and the behavior of animals, particularly humankind. See Gould, "An Evolutionary Perspective on Strengths, Fallacies, and Confusions in the Concept of Native Plants," in Wolschke-Bulmahn, *Nature and Ideology*, 11–19.

39. J. Horace McFarland, "Dolobran—A Wild-Gardening Estate," *Country Life in America*, September 1903, 339.

40. See Virginia Tuttle Clayton, "Wild Gardening and the Popular American Magazine," in Wolschke-Bulmahn, *Nature and Ideology*, 150. Clayton's essay focuses primarily on the relationship of the American middle classes to wild gardening.

41. Ibid., 140, quoted from Eben E. Rexford, "A Garden of Native Plants," *Lippincott's Magazine*, April 1902, 483.

42. Warren H. Manning, "History of Walden Estate of Cyrus H. McCormick," unpublished paper, July 1933, 7, Lake Forest, Ill., Archive.

43. The forward-looking development was designed in 1871 by H. W. S. Cleveland (1814–1900) and William Merchant Richardson French (1843–1914).

44. Manning, "History of Walden Estate," 12.

45. Manning worked for Mrs. Cyrus (Nettie Fowler) McCormick,

Cyrus's mother, and his brother Stanley Robert McCormick at Riven Rock, in Montecito, Calif., and for his sister Mary Virginia on four different estates, in Pasadena, Toronto, Huntsville, Ala., and Cohasset, Mass. For more on the unfortunate life of Stanley McCormick and the role his estate played in it, see the intriguing work of historical fiction, T. Coraghessan Boyle, *Riven Rock* (New York: Viking, 1998). Manning also worked at White Deer Lake, Mich., McCormick's summer retreat, where he created a regional study plan, and he designed the landscape grounds for McCormick Hall at Princeton University in 1925. Manning also designed McCormick gravesites at Graceland Cemetery in Chicago. See WHMA, 63.

46. The first bluff planting occurred 1895–96 and also included Mahaleb cherry, Russian mulberry, and buckthorn, planted in low-quality soil that was obtained at low cost. The surface was covered with swale grass and sedge dug in Quincy, Ill. In 1898 an additional four thousand black locusts were planted.

47. Manning, "History of Walden Estate," 9, 20.

48. Ibid., 12.

49. Ibid., 17. Manning dates his consultation with Miller to 1910.

50. Ibid., 15.

51. In 1916 Stephen Hamblin undertook an arboretum study of Walden, with advice from Charles Sargent and Ernest W. Wilson. See ibid., 45.

52. Manning coined the paradoxical term "new, native plants," by which he meant non-native species that had acclimated to new sites. See WHMA/Hans, 90.

53. Manning, "History of Walden Estate," 52.

54. Harriet McCormick, *Landscape Art, Past and Present* (New York: Charles Scribner's Sons, 1923).

55. Beginning in 1915, the McCormicks also underwrote twelve issues of this conservation- and planning-oriented magazine, of which Manning was director and Stephen F. Hamblin was editor. Among the many contributors were Wilhelm Miller, O. C. Simonds, W. C. Egan, Emil Hollinger, E. O. Orpet (superintendent of Walden), D. Hill, Charles Mulford Robinson, Ralph Rodney Root, Everett L. Millard, Georgia Douglas Clark, and W. M. S. French, director of the Chicago Art Institute. Two other editions of *Billerica* were published (see WHMA, 60); the first covered the Billerica area, and a final series was largely devoted to national resource planning.

56. Only a few remnants of the design exist today. One of these is the Ravello, a pergolalike structure designed by Jarvis Hunt (1859–1941).

57. Manning's work for Rockefeller was limited to advising on house sites.

58. WHMA/Hans, 69.

59. Ibid., 69a.

60. The Harrisburg plan was substantially implemented by 1906. Manning listed the components of the system as Wildwood Park, Reservoir Park additions, Italian Park, Rover Island Parks, playgrounds (twenty were listed), five miles of riverside parks, eighteen miles of parkways, a river shore walk, new intercepting sewer, dam, and many street improvements. See WHMA, 121. Manning returned to Harrisburg often during his career, for a wide range of jobs including several planning projects and designs for the country club, high school, hospital, and private estates.

61. George Manning recalled that his grandfather used the train time to write these articles. George Manning, interview by Jane Roy Brown, Topsham, Me., December 2, 2005.

62. Warren H. Manning, "How to Make a Formal Garden at a Moderate Cost," *Country Life in America*, March 1903, 187.

63. Warren H. Manning, "Wild Garden," in *Cyclopedia of American Horticulture*, ed. Liberty Hyde Bailey, 4th ed. (New York: Doubleday, Page, 1906), 1976–77. William Robinson (1838–1935) was the author of a widely read book, *The Wild Garden*, first published in England in 1870, which likely would have been known to Manning's audience.

64. Ibid., 1976, 1977.

65. Ibid., 1977.

66. Warren H. Manning, "The Two Kinds of Bog Gardens," *Country Life in America*, August 1908.

67. Manning, "Wild Garden," 1977.

68. Manning, "The Nature Garden," 1.

69. William Alexander Lambeth and Warren H. Manning, *Thomas Jefferson as an Architect and a Designer of Landscapes* (Boston: Houghton Mifflin, 1913), 104.

70. For example, Manning and Cyrus McCormick followed the decay of one of the great old trees at Walden, "Old King Cotton," noting more than thirty different tree and herb seedlings sprouting from it. Manning, "History of Walden Estate," 30. For more on Manning's wild gardens, see Karson, "Warren H. Manning."

71. For more on these collaborations see Robin Karson, "A Woman's Place: Ellen Shipman's Gardens Frame a Divided World," *Garden Design*, February–March 1997, 46–48. See also Judith B. Tankard, *The Gardens of Ellen Biddle Shipman* (Sagaponack, N.Y.: Sagapress/Abrams in association with Library of American Landscape History, 1996), 89, 209 n. 3.

72. Manning, "The Nature Garden," 3.

73. Wilhelm Miller, *What England Can Teach Us about Gardening* (Garden City, N.Y.: Doubleday, Page, 1911), 187. This passage is indexed under the phrase "Manning's law," 357.

74. Neckar, "Minnesota Clients," 142–58.

75. Manning to Henrietta Manning, October 27, 1902, Manning Collection, Lowell.

76. Theodate Pope to Alfred Pope, June 30, 1907, courtesy Hill-Stead Archive, Farmington, Conn. "[He] knew I did not like Manning. I told him that made no difference at all—would be *glad* to see him unless he tried to butt in about the locating of [the] school."

77. Fletcher Steele to John Steele, January 27, 1912, Fletcher Steele Papers, Rochester Historical Society, Rochester, N.Y. (hereafter cited as Steele Papers, RHS).

78. Irene Seiberling Harrison, interview by author, Stan Hywet Hall, Akron, Ohio, February 18, 1991.

79. Manning had been commissioned to plan Richmond College, Richmond, Va., in 1898; that project may have given him the contacts for the exposition. He returned to Richmond College to work from 1911 to 1918.

80. Stephen Conant, "Democracy by Design: Warren H. Manning's Contribution to Planning History" (master's thesis, Tufts University, 1984), 29.

81. The company towns in the Upper Peninsula included Munising, Gwinn, Negaunee, North Lake, and Ishpeming.

82. The range of Steele's work for Manning is chronicled in chapter 14.

83. Later Manning employees of note include Wilbur D. Cook Jr., who went on to work with Irving J. Gill on the design of the Dodge House in Los Angeles; Marjorie Sewell Cautley (1892–1954), who worked with Clarence Stein and Henry Wright at Sunnyside Gardens, in Queens, N.Y., and Radburn, N.J.; Helen Bullard (1896–1987); and Clarence Combs (1892–1958), who designed Jones Beach. Other well-known figures listed include William H. Punchard, Carl F. Pilat, Phelps Wyman, Arthur K. Harrison, A. F. Brinkerhoff, Bryant Fleming, and Samuel P. Negus. See "Employee List," Manning Collection, Lowell.

84. Later, the Manse became the headquarters for the Manning Family Association, a genealogical organization that preserves papers and artifacts, which owns it still.

85. The plan collated information about roads, topography, small-lot subdivisions, soil, forest cover, and existing and future reservations, all recorded on maps at the same scale, using techniques pioneered by Eliot. Manning transferred the maps to tracing paper so they could be overlaid and analyzed comprehensively, a planning technique that foreshadowed methods of analysis pioneered by modern practitioners Phil Lewis and Ian McCarg. See Ervin Zube, "The Advance of Ecology," *Landscape Architecture* 76, no. 2 (March–April 1986): 58–67. See also Carl Steinitz, Paul Parker, and Lawrie Jordan, "Hand Drawn Overlays: Their History and Prospective Uses," *Landscape Architecture* 66, no. 5 (September 1976): 421, 444–55.

86. Warren H. Manning, "The Art of Making Landscape Gardens," in *The Standard Cyclopedia of Horticulture*, ed. Liberty Hyde Bailey (New York: Macmillan, 1916), 1786.

87. Wilhelm Miller, *The Prairie Spirit in Landscape Gardening*, reprint of 1915 edition (Amherst: University of Massachusetts Press in association with Library of American Landscape History, 2001), 29.

88. Manning, "The Art of Making Landscape Gardens," 1783. For example, "We are looking and hoping for something distinctive to the art of our country," wrote Thomas Worthington Whittredge in his autobiography, "something which shall receive a new tinge from our peculiar form of Government, from our position on the globe, or something peculiar to our people, to distinguish it from the art of the other nations and to enable us to pronounce without shame the oft repeated phrase, 'American Art.'" See *The Autobiography of Worthington Whittredge, 1820–1910*, ed. John I. H. Baur (New York: Arno Press, 1969), 40.

89. Manning, "Making Landscape Gardens," 1783–84.

90. For more on the "hot fight," see the introduction.

91. Warren H. Manning, "A National Plan Study Brief," special supplement to *Landscape Architecture* 13, no. 4 (July 1923).

92. See Neckar, "Developing Landscape Architecture," 84.

93. See "The City as Client," in *Designs on Birmingham: A Landscape History of a Southern City and Its Suburbs*, ed. Philip A. Morris and Marjorie Longenecker White (Birmingham, Ala.: Birmingham Historical Society, 1989), 46–53.

94. Ibid., 50.

95. By 1920 John Nolen (1869–1937) had become the nation's preeminent planner. For more on Nolen, see Charles D. Warren, introduction to *New Towns for Old*, reprint of 1927 edition (Amherst: University of Massachusetts Press in association with Library of American Landscape History, 2005).

96. See C. Chappell Jarrell, "From Farmscape to Suburban Yard: Robert Jemison, Jr.'s Spring Lake Farms," in Morris and White, *Designs on Birmingham*, 42–45.

97. The study for Mather included twenty-eight maps, four of which covered the twelve-hour running time to Marquette, Mich., by automobile, rail, and airplane. Others recorded winter and summer climate conditions, existing and abandoned railways, highways and trails, wire lines, waterways, air-landing fields, drainage basins, approximate contours, geological and soil conditions, natural vegetation, wildlife, and wildlife sanctuaries. He even included a beaver map. See WHMA, 79.

98. In 1935 Kiley wrote to the *Miami Daily News* in support of Manning's park work there: "Parks, the boon of humanity in the rushy city, will and must be created when and where they are needed. . . . Bayfront Park . . . is an example of what can be created that the people will appreciate." Daniel Urban Kiley, "Plans for Future Miami Envisioned," *Miami Daily News*, June 9, 1935, quoted from Neckar, "Developing Landscape Architecture," 91 n. 55. Kiley did not share Manning's enthusiasm for "associated efforts" such as the ASLA, an organization Kiley disdained his entire life.

99. WHMA, 237.

2. CHARLES A. PLATT

1. For this chapter, I have relied on Keith N. Morgan's seminal biography, *Charles A. Platt: The Artist as Architect* (Cambridge, Mass.: Architectural History Foundation and MIT Press, 1985), and another important work edited by Morgan, *Shaping an American Landscape: The Art and Architecture of Charles A. Platt* (Hanover, N.H.: University Press of New England, 1995). See also Robin Karson, *The Muses of Gwinn: Art and Nature in a Garden Designed by Warren H. Manning, Charles A. Platt, and Ellen Biddle Shipman* (Sagaponack, N.Y.: Sagapress/Abrams in association with Library of American Landscape History, 1995).

2. George Henry Hall, Sanford Gifford, and Jervis McEntree, for example. See Morgan, *Platt*.

3. Morgan, *Platt*, 5.

4. Emily C. Learned to Charles Moore, November 8, 1933, and "Memorial of John H. Platt" delivered at the Century Club, n.d., unpaginated, quoted from Morgan, *Platt*, 7 nn. 13, 14.

5. Learned to Moore, ibid., 7 n. 15.

6. Morgan, *Platt*, 6–7, 8.

7. "An Industrial Experiment at South Manchester," *Harper's New Monthly Magazine* 45 (November 1872): 836–44.

8. Morgan, *Platt*, 9. Platt's other instructors were James Wells Champney and John George Brown. All were genre painters, and Platt would soon reject this type of subject matter.

9. Quoted from Morgan, *Platt*, 11 n. 39.

10. See Erica E. Hirshler, "The Paintings of Charles A. Platt," in Morgan, *Shaping an American Landscape*, 51–73.

11. Ibid., 57.

12. Morgan, *Platt*, 215 n. 57. Morgan cites a letter from Platt to Royal Cortissoz, June 10, 1913.

13. Annie was the daughter of Col. Richard March and Mary Corbin Hoe.

14. Rebecca Warren Davidson, "Charles A. Platt and the Fine Art of Landscape Design," in Morgan, *Shaping an American Landscape*, 81. Davidson quotes Rose Standish Nichols, who was also a resident of the Cornish colony as well as a landscape designer, as noting that "few parts of New England bear so strong a resemblance to an Italian landscape as the hills rising above the banks of the Connecticut River opposite the peaks of Mount Ascutney." (See Nichols, "A Hilltop Garden in New Hampshire," *House Beautiful*, March 1924, 237.)

15. Maxfield Parrish to Daisy Deming, Cornish, N.H., September 3, 1893, quoted from Hirshler, "The Paintings of Charles A. Platt," 73.

16. Keith N. Morgan to author, July 5, 2005.

17. Morgan, *Platt*, 204.

18. Mark Alan Hewitt, *The Architect and the American Country House* (New Haven: Yale University Press, 1990), 63.

19. Morgan, *Platt*, 33.

20. "Where We Get Our Ideas of Country Places in America," *Outing*, June 1904, 352.

21. See Alma M. Gilbert and Judith B. Tankard, *A Place of Beauty: The Artists and Gardens of the Cornish Colony* (Berkeley, Calif.: Ten Speed Press, 2000). The most comprehensive historical article is Frances Duncan's "The Gardens of Cornish," *Century Magazine* 72 (May 1906): 13–19. Also see Susan Hobbs, "Thomas Dewing in Cornish, 1885–1905," *American Art Journal* 17 (Spring 1985): 3–22. Saint-Gaudens (1848–1907) was not alone in his Arcadian enterprise; other American artists were also establishing country lives and experimenting with new forms in houses and landscape. At Olana, in Hudson, N.Y. (where a Persian-influenced house had been designed by Calvert Vaux), Frederic Church put aside his canvases to devote himself to road building, tree planting, and lake digging. Daniel Chester French, a friend of both Church and Saint-Gaudens, who summered in Cornish for a few years, created Chesterwood, in Stockbridge, Mass., from a similar impulse. Saint-Gaudens may have been the first to design a formal landscape for such a retreat, however. All three of these country estates have been preserved and are now open to the public.

22. It should be noted that not all Cornish residents were gardeners, and not all of them were enthusiastic about the topic. Dennis Bunker confided to his wife, "They bore me to death with their houses and their poor little flower beds. It all seems so strange to me this forsaken land." Dennis Bunker to Eleanor Hardy Bunker, July 5, 1890, quoted from Hobbs, "Thomas Dewing in Cornish," 5. According to Hobbs, Daniel Chester French also "found the community too ingrown and self-consciously 'arty.'"

23. Ellen Biddle Shipman, Garden Note Book, 1, Ellen McGowan Biddle Shipman Papers, Department of Manuscripts and University Archives, Cornell University Libraries, Ithaca, N.Y.

24. In Cornish, in addition to Walker's house, his own, and the Crolys', Platt designed Harlakenden House for Winston Churchill (1899), Dingleton House for Emily and Augusta Slade (1899),

and, in neighboring Plainfield, the summer house and studio of Herbert Adams (1903).

25. Herbert Croly (1869–1930) would voice his opinions as editor of *Architectural Record* and the *New Republic* and as author of several books, including *Stately Homes in America* (1903). Somewhat later he also wrote on political topics, in his books *Progressive Democracy* and *The Promise of American Life*, both of which were widely read. In addition he was the biographer of the diplomat Willard Straight, who also summered in Cornish and was later, with his wife Dorothy, an important client of Beatrix Jones Farrand. In his architectural criticism, Croly championed the buildings of John Russell Pope (1874–1937), Howard Van Doren Shaw (1869–1926), Myron Hunt (1868–1952), Wilson Eyre (1858–1944), who designed Stephen Parrish's Cornish house, Elmer Grey (1871–1963), and Harrie T. Lindeberg (1880–1959), as well as Platt's, recommending the restrained classicism that typified the work of these men over the more directly expressed Beaux-Arts formality of Richard Morris Hunt, Carrère & Hastings, and Horace Trumbauer, among others. But Croly was most devoted to Platt, and his enthusiasm both as critic and patron undoubtedly buoyed Platt's confidence and helped propel his quick rise to fame.

26. "Where We Get Our Ideas," 350.

27. Hewitt, *The Architect and the American Country House*, 19.

28. There William Platt likely knew Warren Manning, superintendent of planting for the firm, and he probably also knew Manning's younger brother, William, who was also an Olmsted assistant.

29. Platt to Royal Cortissoz, June 30, 1913, quoted from Morgan, *Platt*, 212 n.17.

30. Frederick Law Olmsted to William Platt, February 1, 1892, quoted from Laura Wood Roper, *FLO: A Biography of Frederick Law Olmsted* (Baltimore: Johns Hopkins University Press, 1973), 433.

31. See Keith N. Morgan, "Al Fresco: An Overview of Charles A. Platt's *Italian Gardens*," introduction to Charles A. Platt, *Italian Gardens*, reprint of 1894 edition (Portland, Ore.: Sagapress/Timberpress, 1993).

32. Platt, *Italian Gardens*, 6–7.

33. Ibid., 93.

34. Eliot wrote, "Evidently our author is not acquainted with W. P. Tuckermann's 'Die Gartenkunst der Italienischen Renaissance-Zeit,' published in 1884, and containing besides the twenty plates and numerous other cuts, some twenty ground-plans and cross-sections of Renaissance villas." Charles Eliot, review of *Italian Gardens*, in *Nation*, December 28, 1893, quoted from Morgan, "Al Fresco," 116.

35. "But after all, works of this kind only appeal to the aesthetic sense; they delight the eye and satisfy the cultivated taste as a beautiful piece of tapestry or pottery does. It is beauty for its own sake. It expresses no sentiment and carries no inner meaning: it does not address itself to the nobler part of our nature as simple natural scenery does." *Garden and Forest*, August 1893, 322.

36. The trend continued. See, for example, Janet Ross, *Florentine Villas* (New York: Dutton, 1901); A. Holland Forbes, *Architectural Gardens of Italy* (New York: Forbes & Co., 1902); Julia Cartwright, *Italian Gardens of the Renaissance and Other Studies* (New York: Charles Scribner's Sons, 1914); Harold Donaldson Eberlein, *Villas*

of Florence and Tuscany (Philadelphia: J. B. Lippincott, 1922); and Rose Standish Nichols, *Italian Pleasure Gardens* (New York: Dodd, Mead, 1926).

37. Joan Platt, manuscript biography of Charles Platt, quoted from Morgan, *Platt*, 219 n. 36. The Elliot property, in Needham, Mass., was designed c. 1895.

38. See Alan Emmet, "Faulkner Farm: An Italian Garden in Massachusetts," *Journal of Garden History* 6, no. 2 (April–June 1986): 162–77.

39. Edward S. Prior, "American Garden-craft from an English Point of View," *House and Garden*, November 1903, 211–15. Prior reviled Platt's garden as "second-hand debris from European museums" and "nail-parings and hair-combings of European styles."

40. Ralph Adams Cram, "Faulkner Farm, Brookline, Massachusetts," *House and Garden*, August 1901, 1–12.

41. Ibid., 1.

42. Wilhelm Miller, "An 'Italian Garden' That Is Full of Flowers," *Country Life in America*, March 1905, 491–92.

43. James Sturgis Pray in *American Architect and Building News* 67 (February 10, 1900), 43 n. 1, also gave the design a passing mention.

44. The architectural historian Rebecca Warren Davidson believes that at Weld Platt was particularly influenced by the Villa Borghese in Rome and by the Villa Castello, which he considered the "most beautiful in Italy." See Davidson, "Charles A. Platt and the Fine Art of Landscape Design," 179 n. 40.

45. See Richard G. Kenworthy, "Bringing the World to Brookline: The Gardens of Larz and Isabel Anderson," *Journal of Garden History* 11, no. 2 (October–December 1991): 224–41. As Kenworthy points out, Platt's Italian garden was one of several specific types on the estate, including a Japanese and a Chinese garden. For a list of other articles on Weld, see Kenworthy, "Published Records of Italianate Gardens in America," *Journal of Garden History* 10, no. 1 (January–March 1990): 10–70.

46. Miller, "An 'Italian Garden,'" 491–92.

47. Keith N. Morgan, "Charles A. Platt and the Promise of American Art," in Morgan, *Shaping an American Landscape*, 20.

48. "Where We Get Our Ideas," 351.

49. Charles D. Warren, introduction to *The Architecture of Charles A. Platt*, reprint of 1913 edition (New York: Acanthus Press, 1998), xiv.

50. Edith Wharton, *Italian Villas and Their Gardens*, reprint of 1904 edition (New York: Da Capo Press, 1988), 5.

51. A discussion of the evolution of the old-fashioned garden can be found in May Brawley Hill, *Grandmother's Garden: The Old-Fashioned American Garden, 1865–1915* (New York: Harry N. Abrams, 1995). Among the most influential American books promoting the use of hardy plants in the border were Alice Morse Earle, *Old-Time Gardens* (New York: Macmillan, 1901), and Helena Rutherfurd Ely, *A Woman's Hardy Garden* (New York: Macmillan, 1903).

52. Louise Shelton, *Beautiful Gardens in America* (New York: Charles Scribner's Sons, 1915). Shelton's book was revised in 1924 and 1928.

53. See Judith B. Tankard, *The Gardens of Ellen Biddle Shipman* (Sagaponack, N.Y.: Sagapress/Abrams in association with Library of American Landscape History, 1996), 43.

54. Fletcher Steele also created later planting designs for two of Platt's gardens, one for Francis T. Maxwell in Rockville, Conn., and one for Mrs. W. H. Schofield, in Peterborough, N.H.

55. For more on Platt's patronage network, see Keith N. Morgan, "Gwinn: The Creation of a New American Landscape," in Morgan, *Shaping an American Landscape*, 121–42.

56. Davidson, "Charles A. Platt and the Fine Art of Landscape Design," 80.

57. According to Morgan, Platt believed that Lutyens had "had more influence towards bad architecture than anyone in England." Schell Lewis, renderer for the Platt office, interview by Henry Hope Reed Jr., August 23, 1958, cited in Morgan, *Shaping an American Landscape*, 167 n. 1. Platt's extremely successful career also came to include institutions. Two of his most ambitious large-scale projects were a plan for Phillips Academy in Andover, Mass., and one for the University of Illinois at Urbana. Platt created a design for the National Gallery of Art in Washington, D.C., in 1924. (The project was never built because Congress failed to allocate funds for it. However, seven other museums designed by Platt were built, including the Freer Gallery of Art in 1913.) He also designed handsome office buildings in Cleveland and New York.

58. Royal Cortissoz, *Monograph of the Works of Charles A. Platt* (New York: Architectural Book Publishing, 1913), viii.

59. Manning challenged this opinion three months later in the same journal. "We believe that to be successful in any one of the professions of architecture, engineering, or landscape architecture, a man must give all his time and attention to the study of his profession, and that he cannot hope for a full measure of success when he attempts to practice more than one profession." Warren H. Manning, "The Field of Landscape Design," *Landscape Architecture* 2, no. 3 (April 1912): 110.

60. Charles Downing Lay, "An Interview with Charles A. Platt," *Landscape Architecture* 2, no. 3 (April 1912): 130.

61. Warren H. Manning, "The Art of Making Landscape Gardens," in *The Standard Cyclopedia of Horticulture*, ed. Liberty Hyde Bailey (New York: Macmillan, 1916), 1784.

62. Herbert Croly, "The Architectural Work of Charles A. Platt," *Architectural Record* 15 (March 1904): 183.

3. GWINN

1. Two sources of biographical information on Mather are Timothy J. Loya, "William Gwinn Mather, the Man," *Inland Seas*, Summer 1990, 117–33; and William G. Mather obituary, *Cleveland Plain Dealer*, April 7, 1951. Gwinn was the subject of my book *The Muses of Gwinn* (Sagaponack, N.Y: Sagapress/Abrams in association with Library of American Landscape History, 1995), which offers readers more detailed and extensive information about the estate and its landscape development. See also Keith N. Morgan, "Gwinn: The Creation of a New American Landscape" in his edited volume *Shaping an American Landscape* (Hanover, N.H.: University Press of New England, 1995). Morgan's account also includes information about the patronage network that spread from Gwinn. See also Keith Morgan and Robin Karson, "Gwinn: William G. Mather's Residence in Bratenahl, Ohio," *Magazine Antiques*, March 1995, 442–54.

2. Burton H. Boyum, "William Gwinn Mather," *Michigan History Magazine*, November–December 1994, 77–79.

3. Ibid., 78.

4. By 1906 Mather had commissioned Manning for extensive work relating to Cleveland-Cliffs in the towns of Gwinn, Ishpeming, Munising, Negaunee, and Marquette, Mich. This work spanned city and town planning, real estate subdivisions, industrial grounds, park design, and home grounds. See WHM Project List, Manning Collection, Lowell.

5. Warren H. Manning to William Gwinn Mather, September 20, 1906, William G. Mather Papers, Gwinn Archives, Gwinn Estate, Cleveland, Ohio (hereafter cited as Gwinn Archives).

6. Manning to Mather, November 14, 1906, Gwinn Archives. In this letter, Manning also urged Mather to hire an architect "from whose work a distinctively American architecture is developing; not men who are clever copyists and adapters of styles that have grown out of European conditions."

7. Manning to Mather, January 4, 1907, Gwinn Archives.

8. Charles L. Freer to Mather, June 28, 1898, cited in Keith N. Morgan, "Gwinn: The Creation of a New American Landscape," 124.

9. Manning to Mather, February 11, 1907, Gwinn Archives.

10. Mather had made a note on Manning's letter, "'Indoors & Out, June 1906' Platt!"—in reference to an article by R. Clipston Sturgis, "Of What Shall the House Be Built?" *Indoors and Out*, June 1906, 101–11.

11. Mather to Manning, May 28, 1907, Gwinn Archives.

12. Manning to Mather, June 10, 1907, Gwinn Archives.

13. Charles Downing Lay, "An Interview with Charles A. Platt," *Landscape Architecture* 2, no. 3 (April 1912): 128.

14. Mather to Charles A. Platt, March 1, 1907, Gwinn Archives.

15. Samuel Howe, "Gwinn, Cleveland, U.S.A.," *Country Life*, May 1916, 565.

16. Platt's design for Gwinn may have been influenced by a design by Carrère & Hastings, Indian Harbor, in Greenwich, Conn. This estate was also sited directly on the water, and some aspects of the architecture (in particular, the gazebo and the curving portico on the rear facade of the house) strongly resemble those at Gwinn. Platt likely knew this project. It was featured in Guy Lowell's *American Gardens*, as was Platt's design for Faulkner Farm, and Platt was often in Connecticut, where he had several projects. Eastover, in nearby New London, one of his largest commissions, was begun in 1906, for George Palmer.

17. Herbert Croly, "The House of William G. Mather," *Architectural Record* 26 (November 1909): 313.

18. Platt was working on three lakeside houses almost simultaneously. In addition to Gwinn, he designed The Moorings for Russell Alger in Grosse Pointe Shores, Mich., and the Villa Turicum for Harold and Edith McCormick in Lake Forest, Ill. In each case, the change in grade from house to water differed, and each led to a different design. The terraces at Gwinn, which negotiated a thirty-foot drop, were more inventive than either the broad, slightly sloping lawns of The Moorings, which were somewhat dull (despite imaginative plantings by Ellen Shipman), or the plunging terraces of the McCormicks' Villa Turicum, which were somewhat derivative.

19. Howe, "Gwinn," 564.

20. Katharine Mather, who was unmarried, lived at Gwinn until William's marriage in 1929. Her role in the design for Gwinn was subdued. For example, her opinion of a large basin in the flower garden fountain, which she liked, was overridden by her brother's concern that it was interrupting a view through the area. See Karson, *Muses of Gwinn*, 111.

21. The attic was later decorated with murals depicting air travel by George de Forest Brush (1855–1941), commissioned by Elizabeth Mather.

22. Karson, *Muses of Gwinn*, 57.

23. Manning to Platt, June 11, 1907, Gwinn Archives.

24. The geographic distance separating Mather, Platt, Manning, local consultants, and contract workers made the construction of Gwinn a complex undertaking, as it was for any comparable country estate. Daily letters and telegrams flew between Mather, Mather's personal secretary (Charles G. Heer), Platt, Platt's engineer (F. H. Henderson), and various contractors and subcontractors. Several local architects, including Abram Garfield, Dercum & Beer, and Bohnard & Parsson, were also used to supervise construction and to design minor buildings on the estate, such as the farm houses. One memorandum, from January 13, 1909, lists fifty-nine workman representing thirteen different contractors at work on the estate that day. See Morgan, "Gwinn: The Creation of a New American Landscape," 131.

25. One of the most important structural elements in the layout was the large stand of trees on the east side of the lawn. The cold clay soil on the bluff was not providing them with the requisite nutrients, and their health was flagging. Manning drained the soil and enriched it with tons of humus, eventually prodding the trees into much more robust specimens. Several of them still grow there today.

26. Frost used California privet to create niches along the long wall that held specimen flowering trees and shrubs, which were underplanted with roses. The long garden wall was covered with vines and climbing roses. Frost's first plans for the herbaceous borders featured perennials, but Mather objected and asked for more annuals, which Platt supplied. The arrangement of plants in the beds was geometric, not the fashionable drift organization recommended by Gertrude Jekyll (1843–1932) and later implemented by Ellen Shipman. Frost worked for Platt for only one year and then departed to work as an assistant at Olmsted Brothers. For more on Frost's design, see Karson, *Muses of Gwinn*, 77–79.

27. Manning to Mather, September 9, 1908, Gwinn Archives.

28. Myron Hunt designed Mather's Pasadena home and landscape, which had a simple vernacular Spanish style. See Winifred Dobyns, *California Gardens* (New York: Macmillan, 1931), pl. 142.

29. Manning to Mather, October 3, 1908, Gwinn Archives.

30. Warren H. Manning, "Planting Notes and Report of Visit to Estate of Mr. William G. Mather," September 16, 1909, Gwinn Archives.

31. Manning to Mather, November 4, 1908, Gwinn Archives.

32. Taylor established his own practice in Cleveland in 1913.

33. Manning to Mather, November 4, 1908, Gwinn Archives.

34. Manning to Platt, September 8, 1908, Gwinn Archives.

35. In 1907 Platt wrote Mather: "I leave the color schemes to be worked out according to what may be obtained, and the longer

this may be left, the better, as I often get valuable suggestions by standing in the rooms when they have reached a certain point of completion." Platt to Mather, May 12, 1907, Gwinn Archives.

36. Mather to Manning, September 15, 1909, Gwinn Archives.

37. Manning to Mather, October 13, 1910, Gwinn Archives.

38. Platt was offered the columns, of Verona marble, "yellowish red and comparatively low in tone," for $700.

39. A compromise of native white pine was reached. Mather to Manning, September 22, 1910, and Manning to Mather, October 13, 1910, Gwinn Archives.

40. For more information on Manning's wild gardens, see Robin Karson, "Warren H. Manning: Pragmatist in the Wild Garden," in *Nature and Ideology: Natural Garden Design in the Twentieth Century*, Dumbarton Oaks Colloquium on the History of Landscape Architecture, ed. Joachim Wolschke-Bulmahn (Washington, D.C.: Dumbarton Oaks Research Library and Collection, 1997), 113–30.

41. Manning, "Gwinn," 32–33. See also Karson, *Muses of Gwinn*, appendix 2.

42. Manning to E. E. Boalt, February 5, 1913, Gwinn Archives.

43. Manning to George Jacques, February 5, 1913, Gwinn Archives.

44. Manning to Mather, May 13, 1913, Gwinn Archives.

45. See Karson, *Muses of Gwinn*, appendix 2.

46. Cornelia Ireland to author, n.d. [summer 1994].

47. J. Horace McFarland, "An American Garden: Dolobran near Philadelphia," *Outlook*, October 7, 1899, 328.

48. These buildings were designed by the firms of Dercum & Beer in 1910 and Bohnard & Parsson in 1911. Platt participated by reviewing the plans. For more on the farm, see Karson, *Muses of Gwinn*, 96–98.

49. Between 1910 and 1912 Mather spent more on plantings, paintings, sculpture, and fountains than he had once contemplated putting into the entire estate.

50. The artist was the son of John Twachtman, Platt's friend. Platt also used murals in his own house in Cornish and a garden building at Faulkner Farm.

51. Louise Shelton singled out Gwinn's gardens as "undoubtedly the most notable in the state." See Louise Shelton, *Beautiful Gardens in America* (New York: Charles Scribner's Sons, 1915), 277–78. A. D. Taylor used an image of Gwinn's pergola as the frontispiece of his book *The Complete Garden* (Garden City, N.Y.: Doubleday, 1921). Gwinn was also featured in Eunice Fenelon, "Open House in the Gardens of Greater Cleveland," *Your Garden and Home*, June 1934, and James M. Fitch and F. F. Rockwell, *Treasury of American Gardens* (New York: Harper and Brothers, 1956). The estate was mentioned as well in Melville Chater, "Ohio, the Gateway State," *National Geographic*, May 1932, 530.

52. Royal Cortissoz, *Monograph of the Work of Charles A. Platt* (New York: Architectural Book Publishing, 1913), v; "The House of William G. Mather," *Architectural Record* 26 (November 1909): 312–20; A. C. David [Herbert Croly], "New Phases in Domestic Architecture," *Architectural Record* 26 (November 1909): 309–12; *National Architect* 2 (September 1912): 22; Frank Miles Day, ed., *American County Houses of To-day* (New York: Architectural Book Publishing, 1912); Aymar Embury II, "Charles A. Platt: His Work,"

Architecture 26 (August 1912): 130–62; Phil M. Riley, "The Spirit of the Renaissance on the Great Lakes," *Country Life in America*, September 15, 1912, 28–30.

53. Howe, "Gwinn," 565, 564.

54. "Woman Manages 55-Acre Estate of W. G. Mather," September 2, 1927, and "Plants—and Dogs—Grow for Her," February 11, 1927, unidentified news clipping, "Gwinn" scrapbook, Gwinn Archives.

55. See William Mathewson Milliken, *A Time Remembered: A Cleveland Memoir* (Cleveland: Western Reserve Historical Society, 1975), 140.

56. Manning to Mather, May 12, 1933, Gwinn Archives.

57. Keith Morgan's seminal monograph, *Charles A. Platt: The Artist as Architect* (Cambridge, Mass.: Architectural History Foundation and MIT Press, 1985), revived interest in Platt's architecture. In recent years there has been increased attention to Platt's etchings, drypoints, lithographs, photographs, drawings, and oil and watercolor paintings. See the essays in Morgan, *Shaping an American Landscape*.

58. See Karson, *Muses of Gwinn*, 135–37.

59. Elizabeth was the founding president of the Garden Center of Greater Cleveland and an active and prominent member of the Garden Club of Cleveland, a Garden Club of America affiliate.

60. Cornelia Ireland, letter to author, n.d.

61. WHMA, 67.

62. Mather's philanthropic activities lie beyond the scope of this book. He served on the boards of all of Cleveland's major cultural institutions and generously supported most of them. See William G. Mather obituary, *Cleveland Plain Dealer*, April 7, 1951.

63. The first mention of Manning's attempt to persuade Mather to turn Gwinn into a public reservation occurs in 1932. Mather responded that "perhaps we are selfish, and perhaps, further, we cannot afford any more to be selfish in this respect. . . . The next time you come out we will have a talk in regard to the matter" (Mather to Manning, December 6, 1932, Gwinn Archives). Five years later, Mather was still reluctant to commit to this plan, but wrote, "Your opinion on all these matters—dreams though some of them may be, yet we should all have dreams—are always welcome with me" (Mather to Manning, June 2, 1937, Gwinn Archives). I have not been able to locate the letters to which Mather referred in his 1937 correspondence. In 1947 several acres of the wild garden were taken by eminent domain for the construction of I-90; only a small portion of it remains intact today.

4. STAN HYWET HALL

1. Several large companies got their start in Akron after the Civil War, including Diamond Match, Quaker Oats, International Harvester, American Tin Plate, and American Sewer Pipe. For more on early Akron and Goodyear, see Hugh Allen, *The House of Goodyear: Fifty Years of Men and Industry* (Cleveland: Corday & Gross, 1949).

2. Raw rubber was imported from Brazil and Africa, and highest quality cotton, an important ingredient in tires at the time, came from the Sea Islands off Georgia or the Nile Valley.

3. Allen, *House of Goodyear*, 12.

4. Three thousand blueprints were created for the house design,

many of which survive. Unfortunately almost all of Manning's landscape plans have been lost.

5. Both Franklin Augustus Seiberling (1859–1955) and Gertrude Ferguson Penfield Seiberling (1866–1946) were Ohio natives.

6. In time, the Seiberlings added several cabins and boathouses to accommodate friends and relatives. According to granddaughter Dorothy Seiberling Steinberg, "The floors were covered with Indian rugs; birch-bark and sweet-grass mats were used at the dinner table; Indian baskets, decorated with porcupine quills and beaded leatherwork filled the houses and a birch-bark canoe, filled with fragrant evergreens, was suspended in a corner of the main lodge." Quoted from Marlene Ginaven, *Not for Us Alone* (Akron: Stan Hywet Hall Foundation, 1985), 58–59.

7. Warren H. Manning to Franklin A. Seiberling, June 23, 1911, Stan Hywet Hall and Gardens Archives, Akron, Ohio (hereafter cited as SHH Archives).

8. Ibid. Manning listed "Trilliums, Hepaticas, Violets, Toothwort, Spring Beauty, Anemones, Lungwort, Water Leaf, Ferns, and the like, that give such a peculiar charm to the old forest."

9. Frank A. Seiberling Jr., "What I Liked about Stan Hywet Hall," undated lecture typescript, 2, author's collection. According to Seiberling's youngest son, F. A. was featured in public exhibitions and advertised, "in good P. T. Barnum manner," as the "boy wonder on skates."

10. Manning to Seiberling, June 27, 1911. Manning noted that Barclay was also a contributor to Bailey's *Cyclopedia* and a superintendent of the Wilkes-Barre park system. This letter was transcribed by Frank A. Seiberling Jr. at the University of Akron on March 22, 1991. The original is no longer in that collection.

11. "Frank A. Seiberling, Esq. Plan of Existing Conditions," no. 908-2, overlaid with "Study for Arrangement of Estate," no. 908-3. Warren H. Manning, Landscape Designer, Boston, Mass., June 22, 1911, SHH Archives.

12. Manning to Seiberling, June 23, 1911, SHH Archives.

13. The glasshouses included two show houses, two propagating houses, several orchid houses, a general plant house, and separate buildings for palms, carnations, chrysanthemums, vegetables, fruits, roses, melons, cucumbers, and ferns, each with its own temperature range.

14. Charles S. Schneider (1874–1932) got his early training in the firm of Mead & Garfield. He also studied at the École des Beaux-Arts. After he resigned from George B. Post & Sons in 1912, he opened an office in Cleveland. As Seiberling attempted to manage the conflicts between the two offices, he wrote Post, "I am only anxious to get my house completed without further difficulty and hope you gentlemen will keep your swords sheathed until this is accomplished." Seiberling to George B. Post, November 24, 1914, SHH Archives.

15. Charles S. Schneider to Seiberling, July 25, 1916, SHH Archives.

16. Blanche Linden-Ward, "Stan Hywet," *Landscape Architecture* 77, no. 4 (July–August 1987): 66–71.

17. The Modern French style was also variously known as French classicism, Parisian Renaissance, or, simply, Beaux-Arts. It dominated the early years of the period but fell out of favor as homeowners discovered how unlivable it was. In the historian Mark

Alan Hewitt's view, it was a collector's style, a distinct reference to Paris and elite standards of taste. For an excellent overview of the cultural context in which the architectural styles and typologies of the period developed, see Mark Alan Hewitt, *The Architect and the American Country House* (New Haven: Yale University Press, 1990), 69–123.

18. In 1915 Seiberling wrote, "I am thru with changes of every character until I can live with the house a year in peace, far removed from contractors, architects, decorators, etc., at the end of which period I may decide to make some changes." Seiberling to Schneider, September 23, 1915, SHH Archives.

19. Harvey S. Firestone in collaboration with Samuel Crowther, *Men and Rubber* (Garden City, N.Y.: Doubleday, 1926), quoted from Clive Aslet, *The American Country House* (New Haven: Yale University Press, 1990), 23.

20. "Idlehour, Estate of Vanderbilt" *Architectural Record* 13 (May 1903): 461.

21. Irene Seiberling Harrison, interview by author, Akron, Ohio, February 18, 1991.

22. Schneider was adamant: "Don't get anything unless you are sure you want it—it must be good to have a place in this house. That does not necessarily mean expensive, but it must have character, style; it should have good lines, color, proportion. It should have use, either as an object of use or as an ornament. Do not let the age of anything get the best of you. Age does not mean that a thing is beautiful." Schneider to F. A. and Gertrude Seiberling, December 29, 1914, SHH Archives.

23. "Guide to the Collections of Stan Hywet Hall, Akron, Ohio," July 1983, SHH Archives.

24. Allen, *House of Goodyear*, 38, 320.

25. "Goodyear Heights," Sales Prospectus, 1913, Goodyear Tire and Rubber Co., Akron, 3.

26. Manning's planting plan, for example, used a dominant tree species on each street, and "one or two shrubs and vines . . . to give the street a distinctive floral character." See Warren H. Manning, *A Step Towards Solving the Industrial Housing Problem*, American City Pamphlet Series, no. 131 (New York: Civic Press, 1913). This idea may have been pioneered by Frederick Law Olmsted Jr. See Susan L. Klaus, *A Modern Arcadia: Frederick Law Olmsted and the Plan for Forest Hills Gardens* (Amherst: University of Massachusetts Press in association with Library of American Landscape History, 2002), 102–3.

27. See Steve Love and David Giffels, "Building Communities," *Akron Beacon Journal*, March 30, 1997. The first phase of Goodyear Heights, completed in 1913, produced about four hundred new homes that sold at an average cost of $3,500. During the second phase, fifteen hundred new homes were constructed and the development was opened to non-employees, although African Americans were barred. *The Wingfoot Clan* (Goodyear newsletter), August 25, 1917, quoted from Love and Giffels, "Building Communities." Large sections of Goodyear Heights still exist as planned by Manning.

28. Firestone Park was laid out by Alling DeForest (1875–1957), who also designed the grounds of Firestone's Akron estate. DeForest also designed George Eastman's estate on East Avenue in

Rochester, N.Y. The latter estate has been restored and is now open to the public.

29. A. D. Taylor to Mr. G. B. Edwards, June 12, 1912, SHH Archives. The letter chronicles many aspects of construction, including the location of roads, grading, surveying, billing of worker expenses, drainage, handling of plants, establishment of a nursery, plant collecting, procurement of manure, and other topics. It finishes, "I wish that you would make every effort to organize and execute this work as speedily as possible and in a most economical manner."

30. Manning to Seiberling, October 23, 1912, SHH Archives. Jens Jensen would get this commission, however.

31. An early letter from Manning to Schneider makes the collaborative process clear. "I am sending you the print of my first pencil study for Mr. Seiberling's property, . . . which represents the approximate location and outline of the house that we discussed on the ground, together with the roads, vistas, yards, gardens, and the like. I am also sending a combination blueprint of this study with the topography, together with a copy of planting list to accompany the study. . . . I would like very much to have your views with reference to the features of this study that connect with the house, and your latest studies, so that we can begin to get together." Manning to Schneider, March 27, 1912, SHH Archives.

32. The apple orchard has been restored to its original configuration. See "Apple Orchard and Drive Restoration," report, Douglas P. Reed, Landscape Architect, June 1, 1995, SHH Archives.

33. The entry court set a domestic tone. When the original elms died, the area lost scale, grace, and charm. Replanting the trees (with disease-resistant varieties found growing as seedlings in one of the old peach orchards) and reducing the area of asphalt drive, introduced when the estate was opened to the public, have resulted in a highly effective recovery of the original tone and appearance. See "Historic Preservation of Landscape and Gardens, c. 1911–16, 1928, for Stan Hywet Hall Foundation, Inc., May 1984," Child, Hornbeck Associates, Inc., Cambridge, Mass., SHH Archives.

34. Manning wrote, "I sympathize wholly with Mr. Schneider's desire to have the garden setting of his house like that of English homes upon which the design of the house was based, but I do feel that we should not make or place gardens in positions where they will impair the value of our fine distant views." Manning to Seiberling, May 25, 1914, SHH Archives.

35. Frank A. Seiberling Jr., "A Concept Rediscovered," unpublished paper, October 24, 1984, 18, author's collection.

36. Manning to Seiberling, June 23, 1911, SHH Archives. There are several invasive species on Manning's list. He was intrigued by the potential for introduced plants to thrive in local conditions. Some of these (bittersweet and goutweed, for example) proved rampant and almost impossible to eradicate.

37. Warren H. Manning, "Park Design and Planting," transcript of lecture to Park and Outdoor Art Association, Louisville, Ky., April 22, 1897, Manning Collection, Lowell.

38. Warren H. Manning, "The Art of Making Landscape Gardens," in *The Standard Cyclopedia of Horticulture*, ed. Liberty Hyde Bailey (New York: Macmillan, 1916), 1784.

39. Frederick Law Olmsted to George W. Vanderbilt, July 12, 1889, quoted from Charles E. Beveridge, "The First Great *Private* Work of Our Profession in the Country: Frederick Law Olmsted, Senior, at Biltmore," in Charles E. Beveridge and Susan L. Klaus, *The Olmsteds at Biltmore* (Bethesda, Md.: National Association for Olmsted Parks, 1995), 3.

40. Seiberling to Schneider, February 25, 1916, SHH Archives.

41. Schneider to Seiberling, February 28, 1916, SHH Archives.

42. "The house was placed and oriented largely with reference to the fine distant view over the valley." Manning to Seiberling, May 25, 1914, SHH Archives.

43. Manning to Mr. N. L. Palmer, March 7, 1916, SHH Archives. This and other important views were re-opened according to recommendations outlined in the Child, Hornbeck master plan cited in n. 33. This plan was implemented under the auspices of then-president of Stan Hywet Hall John Franklin Miller and actively supported by Frank A. Seiberling Jr.

44. Seiberling to Schneider, April 25, 1916, SHH Archives. See also Schneider to Seiberling, July 25, 1916, SHH Archives.

45. The stone basin was carved by Blum & Delbridge, who had also created fountains for Gwinn.

46. In one letter Manning joked, "I wouldn't be surprised . . . if myself, or someone else got a ducking in this basin when starting in a hurry from the house straight to the outlook to enjoy a particularly attractive sunset. Tell Mrs. Seiberling that I might be able to compromise on stepping stones that would enable me to jump across the middle." Manning to Seiberling, February 10, 1916, SHH Archives.

47. Seiberling to Manning, June 16, 1914, SHH Archives.

48. Ibid.

49. One of Manning's letters survives to outline his ideas about the feature: "I would like . . . to make it a little New England Garden in the Japanese style, in which I might have the privilege of selecting just the stones and plants that would be required to carry out the design. I would also like to see a compartment in the garden made up of the material that is to be found in the Snow and Mackinac Island region, using again the characteristic plants." Manning also suggested that he and his wife work with the Seiberlings on designs for lanterns for the garden. Manning to Seiberling, June 25, 1914, SHH Archives. Several drawings by Manning of ornamental rocks and planting vignettes for the new garden survive.

50. T. R. Otsuka, "Terms and Conditions," memorandum on construction of Japanese Garden, n.d., SHH Archives.

51. Warren H. Manning, "List of Plants for Panels in English Garden," March 30, 1915, SHH Archives.

52. Shipman's planting design for the English Garden is discussed in chapter 5.

53. Manning to Seiberling, February 10, 1916, SHH Archives.

54. Love and Giffels, "Building Communities."

55. It is not clear if Seiberling argued that the job should go to Manning. The Olmsted firm may have been first choice as a result of their success with the Cleveland parks system.

56. Olmsted Brothers, Landscape Architects, "Report on a Park System for Summit County, Ohio, Submitted to E. D. Eckroad, President, Metropolitan Park Board of Summit County, 5 October 1925."

57. Stan Hywet Hall was placed on the roll of National Historic Landmarks in 1982.

58. See "Memoranda of Recommendations and Suggestions of Visit of April 20, 1928," Warren H. Manning Offices, Inc. Landscape Design and Regional Planning, 210 Brattle Building, Harvard Square, Cambridge, Mass., April 27, 1928, SHH Archives.

59. Among the several gardens that Manning and Shipman worked on together were three in northeastern Ohio: Amasa S. Mather, Chagrin Falls (1916); Windsor T. White, Halfred Farms, Chagrin Falls (1919); and Willard M. Clapp, Cleveland Heights (1926). For more on their collaborations, see Robin Karson, "A Woman's Place: Ellen Shipman's Gardens Frame a Divided World," *Garden Design*, February–March 1997, 46–48.

60. Irene Seiberling Harrison interview.

61. Gertrude was also active in the Women's National Farm and Garden Association, founded by Clara (Mrs. Henry) Ford.

62. Perennial Planting Plan, May 11, 1929, SHH Archives.

63. Judith B. Tankard, *The Gardens of Ellen Biddle Shipman* (Sagaponack, N.Y.: Sagapress/Abrams in association with Library of American Landscape History, 1996), 118.

64. The English Garden at Stan Hywet was restored in 1991. See John Franklin Miller, "The Restoration of the English Garden at Stan Hywet," in Tankard, *The Gardens of Ellen Biddle Shipman*, 183–88. See also Mary C. Halbrooks, "The English Garden at Stan Hywet Hall and Gardens: Interpretation, Analysis, and Documentation of a Historic Garden Restoration," *HortTechnology* 15, no. 2 (April–June 2005): 196–212.

65. Seiberling Jr., "A Concept Rediscovered," 21. There is more information about Seiberling Jr.'s perspectives on Stan Hywet Hall in Frank A. Seiberling Jr., "Updating Stan Hywet's Grounds and Gardens in the Spirit of Its Builders," undated lecture typescript, author's collection.

66. This work was done under the auspices of John Franklin Miller according to the Child, Hornbeck master plan, 1985.

5. ELLEN SHIPMAN

1. For more on the Colonial-era garden, see Ann Leighton's classics, *Early American Gardens: "For Meate or Medicine"* (Boston: Houghton Mifflin, 1970) and *American Gardens in the Eighteenth Century: "For Use or for Delight"* (Boston: Houghton Mifflin, 1976).

2. Leslie Close, "A History of Women in Landscape Architecture," in Judith B. Tankard, *The Gardens of Ellen Biddle Shipman* (Sagaponack, N.Y.: Sagapress/Abrams in association with Library of American Landscape History, 1996), xiii–xix.

3. See also E. W. Weaver, *Profitable Vocations for Girls* (Chicago: Laidlaw Brothers, 1924).

4. Rebecca Warren Davidson, introduction to Martha Brookes Hutcheson, *The Spirit of the Garden*, reprint of 1923 edition (Amherst: University of Massachusetts Press in association with Library of American Landscape History, 2001), xxvii n.19.

5. *Bar Harbor Record*, September 30, 1896.

6. Mary Bronson Hartt, "Women and the Art of Landscape Gardening," *Outlook*, March 28, 1908, 695.

7. For an excellent discussion of nineteenth-century women and learned professions, see Lillian Faderman, *To Believe in Women: What Lesbians Have Done for America—A History* (Boston: Houghton Mifflin, 1999), 255–73.

8. Charlotte Perkins Gilman wrote "The Yellow Wallpaper" (1892) as an exposé of this type of therapy. For more on the concept of neurasthenia, see Tom Lutz, *American Nervousness, 1903: An Anecdotal History* (Ithaca, N.Y.: Cornell University Press, 1991).

9. Lutz, *American Nervousness*, 82.

10. One of the most successful women landscape architects in this regard was Marjorie Sewell Cautley (1891–1954), a graduate of Cornell University and an assistant in the offices of Warren Manning and the architect Julia Morgan (1872–1957). Cautley was associated with a greater number of large-scale projects than any of her female colleagues. These included Roosevelt Common, a thirty-acre park in Tenafly, N.J., and, somewhat later, Sunnyside Gardens (1924–28), Phipps Garden Apartments (1930, 1935), Hillside Homes (1935), and Radburn (1928–30). In 1937 Cautley suffered a mental breakdown that some have suggested was a result of the strain of her professional associations with strong-minded practitioners, primary among whom were Clarence Stein and Henry Wright. In 1935 she published *Garden Design: The Principles of Abstract Design as Applied to Landscape Composition* (New York: Dodd, Mead, 1935). See Nell Walker, "Marjorie Sewell Cautley," in *Pioneers of American Landscape Design*, ed. Charles A. Birnbaum and Robin Karson (New York: McGraw-Hill, 2000), 47–49.

11. Martha Brookes Hutcheson (1871–1959), Harriet Foote (1863–1951), Grace Tabor (c. 1873–c. 1953), Mary P. Cunningham (d. 1934), Rose Nichols (1872–1960), Rose Greely (1887–1969), and Annette Hoyt Flanders (1887–1946) are among the better-known women practitioners whose practices included primarily flower gardens. There were legions of other women specializing in this arena.

12. Davidson, introduction to *Spirit of the Garden*, viii–ix.

13. There were exceptions to this trend. Percival Gallagher (1874–1934), an associate in the Olmsted Brothers firm, was well known for his flower gardens. Gallagher's c. 1920 work at Oldfields (now a property of the Indianapolis Museum of Art) utilized a tremendous variety of bloom in border gardens arranged around the perimeter of the central oak allée. The grounds of this estate have been restored and are now open to the public. Beginning in 1915, Fletcher Steele would bring considerable inventiveness to the design of the flower garden, eschewing the traditional border format in favor of bolder forms. Steele's work is discussed in chapter 14.

14. Shipman, Garden Note Book, quoted from Tankard, *Gardens*, 53.

15. Tankard, *Gardens*, 5.

16. Shipman, Garden Note Book, quoted from ibid., 12.

17. Ibid., 11.

18. Ibid., 18.

19. Of the three, the most important professional training ground was the Cambridge School, which was established by Henry Atherton Frost (1883–1952) and Bremer Whidden Pond (1884–1959). It eventually became affiliated with Smith College and functioned until 1942, when Harvard began to admit women. For more on the training of early women landscape architects, see Dorothy

May Anderson, *Women, Design, and the Cambridge School* (West Lafayette, Ind.: PDA Publishers, 1980).

20. Shipman amassed a large professional library which included volumes by Jekyll, Robinson, and Mawson.

21. Coffin's career is discussed in chapter 8.

22. See Robin Karson, "A Woman's Place: Ellen Shipman's Gardens Frame a Divided World," *Garden Design*, February–March 1997, 46–48.

23. Fletcher Steele, "Design of the Small Place," in *The House Beautiful Gardening Manual* (Boston: Atlantic Monthly Company, 1926), 10.

24. Shipman eventually found large clusters of clients in Michigan, New York State, Ohio, and North Carolina; she also worked in Illinois, Colorado, Delaware, Florida, Georgia, Kentucky, Louisiana, Maine, Maryland, New Mexico, and Washington. See Tankard, *Gardens*, 189–200.

25. The professional career of Lord and Schryver resembled that of Florence Yoch (1890–1972) and Lucille Council (1898–1964). The garden and architectural photographers Mattie Edwards Hewitt (c. 1870–1956) and Frances Benjamin Johnston (1864–1952) also maintained a professional as well as a romantic partnership. Reaction to these lesbian firms does not appear to have impeded highly successful careers. Other well-known designers who assisted in Shipman's office are Mary P. Cunningham and Agnes Selkirk Clark (1898–1983).

26. Shipman worked on the estate for many years, continuing to advise there after World War II. More than 150 drawings and plans chronicle her work. See Tankard, *Gardens*, 122–26.

27. For more on this project, see Mark Alan Hewitt, *The Architect and the American Country House* (New Haven: Yale University Press, 1990), 80, *82, 85*, 269. See also Tankard, *Gardens*, 132–37.

28. The outstanding example in Shipman's oeuvre is Rose Terrace, for Hugh and Anna (Dodge) Dillman in Grosse Pointe, Mich. It was a measure of Shipman's fame that she won the landscape commission for Detroit's most ostentatious country place, whose house was designed by Horace Trumbauer (1869–1938). The job began in 1931, at the depth of the Depression, and, not surprisingly, the opulence of the Dillmans' mansion became a source of outrage among Detroit's unemployed auto workers, who were among the nation's hardest hit by the faltering economy. Shipman successfully adapted taut, French principles to the lakeside site, but photographs of Rose Terrace—all that remain today of Shipman's design, except for a fragment of fence—suggest that the larger spaces came at the expense of charm.

29. She returned to revise these plantings in 1931, 1935, 1938, and 1946.

30. See Tankard, *Gardens*, 167–174.

31. The Fords wintered in Fort Myers, Fla., where Shipman would soon design a garden for their next-door neighbors, Thomas A. and Mina Edison. This garden was restored in 2006 and is open to the public.

32. The Sterns had turned to Shipman because they were frustrated with David Adler (1882–1949), whom they had originally hired for the project. After Shipman's death, Edith Stern again turned to William Platt, asking for a substantial revision of areas of Ship-

man's garden scheme. His changes brought many new architectural features into the landscape, including a series of fountains on the main vista.

33. The wild garden included plantings by Caroline Dorman (1885–1965), a leading authority on Louisiana wildflowers. Several of Shipman's designs included wild gardens, most of which she designed herself. For more on this aspect of her work, see Tankard, *Gardens*, 143–152. See also the Longue Vue House and Gardens Cultural Landscape Report prepared by Heritage Landscapes and Robin Karson, July 1997. In September 2005 Longue Vue suffered considerable damage from Hurricane Katrina. Large portions of the gardens have been restored, but the long-term health of the soil and its capacity to sustain plantings are still unknown.

34. Shipman's practice slowed during the Depression, and because her designs were highly dependent on plantings, they tended to fade quickly when maintenance ceased, as it did in most of the six hundred projects she completed during her life. At the time of Shipman's death in 1951, few clients had the interest or the fortunes to pursue flower gardens of the type she had designed at Gwinn and Stan Hywet. Yet the architectural framework of many of her gardens survived, and, owing to the publication of *The Gardens of Ellen Biddle Shipman* in 1996, several that were not known to exist have been discovered and restored.

6. BEATRIX FARRAND

1. Paula Deitz, introduction to Beatrix Farrand, *The Bulletins of Reef Point Gardens* (Bar Harbor, Me.: Island Foundation, 1997), xiv. I have relied on several other sources for information about Farrand's career. One of the earliest and still best publications is Diane Kostial McGuire and Lois Fern, eds., *Beatrix Jones Farrand (1872–1959): Fifty Years of American Landscape Architecture* (Washington, D.C.: Dumbarton Oaks Trustees for Harvard University, 1982). Another reliable and well-illustrated collection of essays is Diana Balmori, Diane Kostial McGuire, and Eleanor M. McPeck, *Beatrix Farrand's American Landscapes: Her Gardens and Campuses* (Sagaponack, N.Y.: Sagapress, 1985). There is a great deal of interesting biographical detail in the early chapters of Jane Brown, *Beatrix: The Gardening Life of Beatrix Jones Farrand, 1872–1959* (New York: Viking, 1995).

2. The property eventually included six acres. The Joneses' house was one of twenty-two buildings in Bar Harbor designed by the Boston firm of Rotch & Tilden. Beatrix's parents were already separated by the time it was finished. See Deitz, introduction, xii.

3. Ibid., xii.

4. Mildred Bliss, "An Attempted Evocation of a Personality," in Beatrix Farrand, *Plant Book for Dumbarton Oaks* (Washington, D.C.: Dumbarton Oaks Trustees for Harvard University, 1980), xxi.

5. Mary Bronson Hartt, "Women and the Art of Landscape Gardening," *Outlook*, March 28, 1908, 694–704.

6. "Beatrix Jones Farrand," *Reef Point Bulletin* 1, no. 17, in Farrand, *The Bulletins of Reef Point Gardens*, 112.

7. Charles Downing Lay, "An Interview with Charles A. Platt," *Landscape Architecture* 2, no. 3 (April 1912): 127–31.

8. Beatrix Jones, "Nature's Landscape-gardening in Maine," *Garden and Forest*, September 6, 1893, 378.

9. Laura Wood Roper, *FLO: A Biography of Frederick Law Olmsted* (Baltimore: Johns Hopkins University Press, 1973), 455n. Olmsted's private aside is sometimes interpreted as evidence of his disdain for women in the profession, but there is considerable evidence to contradict this. Olmsted was unusually supportive of women practitioners.

10. Beatrix Farrand, "Book of Gardening," unpublished notebook, 43. Beatrix Jones Farrand Collection (1955-2), Environmental Design Archives, University of California, Berkeley (hereafter cited as Farrand Collection, EDA, Berkeley).

11. Brown, *Beatrix*, 46.

12. Brown covers Farrand's 1895 tour in considerable detail. See ibid., 46–58.

13. Susan Tamulevich, *Dumbarton Oaks: Garden into Art* (New York: Monacelli Press, 2001), 94.

14. Beatrix Jones, "Bridge Over the Kent at Levens Hall," *Garden and Forest*, January 15, 1896, 22, 25.

15. Later the Department of Architecture at Columbia University.

16. See appendix, "Beatrix Farrand's Commissions: 1891–1949," in Balmori, McGuire, and McPeck, *Beatrix Farrand's American Landscapes*, 197–202.

17. Beatrix Jones, "The Garden in Relation to the House," *Garden and Forest*, April 7, 1897, 132–33.

18. *New York Sun*, October 31, 1897.

19. Jones was also the subject of an article in the *New York Herald Tribune*, "New York Society Girl a Landscape Architect," February 11, 1900.

20. In addition to Parsons, Manning, and the two Olmsteds, John Charles and Olmsted Jr., this group included Nathan Franklin Barrett, designer of the town of Pullman outside Chicago and several private estates, including Naumkeag in Stockbridge, Mass; Charles Nassau Lowrie (1869–1939), a park specialist trained as a civil engineer; Daniel W. Langton (1864–1909), the society's only southerner and Lowrie's partner on several municipal parks; O. C. Simonds, educator, author, civil engineer, and landscape architect, who was a designer and the superintendent of Graceland Cemetery in Chicago; George F. Pentecost (b. 1875), an architect and Parsons's occasional partner; and Downing Vaux (1856–1926), Calvert Vaux's son, who worked with his father until the senior Vaux's death in 1895 and then continued in his own diverse practice.

21. See Nancy A. Leszczynski, "Beatrix Farrand: The Development of a Design Philosophy," master's thesis, University of Virginia, May 1991. Leszczynski's analysis focuses particularly on Farrand's fusion of American vernacular and Picturesque traditions with Beaux-Arts formality.

22. Ibid., 16.

23. Between 1902 and 1907 Edith Wharton and George Bucknam Dorr (1853–1944), founder of Acadia National Park (and stepson of Charles Sargent), corresponded about wild garden plantings at The Mount. Dorr was the owner of Oldfarm, a Mount Desert estate, and the founder of the "Wild Gardens of Acadia" and the Mount Desert Nurseries. The extent of the wild garden at The Mount has not yet been determined, but it is clear that such a garden or gardens existed. See Ronald H. Epp, "Wild Gardens and Pathways at The Mount: George B. Dorr and the Mount Desert Island Influence," in *Edith Wharton and the American Garden*, ed. Betsy Anderson (Lenox, Mass.: The Mount Press, forthcoming). During the first decade of the twentieth century, Jones worked for several of the Whartons' wealthy Lenox neighbors in the role typical for women practitioners then—designing plantings for flower borders. At ninety-four-room Elm Court, whose grounds had been laid out by Olmsted c. 1885, she created large herbaceous and rose beds. At Eastover, designed by Francis L.V. Hoppin (1867–1941), of Hoppin & Koen, she had more substantial architectural responsibilities, including an approach drive, terraces, and water features. Farrand's files also contain a plan for Bellefontaine by Carrère & Hastings, but it is not clear that she actually did any design work there. A 1902 job for Anson Phelps Stokes, who moved from Lenox to Darien, Conn., was cohesive and elegant. There Jones fit outbuildings, tennis court, croquet lawn, and formal gardens on a small spit of land in Long Island Sound. The commissions are dated in Balmori, McGuire, and McPeck, *Beatrix Farrand's American Landscapes*, as follows: William Douglas Sloane (Elm Court) 1908; Harris Fahnestock (Eastover) 1910–14; Anson Phelps Stokes (Conn.) 1902. Giraru Foster (Bellefontaine) is undated.

24. Edith Wharton to Morton Fullerton, July 3, 1911, reproduced in *The Letters of Edith Wharton*, ed. R. W. B. Lewis and Nancy Lewis (New York: Charles Scribner's Sons, 1988), 242.

25. Wharton's best-selling novel *The House of Mirth* (1905) was written at The Mount and provided revenue for the creation of the gardens there. The Whartons began wintering in Paris in 1907, and soon Edith became involved in an affair with Morton Fullerton. In 1913 she divorced Edward. See R. W. B. Lewis, *Edith Wharton: A Biography* (New York: Harper and Row, 1975), and Louis Auchincloss, *Edith Wharton: A Woman in Her Time* (New York: Viking, 1971).

26. Edith Wharton, *A Backward Glance* (New York: Appleton-Century, 1934), 125.

27. See Mary Hart Parker, "The Theory and Practice of Garden Design in the Life of Edith Wharton," unpublished paper prepared for the tenth anniversary meeting of the Edith Wharton Society at The Mount, Lenox, Mass., June 1977.

28. Edith Wharton and Odgen Codman Jr., *The Decoration of Houses* (New York: Charles Scribner's Sons, 1897), 192.

29. In 1910 Farrand entered an Architectural League competition with a scheme for "An Ideal Suburban Place." See Beatrix Jones, "Laying Out a Suburban Place," *Country Life in America*, March 1910, 551–52.

30. Beatrix Jones, "The Garden as Picture," *Scribner's*, July 1907, 5, 8, italics added.

31. Ibid., 3.

32. Beatrix Farrand to Mrs. Charles Andrews, October 9, 1937, quoted from Diana Balmori, "Beatrix Farrand at Dumbarton Oaks," in McGuire and Fern, *Beatrix Jones Farrand*, 106.

33. Ibid.

34. David R. Coffin, "Beautifying the Campus," *Historic Gardens Review*, January 2005, 2–8.

NOTES TO PAGES 143–157

35. Ralph Adams Cram to Henry B. Thompson, member of the Princeton Building and Grounds Committee, December 27, 1912, quoted from Diana Balmori, "Campus Work and Public Landscapes," in Balmori, McGuire, and McPeck, *Beatrix Farrand's American Landscapes*, 158.

36. Balmori, McGuire, and McPeck, *Beatrix Farrand's American Landscapes*, 156–59.

37. Ibid., 132–33.

38. At Princeton, Farrand was also the target of an anonymous letter that accused her of combining "too much pleasure with business" and demeaned her abilities in grading and road building. In *Beatrix Farrand's American Landscapes*, Balmori cites this as "Unsigned letter to Charles Hart, Philadelphia" (150).

39. Coffin, "Beautifying the Campus," 6.

40. Ibid., 6–7. Farrand held her position at Princeton until she resigned in 1941. She was also commissioned for design work at Yale (1924–47), Oberlin (1937–46), Vassar (1926–27), Hamilton (1930–35), University of Chicago (1931–45), Occidental College (1937–48), and California Institute of Technology (1928–38). See "Campus Work and Public Landscapes," in Balmori, McGuire, and McPeck, *Beatrix Farrand's American Landscapes*, 127–96.

41. The new house was designed by Delano & Aldrich, who had also designed the Straights' New York City town house at 1130 Fifth Avenue.

42. For more on the project, see Eleanor M. McPeck, "A Biographical Note and a Consideration of Four Major Private Gardens," in Balmori, McGuire, and McPeck, *Beatrix Farrand's American Landscapes*, 40–44. Willard Straight died from influenza in 1918, and Dorothy remarried. She and her new husband, Leonard Elmhirst, hired Farrand to design the grounds of Dartington Hall, their home and school in Devonshire, England. It was Farrand's only work abroad. For more on this important project, see Brown, *Beatrix*, 149–54.

43. Michael M. Laurie reproduces several plans and drawings from the Harkness project in his chapter "The Reef Point Collection at the University of California," in McGuire and Fern, *Beatrix Jones Farrand*, 9–20.

44. Tamulevich, *Dumbarton Oaks*, 30.

7. DUMBARTON OAKS

1. Many of the chronological details presented in this chapter are from Susan Tamulevich, *Dumbarton Oaks: Garden into Art* (New York: Monacelli Press, 2001). More vividly than any others on the topic, Tamulevich's book illuminates Farrand's long involvement with the gardens and with her primary client there, Mildred Bliss. Other sources offer more complex analysis of the design. These include Diana Balmori, Diane Kostial McGuire, and Eleanor M. McPeck, *Beatrix Farrand's American Landscapes: Her Gardens and Campuses* (Sagaponack, N.Y.: Sagapress, 1985); Diane Kostial McGuire and Lois Fern, eds., *Beatrix Jones Farrand (1872–1959): Fifty Years of American Landscape Architecture* (Washington, D.C.: Dumbarton Oaks Trustees for Harvard University, 1982); and Beatrix Farrand, *Beatrix Farrand's Plant Book for Dumbarton Oaks* (Washington, D.C.: Dumbarton Oaks Trustees for Harvard Uni-

versity, 1980). See also Jane Brown, *Beatrix: The Gardening Life of Beatrix Jones Farrand, 1872–1959* (New York: Viking, 1995).

2. Mildred Bliss to Lucy and Ernest [no surname provided], August 24, 1916, Dumbarton Oaks, Research Library and Collections, Washington, D.C. (hereafter cited as Dumbarton Oaks Collection).

3. "I seem to poison [Mildred] after I've been with her for half an hour and she gets perfectly horrid." Wharton, quoted in R. W. B. Lewis, *Edith Wharton: A Biography* (New York: Harper and Row, 1975), 373.

4. See Maureen de Lay Joseph, Mark Davison, and Kay Fanning, *Cultural Landscape Report: Dumbarton Oaks Park, Rock Creek Park, Part I* (Washington, D.C.: National Park Service, 2000), 10–17.

5. Today Casa Dorinda is a retirement home; virtually none of the original landscape design survives.

6. David F. Myrick, *Montecito and Santa Barbara* (Glendale, Calif. Trans-Anglo Books, 1987–1991), 2:420.

7. Mildred Bliss, quoted in Tamulevich, *Garden into Art*, 29. The composition, "A Catechism," was an attempt to reconcile Christian doctrine with contemporary science. In chapter 1, Bliss posed the question "What are you?" Her answer: "I am a conscious human being upon earth and have become so by countless ages of development from the lowest form of life."

8. Beatrix Farrand, "Dumbarton Oaks Gardens," unpublished manuscript, Garden Library and Rare Book Room, Harvard University, Dumbarton Oaks, Washington, D.C.

9. George Burnap (1885–1938) was responsible for many public parks and monuments in the capital city. His best-known work is Meridian Hill Park, 1914; Burnap also designed the planting of Japanese cherry trees around the Tidal Basin.

10. Farrand to Bliss, June 24 and 25, 1922, Dumbarton Oaks Collection.

11. Bliss to Farrand, July 13, 1922, Dumbarton Oaks Collection.

12. No letters between Bliss and Farrand between 1924 and 1930 are in the Dumbarton Oaks archives. Still, it has been possible to trace the design development of many areas of the landscape during this critical period.

13. Farrand to Bliss, May 20, 1923, Dumbarton Oaks Collection.

14. Bliss to Farrand, November 16, 1923, Dumbarton Oaks Collection.

15. Edith Wharton, *Italian Villas and Their Gardens*, reprint of 1904 edition (New York: Da Capo Press, 1988), 46–47.

16. Michel Conan, quoted in Tamulevich, *Dumbarton Oaks*, 96.

17. Balmori, McGuire, and McPeck, *Beatrix Farrand's American Landscapes*, 57, 58.

18. Henry Wotton, *Elements of Architecture* (1624), quoted in *The Genius of the Place: The English Landscape Garden, 1620–1820*, ed. John Dixon Hunt and Peter Willis (Cambridge, Mass.: MIT Press, 1988), 48.

19. This arrangement was somewhat imperiously spelled out in a letter from Mildred Bliss to Farrand. "After much thought, we decided that this is the wisest solution, as it will be the easiest, the most time-saving and the pleasantest way for you and the architect of that group to collaborate. . . . To have him around the corner, in New York, will surely be easier for you both; and it will be

such a pleasure to have the contact with Larry White." Bliss to Farrand, April 16, 1923, Dumbarton Oaks Collection.

20. Farrand, *Plant Book*, 63. An early letter to Bliss also reflects Farrand's wish to avoid any appearance of artifice—not a simple task in a garden of this size and scope: "The wall and steps, while not in any way ambitious or pretentious in scheme, could be a vital part of the plan and if made of fairly large rough stone, perhaps buttressed as many of the old stone walls are and simple in parapet, whether of iron, or stone, or hedged, would hardly give the dressed-up appearance so repellent in many modern gardens." Farrand to Bliss, June 24 and 25, 1922, Dumbarton Oaks Collection.

21. Diane Kostial McGuire, "The Gardens," *Apollo*, April 1984, 43. McGuire points out that the vibrant hues of the roses were intensified by the limited color schemes of the adjacent gardens. Bliss, according to McGuire, considered "the many hues of white to be the essential colour of the garden."

22. Farrand, *Plant Book*, 63.

23. Farrand wrote that the Box (later Urn) Terrace was intended as "an introduction to the Rose Garden, rather than a garden of importance on its own account." *Plant Book*, 59. This narrow terrace was later redesigned by Ruth Havey (1889–1980) to feature an ornate pebble mosaic.

24. Farrand to Bliss, September 11, 1922, Dumbarton Oaks Collection.

25. The oaks in the Green Garden died and have not been replaced. The little Star Terrace was used as an intimate family dining room. In this garden is a plaque with an inscription: "O THOU MAKER OF THE WHELE THAT BERETH THE STERRES AND TORNEST THE HEVENE WITH A RAVISSHING SWEIGH." It was chosen by Farrand and is a phrase from Geoffrey Chaucer's translation of *The Consolation of Philosophy* by Boethius. Several such inscriptions appear throughout the gardens. See Linda Lott, "Garden Ornament in the Dumbarton Oaks Garden: An Overview," August 1996, Studies in Landscape Architecture, Informal Papers, Dumbarton Oaks, Washington, D.C.

26. The Vista posed a difficult challenge for Farrand, who felt it was "one of the most important pieces of planting to be done, requiring both delicacy and solidity of treatment." See Farrand, *Plant Book*, 41.

27. This suggestion is based on Diana Balmori's essay on the gardens. Balmori argues that the Blisses envisioned semipublic functions for these outdoor rooms from the earliest stages of the design and that an awareness of these functions influenced the formal quality of these spaces. See Balmori, "Beatrix Farrand at Dumbarton Oaks," in McGuire and Fern, *Beatrix Jones Farrand*, 101.

28. Farrand, *Plant Book*, 128–29.

29. The Copse no longer exists. The area was selected as the site of a new museum to house the Blisses' art collections, the building for which was designed by Phillip Johnson in collaboration with Mildred Bliss and constructed in 1962.

30. Farrand, *Plant Book*, 67–68.

31. Ibid., 68.

32. Ibid., 69.

33. Brown, *Beatrix*, 140.

34. Balmori, McGuire, and McPeck, *Beatrix Farrand's American Landscapes*, 84.

35. Farrand, *Plant Book*, 83.

36. Ibid., 78.

37. Ibid.

38. Balmori, McGuire, and McPeck, *Beatrix Farrand's American Landscapes*, 61.

39. Farrand, undated manuscript 12, Farrand Collection, EDA, Berkeley.

40. McGuire, "The Gardens," 42–43.

41. Balmori, McGuire, and McPeck, *Beatrix Farrand's American Landscapes*, 120.

42. Farrand warned against substituting another plant: "Nothing will ever be quite as beautiful as the rumpled masses of the Box as they follow the slope of the hill." *Plant Book*, 76.

43. As boxwood has been replaced by other plants and architectural material over many years, the unifying force that it once provided throughout the landscape has lessened.

44. Farrand to Bliss, June 24 and 25, 1922, Dumbarton Oaks Collection.

45. Mildred Bliss, "An Attempted Evocation of a Personality," in Farrand, *Plant Book*, xxiii.

46. The model is in the Farrand papers at Berkeley.

47. Rateau is best known today for the black-and-gold bottle he designed for the perfume Arpège by Jean Lanvin, whose Paris apartment interior he also designed. The platinum bathroom in Linda and Cole Porter's Paris apartment was also Rateau's work. The discovery of Rateau's involvement was made in 1998 by James Carder, archivist at Dumbarton Oaks. Prior to that time, it was assumed that all the designs were the work of Farrand's office. For more information on Rateau, see Frank Olivier-Vila and François Rateau, *Armand-Albert Rateau, un baroque chez les modernes* (Paris: L'Amateur, 1992). See also Lott, "Garden Ornament."

48. James Carder discovered a list of typed comments relating to the drawings which he believes were Farrand's. They range from "perfect" to "to be suppressed." Tamulevich, *Dumbarton Oaks*, 102.

49. For more on Hertrich and the gardens of Henry and Arabella Huntington, see Brown, *Beatrix*, 145–46.

50. Farrand continued to list new projects, including several for Bar Harbor clients and a very large design for Oakpoint, the residence of Harrison Williams, in Bayville, Long Island.

51. Among Farrand's California institutional clients were the California Institute of Technology, Pasadena (1923–38); Occidental College, Los Angeles (1937–40); and Palomar Mountain Observatory Site (1938).

52. McGuire, "The Gardens," 40.

53. Tamulevich, *Dumbarton Oaks*, 149 (no citation provided for letter).

54. Louis Auchincloss, *Edith Wharton: A Woman in Her Time* (New York: Viking, 1971), 186. Wharton's decision to leave her estate largely to Elisina Tyler, the wife of Royall Tyler, Mildred Bliss's first love, came as a shock to Farrand, who litigated for a share of the settlement.

55. "Dumbarton Oaks Capitol Landmark," *Washington Star*, March 25, 1956.

56. Dumbarton Oaks played a historic role in the conclusion of World War II by providing a setting for the conference that led to the formation of the United Nations.

57. Farrand worked for the Blisses on a redesign of the garden there, too. The garden's original design was by Rose Greely.

58. Farrand to Bliss, February 28, 1947, Dumbarton Oaks Collection.

59. Farrand to Bliss, April 7, 1947, Dumbarton Oaks Collection.

60. Farrand to Bliss, May 26, 1947, Dumbarton Oaks Collection.

61. Havey's most spectacular redesign for Dumbarton Oaks, the Pebble Garden, c. 1961, transformed the former tennis court into a large parterre filled with Mexican stones and fountains.

62. Beatrix Farrand, "The Start and the Goal," *Reef Point Gardens Bulletin* 1, no. 1 (August 1946), in *The Bulletins of Reef Point Gardens*, 2.

63. Farrand's library contained approximately 2,700 volumes. See H. Leland Vaughan, appendix B, in Brown, *Beatrix*, 220–21. See also Michael Laurie, "The Reef Point Collection at the University of California," in McGuire and Fern, *Beatrix Jones Farrand*, 9–20.

64. Farrand, "The Start and the Goal," 3.

65. The Beatrix Farrand Society has purchased Garland Farm with the intention of restoring the gardens and opening them to the public.

8. MARIAN CRUGER COFFIN

1. Many of the details of Coffin's early life are drawn from a biographical essay written by Warren Hunting Smith, a boarder in Coffin's New Haven home and later her friend: "Memoir of Marian Coffin," in *Gardens Designed by Marian Cruger Coffin, Landscape Architect, 1876–1957* (Geneva N.Y.: Hobart College, 1958). Another valuable source of information is Clarence Fowler, "Three Women in Landscape Architecture," *Alumnae Bulletin of the Cambridge School of Domestic and Landscape Architecture* 4, no. 2 (April 1932): 7–12. See also Valencia Libby, "Marian Cruger Coffin (1876–1957): The Landscape Architect and the Lady," in *The House and Garden* (Roslyn, N.Y.: Nassau County Museum of Fine Arts, 1986), 24–29. Libby has also written an eloquent essay on Coffin in *Pioneers of American Landscape Design*, ed. Charles A. Birnbaum and Robin Karson (New York: McGraw-Hill, 2000), 64–68. Nancy Fleming, *Money, Manure, and Maintenance* (Weston, Mass.: Country Place Books, 1995), brings together important period photographs of the projects and also provides a near-complete client list, an invaluable resource for researchers.

2. Smith, "Memoir," 2.

3. Fowler, "Three Women," 11.

4. Smith, "Memoir," 2.

5. Valencia Libby, "Henry Francis du Pont and the Early Development of Winterthur Gardens, 1880–1927," master's thesis, University of Delaware, 1984, 67.

6. Fowler, "Three Women," 9. In Hutcheson's case the damage seems to have been reversible; after running a successful practice in Boston for less than a decade, she married, retired, and had a child. For more on Hutcheson, see Rebecca Warren Davidson, introduction to Martha Brookes Hutcheson, *The Spirit of the Garden*, reprint of 1923 edition (Amherst: University of Massachusetts Press in association with Library of American Landscape History, 2001).

7. Fowler, "Three Women," 9.

8. Libby, "Henry Francis du Pont," 70–71.

9. Coffin admired Platt's design; she had a large photograph of Faulkner Farm with her professional papers. Fleming, *Money, Manure, and Maintenance*, 11.

10. Louise and Frank would later create an unusual garden on the grounds of Hagley, the original family estate near Winterthur. See Mac Griswold and Eleanor Weller, *The Golden Age of American Gardens* (New York: Harry N. Abrams, 1991), 143–45.

11. Marian Cruger Coffin to H. F. du Pont, May, 25, 1903, quoted from Libby, "Henry Francis du Pont," 69.

12. Fowler, "Three Women," 12.

13. Smith, "Memoir," 3.

14. Fowler, "Three Women," 12.

15. Marian Cruger Coffin, "A Suburban Garden Six Years Old," *Country Life in America*, February 15, 1912, 19. Elsa Rehmann, *The Small Place: Its Landscape Architecture* (New York: G. P. Putnam's Sons, 1918) 107–17.

16. Rehmann, *The Small Place*, 111.

17. Ibid., 115.

18. Papers in the Winterthur archives list September 9, 1909, and June 4, 1912, as the first and second meeting between H. F. du Pont and Gertrude Jekyll. In 1910 H. F. sent fifty gladiolus bulbs 'America' to Miss Jekyll and the same to her sister, Lady Jekyll, in thanks for his first visit.

19. Coffin wrote about the Boardman garden twice, in *Southampton Magazine* in 1912 and *Architectural Record* in 1916.

20. For example, Alanson L. Daniel's garden, in Wenham, Mass. See Judith B. Tankard, *The Gardens of Ellen Biddle Shipman* (Sagaponack, N.Y.: Sagapress/Abrams in association with Library of American Landscape History, 1996), 50–51.

21. Two years later, Colwell left Coffin's office to open her own Cleveland-based practice. See Fleming, *Money, Manure, and Maintenance*, 20.

22. Coffin to du Pont, September 22, 1919, The Winterthur Library, Winterthur Archives (hereafter cited as Winterthur Archives.) The nature of Coffin's personal relationship with Scheiner is something of a mystery. Her sketches of him in Europe indicate that they traveled there together, which was almost unheard of at the time. He later married.

23. Remnants of Coffin's design survive. A large amphitheater, which was to have nestled in the central grove, was never constructed.

24. Coffin to H. Rodney Sharp, June 2, 1920, Winterthur Archives.

25. Day & Klauder to Coffin, January 23, 1924, Winterthur Archives, quoted in Fleming, *Money, Manure, and Maintenance*, 61.

26. Coffin to H. Rodney Sharp, June 25, 1925, Winterthur Archives.

27. For more on Coffin's role at Naumkeag, see chapter 15.

28. Marian Coffin, note in *Garden Club of American Bulletin*, May 1920, 58.

29. Ibid., 59.

30. Griswold and Weller, *Golden Age of American Gardens*, 94.

31. Enough remnants of this imaginative scheme survive to communicate the rhythm and flow of Coffin's layout. Though much changed, the property survives as a summer camp for the Electrical Workers Union of the Long Island Lighting Company.

32. The term is Mark Alan Hewitt's. See *The Architect and the American Country House* (New Haven: Yale University Press, 1990), 185–88.

33. Ibid., 188–89.

34. Fleming, *Money, Manure, and Maintenance*, 36.

35. "I know Miss Coffin felt these [the Frick and Winterthur estates] to be her two best achievements." Selina Appleyard to H. F. du Pont, March 25, 1957, Winterthur Archives.

36. Coffin felt strong rivalry with Farrand and did not like to speak about her. See Libby, "The Landscape Architect and the Lady," 28.

37. Smith, "Memoir," 5.

38. The renovation is described in Marian C. Coffin and James M. Scheiner, "Our Substitute Castle in Spain," *Country Life in America*, September 1922, 48–49.

9. WINTERTHUR

1. Several details of the early family history in this chapter are based on Jacqueline Hinsley, "Nurturing a Family Tradition," in *The Winterthur Garden: Henry Francis du Pont's Romance with the Land*, ed. Denise Magnani (New York: Harry N. Abrams in association with Winterthur Museum, 1995). Another rich source of information about the Winterthur landscape is Valencia Libby, "Henry Francis du Pont and the Early Development of Winterthur Gardens, 1880–1927," master's thesis, University of Delaware, 1984.

2. As Jacqueline Hinsley points out, du Pont had a model for a colony in his own print shop—La Rochefoucauld-Liancourt's *Voyage dans les Etats-Unis d'Amérique fait en 1795, 1796, et 1797*. The prospectus described a settlement in Genesee, N.Y., similar to the one he hoped to create. See Hinsley, "Nurturing a Family Tradition," 42.

3. Hinsley, "Nurturing a Family Tradition," 46. No date is provided for this letter.

4. Ibid., 46–47.

5. Ibid., 51.

6. Libby, "Henry Francis du Pont," 9.

7. Denise Magnani, "On Becoming a Gardener," in Magnani, *The Winterthur Garden*, 70.

8. H. F. du Pont to Pauline Foster du Pont, May 13, 1896, Winterthur Archives, quoted in Libby, "Henry Francis du Pont," 5.

9. Norman B. Wilkinson, *E. I. du Pont, Botaniste* (Charlottesville: University Press of Virginia, 1972), 102.

10. Libby, "Henry Francis du Pont," 9.

11. H. F. du Pont to Pauline du Pont, October 24, 1901, Winterthur Archives.

12. For a detailed account of du Pont's education at the Bussey Institution, see Libby, "Henry Francis du Pont," 19–27.

13. Ibid., 23, 25.

14. Ibid., 26.

15. Du Pont met Sargent somewhat later; he eventually became a supporter of the Arnold Arboretum. In 1917 du Pont became a member of the Harvard Board of Overseers' Committee to the Arnold Arboretum. He served until 1968, with two brief interruptions, 1923–24 and 1966–67. See Libby, "Henry Francis du Pont," 87.

16. See ibid., 56–59; see also 133–34 and appendix 1, "A Recreated Inventory of Henry Francis du Pont's Horticultural Library Prior to 1927," 196–205.

17. Ibid., 120. Du Pont repeated the same trial with dahlias the following year.

18. Du Pont recommended that new kinds be tried for three years before being planted extensively. Over the course of years he used *Narcissus horsfieldii*, *albicans*, 'Golden Spur,' 'Grandee,' and 'Emperor.' See ibid., 122–23.

19. C. Gordon Tyrrell, "The History and Development of the Winterthur Gardens," *Winterthur Portfolio* 1 (1964): 123.

20. The formal garden was designed by Frank Bissell (c. 1881–1957). Edward Bissell was listed as a practicing architect in Philadelphia during these years; perhaps they were the same person.

21. Libby, "Henry Francis du Pont," 130.

22. Henry Francis du Pont, notebook, "Color Schemes, combinations, Month Gardens A – M," c. 1910, Winterthur Archives.

23. Du Pont was inspired to have formal plans drawn up after seeing those that Marian Coffin had done for his friend William Marshall Bullitt at Oxmoor. He wrote Coffin, "I want to make a similar list of our flower garden and your arrangement is so remarkably clear that I would like to have some one down here follow it." Du Pont to Coffin, April 27, 1911, Winterthur Archives. This work was done by Elizabeth Colwell, the first of many assistants Coffin would employ.

24. Libby, "Henry Francis du Pont," 184 n. 42.

25. Du Pont's first rose order dates to 1906, when he ordered fifty-three varieties from M. H. Walsh, Woods Hole; in 1913 he ordered forty-nine old types from the English specialist Benjamin Cant. By 1924 photographs suggest that the entire rose garden was devoted to pale pink varieties. Du Pont also raised hardy water lilies, beginning in 1908, when he solicited advice from one of the country's experts, Henry A. Dreer, of Philadelphia. See ibid., 131–32.

26. Du Pont to Palisades Nursery, July 23, 1910, and du Pont to E. J. Krug, April 19, 1913, quoted in Libby, "Henry Francis du Pont," 138.

27. The rose garden was destroyed in 1957 when a parking lot was constructed near the Winterthur Museum. "It was either that or the meadow and I think the meadow more important to keep." Du Pont to James Scheiner, July 27, 1957, Winterthur Archives. The other terraces were razed when the Louise du Pont Crowninshield Research Building was constructed, 1967–69.

28. William H. Frederick Jr., "The Artist in His Garden," in Magnani, *The Winterthur Garden*, 19.

29. Libby, "Henry Francis du Pont," 127. The formal garden took 2,000–3,000 Darwin tulips and large quantities of bulbous iris. In 1956 du Pont reported having planted 18,000 iris of "his own division." *Garden Club of America Bulletin*, July 1956.

30. Du Pont bought from Croux et Fils, in France, and from James Veich & Sons, in England. Libby, "Henry Francis du Pont," 94.

31. Henry Francis du Pont, "Azaleas at Winterthur," *Quarterly Bulletin of the American Rhododendron Society*, January 5, 1962, 9.

32. Charles Sargent to H. F. du Pont, May 31, 1919, Winterthur Archives.

33. Du Pont's work on the Azalea Woods continued for many years. The extent of his involvement and the complexity of the scheme are apparent in his speech to the Garden Club of America, deliv-

ered on receiving the Medal of Honor in 1956: "I have also made three new azalea paths, one through the Kaempferi, another combining *Prinsepia sinensis* and three varieties of corylopsis with my Mucronulata, having an underplanting of *Corydalis densiflora*, and adjacent clumps of Lenten hellebores and *Anemone pulsatilla* and *Primula denticulata var. cashmeriana* hybrids. On each side of the third path I am putting some Exbury rhododendrons in tan and cream tones and hybrids and seedlings of Mr. S. A. Everett's and other crosses." *Garden Club of America Bulletin*, July 1956, 64.

34. Coffin to du Pont, May 7, 1948, Winterthur Archives.

35. Ruth Lord, *Henry F. du Pont and Winterthur: A Daughter's Portrait* (New Haven: Yale University Press, 1999), 92.

36. Toward the end of their lives, Sargent and Henry Algernon found an intimate friendship, recorded in their final letters. "Although it is said that really deep and lasting friendships must have their origin in the affiliations of boy-hood or youth," Sargent wrote the Colonel, "I must say that while our relations only began long subsequent to this, I have no friend now living in whom my interest is more cordial and profound." Charles Sargent to Henry Algernon du Pont, August 20, 1926, Winterthur Archives. Henry Algernon du Pont died on the last day of 1926; Sargent died three months later.

37. Du Pont to F. A. Seiberling, September 16, 1919, Winterthur Archives.

38. Lord, *Henry F. du Pont and Winterthur*, 157.

39. Jay E. Cantor, *Winterthur* (New York: Harry N. Abrams, 1985), 113–14.

40. Du Pont to Thomas T. Waterman, 1933, quoted from Cantor, *Winterthur*, 117–18.

41. The beginnings of a new appreciation for American antiques go back to the centennial celebrations of 1876. It rose sharply after 1909, in response to a landmark exhibition hosted by the Metropolitan Museum of Art, the same year that the Walpole Society—which Henry Francis du Pont was later invited to join—was founded by a group of gentlemen collectors. In 1910 the Society for the Preservation of New England Antiquities (now Historic New England) was founded, the first American organization set up to preserve historic buildings.

42. A prime force behind the addition was Robert de Forest (1848–1931), uncle of the landscape architect Lockwood de Forest Jr. In a speech delivered four years after the opening of the new wing, de Forest noted especially the potential influence of well-designed objects on modern-day industry: "Much as I am interested in bringing art to the museum, I am more interested in bringing good art into the home. . . . A beautiful room with harmonious furnishings and fittings can bring calm, joy and happiness." *New York Herald Tribune*, February 4, 1929, quoted in Amelia Peck, "Robert de Forest and the Founding of the American Wing—New York Metropolitan Museum," *Magazine Antiques*, January 2000, 180.

43. In the 1920s, the practice of removing interiors from old houses was widespread; du Pont was aware that it was controversial, nonetheless. He defended the removal of the famous Montmorenci staircase later installed at Winterthur, which had been taken from a house in Shocco Springs, N.C.: "It is much better to have it all in this house than scattered by bits in different houses

all over the country or more probably burned." Du Pont to Thomas T. Waterman, September 4, 1935, Winterthur Archives.

44. Du Pont to Coffin, May 28, 1928, Winterthur Archives.

45. The 1762 house located near Philadelphia was discovered by J. A. Lloyd Hyde, a friend of du Pont's and an antiques dealer. The residence was serving as a Polish club at the time. See Cantor, *Winterthur*, 122.

46. Du Pont to Coffin, December 29, 1928, Winterthur Archives.

47. The boxwood became very large and eventually breached the stairs. They were removed in the 1990s, to the consternation of many. The character of this area of the garden changed drastically as a result.

48. The iris died in 1938 and were replaced by peonies.

49. Du Pont to Coffin, February 21, 1931, Winterthur Archives.

50. Du Pont to Coffin, July 10, 1931, Winterthur Archives.

51. Paul Hensley, "Harry's Other Garden," in Magnani, *The Winterthur Garden*, 133.

52. Elizabeth Mather was also a member, as were Mrs. Charles Platt, Mildred Bliss, and Mrs. Lockwood de Forest II. Mabel Choate was one of the founders.

53. Ruth du Pont to Ruth Hawks Wales, April 18, 1931, Winterthur Archives.

54. Du Pont to Coffin, February 2, 1933, Winterthur Archives.

55. Du Pont to Coffin, April 8, 1932, Winterthur Archives.

56. Du Pont to Coffin, February 16, 1931, and February 21, 1931, Winterthur Archives.

57. Du Pont to Coffin, December 28, 1940, Winterthur Archives.

58. Du Pont to Coffin, February 2, 1933, Winterthur Archives.

59. Coffin to du Pont, May 4, 1933, Winterthur Archives.

60. Du Pont to Coffin, September 24, 1940, and Coffin to du Pont, April 26, 1942, Winterthur Archives.

61. The small garden and terrace featured camellias (pink and red *sasanqua* and *sinensis*) underplanted with *Adonis* and species crocus. A large *Osmanthus heterophyllus* (holly olive) bloomed in late fall.

62. Du Pont to Coffin, February 23, 1955, Winterthur Archives.

63. Du Pont later revised some of Coffin's recommended plantings to ensure a sequence of continual bloom from one end of the garden to the other. See Magnani, "Garden for a 'Country Place Museum,'" in *The Winterthur Garden*, 147.

64. Marian Cruger Coffin, *Trees and Shrubs for Landscape Effects* (New York: Charles Scribner's Sons, 1940), xx.

65. Coffin to du Pont, October 8, 1955, Winterthur Archives.

10. JENS JENSEN

1. Jens Jensen, *The Voice of the Clearing*, quoted from Leonard K. Eaton, *Landscape Artist in America: The Life and Work of Jens Jensen* (Chicago: University of Chicago Press, 1964), 21.

2. Many biographical details in this chapter are based on Robert E. Grese's excellent *Jens Jensen: Maker of Natural Parks and Gardens* (Baltimore: Johns Hopkins University Press, 1992). Grese has also published several shorter studies that I have drawn on here. See his entry on Jensen in *Pioneers of American Landscape Design*, ed. Charles A. Birnbaum and Robin Karson (New York: McGraw-

Hill, 2000), 203–9; "Jens Jensen: The Landscape Architect as Conservationist," in *Midwestern Landscape Architecture*, ed. William H. Tishler (Urbana: University of Illinois Press in collaboration with Library of American Landscape History, 2000), 117–41; and "The Prairie Gardens of O. C. Simonds and Jens Jensen," in *Regional Garden Design in the United States*, ed. Marc Treib and Therese O'Malley (Washington, D.C.: Dumbarton Oaks Research Library and Collection, 1995), 99–123. Another rich source of insight into Jensen's ideas is Eaton, *Landscape Artist in America*. I have also relied on Jensen's own book, *Siftings* (1939; reprint, Baltimore: Johns Hopkins University Press, 1990).

3. Grese, "Jens Jensen: The Landscape Architect as Conservationist," 117.

4. Jensen, *Siftings*, 35–36.

5. Grese hypothesizes that Jensen may also have left because he wanted to escape life on the family farm. Robert E. Grese to author, July 23, 2005.

6. Eaton, *Landscape Artist in America*, 29.

7. "I obtained my love for native plants and my knowledge of their habits by spending my Sundays in search of them in the environments of Chicago, sometimes going as far as one hundred to one hundred fifty miles from this center. In that way I discovered for myself the dunes of Northern Indiana with their rich plant life, the bogs in northern Illinois and southern Wisconsin, the lime and sand stone canyons on the Illinois and Rock Rivers, the majestic cliffs and the extensive river bottoms of the Mississippi and what was left of the varied and beautiful flora." Jens Jensen to Camillo Schneider, April 15, 1939, quoted in Robert E. Grese, "Prairie Gardens," 107.

8. Jensen, *Siftings*, 19–21.

9. Grese, *Jens Jensen*, 7.

10. Ibid., 9, quoted from the 1888 edition of the Annual Chicago West Park Commission Report. The interview was Ragna B. Eskil, "Natural Parks and Gardens," *Saturday Evening Post*, March 8, 1930, 18–19, 169–70.

11. Graceland Cemetery is one of the region's most historically significant landscapes. Its complicated history is well documented in Tishler, *Midwestern Landscape Architecture*.

12. See Robert E. Grese, introduction to O. C. Simonds, *Landscape-Gardening*, reprint of 1920 edition (Amherst: University of Massachusetts Press in association with Library of American Landscape History, 2000). See also Julia Sniderman Bachrach, "Ossian Cole Simonds: Conservation Ethic in the Prairie Style," in Tishler, *Midwestern Landscape Architecture*, 80–98.

13. Somewhat later (1903–11), Simonds worked on the northern extension of Lincoln Park in Chicago, where he continued his nature-based approach to design. Both Simonds and Jensen were members of the Cliff Dwellers and the City Club, where their paths likely crossed often.

14. H. W. S. Cleveland, "The Grand Traverse Region of Michigan," *Atlantic Monthly*, August 1870, 191–95. The best summary of Cleveland's career is Daniel J. Nadenicek and Lance M. Neckar, introduction to H. W. S. Cleveland, *Landscape Architecture, as Applied to the Wants of the West*, reprint of 1873 edition (Amherst: University of Massachusetts Press in association with Library of American Landscape History, 2002).

15. Charles E. Beveridge and Paul Rocheleau, *Frederick Law Olmsted: Designing the American Landscape* (New York: Rizzoli, 1995), 74.

16. Ibid.

17. S. B. Sutton, ed., *Civilizing American Cities: A Selection of Frederick Law Olmsted's Writings on City Landscapes* (Cambridge, Mass.: MIT Press, 1971), 38.

18. Jens Jensen, *A Greater West Park System* (Chicago: West Park Commission, 1920), 20.

19. On a 1929 tour sponsored by the American Civic Association, Manning lauded the "good work" being done by Jensen's Friends of Our Native Landscape "to save all places of beauty and interest that will tie the present and future generations of America to the past, and serve as playgrounds for the people and sanctuaries for wild plant and animal life." See Grese, *Jens Jensen*, 55.

20. Jensen was strongly influenced by the ideas of Raymond Unwin (1863–1940), with whom he was well acquainted. In an address to Chicago's City Club in 1911, Unwin argued that city planning is healthy and sound only "when it is a natural, straightforward, and honest expression of the needs of the community." For more on Jensen's attitudes toward city planning, see ibid., 39–40.

21. Jens Jensen, "Regulating City Building," *Survey*, November 18, 1911, quoted in ibid., 87.

22. Ibid., 42.

23. Cowles's doctoral dissertation, subsequently published as *The Ecological Relations of the Vegetation on the Sand Dunes of Lake Michigan* (Chicago: University of Chicago Press, 1899).

24. Gert Groening and Joachim Wolschke-Bulmahn, "Some Notes on the Mania for Native Plants in Germany," *Landscape Journal* 11, no. 2 (Fall 1992): 120.

25. Ibid, 123. See also Frank A. Waugh, "German Landscape Gardening," *Country Gentleman*, August 25, 1910, 790. For one perspective on the proposal for a scientific basis of garden design and National Socialism in Germany, see Joachim Wolschke-Bulmahn, "The Search for 'Ecological Goodness' among Garden Historians," in *Perspectives on Garden Histories*, ed. Michel Conan, Dumbarton Oaks Colloquium on the History of Landscape Architecture (Washington, D.C: Dumbarton Oaks Research Library and Collection, 1999), 161–80.

26. Jensen to E. G. Liebold (Henry Ford's general secretary) quoted in Grese, "Prairie Gardens," 118.

27. James [Jens] Jensen, "Parks and Politics," *Sixth Volume of the American Park and Outdoor Art Association*, no. 4 (1902), quoted in Grese, *Jens Jensen*, 64.

28. James [Jens] Jensen, "Plan for Hospital Grounds," *Park and Cemetery*, December 1901, 185–86.

29. Grese, *Jens Jensen*, 106.

30. Jensen, *Siftings*, 34. Jensen does not name the project he is describing, but Grese believes that it must have been the Rubens place. See Grese, *Jens Jensen*, 96.

31. Leonard Eaton agrees with Steven Christy's theory that Jensen's signature approach was worked out in 1901–2, in his design for Hermann Paepckes, Indianola, in Glencoe, Ill. Leonard K. Eaton, "Jens Jensen Reconsidered," in *Gateway Cities and Other Essays* (Ames: Iowa State University Press, 1989), 131–32; see also Steven

Christy, "The Growth of an Artist: Jens Jensen and Landscape Architecture," master's thesis, University of Wisconsin, 1976.

32. Eaton, *Landscape Artist in America*, 30.

33. Wilhelm Miller, *The Prairie Spirit in Landscape Gardening*, reprint of 1915 edition (Amherst: University of Massachusetts Press in association with Library of American Landscape History, 2001). Miller also published this garden in "Have We Progressed in Gardening?" *Country Life in America*, April 15, 1912, 26.

34. Jenney was an innovative architect who pioneered the construction of the steel-frame skyscraper, as well as a planner and landscape architect. He planned the West Parks system before the Great Fire of 1871, conceptualizing these large urban parks as a "chain of verdure," in a hybrid approach that straddled the pastoral aesthetic of Olmsted and the gardenesque. Jenney's designs, like Henry Shaw's at Tower Grove Park in St. Louis, included subtropical specimens and features that emphasized the didactic function of plants—both attributes of the gardenesque. Chicago's Central (later Garfield) Park included a conservatory, natural history museum, and botanical garden. Although each of the parks had its own individual character, the sophisticated plantings, architecture, and treatment of water features unified them into a harmonious and consistent ensemble. Jensen would later incorporate hardy plants into Jenney's spatial layout and transform a water feature in Humboldt Park into a lush, teeming prairie river, but he would respect the spatial structure of the layout. For more on Jenney, see Reuben M. Rainey, "William Le Baron Jenney and Chicago's West Parks: From Prairies to Pleasure Grounds," in Tishler, *Midwestern Landscape Architecture*.

35. Grese points out that Jensen successfully built coalitions of knowledgeable and politically influential individuals using many of the same methods as Charles Eliot. Grese, *Jens Jensen*.

36. In addition to founding the highly successful Friends of Our Native Landscape, Jensen organized the Prairie Club, whose Saturday walking trips were intended to introduce people to the beauty of the local landscape as a step toward conserving it. Leaders of these walks were accomplished individuals with wide-ranging backgrounds in the arts and sciences. Among them were Henry C. Cowles (1869–1939), William M. R. French, Walter Burley Griffin (1867–1937), who was both an architect and a landscape architect, the architect Dwight Perkins (1867–1941), O. C. Simonds's daughter Gertrude, and the sculptor Lorado Taft (1860–1936). Jensen also helped found Chicago's Playground Association, whose goal was to provide play areas for the urban poor. He was an active member of many civic groups with progressive social aims. See Grese, *Jens Jensen*, 121.

37. Wilhelm Miller, "Bird Gardens in the City," *Country Life in America*, August 1914, 46–47.

38. Jensen reportedly reassured him that "lesser men would have charged more to ruin the lovely site." Grese, *Jens Jensen*, 99. The Rosenwald home in Highland Park is now the site of Rosewood Park.

39. Photographs of the Simmses' estates were included in P. H. Elwood Jr., *American Landscape Architecture* (New York: Architectural Book Publishing Company, 1924). These represent two of only three naturalistic designs Elwood included among dozens of formal ones. The other was by O. C. Simonds at Graceland Cemetery.

40. Jens Jensen, "Landscape Art: An Inspiration from the Western Plains," *Sketch Book* 6, no. 1 (September 1906): 21–28.

41. Frank A. Waugh, *The Landscape Beautiful* (New York: Orange Judd, 1910), 199.

42. Ibid., 174.

43. See Christopher Vernon, introduction to Miller, *Prairie Spirit*, xiv.

44. Steinway Hall was designed by Dwight Perkins in 1896. Jensen maintained an office there from 1908 through the end of World War I. See Grese, "Prairie Gardens," 102.

45. Robert C. Spencer Jr., "The Work of Frank Lloyd Wright," *Architectural Review* 7 (June 1900): 61. Spencer included two photographs of Wright's design for the Chauncey Williams house.

46. George W. Maher, "The Western Spirit," *Western Architect* 9 (December 1906): 125.

47. Vernon, introduction to *Prairie Spirit*, xxvi n. 34. Jensen was a member of the Chicago Architectural Club.

48. See Grese, "Prairie Gardens," 122–23.

49. Jensen may also have been influenced by Wright and his architectural colleagues in organizing his design approach around a repertory of signature features. He was one of the few landscape architects of the early twentieth century who maintained close ties to architects. Not surprisingly given the personalities involved, the association with Wright was a stormy one. Jensen and Wright worked together on the Avery Coonley house (Riverside, Ill., 1908–17), Avery Coonley School and Kindergarten (Downers Grove, Ill., 1929), Sherman M. Booth house (Glencoe, Ill., 1911–12), and Abby Beecher Roberts house (Marquette, Mich., c. 1936). Each of these projects was fraught with some degree of conflict, and these exceptionally strong-minded designers broke off relations after the Roberts project. See Eaton, *Landscape Artist in America*, 219–22.

50. One other landscape architect whose work was readily identifiable by its signature elements was Charles A. Platt, who was also an architect.

51. See Grese, "Prairie Gardens," 111–15.

52. Wilhelm Miller, "A Series of Outdoor Salons," *Country Life in America*, April 1914, 39–40.

53. In his opening talk at the Twenty-seventh Annual Meeting of the ASLA in 1926, Jensen "called for the use of native plants and the development of 'native styles' to be used in home gardens throughout the country" and "cautioned that imported 'formal' gardens were 'inappropriate to the manner of life of our people.'" Jensen suggested that "landscape architects ought to work to cultivate 'the simple native tastes of this country.'" Then-president James L. Greenleaf "remarked that he doubted if all members of the ASLA would concur." Jensen refused to attend the 1942 meeting, to which he had been invited as guest of honor. Grese, *Jens Jensen*, 28.

54. Robert E. Grese to author, July 23, 2005.

55. Jensen had been recommended to Ford by the architectural firm that had designed the original house, von Holst & Fyfe of Chicago. Marion Mahoney Griffin (1871–1961), wife of Walter Burley Griffin, prepared this design under the firm's auspices. Af-

ter a dispute arose, Ford fired von Holst & Fyfe and hired the Pittsburgh architect William H. van Tine. Grese, *Jens Jensen*, 268 n. 48.

56. Eaton, *Landscape Artist in America*, 126.

57. Grese, *Jens Jensen*, 101 (Alfred Caldwell, interview by Robert E. Grese and Julia Sniderman, Chicago, January 31, 1987).

58. Grese points out that the setting of Ford's house on the River Rouge made it ideal for mosquitoes and that the abundance of songbirds the Fords wanted to attract would also help control these pests. Joseph H. Dodson of Kankakee, Ill., a maker of birdhouses, listed Henry Ford as a client in his advertisements, along with Charles W. Seiberling, John D. Rockefeller, Thomas Edison, and Harvey Firestone. Grese, *Jens Jensen*, 268 n. 49.

59. Ibid., 102.

60. *Horticulture* magazine praised the new rose garden at Fair Lane as "one of the greatest undertakings of the kind ever attempted in this country." See "Rambling Observations of a Roving Gardener," *Horticulture*, January 1, 1930, 9. Clara Ford commissioned Ellen Biddle Shipman to create a new design for the Jensen rose garden. See Judith B. Tankard, *The Gardens of Ellen Biddle Shipman* (Sagaponack, N.Y.: Sagapress/Abrams in association with Library of American Landscape History, 1996), 114–16.

61. Grese, *Jens Jensen*, 102.

62. Most of the interiors of both of the Fords' first two houses were designed by Leonard Willeke (1884–1970). They reflected a strong English Arts and Crafts influence as well as the influence of the German designer Peter Behrens (1868–1940).

63. Grese, *Jens Jensen*, 184, quoting Jensen, *A Greater West Park System*. For more on Jensen's design for Skylands see Jane Roy Brown, "Skylands: A Jens Jensen Landscape in Maine," *Journal of the New England Garden History Society* 10 (Fall 2002): 20–29. The site had been recommended to Ford by John D. Rockefeller Jr., who knew the area well.

64. Jensen to Edsel Ford, September 24, 1924, Jens Jensen Collection, Bentley Historical Library, University of Michigan, Ann Arbor (hereafter cited as Jensen Collection, Bentley). Quoted in Jane Roy Brown, "'Skylands': A Jens Jensen Landscape in Maine, An Interpretive History," unpublished paper for Radcliffe Seminars Landscape Design History Program, May 2001, 87. Brown reports that Jensen used eighty-six different species in his planting plan, sixty of which were native to Maine.

65. In addition to the lodge, designed by Robert O. Derrick (1890–1961), Haven Hill included a gatehouse, chauffeur's house, riding stable, and sheep barn. The approximate cost of these improvements between 1924 and 1926 was $1.1 million. The estate also featured clay tennis courts, a swimming pool, and a 3,000-foot motorized tow-return toboggan run. The sixty-nine-acre lake was created by damming Cedar Creek. See *A Brief Look at Haven Hill History, Edsel and Eleanor Ford's Oakland County Estate*, Save Haven Hill, Inc., n.d.

66. O. C. Simonds, *Landscape-Gardening*, reprint of 1920 edition (Amherst: University of Massachusetts Press in association with Library of American Landscape History, 2000), 223: "These insolent boards, often two stories in height, face many roadways and public parks, and one cannot approach any large city without having the feeling for beautiful landscape continually offended."

67. See Grese, *Jens Jensen*, 106–10.

68. Ibid., 107. Grese cites "An 'Ideal Section' on the Lincoln Highway: Remarks on Beautification and Embellishment," unpublished manuscript, n.d., Jensen Collection, Bentley.

11. EDSEL AND ELEANOR FORD HOUSE

1. The *New York Times* estimated Henry Ford's personal net worth during the mid-1920s to be $1.2 billion. His annual salary was $4.5 million, the equivalent of $50 million today. See Richard Bak, *Henry and Edsel: The Creation of the Ford Empire* (Hoboken, N.J.: John Wiley and Sons, 2003), 120.

2. Sidney Olson, *Young Henry Ford: A Picture History of the First Forty Years* (1963; reprint, Detroit: Wayne State University Press, 1997), 186.

3. Drew Pearson, "Ford Predicts the Passing of Big Cities and Decentralizing of Industry," *Motor World*, August 28, 1924, quoted from Howard P. Segal, *Recasting the Machine Age: Henry Ford's Village Industries* (Amherst: University of Massachusetts Press, 2005), 3.

4. Construction of the River Rouge plant began in 1917. Raw materials for automobiles—timber, coal, iron ore, limestone, rubber, and silica—came from Ford-owned forests, mines, quarries, and plantations throughout the world, shipped to Dearborn via Ford freighters (which could dock at the plant) or transported on Ford-owned rail lines. Comprehensive control of resources, transportation, and assembly had led to unsurpassed efficiency in manufacturing.

5. William A. Simonds, "Rural Factories along Little Streams," *Stone and Webster Journal*, November 1927, quoted from Segal, *Recasting the Machine Age*, 7.

6. Albert Kahn designed most of these factories, but little information has come to light about the landscape designs associated with them. It does not appear that Jensen was involved with the project.

7. "America's Ruggedest Individual Takes a $35,000,000 Crack at Depression," *Life*, May 30, 1938, 38. This article and one by John Bird in the *Saturday Evening Post*, March 18, 1944, brought word of Ford's village industries to the American public. See Segal, *Recasting the Machine Age*, 11.

8. Ford's zest for country life was also apparent in the highly publicized luxury camping tours he took with Thomas Edison, John Burroughs, and Harvey Firestone, the so-called Vagabonds. For several days each summer, the four men communed with nature, chauffeured about from one scenic photo-op to the next. Photographs of these junkets were distributed to newspapers across the nation.

9. Jens Jensen would have a role in the landscape, which he listed as a project in 1935; however, Grese believes that his assistant and son-in-law, Marshall Johnson (1892–1967), probably did the work. Grese to author, July 23, 2005.

10. For more on Greenfield Village and opening day, see Bak, *Henry and Edsel*, 180–86.

11. See W. C. Richards, *The Last Billionaire* (New York: Charles Scribner's Sons, 1948).

12. Edsel Ford had no connection to the unfortunate car that bore his name. It was developed years after his death.

13. *Art in Our Time*, audio track of radio broadcast, WJZ, 10th Anniversary of Museum of Modern Art, May 10, 1939, Benson Ford Research Center, The Henry Ford.

14. Rivera and his wife, Frida Kahlo, arrived in Detroit in April 1932, just after the Ford Hunger March massacre, which had been triggered by a massive demonstration against huge layoffs by Ford workers outside the Rouge plant. Rivera finished the controversial fresco in March 1933 and was paid $22,000 for his work. See Bak, *Henry and Edsel*, 201–3.

15. Ibid., 208.

16. Ibid., 138. Ford's subsequent work on the Lincoln-Zephyr, in 1936, and the Lincoln Continental Cabriolet, in 1939, established his reputation as one of the industry's most imaginative designers.

17. Jens Jensen to Edsel Ford, date illegible. Ford to Jensen, January 10, 1923, Jensen Collection, Bentley.

18. Ford to Jensen, November 10, 1924, Jensen Collection, Bentley.

19. Ford to Jensen, February 12, 1925, Jensen Collection, Bentley.

20. Ford to Jensen, February 19, 1925, Jensen Collection, Bentley.

21. The four Ford children were Henry II (b. 1917), Benson (b. 1919), Josephine (b. 1923), and William (b. 1925). Concern for their security has been cited as a reason for the move to the country estate.

22. Samuel Howe, *American Country Houses of To-Day* (New York: Architectural Book Publishing, 1915), 35–41. Howe's chapter is on Russell A. Alger's residence.

23. For more on the Backus estate, see Robin Karson, *Fletcher Steele, Landscape Architect: An Account of the Gardenmaker's Life, 1885–1971*, rev. ed. (Amherst, Mass.: Library of American Landscape History, 2003).

24. Jensen to A. J. Lepine, November 19, 1926, Jensen Collection, Bentley.

25. Albert Kahn (1869–1942) was born in Westphalia and immigrated with his family to Detroit in 1880. His list of built works is extensive. The last of the factories he designed for Ford was Willow Run (1942), an enormous plant whose construction was overseen by Edsel. The sixty-seven-acre factory proved critical to the U.S. war effort, eventually producing seven hundred B-24 bombers per month—it was the largest aircraft factory in the world, named after a small stream that ran through the Ypsilanti, Mich., property. Kahn also designed several hundred factories for the Five-Year Plan in the Soviet Union.

26. Ford to Jensen, October 21, 1927, Jensen Collection, Bentley.

27. Ford to Jensen, October 26, 1927, Jensen Collection, Bentley.

28. Jensen's high grade for the lawn edge was likely determined by his concern to protect the property from rising lake levels.

29. Ford to Jensen, December 27, 1927, Jensen Collection, Bentley.

30. A. J. Lepine to Jensen, March 29, 1928, Jensen Collection, Bentley.

31. Robert E. Grese, *Jens Jensen: Maker of Natural Parks and Gardens* (Baltimore: Johns Hopkins University Press, 1992), 163.

32. See Karson, *Fletcher Steele*, 135, 182–83, 226, 233, 293.

33. Grese, *Jens Jensen*, 160.

34. Ibid., 157, quoted from Wilhelm Miller, *The Prairie Spirit in Landscape Gardening*, reprint of 1915 edition (Amherst: University of Massachusetts Press in association with Library of American Landscape History, 2001), 17.

35. Jens Jensen, *Siftings*, reprint of 1939 edition (Baltimore: Johns Hopkins University Press, 1990), 34.

36. Jens Jensen, "Landscape Art: An Inspiration from the Western Plains," *Sketch Book* 6, no. 1 (September 1906): 28.

37. Grese, *Jens Jensen*, 166.

38. Darrel K. Morrison, "Jens Jensen," paper delivered at American Horticultural Society Conference, PaineWebber, New York City, January 1990.

39. Grese, *Jens Jensen*, 166, quoted from Jensen and Eskil, "Natural Parks and Gardens," *Saturday Evening Post*, March 8, 1930, 169.

40. Mrs. Elizabeth Gimmler, interview by Patricia Filzen, February 17, 1987. Cited in Robert E. Grese and Miriam E. Rutz, "History and Management Plan for the Grounds of the Edsel and Eleanor Ford House," report, Ford House, Grosse Pointe Shores, Michigan, May 31, 1988, 41.

41. It is unlikely that the council ring indicated on the 1928 plan was built—no remnants of it have been discovered. Originally open to Lake St. Clair and navigable by boat, the lagoon was dammed to serve as a catch-basin for storm water.

42. Rising lake levels have submerged these beaches.

43. Grese believes that some of the shrub plantings may have been installed and then removed, out of security concerns. Grese to author, July 23, 2005.

44. Ford to Jensen, December 1, 1930, Jensen Collection, Bentley.

45. Jensen to Ford, December 10, 1930, Jensen Collection, Bentley.

46. That property still contains examples of Michigan's principal forest types—swamps of tamarack and cedar, beech–maple, oak–hickory, and mixed hardwood, on land that has been largely undisturbed for nearly seventy-five years.

47. The most comprehensive written guide is the cultural landscape report by Robert E. Grese and Miriam E. Rutz, "History and Management Plan for the Grounds of the Edsel and Eleanor Ford House," May 31, 1988.

48. Jensen, *Siftings*, 109–10.

49. "I should be doing great regional parks. That is what I love. That is what I wanted to do. That is the meaning of my life." Reported by Alfred Caldwell, interview by Malcolm Collier, January 1981, quoted from Grese, *Jens Jensen*, 103.

12. LOCKWOOD DE FOREST JR.

1. The notion of California as a unique locale in the second half of the nineteenth century comes from David C. Streatfield: "It was a place that was implicitly associated with new possibilities and the potential for a rich life that could not be experienced elsewhere in the United States. These possibilities included a hedonistic and experimental attitude toward life, an existence that venerated contact with Nature, and an outlook that looked back to and venerated its local past as an alternative to life in an industrialized society." "Where Pine and Palm Meet: The California Garden as a Regional Expression," *Landscape Journal* 4, no. 2 (1985): 61. I am extremely grateful to David Streatfield for his assistance with material relating to California and Lockwood de Forest and have relied heavily on his book *California Gardens: Creating a New Eden* (New York: Abbeville Press, 1994). I have also relied on William

Frederick Peters, "Lockwood de Forest," master's thesis, University of California, Berkeley, 1980, and David F. Myrick, *Montecito and Santa Barbara*, vols. 1 and 2 (Glendale, Calif.: Trans-Anglo Books, 1987–1991).

2. See Kevin Starr, *Inventing the Dream: California through the Progressive Era* (New York: Oxford University Press, 1985), 45. Starr points to a promotional brochure, *Semi-Tropical California*, published by Benjamin Trueman in 1874. "An element of the exotic, of undisciplined luxuriance, had been introduced and it stayed, taking many forms: ostrich farms, riotous planting, extravagances of architecture and design, and, most importantly, displaced semitropicalisms of thought and behavior which would in time make Southern California a place where anything and everything could take hold, and usually did."

3. Church's Persian villa was designed by Calvert Vaux c. 1870. Church added many acres to the hilltop estate and was involved in laying out the grounds, including lakes, vistas, and carriage drives, in the American Picturesque style. The house, grounds, and collections are a State Historic Site in Hudson, N.Y., and open to the public.

4. See Roberta A. Mayer, "The Aesthetics of Lockwood de Forest: India, Craft and Preservation," *Winterthur Portfolio* 31, no. 1 (Spring 1996): 1–22.

5. The firm had two other partners, textile designer Candace Wheeler and Hudson River painter Samuel Colman, and was known as L. C. Tiffany and Associated Artists. The business achieved national prominence when President Chester Arthur commissioned its services to redecorate rooms at the White House. Among other appreciative clients was Mark Twain.

6. Lockwood de Forest III was the youngest of the three children.

7. William Henry Shelton, "The Most Indian House in America," *House Beautiful*, June 1900, 419–23. Van Campen Taylor (d. 1906) designed the house, c. 1887, which still exists at 7 East 10th Street, Manhattan. The most remarkable feature of this facade is a projecting oriel window on the second floor covered with birds, flowers, elephants, crescent moons, and other forms.

8. Susan L. Klaus, *A Modern Arcadia: Frederick Law Olmsted Jr. and the Plan for Forest Hills Gardens* (Amherst: University of Massachusetts Press in association with Library of American Landscape History, 2002). Klaus provides (37–38) a well-integrated picture of Robert de Forest, who was a key figure in the development of Forest Hills Gardens.

9. See Joseph Goldyne, ed., *Lockwood de Forest: Plein-Air Oil Sketches* (New York: Richard York Gallery, 2001).

10. Wright's first cousin Julia Noise was married to Henry de Forest, Lockwood's uncle. Elizabeth de Forest, interview by John Farrell, August 12, 1982, transcript, Santa Barbara Museum of Art, Santa Barbara, Calif.

11. George Kessler (1862–1923) laid out the first section of Roland Park in 1891. John Charles Olmsted became a primary partner in a second planning phase, 1897–98; in 1902 Olmsted Brothers assumed an increasing role there. Thomas W. Sears (1880–1966) established his Philadelphia office in 1917. Details of de Forest's early life are from his obituary, *Santa Barbara News-Press*, March 31, 1949.

12. E. de Forest interview. De Forest stayed in contact with Jones for much of his professional career, seeking her advice on plants, in particular, and she often brought her students down to see his gardens on field trips to Southern California.

13. David C. Streatfield to author, July 6, 2005.

14. The unusual house still exists; it has been converted to apartments. Designed by Lockwood de Forest II, c. 1915, its spare, geometric forms are enlivened by carved wooden panels from India, much like those on the de Forests' home in New York City.

15. Ann Suydam Lewis, *Lockwood de Forest: Painter, Importer, Decorator* (Huntington, N.Y.: Heckscher Museum, 1976), 36. Quoted from Peters, "Lockwood de Forest," 4.

16. Wright Ludington, handwritten note, n.d., from "Italy: Summer of 1921" scrapbook, collection of Kellam de Forest.

17. Of the Villa d'Este, de Forest wrote: "Rushing, roaring, splashing, gurgling water, above and beneath, to the left and right:—water!—it is the dominating feature." Other villas recorded in the scrapbook are Villa Papa Guilio, "assorted" examples at Frascati, Villa Farnese (Caprarola), Villa Palmieri, Villa Collodi, Villa Bernadini, Villa Marlia, and the Villa Medici (Fiesoli).

18. Streatfield to author, July 6, 2005.

19. George Washington Smith, in John Taylor Boyd Jr., "Houses Showing a Distinguished Simplicity," *Arts and Decoration*, October 1930, quoted in Streatfield, *California Gardens*, 155.

20. "Scheme B, 11/23/25. Residence George F. Steedman, Valley Road, Montecito, Calif." Catalogue of Plans and Drawings, Lockwood de Forest Collection (1965-2), Environmental Design Archives, University of California, Berkeley (hereafter cited as de Forest Collection, EDA, Berkeley).

21. Steedman designed and fabricated outdoor chairs in aluminum, and he also worked in silver and wrought iron, creating decorative objects throughout the estate. Later developments in the gardens at Casa del Herrero were overseen by Joe Acquistapace, who began there in 1930 and remained head gardener until his retirement forty-nine years later. See Myrick, *Montecito and Santa Barbara*, 1:207–8.

22. Streatfield, *California Gardens*, 113–14.

23. Ibid., 107.

24. Ibid., 109. See Anne Stow-Fithian, "My Garden of Succulents," *House and Garden*, December 1927, 72–73, 164, 166; "Current Popularity of Cactus," *House and Garden*, January 1928, 100–101, 146, 148; "The Care of a Succulent Garden," *House and Garden*, February 1928, 86–87, 142, 154. George Washington Smith (1876–1930) would add to these gardens in the mid-1920s.

25. See Mrs. Oakleigh Thorne, "When an Easterner Gardens in the Golden West," *Garden Magazine*, April 1921, 178–80. By the 1920s, a movement encouraging the use of native plants had moved into the national mainstream. See, for example, Harold A. Caparn's "Thoughts on Planting Composition," *Landscape Architecture* 19, no. 3 (April 1929): 141–56; and Stanley White, "The Value of Natural Preserves to the Landscape Architect," in *Naturalist's Guide to the Americas*, ed. Victor E. Shelford (Baltimore: Williams & Wilkins, 1926), 8–9. One of the seminal books of the era was Edith Roberts and Elsa Rehmann, *American Plants for American Gardens* (New York: Macmillan, 1929).

26. With her partner Council, Yoch recorded more than 250 commis-

sions during her career. In 1922 she began a large garden in Montecito for Mary Stewart which borrowed heavily from Italy; de Forest was later hired to rework the motor court there. James J. Yoch, *Landscaping the American Dream: The Gardens and Film Sets of Florence Yoch, 1890–1972* (Sagaponack, N.Y.: Sagapress/Abrams, 1989).

27. Olmsted Brothers, however, did a considerable amount of work in California, owing to Olmsted Jr.'s successful contacts there. The firm designed many state parks during the late 1920s and 1930s, as well as several estates. Their greatest concentration of residential projects was at Palos Verdes Estates (c. 1924), where Olmsted Jr. and his wife also owned a home.

28. *Santa Barbara Press*, February 1872.

29. See Victoria Padilla, *Southern California Gardens: An Illustrated History* (Berkeley: University of California Press, 1961).

30. Kevin Starr, *Material Dreams: Southern California through the 1920s* (New York: Oxford University Press, 1990), 270–71.

31. According to Streatfield, de Forest also liked to sail and maintained a home in York Harbor, Me. Streatfield, letter to author, July 6, 2005.

32. The car is now owned by the Santa Barbara landscape architect Sydney Baumgartner; it was given to her by Elizabeth de Forest.

33. Trish Reynales, "The Naturals: Elizabeth and Lockwood de Forest," *Santa Barbara Magazine*, Summer 1995, 42–49, 108. Reynales's article communicates a vivid sense of the de Forests' life in Santa Barbara.

34. Ibid., 45.

35. Ibid., 49.

36. For more on this transition, see David Gebhard, *Santa Barbara: The Creation of a New Spain in America* (Santa Barbara: University of California Museum of Art, 1982).

37. "In Santa Barbara Is a Kitchen," *American Home*, April 1935, 335.

38. Reynales, "The Naturals," 49.

39. The plantings in this garden are described in Lockwood and Elizabeth de Forest, "Christmas in a Santa Barbara Garden," *Sunset*, December 1929, 20–21.

40. This figure is based on Peters's master's thesis. Gail Jansen, director of the Austin Val Verde Foundation, cites 1,500. See Ann Harold, "A Glorious Sight Unseen," *Los Angeles Times*, June 2, 2005.

41. Peters, "Lockwood de Forest," 26. De Forest's papers are held by the University of California, Berkeley. They include several hundred plans and drawings but no correspondence.

42. William Frederick Peters interview of Richard C. Brimer, Grover City, Calif. August 1979. Cited in Peters, "Lockwood de Forest," 28.

43. For example, the Ernest Watson weekend house, Montecito (published in *Sunset* in 1948), and the Nicholas Ludington house and Reese Taylor house, illustrated respectively in *House Beautiful* (1932) and *Country Life* (1936).

44. Meeker was the company's manager. The Meekers' Chicago home had been designed by Charles A. Platt in 1913.

45. Lockwood de Forest, "In the Montecito Valley: A South African Garden in Santa Barbara, California," *Landscape Architecture* 30, no. 2 (January 1940): 55.

46. Gail Jansen, *Lockwood de Forest, Jr.: A Master Revealed*, documentary video, Austin Val Verde Foundation, 2002.

47. David C Streatfield, "Biography of Lockwood de Forest," online archive notes, Environmental Design Archive, University of California, Berkeley. http://content.cdlib.org/view?docId=tf2489n5t4&chunk.id=bioghist-1.8.4.

48. Streatfield, *California Gardens*, 179.

49. De Forest wrote about the "ability to translate experiences from one medium to another" and cited film as a potential source of design ideas. "A scene in a movie may give you an idea for that neglected corner of your garden," he wrote. "The scene does not have to show a garden, but perhaps the design of a bit of floor will suggest a change in the shape of a flower bed and thus complete an otherwise satisfactory composition." "Garden Inspiration," *Santa Barbara Gardener*, November 1937, 2.

50. Yoch, *Landscaping the American Dream*, 65. Yoch and Council were more closely tied to the film industry than most landscape architects. In addition to designing private gardens for movie directors Dorothy Arzner and George Cukor and producer Jack Warner, Yoch also created landscape sets for five movies, *The Garden of Allah* (1936), *Romeo and Juliet* (1936), *The Good Earth* (1937), *Gone with the Wind* (1939), and *How Green Was My Valley* (1941).

51. The articles were unsigned, and although Elizabeth wrote many of them, the design-oriented essays were undoubtedly by Lockwood, whose professional life was focused on design to a much greater degree than was his wife's.

52. The *Santa Barbara Gardener* also included articles on laying out entrance courts, saving native trees, individual species (from lupines to avocados), flower arranging, victory gardens, New York City parkways, and a range of other topics.

53. "The Fear of the Formal," *Santa Barbara Gardener*, March 1927, 2.

54. "Order—Not Stiffness," *Santa Barbara Gardener*, January 1930, 2.

55. Ibid.

56. From 1927 to 1942 and again from 1945 to 1949 de Forest provided design advice there. The botanic garden is in Mission Canyon, north of the city, laid out on thirteen acres donated by Anna Blaksley Bliss, Mildred Bliss's mother. On the design of the large meadow, which is the central feature of the garden, de Forest and Farrand agreed that the space should be kept open and the view to the mountains accentuated. Later, they disagreed strongly over her proposal to create a more formal design in the courtyard adjacent to a new library building. De Forest believed that this landscape (unlike those he was designing for the residences of his private clients) should retain an almost completely naturalistic character. Farrand prevailed, however; her layout is still extant.

57. "Garden Intellect," *Santa Barbara Gardener*, November 1930, 3.

58. "Garden Space," *Santa Barbara Gardener*, October 1932, 1–2.

59. "Garden Inspiration," *Santa Barbara Gardener*, November 1937, 2.

60. "Inspiration," *Santa Barbara Gardener*, July 1933, 2.

61. The *Santa Barbara Gardener* continued to publish articles about native plants, such as the supplemental list of regional species that was prepared by the Museum of Natural History and, a decade later, in 1937, "The Wild Flowers," an article that recommended mass plantings in garden beds based on examples in nature. A 1941 article by Lester Rowntree, "Why Wild Flowers Disappear," laments the effects of uncontrolled fires and overgrazing. The magazine also reported on significant changes in local establish-

ments. Both de Forest and Farrand served on the Advisory Council that year. Florence Yoch and Lucille Council contributed an article, "The Garden of Today," in 1940. As the war loomed in Europe, Lockwood's and Elizabeth's articles focused increasingly on the relationship between successful design and maintenance. They recommended simple layouts for those continuing to design new gardens and an honest reassessment of overgrown informal designs, where exuberant plantings often quickly destroyed all sense of proportion.

62. "Garden Pictures," *Santa Barbara Gardener*, January 1940, 2.

63. Lockwood de Forest, "Opportunity Knocks. This Time Will Landscape Architecture Miss the Bus?" *Landscape Architecture* 36, no. 1 (October 1945): 10.

64. The Mortons were seasonally migrating Chicagoans. Sterling's father, Julius Sterling Morton (1832–1902), was the originator of Arbor Day. He developed a large arboretum in Nebraska City, where the peripatetic Warren Manning also provided advice.

65. Platt designed the original house (1916–18) for Mrs. Henry Stephens. Platt also designed a house for Stephens in Grosse Pointe, Mich., in 1913.

66. No record of this garden exists in de Forest's papers. It is analyzed by Peters, in "Lockwood de Forest," 65–70, who based his assessment on visits to the site and an interview with de Forest's former employee Richard C. Brimer, Grover City, Calif., August 1979.

67. Elizabeth died in 1984.

68. See David C. Streatfield, "The Evolution of the California Landscape: 4. Suburbia at the Zenith," *Landscape Architecture* 67, no. 5 (September 1977): 417–24. California gardens of the post–World War II era were shaped by several convergent forces. These included a rising preference for clean-edged form, a reduction in the size of houses (which put new strain on residential landscapes to provide living and recreational space), and an abundance of new materials, such as plastic and aluminum.

13. VAL VERDE

1. Elizabeth de Forest, interview by John Farrell, August 12, 1982, transcript, Santa Barbara Museum of Art.

2. David F. Myrick, *Montecito and Santa Barbara*, 2 vols. (Glendale, Calif.: Trans-Anglo Books, 1987–1991), 2:244. According to Myrick, the parcel was purchased from Edward Hildreth of Los Angeles.

3. The grapevine purportedly spanned five thousand square feet the year California achieved statehood, 1850. It was cut down and exhibited at the Philadelphia Centennial Exposition of 1876, but its progeny reached almost the same proportions and continued to flourish.

4. The Olmsted firm may also have consulted on the project, as Bertram Goodhue is listed as a Santa Barbara client in the office records (no. 2046). No plans or photographs related to the project have been located, however. According to David C. Streatfield there was an avenue of *Cocos plumosa* along the entry drive, and Gillespie grew another 125 varieties of palms and 25 varieties of acacias. See Streatfield, *California Gardens: Creating a New Eden* (New York: Abbeville Press, 1994), 104.

5. Lockwood de Forest also worked on this project, 1931–32.

6. "Why Palms Belong in Southern California," *Garden Magazine*, December 1922, 187–90.

7. Myrick, *Montecito and Santa Barbara*, 2:269.

8. Gail Jansen to John Gherini, January 7, 1997, Val Verde Archive, Austin Val Verde Foundation, Santa Barbara, Calif.

9. In New England, Goodhue's early residential designs included the Walter Phelps Dodge House, Simsbury, Conn. (1893), Knapp House, Fall River, Mass. (1894), and Merrill House, Little Boars Head, N.H. (1894).

10. During the 1890s, Goodhue's dynamic, somewhat manic personality attracted many well-known figures. A network of artists and cultural figures centered in Boston included Charles Eliot Norton (1827–1908) and Charles Herbert Moore (1840–1930), in addition to Ralph Adams Cram (1863–1942), with whom, according to Cram's biographer, Douglass Shand-Tucci, Goodhue was sexually involved. The heady period came to a somewhat symbolic close with Cram's marriage in 1900. Goodhue married two years later. See Douglass Shand-Tucci, *Boston Bohemia, 1881–1900: Ralph Adams Cram: Life and Architecture* (Amherst: University of Massachusetts Press, 1995).

11. Goodhue also illustrated several books during this period and designed several distinguished typefaces, the best known of which is Cheltenham.

12. Goodhue's independent career was successfully launched when he won a competition for the Cathedral of St. Matthew in Dallas, Texas, and formed a partnership with Cram and Wentworth to realize that commission. Over the course of their long collaboration (which included other partners at various times), Goodhue and Cram designed many fine works, particularly churches and libraries, as well as an important addition to the United States Military Academy at West Point, N.Y. See Richard Oliver, *Bertram Grosvenor Goodhue* (New York and Cambridge, Mass.: Architectural History Foundation and MIT Press, 1983).

13. Details of this trip are given in ibid., 40–41.

14. This work was done under the auspices of Cram, Goodhue & Ferguson, as the firm was known after Wentworth's death in 1897.

15. See Marilyn McMahon, "Paradise Garden," *Santa Barbara News-Press*, April 9, 1987.

16. The architects Myron Hunt and Elmer Grey were also involved at El Fureidis. Hunt is recorded as the supervising architect. Hunt and Grey would later play prominent roles in promoting Goodhue to replace Olmsted Brothers as planner of the San Diego Exposition.

17. "El Fureidis," *House and Garden*, September 1903, 97–103; C. H[oward] W[alker] in *Architectural Review* 10, no. 9 (September 1903): 139–40. See also *American Country Houses of To-day* (New York: Architectural Book Publishing, 1912), 52–58; Henry Hodgman Saylor, "The Best Twelve Country House in America: 'El Fureidis,' Home of J. Waldron Gillespie, at Montecito, California," *Country Life in America*, October 1915, 29–31.

18. Fascination with Persia peaked in Santa Barbara in 1920 with the transformation of Boyland II, a boarding school north of town, into the Samarkand, a thirty-two-acre luxury hotel with extensive Persian water gardens, whose staff wore turbans and curly-toed slippers.

19. See David C. Streatfield, "Where Pine and Palm Meet: The California Garden as a Regional Expression," *Landscape Journal* 4, no. 2 (1985): 65. Streatfield cites Charles Augustus Keeler, *The Simple Home* (San Francisco: P. Elder, 1902).

20. See Herbert Croly, "The California Country House," *Architect and Engineer* 7 (December 1906): 24–39. See also Croly, "The Country House in California," *Architectural Record* 34 (December 1913): 483–85. The more conservative approach Croly advanced did eventually take root in Santa Barbara, largely through the work of George Washington Smith. This treatment was characterized by courtyard fountains, strong axial development, and Spanish Colonial architectural elements, settings that showed robust subtropical plantings to their dramatic best.

21. The Olmsted Brothers had been initially awarded this important commission, but the drama of Goodhue's competing plan, which sited the large exposition buildings at the center of a rocky plateau, prompted the switch.

22. Oliver, *Goodhue*, 122.

23. The Spanish exposition buildings were also much admired and came to exert a strong influence on residential design in Southern California. Goodhue's interest in Hispanic architecture was largely the result of an extensive 1899 trip through Mexico with the Boston-based journalist Sylvester Baxter (1850–1927), who subsequently wrote a ten-volume series, *Spanish Colonial Architecture in Mexico*, illustrated with plans by Goodhue.

24. During these years, Goodhue was also developing the mining town of Tyrone, N.M., for the Phelps Dodge Company. For the residences in the town he turned to adobes for inspiration. Clarence Stein was chief assistant on the project. Between 1913 and 1918 Goodhue was also designing the large Long Island estate of Ormston for J. E. Aldred, representing nearly the opposite extreme in size, architectural pretension, and impact to his work at Días Felicitas. Goodhue identified this as his "Anglomaniac manner." The imaginative gardens of Ormston were designed by Percival Gallagher, of the Olmsted Brothers firm, a particularly gifted plantsman whose work can best be seen today at Oldfields, an estate owned by the Indianapolis Museum of Art.

25. One likely precedent for Días Felicitas is captured in a series of sketches by Goodhue c. 1897 that depict an imaginary Italian estate, the "Villa Fosca," which resembles the Dater house in important respects. In both cases the house orientation capitalizes on opposite views to sea and mountains. There is also, in both cases, a strong contrast between the vernacular front facade and the grander, Italianate rear elevation. And, in both cases, the rear of the house overlooks a formal reflecting pool that lies at a distance below. See Oliver, *Goodhue*, 33, 36–38.

26. Goodhue went on to design other projects in California, including the Montecito Country Club, 1916–17, and a plan for downtown Santa Barbara. One of his last works was the Los Angeles Public Library.

27. The tenants who were renting it at the time, the Peter Cooper Bryces, continued to live there after the purchase, a circumstance that sheds light on the first changes that took place under Lockwood de Forest.

28. Frank J. Taylor, "B1 and the Beanstalk," *Saturday Evening Post*, March 21, 1942, 52. Most clients were not as patient as Ludington. William Randolph Hearst, for example, paid $10,000 to transplant two six-hundred-year-old oaks to San Simeon. Streatfield, *California Gardens*, 122.

29. Elizabeth de Forest later observed that the two men seemed to "spark one another," that both shared an uncanny ability to envision changes to the landscape. E. de Forest interview.

30. For a discussion of the symbolism of the color green and its bohemian meaning in the late nineteenth and early twentieth centuries, see Shand-Tucci, *Boston Bohemia*, 138–44. In support of his interpretation, Shand-Tucci quotes a passage from Gelett Burgess's essay "Where Is Bohemia?" from *The Romance of the Commonplace* (1902), which speaks to the allure of a private place of creativity and sexuality: "One other district lies hidden and remote, locked in the central fastness of Bohemia. Here is the Forest of Arden, whose greenwood holds a noble fellowship. . . . It is a little golden world apart, and though it is the most secret, it is the most accessible of refuges, so that there are never too many there, and never too few."

31. Gail Jansen, interview by author, Val Verde, December 15, 2004. Jansen reports that many actors, producers, and directors were fixtures at Val Verde. Ludington was remembered as a complex person, extremely well read, unfailingly elegant, courteous, and kind. Judith Anderson, describing him vividly in a 1982 interview, by which time he had become reclusive, saw polarities in Ludington's aesthetic sense that she believed paralleled his personality. "That, on the one hand there is a monastic severity to his taste, and on the other hand, there is a luxurious sybaritic indulgence. But what's marvelous to me about his taste . . . although it sometimes verges on the florid, it always stops just short of being too much. It's always just so." Judith Anderson, interview by John Farrell, August 1982, Santa Barbara Museum of Art.

32. Some of the improvements to the bathhouse took place shortly before the elder Ludington's death.

33. Gail Jansen has suggested that Ludington and de Forest were strongly influenced by Hadrian's Villa; Kellam de Forest, Lockwood de Forest's son, concurs.

34. "Lock-wood it be a good plan to 'ave a skilite in each little BOODWAH? What about the tower door being too near th' corner." De Forest wrote "No" after the latter comment. "Sketch Plan for Pool," n.d., folio 1414, de Forest Collection, EDA, Berkeley.

35. Charles W. Eliot, *Charles Eliot, Landscape Architect*, reprint of 1902 edition (Amherst: University of Massachusetts Press in association with Library of American Landscape History, 1999), 259.

36. No plant lists or planting plans for this area of the garden have been found. The plants listed here were noted growing on the site in 1996; obviously, some of these may have been added after Ludington's residency.

37. Elizabeth de Forest, transcript of untitled slide talk, n.d., Santa Barbara Botanic Garden.

38. This piece was reportedly discovered near Hadrian's Villa. Henry J. Seldis, "Harmony in Diversity: Wright S. Ludington," in *The Collector in America*, ed. Jean Lipman (New York: Viking, 1971), 42.

39. The window was designed by Lutah Maria Riggs (1896–1984), who had apprenticed with George Washington Smith.

40. "Wright Ludington Recalls Early Steps in Creation of Art Museum," *Santa Barbara News-Press*, January 10, 1965.

41. Seldis, "Harmony in Diversity," 40. Ludington also patronized modern painters, some of whom he knew personally. He was good friends with Georgia O'Keeffe, who was a visitor to Val Verde. He also knew and collected Alfred Stieglitz. Charles Sheeler, Charles Demuth, John Marin, Stuart Davis, Arthur Dove, Marsden Hartley, Morris Graves, and Mark Tobey were also represented in his collection. Ludington's own moody landscapes owed much to the paintings of Charles Burchfield.

42. Streatfield, *California Gardens*, 186; Mac Griswold and Eleanor Weller, *The Golden Age of American Gardens* (New York: Harry N. Abrams, 1991), 338.

43. "Inspiration," *Santa Barbara Gardener*, July 1933, 2. In the 1940s the columns were painted a range of ocher tones to evoke a sense of great age, contributing further to the stage-set ambience. The change may have come as a result of de Forest's work as a volunteer in the Camouflage Division of the U.S. Air Corps between 1942 and 1944. Ludington worked at Warner Brothers Studio during World War II preparing camouflage plans for airplane plants, and from 1942 to 1946 taught camouflage, so it seems likely that he, too, influenced the painting. Verne Linderman, "Wright Ludington, Part of the Artistic Milieu," *Santa Barbara News-Press*, April 2, 1975.

44. Marguerite Yourcenar, "Reflections on the Composition of *Memoirs of Hadrian*," in *Memoirs of Hadrian*, trans. Grace Frick (New York: Farrar, Straus and Giroux, 1963), 346–47.

45. The fourth of Ganna Walska's six husbands was Harold McCormick, the owner of the Villa Turicum, who married her after he and Edith divorced. De Forest's work there was limited to design advice on a whimsical cactus garden. These estate grounds have been restored and are now open to the public.

46. See Elaine Griscom, "Val Verde's Dr. Warren Austin," *Montecito Magazine*, Spring 1994. Griscom notes that two biographies of Beryl Markham contain portraits of Austin: *Straight On Till Morning* (1987), by Mary Lovell, and *The Lives of Beryl Markham* (1993), by Errol Trzebinski.

47. De Forest was working on a new design for the entry steps to the museum at the time of his death. Lutah Riggs completed this project, which was later dedicated as a memorial to Lockwood and Elizabeth de Forest. De Forest was one of the three founders of the museum, along with Ludington and Buell Hammett, both of whom also attended Thacher School. During his lifetime, Ludington donated more than three hundred pieces to the museum. In addition to classical sculpture, his gifts included works by several modern artists and several pieces of Asian art.

14. FLETCHER STEELE

1. Fletcher Steele, "Background of Culture and Horticulture in the Genesee Valley," in *The Garden Club of America Annual Meeting*, 1941. For more on Steele's background, see Robin Karson, *Fletcher Steele, Landscape Architect: An Account of the Gardenmaker's Life, 1885–1971*, rev. ed. (Amherst, Mass.: Library of American Landscape History, 2003).

2. Fletcher Steele, "Rochester Yesterday and the Day Before," undated lecture typescript, Fletcher Steele Papers, Manuscript Division, Library of Congress, Washington, D.C. (hereafter cited as Steele Papers, LC), 22.

3. Fletcher Steele to Miss Engel, October 10, 1952, Steele Papers, LC.

4. Steele, "Rochester Yesterday and the Day Before," 26–27.

5. Fletcher Steele, "Let Us Go to Cultivate Our Garden" (unpublished essay, n.d.), Steele Papers, RHS, 1–2.

6. Frederick C. Ferry (dean, Williams College), letter headed "To Whom It May Concern," April 22, 1908, Steele Papers, LC.

7. Andrew D. Wolfe, "Fletcher Steele, Individualist," *Brighton-Pittsford Post*, June 6, 1963.

8. See Fletcher Steele, *Gardens and People* (Boston: Houghton Mifflin, 1964), 2.

9. Fletcher Steele, "Westport, Connecticut," undated lecture manuscript, Steele Papers, LC.

10. Steele to Mary Steele, September 2, 1908, Steele Papers, RHS.

11. The questions on the test relating to Charles Eliot: "1. Answer (a) or (b): (a) Give E's definition of the landscape architect. (b) Under what four sets of conditions, according to E., has most landscape been evolved? 2. Answer (a) or (b): (a) What does he conceive to be the ideal relations between the 'landscape gardener' and the architect? (b) At what step of a given undertaking—the development of a house and lot for example—should the landscape architect be called in, and why?" From Landscape Architecture 1, First Reading: Written Test, October 29, 1908, Steele Papers, RHS.

12. Steele to Mary Steele, June 17, 1910, Steele Papers, RHS. The letter was written after Steele had left Harvard.

13. Ibid.

14. Steele to Mary Steele, August 1, 1909, Steele Papers, RHS. Steele wrote the following month about the project in even greater detail. "The final cost was estimated today at $175,000. These things will not all be carried out at once, but the conception is splendid beyond what we see at home even in the most elegant grounds. A vista of a thousand feet of rhododendrons under pines with a glade of purple beeches at the end, to be seen from the main terrace—a lagoon or canoe trail two miles long, dug to do away with mosquitoes principally, roads miles long to reach the house, 18 acres of lawn, which Mr. Stone says he is willing to cover with gold eagles if necessary to get the best turf on the coast—and he will have to in order to get the best, deer park, elk park, formal, ivy, rose and cut flower gardens immediately connected with the house beside all [the] other conveniences and luxuries mean a distinguished residence and grounds even in this land of beautiful homes." Steele to Mary Steele, September 4, 1909, Steele Papers, RHS.

15. Steele to Mary Steele, November 4, 1909, Steele Papers, RHS.

16. Ibid.

17. Steele to Mary Steele, October 5, 1910, Steele Papers, RHS.

18. For more on Manning's office, see chapter 1.

19. After Manning died in 1938, Steele wrote movingly of his mentor, "No one ever had a stronger or better influence on my life than he. No one so well taught me what it was to be truly the

American in thought and deed. His method of studying landscape problems has been for me a permanent model. And while it would be impossible to overestimate the value of his work, yet to me, it will never approach in my dearest memories the value of his nobility of vision, his simple yet sensitive approach to all that was good and beautiful, and his faith in mankind." Steele to Harold Manning, March 9, 1938, Manning Collection, Lowell.

20. Steele to John Steele, January 27, 1911, Steele Papers, RHS.

21. James Sturgis Pray requested a copy of this report in 1920. Steele to James Sturgis Pray, December 13, 1920, Steele Papers, LC.

22. Fletcher Steele, "Europe, 1913" (travel diary prepared for Warren Manning), 1, Fletcher Steele Manuscript Collection, Terence J. Hoverter College Archives, F. Franklin Moon Library, State University of New York College of Environmental Science and Forestry, Syracuse.

23. Ibid., 13.

24. Ibid., 10.

25. Ibid., 15.

26. Ibid., 106.

27. See Karson, *Fletcher Steele*, 246–47, 261–62.

28. Steele to Peter H. Hornbeck, December 29, 1959. Copy of letter given to the author by Peter H. Hornbeck.

29. See Marie Luis Gothein, *A History of Garden Art*, ed. Walter P. Wright, translated from the German by Mrs. [Laura] Archer-Hind (London: J. M. Dent; New York, Dutton, 1928). Gothein discusses new directions in some German gardens that began with exhibitions (at Düsseldorf in 1904, Darmstadt in 1905, and Mannheim in 1907) emphasizing materials over plants. She noted, in 1926, a new generation of garden architects who had come to use plants sympathetically but continued to follow the lead of Muthesius in seeing gardens as outdoor living rooms (*Freilufthäuser*).

30. The garden's planting plan evolved through the years, but it remained almost wholly green. For more on the composition, see Karson, *Fletcher Steele*, 31–33. See also Robin Karson, "Clarity and Elegance: Fletcher Steele's Masterpiece of Design, a Garden Room in Rochester, N.Y.," *Garden Design*, Spring 1989, 40–49.

31. Alexander Calder, *Calder, An Autobiography with Pictures*, 2nd ed. (New York: Pantheon, 1977), 154.

32. For more on Charlotte Allen, see Karson, *Fletcher Steele*, 32–33.

33. Steele to Betty Blossom (magazine editor), July 21, 1953, Steele Papers, LC.

34. Steele to John Steele, January 27, 1927, Steele Papers, RHS.

35. Fletcher Steele, "Westport, Connecticut," n.d., lecture transcript, Steele Papers, LC.

36. Steele to Mary Steele, October 30, 1922, Steele Papers, RHS.

37. Steele, *Gardens and People*, 9.

38. There were also several commissions for churches and some for cemeteries. Steele believed that working for committees led to pallid designs, and because most public jobs required it, he avoided them.

39. Fletcher Steele, "Plant Material," *Garden Club of America Bulletin*, September 1921, 43. Steele continued, "And the effect was as much gayer and brighter than the usual planting as a luminous Monet is more full of light than a Claude."

40. Steele to Betty Blossom, October 9, 1952, Steele Papers, LC.

41. Fletcher Steele, "Aesthetic Principles in the Spring Flower Garden," *House Beautiful*, March 1922, 197. See also Steele, "Plant Material," 41.

42. "Mr. Fletcher Steele," *Town and Country*, December 15, 1926.

43. George B. Tobey, *A History of Landscape Architecture: The Relationship of People to Environment* (New York: American Elsevier, 1973), 198.

44. Steele also addressed these ideas in "The Colonial Garden Today," in American Society of Landscape Architects, *Colonial Gardens* (Washington, D.C.: U.S. George Washington Bicentennial Commission, 1932), 60–68.

45. Fletcher Steele, "Design of the Small Place," in *The House Beautiful Gardening Manual* (Boston: Atlantic Monthly Company, 1926), 12. Steele's piece was illustrated with examples from his own work and gardens by other designers. Many of these were by women, including Ellen Shipman, Agnes Selkirk Clark, Mary P. Cunningham, and Marion Sims Wyeth (1889–1982), an indication of women's prominence in the field at the time.

46. Arthur Asahel Shurcliff (formerly Shurtleff, 1870–1957) was an assistant in the Olmsted office beginning in 1896. He also helped Olmsted Jr. set up the undergraduate program in landscape architecture at Harvard. Shurcliff designed a wide range of projects, including many public works. He is best known for his imaginative re-creation and restoration work at Colonial Williamsburg, where he was chief landscape architect from 1928 to 1941. See Elizabeth Hope Cushing, "Arthur Asahel Shurcliff," in *Pioneers of American Landscape Design*, ed. Charles A. Birnbaum and Robin Karson (New York: McGraw-Hill, 2000), 351–56.

47. Fletcher Steele, "Lisburne Grange," *Garden Club of America Bulletin*, September 1935, 112.

48. After the design was complete, Steele attempted to convince the Sloans to establish Lisburne Grange as a research institute to promote a cross-disciplinary approach to community living, but this never happened. See Karson, *Fletcher Steele*, 243.

49. The Backus estate, which Steele began in 1926, was one of his most complex projects. The plan involved the same jigsaw puzzle–like precision as at Ancrum House, on a much smaller property. Both houses were demolished in the 1960s. Extensive records for both projects are held by Rush Rhees Library, University of Rochester, in the Fletcher Steele Papers, Department of Rare Books and Special Collections. For more on both projects, see Karson, *Fletcher Steele*.

50. The precise nature of this relationship remains elusive. The several references to Cram in Steele's letters to family and clients make it clear that the men saw each other frequently and that they had friends in common.

51. The project is briefly discussed in Karson, *Fletcher Steele*, 101.

52. Steele to Mary Steele, May 27, 1917, Steele Papers, RHS.

53. Fletcher Steele, "Modern Landscape Architecture," in *Contemporary Landscape Architecture and Its Sources*, exhibition catalog (San Francisco: San Francisco Museum of Art, 1936), 23.

54. For more on Steele's response to French modernism, see Robin Karson, "Spheres, Cones, and Other Least Common Denominators: Modern French Gardens through the Eyes of Fletcher Steele," in *Masters of American Garden Design III: The Modern Gar-*

den in Europe and the United States (Cold Spring, N.Y.: Garden Conservancy, 1994). Steele's first article on the topic was "French Gardens and Their Racial Characteristics," *Landscape Architecture* 12, no. 4 (July 1922): 211–23. For more on French modernist gardens, see Dorothée Imbert, *The Modernist Garden in France* (New Haven: Yale University Press, 1993).

55. Fletcher Steele, "New Pioneering in Garden Design," *Landscape Architecture* 20, no. 3 (April 1930): 167.

56. Ibid., 161.

57. Fletcher Steele, "Landscape Design of the Future," *Landscape Architecture* 22, no. 4 (July 1932): 300.

58. For another example, see Marjorie Sewell Cautley, *Garden Design: The Principles of Abstract Design as Applied to Landscape Composition* (New York: Dodd, Mead, 1935).

59. Steele, "Landscape Design of the Future," 300.

60. Steele, "New Pioneering," 177.

61. The Boks were based in Philadelphia. Mary Louise Curtis Bok also founded the Curtis Institute of Music.

62. See Karson, *Fletcher Steele*, 120–25. After convincing the committee to approve the bent-axis plan, Steele took issue with Olmsted's park design, which proposed cutting down a hill that he believed would provide a critical enframement of the view of the harbor. Steele won that battle, too. See Robin Karson, "The Camden Public Library Theater, 1928: Fletcher Steele and F. L. Olmsted, Jr.," *Maine Olmsted Alliance for Parks and Landscapes Newsletter*, Spring 1992, 1, 3–6.

63. The trees were the work of Jan and Joël Martel. For more on Steele's modernist designs, see Karson, *Fletcher Steele*, particularly discussions about the gardens of Claude Branche, James Smithwick, and Helen Ellwanger.

64. Fletcher Steele, "New Styles in Gardening: Will Landscape Architecture Reflect the Modernistic Tendencies Seen in the Other Arts?" *House Beautiful*, March 1929, 353.

65. Steele, "Modern Landscape Architecture," 24–25.

66. Steele bequeathed his professional library to the ASLA, which, in turn, donated it to the College of Environmental Science and Forestry, SUNY, Syracuse. An inventory of this collection is held in the Fletcher Steele Manuscript Collection, F. Franklin Moon Library.

67. Arthur Sylvester worked for Steele from 1932 to 1935. George Campbell was Steele's office manager from 1925 to 1935. For more on Steele's employees, see Karson, *Fletcher Steele*.

15. NAUMKEAG

1. Shadow Brook was designed by the Pittsfield architect Henry Neill Wilson, for Anson Phelps Stokes and Helen Louisa Phelps Stokes. The residence was distinguished largely by its size, four hundred feet in length and one hundred feet deep. The building was sited by Ernest Bowditch (1850–1918), who also created the gardens on the thousand-acre grounds. Bellefontaine, designed by Carrère & Hastings, is considered a masterpiece of site planning, the only Berkshire mansion to be included in Barr Ferree's *American Estates and Gardens* (1904), a bellwether of taste at the time. Literally dozens of other Berkshire mansions were constructed

between the mid-nineteenth and early twentieth centuries, designed by the country's leading architects, among them Peabody & Stearns, Calvert Vaux, McKim, Mead & White, George B. Post, Rotch & Tilden, Delano & Aldrich, Wilson Eyre, H. T. Lindeberg, Charles A. Platt, Henry Bacon, and Guy Lowell. Among the many landscape architects who secured commissions for these properties were Frederick Law Olmsted, James Dawson (1874–1941), as a representative of Olmsted Brothers, Ferrucio Vitale (1875–1933), and Beatrix Farrand. Two sources on the subject are Richard S. Jackson Jr. and Cornelia Brooke Gilder, *The Houses of the Berkshires, 1870–1930* (New York: Acanthus Press, 2006), and Carole Owens, *The Berkshire Cottages: A Vanishing Era* (Englewood Cliffs, N.J.: Cottage Press, 1984).

2. Wilhelm Miller, "Lessons from a Famous Hillside Garden," *Country Life in America*, August 1910, 433. Miller later became an avid proponent of the so-called prairie style. His influence through the period is discussed in the prologue and in chapters 1 and 12. A more extensive discussion of Naumkeag is in Robin Karson, *Fletcher Steele, Landscape Architect: An Account of the Gardenmaker's Life, 1885–1971*, rev. ed. (Amherst, Mass.: Library of American Landscape History, 2003). Also see Karson, "Of Consequence and Caprice: Naumkeag, Haven for Thought and Laughter," *Garden Design*, Spring 1984, 70–77; "The Blue Steps of Naumkeag," *Art New England* 11, no. 7 (July–August 1990): 26–27, 44–45; and "The Designer as Artist," *American Horticulturalist* 67, no. 10 (October 1988): 4–6, 8–9.

3. See Mabel Choate, "Naumkeag Notes," unpublished memoirs, 2-2, Naumkeag House and Gardens, Stockbridge, Mass., Property of The Trustees of Reservations (hereafter cited as Naumkeag Archives). The Barrett design is also discussed in the prologue.

4. Miller, "Lessons from a Famous Hillside Garden," 433. There is also a beguiling description of Barrett's garden at Naumkeag in Samuel Howe, *American Country Houses of To-Day* (New York: Architectural Book Publishing, 1915), 342–45.

5. Joseph Choate to Josephine Choate, July 6, 1883, quoted from Edward Sandford Martin, *The Life of Joseph Hodges Choate*, 2 vols. (New York: Charles Scribner's Sons, 1920), 1:375–76.

6. In New York, the Choates lived in a series of houses, moving to increasingly fashionable neighborhoods uptown, as their wealth grew. From 1863 to 1870, they were at 137 West 21st Street; from 1871 at 50 West 47th Street. In 1929, shortly after her mother died, Mabel Choate purchased a house at 777 Park Avenue.

7. Chesterwood is now a property of the National Trust for Historic Preservation and open to visitors. French designed the landscape with great imagination. French's nephew, Prentiss French, influenced by his uncle's example, became a landscape architect. One of his best-preserved designs is the c. 1933 Stockbridge, Mass., garden for Mrs. Lisbeth Ledyard, in association with a fine house by H. T. Lindeberg.

8. Morgan Bulkeley, "The Choates at Naumkeag," unpublished notes for The Trustees of Reservations, Naumkeag Archives, n.d., 6.

9. Choate, "Naumkeag Notes," 2-2.

10. Bulkeley, "Choates at Naumkeag," 7.

11. Mariana Griswold Van Rensselaer, "American Country Dwellings," quoted in Mark Alan Hewitt, *The Architect and the*

American Country House (New Haven: Yale University Press, 1990), 96. Originally in *Century Magazine* 32 (May, June, and July 1886).

12. Geoffrey Platt, "Narration—Garden Party, Naumkeag," July 21, 1983 (audiotape transcription, Naumkeag Archives), 3.

13. Steele to Charles D. Webster, June 25, 1968, Steele Papers, LC.

14. Choate, "Naumkeag Notes," 2-1.

15. Fletcher Steele, "Naumkeag Gardens Develop," manuscript, May 1947, 1, Steele Papers, LC.

16. Over these years a series of changes were made to the house, including the building of additional bedrooms and bathrooms, and a second-floor porch for the master bedroom. These changes were likely designed by George de Gersdorff (1866–1964), who studied at MIT and the École des Beaux-Arts and then worked for McKim, Mead & White.

17. Joseph Choate to Caroline Choate, August 24, 1894. Quoted in Martin, *The Life of Joseph Hodges Choate*, 1:465.

18. Fletcher Steele, "Naumkeag: Notes on Horticultural Undertakings," Notes for the Horticultural Society Prize Committee, November 3, 1940, Naumkeag Archives.

19. Platt, "Narration—Garden Party," 2. Platt also remembered his father-in-law's panic at the scope and expense of the new gardens being developed under Steele's direction. Since Mabel had no direct heirs, her estate, or whatever remained of it after Steele was finished, would have gone to her brother's children. When she announced that she planned to leave Naumkeag to The Trustees of Reservations, Platt noted that his father-in-law's "pain erupted in a five-page letter—to no avail," adding, "fortunately for all of us today."

20. Steele, "Naumkeag Gardens Develop," 2.

21. Robert R. Crighton was born c. 1891 in Scotland and worked at Naumkeag throughout Choate's life there, continuing after the estate became the property of The Trustees of Reservations.

22. Coffin's plant orders, dated from 1918 to 1921, are in the Naumkeag Archives.

23. Percival Gallagher to Mabel Choate, November 5, 1919, Naumkeag Archives. Gallagher recommended a mix of evergreen ground cover: pachysandra, bearberry, *Taxus canadensis*, *Leucothoe catesbaei*, and periwinkle for the upper slope. At the foot, he recommended a more meadowy mix that included *Lysimachia*, *Galax*, *Itea*, *Cassia*, *Caryopteris*, *Hepatica*, Solomon's seal, and asters.

24. Daniel Urban Kiley, telephone interview by author, April 8, 1988. The story was told to Kiley by Steele when Kiley visited Naumkeag in 1932.

25. Fletcher Steele, untitled essay describing work at Naumkeag, n.d., Steele Papers, LC.

26. Ibid.

27. The martinis are always attributed to Margaret, who kept them pre-mixed in the freezer. Both she and another servant, Rose, are mentioned in memoirs and guests' letters, but these documents do not record the surnames of the two Irish women who made life at Naumkeag a luxury for Choate and her guests.

28. Manuscript sent to Mrs. Charles Marshall, feature editor of *House and Garden*, May 5, 1947, 2, Steele Papers, LC.

29. Steele, "Naumkeag Gardens Develop," 4.

30. I have not succeeded in discovering the title of this exhibition, or its exact dates.

31. Fletcher Steele, "The Temple Garden: The Garden of M. Choate, Stockbridge, Mass.," *House Beautiful*, July 1933. See also Fletcher Steele, "Naumkeag: Miss Mabel Choate's Place in Stockbridge, Massachusetts, Has Been Shaped by Two Generations of Changing Taste," *House and Garden*, July 1947; Fletcher Steele, "The Effective Use of Planting in Landscape Architecture and Gardening," *The Garden*, March and June 1949; Better Homes and Gardens, *America's Gardens* (Des Moines and New York: Meredith Press, 1964); James M. Fitch and F. F. Rockwell, *Treasury of American Gardens* (New York: Harper and Brothers, 1956). The name of the garden was changed from Temple Garden (inspired by a facetious comment by a workman who thought the elaborate design suitable for King Solomon) to Afternoon Garden sometime after 1933.

32. Mabel Choate, "Coal in the Garden," *Bulletin of the Garden Club of America*, July 1939, 79–80.

33. Steele, "Naumkeag Gardens Develop," 4–5.

34. Ibid., 6.

35. Ibid.

36. Ibid.

37. Ibid., 7–8.

38. Steele to Mrs. Roy Hunt, February 27, 1947, Steele Papers, LC.

39. There were thirty-two private gardens listed under the bulletin heading "Garden Club of Santa Barbara and Montecito." Among them were Mrs. Oakleigh Thorne's Las Tejas and J. Waldron Gillespie's El Fureidis. According to David C. Streatfield, Lockwood de Forest usually coordinated these tours. Memo to author, July 5, 2005.

40. On that same trip, Choate recorded a visit to Mrs. Clyde M. Carr's Wyldewoode on Mayflower Road, Lake Forest, Ill., another early Manning wild garden. Jens Jensen also worked for the Carrs, 1913–16.

41. Steele, "Naumkeag: Notes on Horticultural Undertakings," 1–2.

42. After one particularly intense musical weekend, Steele wrote to Charlotte Allen, "Stockbridge was fun, though I don't need to hear any more Mozart for quite a while—say 82 or 3 years." Steele to Charlotte Whitney Allen, August 10, 1944, Steele Papers, LC.

43. In the summers of 2004 and 2005, the lower formal garden at Naumkeag was restored to its 1930s appearance; the marble steps, added in 1948, were also restored.

44. Steele, "Naumkeag Gardens Develop," 7. Choate's notes from the trip are evocative. "Dilapidated and rather neglected, they are on a bigger scale and more formal [than Japanese gardens]. The feeling of space is tremendous. . . . Lots of color, the roofs of the pavilions and temples of tiles of such a color—it makes your heart stand still—yellow, green and sapphire blue. Stone lined pools and moats filled with beautiful tall lotus, pink and white, nodding their heads above the water." Mabel Choate, "Impressions of the East: May–June 1935," typescript, Naumkeag Archives. A different source of inspiration for the garden may be traced to a sketch Choate made, recorded in her Garden Club of America travel book from 1935. It is from Mrs. George R. Carter's Lihinai, in Honolulu, which

bears a striking resemblance to the ornamentation of the Chinese Temple at Naumkeag, constructed two years later.

45. Henry Hoover, interview by author, Lincoln, Mass., January 17, 1988.

46. Fletcher Steele, "The Chinese Garden at Naumkeag," unpublished essay, n.d., Steele Papers, LC, 2.

47. Steele to Charles D. Webster, June 25, 1968, Steele Papers, LC.

48. Platt, "Narration—Garden Party," 3.

49. Steele to Betty Blossom, July 21, 1953, Steele Papers, LC.

50. Steele, "The Chinese Garden at Naumkeag," 1.

51. Steele to Esther Steele, 1949, Steele Papers, RHS.

52. At Naumkeag, the cream-colored industrial rail may have been influenced by Plâs Brondanw, a garden in Wales designed by Sir Clough Williams-Ellis (1883–1978), c. 1908. However, Ellis's design lacked the double semicircles that Steele attached to the front of each landing, which emphasize the layered planes of space. In others ways the resemblance is striking, although there is no evidence that Steele knew Williams-Ellis's garden.

53. Fletcher Steele, "Modern Landscape Architecture," in *Contemporary Landscape Architecture and Its Sources*, exhibition catalog (San Francisco: San Francisco Museum of Art, 1936), 24–25.

54. Steele and Coffin undoubtedly knew each other professionally as well; both were made Fellows of the ASLA in 1918.

55. Marjorie was Ellery's second wife, and with him owner of an important garden at Long Hill, in Beverly, Mass., now open to the public. Sedgwick's first wife was Mabel Cabot Sedgwick (1873–1937), author of *The Garden Month by Month*.

56. Coffin worked for Morgan at Wyndmoor, 1934–35; Steele worked there 1938–40, on the construction of an Orchid Room. For more on Steele's design, see Karson, *Fletcher Steele*, 218–23.

57. The other members of The Three Arts Society were financier Walter Clark, drama critic Walter Pritchard Eaton, sculptor Daniel Chester French, and psychiatrist Austin Riggs. The theater opened in 1928 with a production of *The Cradle Song* and flourished for decades. The company, now known as the Berkshire Theatre Festival, still performs in the original building.

58. Daniel Urban Kiley, interview by author, April 8, 1988.

59. Kiley was generally critical of early twentieth-century design. But he cited one of Steele's articles as a particular influence on his own career and of great significance to the field generally: Fletcher Steele, "New Pioneering in Garden Design," *Landscape Architecture* 20, no. 3 (April 1930): 159–77. Kiley interview.

60. "'Stormfield': Mark Twain's New Country Home," *Country Life in America*, April 1909, 608.

61. Steele to Mrs. Marshall, May 8, 1947, Steele Papers, LC. In this same letter, Steele pointed out that Charlotte Allen had also sold her country house because her town garden provided the same sense of retreat.

62. The Reverend John Sergeant built the house in 1743 for his new bride, Abigail Williams; their son, Dr. Erastus Sergeant, updated it with a Connecticut River doorway in the 1760s. In 1867 the Sergeant farm was sold to David Dudley Field.

63. Steele also advised on the subtle tones of the paint on both the interior and exterior, which was mixed according to old recipes, using an egg base. Henry Hoover recalled that the eggs purchased for the purpose were slightly rotten, and once the paint was applied a horrible stench arose, causing hordes of flies to arrive and stick to all the surfaces. Steele had the paint scraped off and started over again. Hoover interview.

64. John D. Rockefeller Jr. to Mabel Choate, September 2, 1943, Naumkeag Archives.

65. Choate to John D. Rockefeller Jr., September 7, 1943, Naumkeag Archives.

66. Steele also wrote several articles on this theme; for example, "Private Post-War Planning" (Parts 1 and 2), *Garden Club of America Bulletin*, June and September 1944.

67. Choate to Steele, August 21, 1950, Steele Papers, LC.

68. Steele to Esther Steele, September 24, 1950, Steele Papers, RHS.

69. Steele to Mrs. Livermore, March 27, 1948, Steele Papers, LC.

70. The garden was commissioned by Richard and Nancy Turner. Richard L. Turner was the founder of the Landmark Society of Western New York State; Nancy R. Turner served as a vice president of the Garden Club of America and is the founding president of the Library of American Landscape History. For more on the design, see Robin Karson, "Fletcher Steele's Last Vista," *Garden Design*, Spring 1988, 60–65, 80, 82, 84, 93; and Karson, *Fletcher Steele*, 266–73.

71. Fletcher Steele, "The Appeal to the Intelligence," undated, Steele Papers, RHS.

72. Fletcher Steele, *Gardens and People* (Boston: Houghton Mifflin, 1964), 231.

73. Fletcher Steele, "Landscape Architecture," manuscript marked "A-3," March 4, 1942, Steele Papers, LC, 3.

AFTERWORD

1. Garrett Eckbo, telephone interview by author, April 19, 1988.

2. Daniel Urban Kiley to author, July 18, 1995.

3. Norman T. Newton, *Design on the Land: The Development of Landscape Architecture* (Cambridge, Mass.: Belknap Press of Harvard University Press, 1971), 427–28.

BIBLIOGRAPHY

Allen, Hugh. *The House of Goodyear: Fifty Years of Men and Industry*. Cleveland: Corday & Gross, 1949.

"American Country Life and Art." *Architectural Record* 11 (January 1902): 112–14.

American Society of Landscape Architects. *Illustrations of the Work of Members*. 4 vols. New York: J. Hayden Tiss, 1931–34.

Anderson, Dorothy May. *Women, Design, and the Cambridge School*. West Lafayette, Ind.: PDA Publishers, 1980.

"Art and Nature in Landscape Gardening." *Garden and Forest*, May 19, 1897, 191–92.

Aslet, Clive. *The American Country House*. New Haven: Yale University Press, 1990.

Auchincloss, Louis. *Edith Wharton: A Woman in Her Time*. New York: Viking, 1971.

Bachrach, Julia Sniderman. "Ossian Cole Simonds: Conservation Ethic in the Prairie Style." In Tishler, *Midwestern Landscape Architecture*, 80–98.

Bailey, Liberty Hyde. *The Holy Earth*. New York: Charles Scribner's Sons, 1915.

Bak, Richard. *Henry and Edsel: The Creation of the Ford Empire*. Hoboken, N.J.: John Wiley and Sons, 2003.

Baker, John Cordis. *American Country Homes and Their Gardens*. Philadelphia: John C. Winston, 1906.

Balmori, Diana. "Beatrix Farrand at Dumbarton Oaks." In McGuire and Fern, *Beatrix Jones Farrand*, 97–123.

———. "Campus Work and Public Landscapes." In Balmori, McGuire, and McPeck, *Beatrix Farrand's American Landscapes*, 127–96.

Balmori, Diana, Diane Kostial McGuire, and Eleanor M. McPeck. *Beatrix Farrand's American Landscapes: Her Gardens and Campuses*. Sagaponack, N.Y.: Sagapress, 1985.

Baxter, Sylvester. "The Imaginative Element in Landscape." *American Architect and Building News* 59 (January 8, 1898): 11.

Beveridge, Charles E. "The First Great *Private* Work of Our Profession in the Country: Frederick Law Olmsted, Senior, at Biltmore." In *The Olmsteds at Biltmore*, by Charles E. Beveridge and Susan L. Klaus, 1–10. National Association for Olmsted Parks Workbook Series, Vol. 5. Bethesda, Md.: National Association for Olmsted Parks, 1995.

———. "Frederick Law Olmsted's Theory on Landscape Design." *Nineteenth Century* 3, no. 2 (Summer 1977): 38–43.

Beveridge, Charles E., and Paul Rocheleau. *Frederick Law Olmsted: Designing the American Landscape*. New York: Rizzoli, 1995.

Birnbaum, Charles A., and Robin Karson, eds. *Pioneers of American Landscape Design*. New York: McGraw-Hill, 2000.

Blanchan, Neltje. *The American Flower Garden*. New York: Doubleday, Page, 1909.

Bliss, Mildred. "An Attempted Evocation of a Personality." In Farrand, *Plant Book for Dumbarton Oaks*, xi–xiii.

Bliz-Zard, William E. "The Creation of an American Style of Landscape Architecture." *Architectural Record* 47 (January 20, 1920): 93–96.

Boyd, John Taylor, Jr. "Houses Showing a Distinguished Simplicity." *Arts and Decoration*, October 1930, 57–65.

Boyle, T. Coraghessan. *Riven Rock*. New York: Viking, 1998.

Boyum, Burton H. "William Gwinn Mather." *Michigan History Magazine*, November–December 1994, 77–79.

A Brief Look at Haven Hill History, Edsel and Eleanor Ford's Oakland County Estate. Save Haven Hill, Inc., n.d.

Brown, Jane. *Beatrix: The Gardening Life of Beatrix Jones Farrand, 1872–1959*. New York: Viking, 1995.

Brown, Jane Roy. "Skylands: A Jens Jensen Landscape in Maine." *Journal of the New England Garden History Society* 10 (Fall 2002): 20–29.

———. "'Skylands': A Jens Jensen Landscape in Maine, An Interpretive History." Unpublished paper for Radcliffe Seminars Landscape Design History Program, May 2001.

Budd, Katharine Cotheal. "Gardens—Large and Small." *Architecture* 35 (June 1917): 105–11.

Burg, David F. *Chicago's White City of 1893.* Lexington: University of Kentucky Press, 1976.

Burnham, Daniel H., and Francis D. Millet. *World's Columbian Exposition: The Book of the Builders.* Chicago: Columbian Memorial Publication Society, 1894.

Calder, Alexander. *Calder, An Autobiography with Pictures.* 2nd ed. New York: Pantheon, 1977.

Cantor, Jay E. *Winterthur.* New York: Harry N. Abrams, 1985.

Caparn, Harold A. "Thoughts on Planting Composition." *Landscape Architecture* 19, no. 3 (April 1929): 141–56.

"The Care of a Succulent Garden." *House and Garden,* February 1928, 86–87, 142, 154.

Carr, Ethan. "*Garden and Forest* and 'Landscape Art.'" http://www.loc.gov/preserv/prd/gardfor/essays/carr.html.

Cartwright, Julia. *Italian Gardens of the Renaissance and Other Studies.* New York: Charles Scribner's Sons, 1914.

Cautley, Marjorie Sewell. *Garden Design: The Principles of Abstract Design as Applied to Landscape Composition.* New York: Dodd, Mead, 1935.

Chater, Melville. "Ohio, the Gateway State." *National Geographic,* May 1932, 525–91.

Child, Stephen. "Two Decades of Landsacpe Architecture in Retrospect—1910–1930." *Landscape Architecure* 20, no. 4 (July 1930): 267–76.

Choate, Mabel. "Coal in the Garden." *Bulletin of the Garden Club of America,* July 1939, 79–80.

Christy, Steven. "The Growth of an Artist: Jens Jensen and Landscape Architecture." Master's thesis, University of Wisconsin, 1976.

Church, Ella Rodman. *The Home Garden.* New York: D. Appleton, 1881.

"The City as Client." In Morris and White, *Designs on Birmingham,* 46–53.

Clayton, Virginia Tuttle. "Wild Gardening and the Popular American Magazine." In Wolschke-Bulmahn, *Nature and Ideology,* 131–54.

———, ed. *The Once and Future Gardener: Garden Writing from the Golden Age of Magazines, 1900–1940.* Boston: David R. Godine, 2000.

Cleveland, H. W. S. "The Grand Traverse Region of Michigan." *Atlantic Monthly,* August 1870, 191–95.

———. *Landscape Architecture, as Applied to the Wants of the West.* Reprint of 1873 edition. Amherst: University of Massachusetts Press in association with Library of American Landscape History, 2002.

———. *The Public Grounds of Chicago: How to Give Them Character and Expression.* Chicago: Charles D. Lakey, 1869.

Close, Leslie. "A History of Women in Landscape Architecture." In Tankard, *The Gardens of Ellen Biddle Shipman,* xiii–xix.

Coffin, David R. "Beautifying the Campus." *Historic Gardens Review,* January 2005, 2–8.

Coffin, Marian Cruger. Note in *Garden Club of American Bulletin,* May 1920, 58–59.

———. "A Suburban Garden Six Years Old." *Country Life in America,* February 15, 1912, 19–22.

———. *Trees and Shrubs for Landscape Effects.* New York: Charles Scribner's Sons, 1940.

———. "Where East Meets West: A Visit to Picturesque Dalmatia, Montenegro and Bosnia." *National Geographic,* May 1908, 309–44.

Coffin, Marian Cruger, and James M. Scheiner. "Our Substitute Castle in Spain." *Country Life in America,* September 1922, 48–49.

Conant, Stephen. "Democracy by Design: Warren H. Manning's Contribution to Planning History." Master's thesis, Tufts University, 1984.

Copeland, Robert Morris. *Country Life: A Handbook of Agriculture and Landscape Gardening.* Boston: J. P. Jewett, 1859.

Cortissoz, Royal. *Monograph of the Work of Charles A. Platt.* New York: Architectural Book Publishing, 1913.

Cram, Ralph Adams. "Faulkner Farm, Brookline, Massachusetts." *House and Garden,* August 1901, 1–12.

Croly, Herbert. "The Architectural Work of Charles A. Platt." *Architectural Record* 15 (March 1904): 181–244.

———. "The California Country House." *Architect and Engineer* 7 (December 1906): 24–39.

———. "The Country House in California." *Architectural Record* 34 (December 1913): 483–85.

———. "The House of William G. Mather." *Architectural Record* 26 (November 1909): 313–19.

———. "The Lay-out of a Large Estate: 'Harbor Hill,' the Country-Seat of Mr. Clarence Mackay, at Roslyn, N.Y." *Architectural Record* 16 (December 1904): 531–56.

———. "Rich Men and Their Houses." *Architectural Record* 12 (May 1902): 27–32.

"Current Popularity of Cactus." *House and Garden,* January 1928, 100–101, 146, 148.

Cushing, Elizabeth Hope. "Arthur Asahel Shurcliff." In Birnbaum and Karson, *Pioneers of American Landscape Design,* 351–56.

David, A. C. [Herbert Croly]. "New Phases in Domestic Architecture." *Architectural Record* 26 (November 1909): 308–12.

Davidson, Rebecca Warren. "Charles A. Platt and the Fine Art of Landscape Design." In Morgan, *Shaping an American Landscape,* 75–95.

———. Introduction to Hutcheson, *The Spirit of the Garden,* reprint of 1923 edition.

Day, Frank Miles, ed. *American County Houses of To-day.* New York: Architectural Book Publishing, 1912.

Dean, Ruth. *The Livable House: Its Garden.* New York: Moffat, Yard, 1917.

de Forest, Elizabeth. "Old Santa Barbara Gardens and How They Came to Be." *Pacific Horticulture,* Winter 1977–78, 31–36.

de Forest, Lockwood. "Comportment." *Santa Barbara Gardener,* August 1936.

———. "The Fear of the Formal." *Santa Barbara Gardener,* March 1927.

———. "Garden Inspiration." *Santa Barbara Gardener,* November 1937.

———. "Garden Intellect." *Santa Barbara Gardener*, November 1930.

———. "Garden Pictures." *Santa Barbara Gardener*, January 1940.

———. "Garden Space." *Santa Barbara Gardener*, October 1932.

———. "In the Montecito Valley: A South African Garden in Santa Barbara, California." *Landscape Architecture* 30, no. 2 (January 1940): 50–54.

———. "Inspiration." *Santa Barbara Gardener*, July 1933, 2.

———. "Opportunity Knocks. This Time Will Landscape Architecture Miss the Bus?" *Landscape Architecture* 36, no. 1 (October 1945): 10.

———. "Order—Not Stiffness." *Santa Barbara Gardener*, January 1930.

de Forest, Lockwood, and Elizabeth de Forest. "Christmas in a Santa Barbara Garden." *Sunset*, December 1929, 20–21.

Deitz, Paula. Introduction to Farrand, *The Bulletins of Reef Point Gardens*, xi–xxiv.

Dobyns, Winifred. *California Gardens*. New York: Macmillan, 1931.

Doell, M. Christine Klim. *Gardens of the Gilded Age: Nineteenth-Century Gardens and Homegrounds of New York State*. Syracuse: Syracuse University Press, 1986.

Douglas, Ann. *Terrible Honesty: Mongrel Manhattan in the 1920s*. New York: Farrar, Straus and Giroux, 1995.

Downing, Andrew Jackson. *A Treatise on the Theory and Practice of Landscape Gardening, Adapted to North America; with a View to the Improvement of Country Residences*. 2nd ed. New York: Wiley and Putnam, 1844.

Duncan, Frances. "The Gardens of Cornish." *Century Magazine* 72 (May 1906): 13–19.

du Pont, Henry Francis. "Azaleas at Winterthur." *Quarterly Bulletin of the American Rhododendron Society*, January 5, 1962, 9–13.

———. Speech to the Garden Club of America. *Garden Club of America Bulletin*, July 1956, 64.

Earle, Alice Morse. *Old-Time Gardens*. New York: Macmillan, 1901.

Eaton, Leonard K. "Jens Jensen Reconsidered." In *Gateway Cities and Other Essays*, 129–41. Ames: Iowa State University Press, 1989.

———. *Landscape Artist in America: The Life and Work of Jens Jensen*. Chicago: University of Chicago Press, 1964.

Eberlein, Harold D. "Recent Aspects of Garden Design." *Architectural Record* 37 (April 1915): 303–19.

———. *Villas of Florence and Tuscany*. Philadelphia: J. B. Lippincott, 1922.

"El Fureidis." *House and Garden*, September 1903, 97–103.

Eliot, Charles. "Muskau: A German Country Park." *Garden and Forest*, January 28, 1891, 38–39, 41.

———. Review of *Italian Gardens*. *Nation* 57 (December 28, 1893): 491–92.

———. "Waverly Oaks: A Plan for Their Preservation for the People." *Garden and Forest*, March 5, 1890, 117–18.

———. "What Would Be Fair Must First Be Fit." *Garden and Forest*, April 1, 1896, 131–32.

Eliot, Charles W. *Charles Eliot, Landscape Architect*. Reprint of 1903 edition. Amherst: University of Massachusetts Press in association with Library of American Landscape History, 1999.

Elwood, P. H., Jr. *American Landscape Architecture*. New York: Architectural Book Publishing Company, 1924.

———. "Landscape Architecture: An Opportunity and an Obligation." *American Architect* 128 (November 5, 1925): 383–88.

Ely, Helena Rutherfurd. *A Woman's Hardy Garden*. New York: Macmillan, 1903.

Embury, Aymar, II. "Charles A. Platt: His Work." *Architecture* 26 (August 1912): 130–62.

Emerson, Ralph Waldo. "Nature." In *Essays and Lectures*, edited by Joel Porte, 5–50. New York: Library of America, 1983.

Emmet, Alan. "Faulkner Farm: An Italian Garden in Massachusetts." *Journal of Garden History* 6, no. 2 (April–June 1986): 162–77.

———. *So Fine a Prospect: Historic New England Gardens*. Hanover, N.H.: University Press of New England, 1996.

Epp, Ronald H. "Wild Gardens and Pathways at The Mount: George B. Dorr and the Mount Desert Island Influence." In *Edith Wharton and the American Garden*, edited by Betsy Anderson. Lenox, Mass.: The Mount Press, forthcoming.

Eskil, Ragna B. "Natural Parks and Gardens." *Saturday Evening Post*, March 8, 1930, 18–19, 169–70.

Faderman, Lillian. *To Believe in Women: What Lesbians Have Done for America—A History*. Boston: Houghton Mifflin, 1999.

Farrand, Beatrix. "Beatrix Jones Farrand." *Reef Point Bulletin* 1, no. 17. In *The Bulletins of Reef Point Gardens*, 112–14.

———. *Beatrix Farrand's Plant Book for Dumbarton Oaks*. Washington, D.C.: Dumbarton Oaks Trustees for Harvard University, 1980.

———. *The Bulletins of Reef Point Gardens*. Bar Harbor, Me.: Island Foundation, 1997.

———. "The Start and the Goal." *Reef Point Gardens Bulletin* 1, no. 1 (August 1946). In *The Bulletins of Reef Point Gardens*, 2–4.

Fein, Albert. *Frederick Law Olmsted and the American Environmental Tradition*. New York: George Braziller, 1972.

Fenelon, Eunice. "Open House in the Gardens of Greater Cleveland." *Your Garden and Home*, June 1934.

Ferree, Barr. *American Estates and Gardens*. New York: Munn, 1904.

Firestone, Harvey S., in collaboration with Samuel Crowther. *Men and Rubber*. Garden City, N.Y.: Doubleday, 1926.

Fitch, James M., and F. F. Rockwell. *Treasury of American Gardens*. New York: Harper and Brothers, 1956.

Fleming, Nancy. *Money, Manure, and Maintenance*. Weston, Mass.: Country Place Books, 1995.

Forbes, A. Holland. *Architectural Gardens of Italy*. New York: Forbes & Co., 1902.

Fowler, Clarence. "Three Women in Landscape Architecture." *Alumnae Bulletin of the Cambridge School of Domestic and Landscape Architecture* 4, no. 2 (April 1932): 7–12.

Frederick, William H., Jr. "The Artist in His Garden." In Magnani, *The Winterthur Garden*, 19–37.

Gebhard, David. *Santa Barbara: The Creation of a New Spain in America*. Santa Barbara: University of California Museum of Art, 1982.

Gilbert, Alma M., and Judith B. Tankard. *A Place of Beauty: The Artists and Gardens of the Cornish Colony*. Berkeley, Calif.: Ten Speed Press, 2000.

Gillespie, Waldron. "Why Palms Belong in Southern California." *Garden Magazine*, December 1922, 187–90.

Gilpin, William. *Practical Hints upon Landscape Gardening*. London: T. Cadell, 1832.

Ginaven, Marlene. *Not for Us Alone*. Akron, Ohio: Stan Hywet Hall Foundation, 1985.

Goldyne, Joseph, ed. *Lockwood de Forest: Plein-Air Oil Sketches.* New York: Richard York Gallery, 2001.

Gothein, Marie Luis. *A History of Garden Art.* Edited by Walter P. Wright; translated from the German by Mrs. [Laura] Archer-Hind. London: J. M. Dent; New York, Dutton, 1928.

Gould, Stephen Jay. "An Evolutionary Perspective on Strengths, Fallacies, and Confusions in the Concept of Native Plants." In Wolschke-Bulmahn, *Nature and Ideology,* 11–19.

Gray, Asa. *Manual of Botany in the Northern United States.* Boston: J. Munroe, 1848.

Grese, Robert E. Introduction to *Landscape-Gardening,* by O. C. Simonds, reprint of 1920 edition. Amherst: University of Massachusetts Press in association with Library of American Landscape History, 2000.

———. "Jens Jensen." In Birnbaum and Karson, *Pioneers of American Landscape Design,* 203–9.

———. "Jens Jensen: The Landscape Architect as Conservationist." In Tishler, *Midwestern Landscape Architecture,* 117–41.

———. *Jens Jensen: Maker of Natural Parks and Gardens.* Baltimore: Johns Hopkins University Press, 1992.

———. "The Prairie Gardens of O. C. Simonds and Jens Jensen." In O'Malley and Treib, *Regional Garden Design in the United States,* 99–123.

Grese, Robert E., and Miriam E. Rutz. "History and Management Plan for the Grounds of the Edsel and Eleanor Ford House." Report, Ford House, Grosse Pointe Shores, Michigan, May 31, 1988.

Griscom, Elaine. "Val Verde's Dr. Warren Austin." *Montecito Magazine,* Spring 1994. Available online: http://www.austinvalverdefoundation.com/people/warren/.

Griswold, Mac. Afterword to *Fairsted: A Cultural Landscape History,* by Cynthia Zaitzevsky, 123–50. Boston: National Park Service and Arnold Arboretum, 1997.

Griswold, Mac, and Eleanor Weller. *The Golden Age of American Gardens.* New York: Harry N. Abrams, 1991.

Groening, Gert, and Joachim Wolschke-Bulmahn. "Some Notes on the Mania for Native Plants in Germany." *Landscape Journal* 11, no. 2 (Fall 1992): 116–26.

Grove, Carol. *Henry Shaw's Victorian Landscapes: The Missouri Botanical Garden and Tower Grove Park.* Amherst: University of Massachusetts Press in association with Library of American Landscape History, 2005.

Grundmann, William. "The Early Parks of Milwaukee: Lake, Washington, Mitchell, and Kosciuszko, Warren H. Manning's Legacy." Unpublished paper, 1992.

———. "Warren H. Manning." In Tishler, *American Landscape Architecture: Designers and Places,* 56–59.

Halbrooks, Mary C. "The English Garden at Stan Hywet Hall and Gardens: Interpretation, Analysis, and Documentation of a Historic Garden Restoration." *HortTechnology* 15, no. 2 (April–June 2005): 196–212.

Hamerton, Philip. *Landscape.* London: Seely; Boston: Roberts Brothers, 1885.

Hamlin, Talbot. *Forms and Functions of Twentieth-Century Architecture.* 4 vols. New York: Columbia University Press, 1952.

Hartt, Mary Bronson. "Women and the Art of Landscape Gardening." *Outlook,* March 28, 1908, 694–704.

Heilbroner, Robert L. *The Worldly Philosophers: The Lives, Times, and Ideas of the Great Economic Thinkers.* New York: Simon and Schuster, 1967.

Hensley, Paul. "Harry's Other Garden." In Magnani, *The Winterthur Garden,* 129–40.

Hewitt, Mark Alan. *The Architect and the American Country House.* New Haven: Yale University Press, 1990.

Hilderbrand, Gary R. *Making a Landscape of Continuity: The Practice of Innocenti & Webel.* New York: Princeton Architectural Press, 1997.

Hill, May Brawley. *Grandmother's Garden: The Old-Fashioned American Garden, 1865–1915.* New York: Harry N. Abrams, 1995.

Hinsley, Jacqueline. "Nurturing a Family Tradition." In Magnani, *The Winterthur Garden,* 39–61.

Hirshler, Erica E. "The Paintings of Charles A. Platt." In Morgan, *Shaping an American Landscape,* 51–73.

Hobbs, Susan. "Thomas Dewing in Cornish, 1885–1905." *American Art Journal* 17 (Spring 1985): 3–22.

Hofstadter, Richard. *The Age of Reform.* New York: Random House, 1955.

"The House of William G. Mather." *Architectural Record* 26 (November 1909): 312–20.

Howard, Francis. "Making a Garden." *Architecture* 43 (February 1921): 47–48.

Howe, Samuel. *American Country Houses of To-day.* New York: Architectural Book Publishing, 1915.

———. "Gwinn, Cleveland, U.S.A." *Country Life,* May 1916, 132–35.

———. "Home of Mr. W. G. Mather, Cleveland, O." In *American Country Houses of To-day,* 132–35.

———. "Mr. Joseph Choate's Garden, Stockbridge, Mass." In *American Country Houses of To-day,* 342–45.

———. "Prefatory Note." In *American Country Houses of To-day,* ix–x.

Hubbard, Henry Vincent, and Theodora Kimball. *Introduction to the Study of Landscape Design.* New York: Macmillan, 1917.

Hunt, John Dixon, and Peter Willis, eds. *The Genius of the Place: The English Landscape Garden, 1620–1820.* Cambridge, Mass.: MIT Press, 1988.

Hutcheson, Martha Brookes. *The Spirit of the Garden.* Reprint of 1923 edition. Amherst: University of Massachusetts Press in association with Library of American Landscape History, 2001.

"Idlehour, Estate of Vanderbilt." *Architectural Record* 13 (May 1903): 455–94.

Imbert, Dorothée. *The Modernist Garden in France.* New Haven: Yale University Press, 1993.

"An Industrial Experiment at South Manchester." *Harper's New Monthly Magazine* 45 (November 1872): 836–44.

"In Santa Barbara Is a Kitchen." *American Home* 13 (April 1935): 335.

Jackson, Richard S., Jr., and Cornelia Brooke Gilder. *The Houses of the Berkshires, 1870–1930.* New York: Acanthus Press, 2006.

"Jacob W. Manning." *American Gardening* 25 (September 24, 1904): 627.

"Jacob Warren Manning." *American Gardening* 25 (October 1, 1904): 636.

James, Henry. *Collected Travel Writings: Great Britain and America.* Edited by Richard Howard. New York: Library of America, 1993.

Jansen, Gail. *Lockwood de Forest, Jr.: A Master Revealed.* Documentary video. Austin Val Verde Foundation, 2002.

Jarrell, C. Chappell. "From Farmscape to Suburban Yard: Robert Jemison, Jr.'s Spring Lake Farms." In Morris and White, *Designs on Birmingham*, 42–45.

Jekyll, Gertrude. *Colour in the Flower Garden*. London: Country Life, 1908.

Jellicoe, Geoffrey, and Susan Jellicoe. *The Landscape of Man: Shaping the Environment from Prehistory to the Present Day*. New York: Van Nostrand Reinhold, 1982.

Jensen, James [Jens]. "Parks and Politics." *Sixth Volume of the American Park and Outdoor Art Association*, no. 4 (1902): 11–14.

———. "Plan for Hospital Grounds." *Park and Cemetery*, December 1901, 185–86.

Jensen, Jens. *A Greater West Park System*. Chicago: West Park Commission, 1920.

———. "Landscape Art: An Inspiration from the Western Plains." *Sketch Book* 6, no. 1 (September 1906): 21–28.

———. "Regulating City Building." *Survey*, November 18, 1911, 1203–5.

———. *Siftings*. Reprint of 1939 edition. Baltimore: Johns Hopkins University Press, 1990.

Jones, Beatrix. "Bridge Over the Kent at Levens Hall." *Garden and Forest*, January 15, 1896, 22, 25.

———. "The Garden as Picture." *Scribner's*, July 1907, 2–11.

———. "The Garden in Relation to the House." *Garden and Forest*, April 7, 1897, 132–33.

———. "Laying Out a Suburban Place." *Country Life in America*, March 1910, 551–52.

———. "Nature's Landscape-Gardening in Maine." *Garden and Forest*, September 6, 1893, 378–79.

Joseph, Maureen de Lay, Mark Davison, and Kay Fanning. *Cultural Landscape Report: Dumbarton Oaks Park, Rock Creek Park, Part I*. Washington, D.C.: National Park Service, 2000.

Karson, Robin. "The Age of the American Country Place." *Magazine Antiques*, October 2000, 514–23.

———. "The Blue Steps of Naumkeag." *Art New England* 11, no. 7 (July–August 1990): 26–27, 44–45.

———. "The Camden Public Library Theater, 1928: Fletcher Steele and F. L. Olmsted, Jr." *Maine Olmsted Alliance for Parks and Landscapes Newsletter*, Spring 1992, 1, 3–6.

———. "Clarity and Elegance: Fletcher Steele's Masterpiece of Design, a Garden Room in Rochester, N.Y." *Garden Design*, Spring 1989, 40–49.

———. "Conversation with Kiley." *Landscape Architecture* 76, no. 2 (March/April 1986): 50–57.

———. "The Designer as Artist." *American Horticulturalist* 67, no. 10 (October 1988): 4–6, 8–9.

———. *Fletcher Steele, Landscape Architect: An Account of the Gardenmaker's Life, 1885–1971*. Rev. ed. Amherst, Mass.: Library of American Landscape History, 2003.

———. "Fletcher Steele's Last Vista." *Garden Design*, Spring 1988, 60–65, 80, 82, 84, 93.

———. "Gardens of Glory: Recapturing America's Heritage." *Garden Design*, January–February 1991, 36–41.

———. *The Muses of Gwinn: Art and Nature in a Garden Designed by Warren H. Manning, Charles A. Platt, and Ellen Biddle Shipman*.

Sagaponack, N.Y.: Sagapress/Abrams in association with Library of American Landscape History, 1995.

———. "Of Consequence and Caprice: Naumkeag, Haven for Thought and Laughter." *Garden Design*, Spring 1984, 70–77.

———. "Spheres, Cones, and Other Least Common Denominators: Modern French Gardens through the Eyes of Fletcher Steele." In *Masters of American Garden Design III: The Modern Garden in Europe and the United States*, 7–16. Cold Spring, N.Y.: Garden Conservancy, 1994.

———. "Warren H. Manning." In Birnbaum and Karson, *Pioneers of American Landscape Design*, 236–42.

———. "Warren H. Manning: Pragmatist in the Wild Garden." In Wolschke-Bulmahn, *Nature and Ideology*, 113–30.

———. "A Woman's Place: Ellen Shipman's Gardens Frame a Divided World." *Garden Design*, February–March 1997, 46–48.

Kenworthy, Richard G. "Bringing the World to Brookline: The Gardens of Larz and Isabel Anderson." *Journal of Garden History* 11, no. 2 (October–December 1991): 224–41.

———. "Published Records of Italianate Gardens in America." *Journal of Garden History* 10, no. 1 (January–March 1990): 10–70.

Kimball, Fiske. "The American Country House." *Architectural Record* 46 (October 1919): 291–400.

King, Mrs. Francis. *The Well-Considered Garden*. New York: Charles Scribner's Sons, 1922.

Klaus, Susan L. "Frederick Law Olmsted Jr." In Birnbaum and Karson, *Pioneers of American Landscape Design*, 273–76.

———. *A Modern Arcadia: Frederick Law Olmsted Jr. and the Plan for Forest Hills Gardens*. Amherst: University of Massachusetts Press in association with Library of American Landscape History, 2002.

Kowsky, Francis. *Country, Park & City: The Architecture and Life of Calvert Vaux*. New York: Oxford University Press, 1998.

Lambeth, William Alexander, and Warren H. Manning. *Thomas Jefferson as an Architect and a Designer of Landscapes*. Boston: Houghton Mifflin, 1913.

"Landscape Architecture as Seen from the Air: A Series of Long Island Estates, John Russell Pope, Architect." *American Architect* 131 (May 5, 1927): 565–70.

"Landscape Gardening in California." *Architectural Record* 19 (June 1906): 473–74.

Laurie, Michael. "The Reef Point Collection at the University of California." In McGuire and Fern, *Beatrix Jones Farrand*, 9–20.

Lay, Charles Downing. "An Interview with Charles A. Platt." *Landscape Architecture* 2, no. 3 (April 1912): 127–31.

Leavitt, Charles Wellford. "A Half Century of Landscape Architecture." *American Architect* 129 (Jan 5, 1926): 61–64.

Leighton, Ann. *American Gardens in the Eighteenth Century: "For Use or for Delight."* Boston: Houghton Mifflin, 1976.

———. *Early American Gardens: "For Meate or Medicine."* Boston: Houghton Mifflin, 1970.

Leszczynski, Nancy A. "Beatrix Farrand: The Development of a Design Philosophy." Master's thesis, University of Virginia, May 1991.

Lewis, Ann Suydam. *Lockwood de Forest: Painter, Importer, Decorator*. Huntington, N.Y.: Heckscher Museum, 1976.

Lewis, R. W. B. *Edith Wharton: A Biography*. New York: Harper and Row, 1975.

Lewis, R. W. B., and Nancy Lewis, eds. *The Letters of Edith Wharton*. New York: Charles Scribner's Sons, 1988.

Libby, Valencia. "Henry Francis du Pont and the Early Development of Winterthur Gardens, 1880–1927." Master's thesis, University of Delaware, 1984.

———. "Marian Cruger Coffin." In Birnbaum and Karson, *Pioneers of American Landscape Design*, 64–68.

———. "Marian Cruger Coffin (1876–1957): The Landscape Architect and the Lady." In *The House and Garden*, 24–29. Roslyn, N.Y.: Nassau County Museum of Fine Arts, 1986.

Linden, Blanche M. G. *Silent City on a Hill: Picturesque Landscapes of Memory and Boston's Mount Auburn Cemetery*. Rev. ed. Amherst: University of Massachusetts Press in association with Library of American Landscape History, 2007.

Linden-Ward, Blanche. "Stan Hywet." *Landscape Architecture* 77, no. 4 (July–August 1987): 66–71.

Lockwood, Alice G. B. *Gardens of Colony and State*. 2 vols. New York: Charles Scribner's Sons, for the Garden Club of America, 1931.

Longstreth, Richard W. "Academic Eclecticism in American Architecture." *Winterthur Portfolio* 17, no. 1 (Spring 1982): 55–82.

Lord, Ruth. *Henry F. du Pont and Winterthur: A Daughter's Portrait*. New Haven: Yale University Press, 1999.

Lott, Linda. "Garden Ornament in the Dumbarton Oaks Garden: An Overview." Studies in Landscape Architecture, Dumbarton Oaks Informal Papers, Washington, D.C. August 1996.

Loudon, Jane. *Gardening for Ladies*. London: John Murray, 1840.

Lowell, Guy. *American Gardens*. Boston: Bates and Guild, 1902.

Loya, Timothy J. "William Gwinn Mather, the Man." *Inland Seas*, Summer 1990, 117–33.

Lutz, Tom. *American Nervousness, 1903: An Anecdotal History*. Ithaca, N.Y.: Cornell University Press, 1991.

Magnani, Denise "Garden for a 'Country Place Museum.'" In *The Winterthur Garden*, 141–63.

———. "On Becoming a Gardener." In *The Winterthur Garden*, 63–91.

———, ed. *The Winterthur Garden: Henry Francis du Pont's Romance with the Land*. New York: Harry N. Abrams in association with the Winterthur Museum, 1995.

Maher, George W. "The Western Spirit." *Western Architect* 9 (November 1906): 113–15; (December 1906): 125–26.

Manning, Warren H. "The Art of Making Landscape Gardens." In *The Standard Cyclopedia of Horticulture*, edited by Liberty Hyde Bailey, 1783–89. New York: Macmillan, 1916.

———. "The Field of Landscape Design." *Landscape Architecture* 2, no. 3 (April 1912): 108–10.

———. "How to Make a Formal Garden at a Moderate Cost." *Country Life in America*, March 1903, 186–89.

———. "A National Plan Study Brief." Special supplement to *Landscape Architecture* 13, no. 4 (July 1923).

———. *A Step Towards Solving the Industrial Housing Problem*. American City Pamphlet Series, no. 131. New York: Civic Press, 1913.

———. "The Two Kinds of Bog Gardens." *Country Life in America*, August 1908, 379–80.

———. "Wild Garden." In *Cyclopedia of American Horticulture*, edited by Liberty Hyde Bailey. 4th ed., 1976–78. New York: Doubleday, Page, 1906.

"Marian Cruger Coffin." Obituary. *Landscape Architecture* 47, no. 3 (April 1957): 431–32.

Martin, Edward Sandford. *The Life of Joseph Hodges Choate*. 2 vols. New York: Charles Scribner's Sons, 1920.

Masson, Georgina. *Dumbarton Oaks: A Guide to the Gardens*. Washington, D.C.: Dumbarton Oaks, 1968.

Mawson, Thomas Hayton. *The Art and Craft and Garden-Making*. London: B.T. Batsford; New York: Charles Scribner's Sons, 1900.

Mayer, Roberta A. "The Aesthetics of Lockwood de Forest: India, Craft and Preservation." *Winterthur Portfolio* 31, no. 1 (Spring 1996): 1–22.

McCormick, Harriet. *Landscape Art, Past and Present*. New York: Charles Scribner's Sons, 1923.

McFarland, J. Horace. "An American Garden: Dolobran near Philadelphia." *Outlook*, October 7, 1899, 326–33.

———. "Dolobran—A Wild-Gardening Estate." *Country Life in America*, September 1903, 338–42, 365.

McGuire, Diane Kostial. "The Gardens." *Apollo*, April 1984, 38–43.

McGuire, Diane Kostial, and Lois Fern, eds. *Beatrix Jones Farrand (1872–1959): Fifty Years of American Landscape Architecture*. Washington, D.C.: Dumbarton Oaks Trustees for Harvard University, 1982.

McLaughlin, Charles C. Introduction to *Walks and Talks of an American Farmer in England*, by Frederick Law Olmsted, reprint of 1852 edition. Amherst, Mass.: Library of American Landscape History, 2002.

———, ed. *The Papers of Frederick Law Olmsted*, Vol. 1, *The Formative Years, 1822–1852*. Baltimore: Johns Hopkins University Press, 1977.

McPeck, Eleanor M. "A Biographical Note and a Consideration of Four Major Private Gardens." In Balmori, McGuire, and McPeck, *Beatrix Farrand's American Landscapes*, 40–44.

Miller, John Franklin. "The Restoration of the English Garden at Stan Hywet." In Tankard, *The Gardens of Ellen Biddle Shipman*, 183–88.

Miller, Phillip. *The Gardener's Dictionary*. London: C. Rivington, 1731.

Miller, Wilhelm. "Bird Gardens in the City." *Country Life in America*, August 1914, 46–47.

———. "The Fascinating Art of Making Vistas." *Country Life in America*, March 1913, 35–38.

———. "Have We Progressed in Gardening?" *Country Life in America*, April 15, 1912, 25–26.

———. "An 'Italian Garden' That Is Full of Flowers." *Country Life in America*, March 1905, 485–92.

———. "Lessons from a Famous Hillside Garden." *Country Life in America*, August 1910, 433–36.

———. *The Prairie Spirit in Landscape Gardening*. Reprint of 1915 edition. Amherst: University of Massachusetts Press in association with Library of American Landscape History, 2001.

———. "A Series of Outdoor Salons." *Country Life in America*, April 1914, 39–40.

———. *What England Can Teach Us about Gardening*. Garden City, N.Y.: Doubleday, Page, 1911.

Milliken, William Mathewson. *A Time Remembered: A Cleveland Memoir*. Cleveland: Western Reserve Historical Society, 1975.

Milner, H. E. "The Garden in Relation to the House." *Journal of the*

Royal Institute of British Architects, 3rd ser., 4, no. 8 (1896–97): 185–99.

Morgan, Keith N. "Al Fresco: An Overview of Charles A. Platt's *Italian Gardens*." Introduction to *Italian Gardens*, by Charles A. Platt, reprint of 1894 edition. Portland, Ore.: Sagapress/Timberpress, 1993.

———. *Charles A. Platt: The Artist as Architect.* Cambridge, Mass.: Architectural History Foundation and MIT Press, 1985.

———. "Charles A. Platt and the Promise of American Art." In *Shaping an American Landscape*, 3–23.

———. "Gwinn: The Creation of a New American Landscape." In *Shaping an American Landscape*, 121–42.

———, ed. *Shaping an American Landscape: The Art and Architecture of Charles A. Platt.* Hanover, N.H.: University Press of New England, 1995.

Morgan, Keith N., and Robin Karson. "Gwinn: William G. Mather's Residence in Bratenahl, Ohio." *Magazine Antiques*, March 1995, 442–54.

Morris, Philip A., and Marjorie Longenecker White, eds. *Designs on Birmingham: A Landscape History of a Southern City and Its Suburbs.* Birmingham, Ala.: Birmingham Historical Society, 1989.

Morrison, Darrel K. "Jens Jensen." Paper presented at American Horticultural Society Conference, PaineWebber, New York City, January 1990.

Moss, Roger W. *The American Country House.* New York: Henry Holt, 1990.

"Mr. Fletcher Steele." *Town and Country*, December 15, 1926, 32.

Myrick, David F. *Montecito and Santa Barbara.* 2 vols. Glendale, Calif.: Trans-Anglo Books, 1987–1991.

Nadenicek, Daniel J., and Lance M. Neckar. Introduction to Cleveland, *Landscape Architecture, as Applied to the Wants of the West*, reprint of 1873 edition.

Neckar, Lance M. "Developing Landscape Architecture for the Twentieth Century: The Career of Warren H. Manning." *Landscape Journal* 8 (Fall 1989): 78–91.

———. "Warren H. Manning and His Minnesota Clients: Developing a National Practice in a Landscape of Resources, 1898–1919." In Tishler, *Midwestern Landscape Architecture*, 142–58.

Newton, Norman T. *Design on the Land: The Development of Landscape Architecture.* Cambridge, Mass.: Belknap Press of Harvard University Press, 1971.

Nichols, Rose Standish. "A Hilltop Garden in New Hampshire." *House Beautiful*, March 1924, 237–39.

———. *Italian Pleasure Gardens.* New York: Dodd, Mead, 1926.

"Notes on Italian Gardens." *Garden and Forest*, August 2, 1893, 322.

Novak, Barbara. *Nature and Culture: American Landscape and Painting, 1825–1875.* New York: Oxford Universuty Press, 1980.

Oliver, Richard. *Bertram Grosvenor Goodhue.* New York and Cambridge, Mass.: Architectural History Foundation and MIT Press, 1983.

Olivier-Vila, Frank, and François Rateau. *Armand-Albert Rateau, un baroque chez les modernes.* Paris: L'Amateur, 1992.

Olmsted, Frederick Law. *The Cotton Kingdom: A Traveller's Observations on Cotton and Slavery in the American Slave States.* 2 vols. New York: Mason Brothers, 1861.

———. "The Landscape Architecture of the World's Columbian Exposition." *Inland Architect* 22, no. 2 (September 1893): 18–21.

———. "Parks, Parkways, and Pleasure Grounds." *Garden and Forest*, May 22, 1895, 202–3; *Engineering Magazine* 9, no. 2 (1895): 253–60.

———. *Public Parks and the Enlargement of Towns.* Reprint of 1870 edition. New York: Arno Press and New York Times, 1970.

———. *Walks and Talks of an American Farmer in England.* New York: G. P. Putnam's Sons, 1852. Reprint edition, Amherst, Mass.: Library of American Landscape History, 2002.

———. "Yosemite and the Mariposa Grove: A Preliminary Report, 1865." http://www.yosemite.ca.us/library/olmsted/report.html.

Olson, Sidney. *Young Henry Ford: A Picture History of the First Forty Years.* Reprint of 1963 edition. Detroit: Wayne State University Press, 1997.

O'Malley, Therese. "The Evidence of American Garden History: Interpreting American Gardens through Words and Images." In *Keywords in American Landscape Design*, edited by Therese O'Malley, Elizabeth Kryder-Reid, and Anne Helmreich. New Haven: Yale University Press, forthcoming.

O'Malley, Therese, and Marc Treib, eds. *Regional Garden Design in the United States.* Washington, D.C.: Dumbarton Oaks Research Library and Collection, 1995.

Otis, Denise. *Grounds for Pleasure: Four Centuries of the American Garden.* New York: Harry N. Abrams, 2002.

Owens, Carole. *Berkshire Cottages: A Vanishing Era.* Englewood Cliffs, N.J.: Cottage Press, 1984.

Padilla, Victoria. *Southern California Gardens: An Illustrated History.* Berkeley: University of California Press, 1961.

Parker, Mary Hart. "The Theory and Practice of Garden Design in the Life of Edith Wharton." Unpublished paper prepared for the tenth anniversary meeting of the Edith Wharton Society at The Mount, Lenox, Mass., June 1977.

Parsons, Samuel. *The Art of Landscape Architecture.* New York: G. P. Putnam's Sons, 1915.

Peck, Amelia. "Robert de Forest and the Founding of the American Wing—New York Metropolitan Museum." *Magazine Antiques*, January 2000, 176–81.

Pentecost, George F., Jr. "American Gardens." *Architectural Record* 13 (May 1903): 437–52.

———. "The Country Gentleman's Art: Specifications for the Working Out of Landscape Gardening." *Architectural Record* 28 (July 1910): 42–50.

———. "The Formal and Natural Style." *Architectural Record* 12 (June 1902): 174–94.

———. "The Villa Garden." *Architectural Record* 11 (January 1902): 61–68.

Peters, William Frederick. "Lockwood de Forest." Master's thesis, University of California, Berkeley, 1980.

Pitkin, William, Jr. "The Relation between the Architect and the Landscape Architect" (Parts 1 and 2). *American Architect* 117 (March 17, 1920): 327–34; (March 24, 1920): 363–67.

Platt, Charles A. *Italian Gardens.* Reprint of 1894 edition. Portland, Ore.: Sagapress/Timberpress, 1993.

———. "Where We Get Our Ideas of Country Places in America." *Outing* 40 (June 1904): 349–55

Porter, Glenn. *The Rise of Big Business, 1850–1910.* Arlington Heights, Ill.: AHM Publishing, 1973.

Pray, James Sturgis. "The Italian Garden." *American Architect and Building News* 67 (February 10, 1900): 43–45.

Price, Sir Uvedale. *Essay on the Picturesque.* London: J. Robson, 1794.

Prior, Edward S. "American Garden-craft from an English Point of View." *House and Garden,* November 1903, 211–15.

Pückler-Muskau, Hermann Ludwig Heinrich von. *Hints on Landscape Gardening.* Translated by Bernhard Sickert. Edited by Samuel Parsons. Boston: Houghton Mifflin, 1917.

Rainey, Reuben M. "William Le Baron Jenney and Chicago's West Parks: From Prairies to Pleasure Grounds." In Tishler, *Midwestern Landscape Architecture,* 57–79.

"Rambling Observations of a Roving Gardener." *Horticulture,* January 1, 1930, 9.

Rehmann, Elsa. *The Small Place: Its Landscape Architecture.* New York: G. P. Putnam's Sons, 1918.

Repton, Humphry. *The Art of Landscape Gardening.* Edited by John Nolen. Boston: Houghton Mifflin, 1907.

———. *Sketches and Hints on Landscape Gardening.* London: W. Bulmer, 1794.

Rexford, Eben E. "A Garden of Native Plants." *Lippincott's Magazine,* April 1902, 483–88.

Reynales, Trish. "The Naturals: Elizabeth and Lockwood de Forest." *Santa Barbara Magazine,* Summer 1995, 42–49, 108.

Richards, W. C. *The Last Billionaire.* New York: Charles Scribner's Sons, 1948.

Riley, Phil M. "The Spirit of the Renaissance on the Great Lakes." *Country Life in America,* September 15, 1912, 28–30.

Roberts, Edith, and Elsa Rehmann. *American Plants for American Gardens.* New York: Macmillan, 1929.

Robinson, Judith Helm, and Stephanie S. Foell. "Nathan Franklin Barrett." In Birnbaum and Karson, *Pioneers of American Landscape Design,* 10–14.

Robinson, William. *The English Flower Garden.* London: John Murray, 1883.

———. *The Wild Garden.* London: The Garden Office; New York: Scribner and Welford, 1881.

Rogers, Elizabeth Barlow. *Landscape Design: A Cultural and Architectural History.* New York: Harry N. Abrams, 2001.

Roper, Laura Wood. *FLO: A Biography of Frederick Law Olmsted.* Baltimore: Johns Hopkins University Press, 1973.

Rosenzweig, Roy, and Elizabeth Blackmar. *The Park and the People: A History of Central Park.* Ithaca, N.Y.: Cornell University Press, 1992.

Ross, Janet. *Florentine Villas.* New York: Dutton, 1901.

Roth, Leland M. *A Concise History of American Architecture.* New York: Harper & Row, 1979.

Rybczynski, Witold. *A Clearing in the Distance: Frederick Law Olmsted and America in the Nineteenth Century.* New York: Scribner, 1999.

Sargent, Charles S. "The Columbian Exposition." *Garden and Forest,* December 1893, 104–5.

———. "Formal Gardening: Does It Conflict with the Natural Style?" *Garden and Forest,* March 15, 1893, 119–20.

———. "Formal Gardening: Where It Can Be Used to Advantage." *Garden and Forest,* March 22, 1893, 129–30.

———. "Park Work near Boston." *Garden and Forest,* April 29, 1896, 171.

Saylor, Henry Hodgman. "The Best Twelve Country House in America: 'El Fureidis,' Home of J. Waldron Gillespie, at Montecito, California." *Country Life in America,* October 1915, 29–31.

Sclare, Liisa, and Donald Sclare. *Beaux-Arts Estates: A Guide to the Architecture of Long Island.* New York: Viking, 1980.

Sedgwick, Mabel Cabot. *The Garden Month by Month.* New York: F. A. Stokes, 1907.

Segal, Howard P. *Recasting the Machine Age: Henry Ford's Village Industries.* Amherst: University of Massachusetts Press, 2005.

Seldis, Henry J. "Harmony in Diversity: Wright S. Ludington." In *The Collector in America,* edited by Jean Lipman, 36–47. New York: Viking, 1971.

Shand-Tucci, Douglass. *Boston Bohemia, 1881–1900: Ralph Adams Cram: Life and Architecture.* Amherst: University of Massachusetts Press, 1995.

Shelton, Louise. *Beautiful Gardens in America.* New York: Charles Scribner's Sons, 1915.

Shelton, William Henry. "The Most Indian House in America." *House Beautiful,* June 1900, 419–23.

Shepp, James W., and Daniel B. Shepp. *Shepp's World's Fair Photographed.* Chicago: Globe Bible Publishing, 1893.

Simo, Melanie. *Garden and Forest: Traces of Wilderness in a Modernizing Land, 1897–1949.* Charlottesville: University of Virginia Press, 2003.

———. *100 Years of Landscape Architecture: Some Patterns of a Century.* Washington, D.C.: American Society of Landscape Architects, 1999.

Simonds, O. C. *Landscape-Gardening.* Reprint of 1920 edition. Amherst: University of Massachusetts Press in association with Library of American Landscape History, 2000.

Smith, Howard Dwight. "The Relation of the House to the Landscape." *American Architect* 113 (April 3, 1913): 395–404.

Smith, Warren Hunting. "Memoir of Marian Coffin." In *Gardens Designed by Marian Cruger Coffin, Landscape Architect, 1876–1957.* Geneva N.Y.: Hobart College, 1958.

Spencer, Robert C., Jr. "The Work of Frank Lloyd Wright." *Architectural Review* 7 (June 1900): 61–72.

Starr, Kevin. *Inventing the Dream: California through the Progressive Era.* New York: Oxford University Press, 1985.

———. *Material Dreams: Southern California through the 1920s.* New York: Oxford University Press, 1990.

Steele, Fletcher. "Aesthetic Principles in the Spring Flower Garden." *House Beautiful,* March 1922, 197–99.

———. "Background of Culture and Horticulture in the Genesee Valley." In *The Garden Club of America Annual Meeting,* 1941.

———. "The Colonial Garden Today." In *Colonial Gardens,* by the American Society of Landscape Architects, 60–68. Washington, D.C.: U.S. George Washington Bicentennial Commission, 1932.

———. *Design in the Little Garden.* Boston: Atlantic Monthly Press, 1924.

———. "Design of the Small Place." In *The House Beautiful Gardening Manual,* 1–12. Boston: Atlantic Monthly Company, 1926.

———. "The Effective Use of Planting in Landscape Architecture and Gardening." *The Garden,* March 1949, 18–23, and June 1949,

8–12. Reprinted in Better Homes and Gardens, *America's Gardens*. Des Moines and New York: Meredith Press, 1964.

———. "French Gardens and Their Racial Characteristics." *Landscape Architecture* 12, no. 4 (July 1922): 211–23.

———. *Gardens and People*. Boston: Houghton Mifflin, 1964.

———. "Landscape Design of the Future." *Landscape Architecture* 22, no. 4 (July 1932): 299–302.

———. "Lisburne Grange." *Garden Club of America Bulletin*, September 1935, 112–17.

———. "Modern Landscape Architecture." In *Contemporary Landscape Architecture and Its Sources*, 23–25. Exhibition catalog. San Francisco: San Francisco Museum of Art, 1936.

———. "Naumkeag: Miss Mabel Choate's Place in Stockbridge, Massachusetts, Has Been Shaped by Two Generations of Changing Taste." *House and Garden*, July 1947, 68–71, 110–11.

———. "New Pioneering in Garden Design." *Landscape Architecture* 20, no. 3 (April 1930): 159–77.

———. "New Styles in Gardening: Will Landscape Architecture Reflect the Modernistic Tendencies Seen in the Other Arts?" *House Beautiful*, March 1929, 317, 352–54.

———. "Plant Material." *Garden Club of America Bulletin*, September 1921, 40–44.

———. "Private Post-War Planning" (Parts 1 and 2). *Garden Club of America Bulletin*, June 1944, 11–15, and September 1944, 15–18.

———. "The Temple Garden: The Garden of M. Choate, Stockbridge, Mass." *House Beautiful*, July 1933, 21–23.

Steinitz, Carl, Paul Parker, and Lawrie Jordan. "Hand Drawn Overlays: Their History and Prospective Uses." *Landscape Architecture* 66, no. 5 (September 1976): 421; 444–55.

Stone, Bethia. "Val Verde." *Pacific Horticulture*, Summer 1986, 40–42.

"'Stormfield': Mark Twain's New Country Home." *Country Life in America*, April 1909, 607–11, 650, 652.

Stow-Fithian, Anne. "My Garden of Succulents." *House and Garden*, December 1927, 72–73, 164, 166.

Streatfield, David C. "Biography of Lockwood de Forest." Online archive notes, Environmental Design Archive, University of California, Berkeley. http://content.cdlib.org/view?docId=tf2489n5t4&chunk.id=bioghist-1.8.4.

———. *California Gardens: Creating a New Eden*. New York: Abbeville Press, 1994.

———. "The Evolution of the California Landscape: 4. Suburbia at the Zenith." *Landscape Architecture* 67, no. 5 (September 1977): 417–24.

———. "Where Pine and Palm Meet: The California Garden as a Regional Expression." *Landscape Journal* 4, no. 2 (1985): 60–70.

Sturgis, R. Clipston. "Of What Shall the House Be Built?" *Indoors and Out*, June 1906, 101–11.

Sutton, S. B., ed. *Civilizing American Cities: A Selection of Frederick Law Olmsted's Writings on City Landscapes*. Cambridge, Mass.: MIT Press, 1971.

Tabor, Grace. *Old-Fashioned Gardening. A History and a Reconstruction*. New York: McBride, Nast, 1913.

Tamulevich, Susan. *Dumbarton Oaks: Garden into Art*. New York: Monacelli Press, 2001.

Tankard, Judith B. *The Gardens of Ellen Biddle Shipman*. Sagaponack,

N.Y.: Sagapress/Abrams in association with the Library of American Landscape History, 1996.

———. "The Influence of British Garden Literature on American Garden Design during the Country Place Era." In *Masters of American Garden Design III: Influences on American Garden Design, 1895–1940*, edited by Robin Karson, 17–29. New York: Garden Conservancy, 1994.

Tatum, George B. "The Emergence of an American School of Landscape Design." *Historic Preservation*, April–June 1973, 34–41.

Taylor, A. D. *The Complete Garden*. Garden City, N.Y.: Doubleday, 1921.

Thorne, Mrs. Oakleigh. "When an Easterner Gardens in the Golden West." *Garden Magazine*, April 1921, 178–80.

Thornton, Tamara Plakins. *Cultivating Gentlemen: The Meaning of Country Life among the Boston Elite, 1785–1860*. New Haven: Yale University Press, 1989.

Tishler, William H., ed. *American Landscape Architecture: Designers and Places*. Washington, D.C.: The Preservation Press, 1989.

———, ed. *Midwestern Landscape Architecture*. Urbana: University of Illinois Press in collaboration with Library of American Landscape History, 2000.

Tobey, George B. *A History of Landscape Architecture: The Relationship of People to Environment*. New York: American Elsevier, 1973.

Tyrrell, C. Gordon. "The History and Development of the Winterthur Gardens." *Winterthur Portfolio* 1 (1964): 122–38.

Van Rensselaer, Mariana Griswold. *Accents as Well as Broad Effects: Writings on Architecture, Landscape, and the Environment, 1876–1925*. Edited by David Gebhard. Berkeley: University of California Press, 1996.

———. "American Country Dwellings." *Century Magazine* 32 (May 1886): 3–20; (June 1886): 206–20; (July 1886): 421–34. Reprinted in *Accents as Well as Broad Effects*, 223–78.

———. *Art Out-of-Doors*. New York: Charles Scribner's Sons, 1893.

———. "The Artistic Triumph of the Fair-Builders." *Forum* 14 (December 1892): 527–40. Reprinted in *Accents as Well as Broad Effects*, 68–81.

Van Valkenburgh, Michael. *Built Landscapes: Gardens in the Northeast*. Brattleboro, Vt.: Brattleboro Museum & Art Center, 1984.

Veblen, Thorstein. *The Theory of the Leisure Class*. New York: Macmillan, 1899.

Vernon, Christopher. Introduction to Miller, *The Prairie Spirit in Landscape Gardening*, reprint of 1915 edition

———. "Wilhelm Miller: Prairie Spirit in Landscape Gardening." In Tishler, *Midwestern Landscape Architecture*, 174–92.

W[alker], C. H[oward]. "Current Periodicals." *Architectural Review* 10, no. 9 (September 1903): 139–40.

Walker, Nell. "Marjorie Sewell Cautley." In Birnbaum and Karson, *Pioneers of American Landscape Design*, 47–49.

Walker, Peter, and Melanie Simo. *Invisible Gardens: The Search for Modernism in the American Landscape*. Cambridge, Mass.: MIT Press, 1994.

Wanger, Ruth. *What Girls Can Do*. New York: Henry Holt, 1926.

Warren, Charles D. Introduction to *The Architecture of Charles A. Platt*, reprint of 1913 edition. New York: Acanthus Press, 1998.

———. Introduction to *New Towns for Old*, by John Nolen, reprint of

1927 edition. Amherst: University of Massachusetts Press in association with Library of American Landscape History, 2005.

Waugh, Frank A. *Book of Landscape Gardening*. New York: Orange Judd, 1926.

———. "German Landscape Gardening." *Country Gentleman*, August 25, 1910, 790.

———. *The Landscape Beautiful*. New York: Orange Judd, 1910.

———. *The Natural Style in Landscape Gardening*. Boston: R. G. Badger, 1917.

Weaver, E. W. *Profitable Vocations for Girls*. Chicago: Laidlaw Brothers, 1924.

Weidenmann, Jacob. *Beautifying Country Homes: A Handbook of Landscape Gardening*. New York: Orange Judd, 1870.

Wharton, Edith. *A Backward Glance*. New York: Appleton-Century, 1934.

———. *Italian Villas and Their Gardens*. Reprint of 1904 edition. New York: Da Capo Press, 1988.

Wharton, Edith, and Odgen Codman Jr. *The Decoration of Houses*. New York: Charles Scribner's Sons, 1897.

White, Stanley. "The Value of Natural Preserves to the Landscape Architect." In *Naturalist's Guide to the Americas*, edited by Victor E. Shelford, 8–9. Baltimore: Williams & Wilkins, 1926.

Whitehead, Russell F. "Current Country House Architecture: The Pendulum of Design Swings." *Architectural Record* 56 (November 1924): 385–488.

Whittredge, Worthington. *The Autobiography of Worthington Whittredge, 1820–1910*. Edited by John I. H. Baur. New York: Arno Press, 1969.

Wilkinson, Norman B. *E. I. du Pont, Botaniste*. Charlottesville: University Press of Virginia, 1972.

Wilson, Richard Guy, and Dianne H. Pilgrim, eds. *The American Renaissance, 1876–1917*. New York: Pantheon in association with the Brooklyn Museum, 1979.

Wolschke-Bulmahn, Joachim. "The Search for 'Ecological Goodness' among Garden Historians." In *Perspectives on Garden Histories*, edited by Michel Conan, 161–80. Dumbarton Oaks Colloquium on the History of Landscape Architecture. Washington, D.C: Dumbarton Oaks Research Library and Collection, 1999.

———, ed. *Nature and Ideology: Natural Garden Design in the Twentieth Century*. Dumbarton Oaks Colloquium on the History of Landscape Architecture. Washington, D.C.: Dumbarton Oaks Research Library and Collection, 1997.

"Women in Horticulture." *House and Garden*, March 1925, 64–65.

Yoch, James J. *Landscaping the American Dream: The Gardens and Film Sets of Florence Yoch, 1890–1972*. Sagaponack, N.Y.: Sagapress/Abrams, 1989.

Yourcenar, Marguerite. "Reflections on the Composition of *Memoirs of Hadrian*." In *Memoirs of Hadrian*, translated by Grace Frick, 319–47. New York: Farrar, Straus and Giroux, 1963.

Zaitzevsky, Cynthia. *Frederick Law Olmsted and the Boston Park System*. Cambridge, Mass.: Belknap Press of Harvard University Press, 1982.

Zube, Ervin. "The Advance of Ecology." *Landscape Architecture* 76, no. 2 (March–April 1986): 58–67.

ACKNOWLEDGMENTS

Stewardship comes in many forms, and the Library of American Landscape History, under whose embracing wing this book was developed, has, in turn, had the benevolent care of many angels during its fifteen years of existence. No one among them has been as generous, patient, or encouraging as our founding president, Nancy R. Turner. I am deeply grateful to her for believing in LALH and for believing in me.

There are others to thank. I am indebted to John Franklin Miller, one of the founders of LALH and since 2000 its president, a man whose wisdom and goodness have helped guide LALH and keep its mission in focus. Vice president Michael Jefcoat and his wife, Evelyn Jefcoat, have also been instrumental in helping LALH achieve its mission. Their generous financial support for this book and their sophistication and verve have been invaluable. I am also deeply grateful to the LALH clerk, Ann D. Wilhite, our treasurer, Charles D. Warren, and to Elizabeth Barlow Rogers, Mark Zelonis, and our new trustees, John K. Notz Jr. and Ethan Carr, for their support and good work on behalf of LALH. The efforts of these dedicated people, and past board members, including Eleanor Ames, trustee emerita Nesta Spink, and the late Professor Charles C. McLaughlin, have helped LALH to flourish.

Support for this book has come over years from many sources. Early research was underwritten by a grant from the National Endowment for the Arts; travel to the sites and photography were underwritten by the Stanley Smith Horticultural Trust; writing and editing were underwritten by a grant from the High Meadow Foundation and from Furthermore, a program of the J. M. Kaplan Fund. Illustration permission fees and costs of production were supported by generous gifts from Nancy Turner and Michael and Evelyn Jefcoat. I am indebted to these institutions and individuals for making this book possible, as I am to all of those who have so generously supported the LALH program.

I am also grateful to the advisers who have offered guidance, words of encouragement, and other support through the years: Edward L. Blake, ASLA, George W. Curry, FASLA, Julius Gy. Fabos, FASLA, Keith N. Morgan, Cornelia Hahn Oberlander, FASLA, Witold Rybczynski, Robert A. M. Stern, David C. Streatfield, William H. Tishler, FASLA, Suzanne L. Turner, FASLA, and James Anthony van Sweden, FASLA. And, I am grateful to the members of the LALH consulting committee for their good ideas: Carol Betsch, Dean Cardasis, FASLA, Linda Florio, Julia Gaviria, Barbara Shear, Colin Thomson, Molly Turner, and Bruce Wilcox. The enthusiasm of Colin Thomson, director of UBS Art Gallery, was key to the success of the exhibition *A Genius for Place*, as was the very fine design by Linda Florio. We were also extremely fortunate in the remarkable vision of Jacques Charlas, who printed the photographs featured in the exhibition.

The scholarship in this book builds on the work of my colleagues in American landscape history, and I am grateful to them for their assistance and encouragement, which came in many forms. None have been more gracious than Reuben M. Rainey and Daniel J. Nadenicek, who read an early version of the manuscript, communicating enthusiasm for it and also making important suggestions for revisions. Charles C. McLaughlin, who died before the book was completed, also read an early version and shared ideas about how to enrich it.

I am also grateful to Robert E. Grese for his thoughtful and encouraging comments on Jens Jensen and for his help with several illustrations; Keith N. Morgan for his exacting suggestions regarding Charles Platt; David C. Streatfield for his generous suggestions about the California chapters; Diane Kostial McGuire, Gail Griffin, and Linda Lott for encouragement and ideas on my chapters on Beatrix Farrand and Dumbarton Oaks; Valencia Libby, Margaret Lidz, and Denise Magnani for their help with material on Marian Coffin, H. F. du Pont, and Winterthur; John Miller for his comments on the Jensen, Manning, Stan Hywet Hall, and Ford House chapters; and Lance M. Neckar, who has been an ongoing source of insight into Manning. Elizabeth Rogers, who offered copious comments on the introduction and prologue, has also been a source of insight and support throughout. I am particularly indebted to Kellam and Peggy de Forest for sharing information about the work of Kellam's father, Lockwood de Forest, over several trips to California, and for loaning important images of the landscape architect's work.

Many colleagues provided a wide range of help over the years. I am grateful to Mac Griswold for sharing research and perspective gained from her own work; to Patricia O'Donnell, Denise Otis, Melanie Simo, and Catherine Howett for their support and friendship; and to those closer to home, including Clark Dougan, senior editor at UMass Press, and Gerald McFarland, professor of history at UMass, who suggested books that proved critical to certain ideas I have explored here; Dean Cardasis, professor of landscape architecture at UMass, and my associates at Smith College, Nina Antonetti, and Ann Leone.

I am also grateful to Alan Ward for the use of his photographs, to Patrick Chassé for loaning archival images of Maine, to William Frederick Peters for his photographs and plans of the California work; to Townsend Ludington for the use of his uncle's photographs, and to Nancy Angell Streeter for use of images of Ellen Shipman. I thank Rona Schneider for locating a Platt print, and members of the Platt family for the use of important Platt images; Susan Tamulevich for her help with an important Dumbarton Oaks image, and Charles E. Beveridge and Ethan Carr, who assisted in locating an Olmsted plan.

The stewards of the public landscapes featured in this book were also generous, providing access to archives, allowing photography on the grounds, reading chapter drafts, and hunting for missing bits of information and images, without which these stories would have been incomplete. For all these efforts, I thank Lucy Ireland Weller and William Tepley at Gwinn; John Franklin Miller and Don Snodgrass at Edsel and Eleanor Ford House; Mark Heppner, Gary Hartman, Hank Lynch, and the late Carl Ruprecht at Stan Hywet Hall; Gail Griffin and Linda Lott at Dumbarton Oaks; the late Dr. Warren Austin and Gail Jansen at Val Verde; Chris Strand, Margaret Lidz, Denise Magnani, and Thomas Buchter at Winterthur; Steve McMahon, Gordon Clark, and Will Garrison at Naumkeag.

I am indebted to the many archivists who made research for this book possible, including Flora Nyland of SUNY CESF, who is also a wonderful friend; Waverly Lowell and Miranda Hambro at the Environmental Design Archives, University of California, Berkeley; Alix

Reiskind of the Frances Loeb Library, Harvard Graduate School of Design; Malgosia Myc and Karen L. Jania of the Bentley Historical Library, University of Michigan; Janet Parks at Avery Library, Columbia University; Megan Callewaert and Josephine Shea of Ford House; Heather Clewell and Margaret Lidz at Winterthur; Bruce Greer, Mark Heppner, and Margaret Tramontine at Stan Hywet Hall; Martha Mayo at Lowell Center for History, UMass Lowell; Linda Lott and James Carder at Dumbarton Oaks; Tonia Sutherland, Danielle Kovacs, and Mike Milewksi of UMass Amherst; and Tanya Zanish-Belcher, Melissa Gottwald, and William Grundmann at Iowa State University. I also thank Carol Whittaker of The Henry Ford; Jane Katherine Bogden of Spanierman Gallery; Michael T. Steiber of The Morton Arboretum; Lisa Gensel at University of Delaware; and Jane Walsh-Brown at The Prairie Club Archives; special thanks to Julia Bachrach, Chicago Park District.

One of the very first people to read a sample of this manuscript was my friend and LALH author Susan L. Klaus, who urged me to keep going. Others along the way who read and commented helpfully include Julia Gaviria, Joel Ray, and Jane Roy Brown, director of education at LALH. I was fortunate to have as copy editor Katherine D. Scheuer, retired managing editor of Cornell University Press, and, in the last stages, to have the help of the ingenious Mary Bellino, who took the notes and bibliography in hand with the strength of Athena. My son Max Karson, a writer in his own right, helped input editorial revisions.

The design of this book is the work of Jonathan Lippincott, whose talent is apparent on every page of it. I am deeply grateful to him for his patience and sophistication, for everything he did to make the pictures and the words come together with such finesse. Sally Nichols, associate production manager of the University of Massachusetts Press, helped the production along in a thousand ways, with patience and good cheer. Bruce Wilcox, director of the Press and a man of great optimism, provided unwavering support while the manuscript edged toward completion. At every stage of the writing of this book, I was blessed with the exacting perspective of Carol Betsch, a brilliant editor as well as photographer.

In assembling the 483 illustrations, I had the assistance and visual acumen of Carol and the resourcefulness, friendship, and determination of Jane Roy Brown. Neil Brigham, LALH office manager, provided systems for scanning and cataloging images, and much needed humor during this process. I am also grateful to the director of our Warren H. Manning research project, Reid Bertone-Johnson, who took the lead in procuring the Manning images and also helped with graphic changes to the plans; Mackenzie Greer, our intern from the UMass master's program in Landscape Architecture and Regional Planning, who oversaw many aspects of the art log; and Tanya Cushman, who has worn several hats at LALH over the years, including, for this book, research assistant.

I am deeply grateful for the intensely beneficent presences of family and friends over the past decade and a half that I have been working on this project, especially the past year, which has been a particularly challenging one: my parents, Jean and Robert Robinson; my children, Max Karson, Ethan Karson, and Ethan's wife, Tara Robinson; several close friends, especially Marcia Howard and Neil Brigham, Kayla Werlin and Wayne Abercrombie, and Barbara Shear; the understanding staff and trustees of LALH; and others, too, who have helped me through a time of silence and effort, particularly Patricia Gorman-Bishop and Josh Schumer. I owe a particular debt to Walter M. Spink, my professor of art history at the University of Michigan, who encouraged me to explore uncharted territory.

In a very tangible sense, the authorship of this book belongs to Carol Betsch as well as to me. Carol was there from its inception, thinking about the landscapes, taking the luminous photographs, helping decide how to use these images, and then how to trim and tuck and expand the ideas until they all fit together, with precision and grace. All of this occurred in the context of a new life together, laced with a sense of exploration and excitement, grounded in respect and love. It is to her that I dedicate this book.

INDEX

Page references to illustrations are given in italics.

abstraction in landscape design, 263, 267; in Coffin's work, 191, 206, 215; in de Forest's work, 278, 279, 283, 300, 303–4; in Farrand's work, 184; at Ford House, 243, 255, 257, 260; indigenous plantings used in, 324; in Platt's work, 64; in Steele's work, xxiii, 322–24, 334–35; trees used in, 324, 345. *See also* Exposition des Arts Décoratifs et Industriels Modernes

Académie Julian (Paris), 49

Acquistapace, Joe, 384n21

Adams, Charles Gibbs, 289

Adams, Herbert, 52, 366n24

Addams, Jane, influence on Jensen, 227

Addison, Joseph, on reform in taste, 5

Adler, David, 373n32

Aetna Life and Casualty Insurance Company (Hartford, Conn.), 124, *125*, 357

agrarian values, xv, 9, 52; automobile and, 239

Akron Garden Club, 113

Akron Metropolitan District Commission, 111

Akron (Ohio), 110; industrialization of, 369n1; park system in, 111–12; rubber industry in, 89; Stan Hywet acreage bequeathed to, 112–13. *See also* Stan Hywet Hall

Albany (N.Y.), 311

Aldred, J. E. *See* Ormston

Alexander, Kenneth D., 231

Alger, Russell A., Jr. *See* Moorings, The

Algonquin Round Table, 348

Alhambra (Granada, Spain), 274, 316

allées: in Coffin's work, 187, 190; in de Forest's work, 279; at Dumbarton Oaks, 162–64, *164*, 168; at Faulkner Farm, 55; at Gwinn, 79, *80*, *87*, 87; at Naumkeag, *330*, 337, *338*; at Stan Hywet, 95, 97, *97*, *98*, *99*, 104, *104*, 345; in Steele's work, 314, *315*; at Val Verde, 290, *293*, 298

Allen, Atkinson, 313–14; Steele design for (Rochester, N.Y.), 313–15, *315*, *316*

Allen, Charlotte Whitney, friendship with Steele, 314, 343

Allen, Ethan, estate of (North Andover, Mass.), 315–17, *316*, *317*, 319

American Architect and Building News, 14

American Civic Association, 36, 380n19

American Country Homes and Their Gardens (Baker), 56

American Country House, The (Aslet), xiv

American Country House, The (Moss), xiv

American Country Houses of To-Day (Howe), xvi, 80, 243

American Eagle (ship), 195

American Estates and Gardens (Ferree), xvi, 56, 390n1

American Forestry Association, 25

American Gardens (Lowell), 56, 141, 360n21, 368n16

American Home, 277

American Park and Outdoor Association, 36, 229

American Picturesque. *See* Picturesque: American

American Renaissance, xix, 52–53, 134. *See also* World's Columbian Exposition

American Society of Landscape Architects (ASLA), 36; charter members of, xvii, 17, 139, 361n45, 374n20; Fellows at, 189; founding of, xiv, xvii; Jensen and, 236, 381–82n53; Manning as president of, 42, 110; Steele library bequeathed to, 390n66; women in, xiv, xvii, 139, 184

Ames family, 16

amphitheaters, *164*, 323–24, *324*, 337, 345; natural, 62, 69, 97

Ancrum House (Gerry; Delhi, N.Y.), 320–21, *320, 321*, 389n49

Anderson, Isabel and Larz. *See* Weld

Anderson, Judith, 307, 387n31

antiques: Mabel Choate as collector, xxiii, 126; Robert Weeks de Forest as collector, 270; at Dumbarton Oaks, 162, 174; H. F. du Pont as collector, 206–7, 379n41. *See also* Ludington, Wright S.: as art collector; Val Verde

Architect and the American Country House, The (Hewitt), xiv

architects: landscape architects and, xvi, xix, 17, 19, 40, 47, 60, 102, 138; Coffin and Scheiner, 186, 188, 191, 193; Farrand and Cram, 143–44, 157; Farrand and (Lawrence) White, 157, 172, Jensen and Wright, 226, 232, 381n49, Manning and Platt, 60, 62–63, 79; Manning and Schneider, 94, 95, 102, 104, 106, Steele and Cram, 243, 320–22, 340, 356; role in country estate design, 17, 23, 91–92. *See also specific individuals*

Architectural League of New York, 192

Architectural Record, xviii, xix, 56, 80, 141, 366n25

Architectural Review, 232, 287

Architecture, 80

architecture: Arts and Crafts, 143; classical styles of, xxii, 23, 51, 53, 58; English styles of, 92, 124, 243, 262, 321; landscape elements in relation to, xiv, xx, xxii, 17, 18, 20, 47, 142–43; progressive values in, 53, 82; Manning on, 42; regional landscape as inspiration for, 232–33; Spanish Colonial Revivial, 273–74, 276; Steele's interest in, 312; use of term, 359n13; Van Rensselaer on, 14. *See also* Platt, Charles A.; *specific sites*

Arnold Arboretum (Jamaica Plain, Mass.): du Pont as supporter of, 378n15; as horticultural training site, 135, 183, 198; indigenous species at, 15, *15*; Manning and, 26. *See also* Sargent, Charles Sprague

Art and Craft of Garden Making, The (Mawson), xix, 58

Art Deco, 174, 322–23, 346, 352

Art in Our Time (radio broadcast), 241, 260

Art of Landscape Architecture, The (Parsons), xx–xxi

Art Out-of-Doors (Van Rensselaer), 14, 15, 359–60n14

Arts and Crafts: American enthusiasm for, xix, 23; Coffin and, 184, 185; and Cornish, N.H., 119, 171; Cram and, 143; de Forest and, 277; at Dumbarton Oaks, xxii, 164–65, 176; Ford House and, 243, 382n62; formal/classical styles mixed with, xxii, 53; formal/informal combined in, 23; Goodhue and, 286; Jekyll and, xix; Jensen and, 231; local materials emphasized in, 106, 143; plantings of, 171; Shipman and, 120, 124, 125; in Southern California, 275; at Stan Hywet, 90, 97, 106; Steele and, 311

Art Students League, 48

Arzner, Dorothy, 385n50

Aslet, Clive, xiv

Aspet (Saint-Gaudens; Cornish, N.H.), *50*, 52, *52*, 360n21

Associated Artists, 270, 384n5

Atlantic Monthly, 226

Austin, Warren R., 307. *See also* Val Verde

automobile, 184, 237–38, 239

axial design: bent/broken, 267, 320, 323–24, 337, 346, 390n62; cross-axial plans, xix, 3, *4*, 154–57, 191, 209–11; importance of, in Steele's work, 319, 320, 323–24, 337, 345–46, 346, 390n62. *See also* Beaux-Arts design

Babson, Henry, 226; house of (Riverside, Ill.), *226*

Backus, Standish and Dorothy, estate of (Grosse Pointe Shores, Mich.), 249, 321–22, *321, 322*, 389n49

Baile, Margaret H., 174

Bailey, Liberty Hyde: as editor of *Country Life*, xviii–xix; on stewardship of nature, xi; on World's Columbian Exposition, 29. *See also Cyclopedia of American Horticulture*

Baker, Anne, 174

Baker, John Cordis, 56

Ballard, Charles T., estate of (Glenview, Ky.), 185–86, *187*

Balmori, Diana, 143, 376n27

Bar Harbor (Me.), xv, 133, 137, 179, 373n2

Bar Harbor Record, 117

Barnard College (New York, N.Y.), 328

Barnes, Demas, 149

Barnes, Mildred. *See* Bliss, Mildred Barnes

Barr, Alfred H., 323

Barrett, Nathan Franklin, xxiii, 17, 327, 329, 360n21, 361n45, 374n20, 390n4. *See also* Naumkeag

Barry, Patrick, 309

Bassick, Edgar W., *See* Oaks, The (Bridgeport, Conn.)

Bates, William A., 138

Bauhaus design, xiv, 243

Baxter, Sylvester, 387n23

Bayberryland (Sabin; Shinnecock Hills, N.Y.), 190, *190*

Beall, Ninian, 150

Beals, Jessie Tarbox, 123, 189; photograph by, *121*

Beatrix Farrand Society, 377n65

Beauport (Gloucester, Mass.), 206

Beautiful, the, 12

Beautiful Gardens in America (Shelton), 58

Beautifying Country Homes (Weidenmann), xix

Beaux-Arts design, xvi, xix; adaptability to Southern California plants, 274; alignment in, 324; in American architecture, xvi; American integration of, xxi–xxii, 17–18, 23, 273–75; Croly and, 366n25; cultural authority through manipulation of, 23; Jensen critical of, 227; Manning's opposition to, 30; planning style in, 30, 55, 227; Seiberlings and, 92; and social control, 30; Steele's use of, 249; at World's Columbian Exposition, xxii, 17–18, 28

bedding out, 14. *See also* gardenesque; "Shaw's Garden"; Victorian design

Bedford (N.Y.), xx–xxi

Beecher, Janet, 218

Behrens, Peter, 382n62

Bellefontaine (Lenox, Mass.), 327, 374n23, 390n1

Belloc, Hilaire, 193

Belmont (Mass.), 18

Beloochistan Rug Weaving Company (India), 93

Belvedere (Hudson, N.Y.), 181

Berenson, Bernard, 150, 273

Bergson, Henri, 330

Berkshire Playhouse, 348

Berkshire Theatre Festival, 392n57

Berkshires, the (Mass.), 327, 328

Berry, Walter, 183

Beveridge, Charles E., 10, 226, 361n24

B. F. Goodrich Company, 89

Bidermann, Evelina and Jacques, 196

billboards, 237, 382n66

Billerica, 36, 364n55

Billerica (Mass.), 39, *41*, 111

Billerica Garden Suburb (Mass.), 42, *42*

Billerica Improvement Association, 42

Biltmore Estate (G. W. Vanderbilt, Asheville, N.C.), *19, 20*; approach road, 27, *30*; arboretum at, 30, 135; Beaux-Arts style of, xvi, 92; contrasted to World's Columbian Exposition, 20; as country place model, 20; entrance drive, 102; Farrand's visit to, 135–36; forest plantings, 20, 136; genius loci at, 30; Hunt's architectural design of, 19–20; hybrid design style of, 19–20, *20*; Henry James on, 20; landscape plan, *20*; as largest American house, 327; Manning–Olmsted collaboration on, 27, 30, *30*; Olmsted's purposes at, xviii, 19, 30; planning needs for, xvii; scale of, 19, 30; scientific forestry at, 30

biological aesthetics, 228

Birkenhead Park (Liverpool, Eng.), 10

Birmingham (Ala.), 43–44, 361n45

Bissell, Frank, 378n20

Bliss, Anna Dorinda Blaksley Barnes, 137, 149, 151, 176, 385n56

Bliss, Mildred Barnes, xxii, 137, *177*; aesthetic sense of, 151; as art collector, 149–50, 177; Casa Dorinda inherited by, 176; Farrand's landscape scheme proposed to, 152–53; as New Woman, 359–60n14; overseas residence of, 172–74, 176; relationship with Farrand, 152–53, 159, 172–74, 176, 178; residence at Dumbarton Oaks, 176–77; WWI relief efforts of, 150. *See also* Dumbarton Oaks

Bliss, Robert, 149–50, 172, 176–77, *177. See also* Dumbarton Oaks

Bliss, William Henry, 149

Blossom Hill (Wood; Wawa, Pa.), 313, *314*

Blount, Henry Fitch and Lucretia, 150

Blum & Delbridge, 72

Boardman, Albert, estate of (Southampton, N.Y.), 186

Bohnard & Parsson, 368n24, 369n48

Bois-des-Fossés (France), 195

Bok, Mary, 323

Book of Landscape-Gardening (Simonds), 237

Boston Metropolitan Parks, 27–28, 360n15

botanical expeditions, 12, 15, 26

botanizing, 12–13; Manning and, 26, du Pont and, 197; Jensen and, 228

Bowditch, Ernest W., 138, 390n1

Boyland II (Santa Barbara, Calif.), 386n18

Boyle, Richard, 5

Brancusi, Constantin, 334

Brasher, Julia, 270

Brinkerhoff, A. F., 365n83

Bromfield, Reginald, 198

Brooke, Frederick H., 152, 157

Brookline (Mass.), 15–16

Brook Place (Plainfield, N.H.), 124, 171

Brown, Jane Roy, 165, 382n64

Brown, John George, 365n8

Brown, Lancelot "Capability," 198

Brown, Martha Brookes. *See* Hutcheson, Martha Brookes

Browne, Herbert, 54

Brush, George de Forest, 52

Bryant, William Cullen, 4, 47

Bryce, Lloyd Stephen, 191

Bullard, Elizabeth, xvii, 184

Bullard, Helen, 36, 365n83

Bullard, Roger H., 124

Bullitt, William Marshall, 378n23. *See also* Oxmoor

Bunker, Dennis, 49, 52, 366n22

Bunker, Edith Hardy, 52, 58

Burke, E. S., estate of (Chagrin Falls, Ohio), *38*

Burnap, George, 151, 152, 375n9. *See also* Dumbarton Oaks

Burnett, Frances Hodgson, 106

Burnham, Daniel Hudson, 28, 30, 363n17

Burnham & Bennett, 227

Burroughs, John, 382n8

Byne, Arthur and Mildred Stapley, 274

Cadwalader, John Lambert, 134

Calder, Alexander, 314

Caldwell, Alfred, 233

California, Southern: Arts and Crafts in, 275; exoticism and, 383–84nn1–2; gardenesque in, 13–14; post-WWII garden preferences in, 385–86n61. *See also* de Forest, Lockwood

California Institute of Technology, 375n40

Cambridge School of Architecture and Landscape Architecture, 120, 372–73n19

Camden (Me.) Public Library Amphitheater, 323–24, *324*, 337, 345, 357, 390n62. *See also* Steele, Fletcher

Candler, Duncan, 237

Cantor, Jay, 206

Caparn, Harold A., 362n47

capitalism, xvi, 52, 359n8

Carr, Clyde M., estate of (Lake Forest, Ill.) 36, *38*

Carrère & Hastings, xix, 146, 327, 366n25, 368n16, 374n23, 390n1

Casa del Herrero (Steedman; Montecito, Calif.), 273–74, 384n21

Casa Dorinda (Barnes; Montecito, Calif.), 151, 176, 274, 375n5

Cascieri, Archangelo, 331

Caumsett (Field; Long Island, N.Y.), 191

Cautley, Marjorie Sewell, 365n83, 372n10

Cave Hill Cemetery (Louisville, Ky.), 4

Cavendish, Virginia, 325

Cavendish, William Spencer, 12

cemeteries, "rural," xviii, 4, *5*, 6–7, 16, 360n6. *See also* Graceland Cemetery

Central Park (New York, N.Y.), xiii, xvii, xx, 8, *9*, 47, 182, 361nn17, 20

Century Association (New York, N.Y.), 47

Century Magazine, 14

Century of Progress Exposition (Chicago; 1933)

Champney, James Wells, 365n8

Chandler, Abial, 26

Chandler, Joseph, 182

Chase, William Merritt, 48

Chatsworth (Derbyshire, Eng.), 12, 361n31

Cheney, John, 47, 48

Cheney, Mary Elizabeth, 47

Cheney, Seth Wells, 47, 48

Cheney Block (Hartford, Conn.), 48

Cherokee Park (Louisville, Ky.), *28*

Chestertown House (du Pont; Southampton, N.Y.), 192, *192*, 206–7

Chesterwood (French; Stockbridge, Mass.), 328, 360n21, 366n21, 390n7

Chestnut Hill (Pa.), 218–19

Chicago (Ill.), 28, 30; Beaux-Arts style in, 227; Jensen establishes private business in, 224; naturalistic plantings in, 224–25, *225*, 357; park system in, 227–29, 381n34

Chicago Architectural Club, 23

Chicago Art Institute, 251

Chicago Playground Association, 381n36

Child, Stephen, 275; Gould estate, *275*

Children of Flanders Rescue Committee, 150

China: Mabel Choate's notes on, 391–92n44; influence on Farrand, 145; influence on Steele, 335, 340–43, 352

Chinese features, 145, 337–43

Choate, Caroline Sterling, 189, 328

Choate, George, 329–30

Choate, Joseph Hodges, xxiii, 17, 327–28

Choate, Josephine, 329, *329*

Choate, Mabel, *329*, *330*, *352*; Asian tours of, 337–40, 391–92n44; as Barnard trustee, 328; death of, 347, 352; education of, 328; European tours of, 337; guestbook kept by, 346–48; as Naumkeag collaborator, xxiii, 335–37, *345*, 351–52; on Naumkeag construction, 328; as New Woman, xxiii, 359–60n14; Steele first meets, 325; travels with GCA, 335–37; trial plantings of, 337; Washington residence of, 218; as Winterthur visitor, 216. *See also* Naumkeag

Choate, Ruluff, 329

Christy, Steven, 380–81n31

Church, Benjamin, 182, 184

Church, Frederic Edwin, 270, 366n21, 384n3

Church, John Barker, IV, 181

Church, Thomas, 283

Churchill, Winston (novelist), 52, 366n24

City Beautiful projects, 30, 44, 227, 287

City Club, 380n13

Clapp, Willard M., estate of (Cleveland Heights, Ohio), 372n59

Clark, Agnes Selkirk, 347, 373n25, 389n45

Clark, Dana B., 275

Clark, Walter, 392n57

Clayton (Frick; Roslyn Harbor, N.Y.), 191–92, *191*, *192*

Clearing, The (Ellison Bay, Wisc.), 263

Cleveland, Horace William Shaler: design philosophy of, 225–26; Highland Park (Ill.) laid out by, 34; landscape architecture associated with, xix; "landscape architecture" first used as term by, xvii; linked green spaces promoted by, 360n15; Minneapolis park system, 7, 32; naturalist sensibilities of, 6–7; writings of, 226

Cleveland (Ohio): regional park system in, 111; women gardeners in, 85. *See also* Gwinn

Cleveland-Cliffs Iron Company, xvi, 61–62, 83, 368n4

Cleveland Iron Mining Company, 61

client collaboration, xvii, xviii, 131; at Dumbarton Oaks, 152–53, 159, 172–74; at Ford House, 242–43, 245–46; at Naumkeag, 330–31, 335–37; at Straight estate, 145; at Val Verde, 294; at Walden, 34–35

client personality: as design determinant, xxi, 17, 131; in Coffin's work, 189; genius loci and, xxii; in Steele's work, 315, 320, 340

Cliff Dwellers, 380n13

Codman, Henry Sargent: death of, 29, 362n10; as Olmstedian, xix; partnership with Olmsted, xxii, 28–29, 362n10; as World's Columbian Exposition consultant, 28–29; World's Columbian Exposition plan by, xxii, 17–18; writings of, 362n47

Codman, Ogden, Jr., 140, 191

Coffin, Alice Church, 181, 182

Coffin, Julian Ravenal, 181

Coffin, Marian Cruger, xxii, 181–94, *182*, *194*; as ASLA Fellow, 189; as ASLA member, 184; awards received by, 192; birth of, 181; business expansions of, 186–87, 193; career decision of, 182; childhood of, 181–82; circular forms used by, 185–86, 187; color schemes of, 184–85; country estate of, 193; design philosophy of, 183–84, 219–21, 322; early career of, 184–86; education of, 182–84; European tours of, 183, 185; experimental projects, 190–91; Farrand and, 378n36; genius loci and, 126, 219–21; as horsewoman, 181; hospitalization of, 193; marketing strategies of, 188–89; at Naumkeag, 189, 330, 347; as New Woman, 359n14; New York office of, 186–87, 193; fame of, 189, 218; personal style of, 193; plantings of, 171; professional concerns of, 189; progressive sensibilities of, 219; public work overlooked, 357; relationship with clients, 182, 189, 192, 201–3, 218–19; relocation to New Haven, 193; Scheiner and, 377n22; significance of, 221; spatial definition by, 184; staff of, 186–87; Steele and, 347; as Winterthur adviser, 192; Winterthur landscape redesign, 208–16, 219–21; on women in landscape architecture, 117–18; writings of, 185, 188–89

Coffin, Marian Cruger, commissions: Ballard estate (Glenview, Ky.), 185–86, *187*; Bayberryland (Shinnecock Hills, N.Y.), 190, *190*; Chestertown House (Southampton, N.Y.), 192, *192*; Clayton (Roslyn Hills, N.Y.), 191–92, *191*, *192*; Delaware State College, 187–88, *189*; Farnum estate (Norfolk, Conn.), 186, *187*; Gibraltar (Wilmington, Del.), 186, *188*; Hillwood (Wheatley Hills, N.Y.), 190, *191*; The Oaks (Bridgeport, Conn.), 192, *193*; Oxmoor (Glenview, Ky.), 185, *186*; Sprague estate (Flushing, N.Y.), 184–85, *185*; Wing estate (Millbrook, N.Y.), 192, *193*. *See also* Winterthur

Colonial Revival style, xiv, 57, 119, 120, 122, 124, 171, 207, 329, 351

Colony Club (New York, N.Y.), 218

color theory, 311, 317–18

Colt, Mrs. Samuel G., estate of, 145

Colwell, Elizabeth F., 186, 378n23

Combs, Clarence, 365n83

Commission on Country Life, xviii

Community Days, in work of Manning, 30, 42

company towns, xviii, 27, *33*, 40, 42, *42*, 61, 93–94, 311, 365n81, 387n24

composition in landscape design: Beaux-Arts influence on, 183, 184; Coffin on, 181, 219–21; in Coffin's work, 184, 189–90, 209, 211; during country place era, xxi–xxii; de Forest on, 281–83, 385n49; in de Forest's work, 278, 279, 283; Farrand on, 133, 135, 141–42; in Farrand's work, 154, 168, 170, 184, 189–90; Hubbard and Kimbell on, xxi; in Jensen's work, 228, 230, 234, 235; in Manning's work, 31, 39, 70, 77, 87, 102; in Olmsted's work, 11, 12, 30; planting design as element of, xvii, 30, 31, 87, 168, 170, 181, 184, 199, 318; Platt on, 54; in Platt's work, 57, 58, 64, 87; in Shipman's work, 119, 120, 122; Steele on, 323, 325, 346; in Steele's work, 334–35, 351; Van Rensselaer on, 14–15; at Winterthur formal gardens, 200. *See also individual projects*

Compton Wynates (Warwickshire, Eng.), 92

Conan, Michel, 154

Connecticut Land Company, 61, 309

Connecticut River valley, 10, *10*

conservation, xviii, 18, 26; H. W. S. Cleveland and, 226; Coffin and, 189; *Garden and Forest* and, 362n47; Jensen and, 227, 230, 231, 380n3, 381n36; Fords and, 263; Manning and, 26, 36, 111–12, 227, 364n55; H. McFarland and, 33; Steele and, 353. *See also* Trustees of Reservations, The

Constantia (Meeker; Montecito, Calif.), 279, *279*

Contemporary Landscape Architecture and Its Sources (exhibition; 1936), 325

Cook, Wilbur D., Jr., 365n83

Cook County Forest Preserve, 230

Coonley, Avery, 226, 381n49

Cooper, James Fenimore, II. *See* Fynmere

Cope & Stewardson, xix

Copeland, Robert Morris, xix, 7, 360n15

Cornell University, 372n10

Cornish (N.H.), 50–53, *50, 51, 52, 53*, 58, 59, 60, 62, 79, 119, 122, 171, 366nn14, 21, 22, 24, 25

Corrodi, Hermann, 270

Cortissoz, Royal, 59–60, 80

Cotter, E. J., 75

Council, Lucille, 275, 373n25, 384–85n26, 385n50

country estates: agrarian myth and, xv, 52; architectural styles of, xvi, 55–56, 92, 287; designed by artists, 366n21; and conservation, demographic influences on, xv, xvi, 355; functions of, xv; genius loci in, xxi–xxii; impact of WWI on, 111; role of landscape architect at, xvi–xvii; landscape designs for, xiv–xv, xx; as patriotic, 92; and historic preservation, 88; progressive values and, 53; as refuges, xv, 31, 114, 192, 227; scholarship on, xvi; siting of, xv; size reduction of, 112–13; as status symbols, xv

Country Life: A Handbook of Agriculture and Landscape Gardening (Copeland), xix

Country Life in America: Bailey as editor of, xviii–xix; Coffin articles in, 184, 188; de Forest projects in, 385n43; El Fureidis reviewed in, 274; establishment of, 362n47; Gwinn reviewed in, 80–83; Italianate examples in, 141; Jensen projects in, 231; Manning

articles in, 37, 39, 91, 139; Miller articles in, 58; Naumkeag reviewed in, 327; Platt projects in, 56; Steele articles in, 317

country life movement, xv, xviii–xix

country place era, American, x, xi; defined, ix, xiv; economic/social factors of, xiii, xv–xvi; marginalization of, xiv; scholarship on, xiv–xv

Cowles, Henry C., 228, 381n36

Cox, Kenyon, 52

Cram, Ralph Adams: as Ancrum House architect, 320–21; Arts and Crafts aspect of, 143; as Backus estate architect, 321–22; bohemian network behind, 294; collaboration with Goodhue, 386n12; estate of (Sudbury Center, Mass.), 322, *322*; Farrand's disagreement with, 157; Goodhue and, 286, 287; marriage of, 386n10; on Platt, 47, 55–56; Steele and, 320–21, 322, 389n50

Cramer, Ambrose C., 279

Crane, Mrs. Zenas, 145

Crawford, Francis Marion, 134

Crighton, Robert, 330, 391n21

Crile, G. W., estate of (Cleveland, Ohio), *38*

Croly, David Goodman, 53

Croly, Herbert: as architectural critic, 53, 366n25, 387n20; on El Fureidis, 287; estate of (Cornish, N.H.), 53, 62; on Gwinn, 80; influence of, 145; Platt supported by, 53, 60; Shipman and, 119; writings of, 145, 366n25

Croly, Jane Cunningham, 53

Croly, Louise, 62, 119

Cross & Cross, 190

Crosswicks (Newbold; Jenkintown, N.Y.), 139–40, *139, 140*

Crowninshield, Francis (editor of *Vanity Fair*), 340, 348

Crowninshield, Francis (brother-in-law of H. F. du Pont), 183, 197, 348

Crystal Palace (London), 12, 28

Cukor, George, 385n50

Cunningham, Mary P., 372n11, 373n25, 389n45

Custom of the Country, The (Wharton), 149

Cuyahoga Valley (Ohio), 97, 112

Cyclopedia of American Horticulture (ed. Bailey), 37, 42, 100

Daniels, Alanson L. *See* Old Farms

Dartington Hall (Devonshire, Eng.), 375n42

Darwin, Erasmus, 12

Dater, Henry, Jr., 287, 289

Daughters of the American Revolution, 150

Davidson, Rebecca Warren, 118, 366n14, 367n44

Davis, Alexander Jackson, 6, 7

Dawson, Jackson (plant propagator), 26

Day, Frank Miles, xix, 187

Dearborn, Henry A. S., 4, 5

Decoration of Houses, The (Wharton), 140

DeForest, Alling, at Firestone Park, 370–71n28

de Forest, Elizabeth, 276, 277, 280–81, 300, 385n51

de Forest, Emily, 270

de Forest, Henry Wheeler, 270

De Forest, Jesse, 269–70

de Forest, Lockwood, II, 269–70, 271

de Forest, Lockwood, Jr., xxii–xxiii, 176, 269–83; abstraction in design work of, 278, 279, 283, 300, 303–4; ancestral history, 269–70; architectonic approach of, 283; birth of, 270; death of, 283, 307; design philosophy of, 279–80, 281, 282–83, 323; education of, 270–73, 271; European tour of, 271–73, 285, 294; Farrand and, 281, 385n56; framed views of, 279; garden space as redefined by, 282–83; influence of, 283; Italy scrapbook of, 271–73, 272, 273; marriage of, 276; on-site decision-making by, 279; personality/interests of, 276, 276; private practice established by, 271; as Santa Barbara Museum of Art founder, 388n47; self-designed home of, 277–78, 277, 278; three-dimensionality in works of, 323; writings of, 280–83; WWII volunteer work of, 388n43

de Forest, Lockwood, Jr., commissions: Constantia (Montecito, Calif.), 279, 279; Hope Ranch (Santa Barbara, Calif.), 279–80, 280; Lotusland (Montecito, Calif.), 282, 307; Morton estate (Montecito, Calif.), 282–83, 282, 283; Sandyland Cove projects, 279. See also Val Verde

de Forest, Meta, 269–70, 271

de Forest, Robert Weeks, 270, 379n42

Delano, William Adams, 146

Delano & Aldrich, 146

Delaware State College, 187–88, 189

Dercum & Beer, 368n24, 369n48

Derrick, Robert O., 240, 262, 382n65

Design in the Little Garden (Steele), 318

Design on the Land (Newton), x, 356–57

Des Plaines River (Ill.), 226

Detroit Industry (fresco cycle; Rivera), 241

Detroit Institute of Arts, 241

Dewing, Maria Oakey, 52

Dewing, Thomas Wilmer, 52, 59; portrait of Platt, 48

Dexter, Charles O., 201

Diamond Rubber Company, 89, 93

Días Felicitas (Santa Barbara, Calif.), xxii. See also Val Verde

Dickinson, William. See Hope Ranch

Dillman, Hugh and Anna. See Rose Terrace

Dingleton House (Cornish, N.H.), 366n24

Dodge House (Los Angeles, Calif.), 365n83

Dodson, Joseph H., 382n58

Dolobran (Griscom; Haverford, Pa.), 33, 34, 91, 139

Donnelly & Ricci, 93

Dorman, Caroline, 126, 373n33

Douglas Park (Chicago, Ill.), 230

Douglass, Frederick, 28

Downing, A. J., xxii, 3; achievements of, 8; death of, 8; design philosophy of, 4–6, 6, 11; gardenesque methods of, xix; on landscape architecture and morality, xviii; partnership with Vaux, 7–8; planting methods of, 12; publications of, 7–8; urban parks proposed by, 4–5

Downing, Charles, 26

Dropmore (Buckinghamshire, Eng.), 203

Drumthwacket (Princeton, N.J.), 142

Duke Gardens (Durham, N.C.), 124–25, 125, 357

Dumbarton Oaks (Bliss; Washington, D.C.), xxii, 143, 149–79; American influences on, 154; "amusements," 165; architect–landscape architect collaboration, 375–76n19; art museum at, 150, 376n29; Arts and Crafts influences, 164–65, 176; Beech Terrace, 159, 160; Blisses' residence at, 176–77; Box Terrace, 159, 170, 170, 376n23; Box Walk, 153, 169, 170; Charles Burnap at, 151, 152; Cherry Hill, 165, 166; client–landscape architect collaboration, 159, 172–74; Copse, 154, 160–62, 162, 376n29; Crabapple Hill, 165; cutting gardens, 164–65, 170; donated to Harvard, 147, 177; Ellipse, 165–68, 168, 169, 170; existing conditions at, 150–53, 151, 152, 154, 172; Farrand as landscape adviser for, 177–78; Farrand's proposed landscape design, 152–53; Farrand's site inspections at, 150–52; Forsythia Dell, 165; Fountain Terrace, 162, 163; French influence on, 376n47; gardens plan, 154; genius loci at, 154, 168; Green Garden, 159, 160, 177, 376n25; herbaceous borders, 162, 164, 165, 168, 177; Herb Garden Terrace, 168, 170; historic role of, 376n56; house of, 150, 151, 161; house renovation, 152, 157; impact of Depression on, 177; informal plantings, 165; interior design of, 176; Italian influence on, 153–57; kitchen garden, 164, 168, 170; landscape plan of, 151; lawns, 159–62; Lilac Circle, 164, 164; Lover's Lane pool, 162, 164; Mélisande's Allée, 162–64, 164, 168; new buildings proposed for, 172; North Vista, 159–62, 160, 161, 376n26; orchards, 170; ornaments, 172, 173, 174, 174, 175, 376n25; outdoor room, 376n27; ownership history, 150; paths, 152–53, 155, 156; Pebble Garden, 377n61; planting influences, 159, 164, 168–71; planting palette, 376n21; pools, 162, 164, 165, 171, 172; Rose Garden, 157–59, 157, 158, 168, 170, 174, 174, 175, 376n20; spatial alternatives for, 153–54; spatial definition, 170; stairways, 162; Star Terrace, 159; swimming pool, 167; terraces, 151, 152–53, 159; Terrior Column, 172, 173; view, 153, 154, 157, 159, 170, 171, 178; wild garden, 153, 171–72, 171, 177

Dumbarton Oaks Park, 177

Dunes Memorial Fountain, 224

du Pont, Henry Algernon, 182, 196–97, 203, 207, 379n36

du Pont, Henry Francis, xxii, 118; ancestral history, 195–96; as antique collector, 206–7, 240; birth of, 196; childhood/education of, 196–98, 197; Coffin and, 182, 183, 187, 197, 218–19; color schemes of, 201–3, 331; as Delaware State College trustee, 187; design philosophy of, 198; European tours of, 203; marriage of, 198, 203; naturalistic plantings of, 200–203; Sargent and, 378n15; Stan Hywet visit of, 203; summer home of (Southampton, N.Y.), 192, 192, 206–7; trial plantings of, 198, 199–200, 378n18; Winterthur renovations undertaken by, 208; Winterthur supervised by, 198–99, 206, 207–8, 216. See also Winterthur

du Pont, Louise, 183, 196, 197

du Pont, Mary Pauline Foster, 182, 196–97, 198

du Pont, Pauline Louise, 209

du Pont, Pierre, 118

du Pont, Ruth Ellen, 209

du Pont, Ruth Wales, 192, 203, 209, 218

du Pont, Sophie Madeleine, 197

du Pont de Nemours, Eleuthère Irénée, 195–96

du Pont de Nemours, Evelina, 196

du Pont de Nemours, Pierre Samuel, 195

du Pont de Nemours, Victor, 195
Duveen, Joseph, 243
Dybbøl (Denmark), 223, *224*

Eastman, George, 240–41, 370–71n28
Eastover (Palmer; New London, Conn.), *58*, 374n23
Eaton, Leonard K., xiv, 224, 380–81n31
Eaton, Walter Pritchard, 392n57
Eaton Hall (Chester, Eng.), 10
Eckbo, Garrett, 283, 355
Eckhart, Bernard A., 230
École des Beaux-Arts, xvi, xix, 49, 370n14. *See also* Beaux-Arts design
Edison, Mina, 373n31
Edison, Thomas, 240, 373n31, 382n58, 382n8
Edison Institute, 240
Edsel and Eleanor Ford House (Grosse Pointe Shores, Mich.), xxii, 239–64; as abstract work of art, 260; approach drive, 246–47; Arts and Crafts style of, 243; Bird Island, 246, *246*, 247, *247*, *248*, 255; client collaboration in, 242–43, 245–46; cost of, 262; council ring, 383n41; courtyard, *244*; cutting gardens, 249; Fair Lane compared to, 255–57; family life at, 262; Flower Lane, 251, *255*; flower plantings, 251–55; Gatehouse, *247*, 262; grading, 245–46, 255; Great Meadow, 247, 249, *249*, *250*, *251*, *252*, *253*, *260*; as historic house museum, 263; influences on, 243; interior design, 243–45, *245*; Jensen's design plans for, 245–51, *246*, *251*, *257*, 382n64; kitchen garden, 249; house/lake terrace, 255, *260*; maintenance endowment, 263; naturalistic lagoon, 255, *257*, *258*, *262*; "New Garden," 263; paths, 251, *254*; playhouse, *261*, 262; Rose Garden, 245, 249, 251–55, *256*; site of, 243, *245*; size of, 243; spatial sequencing at, 246–49; sunlight/shadow interplay at, 249–51, *252*, *254*, *255*, 257; swimming pool, 245, *257*, *262*; views, *247*, *248*, *249*, *250*, *252*, *253*, 255, *257*, *258*, *259*, *260*, *262*, *264*
Edwardian gardens, 171, 193
Edwards, G. B., 94
Eleutherian Mills, 195–96, *196*
El Fureidis (Gillespie; Santa Barbara, Calif.), 274, *275*, 286–87, *286*, *287*, 386n16
Elias Hasket Derby House (Salem, Mass.), 3
Eliot, Charles, 18–19, 360n2; on art and Nature, 296–98; design philosophy of, 318; Farrand's European tour and, 136; on "fitness," xx, on formal/informal debate, xx; mapping techniques of, 28, 31; as Olmstedian, xix; on Platt's *Italian Gardens*, 54; as Trustees of Reservations founder, 353; writings of, 311, 362n47. *See also* Olmsted, Olmsted & Eliot
Elliot, John, 54, 55
Elliott, Maud Howe, 134
Ellwanger, George, 309
Ellwanger, Helen, 347; Steele garden for, 324, *325*
Elm Court (Sloan; Lenox, Mass.), 374n23
Elmhirst, Leonard and Dorothy, 375n42
Emerson, Ralph Waldo, xi, 4, 6, 26
Engelmann, George, 12–13
England: and American cultural inadequacy, xiv; Coffin's trip to, 185;

Blisses' travel to, 151; Downing trip to, 7; du Pont and, 199, 200, 203; Farrand's trip to, 136–37, *137*; influence on Olmsted, 10; influence on Shaw, 12; as inspiration, 3; landscape design developments in, xix, 4; male flower gardeners in, 118; Picturesque school in, 3, 5; Platt travel to, 49; Stan Hywet model search in, 92, 93; Steele and, 312, 337. *See also* Brown, Lancelot "Capability"; Repton, Humphry; Robinson, William; *What England Can Teach Us about Gardening*
English Flower Garden, The (Robinson), 58
Eolia (New London, Conn.), 145–46, *146*
Erie, Lake, 63–64
Essay on the Picturesque (Price), 11
European travel, 151; by Choate, 337; by Coffin, 183; by de Forest, 271–73, 285, 384n17; by du Ponts, 203; by Farrand, 136–37, *136*, *137*; significance of, 131; by Steele, 311, 312–13, 337
Evarts, Southmayd & Choate, 327
exotic species, 12–14, 38, 189, 274, 318
Exposition des Arts Décoratifs et Industriels Modernes (Paris; 1925), 322–23, *323*
Exposition Universelle (Paris; 1889), 28
Eyre, Wilson, Jr., xix, 366n25
Eyrie, The (Rockefeller; Seal Harbor, Me.), 145, *145*, *146*

Fahnestock, William F. *See* Girdle Ridge
Fair Lane (H. and C. Ford; Dearborn, Mich.), 239, *260*; architect hired for, 381–82n55; house, *234*; Jensen's design plans for, 234–36, 255–57; natural setting of, 382n58; peony garden, *234*; rose garden, *234*, 235–36, *235*, 382n60; Shipman plantings, 125, 235, 382n60; striated rockwork, 234, *234*; view, *234*
Fairlawn Heights (Akron, Ohio), 42–43, *43*, 111
Fairsted (Olmsted; Brookline, Mass.), 15, *16*, 136, *136*
farming: moral benefit from, xv; as element of country estate, xvi, 39; H. Ford and, 240; Jensen and, 223, *224*, 380n5; Manning and, 26; Olmsted and, 9, 10; Steele and, 309, 310
Farmington River (Conn.), *10*
farms, estate: Biltmore, 20; Crosswicks, 139; Dumbarton Oaks, 151, *151*, 172; Eleutherian Mills, 194; Ford House, 243, 251; Gwinn, 67, *78*, 79, 368n24, 369n48; Naumkeag, 348, 351, *352*; Stan Hywet Hall, 90, *90*, 91, 110; Winterthur, 196, 197, 200, 203, 216, *216*
Farnum, Elizabeth E., estate of (Norfolk, Conn.), 186, *187*
Farrand, Beatrix Jones, 133–47, *134*; as ASLA charter member, xvii, 139, 184; birth of, 133; business expansions of, 141, 142, 145–47; in California, 275, 376n51; campus commissions, 375n40; career decision of, 134–35; childhood of, 133–34, 373n2; client base of, 366n25, 376nn50–51; Coffin and, 378n36; color use of, 318; critical marginalization of, xiv; de Forest and, 281, 385n56; design philosophy of, 141–42, 183–84, 189–90, 322; early career of, 137–41; European tour of, 136–37, *136*, *137*; experimental projects, 145; female employees of, 142, 174; final years/death of, 178–79; genius loci and, 126, 154, 168; impact of husband's death on, 178; impact of Wharton's death on, 177; influence of, 182; influences on, 135, 138; informal horticultural training, 135–37, *136*, *137*; marriage of, 144–45; as New Woman, 359n14; New York office of, 142; fame of, 117, 135, 138, 150; Olmsted and, 136; planting palette of, xxii, 376n21; presentation

Farrand, Beatrix (*continued*)

drawings of, 139–40; as Princeton Consulting Landscape Architect, 143–44, 375nn38, 40; relationship with clients, 145, 152–53, 159, 172–74, 178; relocation to California, 176, 193; relocation to Maine, 177; Sargent and, 135; spatial definition by, 170; spatial sequencing in work of, 376n23; water features of, 172; Wharton and, 376n54; on women in landscape architecture, 117–18; writings of, 135, 137, 138, 141–42, 177–78, 362n47

Farrand, Beatrix, commissions: Crosswicks (Jenkintown, Pa.), 139–40, *139*, *140*; Eolia (New London, Conn.), 145–46, *146*; The Eyrie (Seal Harbor, Me.), 145, *145*, *146*; Garrison estate (Tuxedo, N.Y.), 138, *138*; The Mount (Lenox, Mass.), 140–41, *141*, 151, 374nn23, 25; Oheka (Long Island, N.Y.), 146; Princeton University, 142–44, *142*, *143*, 375nn38, 40; Straight estate (Old Westbury, N.Y.), *144*, 145; White House (Washington, D.C.), *144*, 145; Whitney estate (Oyster Bay, N.Y.), 141, *141*. *See also* Dumbarton Oaks

Farrand, Max, 144–45, 177, 178

Faulkner Farm (Sprague; Brookline, Mass.), 54–56, *56*, 80, 183

Federation of Women's Clubs, 150

Ferree, Barr, xvi, 56, 390n1

Field, Marshall, III, 191

Field, Stanley, 36

film industry, 279, 280, 294, 385n50

Firestone, Harvey S., 89, 92, 94, 382n58, 382n8

Firestone Park (Akron, Ohio), *89*, 94, 370–71n28

Firestone Tire and Rubber Company, 89

Fish, Julia, 122, *123*

Fisher, Carl, 237

"fitness" in design, xx, 31, 48, 51, 140, 310, 318

Flanders, Annette Hoyt, 356, 372n11

Fleming, Bryant, 356, 365n83

Flint, Herbert, 41

F. L. Olmsted & Company, 362n10

Flood, James, 13, 14

Flora of Middlesex County, The, 26

flower gardens, xxii; American interest in, 58; as counterpoint to architectural features, 121; as private world, 120; seasonal, 162; Shipman views on aesthetic potential of, 118–19; women associated with, xvii, 85, 117–18, 125, 138, 330. *See also* rose gardens; Shipman, Ellen; *specific sites*

Foote, Harriet R., 235, 372n11

forced perspective, 159, 320, 321

Ford, Benson, *263*, 383n21

Ford, Clara, 235–36, 372n61, 382n60

Ford, Edsel, xxii, *241*, *253*; agrarian values embraced by, 242; death of, 263; as automotive designer, 241, 242; Detroit home of, 236, *236*, 242; as Ford Company president, 236, 242; Haven Hill (Oakland County, Mich.), 237, 382n65; impact of Depression on, 242; Jensen and, 236, 237, 238, 242; Lincoln Highway and, 237, 238; personality/interests of, 241, 261; relationship with H. Ford, 241, 242; Skylands, 236–37, *236*, 242, 251. *See also* Edsel and Eleanor Ford House

Ford, Eleanor, 236–37, 238, 241, 251, 252, *253*, 263, *263*. *See also* Edsel and Eleanor Ford House

Ford, Henry, *241*; agrarian values embraced by, 239, 240, 242, 382n8; as antique collector, 207, 240; Jensen and, 242; Lincoln Highway and, 237; luxury camping tours of, 382n8; Manning and, 94; Model T developed by, 184, 239, 241–42; personality/interests of, 241; personal net worth of (mid-1920s), 382n1; vertical industrial growth by, xvi. *See also* Fair Lane

Ford, Henry, II, *263*, 383n21

Ford, Josephine, 261, *263*, 383n21

Ford, William Clay, 261, *263*, 383n21

Ford Hunger March, 383n14

Ford Motor Company, 239–42; Jensen's commissions with, 236; publicity stunts of, xvi; Rouge plant, 239, 241, *241*; village industries, 239–41, *240*; Willow Run plant, 383n25

Forestier, J. C. N., 273, 322

formal design: Downing on 6; as imperialistic, 6, 8, 227; vs. naturalistic, xi, 19; resurgence in nineteenth century, 17; topiary in, 14; wild gardens as opposition to, 38, 141. *See also* Beaux-Arts design

formal/informal debate, xviii, xix–xxii, 19, 42, 281, 325, 346

Foster, Mary Pauline. *See* du Pont, Mary Pauline Foster

Foster, Victorine du Pont, 197, 198

fountains: P. du Pont and, 118; at El Fureidis, 286, *286*; at Faulkner Farm, 47; at Ford House, 252; at Granada, 273, 316, 332; at Io Viterbo, 137; at Rolling Ridge, 317, *317*; in Santa Barbara, 387n20; at Stan Hywet Hall, 104, *104*, 110; at Weld, 56, *57*; at Winterthur, 199, 209, *211*; at World's Columbian Exposition, *29*, 30. *See also* Dumbarton Oaks; Gwinn; Naumkeag; Val Verde

France, landscape design developments in, 4. *See also* École des Beaux-Arts; French design

Franceschi, Francisco, 275–76, 281

Franklin Park (Boston, Mass.), *12*, 16

Frascati villas (Italy), 51

Frederick, William H., 200

Freer, Charles Lang, 59, 62

Freer Gallery (Washington, D.C.), 59, 367n57

French, Daniel Chester, 328, 360n21, 366n21, 390n7, 392n57

French, Prentiss, 390n7

French, William M. R., 226, 381n36

French classicism. *See* Beaux-Arts design

French design: at Dumbarton Oaks, 376n47; influence on Steele, 322–23, 324–25, 331, 345–46, 353, 355; at Naumkeag, 335; "Three Unities of Garden Design," 325. *See also* École des Beaux-Arts

Frick, Mr. and Mrs. Childs. *See* Clayton

Friends of Our Native Landscape, 231, 380n19, 381n36

Frost, Henry Atherton, 372n19

Frost, Paul Rubens, 58, 69, 85, 368n26

Fulkerson, Mertha, 263

Fullerton, Morton, 140

Furness, Fairman, 348

Fürst-Pückler-Park (Muskau, Germany), *18*. *See also* Pückler-Muskau, Prince Hermann Ludwig Heinrich von

Fynmere (Cooper; Cooperstown, N.Y.), 120–21, *121*

Gallagher, Percival, 330, 356, 372n13, 387n24, 391n23

"garden," use of term, x–xi. *See also* "landscape gardener," use of term

Garden and Forest, xx, 18–19, 54, 135, 138, 362n47

Garden and Home Builder, 188, 191

"Garden as a Picture, The" (Farrand), 141–42

Garden Club of America: Choate's travels with, 335–37, 391–92n44; Coffin as member of, 188; du Pont's speech to (1956), 378–79n33; Gwinn and, 85; E. Mather and, 369n59; Shipman and, 113; Steele lecture to, 325; Walden views and, 35; Winterthur visits of, 208

Garden Club of America Bulletin, 354; Coffin articles in, 180, 188, 189; du Pont and, 378n29; Steele articles in, 317–18

Garden Club of Santa Barbara and Montecito, 391n39

Gardener's Dictionary, The (Miller), 3, *4*

gardenesque, 6, *6*, 13–15; attributes of, 381n34; at Biltmore, 20; defined, 6; Jensen and, 229; Manning and, 75; Picturesque joined with, 6; rise of, xxii. *See also* "Shaw's Garden"; Victorian design

Gardening for Ladies (Louden), 117

Garden Magazine, 58, 188, 285, 317

Garden Month by Month, The (Sedgwick), 200

Garden of the Water Goddess, The (sculpture; Paddock), 106

"Garden of Water and Light" (Guevrekian), 322–23

Gardens and People (Steele), 313

Gardens of Colony and State (Lockwood), 3

Gardner, Isabella Stewart, 183

Garfield Park (Chicago, Ill.), 225, 230, *230*, 381n34

Garland Farm (Farrand; Bar Harbor, Me.), 179, 377n65

Garnier, Tony, 323

Garrison, William Lloyd, Jr., 347

Garrison, William R., estate of (Tuxedo, N.Y.), 138, *138*

Geiffert, Alfred, Jr., 356

Geneva (N.Y.), 181

gender roles in landscape design, 118, 121, 330

genius loci, xxi–xxii; at Biltmore, 30; client's personality and, xxi; Coffin and, 126, 219–21; Downing on, 5; at Dumbarton Oaks, 154, 168; Farrand and, 126, 154, 168; at Gwinn, 87; in Italianate design, xx–xxi; Jensen and, 233–34, 263; modernism and, xxiii; at Naumkeag, 335; as Olmstedian principle, 356–57; outdoor rooms and, 131; Platt and, 48; Shipman and, 126; Steele and, 313, 317, 353–54; use of term, x; view and, 313; at World's Columbian Exposition, 29

geometric approach, xix, 3, *4*, 6, *6*; Beaux-Arts residences and, 17; Coffin's experimentation with, 190–91; exceptions to, 360n2; at Gwinn, 368n26; Shipman's use of, 120, *120*; wild gardens as opposition to, 38

George B. Post & Sons, 91

Georgian style, 57, 67

German landscape architects, 136; and "architectural gardens," 314, 389n29; and Parsons, xx; and plant sociology/ecology, 228, 380n25. *See also* Pückler-Muskau, Prince Hermann Ludwig Heinrich von

Gerry, Angelica. *See* Ancrum House

Gibraltar (Sharp; Wilmington, Del.), 186, 187, *188*

Gill, Irving J., 365n83

Gillespie, J. Waldron, 274, 289, 386n4. *See also* El Fueridis

Gillette, Charles F., 41

Gillies, George H., 191

Gilpin, William, 11

Girdle Ridge (Fahnstock; Katonah, N.Y.), 121, *121*

Golden Age of American Gardens, The (Griswold and Weller), xiv, 304

Goodhue, Bertram Grosvenor, xxii, 274, 294; artistic/cultural network of, 386n10; California institutional projects, 387n26; collaboration with Cram, 386n12; death of, 290; El Fureidis (Santa Barbara, Calif.), 285–87, *286*; independent career of, 386n12; interest in Spanish architecture, 387n23; marriage of, 386n10; Ormston (Long Island, N.Y.), 387n24; as San Diego Exposition planner, 386n16; Tyrone (N.M.) company town, 387n24; Val Verde (Santa Barbara, Calif.), 287–89, 298–300

Goodwin, W. A. R., 207

Goodyear, Charles, 89

Goodyear Heights (Akron, Ohio), 41, 93–94, 111, 370nn26–27

Goodyear Tire Company, 89–90, 111

Gothein, Marie Luis, 389n29

Gottscho, Samuel, 123, 192; photographs by, *191, 201, 203, 208, 209, 211, 215, 218*

Gould, Frederick S., estate of (Santa Barbara, Calif.), 275, *275*

Gould, Jay. *See* Lyndhurst

Gould, Stephen Jay, 363n38

Governor's Palace (Williamsburg, Va.), 3

Graceland Cemetery (Chicago, Ill.), 225, *225*, 380n11. *See also* cemeteries, "rural"

"grandmothers'"/old-fashioned gardens, 52, 58. *See also* Cornish

Gravetye Manor (Robinson; West Sussex, Eng.), 137, *137*. *See also* Robinson, William

Gray, Asa, 13

Great Awakening, xviii

Great Depression, 83–85, 111, 126, 177, 219, 242, 373n28, 373n34

Great Exhibition of the Works of Industry of All Nations (London; 1851), 12, 28

Greeley, Horace, 47

Greely, Rose, 372n11, 377n57

Greene, Charles, 275

Greene, Henry, 275

Greenfield Village (Dearborn, Mich.), 236, 240–41, 382n9

Green Hill (Brookline, Mass.), 183

greenhouse technology, 13

Greenleaf, James L., ix, 356, 381n53

Greensward plan, 8. *See also* Central Park

Green-Wood Cemetery (Brooklyn, N.Y.), 4

Grese, Robert E., xiv, 223, 225, 247, 251, 263, 382n58

Grey, Elmer, 366n25, 386n16

Griffin, Marion Mahoney, 381–82n55

Griffin, Walter Burley, 381n36

Gris, Juan, 260

Griscom, Clement A. *See* Dolobran

Griswold, Mac, xiv, 190, 304

Griswold, Ralph, 36, 190

Groening, Gert, 228

Groton (Mass.), 197

Grounds for Pleasure (Otis), xiv–xv

Grove, Carol, 12

Guevrekian, Gabriel, 322–23

Gwinn (Mather; Cleveland, Ohio), xxii, 36, 59, 61–88; aerial view of, *87*; allée, 79–80, *79, 80*; bosco (little wild garden), 70–73, *71, 72, 73, 74*; *Boy with Dolphin* (Verrocchio), *65*, 79, *83*; as conference center, 88, 369n63; construction of, *64, 67*, 71, 368n24; cost of, 67–69; critical reviews of, 64, 80–83, 369n51; during Depression, 83–85; diverse aesthetic perspectives and originality of, 85–87; entrance drive, 67, *70*; farm buildings, *78*, 79; forecourt, 67, *68, 70*, 79; formal garden, 56, 67, *67, 84*, 85, *86, 87, 87*; fountains, 72, *72, 73*, 75, 79, *86*; Fortuna bronze, 79, *86, 87*; framed views, 64, 279; gazebos, 79, *82*; genius loci, 87; grading, 368n18; greenhouses, 67; house, 63, *64, 67, 68*, 69; interior design, 59, 72, *72*; George Jacques as head gardener of, 67, 71, 72, 75, 76, 83, 85, 87; landscape plan, 63, *63*, 63–67, 368n16; lawn, *66*, 67, 75, 368n25; lions, 79, *79*; loggia, 67, *85*; Manning–Platt conflicts, 60, 72, 75, 79, 85, 86; Manning's narrative history of, 45; Manning's views on, 69, 71, 72; Manship vase, 80, *80*; Mather's opinions of, 71–72, 75, 87; pergola, 72–75, *74*; plantings, 69–71, *69, 70, 71*, 72, 368n26 (*see also* wild gardens); Platt hired as architect of, 62–63; revisions of, 71–72, 75, 85; seawall, 63–64, 79, *81, 82*, 87; Shipman redesign, 85, 125–26; site selection, 62, *62*, 63; stairways, 64, *65*; Albert Davis Taylor as Manning's representative, 41, 312; teahouse, 67, 79, *84*; terraces, 64, *64, 65, 83*, 368n18; vista, 72, 79, *79*; Walden as model for, 34; wild garden, *45*, 72, 75–77, *75, 76, 77*, 79, *88*
Gwinn (Mich.), 368n4

Haddon Hall (Derbyshire, Eng.), 92
Hadrian's Villa, 294, 387n33
Halfred Farms (White; Chagrin Falls, Ohio), 121, *122*, 372n59
halftone printing technology, xviii, 33
Hamblin, Stephen, 41
Hamerton, Philip, 311, 312
Hamilton, William, 208. *See* Woodlands
Hamlin, Talbot, 29
Hanes, Frederick M., 125
Hans, Egbert, 36
Hansen, Anne Marie, 224
Hanson, A. E., 275
Harkness, Edward S. and Mary, 145–46
Harlakenden House (Cornish, N.H.), 366n24
Harper's Monthly Magazine, 14, 56
Harrisburg (Pa.) park system, 36, *37*, 75, 364n60
Harrison, Arthur K., 365n83
Harrison, Irene Seiberling, 40
Hart, Charles M., 190
Hart, James, 270
Harvard University: Arnold Arboretum and, 15; de Forest at, 271; Dumbarton Oaks donated to, 147, 177; du Pont at, 197–98; female applicants to landscape architecture program and, 120, 372n19; first landscape architecture program at, xvii; Steele at, 310–11; undergraduate landscape architecture program at, 389n46
Hastings, Thomas, 146
Haussmann, Georges Eugène, 224
Havemeyer, H. O., estate of (Islip, N.Y.), 361n45

Haven Hill (E. Ford; Oakland County, Mich.), 237, 382n65
Havey, Ruth, 174, 176, 376n23, 377n61
Hawthorne, Nathaniel, 328
Hayden Company, 93
Healy, Harry G., 123, 189
Hecker, Frank J., 59
Heinigke & Bowen, 93
Henry Ford Hospital (Detroit, Mich.), 236
Henry Ford Museum, 240
Hertrich, William, 176
Hesperides (Ludington; Santa Barbara, Calif.), 307
Hewitt, Mark Alan, xiv, xvi, 19–20, 359n10
Hewitt, Mattie Edwards, 122, 123, 188–89, 373n25; photographs by, *123, 191, 192, 318, 319*
Hidcote Manor (Gloucestershire, Eng.), 118
High Cliffe (Backus; Manchester-by-the-Sea, Mass.), 321
High Court (Lazarus; Cornish, N.H.), 51, *51*, 58, 59, 119, 311
Highcroft (Peavy; Lake Minnetonka, Minn.), 32
Highland Park (Lake Forest, Ill.), 34, 226
Hillside Homes, 372n10
Hillwood (Hutton/Post; Wheaton Hills, N.Y.), 190–91, *191*
Himmler, Heinrich, 228
Hints on Landscape Gardening (Pückler-Muskau), xx, 233
Hirshler, Erica E., 49
historic preservation, 357, 379n41. *See also* conservation; landscape preservation; Mission House museum
Hofstadter, Richard, xv, 359n3
Holmes, Oliver Wendell, Sr., 328
Holm Lea (Sargent; Jamaica Plain, Mass.), 135, *135*, 183, 198
Holy Earth, The (Bailey), xi
Home Gardener, The (Church), 117
Hooker, Elon, estate of (Greenwich, Conn.), *39*
Hooker, William Jackson, 13
Hoover, Henry, 325, 340, 345
Hoover, Herbert, 240
Hopedale (Mass.), 27, 311
Hope Ranch (Dickinson; Santa Barbara, Calif.), 279–80, *280*
Hopkins, Alden, 168
Hoppin, Francis L. V., 374n23
Hornbeck, Peter H., 313, 352
horticulture: landscape architects with backgrounds in, 4, 25; landscape architecture vs., 17; popular interest in, xxii; rising interest in, 26, 275; women as suited to, 117
Horticulture, 317, 382n60
Horton, Heath ("Bunny"), 307
Hotel del Monte (Monterey, Calif.), 13
Hotel Potter (Santa Barbara, Calif.), *270*
"hot fight." *See* formal/informal debate
House and Garden, xviii, 55–56, 188, 191, 287, 317
House Beautiful, 188, 270, 317, 334, 385n43
House Beautiful Gardening Manual, 122, 318, 347, 389n45
House of Mirth, The (Wharton), 374n25
Howe, Samuel, xvi, 64, 80–83, 243
Hubbard, Henry Vincent, xi, xxi, 19
Huber, H. F., 93

Hudson River School, xiv, 100

Hudson River valley, 5, 6, 8

Huebner, Herman, 197

Hull House (Chicago, Ill.), 227–28

Humboldt Park (Chicago, Ill.), 228, 230, *230*, 232

Hunnewell, Horatio Hollis. *See* Wellesley

Hunt, Myron, 232, 275, 366n25, 386n16

Hunt, Richard Morris, xvi, 19, 20, 92, 363n17, 366n25

Huntington, Henry, 176

Huntington Art Gallery and Library (Pasadena, Calif.), 176

Huntsman-Trout, Edward, ix, 275

Hutcheson, Martha Brookes, 117–18, 182–83, 372n11, 377n6

Hutchins & Platt, 47

Hutton, E. F. *See* Hillwood

Il Brolino (Stewart; Montecito, Calif.), *280*, 384–85n26

immigration, xv, 207, 227, 359n3

Indiana Dunes State Park, *224*

Indian Domestic Architecture (de Forest II), 270

Indian Harbor (Greenwich, Conn.), 368n16

indigenous/native species: in abstract design, 324; Farrand on, 178; Jensen and, 225, 237, 229, *229*, 380n7, 382n64; mainstream use of, 384n25; Manning's use of, 71; McFarland's notion of, 363n38; patriotism and, 33, 42; in plant collections, 15; vs. non-native species, 28; in *Santa Barbara Gardener*, 385–86n61; in Southern California, 275

industrialism, 52, 239, 359n8

informal design. *See* formal/informal debate; naturalistic design; wild gardens; *specific sites*

Inness, George, 251

Introduction to the Study of Landscape Design (Hubbard and Kimball), xi, xxi

Io Viterbo (Italy), 137

Ireland, Cornelia, 77, 87, 88

Ireland, Elizabeth Ring. *See* Mather, Elizabeth Ring

Ireland, James D., 88

Iron Cliffs Company, 61

Ishpeming (Mich.), 33, 75, 368n4

Italianate style, xxii, 137; American acceptance of, xix; in Coffin's work, 185–86, 209; in de Forest's work, 290, 298, genius loci and, xx–xxi; in Platt's work, xix, 56, 106, 367n44; principles, 209; repertory, in Shipman's work, 124; in Steele's work, 311, 316, 319, 320, 343; in Wharton's designs, 140; at Winterthur, 199, *199*

Italian Gardens (Platt), xix, 54, *54*, 366n34

Italian Renaissance, 23, 58, 140–41, 170–71, 286

Italian Villas and Their Gardens (Wharton), 58, 140, 153–54

Italy: de Forest's trip to, 271, *272*, 273, *273*; Farrand's trip to, 136–37, *136*; Goodhue and Gillespie's travel to, 286; Platt's trip to, 49, 51, 53–54; Steele's travel to, 312

Ives, Albert Ely, 208

Jack, John G., 183

Jackson, Helen Hunt, 276

Jackson Park (Chicago, Ill.), 226

Jacques, George. *See* Gwinn: George Jacques as head gardener of

Jacques, Lillie, 83, *88*

James, Henry, 20, 133, 134, 183

Jamestown Exposition (Norfolk, Va.), 41, *41*

Jansen, Gail, 387nn31, 33

Japanese influence, xx; in de Forest's work, 279; on Mabel Choate, 337; at Stan Hywet, 106, 371n49; at Weld, 367n45

Jefferson, Thomas, xv, 3–4, *4*, 39, 195, 360n3

Jekyll, Gertrude, xix, 58, 137, 138; Coffin visits, 183, 185; color theories of, 198; drift organization and, 368n26; Farrand visit to, 137; influence on Coffin, 184; influence on Dumbarton Oaks, 159, 164, 168; influence on du Pont, 198, 199; influence on Farrand, 138, 139, 145; influence on Shipman, 85, 119

Jemison, Robert, Jr., 44

Jenney, William Le Baron, 11, 225, 381n34

Jensen, Jens, xiv, xix, xxii, 42, 125, 186, 223–38, *224*; birth of, 223; on naturalistic planting in Chicago, 225; Chicago office of, 232, 381n44; as Chicago parks superintendent/landscape architect, 230, *231*, 357; Chicago political corruption and, 228–29; childhood of, 223, *224*, 233; client base of, 231; collaborations with Wright, 381n49; council rings, 227–28, 233, 236, 238, 242; on curves and democracy, 249; design philosophy of, 226–27, 263, 380–81n31; early career of, 225, 228–29; education of, 223–24; elopement of, to United States, 224, 380n5; E. and E. Ford garden, 236, *236*; Ford Motor Co. projects, 236; genius loci and, 233–34, 263; Greenfield Village landscaping and, 382n9; influences on, 228, 229–30; landscape design school founded by, 263; leaves ASLA, 236, 381–82n53; Lincoln Highway plantings, *237*, 238; love of indigenous plants, 380n7; massed plantings of, 249; meadows of, 236, 237, 247–49; midwestern naturalistic design and, 224–26; as nativist, 228, 381n53; fame of, 231, 232; and plant ecology, 228; prairie approach of, 229, 231–34; prairie landscape and, 224–25; prairie walks led by, 381n36; private business established by, 224, 229; progressive sensibilities of, 227–28, 381n36; relationship with clients, 235–36, 242, 261–64; Simonds and, 380n13; spatial sequencing by, 246–49; spatial skill of, 233; "sun openings" of, 249–51; urban parks reshaped by, 230, *230*; writings of, 227, 229, 232, 251, 263

Jensen, Jens, commissions: critical reviews of, 230; marketing potential of, 230; Rosenwald homes (Chicago, Ill.), 231; Rubens estate (Glencoe, Ill.), 229–30, *229*; Spring Station (Ky.), 231, *231*; St. Ann's Hospital (Chicago, Ill.), 229, *229*. *See also* Edsel and Eleanor Ford House

Johnson, Marshall, 263, 382n9

Johnston, Frances Benjamin, 373n25; photograph by, *121*

Johnston, Lawrence, 118

Jones, Beatrix Cadwalader. *See* Farrand, Beatrix Jones

Jones, Frederic Rhinelander, 133, 134

Jones, Katherine, 271

Jones, Mary Rawle, 133, 134, 145

Journal of the Committee on Municipal Administration, 138–39

Joy, Henry B., 237

Kahn, Albert, 243, 245, 382n6, 383n25

Kahn, Otto H. *See* Oheka

Katrina, Hurricane (2005), 373n33

Keeler, Charles, 287

Kellam, Elizabeth. *See* de Forest, Elizabeth

Kellaway, Herbert J., 235–36

Kemp, Edward, 10

Kent, William, 5, 198

Kentworthy, Richard G., 367n45

Kessler, George, 384n11

Kew Gardens (London), 13

Kiley, Dan, 44, 348, 355–56, 392n59

Kimball, Fiske, xi, xv

Kimbell, Theodora, xxi

King, Louisa Yeoman, 318, 347

Kipling, Rudyard, 270

Klauder, Charles Z., 187

Knoll, The (Tarrytown, N.Y.), 6. *See also* Lyndhurst

Kykuit (Rockefeller; Tarrytown, N.Y.), 141

Lachaise, Gaston, 314, *315*

Ladies' Home Journal, 232, 317

La Farge, John, 134

Lake Forest (Ill.), 226

Landscape (Hamerton), 311

"landscape," use of term, x–xi

Landscape Architecture, 43, 60, 283, 317

landscape architecture/design, American: amateurs in, 360n21; as ameliorative force, xix, 10, 11–12, 23, 226; assimilation of previous knowlege and, 318; Coffin on, 219, 221; Downing's influence on, 4–7; as ephemeral, 263; and European prototypes, xiv, xxi, 3, 31, 136, 312, 313; as expression of personality, 19, 189; Farrand on, 135, 138, 142; as fine art, xxi, xxii, 14–15, 31, 42, 48, 97, 100, 221, 365n88; first university programs for, xvii, xix, 15; flower gardens marginalized in, 118; geometric tradition in, 3; historical studies needed in, 356–57; horticulture vs., 17; Manning's significance in, 114; in 1920s, 131; Olmsted as father of, xiii; Olmstedian principles of, xix, xx, 15, 53, 135, 189, 198; perspective in, 257, 260; Platt's influence on, 48, 60; post-WWII, 355; as profession, xvii–xviii, 14–15, 18; professional programs open to women, 120, 182; Progressive-era civic principles in, xviii; publications on, xix (*see also specific titles*); Romantic influences on, 4, 7; scenic preservation in, 18–19; scholarship on, xiv–xv; Steele on role of color, 318–19, 325; theatrical, 280, 290. *See also* Beaux-Arts design; client collaboration; client personality: as design determinant; composition in landscape design; formal/informal debate; gardenesque; gender roles in landscape design; genius loci; modernism; naturalistic design; Prairie School/style; women landscape architects

"landscape architecture," as term, xvii, 359n13

Landscape Architecture, as Applied to the Wants of the West (Cleveland), xvii, 226

Landscape Art, Past and Present (McCormick), 36

Landscape Beautiful, The (Waugh), 230, 232

"landscape gardener," use of term: by Farrand, xvii, 139; by Manning, xvii, 362n8

landscape preservation, xiv, 11, 351, 353, 357; Coffin and, 189, 191;

Eliot and, 18; Ford House and, 263; Choate/Steele and, 351, 353; Dumbarton Oaks and, 147, 177; Gwinn and, 88, 369n63; Winterthur and, 219. *See also* conservation

Landscape Quarterly, 355

Land's End (Newport, R.I.), 140

Lange, Willy, 228

Langton, Daniel W., 360n21, 374n20

Laprade, Albert, 323

Larkspur (Garden at High Court, Cornish) (painting; Platt), *51*

Lathrop, Bryan, 225

Laurel Hill Cemetery (Philadelphia, Pa.), 4

Lawrie, Lee, 287

Lay, Charles Downing, 60

Lazarus, Annie. *See* High Court

Legrain, Pierre-Émile, 323

Lenox (Mass.), xv, 327; Garden Club, 325

Lepine, A. J., 246

Levens Hall (Cumbria, Eng.), 137, *137*

Libby, Valencia, 198

Life magazine, 240

Lincoln Highway, 237; Indiana "ideal section," *237*, 238

Lindbergh, Charles A., 121

Lindeberg, Harrie T., 366n25

Linden Towers (Menlo Park, Calif.), 13–14, *14*

Linneaus, Carolus, 12

Lippincott's Magazine, 33

Lisburne Grange (Sloan; Garrison, N.Y.), 319–20, *319*, *320*

Little & Browne, xix

Little, Browne & Moore, 54–55

Lockwood, Alice G. B., 3, 347

Longfellow, Henry Wadsworth, 7, 26

Long Island (N.Y.), as site of country estates, xv. *See also* Coffin, Marian Cruger: commissions

Longue Vue (Stern; New Orleans, La.), 126, *127*, 373nn32–33

Lord, Elizabeth, 123

Lord, Ruth, 206, 379n35

Los Angeles Public Library, 387n26

Lotusland (Walska; Montecito, Calif.), *282*, 307, 388n45

Loudon, Jane, 117

Loudon, John Claudius, xix, 6, 12, 198

Louisville (Ky.), 28, *28*

Lowell, Guy, xix, xx, 56, 117, 139, 141, 182, 360n21, 368n16

Lowrie, Charles Nassau, 374n20

Lowthorpe School of Landscape Architecture (Croton, Mass.), 120, 123

Ludington, Charles H., Jr., 285, 290, 294

Ludington, Nicholas, house (Montecito, Calif.), 385n43

Ludington, Wright S., xxii; as art collector, 290, 295, 300–303, 307, 388n41; complex personality of, 387n31; death of, 307; European tour of, 271, *272*, 273, *273*, 285, 294; inherits Val Verde, 294; as Santa Barbara Museum of Art founder, 388n47; sells Val Verde, 307. *See also* Val Verde

Lurçat, André, 323

Lyman, Thomas, estate of (Waltham, Mass.), 360n2

Lyndhurst (Gould; Tarrytown, N.Y.), 6, 7, 13, *14*

MacMonnies, Frederick W., 331

Magazine Antiques, 207

Maher, George W., 232

Mallet-Stevens, Robert, 324

Mangold, Ferdinand, 6

Mann, S. Vernon, 146

Mann & McNeille, 93–94

Manning, Harold, 312

Manning, Henrietta Pratt ("Nettie"), 27, 36, 40

Manning, Jacob Warren, 25

Manning, J. Woodward, 36

Manning, Lydia Chandler, 25–26

Manning, Solomon, 26

Manning, Warren H., xix, xxii, 25–45, *26*, *41*, 59, *88*; as ASLA charter member, 374n20; as ASLA president, 42, 110; birth of, 25;
business office of, 41–42; nursery background of, 25–26; client
base of, 36–37, 39–42, 44, 111; collaboration with Shipman, 113,
372n59; death of, 45; design philosophy of, 23, 114, 189; early
career of, 26–27; employees of, 44, 312, 348, 356, 365n83,
372n10; estate layouts of, 39; Farrand's Princeton work reviewed
by, 143–44; on Friends of Our Native Landscape, 380n19; on
garden vs. landscape, x–xi; horticultural repertory of, 38–39; impact of WWI on, 43, 44; marriage of, 27; Mather and, 44–45;
McCormick family and, 363–64n45; National Plan, 43, 44,
110–11; as nativist, 43, 228; as Olmsted employee, 16, 27–31;
Olmsted's influence on, 31, 36, 69, 77, 114; partnership with
brother, 36; planting methods of, 97–100; on Platt, 62–63;
Schneider and, 102, 371nn31, 34; Simonds and, 363n23; as social
reformer, 45, 62, 87–88; solo career begins, 31; Steele as assistant
to, 311–12; Steele on, 388–89n19; "Upper Michigan Land Use
Study" of, 44, 365n98; urban parks designed by, 36, 37, *37*, 75,
364n60; urban planning efforts of, 30, 32, 40, 43–44, 111,
365n85, 368n4; as proponent of wild gardens, 25, 33–36, 37–39,
172; writings of, x–xi, 31, 36, 37–39, 45, 58, 100, 111, 362n47.

Manning, Warren H., residential commissions: Dolobran (Haverford,
Pa.), 33, *34*; Goodyear Heights (Akron, Ohio), 41, 93–94, 111,
370nn26–27; Highcroft (Lake Minnetonka, Minn.), 32; Hooker
estate (Greenwich, Conn.), *39*; Mather summer home (Ishpeming, Mich.), 75; Pinehurst (N.C.), 31, 363n33; Walden (Lake Forest, Ill.), 33–36, *35*, 227; Whittemore estate (Middlebury, Conn.),
31–32, *32*. *See also* Gwinn; Stan Hywet Hall

Manning Family Association, 365n84

Manning Manse (Billerica, Mass.), 41–42, *41*, 110, 311, 365n84

Manship, Paul, 52, 79, *80*

Manual of Botany in the Northern United States (Gray), 13

Mariposa Big Tree Grove, 8

Markham, Beryl, 307

Massachusetts Agricultural College, 228

Massachusetts Horticultural Society, 25, 26

Massachusetts Institute of Technology (MIT), xvii, xix, 120, 182–83,
197, 391n16

Mather, Cotton, 61

Mather, Elizabeth Ring, xxii, 83, *83*, 88, 125–26

Mather, Increase, 61

Mather, Katherine, 67, 368n20

Mather, Richard, 61

Mather, Samuel Livingston, 61

Mather, William Gwinn, xvi, 33; birth of, 61; business career of,
61–62; death of, 88; forebears of, 61; Gwinn construction costs
and, 69; Gwinn revisions demanded by, 71–75; Manning and, 39,
44–45, 62, 71–72, 75, 368n4; marriage of, 83; Platt and, 59,
62–63, 69, 72; progressive policies of, 61–62, 87; summer home
of (Ishpeming, Mich.), 75; "Upper Michigan Land Use Study"
commissioned by, 44, 365n97. *See also* Gwinn

Mawson, Thomas H., xix, 58

Maxwell, Francis T., 367n54

Maxwell family (Rockville, Conn.), 59

May, Ernst, 323

McCormick, Cyrus, Jr., 143. *See also* Walden

McCormick, Cyrus, Sr., 34

McCormick, Edith Rockefeller, 35, 59, 368n18, 388n45

McCormick, Harold, 35, 59, 368n18, 388n45

McCormick, Harriet, 33–34, 36, 227

McCormick, Nettie Fowler, 363–64n45

McCormick, Stanley Fowler, 363–64n45

McCormick, Virginia, 363–64n45

McFarland, J. Horace, 33, 36, 77, 363n38

McGuire, Diane Kostial, 159, 170, 176, 376n21

McKim, Charles, 328

McKim, Mead & White, xix, 328, 363n17

McLaughlin, Charles C., 10

McMillan Plan (Washington, D.C.), 30

McPeck, Eleanor M., 154, 168

Mead & Garfield, 370n14

Meeker, Arthur. *See* Constantia

Melville, Herman, 328

Meridian Hill Park (Washington, D.C.), 375n9

Metropolitan Museum of Art (New York, N.Y.), 207, 270, 379n42

Miami (Fla.), parks in, 365n98

Middlebury (Conn.), 31–32, *32*

Middlesex Fells, 26, *27*

Middlesex Institute, 26

Middleton Place (Charleston, S.C.), 3

Migratory Bird Treaty (1918), 242

Miller, Phillip, 3, *4*

Miller, Wilhelm: Jensen projects chronicled by, 230, 231, 232, 233; on
Naumkeag, 327; prairie spirit and, 233; on Walden, 35; on Weld,
56–57; writings of, xix, 58, 362n47

Milliken, Harry, 186

Milner, H. E., 138

mining industry, xvi, 61–62

Minnehaha Falls (Minneapolis, Minn.), 7, *7*

Minneapolis–St. Paul (Minn.), 32, *32*

Mission House (Stockbridge, Mass.), 351, *351*

Missouri Botanical Garden (St. Louis), 41. *See also* "Shaw's Garden"

Model A, *241*, 245

Model T, 184, 239, 241–42

Modern French style. *See* Beaux-Arts design

modernism: country place era rejected in, xiv; European, as source of
inspiration, 267, 273; forced perspective in, 321; Edsel Ford and,

modernism (*continued*)
xxii, at Ford House, 245, and genius loci, xxii; at Naumkeag, 335; and nontraditional garden materials, 324; spatial composition in, 275, 281–83; at Val Verde, 290

Montecito Country Club, 387n26

Montecito Creek, 286, 289, 300, *302*

Montefiascone (Italy), *273*

Monticello (Jefferson; Charlottesville, Va.), 3–4, *4*

Moore, Charles Herbert, 386n10

Moorings, The (Alger; Grosse Pointe Shores, Mich.), 58, 121, *122*, 368n18

Moraine Farm (Phillips; Beverly, Mass.), 16–17; *16*

Morgan, Frances Biddle, 218–19, 347–48

Morgan, J. Pierpoint, 145, 240

Morgan, Julia, 372n10

Morgan, Keith N., xiv, 47, 57, 369n57

Morris, William, on gardens and nature, 281

Morton, Julius Sterling, 386n64

Morton, Sterling, estate of (Montecito, Calif.), 282–83, *282*, *283*

Moss, Roger W., xiv

Mount, The (Wharton; Lenox, Mass.), 140–41, *141*, 151, 374nn23, 25

Mountain Brook Estates (Birmingham, Ala.), 44

Mount Auburn Cemetery (Boston, Mass.), 4, 5, *5*

Mount Desert Island (Me.), 137, 150

Mount Vernon (Mount Vernon, Va.), 3

Mud Boats on the Thames (etching; Platt), *49*

Muddy River Improvement, 27–28, *28*

Munstead Wood (Sussex, Eng.), 137, 185

Museum of Modern Art (New York, N.Y.), 241, 260, 348

Museum of Natural History, 385–86n61

Muskau (Ger.), *18. See also* Pückler-Muskau, Prince Hermann Ludwig Heinrich von

Nankin Mills (Rouge River, Mich.), 240

National Academy of Design, 48

National Architect, 80

National Arts Club (New York, N.Y.), 184

National Gallery of Art (Washington, D.C.), 367n57

National Geographic, 185

National Park Service, xiv, 9, 42

National Plan (Manning), 43, 44, 110–11

National Trust for Historic Preservation, 390n7

National Zoo (Washington, D.C.), 28

Nation (magazine), 54, 361n25

nativism, 43, 228, 381n53; and Colonial Revival, 122

naturalistic design, 3–4, 8; as Modern style (Downing), 5–6; Olmsted's, 17, at World's Columbian Exposition, 29; compositional challenge of, 141–42; in Coffin's work, 192, defined, xi; in de Forest's work, 277, 286, at Dumbarton Oaks, 171–72; in Steele's work, 319. *See also* formal/informal debate; Jensen, Jens; Manning, Warren H.; Olmsted, Frederick Law; wild gardening; *specific sites*

nature, xxii; as imitation of art, 346; psychological effects of, 10, 361n24; use of term, xi

Nature, 20, 154, 181; art as "mended," 296–98; automobile and ac-

cess to, 239; defined, xi; garden's relationship to, 263; Jensen and, 223

"Nature Garden, The" (Manning), 31

Naugatuck (Conn.), 32

Naumkeag (Choate; Stockbridge, Mass.), xxiii, 327–54; Afternoon Garden (Temple Garden), 281–82, 325, 330–34, *332*, *333*; allées, 337, *338*, *339*; Barrett's landscape design, 17, 327, *328*, 329, 337, 390n4; bequeathed to Trustees of Reservations, 353; Blue Steps, 343, 345, 346, *345*, *346*, *347*, 392n52; Chinese Temple Garden, 337, 340, *340*, *341*, *342*, 343, *343*, 352, *352*, 391–92n44; client collaboration, 330–31, 335–37, *345*; Coffin planting designs at, 189; critical reviews of, 281–82; cultural life at, 337; cutting garden, 343; de Forest on, 281–82, 304; Devil's Gate, 340, *342*; evergreen garden, 337, *340*; flower gardens, 330; formal gardens, 17, *17*, *328*, 337; general plan for, *335*; genius loci at, 335; grading, 334–35, *334*; house of, 328–29, *329*, *353*, 391n16; interior design, 329; land acquisition for, 328; lawns, *334*, 334–35, *334*, *336*; life at, 348; Macmonnies's *Boy with Heron*, 331, *332*, *333*, *335*; name of, 300; Olmsted firm at, 327, 330; Perugino View, 348, *348*; as refuge, 329–30; Ronde Point theater, 337, *337*; Rose Garden, 352, *352*; Steele projects foreshadowing, 319; view, 327, 331, *332*, 334, *334*, *344*, 348, *348*, *349*; visitors, 346–48

Naumkeag Farm, 348–51, *350*

Neckar, Lance M., 40, 43

Negus, Samuel P., 365n83

Nelson, Swain, 225

neoclassicism, 17–18, 20

neurasthenia, 118, 372n8

Nevius, Ethel D., 187

Newbold, Clement B., 139

Newburgh (N.Y.), 5, 8

New Deal, 219

New England Magazine, 56

Newport (R.I.), xv, 8, 195

New Republic, 366n25

Newton, Norman, x, xiv, 356–57

New Women, 118, 359–60n14

New York (N.Y.), 138–39, 184, 270, 390n6

New York Botanical Garden, 124, *125*, 270

New York State Capitol (Albany, N.Y.), 16

New York Sun, 138

New York World's Fair (1939), 245

Nichols, Rose Standish, 52, 366n14, 372n11

Nicolson, Harold, 118

Nolen, John, 365n95

non-native species/exotics: criticism of, 14, 42; de Forest's use of, 274, 279; at Días Felicitas/Val Verde, 289, 300; at El Fureidis, 285; Farrand's use of, 172; Jensen's use of, 229, 245; Manning's use of, 35, 38, 39, 364n52; Olmsted's use of, xvii, 28, *28*; and plant collecting, 13–15; Steele's use of, 318. *See also* indigenous/native species

North Carolina State Normal School, 311

Northcote (S. Parrish; Cornish, N.H.), *52*

North Easton (Mass.), 16

Norton, Charles Eliot, 386n10

Noyes, John, 41

nurseries, 25, 26, 189, 275, 309

Oakland County (Mich.), 237

Oakpoint (Bayville, N.Y.), 376n50

Oaks, The (Bassick; Bridgeport, Conn.), 192, *193*

Oaks, The (Washington, D.C.), 150. *See also* Dumbarton Oaks

Oberlin College, 375n40

Observations on Modern Gardening (Whately), 360n3

Observations sur la Virginie (Jefferson), 195

Occidental College, 375n40

Ochs, Adolph, 241

Ockwells Manor (Berkshire, Eng.), 92, 93

Oheka (Kahn; Long Island, N.Y.), 146, 191

Ohio and Erie Canal, 61

O'Keefe, Georgia, 388n41

Olana (Church; Hudson, N.Y.), 270, 366n21, 384n3

Old Farms (Daniels; Wenham, Mass.), 120, *120, 121*

Oldfields (Lilly; Indianapolis, Ind.), 372n13, 387n24

Oliver, Richard, 286

Olmsted, Frederick Law, 182; achievements of, xiii, xxii; American Picturesque style of, 196; as Century Association member, 47; clash with Sargent, 27–28; client disagreements with, 17; death of, xiii; design philosophy of, 11–12, 15, 23, 226–27, 361n24; early career of, 9–10; Fairsted, 15, *16*, 136; as father of American landscape architecture, xiii, xvii, xix; firm of, 15–16, 362n10; formal layouts by, 360n22; impact of English walking tour on, 10; landscape designs of, xviii, 8, 15–17, *18*, 19–20; Nature and, xi; office of, xvii; park philosophy of, 8–9, 11; planting methods of, 12, *12*; private commissions, 356; as progressive, 10–11, 361n25; retirement of, xiii, 31; writings of, 362n47. *See also* Biltmore Estate; Manning, Warren H.; Moraine Farm; Olmstedian tradition; World's Columbian Exposition; *entries for firm*

Olmsted, Frederick Law, Jr., xix, 31, 323–24, 385n27, 389n46

Olmsted, John Charles, xix, 16, 27, 31, 33–34, 374n20, 384n11

Olmsted, Olmsted & Eliot, 362n10; Faulkner Farm project and, 54–55; influence on Manning, 36; Manning at, 27–31; Olmsted Sr. retires from, 31

Olmsted & Olmsted, 233

Olmsted & Vaux, 8, 11, 226, 233

Olmsted Brothers, 323; Akron (Ohio) park system, 111–12; California commissions, 385n27, 387n21; collaboration with Platt, 58; Frost at, 368n26; at Naumkeag, 330; Oheka (Long Island, N.Y.) landscape plan, 146

Olmstedian tradition, xix, xx, xxi; design elements of, 39; and du Pont, 198; framed views, 279; genius loci in, xv, 356–57; influence on Farrand, 138, 141; Platt's integration of, 48; Manning and, 91; Shipman and, 119

O'Malley, Therese, 3

On Drawing and Painting (Ross), xxi

Orchard, East Hampton (painting; Platt), *49*

Ormston (Aldred; Long Island, N.Y.), 387n24

Otis, Denise, xiv–xv

Otsuka, T. R., 106

outdoor room, 131; in de Forest's work, 283; in Farrand's work, 146, 154, 170, 376n27; in German design, 389n29; garden as, 389n29; in Jensen's work, 233, 234–35, 252–55; in Platt's work, 48; as status symbol, 48. *See also* Naumkeag: Afternoon Garden

Outlook, 33, 77, 117, 134–35, 139

Oxmoor (Bullitt; Glenview, Ky.), 185, *186*

Pabst, Gustav, 36

Paddock, Willard D., 106, 113

Paderewski, Ignace, 93

Paepckes, Hermann, 380–81n31

Palmer, George T. *See* Eastover

Palos Verdes Estates, 385n27

Panama–California Exposition (San Diego; 1915), 287, 300, 386–87nn16, 21, 23

Paris (France): Blisses in, 149–50; de Forest and Ludington travel to, 273; Exposition (1900), 225; Exposition Universelle (1899), 28; Farrand travel to, 136, 177; Platt in, 49; Steele travel to, 313, 322–323. *See also* Exposition des Arts Décoratifs et Industriels Modernes

Park and Cemetery, 229

parks: as fine art, xvii, Olmstedian philosophy of, 8–9; urban, xiii, xviii, 4–5, 40, 138–39, 224, 381n34. *See also individual parks*

Parks & Recreation, 317

Parmelee, James, estate of (Washington, D.C.), 121, *121*

Parrish, Maxfield, 50, 52, 58

Parrish, Stephen, 48–49, 52, *52* (estate), 366n25

Parsons, Samuel B., Jr.: as ASLA charter member, 36, 374n20; Farrand and, 138–39; on genius loci, xx–xxi; as Olmstedian, xix; Pückler-Muskau promoted by, 360n26; visits Muskau, 19; writings of, 362n47

patriotism: country estates as, 92, 355; Henry Ford's collecting and, 240, 322; and landscape, 5, 33, 43, 118, 203; and women in the workforce, 118. *See also* nativism

Patterson, Robert Whitely, 170

Paxton, Joseph, 10, 12, 28, 361n31

Payne, Thomas, 275

Peabody & Stearns, 16, 363n17

Pearson, Drew, 239

Peavy, Frank H., 32

Pennsylvania School of Horticulture for Women (Ambler, Pa.), 120

Penshurst (Kent, Eng.), 137

Pentecost, George F., 374n20

Penwood (Tucker; Mount Kisco, N.Y.), 123–24, *123*

Perkins, Dwight, 232, 381n36

Persia: American fascination with, 386n18; Goodhue and Gillespie travel to, 286; influence at El Fureidis, 274, 287; influence at Olana, 270; influence at Val Verde, 296, 298

Peterborough (N.H.), 367n54

Peters, William, 278

Phelps Stokes, Anson, 374n23, 390n1

Phelps Stokes, Helen Louisa, 390n1

Philadelphia (Pa.), 195, 271

Phillips, John C. *See* Moraine Farm

Phillips Academy (Andover, Mass.), 367n57

Phipps Garden Apartments, 372n10

photography, 36; in advertising, xvii–xviii, 188–89; Platt and, 54; technological improvements in, xviii, 33. *See also specific photographers*

Picturesque: combined with formality, 14; combined with horticultural experiments, 15; combined with Beaux-Arts, 17, 274–75; defined, xix–xx; English, 11, 23; Manning and, 75, 91, 112; at Moraine Farm, 16; Olmstedian/American, xxi, 3, 5–6, *6*, 8, 131, 135, *135*, 196, *196*, *197*, 198, 274–75, 384n3; in rural cemeteries, 4

Pilat, Carl F., 365n83

Pinchot, Gifford, 30, 136, 363n27

Pinehurst (N.C.), 31, 363n33

Pioneers of American Landscape Design (ed. Birnbaum and Karson), x, xiv

Pittsford (N.Y.), 309–10, *310*, 353

Place Vendôme (Paris, France), 313

Plainfield (N.H.), 119–20, 366n24

planning: Jensen and, 227; Manning and, 29–30, 31, 41, 43, 44; Steele and, 311; regional, 40. *See also* urban planning

plant gathering from the wild, 25; for Gwinn, 69, 71, 75; Jensen and, 225; Manning and, 29, 30, 35; for Stan Hywet Hall, 102

plant-hunting expeditions, 12, 26

planting composition. *See* landscape composition

Plâs Brondanw (Wales), 392n52

Platt, Charles A., xxii, 47–60, 48, *48*, 83, 119; architectural education of, 50; architectural style of, 54, 55; education of, 48–49, 365n8; birth of, 47; "blended classicism" of, 57–58; business expansion of, 59; childhood, 47–48; Cornish (N.H.) commissions, 366n24; critical reviews of, 55–56, 59–60; death of, 85, 126; design philosophy of, 135; estate of, 50, *50*, *51*; formal gardens by, 58; framed views of, 279; genius loci and, 48; geometric approach of, 23; influence of, 48; institutional commissions, 367n57; interior designs, 59–60; Italian influence on, 35, 51, 53–54, 140–41, 286, 367n44; Manning and, 60, 79; marriages of, 49, 58; as painter/etcher, 49, *49*, *51*, 270; personality of, 47, 60; as photographer, 54, *54*; renewed interest in, 369n57; scholarship on, xiv; Shipman and, 58, 119–21; significance of, 60; as social reformer, 48, 53; spatial approach of, 57; Steele replantings of designs by, 367n54; wife's death and, 49; writings of, xix, 54, 366n25

Platt, Charles A., commissions: Croly estate (Cornish, N.H.), 53, *53*, 62; Eastover (New London, Conn.), 58; Faulkner Farm (Brookline, Mass.), 54–56, *55*, *56*; High Court (Cornish, N.H.), 51, *51*, 311; The Moorings (Grosse Pointe, Mich.), 58, 121, 122, 368n18; Timberline (Bryn Mawr, Pa.), 58; Villa Turicum (Lake Forest, Ill.), 35, 59, 368n18; Weld (Brookline, Mass.), 56–58, *56*. *See also* Gwinn

Platt, Eleanor, 119

Platt, Geoffrey, 50, 85, 126, 329, 330

Platt, John, 47

Platt, Mary Cheney, 47

Platt, William, 53–54, 85, 126, 373n32

Plutarch, 359n13

Poins House (Shipman; Plainfield, N.H.), 119–20, *119*

Pointe d'Acadie (Bar Harbor, Me.), 27

Pond, Bremer Whidden, 372n19

Pope, Alexander, x, 5, 352

Pope, John Russell, 186, 191, 366n25

Porter, Cole and Linda, 376n47

Port Royal (Philadelphia, Pa.), 208

Post, George B., 92, 363n17

Post, Marjorie Merriweather. *See* Hillwood

Practical Hints upon Landscape Gardening (Gilpin), 11

Prairie Club, 381n36

Prairie School/style, xix; connection to Frank Lloyd Wright, 232; at Humboldt Park (Chicago), *232*, 381n34; Jensen and, 224, 229, 231–32, 233, 234, 356; Miller as proponent of, 233; Olmsted and, 226. *See also* Edsel and Eleanor Ford House

Prairie Spirit in Landscape Gardening (Miller), 36, 230, 233

Pratt, Henrietta Hamblin. *See* Manning, Henrietta Pratt ("Nettie")

Price, Uvedale, 11

Princeton University, Graduate College, 142–44, *142*, *143*, 375nn38, 40

Progressive era, xviii, 270

Pruyn, Mary and Neltje, garden of, 122, *123*

Public Grounds of Chicago, The (pamphlet; Cleveland), 226

Pückler-Muskau, Prince Hermann Ludwig Heinrich von, xi, xiii, xx, xxi, 19, 233

Punchard, William H., 365n83

Putnam, George Palmer, 47

Pyne, Mr. and Mrs. Moses Taylor, 142

Radburn (N.J.), 318, 365n83, 372n10

Rafel Hotel (San Rafael, Calif.), 13

railroads: and access to country estates, xv, 5, 184, 226; as big business, xvi, 62; and rise of industrial city, 11; temporary construction, xvii, 19, 30, 94, *94*; and Santa Barbara, 269; Manning's mapping of, 311; plants transported via, 29, 75, 197

Rateau, Armand-Albert, 174, *174*, 176, 376n47

Raymond Hotel (South Pasadena, Calif.), 13

Reading Nursery (Reading, Mass.), 25, 36

Reef Point (Me.), 133, *134*, 145, 177

Reef Point Gardens Bulletin, *134*, 178

Rehmann, Elsa, 184–85, 187, 189

Reidel, Peter, 281

Renwick, James, Jr., 286

Repton, Humphry, xxi, 11, 198, 233

Rhode Island School for Domestic Industry, 26

Rice, Henry, 335

Richardson, Henry Hobson, 14, 16, 48

Riggs, Austin, 392n57

Riggs, Lutah Maria, 307, 387n39, 388n47

Riley, Phil M., 80

Rivera, Diego, 241, 260, 383n14

Riverside (Chicago, Ill.), 11, *11*, 226

Robinson, William, xix; estate of, 137, *137*; on exotic species, 42; influence on Coffin, 184; influence on Dumbarton Oaks, 164, 168; influence on Winterthur, 200; as wild gardens originator, 38; writings of, 58

Rochester (N.Y.), 28, 309, 313–15, 388n2

Rock City Amusement Park (Olean, N.Y.), *40*

Rock Creek Park, 172

Rockefeller, Abby Aldrich. *See* Eyrie, The

Rockefeller, David, 178

Rockefeller, John D., xvi, 36, 141, 382n58

Rockefeller, John D., Jr.: at Greenfield Village opening, 240; at Mission House museum, 351; Naumkeag and, 334; Williamsburg restoration underwritten by, 207. *See also* Eyrie, The

Rock River (Ill.), *225*

Rockville (Conn.), 59, 367n54

Rogers, Elizabeth Barlow, 8, 360n26

Rogers, James Gamble, 124

Roland Park (Baltimore, Md.), 271, 384n11

Rolling Ridge (E. Allen; North Andover, Mass.), 315–17, *316, 317,* 319, 332

Romanticism, xiii, 4, 7, 8

Roosevelt, Eleanor, 59

Roosevelt, Franklin D., 59, 219

Roosevelt, Mrs. James, 59

Roosevelt, Theodore, xviii, 43, 118, 142

Root, Elihu, 347

Rose, James, 355

rose gardens: Crosswicks, 139, *139;* de Forest garden, 277; Dumbarton Oaks, 152, 157, *157, 158,* 159, 162, 168, 170, 174, *174, 175,* 176, 376n23; Ellwanger garden, 324, *325;* Fair Lane, 125, 235, *235,* 382n60; Ford House, 245, 251, *256, 257;* Hope Ranch, 279; Naumkeag, 352, *352;* Stan Hywet Hall, 97, *109,* 110; White House, *144,* 145; Winterthur, 199, *199,* 378nn25, 27

Rosenwald, Augusta, 231

Rosenwald, Julius and Augusta, 231

Rose Terrace (Grosse Pointe, Mich.), 373n28

Ross, Denman W., xxi, 311, 322

Rotch & Tilden, 373n2

Rotunda (Ford Motor Company), 236, 245

Rouge River, 234, *234,* 382n58

Rowntree, Lester, 281, 385–86n61

Royal Institute of British Architects, 138

Rubens, Harry, estate of (Glencoe, Ill.), 229–30, *229,* 232

Rural Science Series (ed. Bailey), xviii

Rynwood (Salvage; Glen Head, N.Y.), 124, *124*

Sabin, Charles H. and Pauline. *See* Bayberryland

Sage, H. W., 311

Saint-Gaudens, Augustus: as American Renaissance figure, 134; Cornish (N.H.) artists' colony founded by, 50, 52, 366n21. *See also* Aspet

Salvage, Samuel A. *See* Rynwood

Samarkand (Santa Barbara, Calif.), 386n18

Sand Hill Reservation (Akron, Ohio), 111–12

San Diego (Calif.), 287, 300

Sandyland Cove (Carpinteria, Calif.), 279

Santa Barbara (Calif.): earthquake (1925), 276; Goodhue downtown plan for, 387n26; luxury hotels in, 269, *270;* migration of wealthy Easterners to, 269–70; Persia fascination in, 386n18

Santa Barbara Botanic Garden, 176, 281, 385n56

Santa Barbara Community Arts Association, 276, 281

Santa Barbara County (Calif.), 269

Santa Barbara Gardener, 280–83, 385nn51–52, 385–86n61

Santa Barbara Museum of Art, 307, 388n47

Sarah P. Duke Gardens (Durham, N.C.). *See* Duke Gardens

Sargent, Charles Sprague, xix, 15; as Arnold Arboretum founder/director, 26, 135, 159, 201; Coffin and, 182; Dumbarton Oaks plant acquisitions from, 159; du Pont and, 378n15; du Pont (Henry Algernon) and, 379n36; Holm Lea, 135, *135,* 198; Farrand and, 135, 136, 138, 141, 142, 183; as *Garden and Forest* "conductor," 19, 362n47; Olmsted Sr. vs., 27–28, *28;* significance of, 360n20; Winterthur and, 203

Sargent, John Singer, 134

Saturday Evening Post, 93, 225

Sault Ste. Marie (Mich.), 61

Scarborough (N.Y.), 181

scenery, psychological effects of, 10, 361n24

scenic preservation, 18–19, 26. *See also* landscape preservation

Scheiner, James M., 186, *188,* 193, 208, 377n22

Schneider, Charles S.: education of, 370n14; Manning and, 102, 371nn31, 34; as Stan Hywet architect, 91–92, 106, 110; on Stan Hywet interior design, 370n22

Schofield, Mrs. W. H., 367n54

School of Practical Agriculture and Horticulture (Briarcliff Manor, N.Y.), 198

Schryver, Edith, 123, 373n25

Schwab, Charles, 241

scientific forestry: at Biltmore, 19, 20, 30; in *Garden and Forest,* 362n47; at Moraine Farm, 16

Sears, Thomas, 19, 271, 384n11

Sedgwick, Catharine M., 328

Sedgwick, Ellery, 347

Sedgwick, Mabel Cabot, 200

Seiberling, Charles W., 89, 111, 382n58

Seiberling, Frank A., xvi, xvii, xxii; business career of, 89–90, 93, 111; cultural aspirations of, 93, 110, *111;* death of, 114; du Pont and, 203; Goodyear Heights underwritten by, 93–94; Fairlawn Heights underwritten by, 43; land acquisition by, 112; Lincoln Highway and, 237; Schneider and, 92. *See also* Stan Hywet Hall

Seiberling, Frank A., Jr., 95, 114

Seiberling, Gertrude, xxii, *106, 110;* as Arts and Crafts proponent, 90; cultural aspirations of, 93, 110, *111;* death of, 114; garden club memberships, 113, 372n61. *See also* Stan Hywet Hall

Seiberling, Irene, 92, 113

Seiberling, Virginia, *112*

Seiberling Rubber Company, 111

Semi-Tropical California (pamphlet), 384n2

Sessions, Kate, 275

Sexton, Joseph, 275

Shadow Brook (Lenox, Mass.), 327, 390n1

Shadows-on-the-Teche (New Iberia, La.), 126

Shand-Tucci, Douglass, 386n10, 387n30

Sharp, H. Rodney and Isabella. *See* Gibraltar

Shaw, Henry, 12–13, *14,* 381n34. *See also* Shaw's Garden

Shaw, Howard Van Doren, 366n25

"Shaw's Garden" (St. Louis, Mo.), 12–13, *13*, 15. *See also* garden-esque; Victorian design

Sheeler, Charles, 241, 388n41; photograph by, *241*

Shelburne (Vt.), 206

Shelton, Louise, 35, 58, 369n51

Shenstone, William, 198

Shipman, Ellen Biddle, xxii, 39, 118–27, *119*; Arts and Crafts sensibilities of, 120, 124, 125; birth of, 119; business expansions of, 122–23; client base of, 122, 373n25; collaboration with Manning, 113, 372n59; Colonial Revival and, 122; at Cornish, 52; cultivation/maintenance notes by, 113–14; divorce of, 120; early gardening commissions, 119–21; education of, 119; female employees of, 123, 373n25; as flower gardener, 118–19; gender discrimination against, 118; genius loci and, 126; Gwinn formal gardens redesigned by, 85, 125–26; home of, 124, 171; impact of Depression on, 373n34; large-scale commissions, 123–25; marriage of, 119; as New Woman, 359n14; New York office of, *119*, 122; fame of, 123, 124, 389n45; Platt and, 58, 119–21; public work, 124–25; Stan Hywet English Garden redesign, 113–14, *113*, *114*, 125, *126*

Shipman, Ellen Biddle, commissions: Aetna Life roof garden, 124, *125*, 357; Duke Gardens (Durham, N.C.), 124–25, *125*, 357; Fair Lane formal garden planting, 235; Fish garden (Greenport, N.Y.), 122, *123*; Fynemere (Cooperstown, N.Y.), 120–21, *121*; Girdle Ridge (Katonah, N.Y.), 121, *121*; Halfred Farms (Chagrin Falls, Ohio), 121, *122*, 372n59; The Moorings (Grosse Pointe, Mich.), 121, *122*; New York Botanical Garden, 124, *125*; Old Farms (Wenham, Mass.), 120, *120*, *121*; Parmelee estate (Washington, D.C.), 121, *121*; Penwood (Mount Kisco, N.Y.), 123–24, *123*; Pruyn garden (East Hampton, N.Y.), 122, *123*; Rose Terrace (Grosse Pointe, Mich.), 373n28; Rynwood (Glen Head, N.Y.), 124, *124*

Shipman, Louis, 52, 119, 120

Shirlaw, Walter, 48

Shurcliff, Arthur, 319, 389n46

Siftings (Jensen), 263

Simms, E. F., 231

Simms, W. E., 231, *231*

Simonds, Gertrude, 381n36

Simonds, Ossian Cole, xix, 36, 233; as ASLA charter member, 374n20; at Graceland Cemetery, 225, *225*; Jensen and, 233, 238, 380n13; as Lincoln Highway Association adviser, 237–38; Manning and, 363n23; nature-based design approach, 380n13; writings of, 237, 362n47

Sissinghurst (Kent, Eng.), 118

Sketches and Hints on Landscape Gardening (Repton), 11

Skylands (E. and E. Ford, Seal Harbor, Me.), 236–37, *236*, 242, 251

Slade, Emily and Augusta, 366n24

Sleeper, Henry Davis, 206

Sleepy Hollow Cemetery (Concord, Mass.), 6

Sloan, Samuel and Katherine. *See* Lisburne Grange

Small Place, The (Rehmann), 184

Smith, George Washington, 273–74, 387n20

Smith, Thorton, 93

Smith, Warren Hunting, 183

Smith, W. Hinckle, 58

Society for the Preservation of New England Antiquities, 379n41

Song of Hiawatha (Longfellow), 7

Soule, Murphy & Hastings, 273

Soule, Windsor (brother-in-law of Lockwood de Forest Jr.), 273

Southern California Acclimatizing Association, 275–76

Southern Pacific Railroad, 269, 270

Spanish Colonial style, 273, 387n20

Spanish design, Steele on, 343

spatial composition: defined by plantings, 12, 39, 170, 216, 290; defined by water, 172; de Forest on Steele's modern approach to, 281–82, 304; of Humboldt Park (Chicago), 381n34; de Forest's approach, 279, 283; Coffin's approach, 184, 185, 191; at Días Felicitas/Val Verde, 289, 294; at Dumbarton Oaks, 153–54, 159, 164, 170; Farrand inspired by Cram's, 143; at Ford House, 243, 247, 249, 252, 255; French modernist, 322–23; at Gwinn, 87; Jensen's structured by meadows, 233, 236, 254; at Mission House, 351; at Naumkeag, 335; Newton on country place era, 356; Platt on, in *Italian Gardens*, 54; Platt's approach, 57; and response to genius loci, 31, 48, 184; sequencing, 316, 319, 376n23; Shipman's, at Rynwood, 124; Steele's approach, 314, 315–16, *314*, 322–23, 325; at Winterthur, 200. *See also* Beaux-Arts design

Spencer, Robert, 232

Sprague, Charles, 54–55

Sprague, Edward E., estate of (Flushing, N.Y.), 184–85, *185*

Sprague, Mary Pratt, 54

Spring Grove Cemetery (Cincinnati, Ohio), 4

Spring Lake Farm, 44

Springside (Vassar; Poughkeepsie, N.Y.), 8, *8*

Spring Station (Ky.), 231

Standard Cyclopedia of Horticulture (ed. Bailey), xviii

Stan Hywet Hall (Akron, Ohio), xvii, 89–116; allées, 95, 97, *97*, *98*, *99*, 104, *104*, 345; architect hired for, 91–92; architect–landscape architect collaboration, 102, 371n31; Breakfast Room, 110; bridges, 102, *102*, *103*; bridle trails, 111, *112*; commissioned by Gertrude Seiberling, 89; construction of, 94, *94*, 110, 371n29; cost of, 94; cutting gardens, 91, 110; du Pont visits, 203; English Garden, 106, *108*, 110, *110*, 113–14, *113*, *114*, 118, 125, *126*; 372n64; entertainment at, 110, *111*; entrance drive, 94–95; entry court, 371n33; family life, 111, *112*; farm, *90*, 91, 110, 203; formal gardens, 95; fountains, 104, *104*, *110*; *The Garden of the Water Goddess* (Paddock), 106, 113; house, 91, 114, 371n42; impact of Depression on, 111; impact of WWI on, 110–11; interior design, 92–93; invasive species, 371n36; Japanese Garden, 106, *106*, 107, 371n49; lagoon/quarry/wild garden, 91, 97, 98, 100, *100*, *101*, 102, *102*, *103*, *115*; lawns, 91, 95, *96*; maintenance endowment, 114; model search for, 92; modern conveniences, 92; Music Room, 93; name of, 90; orchard, 95; outbuildings, 91, 94, *95*, 110; pavilions, *103*, 104, *104*; plans for, 91, *91*, 95, *95*, 97; public use of, 112–13, 114; recreation at, 90, 111, *112*, 313; restorations of, 44, 113–14, 371n33, 372n64; rose garden, 97, *109*, 110; site conditions, 90–91, *91*; Taylor as Manning's overseer at, 41, 312; terraces, 94, 104, 106, *104*, *105*, *107*, *116*; vegetable gardens, 91,

110; views, 94, 97, 102, *102*, 104, 114, *115*, 371nn34, 42; Walden as model for, 34

St. Ann's Hospital (Chicago, Ill.), 229, *229*

Starr, Kevin, 384n2

Stately Homes in America (Croly), 366n25

St. Clair, Lake, 243, *247*, 255, *258*, *262*, *264*, 321

Steedman, George and Carrie, 273–74, 384n21

Steele, Esther, 347

Steele, Fletcher, xxiii, 218–19, *310*, *322*, *345*, *352*; Asian tours of, 337–40; as ASLA Fellow, 189; birth of, 309; childhood of, 309–10; client base of, 317; client personality, as design determinant, 315, 340; Coffin and, 347; color use of, 318; Cram and, 320–21, 322, 389n50; critical reviews of, 334; design philosophy of, 313, 315, 317–18, 322–25, 353–54; European tours of, 137, 311, 312–13, 313, *313*, 337; existing designs incorporated by, 319–20; family garden of, 310, *310*; flower gardens of, 372n13; on formal/informal design, 325, 346; French influence on, 322–23, 345–46, 353, 355; genius loci and, 313, 317, 353–54; impact of WWII on, 351; influence of, 267, 355–56; Italian influence on, 311, 316, 319, 320; as lecturer, 325; library bequeathed to ASLA, 390n66; on Manning, 40, 388–89n19; at Manning's office, 311–12; on Naumkeag interior design, 329; as Naumkeag visitor, 347, 353; nontraditional garden materials used by, 324; on Olmsted, xiii; outdoor rooms of, 353; personality of, 309, 331; planting palette of, 318, 321–22, 324; Platt gardens replanted by, 367n54; private business established by, 313; public work overlooked, 357; relationship with clients, 314–15, 351–52; semiretirement of, 353; spatial sequencing in work of, 319; three-dimensionality in works of, 314, 322–23, 325; writings of, 122, 313, 317–18, 323, 355, 389n45

Steele, Fletcher, commissions: Allen garden (Rochester, N.Y.), 313–15, *315*, *316*; Ancrum House (Delhi, N.Y.), 320–21, 320–21, *320*, *321*, 389n49; Backus estate (Grosse Pointe Shores, Mich.), 249, 321–22, *321*, *322*, 389n49; Blossom Hill (Wawa, Pa.), 313, 314, *314*; Camden (Me.) Public Library, 323–24, *324*, 337, 345, 357; Cram estate (Sudbury Center, Mass.), 322, *322*; Lisburne Grange (Garrison, N.Y.), 319–20, *320*; Mission House (Stockbridge, Mass.), 351, *351*; Rolling Ridge (North Andover, Mass.), 315–17, *316*, *317*; Wingfield (Mount Kisco, N.Y.), 318–19, *318*, *319*. See also Naumkeag

Steele, John and Mary, 309

Stein, Clarence, 318, 365n83, 372n10, 387n24

Steinway Hall (Chicago, Ill.), 232, 381n44

Stern, Edgar B. and Edith. See Longue Vue

Stevens, Kinton, 275, 285

Stevens, Ralph, 271, 273

Stewart, Mary. See Il Brolino

Stieglitz, Alfred, 388n41

Stiles, William A., 37, 362n47

Stockbridge (Mass.), 327. See also Mission House; Naumkeag

St. Paul and Duluth Railroad Company, 149

Straight, Willard and Dorothy, 366n25, 375n42; estate of (Old Westbury, N.Y.), *144*, 145

Streatfield, David C., 271, 273, 279, 303–4, 383–84n1, 386n4, 388n42

Sullivan, Louis, 226

Sunnyside Gardens (Queens, N.Y.), 365n83, 372n10

Sunset, 385n43

Susquehanna River, 36

swimming pools, xvii; at Allen garden, *316*; at Dumbarton Oaks, 152, 157, *167*; at Gibraltar, 186, *188*; at Haven Hill, 382n65; Jensen's, *231*, 236 (*see also* Edsel and Eleanor Ford House); at Lisburne Grange, 320, *320*; at Winterthur, 209, *209*. *See also* Val Verde

Tabor, Grace, 372n11

Taft, Lorado, 381n36

Tanglewood Music Festival, 337

Tannahill, Robert Hudson, 245

Taylor, Albert Davis, 41, 71, 94, 312

Taylor, Reese, house (Montecito, Calif.), 385n43

Teague, Walter Dorwin, 236, 245

Temple of Vesta (Tivoli), 64

Temple of Neptune, Paestum, *272*

Thacher, John S., 177

Thacher School (Ojai Valley, Calif.), 271, *271*, 388n47

Theory of Pure Design, A (Ross), xxi

Theory of the Leisure Class, The (Veblen), xvi, 227

Thiene, Paul, 275

Thompson, Henry, 143–44

Thorne, Helen, 274

Three Arts Society, 348, 392n57

Tidal Basin (Washington, D.C.), 375n9

Tiffany, Louis Comfort, 270, 384n5

Tiffany & Company, 79

Timberline (Bryn Mawr, Pa.), 58

Tobey, George, 318

Tower Grove Park (St. Louis, Mo.), 12–13, 361n32, 381n34

Town and Country, 318

Towne, John and Nora. See Wingfield

Tranquillity Farm (Whittemore; Middlebury, Conn.), *32*

Transcendentalism, 4, 26, 31

Traquair House (Peebles, Scotland), 165

Treatise on the Theory and Practice of Landscape Gardening (Downing), xviii, 4–6, *6*

Trees and Shrubs for Landscape Effects (Coffin), 191, 219–21

Trueman, Benjamin, 384n2

Trumbauer, Horace, 92, 366n25, 373n28

Trustees of Reservations, The (Mass.), 18, 353

Tucker, Carll. See Penwood

Tudor Revival style, 92, 94

Tufts, James W., 31, 363n33

Tune Agricultural School (Copenhagen), 223–24

Turner, Richard and Nancy, estate of (Pittsford, N.Y.), 392n70

Tüxen, Reinhold, 228

Twachtman, J. Alden, 79, 369n50

Twain, Mark, 13, 348, 384n5

Tyler, Elisina, 376n54

Tyler, Royall, 150

Tyler, William, 150

Tyrrell, C. Gordon, 198

Ulrich, Rudolph, 13–14, 29
Underhill, Francis T., 274, 287
Union Park (Chicago, Ill.), 228, *228*; American Garden, 225
United Nations, 376n56
United States: Americana fervor in, 207, 379nn41, 43; centennial cel-
    ebrations in (1876), 379n41; corporate-capitalist industrialism in,
    51–52, 359n8; country place era in, xiv–xv; immigration to, xiii,
    207, 227, 359n3; impact of automobile on, 239; Jensen's elope-
    ment to, 224; population growth in, 9; rising influence of, xi; ur-
    banization of, xiii, 5, 9; wilderness loss in, xi
United States Military Academy (West Point, N.Y.), 386n12
University of California, Berkeley, 271
University of Chicago, 227, 375n40
University of Illinois, Urbana, 367n57
Unwin, Raymond, 380n20
upper class: agrarian myth and, xiii; country estates commissioned by,
    xi–xii, xiv, xv–xvi; expansion of, xiv, 359n10; Modern approach
    and, 6; parterres and, 85; progressive critiques of, xiv, 227
Upper Peninsula (Mich.), 61, 93, 365n81
urbanization, xiii, 5, 9
urban parks. *See* parks: urban
urban planning, xvii, xviii, 227; Birmingham (Ala.) city plan, 43–44,
    44

Vagabonds, 382n8
Val Verde (Santa Barbara, Calif.), xx–xxi, 280, 285–307; architect for,
    285; art gallery tower, 295; bas-reliefs, 290, *292*; client collabora-
    tion, 294; colonnade, 303–4; courtyard, 295, *296*; as cultural/edu-
    cational site, 307; cultural significance of, 294, 387n31; de Forest's
    additions, 298, 300; de Forest's plantings, 290–94, 300; de Forest's
    revisions, 290, 294–98; entrance drive, 290, *293*, 294; flower gar-
    dens, 289; forecourt, *288, 290*, 298; fountains, 289, 290, *291*, 298;
    garden crew at, 300, *303*; Goodhue's design for, 287, *288*, 289;
    Goodhue's landscape plan, 289, *289*; guest house, 295, *295, 296*;
    house, 287, *288*, 289, *289*; influences on, 287, 290, 294–95; inte-
    rior design of, 289, *289*, 294, *294*; Italianate influence, 298, *298*;
    keyhole rooms, 290, *299*, 300; landscape plan of, *295*; lighting,
    295, *296*; loggia, 300; Ludington (Charles) purchases, 285, 290;
    Ludington (Wright) inherits, 294; Ludington (Wright) sells, 307;
    maze, *304*; paths, 289, *290, 292*, 300, *301*; precedent for, 387n25;
    reflecting pools, 289, 296, *296, 297, 298*, 300, *303, 305*; renaming
    of, 294, 387n30; as rental property, 289–90; service court, 290,
    291; statuary, 294, 295, *296, 298*, 300 (Lansdowne Hermes, Her-
    akles torso, Dioscurus), 303, *303* (Lansdowne Hermes,
    Aphrodite), *304* (Dioscurus), 307; swimming pool, 295–96, *295,
    296, 299*; terraces, 286, *286*, 303–4, *306*; theatrical passages, 290,
    292; view, *286*, 289, *290*, 297, *297*, 304; "What-Not," 297, *298*
Van Brunt & Howe, 363n17
Vanderbilt, Cornelius, xvi
Vanderbilt, George Washington, xvii, 19, 27, 135–36. *See also* Bilt-
    more Estate (Asheville, N.C.)
Van Rensselaer, Mariana Griswold, xiii; Farrand's career and, 134; on
    gardenesque planting fashions, 14–15; as New Woman,

359–60n14; Olmsted's correspondence with, 16; on World's
    Columbian Exposition, 18, 29; writings of, 311, 359–60n14
van Tine, William H., 381–82n55
Vassar, Matthew, 8, *8*
Vassar College, 375n40
Vaux, Calvert, xvii, 366n21; Central Park project and, 361nn17, 20;
    Olana designed by, 384n3; partnership with Downing, 7–8; part-
    nership with Olmsted, 8, 11. *See also* Olmsted & Vaux
Vaux, Downing, xix, 374n20
Veblen, Thorstein, xvi, 227
Vernon, Christopher, xix, 232
Victorian design: Cram's description of, 56; at Crystal Palace, 12; as
    decadent, 207; du Pont's criticism of, 198; Italianate as alternative
    to, xix; at Naumkeag, 330; Seiberling Japanese Garden as, 106;
    wild gardening as alternative to, 38. *See also* gardenesque
Victorian Gothic architecture, 17
Viele, Egbert, 361n17
view, 190; architectural framework for, 138; borrowed, 131; framed,
    279, 304, 320, 321, 348; at Stan Hywet, 371nn34, 42; in Steele's
    work, 313, 316, 318–19, 320, 348, 349
Villa Aldobrandini (Frascati, Italy), 312
Villa Balbaniello (Italy), 273, *273*
Villa Borghese (Rome, Italy), 367n44
Villa Castello (Italy), 367n44
Villa d'Este (Italy), *272*, 273, 320, 384n17
Villa Falconieri (Italy), 319
"Villa Fosca" (imaginary villa), 387n25
Villa Gamberaia (Italy), 55, 273
village industries, 239–40
Villa Lante (Italy), 55, 72, 136, *136*, 137, 273, 312, *313*
Villa Medici (Rome, Italy), 290
Villa Pamfili (Italy), *54*
Villard Mansion (New York, N.Y.), 51
Villa Rufolo (Ravello, Italy), 273
Villa Tachard, 323
Villa Torlonia (Italy), 316
Villa Turicum (Lake Forest, Ill.), 35, 59, *59*, 368n18
Virieux, 198
vista. *See* view
Vitale, Ferruccio, 356
von Holst & Fyfe, 381–82n55
Voyage dans les Etats-Unis de Amérique (La Rochefoucauld-Liancourt),
    378n2

Wagner, Harold S., 111, 112
Walden (Concord, Mass.), 35
Walden (Lake Forest, Ill.), 33–36, *35*, 227
Wales, Ruth. *See* du Pont, Ruth Wales
Walker, Henry, 50
Walks and Talks of an American Farmer in England (Olmsted), 10
Walpole, Horace, 312
Walpole Society, 379n41
Walsh, M. H., 378n25
Walska, Ganna. *See* Lotusland
Ward, Willis, 274

Ware, William, 137

Warner, Jack, 385n50

Warner Brothers Studio, 388n43

Warren, Charles D., 57–58

Washington, George, 3

Washington (D.C.), 8, 30, 375n9

water features, xvii, xix; 172, 275; architectural features as connection to, 209, 297, *298*; in Chicago parks, 381n34; design in relation to, 33, 316 (*see also* Gwinn; Edsel and Eleanor Ford House); in Jensen's work, 233, 237; Miller on charm and, 57; naturalistic/ formal juxtaposed, 209, 211; naturalistic pools/lagoons, 229, *229*, 286 (*see also* Edsel and Eleanor Ford House; Stan Hywet Hall; World's Columbian Exposition); as Olmstedian, 39, 361n24; as organizing spatial element, 172; prairie, 233; in Stan Hywet Hall Japanese garden, 106; reflecting pools, 191, 199, 274, *275*, *286*, *319*, *320* (*see also* Naumkeag: Afternoon Garden; Val Verde); rills, 192 (*see also* Naumkeag: Blue Steps); suggested by natural water, 11, 29; at Villa d'Este, 384n17; water gardens, 274, 287, 322, *323*, 386n18. *See also* fountains; swimming pools

Watson, Benjamin M., 198

Watson, Ernest, house (Montecito, Calif.), 385n43

Waverly Oaks, 18

Waugh, Frank A., 228, 230, 232, 362n47

Webb, Electra Havemayer, 206

Weeks-McLean Migratory Bird Act (1913), 242

Weidenmann, Jacob, xix

Weld (Anderson; Brookline, Mass.), 56–58, *57*, 67, 80, 367nn44–45

Weller, Eleanor, xiv, 190, 304

Wellesley (Hunnewell; Waban, Mass.), 14, *15*

Wendover (Coffin; Watch Hill, R.I.), 193, *194*

Wentworth, Charles Francis, 286

West, Andrew Fleming, 142

Western Reserve, 61

Wharton, Edith: as author, 58, 133–34, 149; in Berkshires, 328; Bliss and, 149; Coffin and, 183; death of, 177; as gardener, 150–51; Platt and, 58. *See also* Mount, The

Wharton, Edward, 140–41

What England Can Teach Us about Gardening (Miller), 39, 58

What Girls Can Do, 117

Wheeler, Candace, 384n5

White, Lawrence, 157, 172, 174–76, 375–76n19

White, Stanford, 17, 48, 55, 328–29

White, Windsor T. *See* Halfred Farms

White House (Washington, D.C.), 64, *144*, 145

Whitney, Edward F., estate of (Oyster Bay, N.Y.), 141, *141*

Whittemore, John H. *See* Tranquillity Farm

Whittredge, Thomas Worthington, 365n88

Wiepking-Jürgensmann, Heinrich Friedrich, 228

Wild Garden, The (Robinson), 200

wild gardens, xvii, xxii, 16–17, 23; and American middle class, 263n40; Babson House (Jensen), 226, *226*; Backus estate·(Steele), 322; Biltmore (Olmsted/Manning) approach as, 20; Crosswicks (Farrand), 139; de Forest on, 281; Dolobran (Manning), 33, *34*; Fair Lane (Jensen), 234–35, *235*; E. and E. Ford gardens (Jensen), 236–37, *236*; formal gardens juxtaposed with, 141,

141, 171, 201, 211; Gibraltar (Coffin), 186; ideal of, 77; Italianate style as opposition to, 137; Harrisburg Parks (Manning), 36, *37*; Longue Vue (Shipman), 126, 373n33; Manning and, x, 25, 31, 33–36, 37–39, *38*, 45, 62, 369n40, 391n40 (*see also specific sites*); Moraine Farm (Olmsted), 16, *16*; The Mount (Wharton), 140, 374n23; The Oaks (Coffin), 192, *193*; restorative appeal of, 23, 33; tasks involved in, 39; Walden (Manning), 33–36, *35*, 227, 364n70. *See also* Dumbarton Oaks: Copse, wild garden; Edsel and Eleanor Ford House; Graceland Cemetery; Gwinn: wild garden; Robinson, William; Stan Hywet Hall: lagoon/quarry/ wild garden; Winterthur: Azalea Woods, Glade Garden, March Bank, naturalistic plantings, vistas, waterfall; World's Columbian Exposition: Wooded Island

Willeke, Leonard, 382n62

William G. Mather (steamer), 83

Williams, Harrison, 376n50

Williamsburg (Va.), 207, 389n46

Williams College (Williamstown, Mass.), 271, 310

Wilmarth, Lemuel, 48

Wilmington and Northern Railroad, 196

Wilson, Ellen Axson, 145

Wilson, Henry Neill, 390n1

Wing, Joseph Morgan, estate of (Millbrook, N.Y.), 192, *193*

Wingfield (Towne; Mount Kisco, N.Y.), *318*, 319, *319*

Winslow, Carleton M., 151

Winterthur (Winterthur, Del.), xxii; aerial views of, *206*, *207*, *208*; April Garden, 219–21, *219*, *220*, 379n63; Azalea Woods, 201, *202*, 203, 378–79n33; Blue Atlas Cedar Circle, *205*; Boxwood Scroll Garden, 215, *215*, 216; Coffin as visitor, 182, 218; cross axis, 209, *209*, 211; cutting gardens, 206; family life, 216, 218; farm/dairy, 196, 197, 200, 203, 216, *216*; formal garden, 199, *199*, 200, 208, *208*, 211, 378n20; Glade Garden, *210*; greenhouses, 206; guiding principles of, 192; house renovation, 207–8, *207*, *208*; house terrace, 209, 211, *211*, *212*, *213*; Icewell Terrace, *214*, 215; impact of Depression on, 219; impact of development at, 378n27; interior design of, 198–99, 206; interior renovations, 379n43; iris garden, 215–16, *215*, 379n48; Italianate plan for, xiv; land acquisitions for, 216; landscape redesign, 208–9, *209*, 211, 215, *215*, 216; Latimeria Gates, *203*, *204*; March Bank, 200, *201*, 203, 215; meadows, 197, *197*, 200, *201*, *203*, 216, *217*; name of, 196; naturalistic plantings, 200–201, *202*, *203*, 208, 209, *210*, 211, *211*, *218*; old carriage drive, *196*; original American Picturesque style of, 196; original construction of, 196; paths, 199, 209, *209*, 215, *215*; pavilions, 209, *209*; pinetum, 203, *203*, *204*, *206*, *218*, *220*, 221; as public museum, 219; as refuge, 219; rose garden, 378nn25, 27; shrub plantings, 215–16; supervision of, 198–99, 206, 207–8, 216; swimming pool, 209, *209*; trial plantings, 186, 198, 199–200, 331; views, 200, *201*, *203*, 208–9, *211*, 215, 216, *216*; waterfall, 209, *210*

Wister, Owen, 118

Wolschke-Bulmahn, Joachim, 228

women: career vs. marriage, 182, 377n6; discrimination against, 118; as gardeners, xvii, 117, 118, 138, 330; higher education of, 328; New Women, 118, 359–60n15

women landscape architects, xiv, xvii, xxii, 117–19, 120, 372n11; in large-scale projects, 372n10; lesbian, 373n25; Olmsted as supportive of, 374n9; prominence of, in period, 389n45; programs for training, 372–73n19

Women's Advisory Council Border (New York Botanical Garden), 124, *125*

Wood, Grahame. *See* Blossom Hill

Woodlands (Hamilton; Philadelphia, Pa.), 208

worker housing. *See* company towns

World's Columbian Exposition (Chicago; 1893), xxii; American Renaissance and, xix, 52–53; architects hired for, 363n17; Beaux-Arts/Picturesque juxtaposed at, 17–18, *18*; Beaux-Arts style of, 55; Farrand at, 135; genius loci, 29; goal of, 363n19; Honor Court, *29*; influence of design, 55; lagoon, 29, *29*, 226; Manning at, 28–30; Massachusetts State Building, 135; plantings at, 29, *29*; Wooded Island, 29, *29*, 106, 226

World War I, 42, 43, 145, 150, 271

World War II, 219, 351, 376n56, 388n43

Wotton, Henry, 154–57

Wright, Frank Lloyd, 59, 92, 226, 232, 381n49

Wright, Henry, 318, 365n83, 372n10

Wright, Lloyd, 275

Wright, Orville, 240

Wurster, William, 277

Wyatt, Jane, 218

Wyeth, Marion Sims, 389n45

Wyman, Phelps, 365n83

Yale University, 375n40

Yellin, Samuel, 93, 152

Yoch, Florence, 275, 280, *280*, 373n25, 384–85n26, 385n50

Yosemite Valley, 8

Ypsilanti (Mich.), Ford Motor Company plant in, *240*

ILLUSTRATION SOURCES

The author is grateful to the following institutions whose credits are abbreviated in the captions for permission to reproduce visual materials in their archives.

Bentley. Jens Jensen Collection, Bentley Historical Library, University of Michigan, Ann Arbor

Dumbarton Oaks. Dumbarton Oaks, Research Library & Collections, Washington, D.C.

EDA, Berkeley. Beatrix Jones Farrand Collection (1955-2), Environmental Design Archives, University of California, Berkeley

Ford House. Edsel & Eleanor Ford House, Grosse Pointe Shores, Michigan

Gwinn. William G. Mather Papers, Gwinn Archives, Gwinn Estate, Cleveland, Ohio

Harvard GSD. Frances Loeb Library, Harvard Graduate School of Design, Harvard University

Naumkeag. Naumkeag House and Gardens, Stockbridge, Mass., Property of The Trustees of Reservations

NPS/FLO. U.S. Department of the Interior, National Park Service, Frederick Law Olmsted Historic Site

NYPL. Robert N. Dennis Collection of Stereoscopic Views, Miriam & Ira D. Wallach Division of Art, Prints & Photographs, The New York Public Library, Astor, Lenox and Tilden Foundations

RMC-Cornell Univ. Library. Division of Rare and Manuscript Collections, Carl A. Kroch Library, Cornell University, Ithaca, N.Y.

Saint-Gaudens NHS. U.S. Department of the Interior, National Park Service, Saint-Gaudens National Historic Site, Cornish, N.H.

SHH. Stan Hywet Hall and Gardens, Akron, Ohio

SUNY ESF College Archives. Photographs are from the manuscript collection of Fletcher Steele held at the Terence J. Hoverter College Archives, F. Franklin Moon Library, State University of New York College of Environmental Science and Forestry, Syracuse, N.Y. Funds from the Graham Foundation for the Fine Arts and Architecture were used to create the Study Print Collection of Steele's client jobs.

The Henry Ford. From the Collections of the The Henry Ford, Dearborn, Mich.

WHM, Iowa State. Warren H. Manning Papers, Iowa State University Library / Special Collections Department, Ames.

WHM, UML. Warren H. Manning Collection, University of Massachusetts Lowell

Winterthur Archives. The Winterthur Library: Winterthur Archives, Winterthur, Del.

A GENIUS FOR PLACE

Designed by Jonathan D. Lippincott. Set in Bembo and Manticore.

Printed in duotone and bound by Everbest Printing, Ltd.

Full-page photographs by Carol Betsch were specially

commissioned for the book and the touring

exhibition *A Genius for Place*.